Modern Europe to 1815

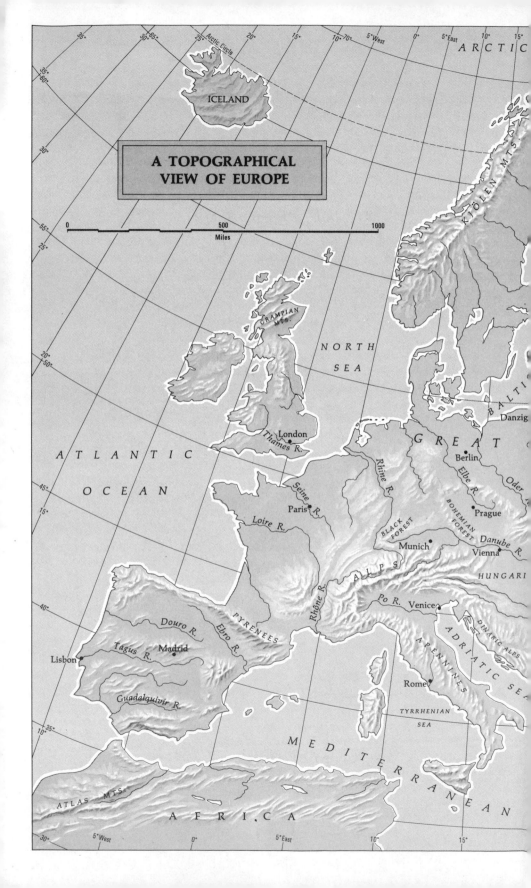

Modern Europe to 1815

PETER GAY
YALE UNIVERSITY

R. K. WEBB
AMERICAN HISTORICAL ASSOCIATION

HARPER & ROW, PUBLISHERS
New York, Evanston, San Francisco, London

Cartography by Harold K. Faye

MODERN EUROPE TO 1815
Copyright © 1973 by Harper & Row, Publishers, Inc.

STANDARD BOOK NUMBER: 06-042283-1
LIBRARY OF CONGRESS CATALOG CARD NUMBER: 72-84327

To the memory of
Richard Hofstadter

Contents

Maps

Preface

All histories are works of collaboration, and this history is a work of collaboration in three ways. It is, first, a collaboration between two authors. For fifteen years we were colleagues at Columbia University, working in allied fields with steadily converging interests. We have criticized each other's manuscripts, talked much about historical problems, and in the process have come to a considerable identity of views, if not always precisely the same conclusions, about history. We planned this book together as a whole. With some exchange of jurisdiction, we have independently drafted those sections in which our chief competence lies, but we have read and criticized our individual efforts so often and so thoroughly that the book has become a truly joint venture.

We have underscored the collaborative nature of this enterprise in a second way, by acknowledging as far as possible our obligations to other scholars. Even the author of a highly specialized monograph must lean heavily on the work of others; all the more, the authors of a general textbook go to school to many specialists. We have used our footnotes to indicate the sources of quotations in the text, and the essays on selected readings, which we have attached to each chapter, record our main debts. Most works in foreign languages have had to be omitted, even though some of them have been of first importance to us; the authors of such works must be collectively acknowledged. Still, we trust that in these ways we have told the student of history something about the nature of the craft he is engaged with. And our dedication will indicate that such a book can owe a sum beyond reckoning to a historian from an entirely different field, whose contribution is the friendship he gave us and the example—scholarly, critical, humane—he set to all of us in a generation, at Columbia and beyond.

This is a more traditional book than the one we set out to write. We have devoted a considerable amount of space to the lives of ordinary people and to popular taste and culture, but even more to the high culture of our Western past—its painting and building, its religious convictions, and its scientific achievements. This difference is to some extent owing to the still tentative stage in which social history finds itself: many of the old sources and forms are no longer quite satisfactory or convincing, and the promising new materials and techniques have not yet yielded up the results in some fields that will allow authoritative generalizations. We had to reckon as well with the insistent and proper claims of traditional political history—reigns and battles and political struggles. We have tried to turn to account the remarkable results of research in these fields in the past couple of decades, and to go, as far as possible, beyond mere narrative to analysis. We have sought synthesis, not compromise.

There has been a third collaboration, a largely invisible debate with our critics. Of those whom we know and can thank by name for their mixture of severity and encouragement, we want particularly to thank Professors John A. Garraty, Orest Ranum, and Gordon Wright, Dr. Patricia Kennedy Grimsted, and Mr. Christopher Thorne. Ruth Gay collaborated not only as a critic but as a contributor in her own right.

Peter Gay
R. K. Webb

a note on the use of this book. To permit the orderly progression of historical argument and a comprehensive view of European civilization, we have organized our chapters and subsections around relatively short spans of time. The maps are grouped together to form small atlases. And the index contains the birth and death dates of all persons mentioned in the text, as well as dates for the reigns of monarchs and popes.

Modern Europe to 1815

Prologue

Europe was made, not born. From the clashes of tribes and creeds, after waves of conquest and migration, through the coalescence of peoples and their reluctant adaptation of parochial customs to a larger pattern, there emerged in the course of the Middle Ages a single European civilization. Of all the lies that men have told about themselves, that of "racial purity" is at once the most pernicious and most absurd: European civilization was a tapestry woven from distinct ethnic, religious, and cultural strands, but none of these strands itself was pure. Europe was a mixture of mixtures.

In that tapestry, two strands predominate: the classical and the Christian. Since the Renaissance there have been fond classicists and anti-Christian polemicists who have seen the true antecedent of Europe in the classical age alone. "The Greeks were the teachers of the Romans," one of those anti-Christians, the philosophe Denis Diderot, told the Tsarina Catherine of Russia, "the Greeks and Romans have been ours."[1] In contrast, pious scholars and historians saw Europe as the product of what they called the Judaeo-Christian

---

[1] Diderot, Œuvres complètes, ed. Assézat and Tourneux (1875-1877), III, 477.

1

tradition—a set of ethical and religious beliefs grafted on to classical literature and thought. Neither of these schools does Europe full justice; indeed, both together, though closer to the truth, fail to account for the whole of Europe's making. Nineteenth-century writers like Heinrich Heine and Matthew Arnold saw Europe poised between "Hellenes and Hebrews," sometimes in collaboration, sometimes in tension, with one another. That view is useful. But it is worth reiterating that both the "Graeco-Roman" and the "Judaeo-Christian" strands of European civilization were complex mixtures. The first included the sophisticated superstitions of Alexandria quite as much as the serene classicism of Athens—astrology *and* astronomy, mysticism *and* philosophy. The second was a volatile combination of Oriental mystery religion, Jewish legalism, and Greek philosophy. Indeed, it was precisely the composite character of the classical and the Christian strains that permitted the peculiar blending of customs that made Europe: unlike as they were, each offered something to the other. In the third and fourth centuries after Christ, devout church fathers were reluctant to give up pagan classical learning (see p. 20). In the 1660s, the great Italian sculptor and architect Gian Lorenzo Bernini designed a church, piously named for Saint Mary of the Assumption, that clearly derived from the pagan Roman Pantheon—yet Bernini was a devout Roman Catholic.[2]

It is not extravagant, then, to think of European civilization as a compromise between compromises, with all the inner tensions and dissonances inescapable in such an arrangement. And, often enough, both smaller and larger compromises failed. There were times, as this book will abundantly show, when classicists and Christians felt themselves torn apart by the incompatible elements; there were times also when classicists faced Christians in sheer and uncomprehending hostility. If, by the fourteenth century, educated clerics and laymen increasingly used the name "Europe" for the culture they all shared,[3] the widespread perception that theirs was a single civilization did not inhibit deep, often lasting divisions. If the struggles of prince against prince, empire against church, class against class became, in a very real sense, family quarrels, this did not make them any less destructive. The history of Europe abounds with economic rivalry, religious persecutions, pitiless warfare. Emerging unity did not preclude diversity.

But, though diversity was often a source of trouble and suffering, it was also a source of Europe's achievement. "European civilization," the French medievalist Marc Bloch has observed, "arose and flowered, until in the end it covered the face of the earth, among those who dwelt between the Tyrrhenian, the Adriatic, the Elbe, and the Atlantic Ocean. It had no other homeland."[4] This achievement is all the more impressive in the light of the relatively scanty resources Europe had at its command. As historians have rarely failed to

---

[2] Howard Hibbard, *Bernini* (1965), 148–150. See p. 227.
[3] See Denys Hay, *Europe: The Emergence of an Idea* (Torchbook ed., 1966).
[4] Marc Bloch, *Feudal Society* (1961), I, xix.

observe, the homeland seems remarkably insignificant. Europe is a mere peninsula, attached to the vastness of Asia and today containing no more than a fifth of the population and a tenth of the land mass of the world. As Americans traveling in Europe sense immediately, Europe, geographically no larger than the United States, is an intimate theater. Trips between major cities or from one frontier to another are strikingly short. The distance from the western tip of Ireland to the Ural Mountains in Russia (commonly taken as the eastern frontier of Europe) is shorter than the distance from San Francisco to New York; the distance from Paris to Berlin or Milan to Warsaw is shorter than the distance from Denver, Colorado, to Lincoln, Nebraska. And still, severely limited in size, numbers, and resources, vulnerable for many centuries to invasions by land and sea, Europe conquered the world, and the conquerors brought their culture with them, for good and ill.

While the history of the modern world is not the history of Europe, it is the history of its Europeanization—or, to use a more comprehensive name, its Westernization. The giant powers of the late twentieth century—the United States, the Soviet Union, and China—are wholly or largely non-European in location and population, but they are wholly (or, despite all protestations, striving to become wholly) Western in their civilization. Their grandiose and terrifying power rests on scientific ideas, military technology, public administration, and styles of thinking invented or perfected in that mere peninsula. The mysterious East of romantic novels is growing less mysterious year by year. All the emerging nations of Asia and Africa, though they retain, revive, and sometimes manufacture distinctive traditions, are becoming more like one another, and more Western, in the process of modernization. The so-called "new" nations resent and often battle their old Western overlords, but they do so with Western weapons and for Western stakes: widespread literacy, high standards of living, a share in world trade and world power. Their very resistance to waning Western imperialism clothes itself in Western slogans: self-determination, nationalism, socialism. The world civilization now emerging in great travail and through repeated explosions will not be European or Western exclusively. The struggle of American blacks for self-respect and self-definition that marks the United States in our time is no mere fad; it is part of that great battle for the right to diversity that will make the world—if it does not destroy the world first—a more interesting and more companionable place than it has ever been. But even in this historic moment, Europe—the West—continues to play a part far greater than its share in land, people, or resources. Europe may be in political decline; ironically, the ever more insistent call for its political unification is a consequence of that decline. But the historical importance of Europe remains unimpaired. It made us—even non-Europeans—what we are today.

Introduction:
The Making of Europe

THE GREEK ACHIEVEMENT

The Greek "Miracle"

The first, and in many respects the finest, exemplars of the mixture that Europe would become were the Greeks. Our enthusiastic, often exclusive preoccupation with the "Greek miracle" is understandable but unjustified. For several thousand years before Homer—the first European immortal—composed or collected the *Iliad* and the *Odyssey*[1] non-European peoples had constructed complex civilizations. Well before 3000 B.C., the Sumerians had mastered the art of cultivating the soil by tapping the waters of the Euphrates. They founded

---

[1] Disputes about the identity of Homer go back to the Alexandrian period, but it was not until 1795, when the German classical philologist Friedrich August Wolf published his *Prolegomena ad Homerum,* that the theory of the multiple authorship of these two epics first gained wide currency. Today scholars agree that there was a single poet named Homer who lived before A.D. 700 and who incorporated into his imperishable poems a number of traditional elements.

walled cities and erected looming temples, introduced the division of labor and an esoteric form of writing. Their successors in the Mesopotamian river valley complicated the political institutions they had inherited, developed higher mathematics, made astronomical observations, and in the Babylonian era—a thousand years before Homer—codified their laws. Their celebrated epic, the *Gilgamesh*, though dominated by myths and strewn with prodigies, offers philosophical reflections on human mortality; the code of Hammurabi shows, by its provisions, that the Babylonians had by this time established a fairly sophisticated and well-defined class system, ranging from slaves to commoners to aristocrats.

Egyptian civilization, which emerged at about the same time, was quite as advanced. Visiting Egypt about 450 B.c., Herodotus shrewdly perceived the country's gravest problem and greatest victory when, in a famous epigram, he called Egypt "the gift of the Nile." The taming of the Nile by irrigation made Egyptian civilization possible, and it was an impressive civilization. In the first dynasties, before 2500 B.c., Egyptians had invented (or perhaps borrowed) a system of writing, devised a relatively reliable calendar, formulated an elaborate set of myths to account for natural events and political rulership, and developed a characteristic style of art. The most imposing of their pyramids—those solemn, seemingly immortal stone monuments rising from the desert sands to celebrate and commemorate the dead—date from the third millennium B.c. They are a triumph of technology: "The Great Pyramid," in particular, the Egyptologist John A. Wilson writes, "is a tremendous mass of stone finished with the most delicate precision. Here were six and a quarter million tons of stone, with casing blocks averaging as much as two and a half tons each; yet those casing blocks were dressed and fitted with a joint of one-fiftieth of an inch—a scrupulous nicety worthy of the jeweler's craft. Here the margin of error in the squareness of the north and south sides was 0.09 per cent and of the east and west sides, 0.03 per cent. This mighty mass of stone was set upon a dressed-rock pavement which, from opposite corners, had a deviation from a true plane of only 0.004 per cent."[2] One need not admire the theology that inspired or the slave system that built the pyramids to recognize the organization and skill required to sustain such an enterprise.

Yet, interesting and impressive as these early civilizations are, their influence on the making of Europe was indirect, largely through the Greeks. These civilizations were, by and large, static; their thinking was wholly dominated by myth; their world was governed by the gods, capricious and demanding deities who needed to be appeased and could never be understood. Whatever science the Egyptians or Babylonians developed was practical, devised to aid in the measurement of land or the celebration of religious ritual. These people reasoned, but their reasoning was, as it were, intransitive; it led nowhere beyond itself. The Greeks were different; the Greeks, in a phrase, invented critical thinking.

[2] John Albert Wilson, *The Burden of Egypt* (1951), 54–55.

To speak in this summary fashion is to invite two misunderstandings. By the time the Greeks had emerged into the classical period—that great epoch of versatile and intense productivity that was to become an object of awe and idealization to modern Europeans—they had experienced a long history of invasions and migrations, of dark ages and renaissances: the Greeks of the sixth and fifth centuries B.C. were an old and thoroughly mixed people. And they did not leap into civilization unaided: the Greek miracle was not a miracle. As they were not reluctant to acknowledge, the Greeks borrowed heavily from their neighbors: artistic motifs and medical learning from the Egyptians, mathematics and astronomy from the Babylonians, the alphabet from the seafaring Phoenicians. What mattered was that they transformed what they borrowed and made it their own.

The precise process of this transformation is obscure, but its meaning for history is decisive; the invention of critical thinking changed the face of the world as profoundly as the mastery over fire and the emergence of writing. Literally, of course, critical thinking was not a deliberate invention; nor was it the monopoly of one man or even of a school. But it came, when it did come, with such stunning rapidity and with such an avalanche of consequences that we can see why the ancients should honor one man, Thales, with the enviable title, Father of Philosophy. Early in the sixth century B.C., Thales of Miletus dared to inquire into the nature of the universe. He thought the world was made up of water; his successors—like Thales, Greeks living on the Ionian islands or on the west coast of Asia Minor—asked the same question Thales had asked and arrived at different theories: Anaximander taught that the universe was composed of opposing elements; Anaximenes, that its basic element was air. These theories, in some degree dependent on Egyptian and Babylonian myths, matter less than the mental set that made the inquiry possible. No Egyptian, no Babylonian, however intelligent or independent, would have enjoyed the mental freedom that allowed escape from the overwhelming weight of his creation myths. Thales' question was a revolution in men's ways of thinking simply because it dared to be a question that had no predetermined answer. Instead of humbly accepting authoritative and tradition-hallowed oracular or priestly pronouncements, the Greeks embarked on a restless search for new knowledge. This search meant an unsparing criticism of accepted stories and implied a new confidence in human powers.

The revolution, as we have seen, came quickly. Thales is said to have predicted the eclipse of the sun in 585 B.C.; Aristotle, the last of the Greek philosophers of the classical age, died in 322 B.C. In these two-and-a-half centuries—a mere moment in time even in the brief history of civilization—the Greeks had laid the foundations not merely of philosophy, but of history, biology, and anatomy, and had enormously advanced the study of geography, mathematics, and astronomy. The names of these modern disciplines, and of others like aesthetics, logic, and metaphysics, are tributes to these pioneers of the mind: they are all Greek words.

This unprecedented and unrepeated explosion of knowledge had a single root: the organization of curiosity into methodical, fearless, often self-corrective inquiry. Nothing, not even a god, was safe from the questioning spirit of the Greeks; while earlier and elsewhere the learned classes had bent their best efforts to celebrate their kings, worship their divinities, and keep their knowledge hidden, the Greeks were ready to criticize all existing forms of government, to attribute the origin of religion to human invention, and thus to make man, rather than the gods, the measure of all things. The two most celebrated Greek philosophers, Plato and Aristotle, were in a sense latecomers; much of their work was a reply to their predecessors. Yet, of course, they matter most to the historian of modern Europe, for their writings, often in fragmentary form, exercised a powerful and almost continuous influence on Western thought. Alfred North Whitehead's oft-repeated remark that all philosophy is a series of footnotes to Plato is an exaggeration that contains a significant kernel of truth. Indeed, a survey of those among Plato's and Aristotle's writings that have come down to us gives a good idea of the comprehensive inquiry into man and nature that the Greeks initiated: politics, ethics, logic, theology, aesthetics, the nature of life and the meaning of death, and perhaps most important, the very nature of thinking itself.

While it would be impossible to expound the philosophical work of Plato and Aristotle in a few paragraphs, even a brief summary will suggest its overwhelming importance for all subsequent European thought. Plato was born in 428 B.C., near the end of the Golden Age of Greek culture, and studied with Socrates, the great gadfly of official Greek philosophy. We shall never know what, if anything, Socrates wrote; we shall never even be sure just what he was like: the descriptions of him that have survived vary enormously. Plato's account is merely the most famous and the most favorable. Socrates' method was ironic questioning; he troubled the souls of complacent thinkers by showing them to be more ignorant than they had thought they were—more ignorant, certainly, than Socrates, who went about proclaiming his ignorance. Plato adopted this technique of clarifying areas of knowledge and ignorance by persistent questioning and of rising inductively to valid generalizations—the dialectic, the Greeks called it—as his literary and dramatic style: all his works are dialogues, and many of these dialogues use Socrates as their witty, eloquent, and always triumphant protagonist. Not surprisingly, Socrates made himself very unpopular, and in 399 B.C. at the age of seventy, he was sentenced to death for blasphemy and for corrupting the youth of Athens. Plato's account of his trial and his courageous death, the *Apology* and the *Phaedo,* both extraordinarily moving works, gave Socrates immortality and transmitted his reputation to Europe as the first martyr to philosophy.[3]

---

[3] In the Enlightenment, Condorcet, in his essay on progress, called the conviction of Socrates "the first crime announcing the war between philosophy and superstition, which still continues today." See Peter Gay, *The Enlightenment: An Interpretation,* vol. I, *The Rise of Modern Paganism* (1966), 82.

While Plato immortalized Socrates and imitated his irony, in other respects he departed from his master: Socrates had turned his attention to the nature of man and the need to understand right conduct; he had been skeptical and even derisive about the ambitious scientific inquiries typical of Greek philosophy in the Golden Age. Plato, on the other hand, inquired into everything. After the death of Socrates, he traveled widely; when he returned to Athens around 387 B.C., he founded a school, the Academy, and wrote works on a wide variety of subjects, including the theory of knowledge, love and friendship, art, ethics, and politics. His great speculative dialogue, the *Timaeus,* which attempts to explain the nature of the universe, ventures into territory Socrates would have disdained to enter. But Plato's most famous dialogue is the *Republic,* which defines an ideal commonwealth in which the able—the philosopher-kings— rule, the brave fight, and the masses of men work and obey.

Plato died in 347 B.C.; he lived long enough to have as his pupil the other great philosopher of the age, Aristotle. Teacher and student have often been contrasted; in fact, much of Europe's intellectual history can be written as a combat between the disciples of Plato and the disciples of Aristotle. But in fact there was more of Plato in Aristotle than later partisans would admit. Their difference was mainly one of mental style. Plato was the poet of philosophy; his dialogues would delight even those who did not fully understand them. He was the playful explorer. Aristotle was more sober, more patient, more prosaic: he was interested in ordering and classifying available knowledge and in establishing conclusions soundly based on factual inquiry. A comparison of his main political work, the *Politics,* with its platonic counterpart, the *Republic,* is instructive: the *Republic* is a bold inquiry into fundamental principles that does not hesitate to use the state and its hierarchical organization as a grand metaphor for the divisions in man's soul; the *Politics,* in contrast, offers carefully differentiated definitions of forms of government derived from a thorough inquiry into the constitutions under which the one hundred and fifty odd Greek city-states lived. But Aristotle, the father of empiricism, was something better than a compiler; his speculations on general principles, the *Metaphysics* (that which lies beyond physics), his writings on biology, on morals, on aesthetics, were as imaginative as they were fact-bound. Plato and Aristotle were indeed latecomers: both thought the world of the city-state to be the ideal, indeed the only possible, world, and this at a time when the city-state was already fading. Aristotle was born in 384 B.C. and lived long enough—to 322—to become tutor to Alexander of Macedon, the prince who would in fact make the world of Aristotle's *Politics* impossible (see p. 12). Yet Plato and Aristotle display not merely the limited vision, but also the vast achievements, of the Greek intellectual revolution.

The historical writings of the Greeks offer added evidence for the profundity and originality of that revolution. Neither the Babylonians nor the Egyptians had developed true history; they had feasted off conventional tales about superhuman kings and active deities, tales uncritically accepted and endlessly retold.[4] The Greeks changed this in its essence. Down to early modern times, those pious Christians who accepted the Bible as literally true celebrated Moses as the first historian. More properly this title belongs to Herodotus, an inquisitive traveler and accomplished geographer, who late in the fifth century B.C. recorded the great clash between the Greeks and the Persians that had taken place a few decades before; with his insatiable curiosity and love of anecdote, Herodotus put down some improbable tales, but his history remains the first coherent and critical report on the past we possess. Only a few years later Thucydides, a cool, masterly analyst of men and events, wrote the history of the internecine war between Sparta and Athens in which he had served; his book remains a model of political history, with man at the center of the stage. It has been suggested that Thucydides borrowed some of his devices from the Greek theater, but he remains a true historian, writing in obedience to the events he has investigated and, in part, experienced.

The Greek elevation of man did not mean the one-sided celebration of man's most distinctive characteristic—his reason—or of his most exalted quality—his heroism. Nineteenth-century scholars, persistent and learned but often genteel, fabricated a sunny Greece, serene, rational, measured in its politics, its art, its ethics. They knew—how could they avoid it?—that the Greek tragedies we have[5] deal with incest, murder, and pitiless divine revenge, but they interpreted these searing plays as appeals to *sophrosyne*—the splendid classical Greek ideal of wholeness, balance, temperance. So they were, but Greek classicism was not cold, remote, dispassionate. On the contrary, it was the hard-won victory over pain and disillusionment and the recognition of man's limitations; it was passionate.[6] What is more, the loftiness of the Greek theater and of Greek speculation in general was punctuated and relieved by irreverence and ribaldry. The tragedies were accompanied by performances of satyr plays filled with scatological language and barracks humor. The Greeks who emerge from the scholarship of our day retain their value as guides to civilized ideals of rationality and moderation, but they are less serene, more earthy, than they had seemed in Victorian dress. And they are also more human and more comprehensible.

The political history of Greece after it emerged from its dark age in the eighth century B.C. accords well with this realistic portrait. The characteristic

---

[4] The ancient Hebrews, on the other hand, were profoundly concerned with history; their very religion is a historical religion. God created the world at a certain moment; the experiences of the Chosen People took place in historical time and receive historical treatment in the sacred records; the Jewish prophets never tire of reminding their people of that history and its lessons. On the other hand, this passion for the past—*their* past—was accompanied by many of the characteristics that marked the mythical thinking of the Hebrews' neighbors: acceptance of conflicting stories, reliance on creation myths, appeal to God as chief actor and cause in history.

[5] The losses are stunning: we have only 7 plays of Aeschylus, although he wrote more than 80; only 7 plays by Sophocles, although he is credited with more than 120; only 19 plays of Euripides, although more than 90 are attributed to him.

[6] This view is now gaining wide acceptance; it informs such a popularization as H. D. F. Kitto's *The Greeks* (rev. ed., 1957).

political unit, the *polis,* dotted the Greek peninsula and was reproduced wherever the Greeks established their colonies.[7] The *polis* might have been the protagonist in one of their tragedies: a noble creature doomed to final disaster by its fatal flaw, a great success ending in a dismal failure.[8] Not merely for classical scholars later, but for its own contemporaries, the *polis* was far more than a political entity. It was a comprehensive community that demanded and deserved men's utmost loyalty; it was the fount of law, the guarantor of social order, the repository of political ideals. This is the meaning of Aristotle's famous definition of man as a *zoon politikon*: man is a being whose nature it is to live in a *polis.* But which *polis?* Like political theorists in later centuries, so the Greeks wavered between two possibilities represented by the two most powerful among their city-states, Sparta and Athens. Sparta, a tight-lipped dictatorship with no nonsense about art and with a passionate devotion to military discipline, came to stand for order; Athens, with its "democracy"[9] and its brilliant cultural life, came to stand for freedom. Those who would later rhapsodize over "the glory that was Greece," normally had the Athens of the fourth century B.C. in mind; it was then that Aeschylus, Sophocles, and Euripides poured out their tragedies; Aristophanes rudely ridiculed what was most sacred; Socrates incensed his fellow citizens with his uncomfortable and unanswerable questions; Phidias sculpted and helped to decorate that newly risen temple, the Parthenon.

Yet the passion that had made the *polis* great—local patriotism—also encompassed its downfall. Early in the fifth century B.C. Greeks had transcended parochial loyalties to beat back a massive Persian invasion; Spartans and Athenians alike had distinguished themselves with brave sacrificial deaths and ingenious naval strategies. But with the threat gone, Sparta and Athens turned on each other in a prolonged and exhausting conflict; the Peloponnesian War ended in 404 B.C. with the total defeat of Athens and with the Greek political structure in danger. Sparta's attempt to play an imperial role in Greece proved a failure, as did all attempts at union in the face of renewed Persian threats, of Rome rising in the west, and of Macedonia in the north. Through much of the fourth century, internecine warfare continued. Thus, by the 340s, Philip II of Macedonia found the Greeks easy prey for his shrewd policy of diplomacy, bribery, war—and patience. By 336 B.C., the year of his death, Philip was master

---

[7] Almost as soon as they entered the light of history, Greek states sent out energetic sailors to western Asia Minor, to the Black Sea, to Sicily and the tip of the Italian boot, and to what is today southern France. Wherever they went they built a *polis:* Syracuse was a *polis* founded about 734 B.C.; Massilia (which we know under the name of Marseilles) was a *polis* founded about 600 B.C. Self-confidence and imperialism, it seems, went hand in hand.

[8] The development of these "city-states" (as we translate that resonant Greek word, *polis,* a little lamely) differed greatly. Most of them began under the rule of tight aristocratic clans and then, in the seventh and sixth centuries, underwent periods of civil strife as the traditional rulers were challenged by popular leaders, the "tyrants."

[9] It hardly needs pointing out that this antique form of popular rule is quite different from our modern ideal: it excluded resident foreigners, women, and slaves—although the Athenians' relatively decent treatment of their slave population astounded and dismayed the Spartans.

of Greece. Alexander, his son and successor, continued and expanded his father's work. The age of the *polis* was over.

The Alexandrian Bridge

After more than two thousand years, Alexander remains an enigma. He was quick, energetic, inordinately ambitious—that much is clear. But was his imagination that of a historic leader or a mere adventurer, his cosmopolitanism the product of ecumenical thinking or simply a love of Oriental luxury?— these remain a matter for controversy. In a series of swift and brilliant campaigns, he defeated the powerful Persians decisively; by 327 B.C. he was at the gates of India. The pupil of Aristotle and the son of a king who, though a "barbarian," had deeply loved Greek culture, Alexander extended the reach of that culture through the scores of encampments and cities, including Alexandria, that he founded all across his vast, if ephemeral, empire. As he extended the sway of Greek civilization, he also diluted its quality. This cosmopolitanism had two faces: it meant not solely the export of one culture, but also the importation of others. And this was to be the quality, too, of the Hellenistic Age that began with Alexander: it was cosmopolitan and eclectic. Yet the age was also a bridge of transmission; much of what later came to be hailed as classical—like the Pergamum Altar or the Laocoön statue—were products of this autumn of Greek civilization.

Alexander died in 323, and with his early death the inevitable happened: lesser men struggled over the great empire that the Conqueror had left behind. After much confused and bloody squabbling for the spoils, three sizable dynasties emerged: the Ptolemies in Egypt, the Seleucids in Asia Minor, the Antigonids in Macedonia. Alexandria stood out as a center of culture with its great libraries and museum, but Athens and Rhodes, too, had schools of rhetoric and philosophy where ambitious barbarians went to polish their manners and expand their knowledge. Hellenistic culture, which dates roughly from the death of Alexander in 323 B.C. to the Roman conquest of the Mediterranean around 150 B.C., was wide if not deep, subtle if not original. In Alexandria especially, urban and urbane poets wrote pastorals proclaiming the virtues of the simple bucolic life they professed to miss but did their utmost to avoid; scholars perfected textual and literary criticism, collected vast libraries, and quarreled over the Greek classics in poetry and drama. It was an age of editors, of commentators, of disciples. Even today the word "Alexandrian" conjures up the precious, the overripe, the slightly tired.

Yet the Hellenistic Age was also a flowering. In the sixth century B.C., Pythagoras and his disciples had developed a mystery cult around mathematics and made some fruitful guesses about numbers; in the fifth century, Leucippus and Democritus had speculated on the atomic constitution of matter. Their tentative but pioneering ideas were carried further by Hellenistic scientists: between 300 and 200 B.C., Euclid laid the foundations of geometry with his immortal *Elements;* Aristarchus of Samos argued that the earth revolves around the sun; Eratosthenes mapped the earth using longitudinal and latitudinal lines and calculated its size with astounding accuracy; Apollonius of Perga studied conic sections and invented such indispensable mathematical terms as ellipse and parabola; and Archimedes of Syracuse discovered specific gravity—hardly an unimpressive list of accomplishments. Of equal importance for posterity— indeed, of particular importance to European civilization in the sixteenth and seventeenth centuries, those centuries of profound intellectual readjustment— were the philosophers of the Hellenistic Age, chief among them the Stoics and the Epicureans.

Stoicism and Epicureanism have been extensively misunderstood. The Stoics were not merely "stoical"; the Epicureans rarely "epicurean." Appropriately enough, both philosophies originated in Athens: Zeno of Cyprus, the founder of Stoicism, came to Athens around 314 B.C.; Epicurus of Samos arrived there about a decade later. The Greek Stoics developed a comprehensive system in which nature and man, physics and ethics, found their appointed places. God is the animating force, the reason, of the universe. He governs the world through comprehensible and unalterable natural laws; and men, who hold in themselves a bit of the divine flame, have the supreme obligation to understand the divine legislation and obey it: "Live according to nature" was the Stoics' central injunction. In this way, they argued, man would gain mastery over his life by gaining mastery over himself. To live according to nature meant to desire only what could be obtained, to regret nothing that was inaccessible, to face pain and loss with courage and resignation, above all, to conquer the fear of death—that was the Stoics' way to man's freedom. The Epicureans, like the Stoics the disciples of the Greek atomists, expressed similar ideas in rather different language. To Epicurus, the aim of life was happiness, but happiness consisted not in swinish self-indulgence and drunken sensuality: that notion was imposed on the Epicureans later by their enemies. The most desirable state was the absence of pain, *ataraxia*—serenity, a kind of sublime indifference to external discomforts or internal turmoil. And Epicurus, whatever others might later charge, exalted the pleasures of the mind over the pleasures of the body.

Stoicism, Epicureanism, and an associated school, Pyrrhonist skepticism,[10] were landmarks in the history of European thought. But they were also symptoms of a society growing weary of the burdens of survival. Plato and Aristotle had thought man's participation in his *polis* his highest duty; the Stoics, the Epicureans, and the Skeptics, living in vast, impersonal empires in which the individual was so obviously without political influence of any sort, taught that man's highest good lies in withdrawal—escape from the world into oneself. Plato and Aristotle had taught men to act; the Hellenistic schools taught them to endure. A civilization dominated by such systematic passivity sooner or later was bound to fall to the energetic, self-confident barbarians at the gate. They were the Romans.

[10] It derives its name from Pyrrho of Elis, contemporary of Zeno and Epicurus, who taught that nothing can be known with certainty and that the only sensible position man can adopt is one of suspended judgment.

ROME: CLASSICS AND CHRISTIANS

The Republic

The Romans were a surprising people who left the modern world a vast legacy. A tribe of peasants and soldiers given to costly civil wars, energetically devoted to imperial expansion, addicted to blood sports, they turned, in their peaceful years, to administration and the law. Our debt to their political arrangements and legal doctrines is obvious. Words we use every day—senator, censor, dictator, empire—are reminders of what the Romans did best. But this is not all: supremely unoriginal in the arts, literature, and science, the Romans were at the same time remarkably willing to learn. Horace put the situation candidly: *"Graecia capta ferum victorem cepit et artes intulit agresti Latio*—Captive Greece captured her savage conqueror and brought the arts to the rustic Latins."[11] The Greeks, of course, had made their varied contributions to literature and science in Greek, and Greek became the obligatory second language of every civilized Roman for centuries after Greek power had been permanently broken. But the Greek heritage survived into the Middle Ages and into modern times mainly in Latin guise. The Greeks had invented rhetoric, but it was Cicero's treatises on rhetoric, little better than compilations of what he had learned from his Greek teachers, that survived—and these treatises were in Latin. Similarly, the first great "Roman" historian was Polybius, a Greek hostage living in Rome. He wrote in Greek, but the subject of his history was Rome's greatness. Once again, in the transmission of an incalculable and invaluable cultural heritage, Europe proved itself a mixture.

The Romans were latecomers among the nations of the Mediterranean. The Italian peninsula had been settled by Indo-European tribes from the Alps and the Danube Valley around 2000 B.C.; their settlements were eclipsed by the appearance of the mysterious Etruscans, probably transplanted from Asia Minor, before 800 B.C. The Romans themselves later dated the founding of their city in 753 B.C., but this, like much else of their early history, is legend: there is evidence that the city of Rome was populated by about 1000 B.C. At first, it seems, the city was governed by Etruscan kings, but then, around 500 or perhaps later (tradition, with characteristic false precision, says 509 B.C.) the Romans rose, expelled their kings, and founded a republic.

The history of the Roman Republic is the history of expansion abroad and class struggle at home. The two, of course, were related: the need for large

---

[11] Epistles II, 1, 156–157. For Horace, see p. 16.

standing armies, for officials and colonists for the conquered territories, put a premium on the kind of leadership the patrician landowners seemed best equipped to provide and checked all possibility of experimenting with democracy. The expansion of Rome from city-state to world power proceeded first slowly, then rapidly; inexorably, the Roman legions subdued the Italian peninsula, the Mediterranean islands, Spain, Greece, then North Africa and Asia Minor, and later, Gaul, southern Britain, and central Europe. By the end of the Pyrrhic Wars in 272 B.c., Rome controlled all of Italy; beginning in 264, with the first Punic War, Rome turned against its great Mediterranean rival, the North African city of Carthage. It took more than a century and three major wars before Carthage was reduced; in 218 B.c. the Carthaginian general Hannibal even succeeded briefly in invading Italy with his elephants. But in 146 it was all over; Carthage was defeated and the city razed to the ground. In the same year, Macedonia became a Roman province.

None of these triumphs brought social peace; on the contrary. At the beginning, the Roman Republic was an oligarchy of patrician families who drew their power from their ownership of land. These landowners had a monopoly of membership in the senate and over its two chief executives, the consuls. Gradually the small farmers, the plebeians, organized themselves, won access to the senate; they made their voice heard as well through their own assembly and their elected representatives, the tribunes of the people. But the centuries of war, in which the plebeians served in the army, reduced their grip on the machinery of government; when they came home from service, they found their farms devastated by campaigns or neglected through their absence, while the patricians, already rich, had grown richer. Class distances grew wider, and the oligarchs consolidated their hold. of the 200 consuls who served Rome between 233 and 133 B.c., 159 came from 20 senatorial families. [12] The self-centeredness and unmitigated greed of the patricians reduced many of the Roman farmers to poverty-stricken tenants or serfs, or brought them to the cities as rootless proletarians. Slavery was widespread; it became the favorite method of recruiting domestic servants and menial laborers on city and farm. In 136 B.c. and again in 101, slaves rose in Sicily, but both rebellions were put down with barbaric severity. And beginning with 133, endemic urban and rural unrest brought social experiments, demagoguery, conspiracies, and for the first time, assassination as an instrument of politics. The brothers Gracchi, who attempted to redress the social balance by a radical redistribution of land, both died violent deaths: Tiberius Gracchus was killed in 133 B.c., Gaius Gracchus in 122 B.c. And Julius Caesar—skillful general, shrewd author, superb politician, a poor but enormously ambitious patrician who had conquered Gaul and invaded Britain—was assassinated in 44 B.c., while he exercised dictatorial control over the dying republic. When in 31 B.c. Octavianus took supreme power, he ended more than a century of civil strife.

[12] Tom B. Jones, *Ancient Civilization* (1960), 347.

The Empire

Caesar Augustus (to give him the name by which Octavianus is best known to history) created an empire in the name of preserving the republic. His long and peaceful reign, which lasted from 31 B.C. to A.D. 14, was a golden age of political calm and literary excellence, and it has come to be known as the Augustan Age with much justice. Every part of Rome's history would continue to dominate man's imagination into modern times: "Rome," wrote Gibbon at the end of the eighteenth century, "is familiar to the schoolboy and the statesman." Tales of the early, legendary kings; the powerful evocation of nature and diatribe against superstition, *De rerum natura,* by the Epicurean poet Lucretius, who died in 55 B.C.; the speeches, letters, the philosophical and rhetorical treatises of Cicero, who was regarded, down to the nineteenth century, as one of the greatest writers of all time—these relics, and others, were the staples on which every educated European could draw with ease. But it was the Augustan Age that furnished posterity with the richest food. This was the time of Vergil, who idealized rural life in his *Eclogues,* gave a more realistic though equally poetic portrayal of that life in his *Georgics,* and created a national, deliberately patriotic epic, the *Aeneid,* about the mythical founder of Rome, which many cultivated readers for many centuries thought greater than Homer's *Iliad.* It was the time of Ovid, who raised erotic poetry to a new high level of wit and grace, and of Horace, the self-confessed Epicurean whose brilliant odes, satires, and epistles celebrate the middle way, the life of good sense and calm enjoyment. And it was the time of Livy, historian and propagandist, whose history of Rome incorporated and immortalized the most fascinating legends surrounding Rome's origins.

Perhaps the greatest work of art the Augustan Age produced was Caesar Augustus himself, coupled with his empire and the peace he began to force on a Mediterranean world gradually being Romanized, the *pax Romana.* Wily, supple, more eager to have the substance of power than its trappings, Augustus set the direction for a unified empire that would last, through many vicissitudes, as a political reality down to the fifth century, and as a dream, a myth, an ideal, down to 1806, when it was finally dispatched by another shrewd man of power, Napoleon Bonaparte (see p. 514). How solidly Augustus had built became evident in the decades after his death: his successors, who included such bizarre psychotics as Caligula and Nero, were so insecure on the imperial throne that they spent more energy despatching their enemies—real or imagined—than governing their state; yet Rome flourished. Around 100, Tacitus, the last of the great classical historians, recorded the antics of these emperors in his powerful, austerely eloquent *Annals* and *Histories.* In the second century after Christ, strictly speaking between 96 and 180, the empire was governed by a succession of five "good emperors"—Nerva, Trajan, Hadrian, Antoninus Pius, and Marcus Aurelius—honest administrators, good soldiers, patrons of the arts, and (for Romans) humane men. In their time the empire reached its greatest extent, the provinces were increasingly brought under the control of Roman law, confidence in the state gradually returned as reigns of terror ceased, and Roman civilization experienced a second flowering. It was a Silver Age, generally thought inferior to the Golden Age that had flourished under Augustus, yet not without merit of its own. But after 180, with the death of Marcus Aurelius, the Stoic on the throne, and the accession of his son, Commodus, these splendid years rapidly came to seem a mere interlude. The third century saw the precipitous decline of Roman civilization and the decisive degeneration of Roman politics. As mystery cults from all over the empire competed for the languid attention of the rich and the passionate devotion of the soldiers, the state itself became more and more an affair of naked force. The army, itself increasingly barbarized, ruled through its chosen vessel, the emperor, whose tenure was precarious and whose life expectancy was short. The year 476 when the barbarian invader Odoacer deposed Romulus Augustulus, the last Roman emperor of the West, is often taken as the end of the empire. But it is no more than a convenient date. On the one hand, the event only confirmed what Romans had long anticipated; and on the other hand, the barbarians embraced much of the Roman civilization. Roman law, the most enduring heritage that the Romans left the European world (see p. 26), went underground in the West but remained a powerful shaping force for the thinking of lawyers, ecclesiastics, and statesmen for many centuries. Even the religion that was to dominate the history of Europe for over a thousand years—presumably worldly and pagan Rome's most implacable enemy—anchored its most influential branch in Rome and spoke, and disseminated, the language of the Romans. Greece, Horace had observed, had conquered Rome, her conqueror. Rome, in turn, would conquer *its* conquerors, and civilize them.

The Origins of Christianity

Probably the least heralded yet most portentous event in the reign of Caesar Augustus was the birth of Christianity. Its founder, Jesus, was born in or before 4 B.C., in the Roman province of Palestine, where he acquired a devoted following with his popular preaching, his bold defiance of religious dignitaries, and reports of his miraculous powers. Like all great innovators, Jesus was a profound threat to established institutions, and his claim to more than human stature opened him to the charge of blasphemy. Around A.D. 30 he was crucified by the Roman authorities. A cult rapidly grew around his sayings, his miracles, and his death. The Jews—of whom Jesus was one—taught that a Messiah, a savior, would come; Jesus proclaimed himself that Messiah and his disciples accepted and propagated his word. From just another Jewish sect the doctrine woven around Jesus, the Christ, [13] developed into a new religion. Like European

---

[13] The name *Jesus* is the Greek version of the Hebrew name Joshua, which means "savior"; the name *Christ* is also Greek, a translation of the Hebrew word *Messiah*, which means "anointed."

civilization Christianity was a gathering of many strands, and its doctrines did not arise ready-made, but developed through several centuries.

The first, in many ways the most important, of these strands was Judaism. Not Jesus alone, but Paul, the organizer and codifier of primitive Christianity, and the other early Christians were Jews. A small nomadic tribe that had finally settled in Palestine in the thirteenth century B.C., the ancient Hebrews had experienced military defeats and long exile, lived in republics and monarchies, built temples and a striking religious system. Indeed, what gives the Hebrews world-historical importance is their religion, which was unique in antiquity: unlike all others, Judaism was monotheistic, legalistic, and historical. According to Jewish teaching, there was one God, who had made a covenant with his people—the Hebrews—and was jealous of their flirtations with other gods. He had created the world and would intervene in the historical process to reward or punish the Jews, to lay down their laws and enforce their obedience. By the time of Jesus, the Jews had developed a sizable historical and legal literature that recorded God's work, the history of the Jewish people, and the hundreds of rules governing diet and prayer and marriage and hospitality by which the Jews obsessively thought themselves bound. Not all was harmony; Jesus' vehement outbursts against the "scribes and Pharisees" were, at least in his mind and the minds of his followers, the rebellion of authentic religion against a legalism that reduced religion to the scrupulous observation of sacred rules. "The letter killeth," St. Paul said, "the spirit giveth life." Yet despite this quarrel (which was, after all, a quarrel within the Jewish family), Christianity as it emerged retained much of the Jewish tradition and of Jewish doctrine. Despite attempts by zealous radical Christians to uproot all Jewish teachings, Christianity would retain the Jewish books of the Bible as divinely inspired authority, and thus the Jewish account of a single God-Father, of his creation, and of his historic work; Christians would come to read much of the Old Testament, especially the Song of Solomon and the sayings of the major prophets, as prefigurations of their own dispensation. The ironic spectacle of Christians despising and persecuting Jews, to whom they owed so much, including their Savior, began fairly early in the history of Christianity. "When I see Christians, cursing Jews," Voltaire wrote in the eighteenth century, "me thinks I see children beating their fathers." [14]

Gradually, Christianity grew beyond the Jewish community. It was Paul, a Jew dramatically converted to Christianity not long after the death of Jesus, who became the first and most significant apostle to the gentiles. On numerous missionary voyages and in eloquent epistles he expounded the new faith and insisted on its universality. When around A.D. 50 the original followers of Jesus met to decide whether all Christians should be circumcised—that is, to profess themselves a Jewish sect—Paul vehemently opposed this policy and carried the day. His voluminous writings soon became, and have remained, a fertile source for Christian doctrine. By the second century, the age of the good Roman

[14] In English, in *Notebooks,* 2 vols., ed. Theodore Besterman (1952), I, 31.

emperors, Christians had formed rudimentary religious communities comprehending laymen and priest, the outlines of a creed and of a sacred service. Jesus' sayings, treasured by his disciples, had made no distinction between rich and poor; if anything, Jesus was more skeptical about the former than about the latter. The first gentile Christians, therefore, were among the deprived, the dispossessed, those to whom the material and cultural glories of the Roman Empire meant little. Then, repelled by the confusing welter of religious fanaticisms, Oriental superstitions, and philosophical nostrums that crowded the empire, a number of educated Romans found the new doctrine more convincing and more consoling than all the others.

Christianity had a concrete and fascinating tale to tell, which explained everything from the creation of the world to its end. The central tale, the martyrdom of Jesus, the Son of God, incarnated among men to take away their sins with his sacrifice and to bring love and the promise of eternal salvation, had an irresistible attraction. While Christian clerics anathematized one another on fine points of doctrine, their sect acquired converts, first among the lower orders, then among the educated. The Roman authorities, annoyed by Christian exclusiveness, subjected the new and growing sect to intermittent persecutions. These persecutions, which reached their peak at the end of the third century under the Emperor Diocletian, were severe enough to give the Christians martyrs to celebrate, not severe enough to inhibit their progress among the imperial population. Early in the fourth century, almost certainly in 312, Christianity won its most important convert: the Emperor Constantine himself. The future of Christianity was assured: in 325, Constantine called an unprecedented ecumenical council at Nicaea, which settled disputed questions of Christian doctrine; in 330, on the site of the ancient city of Byzantium, he dedicated a new city in the eastern part of his empire, Constantinople, to the Virgin Mary. Christianity became the favored religion, and by the fifth century the only religion, of the Roman Empire. The old tolerant attitude that had marked the pagan empire was gone: the upholders of Christian doctrine were nothing less than doctrinaire. In earlier days, the devotee of one religion was content to regard the devotee of another as a benighted outsider; with the ascendancy of Christianity there came a new spirit: the unbeliever was a sinner, to be reproved, corrected, and if necessary, eliminated. This was the price of universality.

The first centuries of Christianity were marked by continuous squabbles over church organization and religious doctrine. This is not surprising. At the heart of Christianity lay a dogma that the Christians themselves announced to be absurd: the Trinity. Against the vehement objections of an articulate minority, the Arians,[15] the Council of Nicaea had laid it down that Jesus, the

---

[15] The most controversial issue animating and exacerbating early debates among Christians was the nature of Jesus. The Arians, named after their founder, the Libyan theologian Arius (ca. 256–336), held that Jesus was the Son and creature of God the Father, neither eternal nor equal in substance with his creator. Arianism was widely popular among the German tribes invading the Roman Empire (see p. 22) and after its condemnation, went underground in Catholic Christendom.

Son of God, was consubstantial with His Father, and thus an equal partner in the Trinity which included as its third component the Holy Spirit. These three components of the Trinity were miraculously separate and united at the same time: three in one. This was to become the orthodox doctrine. Nor is this all: in its totality, Christianity demanded an entirely new conception of man and the universe, life and death, private and public life. The teachings of Jesus and Paul, as developed through four centuries, left no aspect of human activity untouched. The classical world, with all its mysticism and unworldly moments, had celebrated man, this life, and (in the best of times at least) political activity. Christians, too, were ready to live in this world and assign to work its importance and its dignity. While the first Christians had still lived in the vivid hope that the end of the world would come within their lifetime, later Christians resigned themselves to waiting and working and praying. In its essence, though, Christianity reversed the classical order of things: it exalted heaven over earth, eternal life over this life, universal love over patriotism, suffering over success, humility over pride, self-abnegation over sensuality. Perhaps most significant of all, Christianity made belief, not reason, central. The very absurdity of the Trinity, the improbability of Jesus' miracles and resurrection, the great demand made on men's imagination by the conception of a universal God who had made the world and who alone was entitled to worship—all this the Christians proclaimed not apologetically but triumphantly. Some of the church fathers, as later many of the leading Christian clerics, were powerful intellects, but they humbled their reason before their overriding urge to believe the mysteries that Scripture and its chosen interpreters offered them. As St. Anselm was to sum it all up late in the eleventh century: "*Credo ut intelligam*—I believe that I may understand." Here was the great reversal in a phrase: not understanding for the sake of belief, but belief for the sake of understanding.

Such a reversal could only come through and after considerable inner turmoil, and the writings of the greatest church fathers give plain, often moving witness to that turmoil. Classical culture—its philosophy, its poetry, its rhetoric—was a powerful presence to an educated Christian; it was a precious possession as well as a dangerous temptation to put the things of this world above the things of heaven. What was one to do with such an ambiguous legacy? The answer the church fathers gave to this question was to prove of decisive importance to early modern Europe, for it determined the way in which the classical inheritance was to be passed on through the centuries. Origen, in the early third century, and St. Jerome in the late fourth century—both men of wide classical erudition—offered a drastic solution that they had drawn from an Old Testament text: "When thou goest forth to war against thine enemies, and the Lord thy God hath delivered them into thine hands, and thou hast taken them captive, and seest among the captives a beautiful woman, and hast a desire unto her, that thou wouldst have her to thy wife; Then thou shalt bring her home to thine house; and she shall shave her head, and pare her nails; And she shall put the raiments of her captivity from off her, and shall remain in thine house." [16] In other words, shun classical civilization insofar as it provides enjoyment or a philosophy of life; exploit it for Christian purposes and nothing else. Jerome himself, in translating parts of the Old Testament and all of the New Testament into Latin, [17] followed his own prescription to the letter: he used his secular learning for devout purposes.

St. Augustine, the most influential of all the church fathers, whose writings left their mark on the course of Roman Catholicism and on the thinking of the Protestant rebels of the Reformation, solved the same problem with a different metaphor, also from the Old Testament: the children of Israel had left Egypt laden with the treasures of the country that had so long enslaved them; in the same way, he thought, Christians must loot classical culture of what they needed. Augustine was an extraordinary man. Born in Roman North Africa in 354, of a Christian mother, Augustine at first embraced varying forms of pagan belief and lived a worldly life. Then, as he records it in his magnificent *Confessions,* he had a dramatic conversion and put the world behind him. In a long lifetime—he died in 430—he wrote immensely, on dogma, against heretics, about organization, and became bishop of the city of Hippo, not far from where he was born. His main doctrinal opponents were the Pelagians, who took a sunny view of human nature and denied both man's fall and his original sin. In reply, Augustine developed a pessimistic view of man that stressed man's utterly lost condition after his fall, his helplessness without God, and the supreme importance of divine grace, which God could bestow without, as it were, giving his reasons. Calvin, as we shall see, would find this teaching particularly congenial. No one exemplified the great reversal more dramatically than Augustine: in *The City of God,* his greatest and best-known work, he developed the notion of the two cities—the one worldly, corrupt, and lost; the other divine, pure, and saved. Augustine, in his own way a good Roman, thought the Roman Empire to be the finest example of the city of man. But it too was of the devil; it too could make no absolute claim on man's ultimate loyalties—it was too wicked for that. Only the City of God, imperfectly realized on earth by the saintly Christian church and perfectly embodied in God's rule over all the saved, had a right to man's final allegiance. It is only natural that pagans should find such thinking not merely ridiculous, but disloyal and politically subversive as well.

Augustine's *City of God* is a substantial book, but it began as a polemic: in 410 the city of Rome had been sacked by the Visigothic king Alaric, a depressing demonstration of Rome's decay. Hunting for reasons, many pagans charged that the Christians, with their doctrines of humility and unworldliness, had sapped the will to fight. It was against this charge that Augustine wrote, and

---

[16] Deut. 21: 11-13.

[17] This became the basis of the Vulgate version of the Bible that remains the authoritative version of Scriptures for Roman Catholics.

it was in the course of his defense that he developed the conception of the two cities, which would reverberate through the Middle Ages, as popes and emperors struggled for supremacy (see p. 41). Whatever date a historian may choose to signalize the end of the Roman Empire, *The City of God* may serve as a premature, though wholly deserved, epitaph.

INTO THE "DARK AGES"

The Great Restlessness: Migrations and Invasions, 400–700

Ever since Augustine, the decline and fall of the Roman Empire has exercised the ingenuity of commentators. The accusation that prompted Augustine to his strenuous rebuttal found persuasive spokesmen as late as the eighteenth century, but it has few defenders today: historians now treat the triumph of Christianity not as a cause of the decline but as a consequence. The same holds true of the event that provoked this charge against the Christians in the first place: a more effective state system than the empire had become by the early fifth century could have turned back or absorbed the barbarian invasions. The very size of the empire, the long peace, the precarious political structure, the economic decline of once prosperous provincial cities, the endemic unrest among an exploited servile labor force, all these and more doubtless played their part. But it is perhaps more pertinent to ask not why Rome fell, but how, given the inescapable vicissitudes of empires, it could have stood for so long.

Whatever our conclusion, it is clear that the Germanic invasions would have taxed the resources of the most resilient of political organizations. Since the first century after Christ, relations between Rome and its northern neighbors had been intermittently peaceful, sometimes even cordial. Some of the Germanic tribes were steadily on the move and harassed the frontiers of the Roman Empire. But many "barbarians" served in the Roman army, settled in imperial territory, intermarried freely, took positions in the public service, and became good Romans. One of these, the gifted, wily Vandal Stilicho, married the niece of Emperor Theodosius I and around 400 led the troops that prevented a Visigothic invasion of the Italian peninsula. The spread of Christianity after Constantine increased tensions between Rome and the Germanic tribes; partially and superficially Christianized, these tribes normally adopted Arianism (see p. 19) at a time when Arianism was being proscribed in Rome as a heinous heresy. Then, in the 370s, their sporadic wanderings became a general, almost panic-stricken movement. The reasons for these migrations were pressure on the food supply and pressure from the Huns in the East. The Huns were an Asian people, nomadic by habit, formidable cavalrymen. Earlier they had terrorized the Chinese in the East; in the fourth century, probably driven by hunger, they turned westward. Their hordes streamed first into the Volga basin and then into the Danube Valley, then into central Europe. Rome dealt with the menace by paying tribute and employing Hun troops as mercenaries; but by the middle of the fifth century the formidable Hunnish ruler, Attila, invaded Gaul and, in 452, Italy itself. He died the next year, and the Huns disappeared from the European scene as precipitously as they had come, but their legacy—large-scale shifts of populations—remained. One by one, the Germanic tribes wandered across the old imperial terrain. The Visigoths (or Western Goths) were at war with Roman emperors throughout the fourth century, took Rome in 410, then moved to southern Gaul and northern Spain, and established a short-lived kingdom with Toulouse as its first, and Toledo as its second, capital. Meanwhile the Ostrogoths (or Eastern Goths), settled in what is Hungary today and invaded Italy in the late 480s. The Vandals, whose ruthless exploitation of conquered lands became proverbial, came out of central Germany in the fifth century to conquer remote regions; by 406 they were in Gaul, in 409 they entered Spain, and in 429, North Africa; they took Carthage in 435, controlled the Mediterranean trade from African strongholds with their pirate ships, and forced Rome to acknowledge their independence. The Franks moved in the fifth century from the Rhineland into Gaul. And the Saxons, settled on the shores of northern Gaul, with their neighbors, the Angles, invaded the British Isles, first in marauding bands and then, in the middle of the fifth century, as permanent settlers. After Odoacer deposed Romulus Augustulus in 476, a chronicler sadly noted: "And so the Western Empire of the Roman people perished with this Augustulus—and from now on the Gothic kings possessed Rome and Italy." [18] The migrations slowed down, but political turmoil continued. In 489, the Ostrogoth Theodoric overthrew Odoacer; he was acting with the approval of the emperor at Constantinople, but, it turned out, in his own behalf: entrenched by 493, Theodoric made himself ruler of Italy. Then, early in the sixth century, Justinian, greatest of Byzantine emperors (see p. 26) tried to reunite in fact what was still united in law. His success was impressive though temporary: he reconquered North Africa from the Vandals and Italy from the Ostrogoths, and when he died in 565, much of the territory of the old Roman Empire was again under a single command. But three years later, in 568, another Germanic tribe, the Lombards, invaded Italy and undid most of Justinian's work. The barbarian rulers of the West were, by their lights, Christians and Romans, but from Constantinople, by its lights the capital of Rome and of civilization, they looked like upstarts and usurpers. As a military and political, even as a linguistic entity—Greek gradually replaced Latin—

[18] Quoted in J. M. Wallace-Hadrill, *The Barbarian West: The Early Middle Ages*, A.D. *400-1000* (Torchbook ed., 1962), 32.

Byzantium was separate from Rome; by tradition, and in legal fiction, the two remained one. [19]

Then, early in the seventh century, Byzantium was challenged by a new and far more formidable enemy—the Arabs. Their emergence and expansion constitute one of the extraordinary moments in Western history. No one seemed less likely to unite and conquer than the Arab tribes, nomadic for the most part, and even if settled, fiercely particularistic. But there was restlessness and spreading hunger, and among many Arabs, a certain urge toward unity and—the inescapable consequence of unity—expansion. As one ninth-century Arab poet was to put it, candidly:

> No, not for Paradise didst thou the nomad life forsake;
> Rather, I believe, it was thy yearning after bread and dates. [20]

Mahomet was a religious leader whom many followed for religious reasons, but much of the energy that underlay the triumph of his cause sprang from discontent that he galvanized and channeled. Born around 570 in Mecca, Mahomet heard the call to be prophet to the Arabs; his conversion was followed by a series of visions—some ecstatic, most of them supremely convenient—which supplied the outlines of his doctrines and of the political organization it implied. He made converts and enemies; when, in 622, he discovered a plot against his life, he moved from Mecca to the more sympathetic environment of Medina. This "departure"—the *hegira*—was the decisive event in the creation of Islam; the Arab calendar honors it by dating events from that year. In Medina, under the prodding of his followers and critics, Mahomet put his amalgam of prophetic and apocalyptic notions into some sort of order; later, his disciples gathered his revelation in the Koran, the Muslim's sacred book.

As Christianity was the ungrateful child of Judaism, Islam was the ungrateful child of Judaism and Christianity—in particular, Islam took up ideas popular but heretical in Rome and Byzantium alike. Mahomet was a severe, even fanatical monotheist: there is one god, and all the local Arab gods, or the various persons in the Christian Trinity, are chimeras; Jesus, Mahomet insisted, was a prophet, not a divinity. The good Muslim praises his God—Allah—and unconditionally submits himself to his will, recognizes in the terrible history of the world the wickedness of mankind, and prepares himself for the last judgment, which is near at hand, and for the future life, which will be heaven for the believer, hell for the infidel. It is not surprising that Christians should

---

[19] "There are higher things than facts; the Byzantine theory, fanciful as it sounds, was accepted for many centuries by friends and foes alike, and its influence in preserving the very existence of the Empire is incalculable." H. St. L. B. Moss, in Norman H. Baynes and H. St. L. B. Moss, *Byzantium: An Introduction to East Roman Civilization* (1948), 1.

[20] Quoted in Philip K. Hitti, *History of the Arabs from the Earliest Times to the Present* (5th ed., 1951), 144.

think of this "new" faith as just another heresy or that Mahomet should at first seek the cooperation of Jews and Christians living in the Arab world. It was only when they firmly rejected him that he furiously rejected them. Yet Mahomet's fury did not compromise the administrative flexibility of his successors: as in its origins Islam sought to be a comprehensive religion, later, as a conquering imperial power, Islam proved remarkably tolerant of other cultures and other sects.

Mahomet soon controlled Medina, and by 630, Mecca had fallen to him. Two years later he died, to be succeeded by able politicians and ambitious military leaders. The Arab conquest began with the conquest of Arabia itself. Then the world lay open; neither the Persian nor the Roman Empire was in any condition to resist united and energetic soldiers. Syria fell to Islam in 636, Palestine in 638, Egypt in 640, Persia in the 640s; by 669 all of North Africa was in Muslim hands; in 711 they invaded Spain and moved northward. It was not until 732, at the famous battle of Tours, that Charles Martel halted the assault and the wave of Islam receded.

From Justinian to Charlemagne

By the eighth century, then, the Mediterranean world, still the center of civilization, was divided among three large clusters of states, three more or less united empires. The Arabs, with their sprawling new acquisitions, rapidly adapted to, and even refined, the civilizations they found as they spread their soldiers and settlers across the Near East, Africa, and the southwest tip of Europe. Land warriors, they learned how to sail from the Syrians; tribal individualists, they learned how to administer large territories from all the Roman provinces they subdued. And in Alexandria, in Antioch, in Jerusalem, in southern Spain, they found Hellenistic learning and science and fell upon it with a fresh appetite. For the preservation of Greek philosophy, for the elaboration of Hellenistic mathematics, the Arab conquests, far from being a disaster, were a blessing.

In contrast, the German states of the north and west did little to preserve the political, economic, and cultural institutions they had inherited. Far less flexible than the Arabs, they kept up their tribal organization with its stress on local law, personal loyalty, and war as the most highly prized occupation. Cities that had been the pride of the old Roman provinces decayed, trade dried up, and for the most part, each region was reduced to economic self-sufficiency—which is to say, to poverty. In this unpromising soil, the higher arts could scarcely be expected to grow: the number of literate men dwindled with the general depression, and the number of memorable works produced in these centuries was vanishingly small. The most distinguished, perhaps the only, immortal book of those centuries is Boethius' *De consolatione philosophiae,* composed in prison after 510 by a Roman statesman unjustly accused of treason. The work was highly popular with Christian readers for centuries. The *Etymologiae,* by Bishop Isidore of Seville, an encyclopedia composed early in the seventh century in the Visigothic kingdom of Spain, reveals the cultural poverty of the Christian West. Wholly unoriginal, extremely credulous, intently pious, the *Etymologiae* is a crude, unreliable compilation of what little Isidore knew and understood of classical culture. The most lasting contribution the Germans of those centuries made to history was a myth—the myth of democratic self-government which corresponded only very roughly to their tribal elections.

Byzantium, the self-conscious guardian of civilization and Christendom alike, preserved much but created little. Its capital, Constantinople, was a magnificent city, heavily fortified, with splendid churches, palaces and public monuments, and a population that may have approached a million in the tenth century. The most enduring creation to emerge from the Byzantine Empire was characteristically Roman—the Justinian code, which brought together the mass of statutes and edicts, incoherent, inconsistent, often unclear, that together made up Roman law. Justinian acceded to power in 527, and in the next year, at his command, a commission began the great work of sorting out the so-called "new law"—the statutes of the late empire, followed in 530 by another commission detailed to master all the rest, the "old law," which went back into republican times. The result, flawed but immensely impressive, was the *Digest* or *Pandects,* a vast, many-volumed ordering of all the available material, magnificently summarized in a relatively brief textbook, the *Institutes.* If the immediate impact of this labor was negligible, its long-range effect was incalculable: however mixed up with later and irrelevant notions, the Justinian code enshrined the classical ideals of the sovereign ruler and of a public order under law—a set of ideas of great value to the states as they began to emerge from the feudal order, or disorder, from the thirteenth and fourteenth centuries onward.

In religious matters, Byzantium and Rome engaged in what we might call a hostile collaboration. The doctrine of the Trinity, laid down as orthodox at Nicaea and later, confronted wide and continuous challenges: according to orthodox teaching Jesus was a single being with a double nature, divine and human. The Nestorians argued that He was two persons, while the Monophysites would grant Jesus only one nature, the divine. Rome and Byzantium managed to defeat these and other heresies. But then, a series of issues arose to divide the eastern and western branches of the Roman Empire. Byzantine emperors—in this, as in so much else, the heirs of classical Rome—dismissed conflicts between church and state as unthinkable. In practice this meant subjection of clerical to imperial power: in the great iconoclastic controversy that raged in Byzantium from the eighth century on, emperors directly interfered with the popular worship of images, an interference vigorously denounced in the West. [21] Caesaropapism, the political theory that dominated Byzantium, was a sensible reflection of political realities: as the name implies, the ruler was, in his own way, pope. In Rome, meanwhile, different realities produced a different political theory. One by one, the Germanic tribes gave up their Arian heresy or converted directly from paganism to Roman Catholicism. In the 430s and 440s, St. Patrick brought Ireland into the Roman fold; later in that century (tradition says 496) Clovis, king of the Franks, took his tribe from Arianism and paganism into Catholicism; in 596, Augustine of Canterbury came on a mission from Rome to England and effected widespread conversions there; early in the seventh century, the Lombards in Italy, too, chose the Roman persuasion. While at Constantinople clerics continued to assert their equality with Rome, in the West the primacy of the bishop of Rome seemed secure. After all, it was in Rome that St. Peter was reported to have been martyred, and St. Peter was, in Jesus' celebrated pun, the rock on which His church was to be built. The disorders in the western reaches of the empire exposed the bishop of Rome to military and political threats, but it also freed him from imperial domination.

In the fifth century, Pope Gelasius laid down the doctrine of the "two swords." It would have been unthinkable in Byzantium, but it became the rallying point for political controversy in the West for centuries: God, Gelasius argued, had given man two swords, the secular and the religious, each to the proper personage. Now, since spiritual concerns are more exalted than worldly ones, the sword wielded by the religious powers had higher authority. And even before Gelasius wrote, Pope Innocent I had claimed that the popes held the apostolic succession in their hands and that Rome had jurisdiction over Christians everywhere. Self-serving legends strengthened this case: when Attila first approached, then turned back from Rome, pious Christians ascribed Attila's retreat not to the plague among his troops or shortage of supplies, but to the eloquence of Pope Leo I. But stories, no matter how affecting, were not enough: Roman Catholicism profited immensely from the rule of men like Gregory the Great (590-604), the first pontiff to make really serious claims for papal supremacy over all of Christendom and over secular powers alike. Gregory was a courageous statesman, vigorous administrator, scourge of heresy, and enemy to classical culture, and besides, the first monk to be pope. His elevation cemented a long-lasting alliance between monastic orders and the papacy. Ascetic monasticism—the organized retreat from a corrupt world— dated back to the early fourth century; it had received strong intellectual support from the leading church fathers. Early in the sixth century, Benedict founded a new and effective monastic order at Monte Cassino in central Italy,

[21] The iconoclasts—literally, the breakers of images—argued that realistic representations of the Virgin Mary and of Christ were a form of vulgar heresy in which the sheer humanity of sacred figures was unduly stressed; the opponents argued that to forbid representations of Christ was to deny the Incarnation.

and around 529, he laid down what came to be known as the Rule of St. Benedict. It provided for the governance of each monastery by an abbot and imposed monastic discipline and monastic duties—mainly prayer and work— with such clarity and eloquence that other orders soon followed its lead. With Pope Gregory, monasticism entered as a new, powerful element into the amalgam of papal influence. When on Christmas Day, in the year 800, Pope Leo III crowned the Frankish king Charles as emperor, this act reflected the prestige of Rome in the West—the prestige, though not the power: as long as Charles lived, the power was his.

Charles the Great, as he came to be called, had inherited a sizable estate: when he assumed sole rule over the Frankish territories in 771, he was master of what is today France, Belgium, the Netherlands, southern Germany, and Austria. Like his predecessors, Charlemagne cooperated with the papacy, and like them, he mobilized his resources for territorial expansion. In a series of strenuous campaigns, he subdued Lombard Italy all the way to Rome, extended his empire across northern and central Germany to the Elbe, reduced Bavaria to obedience, invaded pagan terrain on the lower Danube, crossed the Pyrenees into the Muslim Empire, took Barcelona, and incorporated a broad strip of northern Spain into his sprawling dominions. Wherever he went, he brought some measure of administrative centralization and Roman Catholicism with him, and for his lifetime at least, there was unity in the West once more, Christian and imperial. The man who came to Rome in 800 to be crowned came as a conqueror, not as a suppliant.

Charlemagne fostered the arts of peace quite as much as the arts of war. His measures to restore trade were rudimentary and paled before the exactions in money and men that his endless wars necessitated. In matters of higher culture he was more successful, though the popular name for his reign, "the Carolingian renaissance," considerably overstates his achievement. Scarcely literate himself, he surrounded himself with literary lights. The intellectual eminence of his reign is a comment on the flatness of the surrounding landscape; still, scholars from all across Europe flocked to his court at Aix-la-Chapelle. And there the palace school under the brilliant direction of the English cleric, Alcuin, and schools set up elsewhere sought to recall the fading glories of classical literature and a pure Latinity. But Charlemagne died in 814, and his "renaissance" died with him: the fire he had tried to light was only a spark, brilliant but ephemeral. When the Frankish historian Einhard wrote Charlemagne's life some time after the emperor's death, he looked back at the last reign with the nostalgia of one who has been expelled from a paradise of learning and greatness.

Charlemagne's empire, indeed, went the way of Alexander's: his son, Louis the Pious, could not hold his inheritance together, and before the ninth century was over, the West was divided once again among a series of small dynasties, which began to define, however roughly, such future states as France and Bavaria. Charlemagne's establishment of a new center of gravity in the north seems now, in long retrospect, the first glimmering of a European civilization, as distinct from the older civilization centered on the Mediterranean. But Europe would have to wait, both as an idea and as a reality. As Charlemagne's empire disintegrated, a new wave of restlessness swept across eastern and central Europe to disturb the tentative balance of powers. In the ninth century, the Magyars moved from the Caucasus across southern Russia into what are today Rumania and Hungary. Like the Huns before them, the Magyars were formidable horsemen and ruthless raiders. They were not stopped until the middle of the ninth century in a series of clashes with Saxonian emperors: Henry I, "the fowler," beat the Magyars at Riade in 933; his successor, Otto I, routed them decisively at the Lechfeld in 955. Confined to Hungary, the Magyars settled there and, around 1000, accepted Roman Catholicism.

The other wanderers were closely associated, though distinct, northern tribes—Danes, Swedes, Norwegians—who began to roam about the year 800. Their terrified victims called them Northmen or Vikings. They were inventive and intrepid sailors, as fierce on land as at sea. With their celebrated long ships, capable of carrying thirty oarsmen and swiftly driven on under huge square sails, the Vikings covered unprecedented distances. They raided Scotland, Ireland, the coast of France, Spain, and Italy. They penetrated deep into Russia, they sailed up the Seine and looted Paris, they briefly took and sacked Cologne and London. They ventured westward into unknown seas, discovered Iceland and Greenland; around 1000 they touched land in America. By the end of the ninth century, they began to settle down in some of the lands they had raided and terrorized before—mainly in Britain and in Normandy. And slowly, almost, one might say, reluctantly, they accepted the civilization about them by accepting baptism in the Roman Church. Yet the Romanization of Western Europe did not in itself produce a revival of civilization. The economic decay and political fragmentation had been too great, the strain imposed by incessant warfare and fearful migrations too severe, to permit such a revival quickly. When historians later looked back on these centuries and called them Dark Ages, they had some reason for using this derogatory epithet.

CHRISTIAN CENTURIES: 1000–1350

Early in the eleventh century, the West began to enjoy a great recovery. For three centuries or more, down to the 1340s, an emerging Europe confronted life with less gloom and more security than before. These are the centuries historians have called the High Middle Ages. The migrations were over. Population increased, and its gradual but uninterrupted growth was at once a cause and a consequence of the slow healing in economic, social, and political life. While the overwhelming mass of Europeans were, and remained, poor peasants, even they found conditions of existence less unstable than they had been. Towns flourished as they had not flourished since the decline of the Roman Empire. Old towns made good their losses in population and trade; new towns were born at strategic spots. Great rulers established great dynasties. In 987, Hugh Capet was elected king of the Western Franks, and his Capetian dynasty, which lasted to 1328, laid the foundations of what is France today. In 1066, William, duke of Normandy, called the Conqueror, invaded England, wrested control from the Anglo-Saxons, and established a particular version of feudal government that would remain unchallenged for a century and a half. This, too, was the age of parliaments—of representative bodies, mainly staffed by magnates, lay and clerical, meeting on occasion to advise the king and vote taxes: the Spanish *cortes,* the French estates, the German diets, the English parliament, date from the twelfth century onward. From being mere servants of the central government, the parliaments would become centers of aristocratic (and, to a lesser degree, urban) power and spokesmen for grievances; the great struggles of early modern history between kings and parliaments, which will mark succeeding chapters of this book, began in the High Middle Ages.

After centuries of dismal desolation, Christian scholarship bloomed once again, with significant assistance from savants but to the greater glory of the Christian god. Men of learning and letters found havens in cities, at courts, and in those new centers of scholarship and professional training, the universities. Architecture and the visual arts, chiefly though not exclusively ecclesiastical in inspiration, brought forth masterpieces and developed distinct styles. The Crusades, which engrossed the attention of secular and religious leaders from the early twelfth century on, were in part disasters and in part cruel farces, but they were also commercial ventures and played their part in that relentless economic and cultural expansion of Europe that would characterize the early modern period. The two swords of church and state, papacy and empire, were often in conflict, but their verbal and sometimes physical combat produced a rich literature in political theory.

The continual and effective threat that heresy posed to the Church of Rome brought persecutions, polemics on faith and obedience, and intermittent efforts at internal reform. In the eighteenth century, anti-Christian historians would deride the High Middle Ages as a time of chaos and credulity; in the early nineteenth century, Romantic historians would look back to the epoch as a time of glory and splendor, of religious unity and exciting personal adventure. Both these characterizations are partial: the High Middle Ages were neither as dismal nor as magnificent as that. But this much is certain: Europe had emerged from the Dark Ages.

Feudal Society

The type of social organization most prevalent in the West in these centuries was feudalism. "A subject peasantry"—this is how Marc Bloch defines its essential qualities—"widespread use of the service tenement (i.e., the fief) instead of a salary, which was out of the question; the supremacy of a class of specialized warriors; ties of obedience and protection which bind man to man and, within the warrior class, assume the distinctive form called vassalage; fragmentation of authority—leading inevitably to disorder; and, in the midst of all this, the survival of other forms of association, family and State."[22] Two terms require explanation here: "fief" and "vassalage." Feudalism was the child of disorganization and decay; later its critics would argue that it was also their father. The Roman political order had rested on the theory, and in its better days the fact, of sovereignty: the sovereign ruler, though responsible for, was not responsible to, the ruled, and the state he governed was a legal, bureaucratic, impersonal entity. As imperial administration collapsed, the sovereign power collapsed with it, and a personal contract emerged as a substitute. This contract was the heart of feudalism; it was a formal acknowledgment of differences in power among men and the need of the weak to obtain security and protection from the strong. The successful—a baron lording it over a province, a military adventurer holding a small castle, or merely the most prosperous farmer in the neighborhood—offered, often imposed, both. As time went by, this system of mutual aid developed into an elaborate ritualized ceremony: the "lord" granted land—a fief or benefice—to his "vassal," who in turn, swore fealty and homage. Both partners in this contract were free men, each had obligations to the other: one to dispense justice and give protection; the other to pay fixed dues, perform stated services, and do military duty.

Feudalism engendered an enormously intricate network of dependence: nearly all lords were also vassals of other, greater lords; nearly all vassals were also lords over other, less powerful vassals. Feudal kings were simply great lords standing in a contractual relationship to their lesser lords: Hugh Capet and his successors ruled not over subjects but over vassals. Thus vassalage tied together areas small and large and imposed obligations on the proudest of men. With the decline (though not disappearance) of a money economy and the increased parochialism of life, feudalism seemed a natural expression of the great fragmentation of authority. Yet feudal institutions differed from region to region. They emerged first in the area of Charlemagne's Empire—Burgundy, central France, and the German Rhineland—and remained most characteristic there. Elsewhere, in England, northern Italy, Spain, central Germany, they assumed special forms; beyond those frontiers, in Scandinavia and Byzantium, they never sank deep roots. The whole system, it can be imagined, was a lawyer's paradise.

Feudal society was larger than the feudal contract. As Marc Bloch's definition makes plain, a subject peasantry was indispensable to the system: someone had to till the soil and weave the cloth that others might carouse and fight and pray at leisure. The peasant did not have the privilege of offering homage: that was reserved to the small elite of landowners and military men.

[22] Marc Bloch, *Feudal Society* (1961), II, 446.

Nor was the manor—the kind of organized village in which most of Europe's peasants lived—a feudal institution: manorialism antedated and outlived feudalism. Yet the two, feudalism and manorialism, had enough in common to sustain and support one another in these medieval centuries. The manor was a large estate, usually comprising several small villages and perhaps a hundred peasant households, held by a lord or a monastery. It included the land reserved for the proprietor—the demesne—which the villagers farmed for him; the land held by the peasants;[23] and the land—forest and pasture—enjoyed in common by all. The lord or his representative normally lived nearby and administered justice over his domain: jurisdiction was strictly local.

The status of the peasant varied from place to place and even within a given manor; few peasants were formally slaves, but most were serfs, bound to the soil by grinding obligations. They had to labor a number of stated days on the lord's land, pay fees for the equipment the lord compelled them to use, work on the roads, repair bridges and buildings, hand over part of their harvest to the lord or the local cleric. In Catholic Europe, the manor was not merely a social, economic, and judicial, but also a religious, unit. The peasant formed a distinct dependent class—he was called villein, *vilain, Holde,* rustic—and he lived in steady fear of losing what little freedom he had. Poverty was built into his life; escape was hard. The peasant was a beast of burden with a host of duties and a handful of rights—the victim of nature, of his crude superstitions, and of his endemic undernourishment. It is true that medieval agriculture made significant improvements. Humble innovations had great consequences. The introduction of a heavy plough permitted reduction of effort and the exploitation of strips of land and types of soil hitherto inaccessible. The harness, another medieval contribution, made horsepower widely available for heavy-duty labor. The three-field system, which appeared in Europe in the time of Charlemagne, by leaving one third of the land fallow for a year, brought more land into cultivation and improved general productivity.[24] But the peasant's life was, for the most part, nasty, brutish, and short. No wonder that on the rare occasion when he rose up, in those brief moments of triumph against the feudal elite—they were never more than brief—he was pitiless in his primitive rage.

The Recovery of Urban Life

Feudalism was in its essence a recognition, indeed a celebration, of decentralization. But the towns that grew up during the feudal centuries were the mark and agent of concentration. In its legal order, its economic pursuits, its styles of

---

[23] Though at the beginning of the feudal age, peasant tenure of land had been "precarious," by the twelfth century it was in effect in hereditary possession. See Henri Pirenne, *Economic and Social History of Medieval Europe* (tr. 1936), chap. III.

[24] For details, see Lynn White, Jr., *Medieval Technology and Social Change* (1962).

thinking, the medieval town was a rival, often an enemy, to the agricultural world around it.

There is no single rule for this urban recovery. Some medieval towns grew on ancient foundations, some clustered near natural harbors, at crossroads, close to natural resources, on navigable rivers, around fortified castles. Towns were the knots formed by the necessities of medieval life: they were the seats of bishops, marketplaces, banking centers, hostels for traveling merchants, bastions of defense, headquarters for officials governing the surrounding region. They were also, notoriously, hospitable to innovation. The townsman was less tied to tradition than the peasant who lived only a few steps away from him—he talked to visiting merchants, his occupational specialization impelled him into literacy, strangers made the strange familiar and thus acceptable. The hatred of novelty and modernity that has characterized conservatives through the centuries has always been accompanied by hatred of the town.

Not unexpectedly, the growth of medieval towns followed the establishment of security and the patterns of trade. Byzantium boasted Constantinople, in which most of its wealth, talent, and urban population were concentrated; the Muslims built cities wherever they went—from Cordova to Cairo and beyond. In Roman Catholic Europe, the first impressive towns grew up in the Mediterranean, on the North Sea, and in Flanders: by around 1300, Milan and Venice surpassed one hundred thousand inhabitants, while leading Flemish cities like Bruges and Ghent rarely exceeded forty thousand. Paris, already a great commercial and intellectual center in those years, had eighty thousand inhabitants, twice as many as London.[25] Clearly, our judgment of what is impressive is a relative one.

Many European towns began as fortified centers of defense—*bourgs*—against invaders or marauders. Then, when life became more secure and commerce more active, settlers burst the bounds of the wall and moved beyond the *bourg* itself to the suburb or *faubourg*. And this suburb, as the Belgian historian Henri Pirenne long insisted, was the real nucleus of most medieval towns: it was in the *faubourg* that traveling merchants or migratory craftsmen settled down to a new kind of stable existence; the great medieval fairs that formed such a distinctive feature of economic life were ways of organizing the migration of goods instead of men.

Once formed and dynamically expanding, the towns developed their own political needs. Their relations with the surrounding countryside and with their feudal neighbors were normally tense, but all needed one another too much to permit unmitigated isolation or incessant warfare. Townsmen, increasingly specialized in their activities, needed food and raw materials from the countryside; the countryside could use some of their finished goods; local lords needed assistance in their struggle against greater, more remote lords. What the towns wanted most was what they called "freedom"—freedom from feudal obligations to neighboring lords, freedom to arrange their own commercial affairs, to regulate apprenticeship, to supervise merchandise, to levy tariffs on incoming merchants or merchandise. *"Stadtluft macht frei*—town air gives freedom" was a celebrated slogan, and it was true enough that once towns won their charters of liberty from a feudal magnate, they could control their own affairs, raise their own taxes, and protect their own residents—even "rustics" who had fled to the town to escape their duties elsewhere. "If a villein come to reside in the borough," so ran a typical twelfth-century declaration of Newcastle-upon-Tyne, "and shall remain as a burgess in the borough for a year and a day, he shall thereafter always remain there, unless there was a previous agreement between him and his lord for him to remain there for a certain time." [26]

Though tearing at the feudal network and jealously ready to fight for all its privileges, the medieval town was by no means destructive of authority. It simply built up its own distinctive structure of authority. Most towns were dominated by small patriciates, open to recruitment from outside or from below, but small in number and authoritarian in temper. From the beginning of the eleventh century, these ruling groups organized themselves into gilds. Some gilds, mainly in the Mediterranean region, were specialized interest groups guarding the privileges of merchants, bankers, clothmakers; others, mainly in the north, were comprehensive social organizations with functions not merely economic but social, political, and even military. Gradually, the southern pattern prevailed: gilds grew into authorized instruments bringing apprentices into the system; regulating the wages, hours, and quality of work; and influencing local government for their own particular purposes. In the early thirteenth century, there was one gild for the cloth industry of Toulouse, and at the end of the century there were five. In the middle of the thirteenth century, there were 101 gilds in the city of Paris alone. [27] The gilds were pressure groups, training centers, monopolies. They were also, in those towns in which lesser trades and industries managed to organize themselves, the way to social status and a certain degree of political influence for the lower orders. Urban life in the Middle Ages was in most respects corporate: men lived huddled together within ever-expanding walls, walked on narrow streets, prayed in crowded churches, with the sounds, sights, and smells of the town all about them. Churches, monasteries, hospitals, orphanages, boastful gild halls—these were the crowded backdrop for colorful festivals, sanguinary uprisings, fervent religious revivals. The medieval town was one center of intellectual ferment. The church was the other.

[26] "The Customs of Newcastle-Upon-Tyne in the Time of Henry I, 1068–1135," in ibid., 138.
[27] Ibid., 64, 65.

The Christian Style

The Middle Ages pursued secular interests as strenuously as one might expect from any advanced complex civilization. But it does not follow that it was hypocritical in its religious professions. Commerce had its uses: the great fairs at Champagne or at Frankfurt, where merchants from across Europe gathered all the year round, the weaving cities of Flanders, or the banking centers in northern Italy underscore the importance that medieval men attached to trade. Work had its dignity: pious sculptors carved representations of handicrafts on cathedral doors. Power on earth was worth fighting for: even pious popes recognized that. The most ascetic of churchmen never thought to turn all Christians into monks and nuns. But in the great chain of being, the universal hierarchy with God at the top and inanimate matter at the bottom, religious concerns had a higher place than secular ones; philosophy was a science, but theology was the queen of the sciences and philosophy its servant. Christianity was not a superstition; in fact it acted, with its bold missions into pagan territory, as the enemy of primitive superstitions. But religion was the overriding, dominant purpose of life, even—perhaps especially—the life of the learned. All important social institutions and private events—birth, marriage, death, holidays (the name is significant), even war—stood under the sign of the sacred. The vogue of giving natural phenomena and literary works an allegorical interpretation illustrates this pervasive turn of mind: all, the book of nature and the books of men alike, were reflections of the divine handiwork, which manifested itself in the world in many marvelous guises. Reason had its part to play but revelation was a purer, more reliable source of knowledge. Science was the devout search for God's traces in the natural world—no wonder it accomplished so little (see p. 232). As St. Thomas Aquinas would put it later in the thirteenth century, in his characteristic Aristotelian fashion: "The natural end of a people formed into a society is to live virtuously; for the end of any society is the same as that of the individuals composing it. But, since the virtuous man is also determined to a further end, the purpose of society is not merely that man should live virtuously, but that by virtue he should come to the enjoyment of God." [28] The church, with its lofty spires and its cruciform shape, dominated the medieval landscape, literally as well as figuratively.

Despite all the energetic, often desperate attempts of Rome to impose unity and uniformity, medieval modes of religious thinking and feeling were often a jangling discord. Many historians have found it convenient to assert, and many students convenient to repeat, that heretics and fanatics were little more than occasional and unwelcome intrusions on the happy and united family of Christendom. But a Roman Catholic Europe, at one in its piety, each

---

[28] *De regimine principum,* quoted by E. F. Jacob, "Political Thought," in C. G. Crump and E. F. Jacob, *The Legacy of the Middle Ages* (1926), 518. For Aquinas and Aristotelianism see p. 39.

believer secure in his place, each worshipping in the same way with the same fervor in the same kind of Gothic edifice, is no more than a picturesque myth. To begin with, the schism between East and West—between the Greek Orthodox and the Roman Catholic churches—which had had its inception in the physical division of the Roman Empire and intensified with the iconoclast controversy (see p. 26) became official and final in 1054. And within Western Christianity itself, heresies were ever-present perils to Catholic claims.

In the twelfth century, two large-scale movements, the Albigensians and the Waldensians, arose in southern and central France and spread their teachings to neighboring Spanish and Italian territories. The Albigensians were an offshoot of the old Manichean tradition that no amount of Christian propaganda and pious persecution had ever wholly silenced: they taught that the world is divided between two forces, good and evil, the first of the spirit and the second of the flesh. Rome, an organized clergy, and the sacraments, the Albigensians insisted, belonged to the wicked world of the flesh; the "perfect" church, in contrast, was in the heart of pure men. In accord with such doctrines, the Albigensians exacted celibacy, pacifism, and communism. The Waldensians, less metaphysical, were almost as ascetic: in their yearning for the simple purity of the primitive Church, they called for poverty and continence. Such unworldly perfection was intolerable, especially since the two movements mustered a following of alarming size; early in the thirteenth century, after a "crusade" called by Pope Innocent III (see p. 43) they were forced underground by vigorous military action and ruthless repression.

But the triumphant conclusion of this crusade was not the end of heresy. There were many preachers like Peter Waldo, the Lyon merchant whose itinerant sermons had given the impetus for the Waldensians—inspired, self-appointed men of God who wandered across Europe, exhorting their followers to reject the flesh and prepare for the end of the world. The line between exceptional sanctity and damnable heresy was thin and shifting. St. Francis and St. Dominic, who early in the thirteenth century founded two great orders of friars who lived in the world by begging, remained firmly within the Roman communion, as did most of their followers; and, by remaining, they validated some of the papacy's claim to spiritual preeminence. But the ostentatious piety and purity of the Franciscans and the Dominicans were an ambiguous support for Catholicism; many troubled believers saw them as a standing reproach to clerical wealth and worldliness, and as a standing invitation to reform.

In the midst of this ferment, the bishop of Rome tightened his hold on the imagination and the religious institutions of the West. In the time of Charlemagne, and for nearly two centuries after, the papacy had been politically impotent, spiritually corrupt, and religiously insignificant; the holders of St. Peter's Chair practiced most of the sins in the calendar, from sexual incontinence to the cynical sale of sacred office, and all in the glare of public indifference or disapproval. Whatever moral and institutional authority the Western church retained rested with a handful of competent and honest bishops. It is significant that the revival of the papacy and the restoration of Western Christendom should begin not at Rome but in eastern France, at Cluny. The Cluniac reform was initiated in 910, with the founding of a Benedictine house. There was nothing novel about its aims and regulations, but in the tenth century a conscientious return to the Rule of St. Benedict (see p. 28) was nothing less than a radical reformation. Soon there were hundreds of monastic houses that followed Cluny and acknowledged its authority, while other independent, new foundations imitated Cluny's pious severity. Monastic celibacy and visible abhorrence of clerical corruption became popular slogans and even popular practices. The papacy, with which Cluny and its daughter houses maintained direct and cordial relations, would benefit enormously from the Cluniac reform. In the midst of papal corruption and impotence, the Cluniacs proclaimed their confidence in Rome. It was a self-fulfilling prophecy: the Cluniacs' confident assertion of papal purity and power helped to secure both. [29]

Other new institutions, the universities, were a rather more ambivalent source of strength to Catholic Christendom. In typical medieval fashion, the universities started as, or quickly turned into, corporations; and, like other corporations, they struggled to obtain charters and jealously watched over the "liberties" they had won. Bologna, founded before 1100 and soon celebrated for its preeminence in the canon law, was organized by the students, who treated their professors strictly as employees; Paris, formally founded around 1200, and the chosen center for theology, was organized by its professors. The universities were battlefields, and the battles did not confine themselves to words: town-gown riots, which claimed numerous victims, were frequent; student-faculty clashes, equally frequent, led to boycotts of classes and migrations of scholars. Students from Bologna set up the University of Pisa; after riots in Paris in 1228 and 1229, students wandered far afield to found new universities elsewhere or, as in Oxford and Cambridge, to swell the tiny number of students already there. There were other battles: between the doctors who were the real professors but few in number, and the masters of arts, lower in prestige, less well trained than the doctors, but numerous and popular within their special provinces—philosophy and science. [30] And there were continuous struggles with the outside world, which supported the universities and sought their support in turn: breeders of bureaucrats and bishops, they fed the spreading apparatus of religious and secular government; centers of debate and new ideas, they were a threat to cautious or autocratic conservatives. "For the popes," Friedrich Heer has written, "the universities were the object of their highest hopes and the occasion of their deepest

---

[29] For later relations of Cluny and the papacy, see p. 42.

[30] It was the masters of arts who were in charge of the seven liberal arts—the *trivium* (logic, rhetoric, grammar) and the *quadrivium* (music, geometry, arithmetic, astronomy).

disappointment." [31] The very qualities that made the universities indispensable
also made them dangerous.

From the eleventh century on, and during the intellectually vigorous
twelfth and thirteenth centuries, Western Christendom had much to debate
about. With the intellectual revival, independent spirits began to object, not to
the truth of Christian revelation—that everyone accepted—but to a naive or
slavish reliance on authority. A small but influential band of "school philosophers"—the Scholastics—boldly began to approach theological issues with
philosophical questions, thus bringing reason into areas from which Augustine
and his followers had banished it long before. Scholasticism goes back to the
ninth century, to John Scotus Erigena, part mystic, part metaphysician, heir of
the Neoplatonists, and for all his mysticism a doughty defender of the place of
reason in religious inquiry. In the eleventh century St. Anselm, an Italian cleric
who ended his long career as archbishop of Canterbury in England, offered a
philosophical proof for the existence of God—the so-called "ontological proof,"
which holds that since we can conceive of God, God must indeed exist. Anselm,
like all the Scholastics, was a devout believer, and he placed belief first—was
he not author of that saying, "*credo ut intelligam*—I believe that I may
understand"? (See p. 20.) But it is significant that he thought it useful, and
possible, to approach one of the profoundest of religious mysteries by the
avenue of philosophical inquiry.

After the Scholastics had fallen into discredit in later centuries, it was easy
to make fun of their abstruse concerns. "How many angels can dance on the
head of a pin?" This is the kind of question that sarcastic critics would consider
typical of Scholastic hair-splitting. Actually, in the High Middle Ages, Scholastic disputes had powerful theological and political reverberations. The great
debate between Realists and Nominalists is one instance of such a dispute that
now interests only the specialist in medieval philosophy but then exercised
educated men everywhere. The Realists argued that universal terms like
"humanity" or "church" referred to real substances, so that individual men or
particular clerics were instances of a greater whole. The Nominalists, on the
other side, held such words to be mere names, linguistic conveniences, and that
individual entities alone were real. While there were Nominalists who were
orthodox, it was Realism that was most serviceable to Roman Catholic doctrine:
it permitted men to accept that strange universal, the Trinity; and that perfect
institution, the church, amidst overwhelming evidence that it was corrupt,
incompetent, or worldly. With Peter Abelard, one of the most inventive of the
Scholastics, whose debating techniques did much to advance the Scholastic
method of argumentation, the practical consequences of such thinking began
to emerge: sometime around 1122, Abelard published his *Sic et Non*, a treatise
that listed statements on 158 questions from the Scriptures and the church
fathers, statements that patently contradicted one another. The lesson Abelard

[31] *The Medieval World* (tr. 1962), 241.

wished to impart was plain: however great the authority of Augustine and Jerome and the other fathers, they had not said the final word on the True Faith; that Faith, indeed, deserved the most scrupulous and most intelligent examination that Christians could bring to bear on it. "By doubting," Abelard said, "we come to examine, and by examining we reach the truth." Here was the new spirit at work. It is not an accident that Abelard should have spent much time in Paris and have been a most popular lecturer there.

Abelard died in 1142. Not long after his death the Christian West received the writings of Aristotle, largely through the mediation of Arabic and Jewish commentaries. The center of diffusion was Muslim Spain. There, by the 1150s, most of Aristotle's chief works, including his *Metaphysics* and his writings on ethics and logic, had been translated into Latin. Aristotle provided exhilarating but also unsettling reading: he was unmistakably a pagan, but his encyclopedic knowledge and his rigorous logic impressed themselves deeply on learned men who, however devout, thirsted for rational discussion. The very source of the Aristotelian revival was suspect: the Arabic translators and commentators, among whom Averroes of Cordova, Abelard's younger contemporary, was only the most recent and most persuasive, proclaimed doctrines wholly unacceptable to Roman orthodoxy. His Christian disciples interpreted Averroes' reading of Aristotle as an invitation to separate philosophy from theology, and thus to complete autonomy for rational inquiry. No school of Christian thought could tolerate that: it was the road to heresy if not outright secularism. Yet the intellectual power of Aristotle and his Arab commentators would not be denied. The first response of the official guardians of Roman Christendom was rejection: in 1210, the University of Paris was enjoined from reading any work of Aristotle or his interpreters; in the 1230s, when it became evident that Aristotle was irresistible, theologians made attempts to prune his writings and to keep what might be useful. But in 1277, there was a great purge at Paris: the Latin Averroists were proscribed, and even the great work of accommodation performed by St. Thomas Aquinas came under severe censure.

By that date, Aquinas had been dead for three years. Like his teacher and colleague, Albert the Great, a Dominican and a professor at Paris, Aquinas was a great controversialist but, beyond that, a great compromiser. The old question that had plagued Christian thinkers as far back as St. Augustine and beyond— what is the place of classical philosophy in the Christian religion? or, more generally, what is the place of reason in theology?—stood at the forefront of his philosophizing. Aquinas opened his most celebrated treatise, the *Summa theologiae,* with an elaborate discussion of just that issue. His conclusion was perfectly orthodox: Thomas was a rationalist in the service of Christianity. The "philosophical sciences," he wrote, "investigated by reason," are fruitful but inferior to the "sacred science of God and the blessed," which discovers its truths through revelation. Hence, he concluded, using a familiar metaphor, theology uses other disciplines, including philosophy, as its *ancillae*—its handmaidens.

Yet Thomas Aquinas was profoundly suspicious of the anti-intellectualism of those who denigrated secular learning, classical philosophy, or rational argumentation as instances of an impious worldliness. Reason and revelation, far from contradicting, complement and support one another. Thus Thomas found it possible to offer rational proofs for most of the truths of Christianity, including the existence of God, the supremacy of the Roman Church, and the hierarchical character of the universe. Through careful dialectical exposition, Thomas states all the objections to the position he wishes to defend and first examines, then refutes them, to allow the Christian truth to stand forth, triumphant and reasonable. Only the central mysteries—the Trinity and the miraculous event of transubstantiation in the mass—were beyond such rational demonstration.

The work of Thomas Aquinas was the finest achievement of Scholasticism: St. Thomas was a moderate without being a waverer. On the delicate question of universals, he was a moderate Realist; on the equally delicate question of political authority, he was a moderate royalist. In explicating the hierarchy of laws under which the world is governed, he put Eternal Law—God's rational wisdom—first and gave prominence to what he called Divine Law—God's special manifestations to man, His revelations. But he found a place also for Natural Law, the divinely prescribed but rationally comprehensible set of unchanging rules by which men and nature live, and for Human Law. Thomas' task was reconciliation.

But after the death of Aquinas, Scholasticism declined. What had been a scrupulous search for distinctions and logical affinities indeed degenerated into a pedantic splitting of hairs. In part, this was because Thomas had built his system so well. But also a new extreme distrust of reason and pagan thinking pervaded the church, and its leading theologians gave reasons for the impotence of reason. Thomism did not revive until the late fifteenth and early sixteenth centuries, just in time to aid those Roman Catholics who sought to preserve learning and rational argumentation amidst the storms of the Reformation and against the pressures of arch-conservatives in the time of the Counter-Reformation (see p. 164). If it took until 1879 for Thomas' system to become the official theology of the Roman Catholic Church [32] it had been the favored philosophical system of Catholic theologians for some centuries before.

The architectonic grandeur of Thomas Aquinas' life work has tempted some historians to liken it to a Gothic cathedral. But all attempts to discover affinities or mutual influences between Scholasticism and Gothic architecture remain speculation. The Christian art of those centuries has a grandeur all its own. Of that art, the Gothic cathedrals are only the most celebrated. Actually, the Gothic style was a relatively late achievement; it emerged with dramatic suddenness around 1140 at the Abbey of St. Denis, near Paris. We do not know the name of its architect; we do know who was responsible for the building:

[32] It was Pope Leo XIII who so declared it, in his encyclical *Aeterni patris*.

Abbé Suger, lover of the arts, biographer, influential advisor to Louis VI and Louis VII of France. There, at St. Denis, Suger's architect brought together the characteristics that other architects had been tentatively and separately employing in churches in and around Paris. The Gothic style, with its flying buttress and, above all, its pointed arch and rib vault [33] was an instant success. Within a few decades tall cathedrals sprang up in central France and in England: Notre Dame of Paris was begun around 1163; Lincoln around 1192; the new Gothic cathedral of Chartres around 1194; Rheims in 1211; Amiens and Salisbury in 1220. The Romanesque style, which the Gothic replaced with such unaccustomed rapidity, had been impressive in its own way: one need only stand in the lofty Romanesque nave of the cathedral at Durham, begun at the end of the eleventh century, or of La Madeleine at Vézelay, built slightly later, to recognize the Romanesque style as something better than pedestrian or earth-bound. With its strong barrel vaults held up by its sturdy piers, the Romanesque church was powerful, stable, secure. The Gothic church in contrast, with its thin piers, its walls pierced by glass, its soaring towers or spires, was a spectacular expression of energy. Everything was calculated to move the eye eastward and upward. Those who commissioned and built them (if not perhaps all those who worshipped there) saw the cathedrals as a spiritual triumph, a symbol of faith, and quite literally, a foretaste of heaven. With the art of cathedral building, the arts of sculpture and of stained-glass making advanced apace: doors, walls, pillars needed decoration that would support and enhance the general impression of lofty sanctity. It has become a commonplace to call these Gothic masterpieces sermons in stones, but this is what they were.

Literature, despite many digressions into worldliness, expressed what the church buildings suggested. Dante's *Divine Comedy*, as imperishable an achievement in poetry as Chartres cathedral is in architecture, was, of course, primarily a poem: Dante, the scholar who wrote his treatises in Latin, put his greatest work into Italian, into the splendid music of the *terza rima*. But the *Commedia* is more than a poem: it is the account of a religious pilgrimage, the voyage of a human sinner through the inferno and purgatory into paradise. It was the destination medieval men all devoutly prayed for.

The Two Swords Drawn: Papacy Against Empire

But men must live. They must work, forget their sorrows in drinking and raucous humor, express their sensuality. Much of the literature of the Middle Ages, though all of it necessarily stood under the sign of Christendom, toyed with heresy and with proscribed notions. The Goliard poets—mainly wandering students and rootless priests—spread their ribald songs, their celebrations

---

[33] For the most convenient definition, see amidst a vast literature, Nikolaus Pevsner, *An Outline of European Architecture* (7th ed., 1962), 89.

of women and drinking, and their impudent assaults on orthodox religion, across Europe from the middle of the eleventh century on. The rich literature of chivalry, composed and sung by the troubadours, though professing piety and soaked in mystical meanings, sang of the complex ritual of courtly love and of heroism in war. Even Dante, perhaps the greatest architect that Christian poetry has ever had, gave respectful hospitality in the *Divine Comedy* to most of the heretical ideas that the popes and the clergy were doing their utmost to extirpate. Nor is this all. The popes, the vicars of Christ on earth, were wholly engaged in the struggle for worldly power. This was doubtless inevitable: power is a limited and scarce commodity, and papal attempts to control territories in Italy, bishops in outlying districts, and nominations to high clerical posts affronted the competing interests of other men. So the papacy, endowed with the spiritual sword, stood with sword drawn through most of the Middle Ages.

The resurgence of the papacy dates from the middle of the eleventh century. Some vigorous Cluniacs became vigorous popes (see p. 37), and the Italian Benedictine cardinal Hildebrand, who became Pope Gregory VII in 1073, had cordial relations with the Cluniac reformers. Hildebrand had been a powerful cardinal in Rome and an effective reformer for decades before his accession. Like his early predecessor and chosen model, Gregory the Great (see p. 27), Gregory VII was one of those rare historical personages who do more than merely embody current tendencies—he set his seal indelibly on Catholic Christendom. But his was a long-range, largely posthumous triumph; the twelve years of his papacy were marked by great claims and great defeats.

In 1059, under Hildebrand's prodding, Pope Nicholas II had decreed that the election of the pope must be taken out of the hands of the Roman nobility and placed into the hands of a college of cardinals; in the same year, under the same prodding, he forbade clerics to marry and declared the appointment to bishoprics to be wholly the pope's business. After his election to the papacy, Gregory VII reiterated these policies. A man of great vigor and great courage, of moderate but useful learning, Hildebrand insisted that the Church of Rome is the guardian of the Christian faith—infallible now and always. The pope, it followed, is sovereign ruler over the church and, being judge of all men, including emperors, can have no earthly judge. Thus, Gregory VII held, the pope alone can call a general synod and alone appoint, depose, or transfer bishops. He can even depose emperors. The emperor of the day, Henry IV, was hardly inclined to bow to such principles. When in 1075 the Synod of Rome officially reiterated the prohibition against lay investiture of bishops, Henry balked. Like many other rulers after him, the emperor was unwilling to surrender the rich patronage and the influence that his right to invest bishops gave him. In 1076, he called a counter-synod at Worms, which obediently deposed Pope Gregory; and, in a strong letter to the pope, he developed his own political theory: the emperor, like the pope, is immediately responsible only to God. Gregory in turn excommunicated the emperor. The great investiture controversy had begun. Faced with a rebellion of German nobles, Henry IV decided to make concessions; he crossed the Alps in midwinter into Italy, and in January 1077, at Canossa, after reputedly standing in the snow for three days, he obtained absolution. "Going to Canossa" was a profound, and became a proverbial, humiliation of the secular before the religious power. But it was Henry's last concession: until Gregory's death in 1085, the emperor made war on the pope and eventually drove him from Rome to die in exile, part guest, part prisoner of his Norman allies. The war of words and arms continued, temporarily appeased in 1122 with a compromise, the Concordat of Worms, which kept the right of investing bishops and abbots in the hands of the church, but specified that insofar as these princes of the church were also feudal landowners—and they all were—their feudal obligations to the secular power, the emperor, would continue in force. It was not until over a century after Gregory's death, with the accession of Pope Innocent III, that his claims were reiterated once again with a sound of real authority.

The importance of Innocent's pontificate lay not in its length—it lasted only from 1198 to 1216—but in its vigor. Innocent did not invent new ideas but acted effectively on old ones. Like Gregory VII, he was tenacious and courageous, an incomparable administrator. He recaptured and enlarged the central Italian lands that had intermittently belonged to the papacy. He reorganized his administration to serve the purposes of a multifarious regime with interests all across Europe. He recognized the potential value of the Franciscans and Dominicans—two orders that had their inception during his reign. He intervened in imperial elections and in domestic politics in several countries as far away as England: by 1213 he had compelled King John, "John Lackland," to grant the lands of England to the Holy See of Rome and receive them back as the pope's vassal. The baronial rebellion that compelled John to affix his seal to the Magna Carta at Runnymede in 1215 grew directly from these concessions to Rome. And in the year of Magna Carta, Innocent assembled the Fourth Lateran Council in Rome, a vast affair crowded with hundreds of princes of the church and representatives of the secular sword; it was at this council that the Church of Rome reiterated its spiritual supremacy over the Christian world. Once again, old ideas received new and definitive formulation: the council declared the sacraments to be "the channels of grace" and the Eucharist—the mass—to be the chief of these channels. It proclaimed the miraculous event of the mass, transubstantiation, as dogma binding on all Christians. It regulated traffic in relics, tightened regulations of monastic life, condemned heresy, and declared the Church of Rome to be one and universal: Gregory VII's political claims were here put into sacred language.

The only conspicuous failure of Innocent III's papacy was the Fourth Crusade, undertaken at the pope's urging. This, too, was an old idea: the notion of crusades had originated in penitential pilgrimages undertaken by Christians to the holy places in Palestine. The early Muslims, tolerant, permitted these pious incursions, but when news came that the Muslim occupants of Jerusalem were persecuting pilgrims and desecrating the Holy Sepulchre, the papacy invited the fighting elite of Europe to take the cross and recapture the Holy Land for Christianity. The First Crusade, preached by Pope Urban II, began in 1095; the Ninth Crusade ended in 1272 with the fall of the last Christian stronghold to Muslim troops. In between, there were official and unofficial crusades, preached and undertaken for a wide variety of reasons. The papacy had religious reasons for seeking the recapture of holy Jerusalem but, as cynics have not failed to point out, some popes at least thought it useful to be publicly identified as the leading champion of Christendom, while other popes, it seems, were pleased to have unemployed and restless European noblemen vent their energies on infidels in the Near East rather than on Christians nearer home. The crusaders themselves ranged across the spectrum of human motivation: sincere believers jostled those lusting for adventure and others hungering for land. Most of the Crusades marched under the highest auspices and were undertaken as military fortunes in the Near East shifted and European settlements there were threatened or reduced. The Fourth Crusade, which briefly marred the rule of Pope Innocent III, is characteristic of their baser aspects. Under pressure from the Venetians, who financed most of the venture, the crusading army first undertook to recapture some Venetian territory in the Balkans, and then in 1204, veered toward Constantinople, took this Christian capital and sacked it, mainly for the Venetians' benefit. Only a few years later, in 1212, another Crusade, this one unofficial, began to assemble in France. Led by a visionary peasant boy, the Children's Crusade gathered thousands of children on the way, but those among them who were not sold into slavery died of hunger and exposure. By that time, the name "crusade" had been perverted to other purposes: it was Innocent III who pressed the military campaign against the Albigensian heretics (see p. 36) and called it a crusade. Thus the very idea of crusades had been widely discredited before the Crusades themselves came to an end in the 1270s. Their part in the expansion of Europe is undoubted; their value, even in that expansion, remains dubious.

The papacy lost more from these excursions than it gained. Innocent III died in 1216 and was succeeded by a number of intelligent and strong-minded popes. But this was the time of the powerful Hohenstaufen Emperor Frederick II, called *Stupor Mundi,* who, in his long reign from 1211 to 1250, vigorously battled the papacy in diplomatic and military arenas alike. The most imperialistic of popes was still to come: Boniface VIII, who succeeded to the Papal Chair in 1294 and promptly asserted papal supremacy over worldly rulers. In 1302, he issued the defiant bull *Unam Sanctam,* which restated, for the last time, the ambitious vision that Gregory VII and Innocent III had seen before him. But Boniface had a redoubtable enemy in Philip IV, the Fair, of France, who threatened to bring the pope to trial. Boniface eluded him: humiliated, helpless, the pope died in 1303. Soon after, in 1309, the papacy moved to the town of Avignon, a papal enclave in southern France, where it was to stay for seven papal reigns, to 1378. It was a shameful interlude, the "Babylonian captivity of the Church," widely interpreted as papal surrender to the power of France and as an abandonment of its spiritual office for the sake of security and splendor. It meant all those things, doubtless, but it also marked a shift in the temper of Europe, the rise of new and powerful entities—the states of the West—and the emergence of that time of glory and trouble, the Renaissance.

SELECTED READINGS

In a field as vast as that covered by this introductory chapter, we can send the reader to only a handful of titles. For antiquity in general, see Tom B. Jones, *Ancient Civilization* (1960). See also Henri Frankfort, ed., *The Intellectual Adventure of Ancient Man* (1946), which deals with the ancient Near East in lucid chapters (the paperback version, titled *Before Philosophy* [1949], omits the ancient Hebrews); Edward Chiera, *They Wrote on Clay* (1938); and Otto Neugebauer, *The Exact Sciences in Antiquity* (2nd ed., 1962), which is excellent. For Egypt, there are Henri Frankfort, *Ancient Egyptian Religion: An Interpretation* (1948), and John A. Wilson, *The Burden of Egypt* (1951). For the early history of the Jews, Salo Wittmayer Baron, *A Social and Religious History of the Jews*, vols. 1 and 2, *Ancient Times* (2nd rev. ed., 1952), is indispensable.

C. M. Bowra, *The Greek Experience* (1957), Hugh Lloyd-Jones, ed., *The Greek World* (1965), and H. D. F. Kitto, *The Greeks* (rev. ed., 1957), are accessible introductions. The emergence of thought in ancient Greece is analyzed in Bruno Snell, *The Discovery of the Mind: The Greek Origins of European Thought* (tr. 1953), and in earlier books by F. M. Cornford: *From Religion to Philosophy: A Study in the Origins of Western Speculation* (1912) and *Principium Sapientiae: The Origins of Greek Philosophical Thought* (1952). For early Greece, see M. I. Finley, *The World of Odysseus* (1954). For economics and politics, see H. Michell, *The Economics of Ancient Greece* (2nd ed., 1957); Victor Ehrenberg, *The Greek State* (tr. 1960), a brilliant treatise; and A. Andrewes, *The Greek Tyrants* (1956). E. R. Dodds, *The Greeks and the Irrational* (1951), is a pioneering study. Werner Jaeger, *Paideia: The Ideals of Greek Culture*, 3 vols. (tr., 2nd ed., 1945), is an aristocratic view of that culture. On Greek science, see George Sarton's exhaustive but pedestrian *A History of Science: Ancient Science Through the Golden Age of Greece* (1952); it should be supplemented by S. Sambursky, *The Physical World of the Greeks* (tr. 1956). On religion, see W. K. C. Guthrie, *The Greeks and Their Gods* (1950), and Martin P. Nilsson, *Greek Folk Religion* (1940). Good introductions to the Greek achievement also include C. M. Bowra, *Ancient Greek Literature* (1933), and H. D. F. Kitto, *Greek Tragedy: A Literary Survey* (3rd ed., 1961). For the Hellenistic world, see M. I. Rostovtzeff, *Social and Economic History of the Hellenistic World*, 3 vols. (1941), a classic; W. W. Tarn, *Hellenistic Civilization* (3rd ed., 1952), a fine survey to be read with Tarn, *Alexander the Great* (1948); Moses Hadas, *Hellenistic Culture: Fusion and Diffusion* (1959), which is, in part, a "democratic" response to Jaeger's *Paideia*.

A good introduction to Roman history remains M. I. Rostovtzeff, *A History of the Ancient World*, vol. II, *Rome* (tr. 1928). Add to this H. H. Scullard, *A History of the Roman World from 753 to 146 B.C.* (3rd ed., 1961); Scullard, *From the Gracchi to Nero: A History of Rome from 138 B.C. to A.D. 68*, (3rd ed., 1970); and Michael Grant, *The World of Rome* (1960). The political transition from republic to empire is brilliantly analyzed in Ronald Syme, *The Roman Revolution* (1939). For the empire, see M. I.

Rostovtzeff, *Social and Economic History of the Roman Empire* (1926), and the more recent A. M. H. Jones, *The Later Roman Empire, 284-602,* 2 vols. (1964). Cyril Bailey, *Phases in the Religion of Ancient Rome* (1932), is very useful; so is H. J. Rose, *Ancient Roman Religion* (1948). M. L. W. Laistner, *The Greater Roman Historians* (1947); S. Sambursky, *The Physical World of Late Antiquity* (1962); and Samuel Dill, *Roman Society from Nero to Marcus Aurelius* (2nd ed., 1911) are all illuminating.

Amid a vast literature on the Fall of Rome and the emergence of Christianity, the following stand out: T. R. Glover, *The Conflict of Religions in the Early Roman Empire* (1909), and Ferdinand Lot, *The End of the Ancient World and the Beginnings of the Middle Ages* (tr. 1931)—both, though old, still full of vitality; Andrew Alföldi, *The Conversion of Constantine and Pagan Rome* (tr. 1948), to be read with Ramsay MacMullen, *Constantine* (1969); A. D. Nock, *Conversion: The Old and the New in Religion from Alexander the Great to Augustine of Hippo* (1933), elegant and comprehensive; Peter Brown, *Augustine of Hippo: A Biography* (1967) and *The World of Late Antiquity from Marcus Aurelius to Muhammad* (1971). In addition to Brown's last-named volume, which moves into the beginnings of the Middle Ages, see H. R. Trevor-Roper, *The Rise of Christian Europe* (1965); H. St. L. B. Moss, *The Birth of the Middle Ages, 395-814* (1935); William C. Bark, *Origins of the Medieval World* (1958); R. W. Southern, *The Making of the Middle Ages* (1953); and, on a special topic, J. M. Wallace-Hadrill, *The Barbarian West,* A.D. *400-1000* (1952).

For medieval history in general, see C. W. Previté-Orton, *The Shorter Cambridge Mediaeval History,* 2 vols. (rev. ed., 1952), which, despite its breathlessness, manages to be sound and authoritative. And see Denys Hay, *Europe: The Emergence of an Idea* (1957). See also, Henri Pirenne, *A History of Europe from the Invasions to the XVIth Century* (tr. 1955). Marc Bloch's masterpiece, *Feudal Society,* 2 vols. (tr. 1961), is indispensable. So is Bloch, *Land and Work in Medieval Europe* (tr. 1967). Social and economic history are well treated in Robert S. Lopez, *The Birth of Europe* (1967); the older, briefer study by Henri Pirenne, *Economic and Social History of Medieval Europe* (tr. 1936), remains useful; see also Pirenne's *Medieval Cities: Their Origins and the Revival of Trade* (tr. 1939), which should be compared with John H. Mundy and Peter Riesenberg, *The Medieval Town* (1958). Among other surveys of more restricted scope, Christopher Brooke, *Europe in the Central Middle Ages, 962-1154* (1964), is outstanding, as is Friedrich Heer, *The Medieval World: Europe, 1100-1350* (tr. 1962). Sir Maurice Powicke, *Medieval England* (1931); F. M. Stenton, *English Society in the Early Middle Ages* (1951); Geoffrey Barraclough, *Origins of Modern Germany* (2nd ed., 1947); R. Fawtier, *The Capetian Kings of France* (tr. 1960); and Charles Petit-Dutaillis, *The Feudal Monarchy in France and England: From the Tenth to the Thirteenth Century* (tr. 1964) are excellent introductions for their respective regions. For the Crusades, Steven Runciman, *History of the Crusades,* 3 vols. (1951-1954), is analytical and narrative.

For religious and intellectual life in the Middle Ages, H. O. Taylor, *The Medieval Mind,* 2 vols. (2nd ed., 1925), remains a valuable introduction. Two books by M. L. W. Laistner, *Thought and Letters in Western Europe,* A.D. *500 to 900* (2nd ed., 1957) and *The Intellectual Heritage in the Early Middle Ages* (1957), deal with the early period. C. H. McIlwain, *The Growth of Political Thought in the West: From the Greeks to the Middle Ages* (1932), may be supplemented with Fritz Kern, *Kingship, Law and the Constitution in the Middle Ages* (tr. 1939); Ernst H. Kantorowicz's provocative study, *The King's Two Bodies* (1957); Sidney Painter, *French Chivalry* (1940); David Knowles, *The Evolution of Medieval Thought* (1962); and Etienne Gilson, *History of Christian Philosophy in the*

Middle Ages (tr. 1955). Among G. G. Coulton's many books, *Five Centuries of Religion,* 4 vols. (1923-1950), gives a scholarly, if secularist survey. Cuthbert Butler, *Benedictine Monachism* (2nd ed., 1961), is valuable, as is Gerd Tellenbach, *Church, State and Christian Society at the Time of the Investiture Contest* (tr. 1940). See also Geoffrey Barraclough, *The Medieval Papacy* (1968); C. H. Haskins, *The Renaissance of the Twelfth Century* (1927); and vol. II, *The Thousand Years of Uncertainty,* A.D. *500 to* A.D. *1500,* of Kenneth S. Latourette's monumental *History of the Expansion of Christianity,* 7 vols. (1937-1945).

Among several valuable surveys of the Byzantine Empire, Norman H. Baynes and H. St. L. B. Moss, eds., *Byzantium: An Introduction to East Roman Civilization* (1948), is highly recommended; other good introductions include Baynes, *The Byzantine Empire* (2nd ed., 1946); J. M. Hussey, *The Byzantine World* (1957); and the outstanding longer work by Georgije Ostrogorsky, *History of the Byzantine State* (tr. 1956). D. J. Geanakoplos, *Byzantine East and Latin West: Two Worlds of Christendom in Middle Ages and Renaissance* (1966), considers cultural and social relationships.

For the Muslim world, see the economical study by Bernard Lewis, *The Arabs in History* (2nd ed., 1958); Philip K. Hitti, *History of the Arabs from the Earliest Times to the Present* (5th ed., 1951); and the controversial Henri Pirenne, *Mohammed and Charlemagne* (tr. 1939). And see G. E. von Gruenebaum, *Medieval Islam: A Study in Cultural Orientation* (1946).

1

The Renaissance in Italy

The Renaissance was everything its name implies: a true rebirth. While it kept alive many ties to the Christian Middle Ages, it renewed ties, dimly remembered or wholly forgotten, with classical antiquity and thus laid the groundwork for modern civilization. The claim the great Swiss historian, Jacob Burckhardt, made for the period over a century ago remains valid: the civilization of the Renaissance was "the mother of our own." [1] The chronological and intellectual distance between that age and our modern age may be considerable, but the connection between the two ages is intimate.

The first to celebrate the dawn of a new day were themselves men of the Renaissance—the Humanists, a new breed of scholars and poets. Passionate antiquarians and reform-minded educators, they saw the revolution they helped to make as a revolution; this awareness in itself gave the Renaissance its distinct character and unique vitality. From the middle of the fifteenth century on, the Humanists proclaimed their own time as an era of renewal in the arts,

---

[1] Burckhardt, who "discovered" the Renaissance as a distinct historical period in his classic *The Civilization of the Renaissance in Italy* (1860), remains the indispensable guide to that age.

49

in literature, and in learning that rivaled, and perhaps surpassed, the classical ages of Greece and Rome they worshiped. Giovanni Boccaccio hailed the revival of poetry and Coluccio Salutati the restoration of literature; Filippo Villani, like the other two a well-known Florentine Humanist, congratulated the painters of his native city on rescuing their art from extinction. [2] It became a commonplace of educated opinion that the world was awakening to a new age of light after nearly a thousand years of barbarous darkness. What Wordsworth said about the French Revolution, the Humanists said about their very different revolution in Italy three and four centuries before him: "Bliss was it in that dawn to be alive, but to be young was very heaven."

The Humanists' pronouncements, with their single-minded exuberance, capture a great moment in the history of Europe. Since the end of the Roman Empire in the West there had been several revivals of the classics, notably at the court of Charlemagne early in the ninth century and in urban centers in the twelfth century. Beginning around 1100, literature, the arts, and philosophy had prospered impressively. But these so-called "renaissances" did not step beyond the circle of traditional culture and styles of thought. The Renaissance that had its inception around the 1330s in Italy was different in kind: it evolved a way of looking at the world and at man in which we may recognize our own.

While it was important and instructive, the confidence of the Humanists tells only part of the story. And the conventional picture of the Renaissance— glittering courts, prosperous cities, sensual paintings, expansiveness every- where—wholly fails to capture the complexity of the age. The peasants and the urban poor, the bulk of Italy's population, lived on in misery; their unvarying routine was broken only by war and famine, and their superstitions survived as though nothing had happened among the educated. Even the educated sometimes saw the novelty around them with deep uneasiness. While the Humanists joyfully rediscovered ancient manuscripts, enjoyed the world of nature and man's inner life, gave voice to such secular passions as the desire for fame and glory, and experimented with a new individualism, there were many who feared all this innovation as a threat to traditional ways of thinking, standards of value, and ideals of conduct. The Renaissance was an age of heroism and crimes, of extravagant hopes and equally extravagant despair; the new individualism proved a source of pleasure and of anxiety. "True tragedy," Burckhardt noted, "which then found no place on the stage, stepped mightily through palaces, streets, and public squares." As Burckhardt also noted, it was in this mixture of freedom and fear, as much as in anything else, that the Renaissance was the mother of our modern age.

[2] Federico Chabod, *Machiavelli and the Renaissance* (1958), 152–153.

THE SETTING
⸺⟨◊⟩⸺

Economics and Politics

In striking contrast with the customary view of the Renaissance, the period began in a time of economic decline and physical devastation. During the very decades in which the Renaissance emerged, a commercial and agricultural depression settled over Europe that did not lift for over a hundred years. Prices declined, popular unrest grew, trade contracted, merchants failed; the Renaissance was the golden age of bankruptcies. Not everyone suffered, of course; some merchants waxed rich in the midst of the general decline, and the shrewd and lucky moneylenders of the fourteenth century, like the Fuggers of Augsburg, became the proud princely banking houses of the fifteenth. Laborers, becoming scarce, sought higher wages, though they rarely got them. But in general, in town and country alike, these were decades of constricted markets, low profits, and widespread famine. The drop in population, which, following three centuries of marked expansion, set in at the same time, was part consequence and part cause of this depression. Neither agricultural techniques nor medical technology could keep pace with the rising population, and so nature did, as it were, wholesale what individuals could only accomplish in small measure through birth control: population was checked and cut back by old scourges—famine, pestilence, and war—raging, it seemed to dismayed onlookers, with unheard-of fury.

The consequences for the Italian cities, and for all of Europe, were catastrophic. In 1347, Italian ships, swarming with infected rats, imported the plague into Sicily. With stunning speed, the Black Death spread.[3] By the end of that year, many thousands had died in the Italian peninsula; by 1348 the disease had reached Spain and France and by 1350 no European state, from England to Poland, was safe. The plague played with Europe as a cat plays with a mouse: it would rise in waves of devastation and then let up, raising false hopes only to dash them as it resumed its lethal work. While the Black Death was at its worst in the fourteenth century, it broke out several times in the fifteenth century as well, and remained an ever-present menace right into the eighteenth century. Its mortal effects were, and remain, incalculable. In

---

[3] The two most prominent forms of the plague were bubonic—named for the buboes, or swellings, produced when it attacked the lymph glands—and pneumonic, which attacked the lungs. Both were highly contagious, the latter more than the former, and both were almost invariably deadly.

Florence, which had reached a population of about ninety thousand during the prosperous 1330s, perhaps fifty thousand died in the single year 1348, and as late as 1380, the population had not yet climbed back to sixty thousand.[4] Boccaccio's celebrated *Decameron* reflects the ravages of the plague in Florence in more than one way: the ostensible reason for the meeting of the storytellers whose one hundred tales make up the book is the plague from which they have fled to a country estate; the preface of the book contains a graphic description of the sufferings in the city itself. Nearby, in the Tuscan city of Pistoia, the population dropped from about eleven thousand to six thousand in 1351; by 1400, it was below four thousand.[5] Elsewhere, in Italy and in other countries, in cities and in the countryside, the devastations were quite as bad: in Bremen and Hamburg perhaps half the population died; England, with a population of about 3,700,000 in the critical year 1348, could count no more than 2,000,000 souls in 1400. Some areas were untouched, some suffered only slightly. But the over-all loss of life across Europe in the first thirty years of the Black Death was no less than 40 percent. The time came when men omitted the regular rites for the dead; they were too dangerous to the survivors.

The mundane consequences were, among other things, an economic decline. At the beginning of the fifteenth century, the total imports and exports at Genoa were down to a fifth of what they had been at the end of the thirteenth century, while the Florentine production of cloth dropped from one hundred thousand bolts a year to about thirty thousand by 1500.[6] The economic depression and the drop in morale were rapid; economic and spiritual recovery were slow. For even when the plague subsided, wars and civil wars continued their own deadly work.

Italy in the fourteenth and fifteenth centuries was a congeries of competing states, often at war. The "Babylonian captivity" of the papacy in Avignon (see p. 44) was a political advantage even if it was a disgrace to the church: "For the first extended period in its history Italy in the fourteenth century was able to go her own way largely undisturbed by the conflict which had troubled her from the eleventh century between the claims of the Roman emperor of the west and those of the leader of the Western Christian church, the pope."[7] The empire was just as impotent. The city-states were therefore on their own to strive for power by seeking allies and plotting the destruction of their rivals. This was the atmosphere that nourished the disillusioned political philosophy of Machiavelli. Many of the states were small towns fighting desperately for a

---

[4] Gene A. Brucker, *Florentine Politics and Society, 1343–1378* (1962), 9, 15n.

[5] See Eugene F. Rice, Jr., in John A. Garraty and Peter Gay, eds., *The Columbia History of the World* (1972), 486–487.

[6] Ibid.; Robert S. Lopez, "Hard Times and Investment in Culture," in Wallace K. Ferguson et al., *The Renaissance, Six Essays* (1962), 40; Karl F. Helleiner, "The Population of Europe from the Black Death to the Eve of the Vital Revolution," in E. E. Rich and C. H. Wilson, eds., *The Cambridge Economic History of Europe*, vol. IV (1967), 1–95 passim.

[7] Denys Hay, *The Italian Renaissance in Its Historical Background* (1961), 58.

measure of independence: in the fourteenth century, the territory of Tuscany alone was divided into the states of Florence, Pisa, Lucca, Siena, Volterra, Arezzo, San Gimignano, and Cortona, to say nothing of the smaller cities.[8] The city-states found themselves trapped in an inexorable cycle. Too small to guarantee food for the laboring masses and to build an army of defense, they were driven to endless wars of expansion to secure land, subjects, and raw materials. These in themselves imposed heavy financial burdens; for since the states could not supply adequate manpower, they relied on mercenaries led by *condottieri*. But these military adventurers, by profession ruthless and by preference rootless, posed new threats; more than one ambitious *condottiere* attempted to take power over the city he had been hired to protect; more than one succeeded. Like the Greek city-states of antiquity, the Italian city-states never solved their most pressing problem: the relation of resources to power.[9]

This tension among the Italian states could not be sustained forever. By the fifteenth century, though wars continued, the Italian peninsula was substantially divided up among five major powers—Venice, Florence, despotic Milan, the Papal States, and the feudal monarchy of Naples—each with its satellites, connected by alliances and divided by implacable rivalries. In addition, a few tough military principalities survived to complicate the situation. The number was small enough to ensure a certain degree of stability—imperialist Milan was the main disturber of the peace in fifteenth-century Italy—but too large to permit hegemony to any single state. A balance of power was purchased at the expense of unity, and the continuing, incurable division of Italy was to make it the victim, at the end of the fifteenth century, of European power politics (see p. 115).

While the pressure of the power struggle drove Italian states toward alliances that would control international conflict, the pressure of the social struggle drove them toward strong-man governments that would control domestic conflict. All across the peninsula, from the fourteenth to the fifteenth century, the drift was from republic to despotism. The pattern was everywhere the same: the city-states lived by trade and were dominated by great merchant families. These mercantile dynasties were united in gilds, allied by marriage, and held together by common interest against common adversaries. But they were also divided by family feuds, commercial rivalries, and competing allegiances to papacy and empire, and these divisions were expensive and exhausting. Factional conflict was exacerbated by class conflict: the great families were in perpetual battle with lesser merchants. They lived in an uneasy, unstable truce with the working masses recruited from the countryside, who inhabited the stinking workers' quarters in the city, and who on occasion, when their grievances became insupportable or when they found an articulate

[8] Ibid., 60–62.
[9] William J. Bouwsma, "Politics in the Age of the Renaissance," in *Western Civilization*, vol. I (3rd rev. ed., 1961), 215.

leader, vented their endemic discontent in riots and general uprisings. The poor of Florence, miserable and oppressed and indispensable, never found their poet as did the English poor, but the vision of *Piers Plowman,* that fourteenth-century allegory, probably by William Langland, would have aptly applied to them:

> The poor may plead and pray in the doorway;
> They may quake for cold and thirst and hunger;
> None receives them rightfully and relieves their
>   suffering.
> They are hooted at like hounds and ordered off.

The great merchants and the middling people thought they could safely disregard the plebs and concentrated instead on fighting one another. The leading families valued security above freedom—or rather, were content to let other freedoms go as long as they were free to make money—and, weary of costly strife, they appealed to outsiders, or to one dominant local family, to establish a temporary dictatorship, which, more often than not, turned into a permanent despotism.

The labels despotism and republic, which go back to Renaissance Italy, must be applied circumspectly: despotisms could be benign, republics oppressive. Yet there were despots of melodramatic villainy, adventurers who followed their impulses unchecked by religious scruples or institutional controls. Some were madmen who let loose their dogs on the population or rolled stones at them from high hills; others were self-willed sensualists or sybarites who indulged their tastes at the expense—literally—of their cities and silenced all criticism by putting their critics to death. Since most rulers had no legitimate claim to rulership and governed simply because they held power, political life was poisoned by plots and counterplots, by rumors, informers, and an air of universal suspicion that invaded even the family. An ambitious brother or son was a potential enemy for the despot, to be watched and, if necessary, eliminated. Inevitably, moral confusion, a sense that everything is permitted, infected subjects as much as rulers. "Once the burghers of a city," Burckhardt reports, "had a general who had freed them from foreign pressure; they consulted daily how to reward him, and concluded that no reward in their power was large enough, not even if they made him lord of the city. At last one of them rose up and suggested: 'Let us kill him and worship him as our patron saint.' And so, we are told, they did." [10]

This chilling story may not be literally true, but it nicely conveys the atmosphere, not merely in smaller states but also in great cities like Milan. Late in the thirteenth century, its leading families turned over the government to a single aristocratic family, the Visconti, who ruled Milan with an iron hand for

[10] Burckhardt, *Die Kultur der Renaissance in Italien: Ein Versuch* (ed. 1958), 21–22, translated by Peter Gay.

a century and a half until they were replaced in 1450 by Francesco Sforza, a brilliant and audacious *condottiere*. The reign of the Visconti was marked by deadly family feuds, enormous cruelty, and successful wars of expansion; it was endurable only because the regime gave the merchants what they wanted— protection and prosperity. The greatest of the Visconti clan, Gian Galeazzo, took power in 1378, embarked on a policy of expansion, and in 1395 bought the coveted title of "duke" from the emperor, giving his rule new legitimacy and prestige. Ten years before, in 1385, he had assumed sole rulership by having his uncle Bernabo murdered, to the surprise of no one—this was Renaissance politics.

Yet some of the despots were men of taste, true men of the Renaissance; Humanists did not have to be hirelings to say that the arts and sciences flourished best under an absolute ruler. There were Renaissance princes who protected painters and scholars for the sake of painting and scholarship. Francesco Sforza of Milan took an informed interest in architecture, imported Humanists to educate his children, and, reversing the bellicose policy of the Visconti before him, made peace with Florence. Federigo da Montefeltro, who governed Urbino from 1444 to 1482, was a characteristic *condottiere* who hired himself and his troops to other Italian rulers and enhanced the fortunes of his family and his small state by adroit diplomatic moves, not excluding marriage. But, as his contemporary biographer, the Florentine bookseller Vespasiano, said of him, Federigo was as brilliant in the arts of peace as in the arts of war. He was a good classical scholar; an amateur theologian; a well-informed patron of architects, sculptors, and painters; a generous supporter of impecunious Humanists; and best of all, a mild duke: his treatment of his subjects "suggested that they were rather his children." His Urbino "was a wondrous sight: all his subjects were well-to-do and waxed rich through labor at the works he had instituted, and a beggar was never seen."[11] Even if we take this panegyric at some discount, Federigo remains the model of the good Renaissance despot.

Conversely, republics were normally tightly constricted oligarchies: in Venice, where nobles alone formed the active political public, the nobility made up less than 5 percent of the population; in Florence, the active citizenry was no larger.[12] Venice, the richest of Italian cities, secure on its remote lagoons since its founding in the sixth century and superbly placed for trade with the East, was run by, and for, its aristocratic merchant families. True, early in the fourteenth century, Petrarch had noted about Venice with some disapproval: "Much freedom reigns there in every respect, and what I should call the only evil prevailing—but also the worst—far too much freedom of speech."[13] But this freedom was possible because the Venetian government secured domestic

[11] Vespasiano, *Renaissance Princes, Popes and Prelates* (Torchbook ed., 1963), 107–108.

[12] William J. Bouwsma, *Venice and the Defense of Republican Liberty: Renaissance Values in the Age of the Counter Reformation* (1968), 60; Felix Gilbert, *Machiavelli and Guicciardini: Politics and History in Sixteenth Century Florence* (1965), 20.

[13] Bouwsma, *Venice*, 93.

peace and boundless wealth; criticism was relatively free because relatively few found grounds for criticism. Besides, the notorious Council of Ten, established in the fourteenth century as a temporary adjunct to its other governing councils, became a permanent watchdog over the political health of the Venetian republic. [14] Operating with commendable dispatch, employing informers and a secret police force, the Council of Ten discovered plots in their incipient stages and sent dangerous men beyond reach—into exile or death. With its doge—that powerless, ceremonial head of state elected for life—with its rotating councils where all were equal, the Venetian constitution symbolized the omnipotence, fulfilled the purposes, and expressed the will of the merchant aristocracy to perfection. Venice secured the kind of loyalty that cannot be bought by fear and lies deeper than mere self-interest.

Florence

Florence was, or liked to think it was, different. While ingenious politicians used the republican Florentine constitution as a screen behind which merchant magnates manipulated the machinery of power, the prevalence of republican rhetoric acted as a check on the oligarchy. Republicanism was an ideal to which the dissident could appeal and which the most ambitious Florentines found it convenient to respect. Even the Medici were too shrewd and too attached to this Florentine ideal to subvert it wholly. At the beginning of the fifteenth century, stung to self-awareness by the aggressive designs of Visconti Milan, Florentine Humanists reexamined their boasted republican tradition: Leonardo Bruni, an impressive polemicist and responsible public official, set the tone with his "civic humanism"—a defense of the active as against the contemplative life. He advocated public service, extolled liberty, and recalled the long-neglected virtues of the ancient Roman Republic. [15] Bruni's civic humanism, developed in the face of foreign danger and in the midst of magnificent artistic vitality, was a characteristic local product. In political theory as in the arts, literature, and philosophy, Florence contributed far more than its share to the making and the glory of the Renaissance.

This contribution was the result of hard work in unpromising circumstances. Florence enjoyed an appealing but insecure geographical situation. Surrounded by the lovely Tuscan hills, bathed in the warm, clear Tuscan sun, the city was cut off from the sea by the hostile republics of Lucca and Pisa. Much of its energy was consumed by wearing, inconclusive wars with these neighbors, too weak to resist Florentine expansion, too strong wholly to succumb to it: while Pisa was added to Florentine territory in 1406, a disastrous campaign against Lucca led to a grave domestic crisis in 1433.

[14] Ibid., 62.
[15] Hans Baron, *The Crisis of the Early Italian Renaissance: Civic Humanism and Republican Liberty in an Age of Classicism and Tyranny* (2nd ed., 1966).

While in the course of centuries Florence experienced political upheavals, the shape of its government down to the end of the fifteenth century was set early in the twelfth, when the gilds emerged as the distinctive political institution of the republic. In 1282, the seven greater gilds—with the bankers, wool merchants, and cloth importers in the vanguard—tightened their grip on power and devised a constitution that, for all practical purposes, excluded nobles from politics and gave the members of the fourteen lesser gilds—the shopkeepers and artisans—token representation. The ruling oligarchy was active, energetic, shrewd; in the course of the fourteenth century, it made Florence into one of the leading banking and trading centers in Europe. For all its internal strains and undeniable thirst for profit and power, the oligarchy was also, in its way, public spirited: in 1427, at a time of public need, it devised a tax assessment, the *catasto,* astonishing in its equity and unprecedented in the burdens it placed on the rich. Twice in the fourteenth century the oligarchs found themselves obliged to make concessions, first, in 1343, to the lesser gilds after an economic crash, then, in 1378, to the disfranchised workers when the wool workers went into the streets to protest increasing pressure from the greater on the lesser gilds. The Revolt of the Ciompi,[16] as the rising of 1378 came to be called, was an experiment in democratizing the oligarchy; it succeeded only for a moment. By 1381, the old families were back to rule undisturbed and to indulge their own rivalries; when in the 1430s the government fell into the hands of the Medici, the event meant a change of personnel but not of policy or political structure.

The history of the Medici dynasty is the history of the Renaissance itself: ruthless, admirable and terrifying, filled with contradictions. The family made its mark in Florentine affairs in the fourteenth century by acquiring wealth and a reputation for liberalism—one Medici had supported the Ciompi—but it was not until 1397 that the family began the ascendancy it would keep for a century, with the founding of the Medici Bank. Giovanni de' Medici, the founder, was a gifted businessman, a bountiful philanthropist, and a popular political leader with a taste for opposition to the oligarchy. His impressive son, Cosimo de' Medici, who assumed management in 1429 after his father's death, used his immense wealth and his father's prestige to equal advantage; he made the family enterprise into a European power and himself into the ruler of Florence. The bank had branches in major Italian and foreign cities, as far away as London; the enormously profitable branch in Rome handled the business of the papacy and of the great Roman families. In 1434, Cosimo took control over Florence, control that ended only with his death thirty years later. His power rested not on any official position but on his wealth, his adroit use of the firm, his manipulation of elections coupled with well-timed sentences of imprison-

---

[16] *Ciompi* is a corruption of the French word *compère,* which the Florentines had heard from French soldiers; it referred to the wool workers and then, by extension, to the working classes as a whole.

ment or exile for recalcitrant opponents, his eminently personal and eminently successful pacific foreign policy, his lavish public benefactions, and—a surprising modern touch—a natural, tactful simplicity that gave him the affection of wide circles in the republic. When the Humanist Pope Pius II visited Florence he noted: "Though Cosimo is practically lord of the city, he carries himself so as to appear as a private citizen." [17] On his death in 1464, Cosimo's fellow citizens placed a short eloquent epitaph on his tombstone: *pater patriae*.

Cosimo de' Medici was a Renaissance man in his vigor and versatility, his genial association with Humanists and earnest study of philosophy, his ambition, and his highly individualistic religious convictions. He was a worldly businessman who went on silent retreats to refresh his soul, a fervent reader of Plato who was also a devout servant of Christ. These qualities, with all their splendor and complexity, reappeared in his grandson, Lorenzo de' Medici, called "the magnificent." Even the legends that soon formed around Lorenzo are typical of his age, for the Renaissance was fertile soil for biography; it reveled in making idols of mere mortals. Cosimo's son, Piero, though sickly, had beaten back a challenge to his family's rule over Florence, but Piero died in 1469, and Lorenzo was called upon to take charge, in business and politics, at the age of twenty. He was young but he was ready: he had absorbed a thoroughgoing Humanist education and the Medici tradition at home, and he had already demonstrated a precocious cool temper and diplomatic skill on a variety of missions. The family business was passing the peak of its prosperity and influence, and Lorenzo did little to arrest the downward trend; his bank declined in company with a general decline in Florentine prosperity and was saved from open bankruptcy only by the French invasions of 1494.

The legends surrounding Lorenzo de' Medici—part invention, part embroidery, part fact—concentrate on his humanism. Like his grandfather before him, he surrounded himself with men of brilliance, generously lent the Humanists books and gave them access to his table, employed painters, architects, and sculptors to embellish his country houses, and fostered talent. Beyond this, he readily gave advice on architecture that other magnates adroitly begged him to give. The list of his friends and employees is practically coextensive with achievement in Florentine culture of his day: the painters Sandro Botticelli and Domenico Ghirlandaio, the philosopher Marsilio Ficino, the poet Angelo Poliziano, the sculptor Andrea Verocchio are only the most famous members of the Medici circle. And Lorenzo was more than a consumer of Renaissance culture: the advice he gave on architecture was worth hearing, he was informed enough in philosophy to discuss it sensibly with the most learned of his Humanist friends, and he wrote verses of which a professional poet would not have been ashamed.

[17] Nicolai Rubinstein, ed., *Florentine Studies: Politics and Society in Renaissance Florence* (1968), 128n, translated by Peter Gay.

Yet Lorenzo's main skill lay in political leadership, his greatest triumphs in foreign policy. His techniques of control were the techniques his ancestors had used: an increasing concentration of power in his hands coupled with attempts to preserve republican appearances, a pacific diplomacy pursued in person with great alertness and physical courage, the forging of family alliances through arranged marriages, and the use of his powerful and attractive presence to bind men to his person. He needed all the skills at his command: the international situation was increasingly unstable, and at home there were rumblings against the "Medici tyrants," partly motivated by authentic republican leanings, but fanned by rival banking factions anxious for power and greedy for profits. In 1478, the Pazzi family, an old dynasty of Florentine bankers, resentful and vindictive, devised a conspiracy to murder Lorenzo and his popular brother Giuliano. The Pazzi conspiracy reads like a Renaissance plot out of a romance, but it was reality: after some changes of plan, and after obtaining qualified assent from the pope, Sixtus IV, who had his own reasons for hating Lorenzo, the conspirators decided to murder the Medici brothers at mass, in the cathedral of Florence. The plot failed: while Giuliano was stabbed to death, Lorenzo, though wounded, escaped with his life. Justice was summary and terrible: more than eighty persons were hanged, including prominent church-men and some innocent bystanders. But Lorenzo came out of the conspiracy and the brief war that followed it with increased power and prestige, more determined than ever to restore and preserve peace in Italy. For the years that remained to him, he devoted himself to this diplomatic task. He succeeded brilliantly; when he died in 1492, the peace of Italy, though precarious, was still intact.

There is something autumnal about Lorenzo's life and work, a sense that nothing, not even the dominance of the Medici, is secure. His most famous verses poignantly capture this feeling of evanescence:

> "Quant' e bella giovinezza
> Che si fugge tuttavia!
> Chi viol esser lieto, sia;
> Di doman non c'e certezza.—

How lovely is youth, how quickly it flies! Let him who will be merry, of tomorrow nothing is sure." [18] This trivial-sounding quatrain accurately predicted the future. Two years after his death, the French invaded Italy, and Lorenzo's son, Piero, fled the city. This was not the end of the Medicis. They reappeared in early sixteenth-century Florence to govern a domain much diminished in importance; but among the newly styled dukes, one, Cosimo, was a ruler of great competence. Others married into royal houses; they appear prominently in the history of France. And two Medicis filled the papal throne: Lorenzo's son Giovanni as Leo X, from 1513 to 1521; Lorenzo's nephew Giulio as Clement VII, from 1523 to 1534. Their tenure seems an ironic commentary on the ambiguous achievement of the Medici dynasty and the pathetic end of the Renaissance: Leo X was, as a true Medici, a great patron of the arts, but he also enjoyed the dubious distinction of presiding over Catholic Christendom at the beginning of its irrevocable splintering by Martin Luther. And Clement VII, though diligent, was inept, and it was during his papacy, in 1527, that Rome was brutally sacked by German and Spanish mercenaries in the employ of Emperor Charles V (see p. 117). The Italian Renaissance ended as it had begun two centuries before in Petrarch's mind—in turmoil.

THE HUMANISTS

Makers of a Style: Petrarch and His Followers

The old view that revolutions are made by great men is now discredited, but a look at the beginnings of the Renaissance almost tempts the historian to rehabilitate it. [19] Petrarch was not the first of the Humanists, but he was for long years the only great Humanist, and others felt impelled to follow his path by the sheer force of his example. Petrarch, eager for fame, would have been gratified at his influence, but astonished also: he aimed to be a poet and a moralist, to follow his talent as he understood it—or rather, as he painfully, all his life, tried to understand it. "You make a orator of me, a historian, philosopher, and poet, and finally even a theologian," he wrote to a friend in 1362. "But," he protested, "let me tell you, my friend, how far I fall short of your estimation. . . . I am nothing of what you attribute to me. What am I then? I am a fellow who never quits school, and not even that, but a backwoodsman who is roaming around through the lofty beech trees all alone, humming to himself some silly little tune, and—the very peak of presumption and assurance—dipping his shaky pen into his inkstand while sitting under a bitter laurel tree. . . . I am not so very eager to belong to a definite school of thought; I am striving for truth." [20] The charm and candor of this self-appraisal made Petrarch into a revolutionary. But he did not quite know it, as Boccaccio would know it soon after. Petrarch was a wanderer by choice, a seeker by temperament, a maker largely by inadvertence.

[19] Hay, *Italian Renaissance*, 68-69.
[20] Petrarch to Francesco Bruni, quoted in Ernst Cassirer et al., eds., *The Renaissance Philosophy of Man* (1948), 34.

The Florentine Francesco Petrarca [21] began his restless life, appropriately enough, in exile. He was born in 1304 near Arezzo, where his father had taken refuge after being banished from Florence for political reasons. Petrarch's contemporary fame rested largely on his poetry—on his Italian sonnets and lyrics, his rhymed Latin letters, and the epic about Scipio Africanus, *Africa*, which he circulated but never finished: in 1341 he was crowned in Rome as poet laureate. But his historical significance lies in two discoveries—his discovery of antiquity and of himself. He was, as Gibbon said four centuries later, "the eloquent Petrarch" who, "by his lessons and his example, may justly be applauded as the first harbinger of day." [22]

Petrarch's discovery of antiquity began with his discovery of some ancients. Forced to study law at Montpellier in France, he found himself instead passionately devouring Cicero and, soon after, St. Augustine; these two writers remained Petrarch's favorite classics all his life. His choice is significant both for what it excludes and what it includes. Petrarch, the great Humanist, never acquired more than a smattering of Greek; to a friend who had sent him a copy of Homer's work he replied sadly: "Your Homer is dumb with me, or rather I am deaf to him." [23] And by giving Cicero and Augustine equal claim to his admiration, Petrarch underscored the religious compromise that most Humanists were to adopt: a continued unquestioning loyalty to the Christian faith coupled with a new understanding for the classics of pagan, especially Roman, antiquity.

Petrarch studied his beloved ancients devoutly but not uncritically. In 1345, in the cathedral library of Verona, he discovered the long-forgotten letters Cicero had sent to his man of business Atticus, to his brother Quintus, and to Brutus. [24] These letters greatly enlarged Petrarch's familiarity with Cicero, who had been up to then a somewhat shadowy figure, a remote if eloquent rhetorician. Cicero's letters elated and depressed Petrarch: Petrarch deplored Cicero's obvious compromises with the sordid business of this world; the unmatched Roman Republican turned out to be in his letters a politician among politicians, a man with ordinary qualities. Petrarch expressed his disappointment quite directly, in a letter to Cicero, which was one of the many bridges to antiquity Petrarch sought to build.

Petrarch's effort to see Cicero honestly, unadorned, is a noteworthy achievement and a revision of scholarly ideals prevalent in his day. The effort implied and exacted the search for more classical manuscripts, the open-eyed study and the meticulous purification of manuscripts already known and of

[21] Petrarch's father was known as Petracco; Petrarch himself appears first to have spelled his name Petracchi and then adopted the more familiar version Petrarca. In English he has always been Petrarch.

[22] Edward Gibbon, *Decline and Fall of the Roman Empire* (1902), VII, 117.

[23] Ernest Hatch Wilkins, *Life of Petrarch* (1961), 136.

[24] Ibid., 51.

those coming to light. In 1428, Leonardo Bruni, Petrarch's admirer and biographer, could justly boast that Florence had restored Latin and even Greek learning and made it possible "to see face to face, and no longer through the veil of absurd translations, the greatest philosophers and admirable orators and all those other men distinguished by their learning."[25] Petrarch's ideal was also a historian's ideal: it was his intent to see Cicero as a man in his own time. He addressed his beloved ancients with easy intimacy across the centuries, but he was aware that it was across the centuries that he was addressing them. Familiarity did not preclude distance; on the contrary, the more accurately the ancient texts came to be edited, and the more texts became available, the more antiquity appeared to be what it had been: a different age, far away in time. This notion was an intellectual innovation of far-reaching significance. For medieval theologians and lawyers the writings of the past, whether clerical or secular, existed in a timeless void, in a pantheon of immortals. Until Petrarch it was understood that Rome had never fallen. Petrarch restored to Europe the historian's priceless gift: the sense of distance and of time. The ancients were intellectually near, historically far; Rome had indeed fallen and given way to a cultural decline from which Europe was only now beginning to emerge. This was the meaning of Petrarch's celebrated claim that between the fall of Rome and his own time a "dark age" had intervened—it was not an assault on Christianity but a historian's attempt to see the past as past.

Petrarch, indeed, had no reason to assail Christianity. His vehement denunciations of the Avignon papacy show him, not an unbeliever, but a lover of Rome and an Italian patriot. St. Augustine was ever with him, even on that famous excursion to Mont Ventoux, not far from Avignon, in April 1336, a date that some historians have offered as the birth of the Renaissance. With his brother, purely for the sake of the adventure and the view from the top, Petrarch climbed the mountain and marveled at the sight below. No medieval man before Petrarch had expressed such secular affection for nature. But as he rested at the summit, he pulled his copy of St. Augustine's *Confessions* from his pocket, and read: "And men go about wondering at mountain heights and the mighty waves of the sea and broad flowing streams and the circuit of the sea and the wheeling of the stars: and to themselves they give no heed."[26] Even his piety led Petrarch to self-absorption.

Petrarch's preoccupation with himself was almost as consequential for the Renaissance as his classical learning. In his letters to the ancients, to friends, and to posterity, in dialogues and in a remarkable self-analysis, the *Secretum,* he explored his motives and his gifts, his vices and virtues, his religious and scholarly vocation. He turned the love of his life into imperishable poetry and thus made the name "Laura" immortal. He recorded his most domestic activities, including the planting of trees, landscaping of gardens, and visits of

[25] Baron, *Crisis of the Early Italian Renaissance,* 417.
[26] Wilkins, *Life of Petrarch,* 13.

friends, thus proclaiming, without even pretending to do so, the importance of the individual. If, as Burckhardt has argued, man in the Renaissance pierced the veil of medieval "illusion and infantile preconceptions," discovered himself, and became "a self-conscious *individual*,"[27] it is in Petrarch that this process is most patent. And it was the individual with all his contradictions on view: Petrarch was the inordinately ambitious poet who decried worldliness, a dweller at courts who proclaimed the pleasures of solitude, a proud political pamphleteer and humble pilgrim, a medieval Christian cherishing the life of contemplation and a Renaissance individualist who embodied the life of action, an enthusiastic proponent of personal and political freedom who spent most of his years with despots like the Visconti in Milan, a perpetual student whose own Greek was rudimentary but who did much to encourage the study of classical Greek in Italy. If modernity is the frank recognition of inner contradictions, Petrarch was a pioneer in modernity.

When Petrarch died in 1374, he was a famous man—the intimate of scholars, the correspondent of emperors, the favorite of princes, the critic of popes. The Humanists of the late fourteenth and early fifteenth centuries were all his followers, including Giovanni Boccaccio, Coluccio Salutati, the Florentine statesman, and Leonardo Bruni. When Bruni wrote his life of Petrarch in 1436, he gave the reason for Petrarch's reputation: he had been the pioneer. "Petrarch was the first who called back to light the gracefulness of the lost and extinguished ancient manner of writing." Even if his effort was imperfect, "still it was he who discovered and opened the path to this perfection . . . surely he did enough by merely pointing the way for those who were to follow after him."[28]

The Recovery of Antiquity

What Petrarch began others completed. In the course of the late fourteenth and early fifteenth centuries, Humanists ransacked the monastery libraries of Europe and found ancient manuscript after ancient manuscript. Petrarch had enlarged the known corpus of Cicero's works; his followers enlarged it further. Salutati found Cicero's *Epistulae ad familiares;* Poggio Bracciolini, the most avid and most successful collector of manuscripts the Renaissance was to know, found a substantial number of Cicero's legal speeches; and in 1421 Gerardo Landriani, the bishop of Lodi, found the complete manuscripts of Cicero's *Brutus, Orator,* and *De oratore.* Bracciolini also brought to light Lucretius' *De rerum natura,* almost unknown for centuries and apparently surviving in a single manuscript. Tacitus, Catullus, Propertius, known only from fragments and by reputation, now took on living form. And with the recovery of

[27] Burckhardt, *Die Kultur der Renaissance in Italien,* 252, translated by Peter Gay.
[28] Baron, *Crisis of the Early Italian Renaissance* (2nd ed., 1966), 267.

manuscripts went care for them. Petrarch was famous for his love of books—
he called his thirst for them his "one insatiable passion,"[29] and his disciples
were as passionate as he. Boccaccio accumulated a magnificent library, and
wealthy amateurs like the Medici eventually made such libraries into public
treasures. Nor was accumulation all: the Humanists, in their thirst for the pure
classical word, edited what they found. Again Petrarch showed the way: while
he was still a young man, he collected all available fragments of Livy's history
of Rome, collated them and commented upon them, to restore, as much as
possible, Livy's own words.[30]

Strictly speaking, the Humanists' discoveries were not discoveries—what
has not been lost cannot be found. But the Humanists' editorial labors, their
joyful announcements of their discoveries to their friends, and their diligent,
patient copying of long and often difficult manuscripts all prove that their
search for books was something more than the idle sport of antiquarians. For
all practical purposes, these ancient manuscripts had indeed been lost: they had
lain unattended and untouched in filthy libraries, often for many centuries. No
one had bothered to read these works, few had bothered even to keep them
clean or keep them intact: when Boccaccio visited the Benedictine monastery at
Monte Cassino, he found its "library" an open space without a door, with grass
growing on the window sills; manuscripts lay about in disorderly piles, covered
with dust, many of them torn and shredded. When Boccaccio, appalled to see
such desecration, asked how this was possible, the monks told him that they
had been in the habit of tearing off strips of parchment and selling them as
psalters or amulets, just to make some money.[31]

The Humanists changed all that; they made these manuscripts accessible
and thus part of general high culture. They did more: they inculcated respect
for learning and for accuracy. Some pagan classical writings had survived the
Middle Ages through the accretion of legends around them and through
allegorical interpretations that turned lascivious poets like Ovid into proper
reading for Christian clerics. If a classical author could not be converted into an
anticipator of Christian doctrine by means of allegory, some obliging monk
would forge the texts that made him so: the Stoic philosopher Seneca, for one,
was supplied with a correspondence with St. Paul—a forgery that Petrarch still
accepted as authentic. All sorts of stories were told of Vergil: he was turned into
a sorcerer, and there were learned theologians who took the *Aeneid* as an
allegory of man's pilgrimage on earth, almost as if the classical poet, born just
a little too soon, had fathomed the kind of teaching Christ would bring.
Gradually, with some missteps and wrong guesses, the Humanists dismantled
such allegories and discredited such legends. The classics were permitted to

[29] Wilkins, *Life of Petrarch*, 57.
[30] Ibid., 16–17.
[31] See Peter Gay, *The Enlightenment: An Interpretation*, vol. I, *The Rise of Modern Paganism*
(1966), 262.

speak in their own voice once again, as ancients and as pagans. This scholarship enormously enriched the culture of the Renaissance and threw doubt on devout efforts to protect the Christian dispensation from pagan impurities. The Humanists' erudition had political consequences: in 1361, Petrarch used his classical learning to discredit claims by Duke Rudolf IV that Austria was a sovereign state. Rudolf offered in evidence privileges granted by Caesar and Nero, but Petrarch proved these charters to be later forgeries. [32] In 1440, in a dazzling display of erudition that had reverberations among historians for centuries, the Florentine Humanist Lorenzo Valla proved that the so-called "donation of Constantine," a gift of the empire that the converted Roman emperor had purportedly made to the pope in the fourth century, was actually composed in the eighth century. Moreover, the Humanists' recovery of ancient works of literature and their affectionate reading of all classics gave unprecedented importance to purity of expression; it became fashionable to condemn the style of theologians and poets who had written before the advent of humanism as mere barbarian efforts. Since manner easily shades into matter, this too had practical consequences: the Humanists were calling attention to new—that is, old—ways of looking at man and the world. The recovery of antiquity was therefore more than the rediscovery of literary masters, interesting storytellers, and matchless poets. It was a prelude to new ways of thinking.

Philosophies and Theologies

There was no single philosophy of the Renaissance, any more than there was a single vision of antiquity. The Humanists placed antiquity into history, but they did not yet know enough about the ancients to give antiquity itself a history—the discrimination among ancient styles in philosophy or in art, or the discrimination between an original doctrine and the commentaries and interpretations of disciples, both familiar exercises to us today, were still impossible in the Renaissance. Those Humanists who wrote on philosophy gave themselves respectable party labels: they were "Platonists" or "Aristotelians" or in the midst of intellectual combat, "Antischolastics." But, in fact, in the time of the Renaissance ancient thought was still incompletely known and often ill-digested. While, from the middle of the fourteenth century on, Greek scholars swarmed across Renaissance Italy, bringing with them knowledge of the classical Greek language and thought, a leading Aristotelian like Pietro Pomponazzi could, in 1516, publish an important treatise on the *Immortality of the Soul* without knowing any Greek. [33] And there were "Platonists" who had never read Plato in the original.

---

[32] Wilkins, *Life of Petrarch*, 176.
[33] Paul Oskar Kristeller, *Renaissance Thought: The Classic, Scholastic, and Humanist Strains* (1961), 42.

Ignorance was compounded by confusion. There had been a good deal of Plato in Aristotle, but after many centuries of philosophical polemics, and since down to the fourteenth century almost nothing of Plato was in Latin, Plato's own teachings had been overlaid by what modern scholars have called Neoplatonism. The Neoplatonists, who began their work at Alexandria in the third century after Christ, concentrated on the mystical and theological implications of Plato's thought at the expense of the rest, and their version of Plato was therefore highly congenial to Christians. Renaissance Humanists did not yet distinguish Neoplatonism from Platonism, and often thought they were expounding the latter when they were expounding the former: Marsilio Ficino, who enjoyed celebrating Plato's birthday with his fellow philosophers of the Platonic "Academy" and holding philosophical discussions on the model of Plato's dialogues, was a conscientious translator of Plato, but his main philosophical treatise, significantly entitled *Platonic Theology*, was a rich and curious mixture of some aspects of Platonism, Neoplatonism, and Thomistic theology—a characteristic product of the Renaissance mentality.

Aristotle was little better off. His writings had remained far better known than Plato's, in part through redactions and commentaries by Arab scholars, and he had been incorporated into Scholastic philosophy by the systematizing mind of St. Thomas Aquinas. But this led some Humanists to attack Aristotle, for to strike at him was to strike at the philosophy of the Scholastics. In the fifteenth century, as the works of Aristotle were carefully disentangled from the writings of his interpreters, there were Humanists who found it possible to despise Scholasticism and to worship Aristotle at the same time, although even then the Aristotle they worshipped was hardly recognizable: Pomponazzi's "Aristotelianism" owes far more to medieval commentators than to the Greek master himself. [34] Beyond all this, the Humanists who criticized the Scholastics for their "barbarism"—by which, incidentally, they did not mean the content of their religious teaching but their style—found themselves in debate with other Humanists who were perfectly content with Scholasticism. In this welter of claims and counterclaims, Paul Kristeller's almost irritated verdict that "the Italian humanists on the whole were neither good nor bad philosophers, but no philosophers at all," [35] seems only slightly too harsh. Not content with losing themselves among ancient doctrines and medieval commentators, many of the Humanists found elements of ancient lore—astrology, magic, mysticism— highly intriguing. A darker, obscurantist tradition, largely borrowed from Hellenistic sources, competed with what we have come to think of as the classical heritage. As the German art historian Aby Warburg felicitously said of Renaissance thought: Athens had to be rescued from the hands of Alexandria. [36]

[34] Ibid.
[35] Ibid., 100.
[36] See Gay, *Enlightenment*, I, 259.

In the midst of this profusion, the Humanists' thought circled around a single problem: how to absorb the rich, bewildering heritage of pagan antiquity into the inherited body of Christian philosophy and theology. Modern historians seeking to differentiate the Renaissance from the Middle Ages have greatly exaggerated the paganism of fifteenth- and sixteenth-century Italy. They have pointed to Valla's Epicurean tract on pleasure, *De voluptate,* and to the immoralities of Renaissance despots. But Valla did not want to exchange Christianity for Epicureanism, he wanted to reconcile the two—it is not an accident that he should have ended his career as a papal secretary. And the lustful, proud, and vicious Renaissance despots were immoral not because they were pagans, but because they were immoral and because there was no one to restrain their appetites. The Humanists were not unbelievers, and they did not do their work for the sake of unbelief, but they made unbelief accessible. Even so, pagan philosophies did not really become significant forces in European culture until the late sixteenth and seventeenth centuries, long after the Renaissance had passed. The Renaissance was not an irreligious or a non-Christian age; it was an age of widening secular concerns. It shows, as Kristeller has put it, a "steady and irresistible growth of nonreligious intellectual interests which were not so much opposed to the content of religious doctrine, as rather competing with it for individual and public attention." [37]

Humbly aware that man is less than the angels but confident that he occupies a worthy place in the scheme of things, the Humanists concentrated their philosophizing on man. Again and again, whatever their particular intellectual loyalty, whether they believed that man's actions are determined by fate or (as some of them did) by the stars or that they are free, whether they were optimistic about man's prospects or pessimistic, the Humanists insistently returned to man's value, man's dignity. Petrarch had given the lead with his life and his writings, and a century later the Florentine Humanist Giannozzo Manetti showed that this was a controversial matter indeed: his sizable treatise on *The Dignity and Excellence of Man* was quite explicitly directed against a treatise on man's misery by Pope Innocent III. Pomponazzi urged that it was man's central task in this world to seek the sphere of moral action most appropriate to him, and in 1486 Giovanni Pico della Mirandola, a precocious disciple of Ficino's, summarized this central concern of humanistic philosophizing in a famous *Oration* on the dignity of man: God, he argued, had created man last of all, after all of the divine gifts had been distributed among God's other creatures. But this was a fortunate fate: it meant that man was free to move freely among all possibilities, to shape himself as he pleased. This unique opportunity imposed a unique duty: to choose the best possible way of life open to mortal man.

One way in which the question of man's place and proper activity presented itself to the Humanists was through the old debate about styles of

[37] Kristeller, *Renaissance Thought,* 72.

life. The ancient Greeks had been the first to confront two conflicting styles—
the active and the contemplative life—and to debate the relative merits of each.
For the Christian, the choice was not hard; while Christian societies had their
secular side—they too needed their peasants, workers, merchants, scribes, and
soldiers—the highest form of existence was embodied in monastic withdrawal
which symbolized the unquestioned preeminence of heavenly over earthly
things. Petrarch had still been enmeshed in this view of life; had he not been
dismayed to find Cicero in the midst of incessant political activity? But here was
one issue on which Petrarch's disciples abandoned their master: they praised
Cicero for his willingness to concentrate his philosophizing on practical
issues—that is, ethics and politics—and to participate in the political strife of
the dying republic. It is this view of Cicero as the practical philosopher that
helps to explain his enormous reputation in the Renaissance, a reputation that
survived, and largely for this reason, into the Enlightenment. The Humanists
who wrote about Cicero—Coluccio Salutati and Leonardo Bruni among
others—admired him as the embodiment of the civic ideal and sought to
emulate him in their own manner of life. But life itself intervened to complicate
the matter. In the middle of the fifteenth century, Marsilio Ficino and his fellow
Humanists in Florence turned their minds to things remote from political action
and counseled withdrawal for the sake of contemplation. But this victory of the
contemplative over the active style was not a purely philosophical victory; civic
humanism was a casualty of the Medici ascendancy. By 1460 in Florence, a call
to political participation would have been interpreted either as a utopian flight
or as an attempt at treachery. Just as philosophy has its effect on life, life has
its effect on philosophy.

Humanist Eloquence and Humanist Education

The Humanists were not—or not primarily—philosophers; they were above all
educators. The very name Humanist originally meant a teacher concerned with
the *studia humanitatis,* the "humanities," which included the study of grammar,
poetry, history, ethics, and significantly, rhetoric. [38] To the Humanists, rhetoric
was never "mere" rhetoric; it was clear and convincing speaking and writing for
the sake of worthwhile instruction. The Humanists liked to quote the ancient
Roman rhetorician Quintilian to the effect that the good orator is a good man
experienced in the art of speech. All subjects lent themselves to eloquence:
Valla's exposure of the "donation of Constantine" (see p. 65) was cast in the
form of a declamation, composed as a formal speech with formal rhetorical
arguments, and larded with shorter speeches inserted into the whole. [39] To be

---

[38] Hanna H. Gray, "Renaissance Humanism: The Pursuit of Eloquence," in Paul Oskar
Kristeller and Philip P. Wiener, eds., *Renaissance Essays* (1968), 201.
[39] Ibid., 213–214.

eloquent was to be effective, to be effective was to educate. Many Humanists were in fact professional educators, and their posts in schools and universities were the pulpits for their ideas. And a number of them, including Leonardo Bruni, published treatises on pedagogy that laid down their ideal and their method.

The moral intentions of this ideal are obvious; after all, educators are, almost by definition, moralists. What was distinctive about the educational ideal of the Humanists was their intense classicism. They argued that all subjects, whether grammar or ethics, must be taught through the classics—a body of writings, it must always be remembered, that included such "classical" Christian writers as St. Augustine and St. Jerome. The Humanists did not believe in progress: the study of morals, of eloquence, of politics, had been brought to such heights among the Greeks and the Romans that all the moderns could do was to find what the ancients had said.

The Humanists' indefatigable efforts at collecting and copying manuscripts, at editing and translating inaccessible classics, were therefore part of their educational program: it was to make available to all civilized men the whole treasure of ancient reflections on all possible subjects. Liberal education—the education worthy of a free man—was thus classical education, a view of schooling that continued to dominate Europe until the advent of democracy and universal schooling in our time.

Posted in their strategic places, the Humanists spread their doctrines through Renaissance society, among the learned and the rich. Technical philosophy, the sciences, mathematics—subjects in which the Humanists did not take great interest—all profited from the Humanists' scholarship, their rescue of texts, and their ideal of clarity. Even manners benefited: Renaissance society was nothing if not sociable, and by the fifteenth century it was clear that social conduct was a moral matter quite as much as a matter of mere "form." Among the moral treatises on manners, the most important and most influential was Baldassarre Castiglione's *Book of the Courtier,* published toward the end of the Italian Renaissance in 1528. Castiglione's courtier lacks the robust directness that had characterized the Florentine ideal of civic humanism, and embodied instead the ideal of the polished universal man who is well read in the classics without showing his learning as a pedant would, who is polite in conduct and entertaining in conversation, who is adept at the arts of music and painting without falling into professional specialization, who presents himself to the world as casual and self-controlled, and who is considerate of others. Burckhardt said that Renaissance rulers had made their states into works of art; Castiglione sought to make man himself into a work of art.

THE ARTS

······⦻······

Art in the Renaissance as Renaissance Art

Art remains, quite literally, the most visible achievement of the Renaissance. Italian cities offer inexhaustible reminders of its magnificence. To walk through Florence is to walk past buildings designed by Brunelleschi, ornamental doors carved by Ghiberti, a cathedral bell tower built by Giotto, statues sculpted by Cellini; to enter its churches is to encounter frescoes by Masaccio and sculptures by Michelangelo. Appropriately enough, modern historians seeking to define the distinctive qualities of this period have appealed to Italian artistic practice and aesthetic theory. This, as we have seen, is not a new idea. The Italians of the Renaissance liked to offer the painting, sculpture, and architecture of their day as proof that theirs was an age of glorious renewal. In the *Decameron,* written between 1348 and 1353, Boccaccio singled out Giotto, who had died only a few years before, for having "restored to light" the art of painting that had languished in darkness for many centuries. This interpretation of the death and rebirth of art, as the distinguished art historian Erwin Panofsky has pointed out, [40] echoes the interpretation that Petrarch had earlier offered for literature; thus, by assimilating the career of painting to that of literature, Boccaccio was postulating a single Renaissance among all the arts. This view became almost a commonplace; it reappears in the *Reminiscences* of the great Florentine sculptor Lorenzo Ghiberti in the middle of the fifteenth century, and was codified in Giorgio Vasari's much-quoted collection of biographies, the *Lives of the Artists,* which first appeared in 1550 and then, in a greatly enlarged edition, in 1568. Vasari prefaces his book with an extensive history of art, recounting how it had risen "from the smallest beginnings" to "the greatest height" in classical antiquity, only to "decline from its noble position to the most degraded status" after the triumph of Christianity and the barbarian invasions of Italy, now at last to be "reborn" and to have "reached perfection in our own times." [41]

The notion that the arts somehow express the style of a whole culture—the spirit of the times or *Zeitgeist*—is far from self-evident and has often been misused. But it seemed obvious at the time that art was indeed an expression of a wider rebirth, and modern research supports the contention that there was a free interplay between painting and poetry, sculpture and classical learning,

---

[40] Erwin Panofsky, *Renaissance and Renascences in Western Art* (2nd ed., 1965), 15.
[41] Giorgio Vasari, *The Lives of the Artists* (Penguin ed., 1965), 46–47.

in the Renaissance. Painters, sculptors, and architects were classical enthusiasts. Ghiberti and Brunelleschi, Donatello and Masaccio, Alberti and Mantegna, went to Rome, sometimes for years, to study classical ruins; like so many Humanists, they pondered and measured the bits of architecture and fragments of sculpture recovered from the earth. Such passionate antiquarianism was still an oddity at the beginning of the fifteenth century; the remains in the Roman Forum, like the classical manuscripts in monastery libraries, had been grossly neglected. But this amateur archeology was contagious; in the 1440s, Flavio Biondo, Humanist and papal secretary, "the father of modern archeology," compiled a catalogue of surviving monuments in Rome, and after him ancient fragments exercised a pervasive influence on artists and scholars alike.

Renaissance artists talked a great deal about imitation. Even a superficial comparison between ancient and Renaissance art shows, however, that their passion for antiquity resulted not in slavish copying, but in a certain inner freedom that permitted them to take up antique and more recent styles in an entirely new way. Filippo Brunelleschi's Foundling Hospital in Florence is one of the finest and most characteristic buildings of the Renaissance, with its slender Corinthian columns, its generous arches, its lucid organization of space throughout. But its inspiration, as Nikolaus Pevsner has shown, came from local buildings of fairly recent vintage, like the facade of the church of San Miniato al Monte, right outside Florence, begun in the second half of the eleventh century. "The Tuscans, unconsciously of course, prepared themselves for the reception of the Roman style by first going back to their own Romanesque Proto-Renaissance." [42] Classicism was the road to artistic independence and, as the artists themselves often proudly said, to nature.

This inner freedom manifested itself in many areas. For centuries, Christian art had turned its back on the beauty of the human body; the rare nudes in medieval art are faint reminiscences of antique figures; they are awkward and seem out of place. Then, in the trecento [43] the antique figure of the winged naked little boy reappeared as the *putto,* the little angel, [44] and at the beginning of the quattrocento, Ghiberti carved a small nude Isaac for a door panel (see p. 76). In 1434, Donatello fully restored the claim of the naked body to man's admiration with his statue of the young David. With its graceful posture, its frank, almost aggressive nudity, the Donatello *David* is a radical break with the Christian tradition. [45] From then on, the nude was domesticated in Renaissance art; later, particularly in Venice, it came to express a voluptuous,

---

[42] Nikolaus Pevsner, *An Outline of European Architecture* (5th ed., 1957), 130.

[43] The Italian way of calling centuries by hundreds—so that the fourteenth century (the thirteen hundreds) is the trecento, the fifteenth century the quattrocento, and the sixteenth century the cinquecento—has been universally adopted by art historians.

[44] Panofsky, *Renaissance and Renascences in Western Art,* 147 ff.

[45] It is a break with antiquity as well; although it is alive with reminiscences of antique bronzes, it is a work of striking originality. Kenneth Clark, *The Nude: A Study in Ideal Form* (1956), 54–55.

single-minded pleasure in the flesh that was wholly alien to the Christian view
of man.

With the new readiness to glory in the human body came a new interest
in the human face: the Renaissance is a great age of portraiture as it is—and for
the same reason—a great age of biography. Patrons had themselves painted on
the walls of their studies or into sacred scenes as donors, or carved in heroic
poses for their tombs. While these portraits strove for idealization (not because
the patron needed to be flattered, but because the classical ideal called for
beauty), they were highly individualized and did not shrink from including
unflattering detail. Even when they were done after the sitter's death—as was
Verrocchio's equestrian statue of the *condottiere* Bartolomeo Colleoni in
Venice, or Ghirlandaio's touching painting of an old man with his grandson—
they strive for characterization, realism, life.[46] Fully participating in this new
individualism, artists depicted themselves with confidence and candor; they
smuggled themselves into group scenes or cast medals of their features for
posterity to admire. Ghiberti, who could say in his *Reminiscences*, boastfully
but accurately, that in his time there were few things in Florence he had not
planned or made,[47] put his portrait into the frame of his bronze doors for the
Baptistry in Florence. There it remains: the bald head surrounded by a fringe
of hair, the shrewd witty face with its compressed lips, distinctive, unique.
Portraits are everywhere in Renaissance art, if we could only read them:
Masaccio's frescoes in Florence are crowded with the features of Humanists,
sculptors, merchants, many of them still awaiting definitive identification. For
the Renaissance artists, pride was not a sin but an inducement to accurate and
virile portrayals.

As Burckhardt noted over a century ago, the discovery of man was
accompanied by the discovery of nature. In medieval art, convincing depictions
of nature were exceedingly rare, and notable because they were so rare; the
loving, accurate representations of vines and leaves on the capitals in Rheims
cathedral have few counterparts. The exploration of nature as a source of
aesthetic pleasure begins with the Renaissance, with Petrarch's excursions and
his meticulous observations on his property. Landscape backgrounds for a
Crucifixion or, as glimpsed through a window, in a portrait or in a depiction of
Virgin with Child came to be exquisitely painted, luminous with brilliant
sunlight and contrasting shade (see p. 87 for Northern, Flemish influences). In
the quattrocento, landscape backgrounds developed into full-scale landscape
paintings; in Renaissance art, the world reappears for its own sake.

Renaissance artists, then, were steeped in the attitudes they found around
them, recorded, and helped to perpetuate. But they participated in the
Renaissance in an even more direct way; many of their works are representations of literary programs drawn up by Humanists, classical myths revived by

---

[46] John Pope-Hennessy, *The Portrait in the Renaissance* (1966), 56–57.
[47] Michael Levey, *Early Renaissance* (1967), 23–25.

Humanists, and philosophical notions propagated by Humanists. Botticelli's two most celebrated paintings, *The Birth of Venus* and *Primavera,* which still strike the viewer with their combination of gravity, grace, and mystery, derive from a poem on the reign of Venus by Poliziano, who, like Botticelli, was part of the Medici circle. [48] Other works of art give pictorial form to contemporary Neoplatonism or accounts of primitive culture. In all respects, art in the Renaissance was Renaissance art.

Art was part of its culture also in its continued dependence on religion. While much patronage came from merchants and princes, the princes of the church remained influential patrons; the Renaissance papacy employed architects to build spacious churches, painters to cover their walls, and sculptors to adorn their chapels. And secular patrons continued to order works of a religious nature—it seemed a good investment in salvation. Giotto's frescoes in the Arena Chapel at Padua were commissioned by Enrico Scrovegni, probably to atone for the vast fortune he had inherited from his father, a usurer. [49] The monastery of San Marco in Florence was restored through the munificence of Cosimo de' Medici, who had Michelozzi rebuild, and Fra Angelico decorate it. Religious themes dominated the arts down to the very end of the Renaissance: Michelangelo's most famous architectural commission is St. Peter's in Rome, his most famous panel painting a Holy Family, his most famous fresco a Last Judgment, and his most famous pieces of sculpture a David, a Moses, a Pietà— the sorrowing Virgin holding the body of her crucified son. Raphael's Madonnas hang in all the major museums of the world; and while Leonardo da Vinci's finest paintings include secular portraits, they include also several Madonnas and, of course, a Last Supper. It is true that the quality of religion changed in the course of centuries; in restless spirits like Michelangelo, Christian belief was infused with Neoplatonic speculations, and the new pleasure in earthly things—in the beauty of bodies, the quality of light, or the vigor of classical stories—gave Renaissance art a pagan quality that sets it off, unmistakably, from earlier Christian art. It has become a commonplace that the supposedly religious art of the Renaissance was pervaded by anachronisms and by worldliness: Adorations of the Kings are set in a Tuscan landscape, Crucifixions are bathed in the light of Umbria, Virgins look like Venetian ladies. It is just as commonplace to say—and just as true—that the loveliest girls in Renaissance art are Madonnas. But this secularization was not a turning away from Christianity; it represented, rather, an enlargement and an enrichment of experience, a certain displacement of emphasis. The antique intrudes more than ever, carnal beauty invades sacred precincts, but for most, if not all, artists in the Renaissance, this meant simply that there were more, and more glorious, ways now of celebrating God's work than ever before. In the early

---

[48] See Warburg as summarized by Panofsky, *Renaissance and Renascences in Western Art,* 191–200.

[49] John White, *Art and Architecture in Italy, 1250–1400* (1966), 204; see p. 74.

twelfth century, St. Bernard had denounced the natural forms he saw carved in cloisters as impermissible worldliness; they were, he said in a striking phrase, "deformed beauty and beautiful deformity—*deformis formositas ac formosa deformitas.*"[50] Two and three hundred years later, the most devout among Renaissance artists did not hesitate to portray the evidence of God's hand in the world—a face, a flower, a tree—with the utmost fidelity. Although sometimes a little unorthodox, and sometimes not very strict in their piety, Renaissance artists remained Christians. Some of them in fact, like Botticelli, were mystics.

Whatever secularization there was in Renaissance art became marked only in the quattrocento; the trecento remains wholly at the service of the Christian story. The painter who dominates the fourteenth century, Giotto, did only sacred scenes. Yet he was in his own way a revolutionary: it is with him that Renaissance art takes its beginning. Giotto's admirers, like Boccaccio, recognized his eminence early; his close friend, Dante, said that Giotto's fame had obscured that of his teacher, Cimabue. For Boccaccio, the revolutionary quality of Giotto's work was an uncanny naturalism: face to face with one of his paintings, "the human sense of sight was often deceived by his works and took for real what was only painted."[51] Like Boccaccio, Vasari saw Giotto as a unique agent—"Giotto alone, by God's favor," had restored painting—and, like Boccaccio, he credited Giotto with a miraculous naturalism: "In my opinion, painters owe to Giotto, the Florentine painter, exactly the same debt they owe to nature, which constantly serves them as a model and whose finest and most beautiful aspects they are always striving to imitate and reproduce." He thought this achievement all the more a "miracle" since Giotto had been born into a "gross and incompetent age."[52] For the men of the Renaissance, Giotto was the Petrarch of painting.

These are only slight exaggerations. Cimabue and Duccio of Siena, both working late in the thirteenth century, had begun to liberate painting from the rigid postures and decorative detail of Byzantine art; their Madonnas appear freer, more natural, than those of their predecessors. But Giotto, an artist of great intuitive invention, moved far beyond his teachers. Compared with their work, his scenes are simple, his dominant figures expressive, his spaces three-dimensional. Giotto achieved his effects by radical means: he places his scenes into a room framed by foreshortened architectural features like columns and roofs; his main actors sometimes appear in the rear of the painting faced by figures shown from the back—both cunning devices to create the illusion of depth. Again, Giotto gives his figures natural postures and, through careful modeling, rounded shapes; the Christ child may hold on to his mother by grasping a finger, and there are real bodies beneath Giotto's draperies. Finally, he composes his scenes with an impressive economy of means, reducing the

---

[50] Quoted in Levey, *Early Renaissance,* 18.
[51] Quoted in Panofsky, *Renaissance and Renascences in Western Art,* 12–13.
[52] Vasari, *Lives of the Artists,* 57.

number of figures, giving each a simple and expressive gesture, and by means of light and shade, placing each solidly within the frame and into appropriate relation to all other figures. Up to Giotto's time, art had striven to express high religious truth symbolically; in Giotto, divine figures, though they are handled no less devoutly than before, appear human. The gain in power and plasticity was enormous.

Giotto's fame matched his pioneering role. He did the Arena Chapel in Padua, a compact group of over forty scenes on four walls, between 1304 and 1313; later he worked in Rome, in Assisi, and in Florence, where in addition to painting, he designed the *campanile* of the cathedral, and where he died, much honored, in 1337.

Civic Art: The Early Quattrocento in Florence

Giotto's genius hovers over the rest of the trecento; meritorious disciples all across Italy—some, like Andrea Orcagna, remarkably gifted—retained Giotto's devices and worked within his limits. The art historian Millard Meiss has conjectured that the Black Death of 1348 awakened a sense of guilt and fear in the fortunate survivors, discouraging experimentation and inviting religious conservatism; certainly, the plague decimated the young, promising artists.[53] Whatever the reasons, it was not until the beginning of the quattrocento that artists outdistanced Giotto. But then change came in a rush: Florence witnessed a concentrated outpouring of creativity in all the arts, which made Giotto's earlier radicalism seem tame.

This beneficent explosion aroused such passionate interest and was so dependent on public participation, that it is not too much to call it a moment of civic art. Florentines had taken pride in their great buildings for centuries; all their art was somehow involved with public events—the gilds' assumption of political power or deliverance from Milanese aggression. The Baptistry, the place not merely of baptisms but of important celebrations and processions, had been started in the middle of the eleventh century, probably on earlier foundations; the legends that formed around this octagonal structure vividly testify to its prominent place in Florentine consciousness. It was the cloth-importers' gild—the most prominent, most powerful, and most affluent of the greater gilds—that was in charge of decorating and preserving the Baptistry. In 1296 the foundations were laid for a new cathedral, next to the Baptistry, and three years later, in 1299, for what is today called the Palazzo Vecchio—both designed by Arnolfo di Cambio. Other structures, only less prominent than these, grew in the city in the course of the trecento, and with all of them the

[53] Millard Meiss, *Painting in Florence and Siena After the Black Death: The Arts, Religion, and Society in the Mid-Fourteenth Century* (1964).

Florentine public—and not the great patrons alone—was intimately engaged; it earnestly debated these buildings, used them for business or worship, paid for them through special taxes. When the artistic explosion came around 1400, Florence was ready—Florence had, in a sense, prepared the way.

In 1401, there was a competition in Florence that brilliantly illuminates the civic nature of its art. In the middle of the trecento, Andrea Pisano had cast two bronze doors for the south entrance of the Baptistry; now the east doors were to be decorated in the same fashion. The gild set the theme for the competition, the sacrifice of Isaac, and seven artists, most of them young, all of them Tuscans, submitted their designs. The debate among the judges seems to have been heated; their verdict was later confirmed by the vote of the whole gild. The judges chose the young Ghiberti, then about twenty, to do the east doors. The only other design that survives, by Brunelleschi, demonstrates that the decision must have been hard, but that it was just. Ghiberti's panels were such a triumph that they were moved to the less conspicuous north entrance, to give Ghiberti room for an even more splendid set of panels. These latter, soon called with pardonable hyperbole, "the doors of paradise," remain in place today, a marvel of refined detail, dramatic clarity, skillful perspective, and a reminder of the importance that Florentine art had for its city.

Filippo Brunelleschi (who, Ghiberti proudly recalled, urged the judges to pass over his design in Ghiberti's favor) went to Rome after this competition and returned years later, a master of the classical idiom and an innovator of genius. One instance of his technical powers was the great dome over the crossing of the cathedral, completed in 1434. His Foundling Hospital, begun in 1419, became a model of the new style (see p. 71); Brunelleschi himself followed it in his designs for the Medici church of San Lorenzo, the Pazzi chapel, and other buildings, while Michelozzi adopted the same combination of slim, virile columns and firm, round arches for his restoration of San Marco. Brunelleschi's Renaissance buildings were vigorously anti-Gothic, a revival of Romanesque with new clarity and delicacy, a renewal, therefore, of a domestic style.

Florentine art of the quattrocento was a collective enterprise; Ghiberti employed over twenty workmen, while artists of lesser stature and renown carried forward what the pioneers had set before them. But two giants deserve individual attention—Donatello and Masaccio. Like the others, Donatello was an eminently public performer: his most popular piece of sculpture, the St. George, was designed for an outside niche at the church of Or San Michele and placed practically at eye level. The young warrior stands, not quite squarely, his shield before him negligently held by the left hand, his finely chiseled features expressive of youth, dignity, alertness, and an almost unbearable tension. As in his many other statues, busts, and reliefs—he was an extraordinarily prolific artist—Donatello here achieves a conquest of reality it would be inadequate to call mere "realism": classical in inspiration, Christian in theme, Donatello's work is modern in its mixture of passion and control, its variety, and its expressiveness, proof of Donatello's freedom to do precisely what he wanted with his materials. Donatello was widely admired, and he influenced painters quite as much as sculptors. Even Masaccio learned from Donatello's early work.

Masaccio's genius invites and defies explanation. His life was as short (1401 to 1428?) as his achievement was unparalleled. He was not a classicist, although antique conceptions reached him indirectly, through his friend Brunelleschi; he was not a medievalist, but he had the wit to learn from Giotto. A comparison of Giotto's work with Masaccio's shows the moment when a change in quantity amounts to a change in quality: Giotto had known tricks of foreshortening and of lending his figures a certain roundness. Masaccio moved beyond tricks to mastery; his paintings are the first statement of the modern vision in art that remained valid for five centuries. Masaccio mastered perspective and anatomy, and design as well: he does not merely copy what he sees, but arranges it with a sure feeling for drama and significance. "To Masaccio especially we are indebted for the good style of modern painting," Vasari wrote, "for it was Masaccio who perceived that the best painters follow nature as closely as possible."[54] It was not nature as the artist found it, but nature artistically shaped—as Alexander Pope would say in the eighteenth century, nature methodized. Masaccio's admirable frescoes in the Brancacci Chapel have a presence, a movement, a convincing naturalness that induced painters from all over Italy to come to Florence, to marvel at Masaccio's work and imitate it. But it is his fresco of the Trinity in the Florentine church of Santa Maria Novella— a work of decisive historical importance—that most eloquently sums up Masaccio's revolutionary achievement. The crucified Christ appears surmounted by the Holy Spirit and God the Father, framed by the standing figures of the Virgin and St. John the Evangelist, and outside the action, by two kneeling donors; the sacred figures are contained within a kind of chapel, beneath a barrel vault of breathtaking depth. The observed perspective is perfect. From then on, whether the debt to Masaccio was direct or indirect, mastery of perspective formed part of the artist's equipment. In Florence itself, such interesting painters as Paolo Uccello continued to experiment with foreshortening, while the wonderfully crowded yet wonderfully organized paintings of the Paduan Andrea Mantegna show how much clear narration and plastic power perspective permitted. With Masaccio and his followers, the old problem of how to make a two-dimensional surface appear three-dimensional had been solved, not in dry academic exercises, but in paintings and plaques of enduring beauty and vitality.

The High Renaissance

While the great Florentine generation passed from the scene at midcentury (Brunelleschi died in 1446, Ghiberti in 1455, and the long-lived Donatello in 1466), a younger generation, only slightly less remarkable than the pioneers,

[54] Vasari, *Lives of the Artists,* 124.

ably took its place: Verrocchio, with his energetic nervous line, recognizable in sculpture and painting alike; Domenico Ghirlandaio, with his cheerful, beautifully painted frescoes which give delight without arousing any complicated feelings and which sometimes suffer from sheer prettiness; Filippino Lippi, son of Fra Filippo Lippi, the distinguished Florentine master, with his charming Madonnas and restless, crowded, almost baroque frescoes; and Sandro Botticelli with his Madonnas, his *Annunciation,* his great allegorical paintings, unmistakable in their sinuous line, their attenuated figures, and their pale, solemn faces.

Then, toward the end of the quattrocento and the beginning of the cinquecento—the period that art historians call the High Renaissance—other cities, mainly Rome, Milan, and Venice, began to produce great artists of their own and attract with irresistible commissions artists born elsewhere. Yet Florence continued to be a setter of styles; the three towering figures of the High Renaissance—Leonardo da Vinci, Raphael, and Michelangelo—all went to school there.

It seems to be impossible to speak of these masters without sounding banal. Even Heinrich Wölfflin, a pioneer of modern art history and a master of cool analytical perception, found it necessary to exclaim: "The progress of Michelangelo through Italian art was like that of a mighty mountain torrent, at once fertilizing and destructive; irresistibly carrying all before him, he became a liberator to a few and a destroyer to many more." [55] Let us grant these artists their titanic stature and summarize their work.

Leonardo da Vinci was the oldest of the three. Born in 1452, he went to Florence in 1466 to study with Verrocchio. His gifts emerged early: Vasari reports that the angel young Leonardo painted for Verrocchio's *Baptism of Christ* was so superior to Verrocchio's own work that the master, conceding the pupil's superiority, never touched paint again. [56] Stylistic evidence alone makes the story appear well founded: the angel has the kind of beauty no other artist, save Raphael, could capture. After working on important Florentine commissions Leonardo moved to Milan in 1482 and stayed there, at the court of Lodovico Sforza, for sixteen years. It was a period of exceptional productivity; it was there that Leonardo painted his *Madonna of the Rocks* and his *Last Supper.* When the Sforzas were overthrown in 1499 by the French invasion, Leonardo left Milan, and, after some wandering, returned to Florence in 1503. This was the decade of the *Mona Lisa.* He died in France in 1519, after some productive years in Milan and Rome, painting, drawing, experimenting, writing (see p. 87).

The range and technical facility of Leonardo's work stretch the vocabulary of the reporter. When Burckhardt sought for an example of the ideal Renaissance man, that universal man who in addition to doing everything did

[55] Heinrich Wölfflin, *Classic Art: An Introduction to the Italian Renaissance,* (2nd ed. tr., 1953), 39.
[56] "Life of Leonardo." See Kenneth Clark, *Leonardo da Vinci: An Account of his Development as an Artist* (1939), 258.

everything well, he singled out Leone Battista Alberti, a member of the great generation in Florence—architect, art theorist, athlete, musician, scientist, prose stylist in Italian and Latin. But then he adds, "Leonardo da Vinci was to Alberti as the completer is to the beginner, the master to the dilettante. . . . The gigantic outlines of Leonardo's being will forever be merely glimpsed from afar." His caricatures are savage and telling; his anatomical renderings, remarkable for their accuracy, are obviously the result of diligent dissections; his drawings of leaves and plants would be at home in a modern book on botany; his architectural designs reveal a major talent in yet another discipline; his brilliant drawings of faces, figures, animals, riders in combat are unexcelled for their tough-minded realism and plastic power: his self-portrait—the full-bearded bald old man, with full lips drawn down, vigorous nose jutting out, and keen eyes peering from beneath bushy eyebrows—is a marvel of candor, old age turned into beauty. Leonardo was a great artist and a great inventor; his mind a marriage of exuberant scientific imagination disciplined by constant experimentation and a severe sense of form.

His paintings, which support this estimate, are perhaps too famous: it is hard to see now that they were innovations in their day or that they realized an unexpected perfection. The *Mona Lisa* is a portrait of a handsome young woman with plucked eyebrows, translucent skin, firm posture, the mysterious hint of a smile, and round though elegant hands—but it is more than that. Leonardo said that "relief is the principal aim and the soul of painting." [57] In this portrait, his principal aim is realized. The *Last Supper* takes a familiar subject into unfamilar regions. Leonardo is so intent on rendering the dramatic impact of Christ's announcement, "One of you will betray me," that the table he uses is too small for thirteen people to sit at—not until Cézanne would art again exact such subordination of realistic detail to painterly purposes. Leonardo sweeps away the traditional ways of rendering Christ or Judas; he bunches the disciples into four gesticulating groups, visibly shocked by the announcement; Christ is absolutely central in the design, serene and alone, lit by the middle window; Judas is marked as the betrayer by the simple device of having his face entirely in the shadows. Damaged as the painting is, it still speaks of its creator's genius.

If Leonardo is universality, Raphael is concentration. No one painted more Madonnas, or lovelier Madonnas, that he. Born in 1483 in Urbino, Raffaello Santi first studied with Perugino, whose orderly, lyrical, somewhat sentimental style dominates Raphael's early work. Then, around 1504, he went to Florence and came under the kind of influence he deserved. Raphael must have known the cartoon Leonardo had exhibited in 1501 of *The Virgin and Child with St. Anne,* a daring, odd, triangular composition with the head of St. Anne forming the apex, and the lamb that the Christ child is straddling, the acute angle at the right. Raphael's Madonnas, which he began to pour out mainly after his move

[57] Quoted in Wölfflin, *Classic Art,* 23.

to Rome in 1508 or early 1509, are alive with a cunning architectural freedom; Raphael organizes the Virgin and Child, or the groupings around the Mother of God, in complex and ever varied triangles: the *Sistine Madonna,* probably his most famous painting, compels the viewer to complete the implicit triangle by moving his eyes from her two worshippers to the Virgin, who stands above them. Raphael was not a master of design alone, he was a master also of color, and his faces, which have won him his enduring popularity, are expressive but calm, beautiful but rarely sentimental.

Raphael was concentrated but not monotonous; in his short life—he died in 1520, at the age of thirty-seven—he designed buildings in Rome; painted some distinguished portraits, including a half-length of Castiglione (see p. 69); and designed a set of ten large cartoons for tapestries which depict scenes from the Acts of the Apostles. And at Rome he decorated the Stanza della Segnatura as well as other rooms in the Vatican; two of his finest murals there are the *School of Athens* and the *Disputation,* both vast, firmly organized compositions classical in their environment and their temper. The first depicts Greek philosophers and their disciples in a fantastic building of lofty receding barrel vaults—the vault of Masaccio's *Trinity* multiplied—the second portrays the fathers of the church in various postures of debate, reading, contemplation, and ecstasy.

Michelangelo lacked Leonardo's scientific passion and Raphael's appealing serenity; he was a tormented genius who converted his sufferings into art, an art that openly discloses the torments its creator has undergone. Michelangelo was a Tuscan; he was born in 1475 not far from Florence and was trained there in the workshop of Ghirlandaio, and under the protection of Lorenzo de' Medici who discovered the young sculptor's talent. While his first, youthful *Pietà,* a brilliant, highly polished, life-size composition of a young woman holding a dead body lightly on her lap, was done in Rome, it was in Florence, on commission from the city, that Michelangelo sculpted his *David,* an outsize statue of a proud young man with huge hands and feet. The details are modeled with superb clarity, the body stands in an awkward posture; the whole is at once impressive and repellent. In spite of this ugliness, Wölfflin has said, "it has become the most popular statue in Florence,"[58] and, one might add, not in Florence alone. Like Leonardo, Michelangelo never descended to mere prettiness. In 1505, Pope Julius II called him to Rome, where Michelangelo sculpted his sitting *Moses* and several *Slaves,* and painted the Sistine Chapel. This chapel is one of the most famous sights in Rome, but it is a sight hard to see: the distant ceiling practically compels the viewer to lie on his back, and the huge *Last Judgment,* which Michelangelo imposed on the chapel wall later, between 1534 and 1541, overpowers the ceiling and the lunettes, with their smaller scenes from the Old Testament, their sibyls and prophets. The whole is rather like his *David*: masterly in every technical detail, impressive in individual scenes, but in many ways unpleasant—an ungainly miracle.

By 1520 Michelangelo was back in Florence on a commission to design and decorate the funeral chapel of the Medici in the church of San Lorenzo. Michelangelo labored on this task until 1534 without quite completing it. His seated sculptures of two minor Medici princes sit in their niches, complete; the Medici Madonna is a perfect specimen of his later style in its harsh beauty; the four recumbent figures of the *Times of Day* are finished enough to compel admiration for their monumentality, the strength of their modeling, and once again, the artist's refusal to make things pretty. In his last years, back in Rome, he turned his attention to architecture and redesigned Bramante's plan for St. Peter's. Upon his death in 1564, he was the most famous artist in the Western world, a legend in his own time.

This legend, based largely on reality, centers around the conflict between genius and society, the free artist in a world of patrons. Michelangelo was an artist difficult to employ and impossible to pass over. The works he completed (and even more, the works he did not complete) testify to his need for vast masses, for twisted postures, and for trying the untried. To organize the curved Sistine ceiling into an articulate whole, to sculpt a group that seems alive and individualized while retaining the general shape of the stone almost undisturbed: these were the problems Michelangelo set himself precisely because they seemed to be insoluble. Dukes and popes treated this prickly genius as an equal, and sometimes as a superior, but never with adequate comprehension. Pope Julius II, who had the wit to employ Raphael, Bramante, and Michelangelo at the same time allowed the last to walk out on him, and begged him to return. He had called Michelangelo to Rome to do his tomb, and then changed his mind. Michelangelo made representations and when he got no satisfaction, simply left for Florence. Julius II, Michelangelo later recalled, sent horsemen after him ordering him to return, but the artist coolly told the pope that he would come back only if he discharged the obligation he had undertaken. It was only to oblige the city of Florence that Michelangelo went back to Rome.[59] In this attitude, as in his art, the ordered relationships of the Renaissance have been disturbed, and a new age, of Mannerism and Baroque, has dawned. The greatest of the Renaissance men, Michelangelo, was also the last.

SELECTED READINGS

Good general treatments of the period are Myron P. Gilmore, *The World of Humanism, 1453–1517* (1952); the informative textbook by Wallace K. Ferguson, *Europe in Transition, 1300–1520* (1963); and G. R. Potter, ed., *The Renaissance, 1493–1520* (1957), the opening volume of *The New Cambridge Modern History.* Denys Hay, *The Italian Renaissance in Its Historical Background* (1961), analyzes the age as a historical and historiographical problem. Among collections of essays, the following may be recommended: E. F. Jacob, ed., *Italian Renaissance Studies: A Tribute to the Late Cecilia M. Ady* (1960); Wallace K. Ferguson et al., *The Renaissance: Six Essays* (1962), which

---

[59] Rudolf Wittkower and Margot Wittkower, *Born Under Saturn: The Character and Conduct of Artists—A Documented History from Antiquity to the French Revolution* (1963), 38–40.

includes an important essay by Robert S. Lopez, "Hard Times and Investment in Culture"; and Ferguson et al., *Facets of the Renaissance* (1963).

Florence has been much written about. Ferdinand Schevill, *History of Florence,* 2 vols. (1936), can now be supplemented by such modern analyses as Gene A. Brucker, *Florentine Politics and Society, 1343-1378* (1962) and *Renaissance Florence* (1969); Nicolai Rubinstein, *The Government of Florence Under the Medici (1434 to 1494)* (1966); and Raymond de Roover, *The Rise and Decline of the Medici Bank, 1397-1494* (1966). Cecilia M. Ady, *Lorenzo dei Medici and Renaissance Italy* (1962), is short, popular, but reliable.

For Venice, somewhat neglected, there is the fine, exhaustive study by William J. Bouwsma, *Venice and the Defense of Republican Liberty: Renaissance Values in the Age of the Counter Reformation* (1968).

For the Humanists, see especially Eugenio Garin, *Italian Humanism: Philosophy and Civic Life in the Renaissance* (tr. 1965), and Paul Oskar Kristeller, *Renaissance Thought: The Classic, Scholastic, and Humanist Strains* (1961), a revised and expanded version of his earlier *The Classics and Renaissance Thought.* Kristeller's shorter essays, collected in *Renaissance Thought II, Papers on Humanism and the Arts* (1965), and his *Eight Philosophers of the Italian Renaissance* (1964), are also extremely valuable. Kristeller, with Philip P. Wiener, has edited *Renaissance Essays, from the Journal of the History of Ideas* (1968), which contains, among many excellent papers, Hanna H. Gray, "Renaissance Humanism: The Pursuit of Eloquence" (pp. 199-216), which places the Humanists into the rhetorical tradition. For lengthy excerpts from the writings of Humanist thinkers, see Ernst Cassirer, Paul Oskar Kristeller, and John Herman Randall, Jr., eds., *The Renaissance Philosophy of Man* (1948), supplied with excellent introductions. Cassirer's *The Individual and the Cosmos in Renaissance Philosophy* (tr. 1963), is a difficult but rewarding survey. For Petrarch, see Ernest Hatch Wilkins, *Life of Petrarch* (1961). Humanist education is well treated in the older but still dependable book by William Harrison Woodward, *Vittorino da Feltre and Other Humanist Educators,* with a Foreword by Eugene F. Rice, Jr. (1897, ed. 1963).

The classical revival in the Renaissance was first placed into its proper context by Jacob Burckhardt, *The Civilization of the Renaissance in Italy;* this book, first published in 1860 and translated in 1878, remains the indispensable classic for this subject, as well as for the idea of "Renaissance" in general. Wallace K. Ferguson, *The Renaissance in Historical Thought: Five Centuries of Interpretation* (1948), surveys the scholarship before, by, and after Burckhardt. See also the reading by Peter Gay, "Burkhardt's Renaissance: Between Responsibility and Power," in Leonard Krieger and Fritz Stern, eds., *The Responsibility of Power: Historical Essays in Honor of Hajo Holborn* (1967), 183-198. One important aspect of Renaissance classicism, "Civic Humanism," has been extensively canvassed in the splendid, though still controversial, volume by Hans Baron, *The Crisis of the Early Renaissance: Civic Humanism and Republican Liberty in an Age of Classicism and Tyranny* (2nd ed., 1966). And see R. R. Bolgar, *The Classical Heritage and Its Beneficiaries* (2nd ed., 1964).

Renaissance art continues to evoke scholarly attention. Michael Levey, *Early Renaissance* (1967), is a suggestive essay; Cecil Gould, *An Introduction to Italian Renaissance Painting* (1957), is a reliable survey. Three volumes in the Pelican series on history of art are indispensable: John White, *Art and Architecture in Italy: 1250-1400* (1966); Charles Seymour, Jr., *Sculpture in Italy: 1400-1500* (1966); and Sydney Joseph Freedberg, *Painting in Italy: 1500-1600* (1971). Erwin Panofsky, *Renaissance and*

Renascences in Western Art (2nd ed., 1965), persuasively connects art history and general history to sustain the idea of a distinct "Renaissance." Heinrich Wölfflin, *Classic Art: An Introduction to the Italian Renaissance* (tr. from 8th German ed., 2nd ed., 1953) remains informative. Vasari's all-important *Lives of the Artists*, first published in the middle of the sixteenth century, has often been presented in excerpts; the recent selection by George Bull (1965) is excellent. Among a vast number of more specialized treatises, the following are perhaps the most important: Millard Meiss, *Painting in Florence and Siena After the Black Death: The Arts, Religion and Society in the Mid-Fourteenth Century* (1964); Kenneth Clark, *Landscape into Art* (1961), especially chaps. I-III, and Clark's spendid essay, *The Nude: A Study in Ideal Form* (1956), which is relevant throughout. John Pope-Hennessy, *The Portrait in the Renaissance* (1966); Sir Anthony Blunt, *Artistic Theory in Italy, 1450-1600* (1962); and Rudolf Wittkower, *Architectural Principles in the Age of Humanism* (3rd ed., 1962) are all valuable. For Leonardo, see Kenneth Clark, *Leonardo da Vinci: An Account of His Development as an Artist* (rev. ed., 1958); for Michelangelo, the bulky volumes by Charles de Tolnay, beginning with *The Youth of Michelangelo* (1943), are indispensable.

For late Renaissance figures like Machiavelli, and for the Renaissance in the North, see the Selected Readings following Chapter 2.

2

The Rise
of the Atlantic States

Beginning in the second half of the fifteenth century, while the artistic and intellectual Renaissance in Italy was at its height, the center of European power shifted from the Mediterranean to the Atlantic states, from the South to the West and, later, to the North. Trade and population began to recover all across Europe, but Italy benefited less than its rivals. This shift was both comprehensive and decisive, embracing economic as much as political affairs, leadership in the realm of the intellect as much as in the realm of belief, and setting a pattern of power that remained relatively undisturbed for over a century.

The most spectacular and, in the long run, most significant evidence for the emergence of the Atlantic states was, of course, the voyages of discovery. The names of the discoverers, their dates and routes, are justly memorable. For many centuries, Western men had been intrepid adventurers, traveling wherever their equipment and an often hostile environment would permit. The motives for exploration had always been mixed, or rather, many. They included the search for souls to save through the Word of the Gospel, the search for spectacular new continents or legendary cities, the search for profits in trade or piracy: for God (as the old saying had it), glory, and gold. Now a fourth motive was added: government. Most of the early expeditions were financed, or at least claimed, by the rulers of the Atlantic states who recognized that control of overseas territories and of their scarce resources could play a part in the struggle for power in Europe.

The first to find spiritual, financial, and political profit in Atlantic exploration were the Portuguese. In the first half of the fifteenth century Prince Henry the Navigator organized meticulous geographical and astronomical studies and financed frequent expeditions, thus markedly increasing reliable knowledge of the eastern Atlantic and the coast of West Africa. Prince Henry, one of his associates said, "had caused seas to be navigated which had never before been sailed, and had discovered the lands of many strange races, where marvels abound."[1] His ambition was greater than his achievement: he had hoped to reach India by sea, but when he died in 1460, his explorers had only reached the Cape Verde Islands off the West African coast. This hardly diminished the importance of Prince Henry's activities; he had laid down the program and pioneered in the marriage of inquiry and practice, astronomy and navigation.[2] But Henry's legacy, like the legacy of European expansion in general, was an ambiguous one: Henry gave the impetus to the formation of a world market in ideas and goods, but while this meant a magnificent enlargement of European horizons, it also meant the organized inception of a great crime for which the West continues to pay today. In the 1440s some of Henry's voyagers to Africa began to trade in slaves.[3]

Occupied nearer home in the 1460s, the Portuguese let Henry's efforts lapse for a few years, only to take them up again in the 1470s; they intensified them further after 1481, with the accession of John II. Their careful accumulation of knowledge and piecemeal reconnaissance now paid gratifying dividends: Bartolomeu Dias rounded the Cape of Good Hope early in 1488, and between 1497 and 1499 Vasco da Gama made a spectacular voyage to India; he returned, two of his four ships and many of his crew gone, but with a cargo of spices estimated at sixty times the cost of his venture.[4] The Portuguese were not slow to apply the lesson of da Gama's profitable expedition. Nor were they alone. When around 1483 King John of Portugal refused to finance Christopher Columbus' projected voyage to the East by means of going westward—a proposal based on the assumption that the earth is round—Columbus turned to the Spanish court for help and finally persuaded Queen Isabella to sponsor his voyage. On October 12, 1492, Columbus' expedition sighted land—not Asia, as he fondly believed, but America, specifically the Bahamas. This was only the first of his four voyages to the Americas; in later expeditions Columbus

[1] Myron P. Gilmore, *The World of Humanism, 1453–1517* (1952), 24.
[2] Ibid., 23.
[3] This was not the *absolute* beginning, since after A.D. 1000 slaves were brought to Europe by Crusaders. See E. E. Rich, "Colonial Settlement and Its Labour Problem," in *Cambridge Economic History of Europe*, vol. IV (1967), chap. 6.
[4] Gilmore, *World of Humanism*, 26.

discovered Puerto Rico, Jamaica, and other Caribbean islands; Trinidad and portions of South America; and Central America. Like many other pioneers, Columbus, Admiral of the Ocean Sea, did not quite know what he had done. To the day of his death in 1506, he thought he had been exploring the easternmost coast of Asia. Perhaps there is a certain rough justice in the fact that America was to be named not after her discoverer but after Amerigo Vespucci, a Florentine who had made two voyages to America around 1500 and seems to have been the first to assert in print that it was a new continent and not India.

England and France entered the competition for discovery a little later, timidly at first, allowing merchants to finance the expensive voyages: under Henry VII of England, before 1500, John Cabot and his son Sebastian discovered Newfoundland and New England; by the 1520s, the French took an interest in Canada. But it was Spain, for a century the greatest power in Europe, that supported the most decisive of the voyages. The name Christopher Columbus will forever be attached to that of Queen Isabella; in 1513, the Spaniard Vasco Nuñez de Balboa discovered the Pacific Ocean; and between 1519 and 1522, the Portuguese Fernão de Magalhães, better known by his English name Magellan, in the Spanish service, led an expedition that circumnavigated the globe. From then on the expansion of European culture into a world culture—for good or ill—was only a matter of time.

But it *was* a matter of time. The full significance of the discoveries did not immediately appear: their economic, social, and intellectual effects belong not to the history of the late fifteenth, but to that of the late sixteenth century (see p. 206). This was a time of fundamental change on the European scene, but its direct impulse came in and from the realms of ideas, technology, economics, and politics. "The three great elements of modern civilization," Thomas Carlyle observed in the nineteenth century, were "Gunpowder, Printing, and the Protestant Religion." The first of these, a medieval invention, symbolized military power in political affairs; the second and third of these originated not in Italy but in the North, and were in part the instruments, in part a repudiation, of the Northern Renaissance.

THE NORTHERN RENAISSANCE

The Arts

The Northern Renaissance flourished later than the Renaissance in Italy. Its most celebrated Humanist, artist, and scientist—Erasmus, Dürer, and Copernicus—did their enduring work after 1500 (for early modern science, see p. 233). This late date suggests that the Renaissance originated in Italy and expanded northward, to spawn a Renaissance there. The evidence in favor of this view is impressive. Leonardo da Vinci, who died in France, and lies buried at the French château of Amboise, did little in his last years in the service of Francis I, but the French king's eagerness to have this great Italian with him indicates how much prestige the Italian Renaissance had for its northern admirers. Albrecht Dürer was only one, and the greatest, among northern painters to enter the ambiance of Italian artists and theoreticians; when he said, in perfect candor, that the rebirth of the arts had begun in Italy, with Giotto, he was voicing an accepted opinion.[5] English and French Humanists traveled to Italy, Italian Humanists traveled to France and England, and in these exchanges it was understood that the Italians were the teachers, the northerners their disciples.

But there were areas where the flow of influence also went in the opposite direction. Vasari credited the early fifteenth-century Flemish painter Jan van Eyck with the invention of oil-painting, and even if Vasari is not literally right, it remains true that Italian artists welcomed and imitated van Eyck's technical improvements. And the Flemish painters of the early quattrocento were more than technicians for the Italians: they learned a great deal from van Eyck's powers of accurate pictorial observation and meticulous brushwork. When in the 1450s the Genoese Humanist Bartolommeo Fazio compiled his collection of famous men, he included two Flemings among the four painters on his list and called one of these—Jan van Eyck—"the first painter of our century."[6] This, from an Italian, was high praise.

Apart from these exchanges, the arts of the Northern and Southern Renaissances also developed with a certain independence of one another. Dürer's woodcuts reflect the religious turmoil in Germany perhaps even more than the artistic principles he studied on his Italian visits. The Flemish painters of the fifteenth century employed their newly found pleasure in light, landscape, and three-dimensional modeling to depict traditional subjects in traditional ways: it is impossible and in fact meaningless to decide whether a Deposition by Rogier van der Weyden, or a Crucifixion by Rogier's greatest pupil, Hans Memling, should be called a late Gothic or an early Renaissance work. The world of nature invaded these luminous Flemish paintings, but their religious feeling seems more conservative, more continuous with medieval piety, than contemporary Italian feeling.

In Italian art, religious sentiment emerges most forcefully in the quiet figures of Fra Angelico and the pale Madonnas of Botticelli; but in the North some painters dwelled on the horrible glory of Christ's Passion with such fervor and such ecstasy that their work has been called, without any sense of anachronism, "expressionist."[7] The best known document of this frenzy is the Isenheim altarpiece, by Mathis Gothardt-Neithart, better known as Matthias Grünewald, painted between 1513 and 1515. It consists of several panels, the

---

[5] See Erwin Panofsky, *Renaissance and Renascences in Western Art* (2nd ed., 1965), 30.
[6] Erwin Panofsky, *Early Netherlandish Painting: Its Origins and Character*, 2 vols. (1953), 1–2.
[7] Otto Benesch, *The Art of the Renaissance in Northern Europe: Its Relation to the Contemporary Spiritual and Intellectual Movements* (rev. ed., 1965).

most famous a Crucifixion which shows the crucified Christ noticeably larger than his swooning mother and St. John the Baptist; His twisted body is riddled with wounds and beginning to assume the color of decay; His blood flows freely; His head, lacerated by the crown of thorns, lolls helplessly on one side; His mouth is open; His hands are cruelly contorted. The whole seems like an aggression against the spectator, a pressing invitation to participate in the Lord's sufferings that will not be denied. This altarpiece, glorious and disturbing, records the religious travail of the North, to which the Reformation was a response and a resolution (see p. 127).

In portraiture, too, the North reached independent heights that rivaled those of Italy. Thanks to Lucas Cranach the Elder, Hans Holbein the Younger, and Albrecht Dürer, we vividly know what the leading actors on the stage of German and English history in these times looked like—we have splendid portraits of reformers, kings, and scholars. Erasmus' personal vanity in particular—he greatly enjoyed having his features fixed in pencil, brush, or metal—served the curiosity of later historians: Massys, Dürer, and Holbein portrayed him over and over again. And these artists sought their models not in the great alone, but among the humble as well, with their careworn faces and workworn hands—pious, ordinary men and women made immortal because immortal artists took the trouble to record their features.

It is in the art of Albrecht Dürer that the divergent streams of the Northern Renaissance flow together, harnessed by one man's technical skill and sheer talent. Dürer owed to the Italians his discovery of pagan antiquity and instruction in proportion, but his inspiration is pure German piety in the time of Luther; he was a scientist in art and a seeker in religion: he inquired after the laws of perspective and the true faith with equal earnestness. Born in 1471 in Nuremberg, the son of a goldsmith, Dürer early acquired, and on his travels rapidly extended, the professional deftness to which his engravings and woodcuts still testify. He did series of woodcuts on religious subjects, painted altarpieces, and drew portraits. But his most enduring works are his great engravings, like his *Knight, Death and the Devil,* or his still mysterious *Melancholia I.* Dürer's copperplate is crowded with incident, but rarely overwhelmed by detail; he boldly captures his figures in vehement motion and in difficult foreshortening. Not all of Dürer's work was tempestuous: his engraving *St. Jerome in His Study* depicts the saint reading serenely in a large, sunlit room, his lion somnolent at his feet, the whole breathing a tranquility, order, and saintly industriousness that contrast with the turmoil of Dürer's agitated portrayals of the horsemen of the Apocalypse.

Printing

When Dürer died in 1528, artists, scholars, and the educated lay public were living in a new world, transformed beyond recall by the advent of printing. Dürer himself illustrated printed books, and so did other leading artists. But the aesthetic appeal of books, although pleasing, was a secondary element in the printing revolution—its primary significance lay in the rapid multiplication and distribution of information, which produced rapid decay of the handicraft of copying and a decisive decline in the oral tradition.

Like the discovery of America and the circumnavigation of the globe, the invention of printing was a great moment in man's history whose revolutionary import became evident only with the passing of years. "The coming of the printed book did not immediately produce substantial changes in taste and outlook."[8] Resistance on the part of many Humanists, mainly on aesthetic grounds, was vigorous: in his biography of Federigo da Montefeltro, duke of Urbino (see p. 55), the Florentine bookseller Vespasiano spends several pages listing the duke's books, and then adds: "In this library all the books are superlatively good, and written with the pen, and had there been one printed volume it would have been ashamed in such company."[9] The Humanists had not developed their celebrated handwriting for nothing, and it is not an accident that the first printing types were careful imitations of these Renaissance hands. "The weary copyists . . ., not those who made a living copying, but the many who had to copy a book to possess it," Burckhardt observes, "were jubilant at the German invention." At the same time, as Burckhardt does not neglect to note as well, the new invention inevitably produced a fearful reaction on the part of the powerful; printing brought preventive censorship in its train.[10] Every instrument of human progress, it seems, exacts its price.

When Johann Gensfleisch zum Gutenberg of Mainz perfected or invented printing by movable type in the 1440s—the precise sequence of events and influences remains, and must always remain, somewhat obscure—the idea of multiplying information mechanically was not new. But in the hands of Gutenberg and of the financiers and printers associated with him, the convenient new device spread rapidly. The Gutenberg Bible, set from 1452 on and published in 1456, remains the most precious relic of these heroic days. While the cultural effects were not immediate, the technical transformation was indeed nothing less than a revolution; this was not handwriting speeded up, it was a new mode of communication altogether: "A hard-working copyist," Elizabeth L. Eisenstein has said, "turned out two books in little less than a year. An average edition of an early printed book ranged from two hundred to one thousand copies. Chaucer's clerk longed for twenty books to fill his shelf; ten copyists had to be recruited to serve each such clerk down to the 1450s, whereas one printer was serving twenty before 1500."[11]

The phenomenal growth of the printing industry reflects the widespread hunger for books. The spread of lay learning, at once cause and effect of the

[8] Hans Baron, "Fifteenth-Century Civilisation and the Renaissance," in *The New Cambridge Modern History*, vol. I, *The Renaissance, 1493–1520* (1957), 53.

[9] Vespasiano, *Renaissance Princes, Popes, and Prelates* (Torchbook ed., 1963), 104.

[10] See Jacob Burckhardt, *The Civilization of the Renaissance in Italy* (1860, ed. 1945), 118.

[11] "Some Conjectures about the Impact of Printing on Western Society and Thought: A Preliminary Report," *Journal of Modern History*, XL, 1 (March 1968), 3.

Renaissance mentality, called for reading material in ever larger quantities, and printers across Europe soon supplied it. Mainz, Gutenberg's home city, was the first center; before 1460, there were printers in Bamberg and Strasbourg; by the early 1470s, the major German and Italian cities all had printing presses, and by the early 1480s, so did Stockholm and Valencia, Budapest and Antwerp, Cracow and Paris. [12] Printing was an industry calling for considerable capital; it was part not merely of the intellectual, but also of the commercial, revolution of the age.

For the Humanists who accepted printing—and gradually more and more of them did—it meant a wide public for their editions of classical authors and for their writings: Erasmus, who in his wandering life spent eight months in 1508 with the Venetian printer Aldus Manutius, was thoroughly modern in his quick recognition and shrewd exploitation of movable type. He wrote quite deliberately for the press, with gratifying results. His European reputation, already established, grew with the thirty-four editions of his *Adages* and the many thousands of copies that were sold all over Europe of his *Praise of Folly* (see p. 94). The ancients—both the pagan and the Christian classics—became available to a new reading public, and as scholars enjoyed the new audience printing gave them, this audience in turn provided a stimulus for further scholarly efforts.

But this was by no means all. As today so at its very beginning, printing mainly served a public that had no interest in scholarship. Printers turned out textbooks, books of devotion, collections of saints' lives, and political tracts in impressive quantities. "Printing," Luther said, "was God's highest act of grace," [13] and this single observation, made about half a century after printing had been invented, illuminates its cultural possibilities. The printing press, after all, was a docile and neutral instrument. It could produce a learned edition of St. Jerome but also, and with far less trouble, an inflammatory broadside or a papal indulgence. Printing made information immeasurably easier to produce and disseminate; truths and lies traveled faster and further than ever before. In the long run, the invention radically altered the tone and even the content of political and social life, the mode and matter of education, the distribution of fashion, and man's very way of perceiving the world. The effects were incalculable and, in the early modern centuries, no one even tried to calculate them. All one could say was said by Bacon early in the 1600s: the three inventions that the ancients had not known and that had "changed the appearance and state of the whole world," he wrote, were gunpowder, the compass, and printing. [14]

---

[12] S. H. Steinberg, *Five Hundred Years of Printing* (Penguin rev. ed., 1966), 44–45.
[13] Quoted in Eisenstein, "Conjectures about the Impact of Printing," 34.
[14] Aphorism 129 of *Novum Organum*. Quoted in Eisenstein, "Conjectures about the Impact of Printing," motto on p. 1.

Northern Humanism

If printing was a unique contribution of the North to the Renaissance, northern humanism, although not unique, was distinctive. Its single-minded campaign to purify religion has earned it an epithet of doubtful validity: "Christian humanism." It is doubtful because the Italian Humanists, for all their flirtations with esoteric doctrines, remained Christians too; it is doubtful also because the northern Humanists, for all their intentions, sometimes strayed perilously close to infidelity.

Moreover, it is plain that French, British, German, and Netherlands scholars acted under the impress of ideas and personalities native to the Mediterranean regions. By the 1480s, Paris was saturated with Italian and Greek Humanists teaching Greek and denigrating Scholastic philosophy. The two most influential figures in the French Renaissance, Guillaume Budé and Jacques Lefèvre d'Etaples, eagerly consumed these southern dispensations; Lefèvre in fact absorbed Italian teachings quite directly in Florence and Padua. The same is true of English Humanists: William Caxton, the most distinguished printer in the country—and in this movement, printers were not simply technicians or businessmen but influential molders of learned opinion as well—resorted to Italian scholars in England as editors and advisers;[15] and the leading English Humanists—John Tiptoft, William Grocyn, Thomas Linacre, John Colet—all studied in Italy during the second half of the fifteenth century and bore the marks of Italian tastes and Italian scholarship. Sir Thomas More, the exemplar of English humanism—the English Erasmus—is only an apparent exception. He never set foot in Italy, but he acquired the methods and aims of the Mediterranean Renaissance through his circle of learned friends and through Italians resident in England.

The German Humanists, too, beginning early in the fifteenth century with the versatile theologian Nicolas of Cusa and ending a century later with the political knight Ulrich von Hutten (see p. 133), looked to the South for instruction and inspiration; they disseminated their new learning at courts and in universities, in literary societies and academies. The members of these societies encouraged the study of antiquity, the writing of Latin verse, the study of the German past—and one another.[16] Perhaps the best known of these informal but influential groups centered around Mutianus Rufus at Erfurt, and Rufus was a disciple of the Florentine Neoplatonists.

Yet all across northern Europe the Humanists applied what they had acquired on their memorable journeys—the doctrines of Neoplatonism, the restored works of Aristotle, respect for precise scholarship, and Greek—in their

[15] R. Weiss, *Humanism in England During the Fifteenth Century* (2nd ed., 1957), 139, 172, 176.

[16] See R. Weiss, "Learning and Education in Western Europe from 1470 to 1520," in *The New Cambridge Modern History*, vol. I, *The Renaissance, 1493-1520* (1957), 117.

own way and for their own purposes. The German movement nourished, and was nourished by, a series of new Humanist universities—between 1450 and 1510 there were eight new foundations, including Wittenberg in 1502—and fed the stream of religious discontent that was to become the German Reformation. [17] Elsewhere, too, northern Humanists wrote treatises and founded institutions in the service of a purified Christian faith. Their very ideal of learned piety—docta pietas—had first been proclaimed by the Italian Petrarch, but in the North it acquired special force. The northern Humanists were certain that the shortest and perhaps the only path to true religion was through scholarship. Accurate learning alone could clear away the trivia, the superstitions, and the worldliness that had accumulated around Christianity and that were threatening to choke it. The truth would make men pious, and the truth lay in the sacred texts themselves; in the Scriptures carefully read, devoutly interpreted, and accurately translated; and in the writings of the church fathers, printed and edited with religious care. Secular learning—the study of languages, the law, and the natural sciences—were forms of, and often preparations for, authentic piety. The northern Humanists did not denigrate religious feeling and did not doubt miracles; they were not unbelievers in clerics' disguise. But they saw danger in the general sway of ignorance, and a place for the exercise of the intellect—was not reason itself, honestly and humbly used, a divine gift?

Since these scholars were as eager to disseminate their knowledge as they were to acquire it, they were all educators. And their energetic pedagogy was anything but remote or neutral: in the inflamed political and religious situation around 1500, it was a force for reform, even toward revolution. "We should actively rejoice at the felicity of this age," Robert Gaguin exclaimed in France in 1496, "in which, although many other things have perished, many men of genius are nevertheless incited, like Prometheus, to seize the splendid torch of wisdom from the heavens." [18] Guillaume Budé was one of Gaguin's Prometheuses: his treatises and commentaries on Roman law and money, his translations from Plutarch, are filled with calls to remember prudence in the pursuit of wisdom, to heed the lessons of history, and to reform contemporary institutions in accord with intelligence. His most direct contribution to education, however, was his persistent lobbying with Francis I in behalf of a new university that would break with the traditional restrictive, corporate organization of the medieval university in behalf of an open and free pursuit of knowledge. First broached in 1517, the Collège de France was established about 1530, with its chairs first in Greek and Hebrew, later in mathematics and Latin; it was a tribute to Budé's patient nagging and Humanist ideals. Lefèvre d'Etaples, meanwhile, inspired by Italian Aristotelians, lectured on Aristotle in Paris and published a commentary on him. Urged on by the desire to make available authentic texts, he translated church fathers and portions of the Bible

---

[17] Hajo Holborn, A History of Modern Germany, vol. I, The Reformation (1959), 106.
[18] Eugene F. Rice, Jr., The Renaissance Idea of Wisdom (1958), 94.

into Latin and brought out a French version of the New Testament in 1523. A prolific writer and editor, he also wrote commentaries on the Epistle of Paul and the Four Gospels. Lefèvre was a characteristic transitional figure. He was a sound scholar prone to mystical experiences; he exposed some pious forgeries but perpetuated others; several years before Luther, he placed special weight on faith and encouraged the reading of Scriptures, but he would have nothing to do with Luther or other reformers. Lefèvre d'Etaples, like many other northern Humanists, was a heretic but not a Protestant; his scholarly contributions are undeniable, but others, more radical than he, would reap the benefits of his labors and draw the conclusions he had only implied.

In England, Humanist learning penetrated the court and the church. It even touched the universities: this was a time of college foundations, mainly at Cambridge, devoted to the study of the ancient languages, including Hebrew. The Humanist message was carried to wide reaches of society by an impressive collection of scholars, nearly all of them in holy orders. The career of John Colet is representative. Born in London around 1467 of a substantial family, he became a priest, but while his eyes were on higher things, he did not neglect the blessings of reason. With inherited money he opened St. Paul's School in 1512, dedicated to the realization of *docta pietas* (see p. 92). Even more significant, perhaps, for the cause of Christian learning were his public lectures on the Epistles of St. Paul, which he delivered to large and distinguished audiences at Oxford in 1496. One modern student has not hesitated to call these lectures on 1 Corinthians and Romans, "a milestone in the history of Christian scholarship." [19] Medieval exegetes, delighting in number mysticism, allegorical readings, and obscure depths beyond obscure depths, had treated sacred texts as material for elegant or esoteric dialectical games. Colet broke with all this, and the effect was electrifying. He was not a modern rationalist or a radical philologist; compared with other Humanists of his time he was not even much of a classicist. But his devotion, which has something mystical about it, was directed at the plain sense of the texts; he cut through logic-chopping and the manufacture of allegories to the meaning of St. Paul's message, its historical context, and the moral lesson it held for the time of Colet and his hearers. And this reform of method led to a demand, by Colet and his friends and disciples, for larger reform—in church and state alike. More than in the Mediterranean world, Humanism in the North was thoroughly political.

Erasmus and More: Two Humanists in the World

John Colet made memorable contributions to Christian scholarship, but his greatest achievement was doubtless Desiderius Erasmus. [20] He found Erasmus

---

[19] E. Harris Harbison, *The Christian Scholar in the Age of the Reformation* (1956), 58.
[20] For what follows, see Harbison, *Christian Scholar*, 61, 69–78; Johan Huizinga, *Erasmus of Rotterdam* (tr. 1952).

a brilliant classicist without inner direction; he left him launched on a career of scholarly productivity and humane propaganda unequaled in his time.

Erasmus was born at Rotterdam, probably in 1466, an illegitimate child. Educated by an influential lay fraternity, the Brethren of the Common Life (see p. 128), he early made a misstep that took many years to rectify: around 1488 he took monastic vows. Until he met Colet he was not certain of his vocation, but he was certain that he had no vocation for the clerical life. He secured permission to study at the University of Paris, and with his first long stay there, beginning in 1495, he moved from one center of scholarship to another. Erasmus' peripatetic career testifies to the cosmopolitan quality of the Renaissance style; where there was a Humanist, Erasmus was at home. He visited England three times, he stayed at Louvain and Venice, and he ended his years at Basel, where he died in 1536, one of the most famous men in Europe, a private citizen of doubtful ancestry who had made his fame with his pen alone.

When Erasmus met Colet and other English Humanists on his first English visit in 1499, his erudition was already impressive. What Colet did for him was to channel his talents, to prove to him that learning and piety, even wit and piety, were by no means incompatible. Every reader of Erasmus has been impressed by his cool temper, that almost ostentatious moderation which he erected practically into a philosophy. If there were deep crises in his emotional and spiritual life, Erasmus knew how to keep them private. In his adolescence, he had been passionately attached to a friend and been rebuffed; from then on his letters contain no more intimate revelations. He was fastidious beyond the normal, but if his passion for cleanliness is indeed a neurotic symptom, he turned his neurosis to good purpose. He spent his life seeking to cleanse thinking, to purify texts, to bring the fresh air of decency and good sense into the affairs of the world.

Erasmus was both a scholar and a popularizer, and sometimes both at once. His first major work, the *Adages (Adagiorum collectanea)*, published in 1500 and often reprinted and greatly enlarged, consisted of a vast collection of sayings from the classical writers supplied with full annotations—all, of course, in Latin. The work made Erasmus famous and humanism popular. "Until this time the humanists had, to some extent, monopolized the treasures of classic culture," Johan Huizinga has written, "in order to parade their knowledge of which the multitude remained destitute, and so to become strange prodigies of learning and elegance. With his irresistible need of teaching and his sincere love for humanity and its general culture, Erasmus introduced the classic spirit, in so far as it could be reflected in the soul of a sixteenth-century Christian, among the people."[21] The phrase "the people" should be taken in a restricted sense; the many were still illiterate, and to many who could barely read, Latin was still an alien tongue. Still, Erasmus pioneered in making classical education general by taking the classics out of the realm of mystery open to a few initiates

[21] Huizinga, *Erasmus*, 39.

alone. The vast success of his book was a tribute at once to the powers of the printing press and to his lively Latin style. Erasmus' great edition of St. Jerome and his corrected edition of the Greek New Testament, both published in 1516, reached a smaller public, but they were daring appeals to the text in defiance of tradition, all the more so as Erasmus joined to his Greek text of the Scriptures a Latin translation that varied considerably from the accepted Vulgate version.

Erasmus sought to disseminate his religious and social ideas in a wide variety of ways: his vast correspondence with publishers, cardinals, kings, and Humanists and his didactic treatises, like the *Manual for a Christian Knight* of 1503 and the *Education of a Christian Prince* of 1515. The most celebrated of these writings, the one book by Erasmus that is still widely read, is *The Praise of Folly* (1509), a lighthearted satire that says humorously what his other writings say, though with wit, gravely. Its original title, *Moriae encomium,* with its punning reference to Thomas More, reveals its origin: Erasmus conceived the book on his way to More's house, and wrote it there. Cast, like Valla's critique of the Donation of Constantine (see p. 65), in the form of a declamation, *The Praise of Folly* once again displays the hold of classical rhetoric on the Humanists. Cheerfully speaking in its own behalf, Folly declares itself necessary to human happiness, indeed human existence, and in the course of its demonstration surveys the contemporary world with a keen eye for its failings. All professions are legitimate targets for Erasmus' gentle yet biting scorn, but most of all the clergy, with their worldliness, their ignorance, their elevation of ritual over faith.

In *The Praise of Folly,* we penetrate to the core of Erasmus' thought. As the aim of scholarship must be to free texts from corrupt readings and ignorant misinterpretations, so in life the aim is to find the essence of things by discarding its trappings. This is what Erasmus meant by what he called "the philosophy of Christ"; his religious thought is a distillation of Christian morality at its purest. This set him apart from mystics or from unquestioning followers of Rome—some thought, in fact, from religion altogether. It is undeniable that the perfect marriage of antiquity and Christianity, consummated in Erasmus' mind, made him a stranger to religious fervor. Eventually, his way of thinking set him apart from the Reformers as well. He prized Christian unity too highly to participate in its destruction, cultivation and moderation too highly to enjoy the coarse fanaticism of Luther and his followers. While at first he welcomed Luther as a surgeon called by God to cure the corruptions of the Renaissance papacy, he later polemicized against him. It was this moderation that led Erasmus even to ridicule fellow Humanists for demonstrating the "purity" of their Humanism by slavishly imitating Cicero.

Strong spirits have always found Erasmus too mild for their tastes, but there is something vastly appealing about this self-made scholar and moralist, inveighing against corruption, superficiality, fanaticism, stupidity, and the love of war, and championing tolerance, reasonableness, accuracy, generosity of mind, and decency. Yet in the world of the Reformation, Erasmus was in the end a misfit, distrusted by Catholics for the tepidness of his support and detested by Protestants (whose cause he had done so much to advance with his criticisms and his scholarship) for his refusal to join them. In immoderate times, moderate men are sadly out of place.

Just as sadly, in an unprincipled world a man of principle is out of place. This is the lesson that forces itself on the student of Sir Thomas More. In the extravagant portrait Erasmus drew of him in a letter to Hutten, he appears a man "born for friendship," simple in his tastes, a charming and witty host, a generous husband and father, "the common advocate of all those in need," an excellent speaker, a consummate classicist versed in Greek, Latin, pagan and Christian writers alike, a splendid stylist, a good man even at court—"and then there are those who think that Christians are to be found only in monasteries!" [22] Born in 1478, More came under the beneficent influence of Colet; the passionate humanitarianism of his *Utopia* owes much to Colet's articulate practical charity. Unlike most of the other English Humanists, More was not a cleric but a lawyer; yet his piety was as fervent and his scholarship as accurate as that of any priest. And he wrote, both English and Latin, better than anyone else in his day. His rise was rapid and his career, first as a lawyer and then as a statesman, was distinguished; Henry VIII employed him on diplomatic missions and in 1529 appointed him to his highest post, lord chancellor. But in the midst of his legal and public activities More never forgot his humanism; at Oxford, his university, he defended the teaching of Greek against detractors who feared that such Humanist interests would lead to impiety.

More's greatest work, a fine late flower of Renaissance humanism, is *Utopia*, published in 1516, a satire and program that has given its name and form to a large genre of writings for four and a half centuries. Erasmus, who had reason to know its author's intentions, said that it "was published with the aim of showing the causes of the bad condition of states; but was chiefly a portrait of the British State, which he has thoroughly studied and explored." [23] The first book, written last, is a vehement indictment of war, the idle rich, an unjust social system that first turns men into thieves and then cruelly punishes them, and the enclosure movement which has led the mild sheep of England to grow voracious and wild, so that (in More's savage simile) they eat men, and "devour whole fields, houses, and cities." [24] The second book, written first, portrays a perfect commonwealth, rationally divided into regions and cities, reasonably and justly governed, tolerant of religious dissent, and above all, free from the curse of private property. Some critics have dismissed these utopian proposals as a Humanist's intellectual pastime or as the longing of a reactionary for the medieval communal ideal that was being destroyed by nascent capitalism. On the other side, Socialists have hailed them as an early version of

[22] July 23, 1519, in selected letters appended to Huizinga, *Erasmus*, 231–239 passim.
[23] Letter in Huizinga, *Erasmus*, 238.
[24] *Utopia*, 175.

their own designs. While there is some point to the Socialist view of More, both parties are wrong: More was neither a belated Scholastic nor a premature Marxist, but a keenly observant student of his own time and a radical reformer. [25] And his satire was not a game; it was serious—satires usually are.

As soon as he accepted employment under Henry VIII in 1518, More was compelled to recognize that he could not act in government and realize the principles he had so seriously advocated; neither toleration nor communism seemed a possibility in the world of sixteenth-century England. Then came Henry VIII's divorce and his break with Rome (see p. 154), both incompatible with More's legal and religious principles. He retired from office, refused to take the required oath of supremacy, and paid for his principles with his life. In 1535 he went to his execution, his wit unimpaired to the end. Speaking from the scaffold, he told the throng that he "died the King's good servant but God's first." [26] They were brave and potent words, but they could not hide the reality that had brought him to his fall. Politics was made by ideas, but in the clash of the two, politics must win.

THE ORGANIZATION OF POLITICAL ENERGIES: THE GREAT POWERS

Among the forces that gave France, Spain, and England preeminence in Europe around 1500, the weightiest was the capacity of their rulers to consolidate their hold and their holdings. Most of the institutions they manipulated and modified were centuries old; ancient rivalries were scarcely appeased; competing centers of power at home and implacable enemies abroad continued to limit their range of action; economic and, soon enough, religious divisions threatened to disrupt precarious order. But amid the confusion of old and new and the endemic conflicts, there began to emerge in these great powers, still faint yet recognizable, the lineaments of the modern state.

The state, to put it baldly, exists for two purposes: to keep order and to make war. Of course, neither of these is as simple as it sounds. Keeping order is something more than the mere repression of the poor and the rebellious; it includes the administration of justice, the distribution of charity, the supervision of the economy, and until quite recent times, the safeguarding of the dominant religion. Similarly, making war is not merely the search for territory or supremacy by force of arms; it includes economic penetration and diplomatic maneuvering. To trade and to negotiate, one might say, playing a variation on

---

[25] We here agree with the position of J. H. Hexter, *More's "Utopia": The Biography of an Idea* (1952), and dissent from Gilmore, *World of Humanism*, 136–137.

[26] Raymond Wilson Chambers, *Thomas More* (1958), 349.

a famous saying of Clausewitz's, are to carry on war by other means. To complicate things further, the precise relationship between the two purposes of the state is far from obvious and continues to be a subject of vigorous controversy among historians: Ranke and his followers have insisted on the primacy of foreign over domestic policy, Marx and *his* followers on the primacy of domestic over foreign. No dogmatic answer will hold in all situations. War, even successful war, may produce famine, tax revolts, or political crises at home. Besides, the state may keep order for the sake of making war—an obedient kingdom is the best possible base for the raising of money and men; or it may make war for the sake of keeping order—foreign distractions can usefully divert attention and energies from domestic troubles, and foreign conquest often brings welcome booty. Finally it is worth noting that the instrumentalities of the state—the military machine or the bureaucracy—feed upon their own prosperity. An army increasing in size and competence, far from giving the desired security, may spur statesmen on to more ambitious plans and bigger wars than ever before; a growing bureaucracy, designed to master complex problems of administration, will create even greater complexities to administer. No general ever cheerfully dismissed his troops; few bureaus have abolished themselves. Solutions turn out to be problems.

The emerging Atlantic powers confronted all these difficulties; they rose to preeminence because they had solved earlier difficulties. They were large enough, rich enough, and unified enough to conduct their business. This, precisely, was what the political entities of medieval Europe had been unable to do. Feudal units were normally manors with a few farms attached, overgrown villages, clusters of villages, or in a few instances, sizable baronies—centers of resistance to effective centralization. They were too small or too unruly to curb international anarchy; in many respects, indeed, they were its cause. In contrast, the great units, empire and papacy, were too large to curb internal anarchy, too loosely organized and too weak, especially in the extremities, to control their rebellious vassals (see p. 112). The great powers of the fifteenth century redistributed power to their own advantage by curbing the independence of the small manorial lords, defeating and disarming proud feudal barons, disregarding or manipulating the empire, and defying the claims of the papacy to sole control over clerical organization. The power these states got was power they took away from others.

Historians have given the great powers of 1500 a single name: "the new monarchies." But both their prehistories and their organization were quite different. France, the originator of feudalism, gathered the large domains it controlled at the end of the Renaissance through war, diplomacy, purchase, inheritance, and adroit marriages. Spain emerged from the laborious reconquest of the peninsula from the Muslims and a marital union of two dynasties; it was united only in policy, not in law. In contrast, England, though rent by persistent civil conflict, was unified in territory and institutions. And while there *was* something new about these monarchies—the sheer weight of their power abroad, the tightening control over the feudal nobility at home—at least the French and English monarchs who wielded that power and exercised that control did not lack for precursors: Edward I of England and Philip the Fair of France, contemporaries and rivals at the end of the thirteenth and the beginning of the fourteenth centuries, gathered as much executive power into their hands, and asserted as much sovereignty [27] as poor roads, slow communications, stubborn aristocrats, and entrenched ecclesiastics would permit. "Through his whole existence," writes Leopold von Ranke about Philip the Fair, "there already blows the piercing draft of modern history." [28]

France: Consolidation of a Kingdom

Philip the Fair died in 1314, after a long and effective reign, marked by acquisition of territory, centralization of government, defeat of papal claims to rights over the French church, ruthless tax exactions, and vicious but profitable persecutions of the Templars [29] and the Jews. Louis XI, the first of the new monarchs, came to the throne in 1461, and completed what Philip the Fair had begun. But the line connecting these two kings is a long, sagging curve, for in that century and a half royal authority and the French economy gravely declined, only to be restored, gradually and painfully, in the first half of the fifteenth century.

The most visible disaster of this period was the intermittent conflict that occupied England and France from 1338 to 1453, the so-called Hundred Years' War. English kings laid claim to territory controlled or coveted by France, and to give weight to that claim, to the crown of France itself. The war fluctuated through four distinct phases. The first, ending in 1360, was a period of English victories, well-meaning but futile attempts at administrative reform in France, the ravages of the Black Death (see p. 51), and the great peasant revolt of 1358, the jacquerie, a protest against the exactions of the war. The second phase began with the accession of Charles V, who anticipated Louis XI by his capable administration in fiscal and military matters. But his reign proved a mere interlude; with his death in 1380 came the third and, for the French, most disastrous phase of the war, lasting until 1422, when Henry V, their most formidable invader, suddenly died. This was a period of civil war, of bloody feuds among great nobles proving, if further proof were needed, that feudalism

---

[27] The thing, not the word—that was not invented, or revived from Roman law, until the late sixteenth century.

[28] *Französische Geschichte*, vol. I (ed. 1957), 26.

[29] The Templars were a military religious order, called, from their Jerusalem foundation, Knights of the Temple of Solomon. They emerged early in the twelfth century, during the Crusades, and rapidly grew rich and powerful, a favorite with chivalric nobles. Solidly established across the Christian world, and increasingly worldly, they acted as bankers and aroused both genuine disapproval and envy. Philip the Fair's proceedings against them between 1308 and 1314 claimed a religious basis, but the results were eminently rewarding, largely in a financial sense.

bred anarchy. As usual, the poor paid for the sport of the rich; starvation, always endemic, became epidemic in these years: "And on the dunghills of Paris . . . you could have found ten, twenty, or thirty children, boys and girls alike, dying there of hunger and cold, and no heart could be so hard as to hear their cries at night—'Ah! I die of hunger'—without pitying them; but the poor administrators were not able to help them, for they had no bread, nor wheat, nor fuel."[30] It was only in the final phase that France recovered her vigor and her territory and paved the way for the work of Louis XI.

Charles VII, a weak man whose only strength was the strength of others, was crowned at Rheims in 1429 under the watchful eye of Joan of Arc, who had so miraculously rallied French morale and presided over the French relief of Orléans in the same year. Joan was captured in 1430, turned over to the English, tried, and burned at the stake in 1431; and the king she had raised from a despised puppet to a real monarch did nothing to save her. On the other hand, he discarded the favorites who had been so ruinous to him in earlier years and now followed sound advice—having been called the King of Bourges he was now called Charles the Well-Served. In his long reign—he died in 1461—the decay of the medieval political system was, as it were, made official. The great nobles, the rich cities, and the representative estates were brought to heel. Charles VII took the collection of taxes into his own hands, made the beginnings of a permanent army under royal control, and proclaimed, in the Pragmatic Sanction of Bourges,[31] in 1438, the superiority of church councils over the papacy and the right of French ecclesiastics to select their own bishops. This bold declaration of independence of the French church from Rome was, in actuality, a declaration of the submission of French clerics to the French crown. It was also a firm statement of what came to be known as Gallicanism: the claim that in Catholic Christendom, the French crown had special privileges, amounting almost to sovereignty, over the clerical establishment in its own boundaries.[32]

The test of these vigorous policies came in 1440, with a rebellion of great dukes. It was crushed, and Charles VII used the opportunity to enlarge his domains with the lands of the rebels. Class society, even caste society, remained alive, but an elite of lawyers, merchants and petty nobles acquired a new political prominence. Feudalism as a force was dying. "To be sure," writes the French historian Georges Duby, "there remain some dependencies, groups of armed men, private castles, and powerful habits of insubordination, and for a long time to come these will make themselves known through rebellions and

---

[30] Georges Duby and Robert Mandrou, *A History of French Civilization from the Year 1000 to the Present* (1964), 171.

[31] The term "pragmatic sanction," which recurs in European history, originated in Roman law; it refers to a ruler's decision of vital importance claiming the status of a fundamental law; among later pragmatic sanctions, that of 1713, modifying the Hapsburg succession, is possibly the best known (see p. 389).

[32] Gallicanism punctuates French history; it reemerged with special force in the reign of Louis XIV (see p. 306).

outbursts of impatience running from end to end of the kingdom. . . . But henceforth these rebellions are merely short-lived, unimportant clashes, *guerres folles*. No longer is France the sum of her manors: now the realm belongs, truly, to the king."[33]

The reign of Louis XI confirms this assessment. The feudal barons, several of them connected by ties of blood to the royal house, continued to hold sizable territories, harbor undiminished aspirations, and cherish unappeasable resentments. The most considerable of these barons was the duke of Burgundy. His land was rich and his territory extensive: in the reign of Louis XI, it stretched from Dijon in the south northward across what is today Lorraine, Luxemburg, and most of Holland and Belgium. Endowed with fertile farm lands and opulent trading cities, the duchy, although an appanage of the French crown, was in effect an independent state and a real threat to France. This threat increased in 1467, when Charles le Téméraire succeeded to his sprawling duchy. He is usually called Charles the Bold in English, but his French appellation is more justly rendered as Charles the Rash. In the dazzling constellation of major European monarchs, Charles of Burgundy is a star of a lesser order, but for the decade of his reign—he was killed in 1477 by Swiss troops in French pay—he flashes across history like a meteor, proud, unbending, with a rage for magnificent show and an unquenchable thirst for immortality: "He desired great glory," the historian Philippe de Comines, his contemporary, reports, "which more than anything else led him to undertake his wars; and longed to resemble those ancient princes who have been so much talked of after their death."[34] His intention was nothing less than to establish a "middle kingdom" by rounding out his territories in the center of his thin, stretched-out domain.

Compared with this glittering dreamer, Louis XI of France seemed at a decisive disadvantage. Charles the Rash gave him the nickname "the universal spider"; that it should have gained general currency is a commentary on the impression Louis XI made on the men of his day. Impatient for power, he had participated in the Praguerie and had been exiled to the provinces for his share in the revolt against his own father. Ill-favored in body and unprepossessing in appearance, he compensated for his physical defects, and confirmed his bad reputation by exploiting his resourceful and ruthless intelligence. The contradictions that haunt all men haunted him more than most. He was characterized (as Ranke aptly puts it) by "generosity and greed, incautious trust and an ever-active, unappeasable suspiciousness, a nervous timidity under pressure and an absolute confidence, in fortunate moments, that they would last. Respect for the individual vanished in the face of his concern for the whole; justice and cruelty became one." He did great things, but no one was grateful to him, for he was without "all higher moral qualities. He made a kingdom great, but he lacked all personal greatness."[35]

[33] Duby and Mandrou, *History of French Civilization*, 187.
[34] Johan Huizinga, *The Waning of the Middle Ages* (ed. 1956), 72.
[35] Ranke, *Französische Geschichte*, 43.

In foreign policy, his skill and determination served Louis well. The end of the Hundred Years' War, and the Wars of the Roses, which kept the English occupied at home, were favorable preconditions for expansion. Charles of Burgundy left only a female heir upon his death in 1477, and after some fighting and much negotiating, Louis managed to add the province of Burgundy and, later, Artois and Franche-Comté, to the domains of France. In 1481, when the Angevin line died out, Louis inherited the rich provinces that had belonged to the house of Anjou: Maine, Bar, Anjou, and Provence. The territories Louis acquired for France were not simply favors that timely deaths and childless rivals threw into his lap: he had to fight for every inch of land in the field and at the conference table.[36] Such luck comes only to the able.

In domestic matters, Louis followed and developed the policies of his father. Characteristically, he called the Estates, first called by his great predecessor Philip the Fair in 1302, only once, in 1468, and for the same reason: not to participate in his government but to give him support and ratify his policies. He staffed his council with petty nobles and lawyers who would give him sound advice without seeking to circumscribe his authority. He imperiously supervised the courts and refused to countenance any independence on the part of judges, let alone grant them the share in the making of policy they liked to claim as a right. He controlled church appointments more firmly than any of his predecessors and dispensed this lucrative patronage himself. He vigorously protected industry and trade—not always to the satisfaction of those he presumed to protect, for his policies always were expensive. He encouraged trading companies, supported mining, and in some respects anticipated the policies of mercantilism—the use of state power to encourage the economy for the sake of increasing state power—that was to become so typical of seventeenth-century policy (see p. 300). When Louis XI said on his deathbed in 1483, "Under us the crown has not been diminished, but rather it has gained and grown," he could with justice apply this remark to domestic as well as to foreign affairs.

How solidly he had built emerged most clearly after his death. His son and successor, Charles VIII, was a boy of thirteen, and unappeased nobles and restless subjects alike thought the regency a good time to reverse the trend toward absolutism. They were wrong: the confused intrigues and uprisings, derisively called *guerres folles,* and an inconclusive meeting of the Estates General in 1484, only left the crown more firmly entrenched than ever. In 1491, three years after the death of the duke of Brittany, Charles VIII married the duke's daughter, Anne, thus adding another coveted territory to France. When he invaded Italy in 1494, the resources of a large, populous kingdom, heavily taxed and in general obedient, were at his disposal.

[36] But note the warning of Gilmore not to modernize Louis XI too much *(World of Humanism,* 82–83).

Spain: The Marriage of Castile and Aragon

One of Louis XI's most galling failures in foreign policy was his inability to prevent the marriage between Ferdinand of Aragon and Isabella of Castile in 1469. If anything, his aggressive posture did much to speed it. With that marriage, hastily concluded to circumvent widespread opposition to the match, Spain was launched on its march to the status of a great power. The union of Ferdinand and Isabella was dictated by reason; it joined the heirs to the two largest, richest, and most populous portions of the peninsula. There was about it, as the English historian J. H. Elliott has written, "a dynastic logic which reached back to a period long before they were born." [37] That logic, as Elliott says, was dynastic rather than modern: the marital union of the two houses united only those two houses, not the territories they controlled. Like the other "new monarchs," Ferdinand and Isabella did not set out to destroy traditional patterns of kingship; they joined patrimonies, but kept their portions distinct. Domestic and even foreign affairs continued to be regarded as mainly the business of Castile or Aragon, and the institutions of these realms were untouched. When the couple acted in concert, as they often did, they acted like intimate allies, never as rulers of a single state. The marriage was an effective way of joining two branches of a single Castilian dynasty [38] and of freeing the energies of militant Christians to complete a long-delayed crusade; it was the signal for the final *reconquista* of Spain.

At the time of the marriage the Muslim holdings in Spain consisted of the Kingdom of Granada, a modest patch of ground just east of the southern tip of the peninsula. Early in the tenth century, the Moors had held practically all of Iberia, but in the twelfth and thirteenth centuries, Christian troops had slowly pushed them toward the south: the compact Kingdom of Granada was the last remnant of the great Moorish offensive in Europe. The shape of the Spanish map had remained unaltered for over a century and a half; while Castilians and Aragonese were busy with foreign adventures and domestic conflicts they paid little attention to the infidel in the south. Nor did the efforts made in the 1450s to renew the *reconquista* come to very much. The idea of a crusade against unbelievers was in the air, but it needed vigor, intelligence, resources, and common action to become a reality.

Ferdinand and Isabella supplied all four. Upon the death of her brother Henry IV in 1474, Isabella styled herself Queen of Castile, but she had to fight a civil war, sometimes of serious dimensions, before her title was honored; opposition was not eliminated until 1479. In the same year Ferdinand succeeded to the throne of Aragon. The two crowns now turned to the *reconquista* in earnest. They achieved it in piecemeal but rapid fashion. In ten years, between

[37] *Imperial Spain, 1469–1716* (1963), 6.
[38] The house of Aragon had died out in 1410, and in 1412 a member of a Castilian house had ascended the Aragonese throne.

1482 and 1492, the Kingdom of Granada was overpowered. The defeated Moors, at least for the moment, were left in peace, to live their lives and practice their religion. [39]

The Spanish Jews were not so fortunate. In March 1492, shortly after their victory over the Moors at Granada, Ferdinand and Isabella issued a decree that ordered all Jews expelled from Castile and Aragon within four months. Perhaps as many as one hundred fifty thousand Jews left the Spanish lands, among them a number of Jewish converts to Roman Catholicism (known as *conversos* or *maranos*) whose sincerity had come into question. [40]

The Jews of medieval Spain had participated actively and constructively in the cultural and economic life of their countries; many of them had converted to Catholicism from conviction not fear, some of them had intermarried—Ferdinand himself was partly Jewish—and found Spanish society and professional life open to them. There had been sporadic anti-Jewish outbursts; during the Black Death and in times of economic distress fanatical priests had aroused general hatred for the outsiders, and in 1391 there had been a massacre of Spanish Jews across the peninsula. By the middle of the fifteenth century, the first racial laws requiring *limpieza de sangre* (pure blood) had excluded Jews from office in the city of Toledo. [41] The triumph of Ferdinand and Isabella over the Moors strengthened the feeling—scarcely national, partly racial, wholly irrational—that Spain must be purged to reach its true greatness; it was a signal not to relax, but to intensify, this great crusade for religious and racial purity. At least in part, the Spanish monarchs were driven to the expulsion of the Jews by their own successes.

This was the first irony of the expulsion. The second was that by depriving Spain of loyal merchants, bankers, and physicians, it threatened Spanish economic, intellectual, and scientific life at the very moment Spain was launching its great career as an empire. [42] There was yet a third irony: one instrument of the anti-Jewish policy was the Tribunal of the Holy Office, the Inquisition, an old institution put on a regular footing in Spain in 1478. It was designed to guard the purity of the Christian religion in Ferdinand and Isabella's domains, and at least one group favoring the institution had been influential *conversos*, anxious lest their position be imperiled by false converts. [43]

---

[39] For later Morisco policy, see pp. 174, 198.

[40] The familiar distinction between Sephardic and Ashkenazic Jews has its origins in the expulsion. The descendants of the Spanish Jews, who settled across Europe, northern Africa, and the Near East, came to be known as Sephardim, and to be contrasted with the Ashkenazim—a word of obscure and disputed origins that acquired the meaning of "German" and, by extension, "eastern European."

[41] Elliott, *Imperial Spain*, 95.

[42] Ibid., 99.

[43] The precise role of the Inquisition in Spain remains a matter of some discussion. It now seems doubtful that, as some earlier historians used to assert, the rulers of Spain designed the

The expulsion of the Jews was an act of politics, but it was also an act of piety. In these years as later, Spain was the proverbial bastion of the faith: in view of the worldliness that infected the Renaissance papacy (see p. 110), the old cliché about being more papist than the pope applies quite literally to Spain. But their fervent religious feelings did not stop Ferdinand and Isabella from acting decisively against the Spanish clergy. As in other kingdoms, quite as Christian or nearly as Christian as Castile and Aragon, in Spain, too, the state treated the church as a powerful rival to be mastered before it could be considered a congenial ally to be aided and a spiritual guide to be followed. The Spanish church was enormously rich, exceptionally privileged, and hence extraordinarily independent. It enjoyed an annual income of more than six million ducats, while individual prelates, like the archbishop of Toledo, had an income of eighty thousand ducats a year;[44] it owned vast tracts of land for the most part free from taxation; its great dignitaries acted precisely like feudal nobles, with their castles, their private armies, their "dynastic" ambitions. After prolonged and often embittered controversy, reaching all the way to the pope, Ferdinand and Isabella reduced the independence of these proud and powerful clerics, more barons than bishops: they assumed the right to name bishops, first in the conquered kingdom of Granada, later in the conquered territories overseas;[45] diverted part of the exactions of the church to their own treasury; intervened in the administration of clerical affairs; and supervised the conduct of clerical personnel, who, for all of Spanish piety, badly needed supervision.

This ecclesiastical policy, which the Spanish monarchs enforced with consistent vigor, was part of a general effort at mastering their sprawling and disparate domains. To achieve this mastery, they revived and transformed some old institutions. They reduced the anarchy rampant in the cities by strengthening the *corregidor,* a royal official who supervised municipal government; they further brought order into local chaos by reviving the *santa hermandad.* In the Middle Ages, these holy brotherhoods had been strictly local police forces; with the decree of 1476, they were staffed by the localities but controlled by the crowns. In a land overrun with brigands and robbers, the *hermandades*—at the same time policeman, judge, and executioner—armed with wide powers, animated by fresh zeal, and acting with notorious ferocity, appeared necessary and were soon effective. As elsewhere, so in the Spanish world, the united

---

Inquisition as a political weapon to tighten the crown's control over their lands or to speed the unification of their territories. The ostensible purpose of the Inquisition—to supervise the purity of the faith—was also its actual purpose. But, as Elliott has said, "in a country so totally devoid of political unity as the new Spain, a common faith served as a substitute, binding together Castilians, Aragonese, and Catalans, in the single purpose of ensuring the ultimate triumph of the Holy Church." Thus it compensated, "in some respects for the absence of a Spanish nationhood" (*Imperial Spain,* 97).

[44] Elliott, *Imperial Spain,* 88.

[45] It was not until 1523 that the process was completed, when Charles V won the privilege of naming bishops all across Spain.

crowns firmly believed in an aristocratic, steeply graded society, but they
asserted their authority over great nobles, sought and found sources of taxation
that needed approval from no assembly, and chose able men from the middling
strata to serve them: "They took care," one contemporary wrote, "to appoint
discreet and capable officials, even though they were only of middling rank,
rather than important figures from the principal houses." [46]

Ferdinand and Isabella's proceedings against the Spanish church were thus
anything but a sign of impiety. Machiavelli thought Ferdinand acted "under the
pretext of religion," [47] but Machiavelli, although he understood a great deal,
could never understand the complexity of the religious mind. It cannot be
repeated too often that men could be truly devout and yet attack the church;
indeed—and this was to become a pervasive theme during the Reformation—
men could attack the church *precisely because* they were truly devout.

Historians of Spain like to point to the year 1492 as a decisive year for their
country. They are right: the defeat of the Moors, the expulsion of the Jews, and
the discovery of America were linked by more than coincidence. They were
steps in the precarious unification of Spain around the conquest of territory,
fanatical religious convictions, and the search for empire, and it was the last of
these that was made realistic by the first two. Ferdinand and Isabella enjoyed
a long reign—the queen of Castile died in 1504, the king of Aragon in 1516—
and in their time they molded the institutions and gathered the resources that
would make Spain into the first power in Europe. [48] Modernity comes in strange
ways. These monarchs made a country they did not envisage and conquered an
empire they could not oversee; they were new monarchs acting on traditional
principles and medieval ideals.

England: The Triumph of the Tudors

When Henry Tudor usurped the throne of England in 1485, he could look back
on nearly two centuries of political instability. For ordinary Englishmen and
women, doing their daily chores, the interminable squabbles among nobles
may have seemed remote and even trivial—the kind of game aristocrats,
trained only for fighting and professionally incapable of working, would play
to pass the time. Even the long and wearisome Wars of the Roses (1455–1485)
scratched only the surface of English society. "The fighting was sporadic," as
the English historian S. T. Bindoff puts it, "the armies small, the material losses
inconsiderable." Yet, he adds, "anarchy is a dangerous pastime," as "four
centuries of heroic efforts by kings and statesmen to establish the reign of law
seemed in danger of being brought to nought amid a surfeit of kings and a

---

[46] This is from Elliott, *Imperial Spain*, 80, quoting other sources.
[47] *The Prince* (1532), chap. xxi. For Machiavelli, see p. 118.
[48] For the Spanish Empire, see p. 170.

shortage of statesmen."[49] Dangerous as it was to society, anarchy was particularly dangerous to kings and aspirants: of the nine Plantagenets who had reigned in England after the death of the great Edward I in 1307, only four died a natural death.

Let us read the dismal roll: Edward II, deposed in 1327 and murdered; Edward III, died of natural causes in 1377; Richard II, forced to abdicate in 1399, died a year later in prison, murdered; Henry IV and his son Henry V, the hero of Agincourt, died natural deaths, the first in 1413, the second in 1422; Henry VI, deposed in 1461, imprisoned, and finally murdered in 1471; Edward IV, died of natural causes in 1483; Edward V, a twelve-year-old boy, deposed and murdered, under circumstances that still exercise historians and amateur detectives, in 1483; Richard III, died on Bosworth Field in battle against Henry Tudor, in 1485. This catalogue, dismaying as it is, does not even tell the whole story of vendettas, the abuse of Parliament for purely partisan purposes, slanders, plots, poisonings. Shakespeare's famous line, which he lends to Henry IV, "Uneasy lies the head that wears a crown," was true in a more literal sense than its author had meant to convey. It was a cruel world of proud men and women, of bellicose landowners and ambitious officials who knew that defeat exacted only one price: death. The Wars of the Roses were essentially a family feud between two branches of the Plantagenet dynasty, the white rose of the Yorkists and the red rose of the Lancastrians. The triumph of Henry Tudor was the triumph of Lancaster.

But it did not bring immediate peace. As Henry could not help seeing in the light of recent history and current challenges, his greatest problem was survival itself. His title to the throne, like everyone else's, was doubtful, and Yorkist claimants did not give up their pretensions. For the first half of his reign—down to 1499, when the main Yorkist pretender, young Warwick, was executed for treason—Henry VII faced invasions and melodramatic conspiracies. He surmounted them by a combination of intelligence, adroitness, and hard work. His marriage to a member of the competing house, Elizabeth of York, typical of his shrewdness, was not enough to appease those who felt hungry for, and cheated out of, power.

Hence Henry used other means, all of critical importance for the rise of the modern English state. One of these, a welcome departure, was relative clemency: in more than one uprising, the king brought only the leaders to the scaffold and sent the followers back to their ordinary lives. But beyond this, Henry laid hands on time-honored institutions. Characteristically, he kept their name but changed their role. He did not destroy the common law, local government, or the Parliament, but instead bent them to his purposes. The chief menaces to political stability were the great feudal nobles, equipped, as wealthy landowners, with the means and the manpower to form private armies of the retainers they maintained and who wore their masters' livery. The

[49] *Tudor England* (1950), 8.

common law courts, which had been used against them in the past, were unwilling and unable to control these magnates: the courts were mired in legalism, ridden with corruption, and enfeebled by fear of the great. Henry VII was both willing and able. He restored local government, badly neglected under his predecessors, by strengthening the justices of the peace, carefully and diligently supervising the appointment of these magistrates. This duty of appointment, among all his duties, Henry took most seriously of all.[50] He centralized executive power in his councils—the flourishing of conciliar government, which marks the Tudor epoch, begins with him—and increasingly staffed them not with great lords but with lesser aristocrats and landed squires. By surrounding himself with men who owed him everything and on whose unwavering loyalty he could count, Henry VII employed a technique of absolute government that was becoming widespread (in Spain, for example; see p. 105), and that Louis XIV of France would bring to perfection a century and a half later. He created a court of the Star Chamber,[51] an offshoot of the judicial work of his council, defined by act of Parliament in 1487. The court settled disputes among the great, gave judgment in riots and other unlawful assemblies, and enforced the prohibitions against "livery and maintenance".[52] It acted, that is, against the powerful subjects before whom the common law courts had stood in awe. Hated as it came to be under the Stuarts (see p. 272), under the early Tudors the Star Chamber was popular, at least with the people. Finally, Henry VII adroitly used Parliament. He called it when he needed it— between 1485 and 1497 it met ten times—and sent it home when it had passed the legislation he wanted and when he was militarily and financially secure: After 1497 it met only once more during his reign, in 1504.[53]

To break the power of the feudal aristocracy was a notable achievement, but Henry was not satisfied with that. He wanted a prosperous crown and a prosperous country, and he produced both. A poor crown is a dependent crown, and Henry wanted independence. He managed the crown lands to yield greater returns, enlarged his patrimony by confiscating the lands of nobles partisan to Richard III, diligently collected feudal dues, effectively collected taxes, and derived large profits from customs duties and court sentences imposing fines and granting pardons: Henry VII, quite literally, made justice pay. At his accession, the crown took in £52,000; twenty-four years later, at his death, its income had nearly tripled to £142,000.[54] But Henry also took care of his subjects, especially the merchants. In 1496, he granted a charter to John

---

[50] Ibid., 58.

[51] So called after a chamber in the palace of Westminster, where it met, under a ceiling decorated with stars.

[52] "Livery" was the practice of keeping uniformed retainers, small private armies; "maintenance" was the equally obnoxious practice of the powerful to press unjust claims in court by means of threats and outright violence.

[53] Bindoff, *Tudor England,* 63.

[54] Sir David Lindsay Keir, *The Constitutional History of Modern Britain, 1485-1951* (5th ed., 1955), 12.

Cabot to explore, and take possession of, territories in North America; in the same year, he concluded a trade treaty with the Netherlands that hardened the monopoly of London merchants on the profitable cloth trade with Antwerp; and he further protected and regulated domestic manufacture. These enactments were less a system of economic policy than the groping of an intelligent monarch with an emerging commercial capitalism;[55] as such, they are another element in Henry's successful campaign to restore England to order, centralize political power, and make the country prosperous. Not even Henry VIII, his flamboyant and neurotic son, could undo it all (see p. 154).

THE ORGANIZATION OF POLITICAL ENERGIES: PAPACY AND EMPIRE

The Papacy as a Political System

While France, Spain, and England took the center of the political stage late in the fifteenth century, other political systems continued to play considerable roles in the making of history. Events in Rome or at Wittenberg reverberated across Europe.

One of the most remarkable of these systems was the papacy. In the eyes of European statesmen, no matter how devout, it was a state like any other. It is true that the church had a special hold on men's minds in medieval and early modern Europe, but when its kingdom was evidently of this world, secular princes could not afford to overlook its activities. And from the thirteenth century on, precisely as the involvement of the church in the world—in its politics, its luxuries, its corruptions—became overwhelming and disturbing, the capacity of the papacy to influence events markedly declined. This combination of visibility and impotence was irresistible: ruler after ruler deprived Rome of the right to appoint bishops, tax the local clergy, or take appeals from local courts.

By 1417, when a comparatively united church agreed to elect the Roman cardinal Otto Colonna to the papal chair, the long decline of the papacy seemed to have been arrested. For over a century it had undergone humiliation at the hands of grasping princes, a glittering captivity at Avigon under French pressure, and most dismaying of all, a discreditable schism in which two, and later three clerics had claimed to be the sole vicar of Christ (see p. 44). The Council of Constance, convoked in 1414 to deal with disorders in the church, combat heresy, and restore unity, had three popes on its hands: the aged Gregory XII, the Avigon claimant Benedict XIII, and the egregious John XXIII,

[55] See Bindoff, *Tudor England*, 64.

"the most profligate of mankind," as Gibbon, with malicious accuracy, describes him. Gregory resigned, Benedict was deposed, and John imprisoned: "He fled," Gibbon writes, "and was brought back a prisoner; the most scandalous charges were suppressed; the vicar of Christ was only accused of piracy, murder, rape, sodomy, and incest."[56] After such leadership, the resumption of papal residence at Rome and the elimination of rivals seemed the most far-reaching of reforms. But the Renaissance popes who followed the Great Schism resisted the drastic purge that was so obviously essential for the health of organized Christendom. For the first half of the fifteenth century, a series of church councils made solemn efforts to assert their superiority over the pope: "This synod," the Council of Constance affirmed and, in 1432, the Council of Basel reaffirmed, "lawfully assembled in the Holy Ghost, and forming a general council representing the Catholic Church, has its power directly from Christ, and everyone, of whatever rank and office, even the Pope, is obliged to obey it in matters touching the faith, in the removal of the Schism, and in the reformation of the church in head and members."[57] Clerical vices were prevalent and palpable: simony—the selling of church offices; indulgences—the selling of salvation;[58] pluralism—the profitable occupancy of several benefices; and concubinage—the widespread practice of priests too weak (or too strong) to obey the church's rule demanding celibacy. The conciliar movement enlisted some of the finest minds of Christendom, including Nicolas of Cusa, but after an effort of thirty years, it failed. The popes temporized: they agreed on the need for reform but rejected the political theory of the reformers. When the acrimonious Council of Basel was dissolved in 1449, the papacy had reasserted its sovereignty over the church. Flushed with victory, it staged a jubilee in 1450, and the need for concessions being over, made no reforms. Precisely like other states, the papacy sought to secure its hold on its territories and absolute authority over its constituencies. Half a century later, Martin Luther would make the papacy pay, not so much for its monarchical aspirations as for its self-confident and short-sighted neglect of its spiritual office.

While few of the Renaissance popes were admirable spiritual guides to Christians across Europe, many of them were characteristic Renaissance men, with all the good and evil consequences this implies. Nicholas V, a Humanist who had been librarian to Cosimo de' Medici, founded the Vatican Library and surrounded himself with such fellow Humanists as Lorenzo Valla and Leone Battista Alberti. Pius II, who is one of the heroes of Burckhardt's *Civilization of the Renaissance in Italy*, was a reformed worldling and poet who distinguished

---

[56] *Decline and Fall of the Roman Empire* (1787, ed. J. B. Bury), VII, 288, 289.

[57] George H. Sabine, *A History of Political Theory* (rev. ed., 1950), 323.

[58] This, of course, is what the Protestants later came to call it; precisely and officially, indulgences, first introduced in 1300 by Boniface VIII to raise money, were considered supplementary expiations of sin, added to the sacrament of penance. To gain an indulgence, by prayer or by purchase, was to "make satisfaction."

his tenure with a fine autobiography and an elegant correspondence. Sixtus IV was one of the most lavish among Renaissance patrons; he began construction of the Sistine Chapel and brought painters like Botticelli and Ghirlandaio to Rome. But with the reign of Sixtus, the worldly papacy added to the innocuous patronage of artists the vicious patronage of relatives. Sixtus' midcentury predecessors—Pius II's reign had ended in 1464—had still taken their responsibilities with the utmost seriousness. The Turks' capture of Constantinople in 1453 had moved the vicars of Christ to proclaim a crusade against the infidel at the gates, and Pius II, disappointed in the poor response his call for a crusade received among Christian princes, even outfitted his own fleet. But Sixtus cared more for his family than for larger issues; he made nepotism, one of the most glaring vices of the papacy, into a system. Six of Sixtus' cardinals were close relatives, three of them his nephews. "One alone—Giuliano della Rovere—" the Catholic historian Philip Hughes exclaims, scandalized, "held eight bishoprics in four different countries, besides various abbeys!"[59] Giuliano's influence in Rome was almost unparalleled. After his uncle's death in 1484, he remained to dominate his successor and finally obtained the papal tiara himself in 1503. As Julius II, he proved to be as energetic and militant as a *condottiere*. "He would have been a pope worthy of the highest renown," the great sixteenth-century Florentine historian Guicciardini said of him, "if he had been a secular prince or if the care and diligence he showed in glorifying the church in the temporal sphere and through the art of war had been used to glorify it in the spiritual sphere through the arts of peace."[60] Even to Italians hardened in the ways of the world, the spectacle of warrior-diplomat-popes seemed a little inappropriate.

The lust for political power, artistic display, and family influence reached its climax with Alexander VI, the Borgia pope, Giuliano's rival and predecessor. Among Alexander's unusual distinctions is the fame—or the notoriety—achieved, with his active support, by two of his illegitimate children, Lucrezia and Cesare Borgia. Alexander made no secret of his sensuality and his greed, even as pope. While the most scandalous rumors about his conduct, like his supposed incest with his daughter Lucrezia, have been traced to the malicious gossip of disappointed office seekers, the truth about Alexander's debauchery and abuse of office for political purposes and private gain was dramatic enough. "Of all the pontiffs who ever reigned," Machiavelli coolly appraised him, "Alexander VI best showed how a Pope might prevail both by money and by force."[61] It was popes like Alexander VI and Sixtus IV who moved Erasmus to excoriate, in *The Praise of Folly*, the "scourges of the human race."

---

[59] *A Popular History of the Catholic Church* (Image Book ed., 1954), 157; note to Pazzi conspiracy in chap. I.

[60] Quoted by R. Aubenas, "The Papacy and the Catholic Church," in *The New Cambridge Modern History*, vol. I, *The Renaissance, 1493–1520* (1957), 84.

[61] *The Prince*, chap. XI.

By and large, the Renaissance popes were an effective group of men, normally with exquisite taste, consummate diplomatic skill, and, like Julius II, personal bravery. But, especially from Sixtus IV on, they walked like dreamers through an earthquake. In the midst of outbursts of popular fanaticism, large-scale heresy, foreign invasion, and the Turkish menace to Christendom, they looked to their property and haggled with painters. In the century and a half after the Great Schism had been healed, the popes regained some of their political power, firmly secured the papal states around Rome, amassed immense wealth for their families, and procured for the world imperishable works of art. But the papacy was not to recover much of its spiritual authority until the second half of the sixteenth century, with the austere and militant Counter-Reformation (see p. 164).

The Empire: Decline and Recovery

The decline and recovery of the empire—the Holy Roman Empire—preceded those of the papacy, but its capacities never matched its claims, not even in the early sixteenth century under the Emperor Charles V. Voltaire's famous quip that the Holy Roman Empire was neither holy, nor Roman, nor an empire was absolutely on target. The empire was a confused conglomerate. It contained more than two thousand imperial knights who held anything from a tiny patch of land to a castle with surrounding terrain and owed allegiance to none but the emperor himself; dozens of ecclesiastical principalities usually dominating a wealthy city and its hinterland; perhaps three score free cities; and a few small independent countries like Bavaria or Saxony or Brandenburg. The political, geographical, and constitutional confusion that characterized this patchwork is illustrated by the sheer impossibility of giving precise numbers for these constituent parts and by the arbitrary way in which some were represented in the imperial parliament, the Reichstag, and others not. In the hands of exceptional emperors, this miserable memory of a greater past might muster some political unity and military strength, but such exceptional emperors were just that—exceptional. The emperor could call on his Reichstag to vote him financial supplies or troops against foreign enemies, but if no money or troops came, he was powerless to compel their presence. The very procedure for choosing an emperor—determined in the Golden Bull of 1356 to be by majority vote of seven electors— [62] underscored the intentions of the emperor's great subjects to keep the substance of power in their own hands and leave their overlord with its trappings.

Then, in 1438, though not at first by design, this elective aristocracy became something like a hereditary monarchy, when the king of Bohemia and

---

[62] The archbishops of Mainz, Cologne, and Trier; the king of Bohemia; the elector of Saxony; the margrave of Brandenburg; and the count palatine of the Rhine.

Hungary, a Hapsburg, was elected Emperor Albert II. From then on, to the ignominious end of the empire in 1806, Hapsburgs were chosen as emperors. [63] They brought to the imperial crown the kind of authority that only extensive lands and impressive wealth can bestow.

The Hapsburg dynasty emerges into the light of history in the tenth century, with family holdings in Switzerland and Alsace. By the thirteenth century Hapsburgs had amassed great estates in Austria, Bohemia, Carinthia, and Styria, and in succeeding centuries these domains, with Hungary added, became the heartland of Hapsburg power. When Albert II died in 1439, his distant cousin Frederick became Emperor Frederick III and was succeeded, after a long reign, by his son Maximilian I in 1493. As king of Rome, he had already been wielding considerable power since 1486; as emperor—intelligent, impressive, and popular—he first aroused, and soon disappointed, great expectations. But what he could not do for his realm, he did for his family, and significantly enough, he did so by pursuing the policies and methods that his ancestors had used: he made advantageous marriages. The Hapsburgs' adroitness in adding desirable territory by uniting their house with eligible heirs and heiresses gave rise to envious jokes. Every self-respecting textbook quotes the famous Latin quip: "*Bella gerant alii, tu felix Austria nube*—Let others wage war, you, happy Austria, marry," a quip that concludes with the observation that what others obtained through Mars, the Hapsburgs obtained through Venus. But marriage is no joke; for the Hapsburgs, in any event, it was a favorite means of enlarging domains with a minimum of cost. Albert II had acquired Hungary by marrying the daughter of the king of that country. Frederick III gave the Hapsburgs a grip on Western Europe by marrying his son Maximilian to Mary of Burgundy, daughter of Charles the Rash (see p. 101). When Maximilian became emperor, he brought this pacific dynastic imperialism to a climax with a spectacular union between his son Philip and Joanna, the daughter and heiress of Ferdinand and Isabella. Charles, the eldest son of this couple, was to become Emperor Charles V, holding, overseeing, if not wholly controlling, lands stretching from Central America to the gates of Turkey. Spanish America, Spain, the Netherlands, Italian territory, Austria, Bohemia, Hungary, all gathered into a single, if somewhat tenuous family property by means of marriage: it was a great tribute to the institution.

Besides covering Europe with his family and his in-laws, Maximilian laid the foundations for the Austrian state. In several provinces he set up governing councils responsible to the crown, and he reorganized and strengthened the central administration. He liked to say that he preferred being a powerful duke of Austria to being the impotent emperor of the Germans. [64] One can see what

---

[63] For the record we must note a single brief interlude: from 1742 to 1745, Charles Albert, elector of Bavaria, of the house of Wittelsbach, was emperor as Charles VII.

[64] See R. G. D. Laffan, "The Empire under Maximilian I," in *The New Cambridge Modern History*, vol. I, *The Renaissance, 1493–1520* (1957), 210.

he meant: the constituent elements of the empire were too strong, and in consequence the empire itself was too weak, to make real imperial government possible.

The reasons for this impossibility lay in the course of German history. With the death of Emperor Frederick II in 1250, the German territories had fallen into an anarchy lasting a century or more; it was a time of foreign interventions and domestic disorders. As French and English history testifies, feudalism had been a centrifugal force everywhere; in the German lands its divisive power was greater than anywhere else. When in the fourteenth and fifteenth centuries German rulers and statesmen painfully restored a measure of order, they did so by strengthening local territories, coming to terms with local estates, raising local armies. Reform meant a stronger state of Saxony or a stronger city of Frankfurt, rather than a united Germany. There was an emerging sense of Germanness everywhere, a consciousness that found its expression in that odd term "German nation" that was appended to the older name "Holy Roman Empire" in the fifteenth century.[65] But this was, if anything, a cultural rather than a political nationalism; no one, no matter how far-seeing, drew the consequence that Europeans of the nineteenth century would have found inescapable: that cultural unity implies and demands political unity. Despite these obstacles, Maximilian preserved the empire largely if not wholly intact. His Swiss subjects escaped imperial control by their rebellion of 1499, and other lands, like Holstein in the north and those controlled by the Teutonic knights in the east, came under foreign domination. And he preserved a certain imperial influence in European affairs.

But the future lay with France, Spain, and England; with states growing within the empire (like Prussia); with the Hapsburg domains themselves (lying partly within and partly outside the empire); and with the looming giant of the East, Russia. This was so not because these states were modern or national while the empire was medieval and dynastic. The emerging states, too, derived their authority from traditional sources, and their royal houses were firmly committed to the principle of dynasticism. But the empire was too scattered in its territories, too diverse in its populations, too indefensible in the flatlands, surrounded by too many voracious neighbors, and subdivided too finely into thousands of units, each jealous of its prerogatives, to forge the parts into a whole. What marriage had done, diplomacy, rebellion, and war would in the long run undo. Mars was not wholly powerless in the hands of Venus after all.

WAR AND REALISM IN ITALY

Italy as Battleground

The Italian wars demonstrate how vulnerable small states had become to the ambitions of great powers. And—an illustration to warm the hearts of moralists—the conduct of Italian statesmen during these wars demonstrates that selfishness and cynicism often have disastrous consequences.

When in 1494 Charles VIII of France crossed into Italy with an army of forty thousand men, he set a pattern for French foreign policy that he and his two immediate successors, Louis XII and Francis I, would follow for half a century. Italy (to use language Machiavelli might have used) was like a beautiful young woman—too seductive to be left intact, too weak to defend herself, a temptation irresistible to rulers trained not to resist but to yield to such temptations. The reasons for Charles' intervention were old: a combination of claims to Naples by the house of Anjou and pressing invitations to the French by Italian politicians to rescue them from other Italian politicians. What was new was the capacity of France for large-scale adventures, mobilized by young Charles VIII, whose chivalric imagination was unchecked by intelligence. Charles was dazzled by grandiose plans to seize Naples as a base for a crusade against the Turk, and there were disturbing, well-founded reports that he meant to retake Constantinople, liberate Jerusalem, and make himself emperor of East and West. [66] Political refugees at the French court stirred him into action. The embittered Cardinal Giuliano della Rovere, whose bid for the papacy had been defeated by the Borgia faction, urged Charles into Italy; other exiles told him that the Angevin party at Naples was being persecuted and ardently hoped for his coming. Then Lodovico Sforza of Milan, fearful of Neapolitan intervention in his affairs, declared himself the ally of France and associated himself with those Italians interested in seeing Charles seize the crown of Naples to which the French had such a dubious claim. Lodovico's precise expectations remain unclear. He thought either that the mere threat of the French presence would deter his enemies or that the French, having done his work for him, would limit their Italian intervention to Naples itself.

In either case he was mistaken. Backed by agreements with Ferdinand of Aragon and Emperor Maximilian, both expensive to France, Charles invaded

---

[66] J. R. Hale, "International Relations in the West: Diplomacy and War," in *The New Cambridge Modern History*, vol. I, *The Renaissance, 1493–1520* (1957), 263–264, 295–296.

Italy in September 1494. The internal divisions that bedeviled most Italian states materially aided his campaign; each ruler treated him in accord with his own partisan interest. Accordingly, Charles met with little resistance, and by February 1495 he was in Naples. His triumph was his undoing: alarmed at French dominance over Italy, and outraged by the conduct of French troops and military governors, his enemies formed the Holy League in 1495, designed to expel the invader. Even Charles' former supporters, the emperor and Spain, joined the league, which also included Milan, Venice, the papacy, and in the following year, the English. It rapidly achieved its objectives: by 1496 all Italy was free of French troops.   *allies turned on him*

In 1499, the French were back in Italy. The second scenario was reminiscent of the first, only this time the French king was Louis XII, who had ascended the throne the year before, and his claim was to Milan. But once again, the Italians thought only of their immediate interests. "Before 1494," the English historian Cecilia M. Ady has said, "they were confident that the French would not come; after Charles' withdrawal they flattered themselves that the French would not stay; the chief thought in their minds was how Louis's intervention could best be used to their individual advantage." [67] The Venetians supported the far-fetched French claim in the hope of territorial gains at the expense of Milan; Florence favored French designs to advance its own design of retaking Pisa; most cynical of all, Pope Alexander VI abetted Louis' Italian plans and his desire for a divorce in return for French support for the ambitious secular career of his son, Cesare Borgia, that impious cardinal turned ruthless duke. Power politics could go no further, and sink no lower, than this.

For a time they French did well. By 1500, after shifting fortunes, they held Milan; Lodovico Sforza was taken and spent the rest of his days in French captivity. In the same year, Louis agreed with Ferdinand of Aragon to divide up the Neapolitan kingdom between France and Spain, and in 1501, French troops were in Naples once again. But the allies fell out, as allies will, and by 1504, Naples was in Spanish hands. After complex fighting across the peninsula, a second coalition finally compelled the French to yield their Italian holdings. By 1512, the French had evacuated Milan, and a last desperate attempt to recoup their losses led to a French defeat at Novara in 1513, and to tenuous peace. In consequence, the Sforzas returned to Milan, and the Medici, who had been expelled in the wake of the first invasion of 1494, to Florence. The lesson was inescapable: domestic power in Italy depended on the fortunes of war, and those depended on foreign states.

Where Charles VIII and Louis XII had failed, Francis I failed as well. Three successive invasions of Italy—in 1515, the very year of his accession, in 1524, and in 1527—only ended in 1529 with the Treaty of Cambrai, in which the French gave up all their Italian claims, a renunciation confirmed, after further tentative probes, in 1559, with the Treaty of Cateau-Cambrésis (see p. 163). Meanwhile, Italy had turned into one theater of war among several, as two great dynasties, Valois and Hapsburg, battled for hegemony. Reduced to a battle-ground, Italy suffered the ultimate humiliation of becoming, by the 1520s, merely a secondary battleground (see p. 60).

The New Realism: Machiavelli

Though in many respects more a symptom than a cause of transformation, the wars that began in 1494 and ended, more or less, in 1529, stimulated far-reaching changes in styles of warfare and diplomacy and modes of thinking about international and domestic affairs. The rise of the infantry and the increasing importance of portable firearms diminished the relevance (while it increased the beauty) of armor and reduced (while it did not eliminate) the work of cavalrymen in battle. The shift to infantry had been pioneered by the Swiss, who continued to export their able-bodied men to mercenary contin-gents all across Europe. "The Swiss, whose defeat of the Burgundian cavalry at Grandson and Morat in 1476 had caused such general concern among military men, fought in compact squares of about 6,000 men, eighty-five shoulder to shoulder, on a hundred-yard long front, and seventy ranks deep. The success of this formation depended on rigid discipline and strict drill. Nothing could be allowed to divert the pressure or resistance of the square till it was crippled or victorious; no prisoners could be taken, the wounded were ignored. A cavalry charge at such a square met first a solid hedge of steel, the pike heads of the first four ranks, then halberds, taking advantage of broken order to stab at close quarters or to grapple from the flank and hook a horseman down, then at the centre of the square broadswords which could swing at a man still mounted or be grasped below the hilt to thrust at those unhorsed. An infantry charge was met first by ranks of halberds which struck down the points of the pikes, then by row after row of pikes in front and in the flanks by swordsmen and crossbows and arquebusiers issuing from the centre and rear of the phalanx." [68] These tactics, as contemporaries noted, came into their own in, and through, the Italian wars. "Before 1494," writes Guicciardini, with Machiavelli the keenest observer of his day, "wars were long, campaigns were relatively bloodless, and methods of conquest were slow and difficult. And although artillery was already in use, it was handled so unskillfully that it did little damage. Thus, those who held power stood in little danger of losing it. When the French came to Italy, they introduced such efficiency into war that, up to 1521, the loss of a campaign meant the loss of a state." But, as Guicciardini also observed, new tactics of attack produced new ingenuity in defense: "Rulers now have the same security they had before 1494, but for a different reason.

[68] Hale, "International Relations in the West," 284.

Then, it was due to the fact that men were unskilled in the art of offense; now, to the fact of knowing well the art of defense."[69]

Like the art of war, the art of diplomacy was greatly refined during these decades. The old method of handling international relations through special envoys and the occasional meeting of princes was simply inadequate in a Europe bound together by a network of alliances, intricate dynastic arrangements, shifting enmities that might engage troops far from home, and commercial relations as complex and sometimes as acrimonious as political competition. The period of the Italian wars saw the proliferation of permanent missions, which had been tried by a few states before and now became general practice. Sir Henry Wotton's celebrated definition of an ambassador—"an honest man sent to lie abroad for the good of his country"—dates from 1604, but it might well have been coined a hundred years before.

Modern historians think of these decades as the end of an epoch and the beginning of another. Acute observers at the time obviously thought the same thing. The Italian wars raised old questions in a new and most acute form: What are the stakes of fighting and negotiating? What are proper moral and constitutional constraints on political action? What is the place of self-interest in politics? What, indeed, is the function of state and the state system? Princes of the church had appealed to the sword, secular princes had blatantly placed private profit above public good. And it was sadly plain that the Italian state system had failed. True, the French had been expelled from Italy, but this was no cause for rejoicing: Italians had connived at their coming; Spaniards, Swiss, and Germans had engineered their going. In the second half of the fifteenth century the Italian powers had worked out a relatively pacific arrangement among its five largest constituent states, a miniature balance of power. That balance was a foretaste of the larger balance at which European statesmen would aim for centuries, and which would dictate the formation of coalitions against those—from Louis XIV to Adolf Hitler—who would seek to destroy that balance in search of hegemony. But the smaller Italian balance had proved inadequate to keep Italy from being victimized by larger, more powerful states. It was not until the second half of the nineteenth century that Italy would once again control her own affairs.

These were all agonizing matters, and these are the raw material that Machiavelli worked into his political theory. Niccolò Machiavelli wrote for the sake of practice, out of a fund of personal experience, enriched by purposeful reading in the classics. He was born in 1469, to a poor but patrician family and was tied all his life to the turbulent affairs of his beloved Florence. From 1498 to 1512, while the Medicis were in exile, he held a post in the chancellery in Florence. He went on diplomatic missions—his low estimate of human nature rests on intimate and lengthy experience with statesmen and rulers. He raised

[69] Francesco Guicciardini, *Maxims and Reflections of a Renaissance Statesman* (tr. 1965), 57–58.

troops for the defense of Florence, acting on his conviction that mercenaries are the death of republics and that only militiamen preserve freedom. Then, when the Medicis returned in 1512, he was dismissed, imprisoned, and sent out of the city.

This was dreadful exile for him. He would rise early (as he describes his life in his most famous letter), inspect his estate, talk with farmers, do desultory reading. "When evening comes, I return home and go into my study. On the threshold I strip off the muddy sweaty clothes of everyday, and put on the robes of court and palace, and in this graver dress I enter the antique courts of the ancients where, being welcomed by them, I taste the food that alone is mine, for which I was born. And there I make bold to speak to them and ask the motives of their actions. And they, in their humanity, reply to me. And for the space of four hours I forget the world, remember no vexation, fear poverty no more, tremble no more at death: I am wholly absorbed in them. And as Dante says that there can be no understanding without the memory retaining what it has heard, I have written down what I have gained from their conversation, and composed a small work *De Principatibus,* where I dive as deep as I can into ideas about this subject, discussing the nature of princely rule, what forms it takes, how these are acquired, how they are maintained, why they are lost." [70] To his death in 1527, the rest of his life, filled with talk about political theory and restless activity, was one long effort to find employment suitable to his talents. He wrote his books—his comedies, his history of Florence, his long essay on the art of war, and his two classics in political theory, *The Prince* and *The Discourses on the First Ten Books of Livy,* all distinguished by his virile mind and brilliant style—as a substitute for, and a way back into, the action he craved. However he felt about his later years, we have reason to be grateful to the political fortunes that gave him the unwelcome leisure to do his immortal work. [71]

The controversy over the meaning of Machiavelli's political thought has raged for over four centuries. He has been portrayed as a scientist, a patriot, and a devil. Some of his admirers, pained by the harsh tone and ruthless prescriptions of *The Prince,* have read it, not as a handbook for tyrants but as a satire on tyranny. There have been desperate admissions that the teachings of *The Prince* and those of *The Discourses* are irreconcilable, and ingenious efforts to reconcile them. But, as Gilbert has said, "Machiavelli's contemporaries would have found the seeming disparity of his subject matter less astounding and less objectionable than we do. . . . The contrast between *The Prince* and *The Discourses* is more apparent than fundamental; in both works the problem of political leadership is clearly a basic issue." [72] Machiavelli's political thinking reflects the sober response of a disillusioned, clear-eyed

---

[70] Quoted by J. R. Hale, *Machiavelli and Renaissance Italy* (1963), 130.

[71] See Felix Gilbert, *Machiavelli and Guicciardini: Politics and History in Sixteenth-Century Florence* (1965).

[72] Ibid., 188.

observer witnessing a new rootless age. His two masterpieces deal with Machiavelli's greatest, his only love: politics, or more precisely, human nature in politics. As a Humanist, Machiavelli is ready to apply the lessons that classical antiquity has to teach; as an innovator, proudly aware that his enterprise is unprecedented—"I have resolved to open a new route," he said, "which has not yet been followed by anyone"[73]—he sought for the laws that would make politics into a science. Clearly he preferred a republic to a tyranny; *The Discourses* breathe his distaste for plutocracies and his admiration for sturdy, self-governing commonwealths. He knew, as all men of the Renaissance knew, that fortune is fickle and powerful, and that the most resolute vigor and the most cunning foresight will fail if fortune frowns. But this was no excuse for passivity; it was, on the contrary, a call for the exercise of *virtù*—of energy, of patient, vigorous, and intelligent action. He was convinced that men are by nature bad: Machiavelli shows that one does not have to be a Christian to be a pessimist about human nature. *The Prince,* with its imaginative transformation of Cesare Borgia into a kind of ideal ruler and its cold advice on how to succeed in the jungle of the political world, voices this pessimism on every page. "Men must either be caressed or else annihilated; they will revenge themselves for small injuries, but cannot do so for great ones."[74] And again, "A prince being thus obliged to know well how to act as a beast must imitate the fox and the lion, for the lion cannot protect himself from traps, and the fox cannot defend himself from wolves. One must therefore be a fox to recognize traps, and a lion to frighten wolves. Those that wish to be only lions do not understand this. Therefore, a prudent prince ought not to keep faith when by doing so it would be against his interest, and when the reasons which made him bind himself no longer exist. If men were all good, this precept would not be a good one; but as they are bad, and would not observe their faith with you, so you are not bound to keep faith with them."[75] And yet this clinical intelligence that could draw such lessons and give such advice also had its passions. In the last chapter of *The Prince,* which remains as controversial as the rest of the book, Machiavelli suddenly draws yet another lesson from the dreadful time of the Italian wars. In a passionate outburst, reaching back to the very beginning of the Renaissance, to Petrarch, he calls for a liberator who will drive the barbarians from Italy. "This barbarous domination stinks in the nostrils of everyone."[76]

If Machiavelli's world of grasping princes, immoral popes, craven peoples, wholly ruled by self-interest and always ready for murder, does not awaken our admiration, Machiavelli's effort to portray and penetrate it does. His political theory belongs with the magisterial achievements of the Renaissance, with

[73] "Introduction," First Book of *The Discourses* (Modern Library ed.), 103.
[74] *The Prince,* chap. III.
[75] Ibid., chap. XVIII.
[76] Ibid., chap. XXV.

Leonardo's portraits or Michelangelo's sculptures. In Machiavelli's books the modern world stands before us; political power has been secularized, freed from religious direction and moral restraint, become an end in itself. *The Prince* and *The Discourses*, sometimes explicitly, always implicitly, are involuntary tributes to the rising Atlantic states. They are heralds of the age to come. Yet in one respect they are curiously incomplete: with all his gift for observation, Machiavelli treated religion as merely a mode of manipulating superstitious populaces. There is no sign in his work of the upheaval through which he was living, the greatest revolution the Christian church had known until then, or has known to this day.

SELECTED READINGS

For the expansion of Europe, see the magisterial volume by Samuel Eliot Morison, *The European Discovery of America*, vol. I, *The Northern Voyages, A.D. 500-1600* (1971). Morison's biography of Columbus, *Admiral of the Ocean Sea* (1942), is definitive. Other excellent titles include Boies Penrose, *Travel and Discovery in the Renaissance, 1420-1620* (1955); John B. Brebner, *The Explorers of North America, 1492-1806* (1933); and J. H. Parry, *The European Reconnaissance* (1968), with selected documents and a fine bibliography. J. H. Elliott, *The Old World and the New, 1492-1650* (1970), traces the interaction of conqueror and conquered.

For the arts in the Northern Renaissance, see Otto Benesch, *The Art of the Renaissance in Northern Europe* (rev. ed., 1965); John Pope-Hennessy, *The Portrait in the Renaissance* (1966), which contains material on Holbein, Dürer, and other northern artists; the brilliant studies by Erwin Panofsky: *The Life and Art of Albrecht Dürer* (4th ed., 1965) and *Early Netherlandish Painting: Its Origins and Character*, 2 vols. (1953); and Theodor Müller, *Sculpture in the Netherlands, Germany, France, Spain: 1400-1500* (1966).

Northern Humanists are well treated in E. Harris Harbison, *The Christian Scholar in the Age of the Reformation* (1956). For more, see Raymond Wilson Chambers, *Thomas More* (1958), and J. H. Hexter, *More's "Utopia": The Biography of an Idea* (1952). Johan Huizinga, *Erasmus of Rotterdam* (tr. 1952), and the fuller biography by Preserved Smith, *Erasmus: A Study of His Life, Ideals and Place in History* (1923), may be supplemented with John C. Olin, ed., *Christian Humanism and the Reformation: Selected Writings of Desiderius Erasmus* (1965), and Roland M. Bainton, *Erasmus of Christendom* (1969). R. Weiss, *Humanism in England During the Fifteenth Century* (2nd ed., 1957), sets the background. Equally interesting is Fritz Caspari, *Humanism and the Social Order in Tudor England* (1954). For French humanism, above all, Eugene F. Rice, Jr., *The Renaissance Idea of Wisdom* (1958). Louis Battifol, *The Century of the Renaissance* (1916), on France, is now rather antiquated. For the importance of printing, see S. H. Steinberg, *Five Hundred Years of Printing* (2nd ed., 1966), and polemical articles by Elizabeth L. Eisenstein, notably "Some Conjectures about the Impact of Printing on Western Society and Thought: A Preliminary Report," *Journal of Modern History*, 40 (March 1968), 1-56.

For the rise of the Great Powers see, for France, the relevant chapters in Georges Duby and Robert Mandrou, *A History of French Civilization from the Year 1000 to the Present* (tr. 1964); vol. I of Charles Guignebert, *A Short History of the French People*,

2 vols. (1930); and J. Russell Major, *Representative Institutions in Renaissance France* (1960). For England, A. R. Myers, *England in the Late Middle Ages* (1964); the opening chapters of S. T. Bindoff, *Tudor England* (1950); J. D. Mackie, *The Earlier Tudors* (1952); V. H. H. Green, *The Later Plantagenets: A Survey of English History Between 1307 and 1485* (1955); and Lacey Baldwin Smith, *Tudor Prelates and Politics* (1953). For Spain, the best coverage is in the early chapters of J. H. Elliott, *Imperial Spain, 1469–1716* (1963). See also, H. Mariéjol, *The Spain of Ferdinand and Isabella* (tr. 1961). J. Vincent Vives, *An Economic History of Spain from the Earliest Times to the End of the Nineteenth Century* (tr. 1969), is brilliant.

General treatments of politics and culture in these decades have been listed in the Selected Readings for Chapter 1. Most relevant here are Myron P. Gilmore, *The World of Humanism, 1453–1517* (1952), and G. R. Potter, ed., *The Renaissance, 1493–1520* (1957). See also Denys Hay, *Europe in the Fourteenth and Fifteenth Centuries* (1966). To these should be added the splendid survey by Garrett Mattingly, *Renaissance Diplomacy* (1965).

The decline and revival of the empire is traced in Hajo Holborn, *A History of Modern Germany*, vol. I, *The Reformation* (1959). Two books by F. L. Carsten bring modern scholarship to bear on early modern Germany: *The Origins of Prussia* (1954) and *Princes and Parliaments in Germany* (1959). For Machiavelli the best among a large literature is Felix Gilbert, *Machiavelli and Guicciardini: Politics and History in Sixteenth-Century Florence* (1965); see also J. R. Hale's sketch, *Machiavelli and Renaissance Italy* (1963).

3

The Shattering
of Christian Unity

Outsize figures—Martin Luther, John Calvin, Emperor Charles V, Henry VIII of England—loom over the age of the Reformation like so many giants. Yet the Reformation was not the work of a few individuals, no matter how titanic their stature. Fortune was on their side. There had been self-willed rulers before, but they had always somehow remained within the communion of Rome. There had been uncompromising religious rebels before, but they had never produced the effective and irremediable[1] shattering of Christian unity. Luther, Calvin, Zwingli, and their followers were the right men at the right time; economic, political, and social developments gave them what had been denied their predecessors: the opportunity to construct a viable alternative to Roman Catholicism

[1] It seems safe to say now, more than four centuries later.

PRECONDITIONS FOR RELIGIOUS REVOLUTION

From Wyclif to Hus

To speak of the Reformation as a shattering of Christian unity is in an important sense misleading. As we have noted in some detail, Christendom had been deeply, often furiously, divided for centuries, long before Martin Luther made that division final (see p. 35). To say this is not to diminish Luther's historical importance—to the extent that an individual can ever change the course of events, he did—but simply to place him into the stream of time. Luther himself never denied that he had ancestors and allies in his great enterprise.

Among these ancestors, John Wyclif in England played a decisive part; he was John the Baptist to the Reformation. Wyclif's shift from orthodoxy to heresy, motivated as it was by a peculiar mixture of religious rage and private interest, of desire for institutional reform and theological purification, prefigures the life and work of Martin Luther. Wyclif's very ideas—his stress on faith and on man's direct relation to God—are early versions of Protestant doctrines. Born in Yorkshire around 1328, Wyclif first achieved prominence as a prolific, wholly respectable scholar, with close ties to Oxford. He entered religious controversy as a propagandist for the antipapalism of the English Crown in the early 1370s. But this was a financial rather than doctrinal squabble. The government wanted good reasons why money should not leave England, and Wyclif supplied them. Politics led into theology, as in that time it often did; by the mid-1370s, Wyclif was defending the right of the laity to control the property of the church. Then, at the end of the 1370s and the beginning of the 1380s, Wyclif became a thoroughgoing theological revolutionary.

Advancing age, ill health, frustrated ambitions, and the scandal of the Great Schism, then in its inception, probably all contributed to Wyclif's growing radicalism. But his teaching was greater than his motives. As Wyclif himself insisted—this was a favorite argument of reformers, radicals, and revolutionaries down to the eighteenth century—he had no wish to innovate and every wish to restore. His model was the pure early church of primitive Christendom, unencumbered by complex organization or doctrinal accretions of dubious origins and equally dubious worth. The heart of Christian faith was the Scriptures. This heretical doctrine was to find loud echoes in sixteenth-century Protestantism. The Bible alone has divine authority. By devout and careful reading, a Christian layman can work toward goodness and even hope for salvation. "He who reads the Scriptures of God," one of his followers said, speaking for them all, "will find God, and his good living is like the light of the lamp before the eyes of his heart, and will open the way to truth."[2] The supremacy of the Bible meant the fallibility of all clerical institutions, including the papacy; the true church, Wyclif reasoned, is invisible. He went further. While he was neither consistent nor clear in his writings—his mind has been called both academic and unsystematic—and worked out only some of the implications of his ideas, he laid hands (profane hands, Rome thought) on some of the most cherished ideas of Catholic Christendom: free will and the mass. The true invisible church consists of the saved, the "elect," and God has chosen them in advance. And what happens during mass, though miraculous, is not precisely what Rome said. Wyclif seems to have become so hostile to Rome, so suspicious of the manner in which articles of faith had been manipulated to the profit of sinful men masquerading as humble servants of Christ, that he could no longer accept the doctrine of transubstantiation. Faith was more important than ritual (see p. 132). Indeed, to Wyclif and his excitable disciples, the visible church, disfigured by monks across Europe and the pope in Rome, was a gathering of antichrists.

That the lords and beneficiaries of the visible church should have taken offense at Wyclif's teaching is only human. In a Christian world no one, especially not the man who occupies the papal chair as Christ's vicar, likes to be called antichrist. But while the papacy condemned Wyclif's doctrines as heretical, it could not get its hands on him. He had loyal support among the clerics at Oxford and across England; he had strong, if, in his last years, waning, support at the court. "Heresy," V. H. H. Green has aptly said, "is a more dangerous ally than anti-clericalism, both in this world and . . . in the next."[3] Hence Wyclif died peacefully enough, at home, in 1384. Roman Catholicism took posthumous if ineffectual revenge: the Council of Constance solemnly condemned Wyclif's teachings (see p. 109), and in 1428 his bones were dug up and burned. But his teaching, though more or less underground, survived through the fifteenth and into the sixteenth century with the Lollards; they form part of the stream of heresy that was to swell into the broad river of the Reformation.

The Lollards, Wyclif's disciples, are as interesting as he.[4] Down to the seventeenth century, when documentation becomes more abundant, the poor erupt into historical visibility mainly in riots, rebellions, and religious upheavals. Lollardy began, not as a poor man's movement, but at Oxford, under the direct influence of Wyclif's lectures and books. But academics are rarely

[2] Put into modern English, slightly paraphrased, from V. H. H. Green, *The Later Plantagenets: A Survey of English History Between 1307 and 1485* (1955), 199.

[3] *Later Plantagenets,* 195.

[4] The name "Lollard," writes A. G. Dickens, was applied "to the sect in a sermon by the Irish Cistercian Henry Crump" in 1382. "A Middle Dutch word meaning 'mumbler' or 'mutterer' of prayers, it had long been applied to the Beghards and other Netherlandish pietists whose orthodoxy was suspect" (*The English Reformation* [1964], 23–24).

persistent revolutionaries; one learned Lollard after another recanted and rejoined the orthodox communion. But what Lollardy lost in intellect it gained in vehemence and tenacity. It soon spread to the country, to receptive squires, urban merchants, even members of the House of Commons, and a few aristocrats. Finally, early in the fifteenth century, itinerant preachers enlisted segments of the urban and rural proletariat. Support for Lollard doctrine was as varied as the doctrine itself; some followed it because they wanted clerical reform; others because they saw profit, both to themselves and the common-wealth, in the expropriation of the wealthy English church; still others, the most radical and least tractable, fervently hoped for a reform of the articles of faith and the restoration of primitive Christianity, when men had faced God as humble children, without priestly intermediaries. Lollardy was confined to no single class: Sir John Oldcastle, who plotted a pathetic Lollard uprising in 1414, was a close associate of King Henry V. But in the end most of the Lollards were poor, rescued from total anonymity only in the town records that list their names and the price of the faggots needed to burn them. The movement went underground but not out of existence: there are records of sporadic burnings of Lollards right into the time of the English Reformation.

Wyclif's influence spread from England to the Continent; the other great heresiarch before Luther, Jan Hus, was obviously and deeply in Wyclif's debt. Hus, born around 1369, was, like Wyclif, a prominent priest and scholar—for a time he served as rector of his University of Prague. Like Wyclif, he was an orthodox believer for much of his life, and once again like Wyclif, he was moved to heresy by clerical abuses. Soon Hus's rhetoric grew extreme: he applied the favorite epithet of heretics—antichrist—to Rome. In 1410 he was excommunicated, but his local popularity, in which nascent Bohemian nation-alism and anti-German sentiment played a prominent part, remained undimin-ished, and Hus continued his provocative preaching. On matters of doctrine, Hus was less radical than Wyclif: while he insisted on the fallibility of the pope—those who proclaimed his infallibility were also antichrists—and on the primacy of Scriptures, he conceded that a pure clergy or a pure written tradition could have their uses.[5] On the mass, too, Hus was relatively cautious: his moderate followers, the Utraquists,[6] whose views did not markedly differ from Roman Catholic teachings, accurately preserve his own views.

Hus was both a political and a religious storm center. He stood for Bohemian particularism quite as much as for independence from the papacy. His fate was certainly shaped by the exigencies of politics. Emperor Sigismund first protected Hus and then betrayed him: he lured Hus to the Council of

---

[5] See Heiko Augustinus Oberman, *The Harvest of Medieval Theology: Gabriel Biel and Late Medieval Nominalism* (1963), 376.

[6] The name derives from the Latin term for their demand for the mass "in both kinds"—*sub utraque specie.*

Constance with an imperial safe-conduct, which induced Hus to leave the safety of Bohemia for the treacherous soil of Constance. At the council, Hus found himself in a difficult position. He refused to repudiate Wyclif but refused, at the same time, to admit he was a heretic. Reasonably enough, he was willing to reformulate many of his ideas, but he insisted that Christ, not Peter, was the rock on which the church had been built, and he would not submit to the humiliating conditions his examiners sought to force upon him. The end was inevitable: in July 1415 he was burned at the stake, with the heretic's hat on his head.

The execution was stupid as well as vicious. Its consequence was not an end to heresy in central Europe, but war. In a series of brilliant forays, Bohemian troops defeated all crusading armies sent against them; the Hussite wars, fought sporadically from 1418 on, finally ended with a compromise, the so-called Compactata of 1436, which largely excluded Germans from Bohemian affairs and gave the Hussites the kind of Utraquist mass they had asked for. And this was not all. By handing the Wyclifite heresy a martyr on the Continent, the papacy had given the forces of reform a figure to admire and to exploit when the time of the Reformation came.

Piety Beyond the Pale

The great heresies that beset fourteenth- and fifteenth-century Europe were expressions of class hatreds, economic distress, local particularism, and political aspirations, but the dominant component of these movements was what the heretics claimed it to be—religious. To put it in another, perhaps more precise way, in the centuries preceding the Reformation, social, economic, and political discontents took religious forms. They could hardly do anything else: with the rare—extremely rare—exceptions of a few disenchanted intellectuals like Marsiglio of Padua (see p. 128), all men saw the world in religious terms. Utopians cast their visions of social regeneration in religious language, not from convenience but from conviction. Economics and politics were not yet separated from religion, even in thought.

It is only in recent years that historians like Johan Huizinga have taught us to appreciate the extent and intensity of the religious malaise that darkened the face of Europe in the time before the Reformation. Ecstatic visions of the blessed kingdom on earth alternated with gloomy preoccupations with death; art historians have singled out the emergence of obsessions with the Dance of Death, social historians the witch craze which held in its deadly grip both the poor deranged beings who actually believed themselves to be witches and the inquisitors who ferreted them out and burned them by the thousands. Christians translated their helplessness and despair into the conviction that the land was overrun by devils who conjured up plagues and crop failures—there was nothing abstract in this late medieval quest for scapegoats. The Jews were the most prominent victims of this displacement, and it was not the illiterate alone who persecuted them: learned theologians denounced the Jew as Anti-Christ, called for his conversion or, more often, his extirpation, and manufactured charges of ritual murder that would never wholly disappear from the popular mythology of the Western world.

The range of religious belief was enormously varied—from naive credence in tales about witchcraft to involved theories about the influence of the stars, from primitive visions of heaven on earth to abstruse philosophical speculations about the nature of reality and the course of history. Among the most modern of heretics was Marsiglio of Padua, whose *Defensor Pacis* of 1324 anticipates secular political ideas of the seventeenth century. A polemic serving Emperor Louis the Bavarian in his controversy with Pope John XXII, *Defensor Pacis,* like other tracts of the time, defends imperial institutions against papal claims to supremacy in worldly as well as spiritual matters. But Marsiglio went beyond his time. Almost alone in using rationalistic methods in inquiry, he argued for the total autonomy of the secular power, a monopoly of legal and coercive authority for the state, the equality of all priests, the equation of the church with the whole body of Christendom, and—an idea that Wyclif and Hus would take up—the supremacy of Christ, rather than the pope, in and over the church. For centuries after, Marsiglio's bold propositions served not merely the anticlerical assertions of pious men, but the wider claims of secularists.

The English Franciscan William of Occam, Marsiglio's ally in the antipapal cause, fed the stream of heresy also in another way. In the early fourteenth century the dominant philosophical direction in Western Christianity was Scholasticism, a school which placed considerable trust in the power of reason to prove the existence of God and the necessity of Catholic institutions. Occam—to use modern words for him—was a nominalist and an empiricist. He denied substantive reality to universal terms like "Church" and held that they were but names. Only individual things are real. This was of considerable philosophical importance, but it was his empiricism, his insistence that our knowledge comes from experience alone, that helped to undermine the confidence of Christian believers in the power of reason to prove the existence of things that were higher than reason. Nothing, not even the existence of God, could be demonstrated.

William of Occam should not be read through modern spectacles. He was not an unbeliever. Quite the contrary: Occam sought not to discredit God but to exalt him by vastly widening the gulf between the creator and his creatures, a gulf the Scholastics had tried to bridge with their rational arguments. Only a handful took Occam's skepticism as a guide to irreligion; most of his readers—and his influence was enormous and lasting—interpreted his assault on the powers of reason as an invitation to practical piety, to mysticism, and to a new trust in a sheer faith that operated without, and often against, the evidence of reason. In 1349, Occam, like so many thousands of others, succumbed to the Black Death, but a century and a half later Martin Luther hailed him as "my dear master."[7]

Most troubled Christians needed headier fare than disputes over the theory of knowledge. In the fourteenth century, in England, the German states, Flanders, and northern Italy above all, but elsewhere as well, individual believers turned away from formal theology to establish personal relations with the deity through mystic union. One of these, Johann Tauler, later exercised significant influence on young Martin Luther struggling for light. By definition, the mystical experience is intimate and private, but the mystics did not disdain to record their visions in ecstatic writings, and these induced others to reexperience them. The church found it hard to establish a consistent policy for these exceptional believers; Christianity, after all, insisted on the essentially nonrational character of religious experience, but an organized church that proclaimed itself, as Roman Catholicism proclaimed itself, the chosen intermediary between God and man, could only view with some suspicion the devout who took their own road to God. Hence Rome excommunicated some of the mystics and canonized others.

One offshoot of mysticism relatively safe to the established clerical order—"mysticism by retail," it has been called[8]—was the tendency among devout Christians before the Reformation to reject theological controversy to concentrate on charity. The best known of these were the Brethren of the Common Life, founded late in the fourteenth century. The brethren lived in common quarters but, not being monks, remained in the world; they devoted themselves to doing charitable works, nursing the sick, studying the Scriptures, and teaching the young. Their fervent, practical piety, which came to be called the *devotio moderna,* was only an indirect precursor of Protestantism: where Luther and his followers would stress faith, the practitioners of the "modern devotion," though their faith was ardent, stressed works. But they, too, prepared the way for religious upheaval; they laid the foundations, as Huizinga has said, both "in the northern Netherlands and in lower Germany, for a generally diffused culture among the middle classes; a culture of a very narrow, strictly ecclesiastical nature, indeed, but which for that very reason was fit to permeate broad layers of the people."[9] Many famous men went through their schools, including Nicolas of Cusa, Thomas à Kempis, and Erasmus, all of whom studied at the brethren's school at Deventer. The most familiar work to emerge from their circle, *The Imitation of Christ,* perhaps by Kempis, perhaps by Gerhard Groote, the founder of the movement, is the most widely read devotional tract ever written; in lucid and simple language and without recourse to theological quibbles and doctrinal subtleties, it calls Christians to pious communion with their Savior.

---

[7] G. G. Coulton, *Studies in Medieval Thought* (1940), 190.
[8] Johan Huizinga, *The Waning of the Middle Ages* (ed. 1956), 225.
[9] Johan Huizinga, *Erasmus of Rotterdam* (tr. 1952), 4.

Other spirits in these terrifying times could not respond to the world by devotion and charity. Finding their life unbearable, Christians by the thousands thirstily consumed prophecies of a new world to come. [10] Extravagant pessimism invited and produced extravagant optimism. The first Christians had expected the return of Christ within their lifetime; sporadically after that, century after century, prophets had prophesied the end of history, the Second Coming. In the late twelfth century, this vision found authoritative expression in the writings of Joachim of Flore, a Calabrian priest who was at once a hermit and the friend of popes. No millenarian either before or after him has ever been so orderly in his system. Neatly, everything fell into three parts: there were, Joachim taught, three ages of man. The first reached from the creation to the coming of Christ—roughly 1260 years. The second began with Christ and would end around 1260, to give way to the third period in which mankind would witness the great struggles that must precede the victory foretold in the Apocalypse. Each of these three periods had its characteristics: the first, the age of the Old Testament, was under the sign of the Father; it was the reign of law, and thus of men's fear and servitude. The second, the age of the New Testament, was under the sign of the Son; it was the reign of faith, and thus of filial obedience and belief. The third, the age to come, would be the age of what Joachim called, from a passage in Revelation, the "everlasting gospel." It would be under the sign of the Spirit and would usher in the reign of charity. This was the glorious future, a time of universal poverty, spirituality, and freedom when the bonds of human institutions like church and empire and marriage would be cast off. Mankind would unite in a universal monastery and live in joy and spiritual happiness to the Last Judgment.

These Joachimite notions spread from country to country and survived refutations and persecutions. In the German states, Emperor Frederick Barbarossa and his grandson, Frederick II, became the subjects of hopeful legends: they would rise again and lead Christendom to a future of untold bliss. Extremists among the Franciscans in the fourteenth century, the radical wing of the Hussites in the fifteenth century, saw the world ready for the Second Coming; in 1501, Christopher Columbus proclaimed himself the "Joachimite messiah." [11] The vision never disappeared—the English Puritans in the seventeenth century entertained hopes of the Messiah, and in our own time the Nazis would enact a hideous parody of the "Third Reich" that Joachim of Flore had foretold, with wholly different intentions, almost eight centuries before. Men in deep trouble will believe almost anything. The period of the Reformation itself was marked by these expectations: the Anabaptists and their most pitiless adversary, Martin Luther, shared, if they shared little else, millenarian visions. (see p. 143).

(see p. 143).

[10] On this point see H. G. Koenigsberger and G. L. Mosse, *Europe in the Sixteenth Century* (1968), 87.
[11] Ibid., 94.

Lighting the Fuse: Luther's Europe to 1517

It is the most extraordinary quality in that extraordinary man, Martin Luther, that he contained within himself most of the strands of thought and passion traversing Europe in the fifteenth and early sixteenth centuries. He joined, at least for some years, in the mystics' millenarian hopes: the fantasy that Christ's thousand-year reign was about to begin. He had his own personal encounters with the devil, suffered fearful attacks of indecision, absorbed the humble skepticism of Occam, shared in northern Humanist learning, longed for the cleansing of his church, and became involved—somewhat against his will—in the social struggles of which the Reformation was in part the cause, in part the expression. The miracle is that after long and heartrending suffering Luther brought coherence to this diversity of ideas, fears, and hopes.

Martin Luther was born in the Saxon town of Eisleben, in 1483, the son of a peasant grown prosperous in the mining of copper. He became an educated man—few Germans more than he—but he always retained the impress of his background; his pungent, often rude speech, his coarse humor, his delight in proverbs, his vehement prejudices and quick calls for violent remedies contrast sharply, indeed painfully, with the urbanity of his great contemporary, Erasmus. His schooling, at Eisleben and at the University of Erfurt, was sound and conventional. He was destined for the law, but in 1505, after a bolt of lightning threw him to the ground as he was walking to Erfurt, he vowed to become a monk. His father was dismayed and infuriated, but Luther was firm. The lightning was no more than the dramatic occasion of his conversion; he had long been wrestling with the state of his soul.

Luther entered the Augustinian order at Erfurt and proved, by all reports, a brilliant but troublesome brother. He insisted on confessing, at great length and on every possible occasion; his fellow clerics, no cynics, thought his search for holiness extravagant and almost absurd. But Luther was in earnest: the sense of his unworthiness and of the chasm that inexorably divided him from his angry God, haunted and terrified him. "Though I lived as a monk without reproach," he recalled much later, "I felt that I was a sinner before God with an extremely disturbed conscience. . . . I did not love, yes, I hated the righteous God who punishes sinners, and secretly, if not blasphemously, certainly murmuring greatly, I was angry with God." [12] He was certain he was damned. It is too easy to say he was a guilt-ridden neurotic—many people are, and do not achieve what Luther achieved. Luther translated his sufferings into a new vision that changed the face of Europe.

The precise course of Luther's religious development, his liberation from despair, remains a matter of some debate. It is certain that it involved prayer, philosophizing, profound and private religious experiences, and above all

---

[12] "Preface to Latin Writings" (1545), in John Dillenberger, ed., *Martin Luther: Selections from His Writings* (1961), 11.

reflection on the Scriptures. Despite his obtrusive anguish, his superiors trusted him. In 1508 they sent him to the University of Wittenberg as a lecturer; in 1512 he took the doctorate in theology there and began his celebrated lectures on the Bible: on the Psalms, on Romans, and on Galatians. Whatever they taught others, these lectures taught Luther what he desperately needed to know. The book that had plunged him into despair now gave him relief. "At last, by the mercy of God, meditating day and night," he recalled later, "I gave heed to the context of the words, namely, 'In it the righteousness of God is revealed, as it is written; He who through faith is righteous shall live.'[13] There I began to understand that the righteousness of God is that by which the righteous lives by a gift of God, namely by faith. . . . Here I felt that I was altogether born again and had entered paradise itself through open gates."[14] The traditional Catholic faith, which stressed the conjunction of faith and works and insisted that man seek to earn salvation, now was confronted by the sublime passivity of the believer who puts himself into the hands of the Savior: the Protestant doctrine of justification by faith alone—*sola fide*—was born, and with it a new era in European history. Probably by 1516, certainly a year or two later, Luther's new vision was clear and, despite recurring bouts of despairing uncertainty, secure.

The world in which young Luther was laboring to attain religious light was, as usual, in turmoil, but perhaps in graver turmoil than usual. We have pointed to the destructive effects of the Italian wars, the unmeasured ambitions of secular rulers, the disruptive consequences of heresy, and the much-criticized conduct of Renaissance popes (see p. 110). But there were some new and explosive ingredients in the familiar mixture. The Renaissance popes were perhaps no worse than earlier popes, but they were more open about their political and financial manipulations than their predecessors, and they alienated many ambitious men by their very successes against the Councils and their very concentration on Italian affairs. Complaints against the laziness of priests, their lust, their ignorance, their greed for lucrative offices, were very old indeed; there are texts from clerical reformers of the thirteenth century that sound like the inflammatory tracts written in Luther's day. What was new was the general virulence of antipapal and anticlerical sentiment; what was new was the printing press, which distributed manifestos, tracts, pictures with unprecedented effectiveness. Both the makers and the critics of scandals were more public than ever before.

As the strange interlude of Savonarola shows, discontent with the papacy was not a monopoly of the North. The Dominican friar Girolamo Savonarola, one of the most remarkable religious zealots of all time, first came to Florence in 1482, but his first preaching mission there was not a success. When he returned to preach in 1490, he had learned to trust his charismatic presence, developed his oratorical powers, and hit upon his single theme. That theme was

---

[13] Rom. 1:17.
[14] Dillenberger, *Martin Luther*, 11.

sin: the wicked luxury of the laity, the unforgivable corruption of the church, the need for universal reform and the opportunity for such reform—now. In 1494, when Charles VIII invaded Italy, Savonarola hailed him as "an instrument in the hands of the Lord who has sent you to cure the ills of Italy." [15] In that year, as the Medici fled, Savonarola identified himself with the popular regime in Florence; in his short ascendancy—many have called it a dictatorship—religion and politics fused to perfection. The same combination would destroy him: Florentine plutocrats and, once he had become sufficiently aroused, Pope Alexander VI cordially hated the gaunt, fierce-eyed preacher who wanted to deprive laymen of pleasure and clergymen of wealth.

Like other preachers of humility, Savonarola had his share of pride: if Florence was now entering the millennium of purity, who, after all, was the savior who had stood up to antichrist? Like other saintly reformers, he was intolerant—certainly he enjoyed his hold over his audiences. His short reign produced some rather peculiar spectacles in luxury-loving Florence. Smarting under his words and afraid of his supporters who were as fanatical as he, the elegant and the vicious assumed simple dress and abandoned, or concealed, their pleasures. In 1497, and once again in the following year, Savonarola presided over a "burning of the vanities," big public bonfires in which dice, carnival dresses, lascivious pictures, and other symbols of sin were solemnly consigned to the flames. [16] But in the long run Savonarola could not hold his public; his support dwindled as rapidly as it had grown, and he was first excommunicated, and then in 1498 burned at the stake, his two chief lieutenants by his side.

The Savonarola intermezzo is richly instructive. It illustrates, once again, the fatal conjunction of politics and religion, the persistent appeal of traditional rhetoric, and the height of passion that millenarian appeals could arouse—even in Italy. This is a useful reminder of a neglected fact. A look at the religious map of Europe, say in 1600, suggests a generalization about the course of the Reformation that would in fact be wrong. Because Italy and the regions nearest it retained—or in some instances regained—their loyalty to Rome, this does not mean that unrest and heresy were weakest in Italy and strongest in the outermost reaches of Christendom. Both were everywhere; the eventual disposition of religious allegiance depended on other forces.

Yet it remains true that in the North, particularly in the German states, discontent with the church was closest to the point of revolutionary action. German Humanists, in the new universities and in their polemical writings, inveighed against the papacy, lampooned the Scholastics, defended the new learning, and proudly felt themselves to be German imperialists tired of Roman domination. With Ulrich von Hutten, the wandering knight who put his chivalrous values in the service of German humanism, the search for religious

[15] Ferdinand Schevill, *Medieval and Renaissance Florence,* 2 vols. (Torchbook ed., 1963), 444.
[16] Ibid.

purification grew from outspoken, often scatological criticism of the clergy and from vehement support of the "German" emperor, to acceptance of religious revolution. "While Hutten," Hajo Holborn has written, "merged the popular resentment against Rome . . . with the humanistic opposition to the theologians, he was in his heart not unmindful of the need for a more comprehensive spiritual power to broaden the basis of the struggle with the Romanists."[17] Once he had grasped the meaning of Luther's cause, Hutten ranged himself on Luther's side.

Luther was to find many other allies, among them, to his embarrassment, the German peasantry. Peasant unrest was endemic in early modern Germany; in 1502, there was a large-scale peasant rising in the southwest, the *Bundschuh*.[18] The peasants fondly recalled earlier days when taxes were lower, income was higher, and respect for the peasant was greater. In their minds nostalgia for the past and millenarian hopes for the future coalesced. Corrupt priests must be driven out, life under the old divine law where men were equal must be restored. Credulous, ill-organized, and ill-equipped, the rebels were no match for the troops sent against them, but they did not give up easily. In 1517 famine conditions brought a new *Bundschuh rising*, more alarming than any before. It was a fateful year. Politically, religiously, socially, Germany was ready for rebellion. The wood was dry, the tinder was laid. All that was needed was someone to light it.

THE LUTHERAN REFORMATION

From Rebel to Revolutionary

On October 31, 1517, Martin Luther affixed ninety-five theses to the door of the castle church at Wittenberg. They were a protest against the Dominican commissary Johann Tetzel, who was traveling about the country selling indulgences. The issue of indulgences had long been the subject of ill-tempered debate; objections to the practice had multiplied since the reign of Pope Sixtus IV, who had extended it in 1476 to apply to the time that sinners would have to spend in purgatory. The old logic of indulgences—that Christ and the saints had built up a "treasure of merits" on which ordinary mortals could draw—now became a blatant excuse for collecting money for all sorts of secular purposes: Tetzel was circulating around Wittenberg as an agent of Prince

---

[17] *A History of Modern Germany,* vol. I, *The Reformation* (1959), 112.

[18] The *Bundschuh* is the low shoe the peasant wore, laced above the ankle with a string, in contrast with the riding boots favored by the aristocracy (see Holborn, *History of Modern Germany,* vol. I, 62). This is not the last time that an article of clothing gave a name to a revolutionary group: for the *sans-culottes* in the French Revolution see p. 480.

Albert of Brandenburg, archbishop of Mainz and thus primate of Germany, to raise funds for the rebuilding of St. Peter's in Rome. [19] For Luther the issue was particularly sensitive. He knew, from his own harrowing experience, that the road to redemption was hard, and here was a scandalous preacher collecting money on the pretense that redemption was easy—and cheap. [20]

Luther's theses—the "Disputation on the Power and Efficacy of Indulgences"—were moderate in tone. They were an invitation to a scholarly disputation in the traditional manner, written "out of love and concern for the truth, and with the object of eliciting it." [21] They argued that "the entire life of believers" should be one of "penitence," and that ways of evading this obligation, like the treasure of merit, were invalid. "Any Christian whatsoever, who is truly repentant, enjoys plenary remission from penalty and guilt, and this is given him without letters of indulgence." [22] Perhaps Luther was being offensive when he suggested that the pope should "liberate everyone from purgatory for the sake of love (a most holy thing)," rather than "for money, a most perishable thing, with which to build St. Peter's church, a very minor purpose." [23] But Luther's theses were only implicitly heretical. And they were in Latin.

But then translators put the ninety-five theses into German and printers distributed them by the thousands. Almost overnight, a scholar's protest grew into a popular cause. In October 1518, Luther was ordered to discuss his views with the Dominican Cajetan, the cardinal legate, but the conversation broke up in disagreement and ill-feeling over the meaning of the word "treasure." Luther and his friends realized that Pope Leo X would soon act against him, but in December 1518 Frederick the Wise, elector of Saxony, told the papacy that Luther was under his protection. Luther was fortunate in the timing of his rebellion: Emperor Maximilian was dying (he was, in fact, to die in January 1519), and neither the imperial nor the papal party could afford to antagonize Frederick, whose vote they wanted. The election of Maximilian's successor took place in June 1519; Charles of the house of Hapsburg became emperor, "after an election conducted with the publicity of an auction and the morals of a gambling hell." [24]

---

[19] Frivolous as this ostensible purpose was, the actual reason for the indulgences proclaimed by Albert was more frivolous still. His drive to collect posts had involved him in huge expenditures for fees and placed him in debt to the Fuggers. By a secret agreement with the Roman curia which did not become public until much later, Albert agreed to repay the Fuggers with half of the proceeds from the indulgences and hand over the other half to Leo X for St. Peter's. One can imagine how Luther would have couched his theses if he had known *this*.

[20] On this point, see E. G. Rupp, "Luther and the German Reformation to 1529," in *The New Cambridge Modern History*, vol. II, *The Reformation, 1520-1559* (1958), 77.

[21] Theses, introductory paragraph, in Dillenberger, *Martin Luther*, 490.

[22] Thesis No. 36, in Dillenberger, *Martin Luther*, 494.

[23] Thesis No. 82, in Dillenberger, *Martin Luther*, 498.

[24] R. H. Tawney, *Religion and the Rise of Capitalism* (1929), 79; quoted in Joel Hurstfield, ed., *The Reformation Crisis* (1965), 2.

The undignified wrangle made the case of Luther recede into the background, but the issues he had raised were too inflammatory to remain dormant for long. In July 1519, at Leipzig, Luther engaged in a fundamental and seemingly interminable debate with Johann Eck, a formidable theologian and an adroit antagonist who drove Luther into admission of heresy. Under the pressure of events, Luther's religious thinking had been evolving rapidly. What he had called "our theology" in Wittenberg before 1517 was still compatible with orthodox belief, and his rebelliousness against clerical authority in 1517 and 1518 smacked of a Conciliarist position—out of favor but not precisely heretical. Now, with Eck, Luther went beyond anything he had said or written before. Eck charged Luther with following "the damned and pestiferous errors of John Wyclif," and "the pestilent errors of Johann Hus." [25] In reply, Luther vehemently denied "the charge of Bohemianism," and criticized the Hussites for creating a schism in the church. But he acknowledged that "among the articles" of Hus he found "many which are plainly Christian and evangelical." [26] Neither councils nor popes could establish articles of faith—"these," Luther argued, "must come from Scripture." [27] This was true particularly because the papacy was a human, not a divine, institution. Papal decretals purportedly dating back to the early days of Christianity and asserting the opposite were, Luther asserted, plain forgeries. It was equally plain that Luther had read himself out of the Roman communion. Nor did he stop with the fragmentary theology he had developed at Leipzig under the prodding of Eck. By February 1520 he could say: "We are all Hussites without knowing it." [28]

Rome knew it. In June 1520 Leo X issued a bull condemning his writings. If he did not recant within sixty days, he would stand an obstinate heretic, a withered branch on the tree of Christendom. The proscribed man did not waver. In December, in a flamboyant gesture of defiance, he publicly burned the papal bull, together with books on canon law. In the months before, he had set down his new-won clarity for the world to read in a trio of tracts which, different as they are in tone and purpose, belong together. The whole of the Reformation is in them. The first of these tracts, *An Appeal to the Christian Nobility of the German Nation*, rehearses the grievances of German Christians against Rome and the familiar list of complaints against clerical conduct—boldly, plainly, effectively, and it must be added, exhaustively. But, beyond that, in his *Appeal* Luther advanced his uncompromising doctrine of the priesthood of all believers. "The Romanists," he wrote in the slashing polemical manner characteristic of him, have "very cleverly" protected their privileged position with three paper walls, so far impregnable. They have argued that secular power has no jurisdiction over clerical institutions, that there is no point

---

[25] See Roland H. Bainton, *Here I Stand: A Life of Martin Luther* (1962), 89.
[26] Ibid.
[27] Ibid., 90.
[28] Ibid., 92.

in citing Scriptures against them since the pope alone is competent to expound Holy Writ, and that the threat of a council is empty since after all only the pope can convene such a council. What was inscribed on these three walls was the separation of Christendom into two distinct classes, the secular and the religious. But this separation, Luther insisted, was only "a specious device invented by certain time-servers." In fact, "all Christians whatsoever really and truly belong to the religious class, and there is no difference among them except in so far as they do different work." This is so because "we have one baptism, one gospel, one faith, and are all equally Christian." Baptism "consecrates us all without exception, and makes us all priests." [29] Since in its sublime arrogance, Rome has failed to observe this essential principle of true Christianity and continues to manipulate believers to its own profit, the time has now come for German Christians to turn to the only true source of authority— Scriptures—and take the cause of reform into their own hands. Luther's copious list of "twenty-seven proposals for improving the state of Christendom" calls for the dismantling of nearly the whole structure of "Romanism" including indulgences, the Holy Office, the pope's assertion of authority over secular affairs, pilgrimages, unbreakable vows, excessive masses and holidays. Centuries-old longings of pious heretics are here gathered into one grand, impressive program.

Luther had addressed the first tract to the German nobility in German. He addressed the second, *The Babylonian Captivity of the Church*, to the clergy, in Latin. In the opening paragraph, he testified to the rapid and decisive shift in his thinking; as late as 1518, only two years before, he had still been "entangled in the gross superstitions of a masterful Rome." [30] Now he had thrown them off. In his address to the German nobility he had sought to destroy Roman institutions; in his address to the clergy he sought to destroy Roman beliefs. He denied that there were seven sacraments (the Catholic complement); instead, "for the present," he propounded three: "baptism, penance, and the Lord's Supper." [31] Of these, as Luther recognized, the Lord's Supper was "the most important of all." By eliminating such sacraments as ordination and extreme unction, Luther was reaffirming his doctrine that all believers are priests and that therefore no special qualities inhere in professional clerics. But while retaining the Lord's Supper, Luther took care to distinguish his interpretation of that sacrament from the Roman version. First of all, the laity must have restored to it what the Roman curia had so wickedly taken away: the mass in both kinds. The communicant must receive not merely the bread, but the wine as well: "To deny both kinds to the laity is impious and oppressive." [32]

---

[29] In Dillenberger, *Martin Luther*, 406–408.

[30] Ibid., 250.

[31] Actually, as Luther writes later in this tract, only two of these, baptism and the Lord's Supper, are divinely instituted. Penance is merely "a means of reaffirming our baptism" (in Dillenberger, *Martin Luther*, 359).

[32] In Dillenberger, *Martin Luther*, 263.

Secondly, the mass is not a sacrifice but a testament, and the sole precondition for its worthy observation is faith: "Of all for whom the mass has been provided, only those partake of it worthily whose consciences make them sad, humble, disturbed, confused, and uncertain." The mass is the testament of Christ which takes away sin only if men "cling to Him with unwavering faith. . . . If you do not believe this, then never, nowhere, by no good works, and by no kinds of efforts, can you gain peace of conscience."[33] Finally, what happens at mass is not transubstantiation; that notion is a "human invention" defended by overly clever Scholastics like Thomas Aquinas who base themselves on a misunderstanding of Aristotle—"thus building an unfortunate superstructure on an unfortunate foundation." Christ, Luther believed, is mysteriously present in communion—"consubstantiation." But at the same time, Luther was concerned to allay the tender consciences of those who thought, following the plain meaning of the Scriptures, that bread remained bread, and wine, wine. "Here I shall be called a Wycliffite and six hundred times a heretic. But what does it matter? Now that the Roman bishop has ceased to be a bishop and has become a dictator, I fear none of his decrees at all; for I know that he has no power to make a new article of faith, nor has a general council."[34] Luther squarely placed the burden of faith on the conscience of the individual Christian.

Luther completed this structure of argument in his third great tract of 1520, *Of the Liberty of a Christian*. Shaped as a letter to Pope Leo X, it is far shorter than the other two and more pacific in tenor. But, however edifying its tone and conciliatory its intention, its doctrine is clearly heretical. Men must live among ceremonies and do good works, but both are the consequences and not the conditions of faith. Works produce hypocrites; faith alone justifies. Works have no power to give men the healing belief in God, or honor Him, or unite men with Christ; faith alone can do all three. "Works, being inanimate things, cannot glorify God, although they can, if faith is present, be done to the glory of God."[35] The liberty of a Christian—that is, of a man of faith—brings glorious works in its train: "Behold, from faith thus flow forth love and joy in the Lord, and from love a joyful, willing, and free mind that serves one's neighbor willingly and takes no account of gratitude or ingratitude, of praise or blame, of gain or loss."[36] All else, no matter what learned theologians might argue, is bondage. It was Luther's purpose in these three tracts to free man from such bondage.

This was precisely what the clerical authorities feared. Luther had apostrophized Leo X as "most excellent Leo" and hailed Charles V as "a young

[33] Ibid., 291.
[34] Ibid., 265–267.
[35] Ibid., 62.
[36] Ibid., 75–76.

man of noble ancestry" whom God had given to the world, but neither pope nor emperor was appeased by Luther's rare excursions into diplomatic manners. On January 3, 1521, Luther was excommunicated. But he was not without protection. The papal nuncio in Germany reported that nine tenths of all Germans cried "Luther," and the other tenth, "Death to the pope."[37] After complex maneuverings on all sides, Luther was bidden to appear at Worms, at the first imperial diet of Charles' long reign. Luther was courageous and tenacious, but he could go to Worms confident that he would not share Hus' fate; the attention of the world—and, more important, of sympathetic German princes—was centered on him, guaranteeing that the imperial safe-conduct would be honored. In April, Luther presented himself before a crowded assembly including princes and bishops and the emperor himself. Sternly, he was asked two questions: Did he acknowledge the books that were heaped up on a table before him? He did. Did he defend what he had written there? He wanted time to think it over. His examiners gave him one day, and Luther's second hearing has remained, in history and in myth, one of the decisive moments in European history. With the skill of a politician, Luther turned a trial into a triumph. He distinguished among his many writings, regretted the personal attacks he had permitted himself, and appealed to the Germans in the audience by inveighing against the foreign tyranny that was devouring his nation. And he sturdily refused to recant any of his theological opinions: "Unless I am convicted by Scripture and plain reason—I do not accept the authority of popes and councils, for they have contradicted each other—my conscience is captive to the Word of God. I cannot and will not recant anything, for to go against conscience is neither right nor safe. God help me. Amen."[38] Adroitly, Luther had spoken in German, but upon request he reiterated his stand in Latin, and walked out.

Luther, his safe-conduct intact, underwent further private hearings, but in May, after he had left, the diet voted the Edict of Worms accusing him of Bohemianism, denying the sacraments, sullying sacred institutions, and encouraging rebellion. By decree of the governing body of the empire he was an outlaw. His temporal overlord, Elector Frederick of Saxony, saw it otherwise; while Luther was on his way home, Frederick's men kidnapped him and hid him at a remote stronghold, the Wartburg. Isolated in the castle—for a time his anxious supporters feared him dead—and released from almost unbearable strain, Luther experienced some terrible depressions and terrifying confrontations with evil spirits. The wall against which he hurled his ink-well at the devil was to become a tourist attraction. But he soon regained his spirits and began

[37] Bainton, *Here I Stand,* 130.

[38] These are the words quoted in the report of the meeting. Ironically enough, his most famous words, which have given titles to books and been endlessly repeated—"*Hier stehe ich, ich kann nicht anders*—Here I stand, I can do no other"—were added later to the printed account of the day.

to write again—letters, tracts, and most important, his German translation of the New Testament.

His cause was prospering. The rich mixture of religious, social, and political elements that had distinguished the Reformation from the beginning became, if anything, richer than before. True, some leading Humanists fell away; drawn at first by Luther's undeniable good will and reforming zeal, they were soon put off by his unwillingness to compromise, his growing impatience with disagreement—the occupational hazard of the prophet—and his invectives. Erasmus, to whose scholarship Luther was considerably indebted, temporized on Lutheranism for years and thus lent it some of his enormous prestige, but in 1524 his distaste for, and disagreements with, Luther came into the open. Ostensibly the break came over the philosophical issue of free will versus determinism; actually, it was a clash of temperaments and essential aims. The bull-headed, assertive dogmatist with a single cause could not peacefully coexist for long with the urbane skeptic and compromiser.

On the other hand, Luther found fanatical and often unwanted supporters all across Germany. In 1522, the year Luther emerged from hiding and returned to Wittenberg to preach, a band of imperial knights waged a scattered series of feuds against the "Romanists" in Germany, raiding monasteries, plundering abbeys, and assaulting well-fortified ecclesiastical cities. The princes crushed their efforts, and their leaders died—Franz von Sickingen in battle in 1523, Ulrich von Hutten in exile in the same year. Romantic anachronisms that they were, the knights in their last flickering bid for power courted, and found, disaster.

The imperial cities and the princes induced to join Lutheranism fared much better. For them, power, profits, and piety harmonized splendidly. To assume full sovereign rights over one's territory—to gather ecclesiastical establishments into a state church that would obey the dictates not of pope or emperor but of the local patriciate or local prince—made it possible to eliminate Roman influence, expropriate the property of monasteries or cathedral chapters, and keep at home the money the faithful had been sending to Rome for centuries. By the mid-1520s, two imperial electors—of Saxony and Hesse—had joined the Lutheran cause. So had Albert of Hohenzollern, grand master of the Catholic Order of the Teutonic Knights, who converted at Luther's urging and took the territories under his control—East Prussia and Brandenburg—into the Protestant camp. Many of the imperial cities, including Nuremberg, Bremen, Erfurt, and Gotha, all populated by literate and independent-minded men who were a receptive audience for the outpouring of Luther's prolific pen, turned Protestant as well. But by 1525, its very success had brought Lutheranism to the edge of disaster: the peasants, inflamed by Luther's teachings, had risen to claim their share of the new dispensation at hand. [39]

[39] For Lutheranism after 1525, see p. 144.

The Radical Reformation

In 1521, while the Diet of Worms was weighing its edict against Luther, the city was plastered with placards bearing the symbol of peasant rebelliousness, the *Bundschuh*. In 1524 and 1525, with the short-lived, ill-starred Peasants' War, the emerging alliance between religious reformation and social rebellion briefly flourished and quickly collapsed.

"The French Revolution," as Hajo Holborn has observed, "was not caused by the philosophy of the Enlightenment, nor was the so-called Great Peasants' War caused by Lutheranism." Despite frequent defeats and ferocious reprisals, peasants had continued to engage in sporadic protest ever since the *Bundschuh* had first unfurled its defiant flag. "But," Holborn continues, "the new ideas gave the peasants' movement principles that enabled it to organize beyond the local sphere and to present its aims as part of a universal and national reform."[40] The regions in which the great war originated in 1524 are significant: southwest Germany, in the Black Forest, near the Swiss territories that were rapidly falling into the hands of reformers, and near the walls, in the shadow, of imperial cities that had embraced Protestantism. Soberly, the rural rebels held greed, cruelty, even millenarian hopes in check. The best known formulation of their demands, the *Twelve Articles of the Peasantry*, began, in good Lutheran fashion, with the pacific salutation, "To the Christian Reader Peace and the Grace of God through Christ," and concluded with the modest proviso that if any of the demands "should not be in agreement with the word of God," the peasants would "willingly recede" from them. What the rebels asked for was reasonable enough: a clergy elected by, and responsible to, its congregation and capable of preaching the Divine Word plainly, "pure and simple, without any human addition, doctrine or ordinance"; an end to excessive services, fees, and rents exacted by the lords; an end as well to the nobles' appropriation of woodlands and to their burdensome monopoly on hunting and fishing rights; an end above all to serfdom. This was the way the Swabian tanner, Sebastian Lotzer, who wrote the *Twelve Articles*, chose to understand Luther's doctrine of Christian freedom.

For a time the conciliatory attitude of the rebels, coupled with the craven fears of the lesser rulers, produced an aura of possible compromise and peaceful social adjustment. But the social fear drove the greater princes not toward concessions but into resistance. As men with great privileges to defend and the power to defend them, they refused to deal with the rebels at all or dealt with them only to gain time to raise their own armies. As princely resistance stiffened, the revolt spread northward, mainly in the Rhineland, grew more violent in its methods and more radical in its aims. The peasants never had a chance for victory. Though filled with brave and experienced soldiers, their

[40] *History of Modern Germany,* vol. I, 170-171.

forces were scattered and amateurish; they had no horses, no alliances, no long-range aims. While by April 1525 the number of rebellious peasants exceeded a quarter of a million, by May and June their movement was in disarray. First came routs, then came retribution, an outburst of wilful mass slaughter that blighted the German lands for decades. The traditional devices of criminal procedure—torture, mutilation, hanging, burning, decapitation—were applied in city after city with wanton energy and on an unprecedented scale. When Würzburg was recaptured by Bishop Conrad, "the event was celebrated with the execution of 64 citizens and peasants. Then the bishop made a tour of his diocese, accompanied by his executioner, who took care of 272 persons." [41] The ruling orders, back in control, were repaying their hapless victims for the months of shameful panic in which they had lived. No reliable figures exist or can exist, but it is estimated that a hundred thousand peasants were killed in battle and after; the number of cripples who survived is incalculable. It was, as Hajo Holborn has said, "one of the most shameful chapters in German history" [42]—one of the most shameful chapters, but not the most shameful.

Infatuated with Luther, whom they regarded as one of their own, the peasants did not anticipate that Luther would turn against them. They should have anticipated it. In his published writings he had always insisted, with perfect consistency, that the political authorities must be obeyed. Late in April 1525, when the peasants seemed on the verge of victory, Luther assailed both princes and rebels in his *Friendly Admonition to Peace Concerning the Twelve Articles of the Swabian Peasants*. He urged the princes, whom he blamed for the outbreak of the revolt, to grant the peasants what they deserved to allay their "intolerable grievances." At the same time, he berated the peasants for taking the sword. "Because you boast of the divine law and act against it, He will let you fall and be punished terribly, as men who dishonor His name." [43] Then, in May, after his attempts to calm rebellious peasants in Thuringia had embarrassingly failed, Luther dashed off a far more one-sided and far coarser exhortation to the princes, *Against the Murderous and Thieving Hordes of Peasants*, in which he declared the rebels "outside the law," worse than murderers, who had brought "murders and bloodshed" to the land, "made widows and orphans," and turned the social order upside down. "Therefore, let everyone who can, smite, slay, and stab, secretly or openly. . . . It is just as when one must kill a mad dog; if you don't strike him, he will strike you, and the whole land with you." [44] The princes had been unwilling to listen to Luther's call for social reform; they cheerfully obeyed his call to vengeance.

As by 1525 Luther had vehemently repudiated the social radicalism that had been encouraged by his example, so he had divorced himself from the

---

[41] Bainton, *Here I Stand*, 220.
[42] *History of Modern Germany*, vol. I, 170–171.
[43] Quoted in Hans J. Hillerbrand, ed., *The Protestant Reformation* (1968), 74.
[44] Bainton, *Here I Stand*, 217.

religious extremism that had for some years drawn inspiration from his work. The most interesting of his early extremist adversaries was Thomas Münzer, like Luther a Saxon and, like Luther, a well-educated cleric. For a time he professed himself Luther's disciple, but by 1524, he was denouncing Luther as a sensualist, a false prophet, and a servile truckler to temporal authority. He rejected all authority including Scriptures—"Bible, Babel, bubble!"—and insisted that the true Christian must wait, as the first Christians had waited, for direct divine inspiration. "The letter killeth, but the spirit giveth life." [45] Wherever Münzer preached, he attracted a fierce following among the disinherited of the world, urging them to turn their back on the fat, self-satisfied compromiser Luther and to overthrow the oppressive social order. His presence in Saxony helped to precipitate the peasant uprisings there; Luther's brutal accents in his diatribe against the "murderous and thieving hordes" were partly an expression of his rage against Münzer. Finally, in May 1525, following a decisive defeat of his peasant troops, Münzer was captured, tortured, and beheaded.

In Thomas Münzer religious extremism and social protest coalesced. In other sectaries of the time, like the Anabaptists, religious enthusiasm predominated. [46] The precise early history of the Anabaptists remains somewhat uncertain; Münzer, who rejected all baptism, seems to have had some influence on the discussions about infant baptism that divided Wittenberg in 1521. But the first significant center for the doctrine was Zurich (see p. 147). The reformer Ulrich Zwingli had gained control there in 1523 and found himself almost instantly in debate with the Protestant left wing. Some new Protestants, led by the "noble and learned young" Conrad Grebel, [47] insisted that baptism be given only upon profession of faith. Their following was considerable; numerous troubled citizens of Zurich refused to have their children baptized, although the city council, dominated by Zwingli's views, ordered them to comply with infant baptism. By 1525, the Anabaptist leaders were in prison or in exile. But the movement, cruelly persecuted wherever it went, spread and flourished, a sincere and touching Christian underground. [48]

The religious program of the Anabaptists was simple and straightforward. But the turmoil of the Reformation cast up other preachers, other sects, each with his own particular version of Christianity. The confusion of tongues against which Roman Catholic partisans had warned, once the Protestant contagion was allowed to spread, was not long in showing itself. Andreas Karlstadt, Luther's colleague at the University of Wittenberg and for some time his rival in popularity, developed a stridently anti-intellectual, populist Protes-

---

[45] 2 Cor. 3:6.

[46] The word is derived from the Greek prefix *ana,* meaning again or anew, marking the central doctrine of the sect, that true baptism can be administered only to adults.

[47] See Ernest A. Payne, "The Anabaptists," in *The New Cambridge Modern History,* vol. II, *The Reformation, 1520–1559* (1958), 120.

[48] For its development after 1525, see p. 144.

tantism; he professed to prefer the wisdom of illiterate peasants to the disputations of scholars and sought to banish images and music from the churches. Other sectarians excluded outsiders from the blessings of their teachings. Still others wandered about the countryside foretelling the millennium. Like many revolutionaries, Luther would discover that he could not confine the revolution he had made within the boundaries he himself had chosen; like many revolutionaries, he found his own extreme left—those who wanted to drive his logic to its conclusion—troublesome, detestable, and dangerous.

Spreading the Word: Luther's Europe After 1525

The year 1525 was decisive for Martin Luther. In that year his breach with Erasmus, with social radicals, and with religious extremists became final and irreparable. In that year, too, he put an end to monasticism in his church: he married. The time that was left him—he died in 1546, after some ill-health—was a time of significant and tireless activity: he defined the relations between church and state, wrote hymns and catechisms that became the classics of his confession, watched the travail of Lutheranism within, and the expansion of Lutheranism beyond, the frontiers of his Germany.

Anabaptism continued to be a holy plague. Driven from Zurich, the sect took refuge in Moravia, in some Hapsburg territories and some German cities, and found new supporters. The authorities hounded these pious rebaptizers, exiling them, burning them, and in an unconscious form of poetic justice—or, rather, injustice—drowning them. In 1527, a group of Anabaptists met in Switzerland and adopted what came to be called the Schleitheim Confession, which reiterated the Anabaptists' insistence on baptizing only those who "walk in the resurrection of Jesus Christ"; reduced the Lord's Supper to a "memorial" occasion and restricted it to the baptized; and abjured the use of violence for themselves. [49] This profession of faith remained the heart of the Anabaptists' program across northern Europe. A large-scale tragedy awaited them. In 1533, Anabaptists had managed to secure control of the German city of Münster. Sympathizers from the Netherlands, hearing the good news, tried to join their brethren, in vain; they were rounded up and judicially murdered. While the city was besieged, the holy remnant within expelled Catholics and Lutherans, baptized adults, preached community of property, and at the urging of their young leader John of Leyden, began to practice polygamy. John of Leyden, whose sanity gave way under the pressure of events, took a total of sixteen wives, had one of them executed, and finally had himself crowned king. In the early summer of 1535, this modern caricature of an Old Testament common-

---

[49] The seven points are summarized in *The New Cambridge Modern History*, vol. II, *The Reformation, 1520-1559* (1958), 125.

wealth was taken. Most of the defenders were butchered, the leaders tortured and executed in leisurely and edifying fashion. In the late 1520s Luther had still urged the authorities to deal mercifully with harmless Anabaptists; now, his patience gone, he said nothing.

Not all was turmoil and trouble. Lutheranism spread. In the 1530s other German cities, including Frankfurt am Main and Augsburg, joined the earlier converts. There were many states now, large and small, with a stake in the new order: they had confiscated church properties that they would on no account surrender. In 1530, Charles V called an imperial diet at Augsburg to clarify the religious situation of the empire. It was clarified beyond his desires. The Lutherans, led by the moderate Humanist Philip Melanchthon, drew up the Augsburg Confession which, despite its compromising tone, made the division between Catholics and Protestants obvious and irreparable. For some years there was confessional peace. It is a token of the complex political situation that German Protestant rulers, conscious of their membership in a Holy Roman Empire headed by a Roman Catholic prince, supported Charles V during the early 1530s to ward off a new threat from the Turks. True, in 1531 German Protestant princes, joined by German Protestant cities, set up the Schmalkaldic League which undertook to defend their faith in all their lands.[50] But war within the empire did not erupt until 1546, the year of Luther's death, only to be settled nine years later, in 1555, with the Peace of Augsburg, which gave the Lutherans what they wanted—the right to determine their own religion in their own states (see p. 164).

Other countries, meanwhile, had swelled the Lutheran avalanche. Lutherans made many converts and exerted widespread influence in France and England although neither was to become a Lutheran country (see pp. 177 and 184). The Swiss reformers were inspired by Luther's ideas and heartened by Luther's success, though they remained an independent strain of Protestantism (see p. 147). In Luther's lifetime, there were to be Lutheran settlements in Transylvania, the Baltic regions, small areas of Poland, and far more significantly, in Scandinavia. Before 1525 preachers who had been in direct touch with Luther himself preached in Denmark, and by 1537 the Danish crown established a Lutheran state church. Having taken full control of Norway the year before, King Christian III of Denmark also gradually introduced Lutheranism into his Norwegian lands. In Sweden, which had secured independence from Danish overlordship in 1521 under the leadership of Gustavus Vasa, Lutheranism was imposed by Gustavus (crowned king in 1523). A Lutheran preacher, Olaus Petri, who married in 1525 (the year his model Martin Luther took the same step), exercised enormous influence over his country and his king. Petri

[50] The name of the league is drawn from the town of Schmalkalden, where the negotiations for its formation took place in late 1530 and early 1531. Its most prominent members were Landgrave Phillip of Hesse, the duke of Brunswick, the elector of Saxony, the cities of Strasbourg, Bremen, and Ulm, joined later by Göttingen, Hamburg, and Rostock, and in 1537, by the major city-states of Frankfurt, Hanover, and Augsburg. See *New Cambridge Modern History,* vol. II, 350.

published popular books of Lutheran devotion, preached endless Lutheran sermons, participated in a Swedish translation of the New Testament, and wrote a Swedish mass. While Gustavus Vasa largely expropriated the church in 1527, Lutheranism proved a slow growth confronting sturdy resistance. It took decades, punctuated by rebellions and interminable efforts at persuasion, before Lutheranism was really established in Sweden. But once it was secure, it was unassailable.

The Lutheran Paradox

It was the essential aim of Luther's reformation to restore the direct, primitive Christian relationship between God and man. Man was to feel all the weight of his sin, all the terror of his perdition, all the glory of his faith, unencumbered by mere human intermediaries. Luther's attack on the Roman Catholic hierarchy was only in small part, and mainly at the beginning of his mission, an attack on secularism, corruption, nepotism, bureaucratic stupidity. It was an attack, rather, on a human institution that had dared to interpose itself between God and man and to claim the right of mediating in a situation in which no mediator, except Christ, was welcome. The political and economic profits accruing to those confessing themselves Lutherans—and they were, for many, considerable—should not obscure the profound inwardness of Luther's teachings. The extremists who arose so widely, and so wildly, in the wake of Luther's break with Rome, testify to the emotions that his preaching, his writing, his very presence unloosed in pious and disoriented men. If—as many reasoned after 1517—there was to be no pope, no separate priesthood, no pilgrimages, no interceding saints, there was no need for formal clerical institutions at all. Faith in God and a divine sign in man were all a true Christian needed; or, as others, less individualistic, put it: the communion of saints was sufficient unto itself.

But this was not Luther's view, even though some of his early pronouncements could be interpreted in this way. His lifelong ideal was the communion of saints, united in the invisible church of the faithful. But the experiences of 1524 and 1525, as well as inexorable political realities, drove Lutheran rulers, and Luther himself, into a less exalted conception of church and state. In a world of hostile Catholic neighbors and excitable fanatics at home, the secular princes and city governments came to assume the position of little popes within their territories. No longer a universal autocracy governed by Rome, the church became a local autocracy governed by its duke or city council. As Luther's political thought developed in response to external events, it became clear that the state must assume certain functions, notably education and welfare, that had once been the province of the church, and must supervise, moreover, the good conduct and uniform practice of churchmen. Luther did not think rulers free from sin; on the contrary, he frankly told them over and over again how subject they too were to human failings and how liable they too were to damnation. But Luther took seriously St. Paul's injunction that the powers that be are ordained of God; it followed that a Christian owed his state obedience, and nothing but obedience. A true Christian man was a free man, but Luther interpreted this freedom in a subjective sense. He was free in his heart, no matter how oppressive the regime under which he might live and suffer. Thus Luther, the great liberator, became the great proponent of state churches subservient to state governments. And so, when Protestantism began its march across Europe, Lutheranism traveled far less well than Calvinism. It was Calvinism, not Lutheranism, that seemed made for export. [51]

THE SWISS REFORMATION

Zwingli: Protestantism in Zurich

The Swiss Reformation, dominated by that austere logician, John Calvin, arose partly on its own impulsion, largely as a response to Luther. The precise proportions of its independence and dependence are, like all such subtle affairs, impossible to settle with precision; nor does it much matter: the ideas were in the air. Ulrich Zwingli, who set the Swiss Reformation in motion, was an Erasmian Humanist and a learned student of the Old Testament; he knew the Neoplatonists of Florence and the church fathers. He later claimed that he had taken the road to reform before he had heard of Luther: "I object to being called Lutheran by the papists; for I did not learn Christ's teaching from Luther but from the very word of God." [52] The claim can neither be substantiated nor refuted, but it is certain that Zwingli studied Luther's progress closely and admired it greatly. Born in 1484, Zwingli entered the priesthood in 1506; in 1518 he was called to Zurich. When he began to preach there on January 1, 1519, his heresy was dramatically obvious. In his sermons and his writings, he rapidly developed his Protestant theology until, in 1525, he was ready to summarize his teachings in his main work, the *Commentary on True and False Religion*: scriptures are the sole authority a Christian must accept; Roman sacraments, festivals, institutions are devilish inventions; the spirit is essential, trappings like church music are nothing. By the time he wrote the *Commentary,* he and his party had been in control of Zurich's political and religious affairs for two years. The clergy were allowed to marry; Catholic religious houses were closed;

---

[51] Holborn, *History of Modern Germany,* vol. I, chap. 8.
[52] Quoted in Hurstfield, *Reformation Crisis,* 35.

local churches were cleansed of relics and organs; the mass was abolished; and Zwingli instituted a new order of preaching, a new church service, a new ritual of baptism.

All this, a few details apart, was compatible with Luther's teachings. Only one issue remained, and that an important one: the meaning of the Lord's Supper. In his *Commentary,* as in many sermons, Zwingli employed a good deal of metaphysical and philological ingenuity to prove that the bread and wine of the mass were simply a commemoration, a symbol of God's covenant with man. Zwingli was so intent on asserting the distance between matter and spirit that he rejected, almost with disgust, any intimation that merely physical things like bread and wine could ever embody, even vaguely, such spiritual things as the body and blood of Christ. Thus he repudiated not merely transubstantiation, but also Luther's teaching of the "real presence"—consubstantiation.

This issue occupied Zwingli above all others. It is true to say, with Owen Chadwick, that "in his early years as a Reformer he and his friend Oecolampadius of Basle were so engaged upon saying what the Lord's Supper was not, that they rarely and reluctantly attempted to describe what it was."[53] His single-minded zeal led Zwingli into direct confrontation with Luther. In 1529, Landgrave Philip of Hesse, anxious to forge a united Protestant front, brought together a glittering galaxy of reformers: Zwingli and Luther came, as did Oecolampadius, Melanchthon, Bucer of Strasbourg, and some others. They settled much and at least did not break up in mutual animosity. But on the Lord's Supper, on which Luther in earlier years had been so pliable, no agreement proved possible: Luther strongly insisted on reading supernatural meaning into Jesus's words, "This is my body"; Zwingli insisted, quite as strongly, that they meant simply, "This signifies my body." The union of Protestants, however desirable politically, failed to materialize. The Lutheran, and what came to be called the Reformed church, continued to coexist, compete, and often enough, conflict with one another. In 1531, two years after this Colloquy of Marburg, Zwingli died, "sword and battle-ax in hand,"[54] at Kappel, in a battle between Zurich and Catholic Swiss cantons. The Zurich Reformation was fortunate: Zwingli's long-lived successor, Henry Bullinger, kept Zwingli's work alive, both in Zurich and, largely by correspondence, elsewhere. But Zwingli's and Bullinger's dream of an all-Protestant Switzerland never became reality.

Calvin: Protestantism in Geneva

What Zwingli failed to do in Switzerland, another Swiss reformer—or, rather French reformer active in Switzerland—succeeded in doing across much of

[53] Owen Chadwick, *The Reformation* (1964), 79.
[54] Ibid., 80.

northern Europe.[55] John Calvin developed a rigorous theology, a widely admired church, a persuasive moral doctrine, and a set of justifications for his faith that impressed the scholar and moved the plain man. Calvin was a remarkable theologian, but he was not a theologian alone; he was, in addition, a Humanist and a lawyer, and his extensive, versatile philological and legal training gave his thought on divine things its unique strength. He read the Scriptures with the eyes of a scholar;[56] he served Protestantism as learned counsel, as if it were a case he must win.

He found his opportunity in permanent exile. Probably in 1533, Calvin had turned Protestant; he remembered his conversion as a sudden experience, a blinding insight that dispelled his obstinate adherence to error and calmed his fear that apostasy might destroy the church. Once he was a heretic, his life was in danger, and he left France to settle at Basel. There he wrote and, in 1536, published *The Institutes of the Christian Religion*, destined to become a classic of Protestantism. In the same year, Guillaume Farel, who was leading the Reformation in Geneva, imperiously invited Calvin to apply his administrative talents to the Protestant cause in that divided city-state. "When I first came into this Church," Calvin recalled later, "there was almost nothing there. They preached and that was all. They sought out the idols indeed, and burnt them, but there was no reformation. Everything was in tumult."[57] It was a muddle only a lawyer could have loved, or resolved.

In the Geneva of 1536, the Protestants were a dominant and embattled minority. In the embittered disputations between Catholic and Reformed theologians that had brought the republic to the verge of civil war, reformers had carried the day; in 1533, the Catholic bishop had left; by 1535, against the objections of the Catholic majority, the city government had abolished the mass. But staunchly Catholic Savoy (a powerful and aggressive neighbor), Roman Catholics within Geneva, and a desperate shortage of qualified leadership in Farel's party placed the Reformation in Geneva in a precarious position. Then Calvin began to organize the Protestant forces with all the subtlety of a scholar, decisiveness of an attorney, and self-assurance of a believer who knows that he is right. Calvin was everywhere; the outlines of a city of the saints, which he would later impose on Geneva, rapidly emerged.

---

[55] Calvin was born in 1509 at Noyon in Picardy as Jean Cauvin, but it is by the abbreviated version of his Latin name Calvinus that he is universally known.

[56] Calvin insisted that the Scriptures were God's inestimable gift to man, superseding all merely human efforts at comprehending His will. The authority of the Bible is therefore nothing less than divine, and Calvin made much—more than Luther did—of the Old Testament. Accordingly he condemned both the Roman Catholics, who relied on tradition and priestly interpretation, and the radical enthusiasts, who relied on inspiration. At the same time, "he accepted like any other humanist the need for historical and textual criticism" (A. G. Dickens, *Reformation and Society in Sixteenth-Century Europe* [1966], 156).

[57] Quoted in François Wendel, *Calvin: The Origins and Development of his Religious Thought* (1963), 49n.

Too rapidly. While Calvin's aims pleased the city, his speed and his methods did not; in 1538, accordingly, he was asked to leave Geneva. Farel left with him.

For three years, Calvin lived in Strasbourg, watched the Reformation at work there, read and wrote extensively including a second much enlarged version of his *Institutes,* and elaborated his theological, ecclesiastical, and political views. Then, in 1541, after abject appeals by the Genevan council, once again controlled by his friends, he returned, on his own terms, not quite, but seeking to become, a holy dictator. Once installed, Calvin moved without hesitation. His clerical ordinances setting up a Calvinist church appeared in the same year; other ordinances, penetrating into every aspect of life, appeared soon after. Calvin preached and wrote, recast his *Institutes,* decimated and gradually silenced his opponents. When he died in 1564, his mastery over his republic absolute, Geneva had become the headquarters for spreading his militant faith.

The three rocks on which Calvin built his church were the majesty of God, the mercy of Christ, and the vigilance of the faithful. The rigor of Calvin's logic, the harshness of his doctrines, and the dour aspect of his Geneva, have impelled many of his later readers to visualize him as a gloomy Scholastic obsessed by the rage to dominate and by man's utter, sinful wretchedness. But, it has rightly been said, "No summary does Calvin justice." While it will not do to "soften the message of Calvin," it is essential to remember that Calvin was "vitally concerned with divine mercy and redemptive power, as well as with the more fearful aspects of the divine plan. To neglect these moving, impressive passages would be to barbarize a great theologian and reduce him to the level of his least enlightened followers." [58] This much said, Calvin's God remains an awesome, remote, terrifying, wholly self-willed paternal figure. In man's fallen state, the direct consequence of Adam's sin in Eden, he cannot encompass his salvation or even understand God's decrees. He cannot earn heaven: like Luther, Calvin firmly rejected the notion that works could in any way influence man's ultimate fate. Among God's dark decrees, inaccessible to human reason and unchangeable by human action, the one that aroused most discussion in his day was Calvin's doctrine of election and reprobation. It was important to him, though not nearly so important as it would become to his disciples, the Puritans. God, Calvin reasoned, had decided from all eternity to elect some to salvation and assign others to eternal damnation. While God had conceived this decree in perfect foreknowledge of man's conduct, foreknowledge was not the cause of His decree: to explain God's permanent and irrevocable decision by foreknowledge was to infringe on His majesty by reducing His freedom. "If we ask why God takes pity on some, and why he lets go of the others and leaves them, there is no other answer but that it pleases him to do so." [59] This, in all its stark simplicity, was Calvin's famous doctrine of predestination; it had been implied

---

[58] Dickens, *Reformation and Society,* 157–159.
[59] Quoted from Calvin's Sermon on Ephesians 1:3–4, in Wendel, *Calvin,* 272–273.

or obliquely stated by many other earlier theologians, notably St. Augustine, but never with such uncompromising precision.

Yet it is worth noting—and this brings us to the second aspect of Calvin's doctrine—that the chapters of the *Institutes* in which Calvin discusses election and reprobation are in Book III, which deals not with the majesty of God but with the grace of Christ. It was not a matter of lamentation that most men should be damned, but a matter for rejoicing that a few men should be saved, for by his original sin man had forfeited all claim to divine consideration. The salvation of any was therefore an act of superhuman mercy; it could be justified only by the sacrifice Christ had made on the cross. Christ had died for the elect. While "the whole human race perished in the person of Adam," Christ, the sole mediator, had, through his death, taken away "penalty and guilt"[60] from some.

The psychological and social consequences of this doctrine were not apathy but incessant labor, not heedless sinning but austerity; far from drawing lessons of despair or libertinism, Calvinists drew instead incentives for strenuous efforts and a sturdy (it seemed, to their many adversaries, smug) self-confidence. The reason for this perhaps surprising result lay in Calvin's conception of outward signs. Not even Calvin was arrogant enough to claim that he and his followers were definitely saved. But it seemed at least highly probable. While no one could be certain of his own, or anyone else's, fate, there were indications, divinely bestowed hints, on which men could place some reliance. To lead a sober Christian life, work hard, dress quietly, eschew giddy entertainments, worship God in the correct—that is to say, the Calvinist—manner, was to confirm, as much as mere mortals could confirm, one's sense of being among the elect. Calvin's social and religious thought here join: man could be godly in his worldly calling, in his profession as a merchant, quite as much as a minister was godly in his preaching.

As historians have not failed to note, in the effort to turn Geneva into a city of saints, Calvin made it into something of an armed camp. As a Humanist, Calvin respected literature and the arts, but he was wholly without patience for a life of pleasure or self-indulgence. From the beginning he insisted that the community must control the moral life of Genevans in the most minute detail and guarantee observance of the orthodox faith in the most rigid fashion. As his power grew, the association of ministers, the consistory, followed his lead. The reports of repression sound like tendentious stories invented by Calvin's enemies, but they are fully documented. The consistory disciplined Genevans for dancing, for making noise or laughing during divine service, for speaking out on touchy issues (one Genevan was penalized for complaining that the influx of French refugees had raised the cost of living, another for objecting to the death penalty imposed on religious dissenters), or even for owning a copy of the romance *Amadis of Gaul.*[61] Calvin might have to contend with a

---

[60] *Institutes of the Christian Religion*, II, 6, 1; and III, 4, 30; ed. John T. McNeill (1960), 340, 657.
[61] For these and similar cases see Wendel, *Calvin*, 84, and Williston Walker, *John Calvin: The Organizer of Reformed Protestantism* (1906), 304 ff.

recalcitrant city government—despite his reputation as a dictator he always found vigorous local opposition—but at least he could act with a high hand against moral offenders and theological dissenters. His reign in Geneva is punctuated by acts of repression, at least unpleasant and at worst tyrannical. After a long controversy in the mid-1540s, Calvin succeeded in procuring the expulsion of the French reformer Sebastian Castellio with whom he had become embroiled over the canonical status of the Song of Songs. Far grimmer was the case of the Spaniard Michael Servetus, a provocative, somewhat unbalanced religious radical who professed antitrinitarian views as offensive to the Calvinists as they were to the Roman Catholics to whom they were originally addressed. In 1553, seeking refuge, Servetus made the mistake of entering Genevan territory. He behaved as offensively as he could; he was arrested at Calvin's instigation, tried for blasphemy at Calvin's urging, and put to death with Calvin's approval, though at the end Calvin objected to the mode of executing Servetus—burning alive—in vain. The incident shows, if it shows anything, that Calvin's hold over his city was not complete even as late as 1553, and it shows, also, that Calvin was a man of his day.

Calvinism for Export

Despite all this, and partly because of all this, Calvinism was a faith with a future, and not in Geneva alone. Geneva was deluged with Protestants from all across Europe, curious scholars and desperate refugees, from Scotland and Poland, France and England, the Netherlands and Germany. When they returned home, they were fired with the determination to make other Genevas. In 1559, the bishop of Winchester spoke for chagrined Roman Catholics everywhere: "The wolves be coming out of Geneva and other places of Germany," he said, "and have sent their books before, full of pestilent doctrines, blasphemy and heresy to infect the people." [62] Wherever else the Protestant wolves might come from, Geneva was evidently first, and worst. Thucydides had proudly called Athens the school of Greece; John Knox, the great Scottish Calvinist, proudly called Geneva "the most perfect school of Christ that ever was on earth since the days of the Apostles." [63]

One influential source of Calvinist instruction was Calvin's masterpiece, *The Institutes of the Christian Religion*. With its lucid Latin and perspicuous organization, it found many grateful readers. In 1541, Calvin himself translated the second edition into French, thus greatly enlarging its public, and the definitive version of 1559, also in Latin, was immediately translated as well. The second source was the example of the Calvinist community, sober, self-

---

[62] Quoted from J. E. Neale, *Elizabeth I and Her Parliaments* (1953), 57, by J. H. Elliott, *Europe Divided, 1559-1598* (1968), 31-32.
[63] Quoted in Hurstfield, *Reformation Crisis*, 43.

respecting, dominated by preachers and merchants and craftsmen confident in their calling; here was a community at once pious and worldly, a model to those who wanted to follow Christ without quite turning their backs on Mammon. Finally, there was the Calvinist church organization; it had a definite shape in Geneva itself, but Calvin, in his discussions and correspondence with foreigners, showed himself reasonable and flexible: he was persuaded that local differences might require differences in structure. It has often been observed, and with justice, that while Calvinism was far from democratic in its political and ecclesiastical ideas, it promoted, however indirectly, the progress of democracy. While Calvin himself sought to convert Geneva into a theocracy, his doctrine that church and state govern separate spheres induced, in many Calvinist communities, a congregational system, in which the church members chose their ministers and in which the ministers were subject, in worldly matters, to the magistrates. These were local variations which Calvin himself sanctioned and encouraged.

But there was one respect in which Calvinism survived and flourished abroad not because it obeyed, but because it abandoned, Calvin's explicit teachings—in the area of political theory. Calvin himself had taught passive obedience. The exceptions to his severe injunction, duly recorded in his *Institutes,* were so exceptional as to be, for Calvin himself, almost meaningless. In a political order equipped with magistrates whose explicit duty it was to resist tyranny, such resistance was permissible. And there might be an inspired individual, obeying God's direction, overthrowing the tyrant. But in general, men must bear even the infidel—only God should punish the wicked king. This was an obvious political theory for a party in power; Calvinists in a minority position must revise this theory or perish. They chose to revise it: John Knox in Scotland and a series of Calvinist writers in France laid down the conditions under which resistance to the wicked king was not merely permitted but commanded. This tenacious will to live was among Calvinism's most appealing traits.

THE ENGLISH REFORMATION

The Dynastic Issue

On the Continent, the Reformation began with religion and ended in politics; in England, it began with politics and ended in religion. In 1509, when Henry VIII ascended the throne to succeed his father, Henry VII, Lollard piety, Erasmian philosophy, and popular anticlericalism were in the air; they were soon joined, first by Lutheran, then by Calvinist, heresies. Doubtless these religious forces would have compelled some form of rebellion against Rome in

England, but the English Reformation took its particular course because the king of England wanted—needed—a divorce.

Henry VIII is a curious, and remains a controversial, figure. Profligate, lecherous, cultivated but not civilized, eager to govern but impatient with the routine of administration, imprudently militant in foreign affairs, and incapable of sustaining frustration, he was nevertheless thoroughly alert to his situation. He was the second of a disputed line, heir to a throne his father had usurped, and his primary concern was to sustain the Tudor dynasty. For this purpose he needed a son, but his queen, Catherine of Aragon, the victim of repeated disasters—miscarriages, stillbirths, infants dying—had given him only a daughter, Mary. It was, Henry feared, not good enough. He was not above toying with Lutheran ideas and negotiating with Lutheran leaders to frighten Catholic clerics from whom he wished to extract concessions. But he was not a Lutheran or any kind of Protestant. Indeed, in 1521 he published a polemic against Luther in defense of the Catholic sacraments, for which the Pope granted him and his successors the title of *defensor fidei.* [64] The irony is too obvious to have gone unnoticed: whatever Protestantism was to come to England would come against his intentions. Next to the Renaissance popes, Henry VIII of England was the most effective unwitting agent the Reformation had.

When Henry married Catherine in 1509, he had earlier obtained a papal dispensation, for his chosen wife was the widow of his brother Arthur, a marital union explicitly forbidden in the Old Testament. It had been a strictly political choice: Henry VII had insisted on it because he was intent on retaining the Spanish dowry and the Spanish alliance for England. As Catherine failed and failed to produce a viable heir to the throne, the grim prohibition of Leviticus seemed nothing less than prophetic: "If a man takes his brother's wife, it is impurity; he has uncovered his brother's nakedness, they shall be childless." [65] It is naive to suppose that Henry wanted a divorce because he wanted to gratify his lust; as he had repeatedly demonstrated during his marriage, he did not need a divorce for that. He was brooding over his dynasty, and he came to regard Catherine's tribulations as divine punishment. Accordingly, in 1527 he applied to Pope Clement VII for a dispensation; the marriage that one pope had legitimized, another pope was now to dissolve.

Clement was in a difficult position. There was no question of his competence in the matter; it was common practice to release the powerful and the rich from marriages that did not suit them. But the pope was in the hands of Charles V, and Catherine of Aragon was the emperor's niece and under his

---

[64] He published, but did not write it by himself. "There is not much proof that the King had either learning or leisure enough to produce the *Assertio Septem Sacramentorum Adversus Martin Lutherum.* It is probable that the royal author had considerable assistance from More, Fisher and Lee and that the texts of Scripture, the linguistic evidence from Hebrew and Greek, the patristic citations and much of the argument were supplied by others" (E. G. Rupp, *Studies in the Making of the English Protestant Tradition* [1947], 90).

[65] Lev. 20:21; Revised Standard Version.

protection. Thus Cardinal Wolsey, Henry's much-feared, much-hated chief minister maneuvered and remonstrated in vain: the pope delayed and prevaricated. Henry lost his patience and Wolsey his post, and in November 1529, Parliament met to encompass at home what the king had failed to obtain abroad. The legislation that the Reformation Parliament passed in its long existence—it met in numerous protracted sessions until 1536—was like an avalanche, moving less by a deliberate plan than by its own growing momentum. Down to 1532, its acts were mostly directed at controlling the English clergy and intimidating the pope. Then Anne Boleyn, Henry's long-time mistress, became pregnant. In April 1533, Thomas Cranmer, recently appointed archbishop of Canterbury and one of the king's most assiduous servants, became the last court of appeal in clerical matters—the tie with Rome was loosened. And in May Cranmer gave the king what Clement had refused: he annulled Henry's marriage to Catherine. In June, Anne was crowned queen of England, and in September she gave birth. It was a girl: Elizabeth. But Henry persevered in his course. In 1534 he induced Parliament, astutely managed by Thomas Cromwell, to pass a whole series of enactments culminating in the Act of Supremacy which laid down that the king of England "is and ought to be the supreme head of the Church of England."[66] There was scattered, but only scattered, resistance: the two most prominent Englishmen to refuse to take the oath of supremacy—Sir Thomas More and John Fisher, bishop of Rochester—were beheaded in 1535. The king was supreme in more than name.

In 1536, Henry demonstrated this supremacy by adopting a policy profitably pursued on the Continent by princes won over to Protestantism: he expropriated the monasteries. In the previous year Cromwell had ordered inquiries into the financial position and the moral conduct of the English church, and to no one's surprise, he found what he was seeking and what he did not find he invented. Using the revelations as a convenient pretext, the king had about four hundred smaller monasteries dissolved, and in the next three years, in gradual but rapid steps, he put his hands on the larger houses. Monks were pensioned off, many of the nuns found husbands, abbots and priors obtained often lucrative posts in the English church. But the ultimate social consequences of the dissolutions were vast and unforeseen; they far transcended the shift of some ten thousand regular clergy from one place, or post, to another. The dissolution eliminated centers of resistance to royal policy and gave the crown undreamed-of wealth. Wasting his substance in splendor, gifts, and war, Henry could not hold on to what he had grasped, and in the end the Crown was as dependent on Parliament for supplies as before. But between 1536 and 1547, the year of Henry's death, he had realized more than £1.5 million from the sale of church properties.[67] The most far-reaching consequence of the dissolution, however, was its aid in creating and fostering a class

---

[66] See S. T. Bindoff, *Tudor England* (1950), 95.
[67] Ibid., 114.

of middling landed proprietors, the gentry. The courtiers and speculators who acquired church lands in the earliest distributions rapidly sold them, chiefly to prosperous farmers and younger sons of country gentlemen.[68] Thus the Henrician dissolution produced a subterranean social revolution that its author had not foreseen and would hardly have liked.

The Infiltration of Protestantism

It was obvious to all but Henry VIII that he could not for long contain, let alone throttle, the religious revolution he had unloosed. To deny the supremacy of the pope, to erase the monasteries and nunneries after first thoroughly maligning them, to conduct talks with Luther and Melanchthon, and to marry again and again for an impressive total of six marriages, was to act like anything but a Catholic king, to give public support to antipapal passions, and awaken the impression that the king of England was in company with rebellious Protestant princes on the Continent.[69] Such conduct could only give English reformers a certain measure of hope.

Henry did his best to disappoint it. He made it painfully clear that while he had departed from Rome he had little intention of departing from the Catholic faith. True, he responded violently to Catholic unrest. In 1536, in Lincolnshire and Yorkshire and the whole northeast of England, a mixture of parochial resistance to London and nostalgia for medieval monasticism produced a confused and short-lived series of risings, the Pilgrimage of Grace, which the government repressed with little difficulty; the rebels' leader, Robert Aske, was executed in 1537 despite a royal promise of pardon—Henry was nothing if not unscrupulous. But on the other side and, to the king, just as alarming, there was a marked drift toward Protestantism: powerful public figures like Thomas Cromwell and Thomas Cranmer found themselves in sympathy with Luther's teachings. English Bibles, tendentiously translated by William Tyndale and Miles Coverdale and pointedly patronized by Cromwell and Cranmer, became influential agents in the dissemination of Protestant

---

[68] See David Knowles, *The Religious Orders in England,* vol. III, *The Tudor Age* (1961), 399.

[69] Henry's six marriages were more than a tragicomedy, although they were also that. They were part of the great political and religious struggle that went on in his realm during his long reign. In 1536, after she had had a stillbirth, Anne Boleyn was tried for adultery (on trumped-up charges, it would seem) and beheaded. Henry's third wife, Jane Seymour, finally gave him the son he longed for, Edward, but she died in bearing him. Free to marry again, Henry this time chose (or was persuaded by his chief minister, Thomas Cromwell, to choose) for diplomatic reasons. Anne of Cleves, daughter of the duke of Cleves, was the symbol of a Protestant alliance against the powerful Catholic Emperor Charles V, but Henry found Anne distasteful and the alliance unprofitable, and so he divorced his fourth wife soon after marrying her, in 1540. Cromwell, the architect of the king's Protestant policy, fell with the divorce and was executed shortly after. Catherine Howard, Henry's fifth wife, marked the decline of the Protestant faction and the rise of the Catholic clan of Norfolk, but when Henry had her executed in 1542 for "treasonable unchastity," this meant the end of the "conservatives." Henry's final marriage, to Catherine Parr, a devout and moderate Protestant, was peaceful and lasting—Catherine had the unique experience of outliving her dangerous husband.

ideas. The king liked none of it; in the early 1530s a few of the Cambridge reformers and a number of hapless Anabaptists were burned at the stake, and in 1539, at the king's insistence, Parliament passed the Act of Six Articles. It was uncompromisingly Catholic. It declared transubstantiation, mass in one kind, celibacy for the clergy, the vow of chastity, and auricular confession to be the belief and practice of all Englishmen and threatened to enforce those doctrines with savage penalties. Anyone caught denying transubstantiation was to be burned at the stake and have his property confiscated, with no pardon for recantation. [70] But Henry VIII was a king of England before he was a champion of orthodoxy; in his last years he proceeded cautiously against Protestant dissent and protected Cranmer, for all his Lutheran leanings, against his vocal enemies. The Protestants moved ahead cautiously, in private Bible readings, in discussions about a new prayer book, awaiting their opportunity.

It came in 1547, with Edward VI, Henry's son by Jane Seymour. Edward was ten at his accession and had been raised, on his father's command, by distinguished reformers. Like all minorities, Edward's short reign—the young king died in 1553—was marred by the jockeying of great families greedy for power. The king's first protector, the duke of Somerset, held control until 1549 when he was supplanted and eventually brought to the scaffold by his rival, the earl of Warwick. [71] But neither the political squabbles of the magnates nor Warwick's short-lived return to the repressive policies of Henry VIII slowed down the impetus of the reformers. Among Somerset's first acts was the repeal of Henry's treason laws, the Six Articles, and of all restrictions on the dissemination of the English Bible. Cranmer, now a little freer to maneuver, cautiously imposed a new service on all English churches; in the following year, somewhat more boldly, he got Parliament to accept a new *Booke of the common prayer and administracion of the Sacramentes, and other rites and ceremonies of the Church after the use of the Churche of England.* Imposed on the country, and then drastically revised in 1552 to catch up with the revolutionary reformist mood of much of the country, the Book of Common Prayer, even in its celebrated second version, remains typical of the Anglican attitude toward doctrinal questions: majestic and memorable in tone, it was conveniently obscure about important doctrinal details, claiming to be truly Catholic while incorporating many significant features of the Protestant revolt on the Continent. The austere monopoly of that book was part of the great dismantling of Catholic observances that characterized Edward's short reign: Catholic images and books were ordered destroyed, the service was given new simplicity, the mass was translated into communion, priests were transformed from vessels of grace into appointed officials. All was still flux; the building of Anglicanism, still incomplete, was on its way to completion. But Edward was dying, and after a mad, abortive scheme to substitute Jane Grey for Mary Tudor predictably

---

[70] See Dickens, *English Reformation*, 177.
[71] Warwick is perhaps better known by the title he acquired in 1551, as the duke of Northumberland.

failed, Mary became queen of England, and the course of the English
Reformation was dramatically reversed.

From Mary to Elizabeth

In company with other celebrated epithets, the name Bloody Mary, bestowed
on Mary Tudor in pure hatred, is only three quarters deserved. Protestant
propagandists aside, historians agree that Mary was kindly in her personal life
and on numerous occasions generous with mortal enemies. But like her half-
brother, she brought her education into her reign and, being the proud
daughter of Catherine of Aragon, she was half Spanish and all Catholic. And
unlike her father she acted from religious rather than political principles—she
was doctrinaire rather than flexible. Her own father-in-law, Charles V, who
married her to his son Philip in 1554, disapproved of the persecutions she
unloosed on her realm: as Catholic as Mary, but more politic, he distrusted a
policy that would divide and weaken a country that could be useful to him.

Heedless and pious, Mary persecuted the Protestants with all the calm
confidence of a believer doing the Lord's work. By the end of 1554, her
Parliaments had repealed the reform legislation[72] enacted by Henry VIII and
Edward VI, while her distant kinsman, Cardinal Reginald Pole, returned to
England as papal legate bringing the pope's absolution with him. Her
Parliament under control, her political enemies dead, her predecessor's spiritual
guides in the Tower, Mary could now undertake her purification in all earnest.
Cranmer and other Protestant bishops died by burning, disdaining to take
flight; about three hundred others, most of them humble workmen and
artisans, some sixty of them women, died with them, for the most part with
exemplary courage, stubbornly loyal to their heresies and saying memorable
things at the stake. Around eight hundred Protestants fled abroad, settling in
Frankfurt, in Strasbourg, in Geneva, to celebrate the English martyrs, hammer
out their theological doctrines, and quarrel with one another.

To our century, stained by vaster horrors, the number of Mary's victims
seems modest. The persecution was, in fact, too small to eradicate Protestantism in England.[73] But what made it so notorious, what gave Mary her
unenviable epithet, was its solitary prominence in the queen's policy. She
seemed untouched by the Catholic spirituality burgeoning abroad in response
to the Protestant challenge; her burnings at the stake were unaccompanied by
any inner fire that might rekindle traditional Catholic religion in England. Men
might be intimidated by the threat of the stake; it did not turn them into fervent
believers. Besides, the queen found herself powerless to reverse the policy that

---

[72] For the single exception, the land settlement, see p. 155.

[73] In the century and a quarter before 1529, some one hundred Lollards had been burned for
their religion; in the first twenty years of the English Reformation, the figure was sixty; and during
Elizabeth's reign there were about two hundred Roman Catholic victims. The rate of executions was
thus noticeably higher. For the figures, see Bindoff, *Tudor England*, 177.

had despoiled the monasteries under her father. No effort on her part could induce Parliament to return the church lands to their original owners. It was technically impossible to trace properties to their original owners, and in any event present owners would give up nothing. With his dissolution of the monasteries Henry had, without wishing it, given thousands a stake in Reformed England. And finally, by burning some Protestants and allowing others to escape, Mary gave those others a rich opportunity for celebrating the martyrs she had made. In 1559, the year after Mary's death, John Foxe, one of the exiles, published a Latin account of the sufferings his fellow Protestants had undergone; in 1563, he published the first English version of his *Actes and Monumentes*. It became widely known as Foxe's Book of Martyrs and remained for many years the most popular book—for some people, aside from the Bible, the only book—they read. [74] In the course of her reign, Mary had made herself generally hateful with her Spanish marriage even among those whom the persecutions left indifferent. After her death, Foxe, with his lurid woodcuts, his circumstantial, stirring reports of the burnings, and his placement of the Marian interlude amidst the eternal struggle between God and the devil, made Mary into a byword of satanic cruelty. Her reputation helped to determine English policies for centuries after. With such an enemy, Protestantism scarcely needed a friend.

Still, English Protestants were delighted to see Mary die in 1558; the bonfires they lit in the streets were perhaps as much for her disappearance as for the advent of her half-sister, Anne Boleyn's daughter. Elizabeth's precise religious position was unknown—it still is—and she had good military and diplomatic reasons for proceeding with caution. Her very hold on the throne was uncertain and needed to be secured. She was a woman and (at least Catholics professed to believe and soon began to murmur) of illegitimate birth. But there was no doubt that her accession would make the Marian return to Rome a mere interlude. In 1559, she moved, and by 1563, the shape of what has come to be called the Elizabethan Settlement had emerged. The English crown was "the only supreme governor" in ecclesiastical as well as temporal matters. [75] The exiles had come home, not, it turned out, to be quiet but to agitate for the purification of the Anglican church and to eradicate from it all traces of what appeared to them, not without justice, Roman beliefs and practices. In 1563, a convocation passed the Thirty-Nine Articles of the Church of England; they

[74] Foxe is one of the first beneficiaries of printing to celebrate its vast merits: "The Lord began to work for His Church not with sword and target to subdue His exalted adversary, but with printing, writing and reading. . . . How many printing presses there be in the world, so many blockhouses there be against the high castle of St. Angelo, so that either the pope must abolish knowledge and printing or printing at length will root him out" (quoted in William Haller, *The Elect Nation: The Meaning and Relevance of Foxe's Book of Martyrs* [1963], 110).

[75] Note that Henry VIII had proclaimed himself "the only supreme head" rather than "governor." "This qualitative difference in the wording, be it noted, sacrificed nothing of the substance of power, but it was intended to soften the impact of the measure on the catholic conscience, and to make the transference of ecclesiastical power to the Crown as little obtrusive as possible" (J. B. Black, *The Reign of Elizabeth, 1558–1603* [2nd ed., 1959], 16).

became the law of the land eight years later—Elizabeth was the most circumspect of monarchs. This statement of Anglican belief has often been called ambiguous. The charge is true but the ambiguity was deliberate; it was designed to invite as large a number of Englishmen as possible to join the Anglican communion. Ambiguity was an act of statesmanship, a typical expression of Elizabeth's canny political sense. It was typical as well for the time, a time of groping for settlements that would make the stake and the hangman unnecessary. Yet it was not wholly a success. Far too many Englishmen, including a variety of Puritans and permanently disgruntled English Catholics, wanted only clarity. As Elizabeth would discover in her long and glorious reign (see p. 183), for the truly devout, compromise was at best unacceptable, at worst the work of the devil.

SELECTED READINGS

The preconditions for the religious revolution are set out in a variety of studies. Paul Vignaux, *Philosophy in the Middle Ages: An Introduction* (1959), and G. G. Coulton, *Studies in Medieval Thought* (1940), are two of many volumes exploring the medieval background. To these should be added Meyrick H. Carré, *Realists and Nominalists* (1946); David Knowles, *The English Mystical Tradition* (1961); and Heiko Augustinus Oberman, *The Harvest of Medieval Theology: Gabriel Biel and Late Medieval Nominalism* (1963). The prehistory of the German Reformation can be followed in Ulrich von Hutten and others, "Letters of Obscure Men," collected in *On the Eve of the Reformation* (tr. 1909 and ed. 1964, with an introduction by Hajo Holborn). From the Roman Catholic point of view, Philip Hughes, *The Revolt Against the Church: Aquinas to Luther* (1947), says the essential.

Among many general treatments of the Reformation, see above all, Owen Chadwick, *The Reformation* (1964); A. G. Dickens, *Reformation and Society in Sixteenth-Century Europe* (1966); G. R. Elton, ed., *The Reformation, 1520–1559* (1958), the second volume in *The New Cambridge Modern History*; and Elton, *Reformation Europe, 1517–1559* (1963). Hans J. Hillerbrand, ed., *The Protestant Reformation* (1968), is a judicious collection of documents; Joel Hurstfield, ed., *The Reformation Crisis* (1965), has some helpful essays. H. G. Koenigsberger and G. L. Mosse, *Europe in the Sixteenth Century* (1968), though a general text, has some excellent chapters on the Reformation. E. Harris Harbison, *The Christian Scholar in the Age of the Reformation* (1956), lucidly surveys Luther, Calvin, and other leading thinkers. The old study by Karl Holl, *The Cultural Significance of the Reformation* (tr. 1959), retains its value. See also J. S. Whale, *The Protestant Tradition* (1955). From a Roman Catholic perspective, see especially Josef Lortz, *How the Reformation Came* (1964), and Philip Hughes, *A Popular History of the Reformation* (1957).

Martin Luther has attracted numerous biographers. Roland H. Bainton, *Here I Stand: A Life of Martin Luther* (1962), is comprehensive, but neglects Luther's connections with the apocalyptic tradition. Heinrich Boehmer, *Martin Luther: Road to Reformation* (tr. 1946), treats the young Luther in detail, as does E. G. Rupp, *The Progress of Luther to the Diet of Worms* (1951), and, from a psychoanalytical perspective, Erik H. Erikson, *Young Man Luther: A Study in Psychoanalysis and History* (1958). A. G. Dickens, *Martin Luther and the Reformation* (1967), is short and excellent.

So is V. H. H. Green, *Luther and the Reformation* (1964). Lucien Febvre's biography, first published in 1929, repays reading. So does the fine biography by Ernest B. Schwiebert, *Luther and His Times* (1950). Hajo Holborn, *A History of Modern Germany*, vol. I, *The Reformation* (1959), places Luther into his age and his times. Clyde Leonard Man-schreck, *Melanchthon, The Quiet Reformer* (1958), ably sums up the career of Luther's powerful associate. It should be read in conjunction with Lewis Spitz, *The Religious Renaissance of the German Humanists* (1963). For the radical German reformation, see Hajo Holborn's biography, *Ulrich von Hutten and the German Reformation* (tr. 1937); George H. Williams, *The Radical Reformation* (1962), a massive treatise; and Franklin H. Littell, *The Anabaptist View of the Church* (1958). Norman Cohn, *The Pursuit of the Millennium* (rev. ed., 1964), begins with the Middle Ages, but does much with extremists in the sixteenth century.

For the Swiss reformers the literature is less ample than for Luther, but ample enough. S. M. Jackson, *Huldreich Zwingli* (1901), is now old but remains important; Oskar Farmer, *Zwingli, The Reformer* (1952), is a skimpy condensation of an authoritative biography available in German in three volumes (1943, 1946, 1960). For Bucer, see Hastings Eells, *Martin Bucer* (1931). The best modern biography of Calvin is François Wendel, *Calvin: The Origins and Development of His Religious Thought* (tr. 1963). R. N. Carew Hunt, *John Calvin* (1933), is also worth reading. The early chapters of John Thomas McNeill, *The History and Character of Calvinism* (1954), are relevant here. For Calvin's state, see William Monter, *Calvin's Geneva* (1966), and Robert Kingdon's important monograph, *Geneva and the Coming of the Wars of Religion in France, 1555–1563* (1956). For Calvin's victim, Servetus, see Roland H. Bainton, *Hunted Heretic: The Life and Death of Michael Servetus* (1953). John Calvin and Jacopo Sadoleto, *A Reformation Debate* (ed. John C. Olin, 1966), is an interesting document.

The history of the English Reformation begins with the dynastic issue. Among many general histories of the period, S. T. Bindoff, *Tudor England* (1950), is crisp and accurate. See also F. M. Powicke, *The Reformation in England* (1941). Garrett Mattingly, *Catherine of Aragon* (1942), is an elegant biography that reaches wider and deeper than its ostensible subject. G. R. Elton, *The Tudor Revolution in Government: Administrative Changes in the Reign of Henry VIII* (1959), is controversial but useful. Among general surveys, A. G. Dickens, *The English Reformation* (1964), is masterly. To this one may add E. G. Rupp, *Studies in the Making of the English Protestant Tradition* (1947), which concentrates on the reign of Henry VIII. For that ruler, we are fortunate in two recent biographies: the general account by J. J. Scarisbrick, *Henry VIII* (1968), and the penetrating psychological study by Lacey Baldwin Smith, *Henry VIII: The Mask of Royalty* (1971). Another approach to the English Reformation is through the leading figures (normally the victims) of Henry's reign. See Jasper Ridley, *Thomas Cranmer* (1962); A. G. Dickens, *Thomas Cromwell and the English Reformation* (1959); and above all Raymond Wilson Chambers, *Thomas More* (1958). Among a large literature on More, see J. H. Hexter, *More's "Utopia": The Biography of an Idea* (1952). David Knowles, *The Religious Orders in England*, vol. III, *The Tudor Age* (1961), deals authoritatively with the dissolution of the monasteries. James Kelsey McConica, *English Humanists and Reformation Politics* (1965), is a general account. Christopher Morris, *Political Thought in England: Tyndale to Hooker* (1953), surveys the ideas dominating English politics in the critical decades, while William Haller, *The Elect Nation: The Meaning and Relevance of Foxe's Book of Martyrs* (1963), brilliantly treats English Protestants under Bloody Mary.

4

Dominance and Decline of Spain

EUROPE AFTER THE REFORMATION

A Moment of Settlement and Regrouping

The Europe of 1560 was a Europe at peace. The diplomatic and religious settlements that ended half a century of fighting among and within states were little better than truces, soon to be broken by bigger and better conflicts. But especially in the sphere of religion, these settlements represented the dawning of an awareness—no more—that all attempts at reunion were bound to fail, that Protestants and Catholics, Calvinists and Lutherans, would have to learn to live together in some fashion. Many rulers and statesmen continued to act in defiance of this insight; many whose profession it was to preach the true religion would insist that the truth could survive only if falsehood were extirpated. But their failures in the next decades would prove that the pose of crusader was outmoded, the time of crusades, over. The Spaniards would be the last to know this.

The Spaniards' tenacious desire to impose Catholic uniformity on their world reflected their particular national and religious experience and their powerful position in Europe. The Treaty of Cateau-Cambrésis, concluded in 1559, ratified Spanish victories on the diplomatic and military battlefield. It settled, or at least controlled, the endemic warfare between Europe's two greatest dynasties, Hapsburg and Valois. It put an end to France's Italian ambitions for two centuries and a half, until the advent of Napoleon Bonaparte. Francis I had been badly beaten at Pavia in 1525, and checked in 1529 by the Treaty of Cambrai (see p. 116), but to the end of his reign in 1547, he had made intermittent forays against Hapsburg possessions in the Italian peninsula. The slightest pretext, the smallest opportunity, mobilized French troops and French greed: in 1536, Francis I had managed to take and hold Savoy and Piedmont. His son and successor, Henri II, continued the anti-Hapsburg policy, mainly in Germany. But while an exhausted Spain went bankrupt in 1557, France, just as bankrupt, was even more exhausted, and Cateau-Cambrésis mirrored their respective resources. While the French held on to the imperial cities of Toul, Metz, and Verdun, which they had occupied in 1552, they conceded to Spain continued control over its Italian territories, evacuated Piedmont, and left the Spaniards in possession of Franche-Comté.[1] Thus the Spanish Hapsburgs, closely allied with the Austrian Hapsburgs, straddled Europe while France was left weakened and confined.

Emperor Charles V, in many respects the architect of Cateau-Cambrésis, did not live to see his triumph. Aged beyond his years and excessively disheartened, he had abdicated his many posts in 1555 and 1556, retired to the country in Spain, and died there in 1558. Charles was a tragic figure, a missionary for two anachronisms—universal empire and universal Catholicism. He was intelligent without being brilliant, impressive solely by an act of will, ridden with his duty, and imbued with his imperial destiny. The very size of his empire worked against him: it was too large, too diverse, to be kept easily under control, and his enemies were too numerous and too formidable to be permanently kept down. As a Hapsburg, Charles held Spain, the Netherlands, Naples and Milan, and the Austrian lands; as emperor, he held the Germanies. Hence he had to fight everyone: the Ottomans on the eastern frontier, rebellious coalitions of German states, restive Spaniards who thought him a Burgundian foreigner, to say nothing of France. The way Charles disposed of his dominions in 1555–1556 (he handed his Spanish possessions to his son, Philip II, and the imperial lands to his brother, Ferdinand I) suggests that he had become aware just how unmanageable his sprawling domains were.

Among the most intractable problems of Charles' beleaguered reign was the German problem, which was, in large part, a Protestant problem. Intermit-

---

[1] The Treaty of Cateau-Cambrésis also included an agreement between France and England under which the French would keep Calais, England's last continental foothold, which the French had retaken in Mary Tudor's reign.

tently, Charles offered concessions German Protestants deeply desired—the communion in both kinds and the right of priests to marry—but by about 1540 he recognized that his attempts at conciliation did not appease the Protestants and only aroused devout Catholics against him. From that time on he schemed to close out his wars elsewhere that he might crush German resistance. By 1546 he was ready. In a short war, ending in 1547, he easily defeated the Schmalkaldic League (see p. 145). But his victory was inconclusive. While it weakened the military and political power of German states for a time, it left Protestant inroads unaffected: neither the defeated states nor those Protestant states that did not belong to the league returned to Catholicism. The great banking firm, the Fuggers, who had helped to elect Charles with enormous loans in 1519, now warned that their patience with him was wearing thin. And in 1552, when war flared up again in Germany, he had insufficient resources to win it. Significantly, Charles' Protestant enemies had Roman Catholic allies, among them Henri II of France, proving, if further proof be needed, that religion was no longer the sole determinant of a nation's foreign policy.[2] At last, reluctantly, Charles agreed to the Diet of Augsburg in 1555, which produced a far-reaching religious settlement. The Peace of Augsburg granted each Lutheran and Catholic prince the right to determine the religion of his own country, a policy later summarized in a famous Latin phrase: *cuius regio, eius religio.* True, the peace excluded the Calvinists and included pious hopes of fostering religious unity in the German lands. But in effect, claiming to be a step to unity, the peace guaranteed the persistence of political and religious fragmentation in Germany for a long time to come. And there were forces in Roman Catholicism that would not accept the new religious realities as permanent.

Catholic Reform and Counter-Reformation[3]

Even before Martin Luther's rebellion there had been voices demanding institutional reforms in the Roman communion; after Luther's cause had proved indestructible, these voices redoubled in volume and anxiety. Urbane

[2] Francis I had made this painfully clear earlier, in the late 1520s, when he had negotiated and achieved a cordial understanding with the Ottomans, whose aid he wanted in his struggle against his fellow Catholic, Charles V.

[3] It is important to note that the very names historians use for this epoch are controversial. For Roman Catholic historians, the Protestant Reformation is the Protestant Revolt and the Catholic Counter-Reformation the Catholic Reformation. The implications of such names should be obvious: Roman Catholicism, they argue, was faced early in the sixteenth century with a major rebellion which was not a reform but a departure from the truth; and the efforts of Catholic rulers and ecclesiastics to bring order into their affairs was not a *counter*-reformation because it sprang from internal impulsions. We have retained the traditional names because they seem to us to do justice to the historical realities. Some recent historians have offered a useful terminological amendment: they speak of Catholic Reformation or Catholic reform when these internal reforms are in question, and use the old term Counter-Reformation when Catholic actions seem to be a response to Protestant pressures. We have adopted this device here. See G. R. Elton, *Reformation Europe, 1517-1559* (1963), 176-197; and J. H. Elliott, *Europe Divided, 1559-1598* (1968), 145-174.

disciples of Erasmus and strict followers of old, long-neglected vows alike pressed for an internal purification that would equip the faithful for battle with the Protestant rebels while leaving the essentials of the Roman theology and Roman hierarchy untouched. The urgency of reform was indeed obvious: Lutheranism was making inroads even in Italy; some old and some new heresies were gaining adherents among troubled and intelligent men; there was remarkably widespread interest in the radical antitrinitarian heresy of Socinianism (so-called after two Italians, Lelio Sozzini and Fausto Sozzini), which denied the divinity of Jesus. Beginning in 1522, with Adrian VI, the age of the Renaissance papacy was over; the new popes were more austere, more purposeful, than their flamboyant predecessors. True, during his long reign (1534–1549), Pope Paul III revived in some measure both worldliness and nepotism, but even he could not deny the call for reform; while he was intensely interested in advancing the fortunes of his family, he also appointed scholars and clerical reformers to the highest posts and sympathetically supervised their work.

Sincere as they were, the efforts at self-criticism and amendment were scarcely radical. The reformers were high-minded, hard-working, unimpeachably pious, and their notions conformed to their character: they were eager to cleanse the church of abuses but defensive in the face of heresy all about them. Their conservatism emerges plainly from one of the most famous documents the Catholic reform produced, the *Consilium de Emendanda Ecclesia*, a report published in 1537 by a commission that Paul III had appointed in the previous year. It included such distinguished men as Reginald Pole (see p. 158); Gasparo Contarini, a devout Venetian aristocrat, a diplomat of wide learning and generous spirit; and Gian Pietro Carafa, an energetic, fiercely aggressive cardinal whose later pontificate as Paul IV (1555–1559) was to mark a high point in the repressive Counter-Reformation. The rhetoric of the *Advice on Reforming the Church* was brave and bold; it pleased the Protestants enormously. It excoriated corruption, evil counselors, lazy priests, and profiteering bishops and did not exempt the papacy from its strictures. But beyond calling for an end to such abuses (and what candid churchman could do less?) the *Consilium* also called for the censorship of books, tight control over philosophical speculation, and elimination from the schools of such pernicious works as Erasmus' *Colloquia*. For these reformers freedom was as great a vice as corruption.

Purity, piety, and control, the governing themes of the *Consilium*, also were, or soon became, the moving forces behind the new orders that were to furnish the shock troops of the Counter-Reformation. The history of Roman Catholicism is dotted with the founding of new clerical orders and the decay and regeneration of old orders. While the picture was far from uniform, during the age of the Reformation religious orders were generally in disarray; the worldliness of the papacy had not left them untouched. Hence in the first years of the Catholic Reformation there was much doubt which policy would best advance the cause of purification: the creation of new or the suppression of old orders. [4] The enthusiasm, patience, and devotion of a few, driven by the fervent desire for a holy life and the accompanying desire to win others to it, wore down the skepticism of the popes and their advisors. Soon the few became many, and the first half of the sixteenth century saw the creation of several new orders destined to affect the religious history of Europe in the most profound way. All these orders had difficulty being accepted and accredited; conservative supporters of the old hierarchy saw them as dangerously independent, given to private interpretations of important doctrinal issues and possibly schismatic. Yet all of them managed to convince the authorities that their intention was pure, their faith correct, and their organization effective.

One of these new orders, the Capuchins, grew out of an older one, the Franciscans. Its founders, Italian priests, vowed to take St. Francis' precepts seriously, to live in absolute poverty and do charitable works. Founded in the 1520s, ridden with internal strife, and endangered in 1542 by the desertion of their superior, Bernardino Ochino, to the Lutherans, the Capuchins survived these trials to establish themselves as an independent order and, by the 1570s, to spread abroad from Italy. In contrast, the Theatine order was too strenuous and inward-looking to achieve the Capuchins' popularity: leading lives of intense piety, forming centers of exalted discussion, and doing works of difficult charity, the Theatine priestly communities remained a small elite of Catholic Puritans. [5] New as these orders were, the religious impulse that animated them was conservative: it was to restore an earlier unblemished ideal. Their institutional arrangements were also forced into a conservative pattern; thus the Ursuline community, founded in 1535 by and for women to lead lives of good works and exemplary piety in the world, was before long transformed into a regular order of nuns with habits and houses.

The most famous and most significant of the new orders was the Society of Jesus, founded not (like all the others) by an Italian, but by a Spaniard, Ignatius Loyola. [6] Born in 1491 into an aristocratic family, he led the life of the typical worldling—soldiering and womanizing—until he was laid low in 1521 by a painful, slow-healing leg wound received in battle. During his extensive and involuntary leisure he avidly read devotional books and experienced a religious conversion. When he emerged from his hospital bed he was an avowed servant of God. Loyola, who never did things by halves, prepared himself meticulously for his new vocation. He confessed his sins—as he said later, he had many sins to confess—and spent eight months buried in the small Catalonian town of Manresa, doing severe penance and having religious visions. His self-discipline became absolute; later he imposed the same discipline on others.

The earliest expression of Jesuit discipline dates from this period: the first

---

[4] See *The New Cambridge Modern History*, vol. II, *The Reformation, 1520-1559* (1958), 277.
[5] Ibid., 287.
[6] Loyola's original name was Don Inigo Lopez de Loyola; his origins were, strictly speaking, Basque.

draft of a handbook, the *Spiritual Exercises*, which Loyola periodically revised, put into final shape in 1541, and published in 1548, eight years before his death. "It is not a book to be read," Owen Chadwick has said. "If it is not used experimentally, it is nothing."[7] Its point is to train the mind, to direct attention to man's sinfulness, and, by contrast, to God's grace. From solitary, silent contemplation will come the decision to live for Christ, in total self-denial and total obedience. If the church teaches that white is black, the Jesuit must believe it. This phrase, all too famous, was unfortunate: designed to dramatize the need for absolute obedience, it instead gave generations of hostile critics the impression that Jesuits were a band of trained liars and sworn enemies of rationality—which is to say, a wrong impression.

Loyola was still groping. In 1523 he went to Jerusalem on a pilgrimage and sought to join the Franciscans, in vain. On his return to Barcelona, he considered various courses; ever alert and self-critical, he saw that he must first get the education he had neglected in his worldly days; he attended Spanish universities and then, in 1528, went to Paris, where he studied for seven years. It was there, in 1534, that he took a vow to live in poverty and chastity and to serve God wherever He should need him. Six of his disciples took the vow with him: Loyola, from his youth, had exercised charismatic power over men. Finally, in 1540, Pope Paul III, after some hesitation, established Loyola's band as the Society of Jesus. It was different from all other orders. Its sole head, the general, was chosen for life. Its members had to pass through several stages—a two-year novitiate, an indefinite period of training, the "scholasticate," and another one-year probationary period—before they were admitted to formal membership. Its purposes were to spread the word of Christ through missions, to counter the threat of Protestantism, and to serve as the educators of the young—this last, the least of Loyola's aims, actually became the most prominent as time went on. It produced an odd paradox: "No one could be less truly called a 'child of the Renaissance' than Ignatius who had early and decisively rejected the Erasmian outlook; but it was the Jesuits with their high academic standards in Latin and Greek who incorporated much of the scholarship and not a little of the humanistic spirit of the classical Renaissance into orthodox Catholic education."[8] Jesuits would educate much of Europe for over two centuries, including, in the eighteenth century, their wittiest and deadliest enemies (see p. 441). Their cultivation and urbanity throw serious doubts on the ubiquitous metaphor of the Jesuit "soldier of Christ." The Jesuits were not monastics, of course, and they took an active role in the world; but their rhetoric to the contrary, they were not military but militant.[9] Yet the

---

[7] Owen Chadwick, *The Reformation* (1964), 257.

• [8] H. O. Evennett, "The New Orders," in *The New Cambridge Modern History,* op. cit., 297.

[9] "Yet the conception of Jesuit obedience as essentially military is not the whole truth. The amount of care for individual temperaments which the constitutions specifically require to be shown by superiors, and which is exemplified in Ignatius's own skill in dealing with his subjects, is very remarkable, and many early Jesuits showed a truly Renaissance variety and independence of character within the society's prudent and elastic framework" (Evennett, "New Orders," 295-296).

Jesuits were, without doubt, energetic and highly visible. There were Jesuits at the shoulders of kings and chancellors, Jesuits on the ships that conquered distant territories, Jesuits on the frontiers of the Protestant North and in the midst of religiously divided lands. Unafraid of the world, seeking prominence, and always, in all things, fiercely loyal to the popes and their policies, they would gather unto themselves a special admiration and a concentrated hatred, neither of which they wholly deserved.

From Reform to Repression

As Catholic morale recovered from the first shocks of the Lutheran assault, the desire to extirpate dissent or to treat mere dissent as outright heresy recovered with it. The reform proposals of 1537, the Consilium (see p. 165), had shown the reformers in no way averse to censorship, but they had at least been willing to see the sources of Catholic distress in themselves. As time went by, the balance of policy shifted away from self-criticism to the suppression of others, from compromise to dogmatism, from reform to repression. To be sure, Lutherans, Calvinists, Anglicans were no less hostile to the idea of toleration than the Catholics: toleration implied, after all, that the doctrines of heretics might be correct or that the full truth was not known—two ideas that all but a handful of philosophers found unthinkable. But it was the Catholics who developed the best-known of all repressive agencies, the Inquisition. It alone became proverbial for its ruthlessness, its cruelty, its unrelieved bigotry.

The idea of an inquisition into belief, backed by the power to extract confessions of heresy, dates back to the great waves of Waldensian and Albigensian heresies in the twelfth and thirteenth centuries, but it was put on a regular footing in Spain, under Ferdinand and Isabella, in 1478 (see p. 104). It employed spies and informers, customary tortures, and unaccustomed pressures—endless delays, sowing of universal distrust, and the weapon of disgrace for whole families—to check on, and to check, suspected religious disloyalty among recent converts to the true faith, whether former Jews or Muslims. In 1542, upon the urging of Cardinal Carafa, a papal bull established an Inquisition in Rome, the Holy Office, which centralized all local tribunals under a single committee of six inquisitors-general, all cardinals. Carafa was among them. Its powers were extensive: they included the right to imprison suspects and to execute heretics. [10] Centralization of the Inquisition brought uniformity and effectiveness. It also brought control over publications. In 1543, Carafa listed books and publishers he thought dangerous, though it was not until 1559, while he held supreme power as Pope Paul IV, that the full-fledged Index, the notorious *Index Librorum Prohibitorum,* was inaugurated. It was to be often revised and republished, to keep up with new heresies; one of its entries

[10] Chadwick, *Reformation,* 269.

prohibited the reading of the *Consilium of 1537* in which Carafa had participated. [11]

The course of the Council of Trent, convened after many delays in 1545, testifies to the hardening of the Catholic position. Its calling was a victory of Charles V over a reluctant Paul III; the emperor hoped it might bring reform and, perhaps, accommodation with Protestantism; the pope feared it might mark a return to conciliarism and compromise with the devil. Both hopes and fears were groundless. In three protracted, often adjourned sessions—the council met from 1545 to 1547, 1551 to 1552, and 1562 to 1563—the Italian prelates, ably seconded by the Jesuits, dominated the proceedings. Except for pushing through some perfectly traditional resolutions against financial and organizational abuses, the reforming party was outgeneraled and outvoted on every point. When in January 1564 the Tridentine decrees were published, there was rejoicing among dogmatists everywhere: the Roman church had refused to compromise on any of its crucial doctrines—whether transubstantiation or the importance of works, the denial of private judgment or insistence on clerical celibacy—and, on the contrary, firmly reiterated and meticulously clarified the Catholic position on these and other points of doctrine, discipline, and organization. The papacy emerged stronger than ever, having now the added authority of conciliar confirmation. While there was some resistance in Spain and France to those provisions of the Tridentine decrees that seemed to infringe the rights of the crown over its churches, the confirmation of the old doctrine and the old church was welcome throughout all the Catholic territories. Religious reunion of Christendom was now impossible, and only two courses were open: a crusade to impose a single faith on the other half of Europe, or the decision to live together somehow, permanently divided.

SPAIN'S ASCENDANCY

During much of the sixteenth century, relations between Spain and the papacy were strained; they improved only in the 1560s, when common interests outweighed causes for conflict. Despite these strains, Spain never ceased to regard herself as the supreme fortress of Christendom; while at home the Spanish Inquisition solicitously shielded the faithful from the contamination of modern ideas, abroad Spain played the role of defender and disseminator of the true faith.

---

[11] See Elton, *Reformation Europe,* 189-192. The Protestants, it is worth repeating, had their own inquisitions into belief and their own lists of forbidden books, but the great variety of practice in the Protestant territories and the often decentralized organization of the churches permitted thought far greater latitude than it was to have in the Italy and the Spain of the Counter-Reformation.

The Spanish Overseas Empire

From the beginning of their overseas explorations (see p. 85) Spaniards had found their solemn religiosity a problem. To be the privileged bearers of the Christian message to the heathen was an excuse for imperialism, but it was also an obstacle—a cover for, but also a restraint on, cupidity. The Spanish conquerors were unused to manual labor and reluctant to do in the Caribbean what they would scorn to do in Aragon and Castile. Hence, on the West Indian islands discovered and settled by Columbus, they enlisted the Indian natives in a system of forced labor much like slavery—much, but not quite: it was disguised by a legal device called the *encomienda*, an adaptation of the Spanish experience with conquered territories on the Iberian peninsula. *Encomienda* was in legal theory a system of mutual obligation, a distant cousin of feudal relationships. The Spanish overlord, or *encomendero*, could exact labor and commodities from "his" Indians, and owed them in return military protection and religious instruction. There were pious Spaniards, including Queen Isabella herself, who insisted on decent treatment for Spain's new subjects,[12] but it can be imagined how little her instructions meant in remote territories. There, only the conquered were compelled to fulfill their side of the "bargain."

Equally grave, perhaps graver, problems of conscience arose when the Spaniards moved to the American mainland. In 1519, Hernando Cortes, the first and greatest of the Spanish *conquistadores*, began the conquest of Aztec Mexico. By 1520, the Aztec emperor, Montezuma II, was dead; by 1521, Mexico City was in Cortes' hands, and Mexico became not a foreign country to be conquered but a Spanish territory to be administered. Francisco Pizarro, after some unsuccessful attempts in the 1520s, reached Peru in the early 1530s and undertook the protracted "pacification" of the Inca empire. These conquests were extended romantic tales, glorious and terrible, in which fact rivals fiction. Like all men, the *conquistadores* were rent with inner contradictions; unlike other men, they gloried in them. Their mentalities had been shaped by romances, and their hunger for conquest overseas was sharpened by social and financial aspirations at home. Once in the Americas, they acted out a high drama of adventure in which piety and treachery, an unmeasured appetite for life and a reckless courtship of death, kindness and cruelty, high ideals and the most sordid scramble for profit, were curiously intermingled. "We came here," wrote Bernal Díaz del Castillo, historian and Cortes' friend, "to serve God and the king, and also to get rich."[13] When Cortes and his men encountered

---

[12] The good queen should not be sentimentalized. "Her condemnation of Indian slavery—a condemnation frequently cited by her modern admirers—" writes Charles Gibson, the leading modern authority on Spanish America, "was neither uncompromising nor disinterested. On a number of occasions the queen countenanced, and even demanded a share in, the trade of Indian captives as slaves" (*Spain in America* [1966], 51).

[13] Quoted by J. H. Elliott, *Imperial Spain 1469–1716* (1963), 53, from Lewis Hanke, *Bartolome de las Casas* (1951), 9.

Montezuma's envoys, they received the Indians' gifts with unmasked excitement: "When they were given these presents," one Indian contemporary reported, "the Spaniards burst into smiles. . . . They picked up the gold and fingered it like monkeys. . . . Their bodies swelled with greed, and their hunger was ravenous. They hungered like pigs for that gold." [14]

Their hunger was not always so unconcealed. The *conquistadores* carried with them a legal document much like an injunction, the *requerimiento,* which they were supposed to read aloud to the opposing Indians before battle. It is a classic in man's long history of rationalization: the Indians could usually not hear the reading of this "requirement," nor would they have understood it. But the mere reading of its provisions calmed the Spaniards' conscience. It enjoined the Indians to submit themselves to Spain, the papacy, and the Roman Catholic church; if they refused, the death and devastation that would follow were their own responsibility.

This was not all. The Spaniards settled and exploited the territories they conquered and, for the most part, though they supplemented the local pool of labor with black African slaves, they relied heavily on the natives to till the fields and work the mines. The *conquistadores* decisively subdued the native populations. They had weapons on which the Indians could look only with superstitious awe: firearms, horses, superb military discipline, seemingly unlimited self-confidence, and alcohol. Moreover, the empires that the Spaniards overthrew were themselves relative latecomers and often deeply divided internally; hence the *conquistadores* could count on native allies. Nor were the Incas and Aztecs particularly beloved: they too had taken slaves, and they practiced human sacrifices. In consequence, many Indians humbly, but with justification, asked the Spanish crown to recognize and reward their services. The Spaniards brought disease and the Inquisition, but they also brought techniques of raising food and governing territories, universities and Christian humanity, all unknown in the Americas. Thus the history of the Spanish overseas empire is part of a larger history: the expansion of the West over the rest of the world.

While the bestiality of the Aztec rulers served many Spaniards as an excuse for their expansion into Latin America, there were Spanish Christians whom the conquests made profoundly uneasy. As early as 1511 the Dominican friar Antonio de Montesinos had startled his fellow Spaniards on the Caribbean island of Hispaniola with his bold rhetorical question: "Are these Indians not men? Do they not have rational souls? Are you not obliged to love them as you love yourselves?" [15] Others disagreed, but the Christian conscience of Spain was awakened, and in 1550 Charles V actually ordered a cessation of all further conquests while Bartolome de las Casas, bishop in Mexico and for many years

---

[14] Miguel Leon-Portilla, ed., *The Broken Spears: The Aztec Account of the Conquest of Mexico* (tr. 1962); quoted in Gibson, *Spain in America,* 37.

[15] Quoted in Lewis Hanke, *Aristotle and the American Indian* (1959), 15.

the spokesman for the Indians, debated the question with Juan Gines de Sepulveda, an Aristotelian scholar, who used arguments that later advocates of slavery would also find enormously convenient: the Indians were specimens of what Aristotle had called "natural slaves," and wicked idolators and inhuman cannibals to boot. Moreover, being conquered by Spaniards exposed them to the blessings of the true religion, legitimate government, and humane treatment. Las Casas won the debate; the atmosphere was in any case favorable to his side: Indian slavery had already been outlawed in the Spanish territories, and while exploitation continued and the reduced availability of Indians for the most unsavory labor only led to a rise in the importation of African Negroes, there was at least some easing of the Indians' lot by midcentury. But even this modest claim must be kept modest indeed: mistreatment of natives continued, and epidemics swept the Indian populations vulnerable to the ravages of smallpox and other scourges. In 1548, when the Indian population in Spain's American territories had already been much reduced, it was estimated at 6.3 million; in 1580 it was down to 1.9 million.[16] Nor was the government's attack on the *encomienda* system purely a humane reflex. The crown was concerned to secure its control over its remote outposts, and it could do so only if it permanently weakened the semifeudal, relatively independent centers of power that the *encomiendas* became.[17]

The Spanish Empire in Europe

Spanish expansion overseas was to have profound consequences at home. Those *conquistadores* who survived the rigors of the New World—the risks of battle, the climate, and treachery—came home to claim titles for their services. Then, from the 1530s on, the settlers began to send home silver from the rich American mines; the greatest of these, Potosí in what is today Bolivia, was discovered in 1545. Despite its almost inaccessible site twelve thousand feet above sea level, the Spaniards exploited it heavily. Potosí silver changed the economic fate of Spain and the economic face of Europe—but not immediately. It was not until the reign of Philip II that the effects of Spain's overseas possessions became apparent.

Philip II, who accepted the crown of Spain and Spain's possessions in 1556 (see p. 163), seemed, but only seemed, in every respect the antithesis of Charles V. Actually Philip II and his father, whom he revered, were alike in what counted: both were driven by their religious fervor and by an overwhelming sense of public duty. They differed mainly in their attitude toward Spain. Charles V (who was Charles I in Spain) was a Burgundian who at the beginning

---

[16] See J. H. Parry, *The Spanish Seaborne Empire* (1966), 219–220. As Parry points out (p. 220), the epidemic of 1576–1579 "destroyed one optimistic illusion about labour in the Tropics: the mortality among Negroes was at least as severe as that among Indians."

[17] This point has been persuasively argued most recently by Elliott, *Imperial Spain,* 63–64.

of his reign spoke no Spanish and had few Spaniards in his entourage; he aroused mainly hostility when he arrived to take over his Spanish realm, and in 1520 and 1521, he was compelled to crush a revolt against him in Castile. He won the trust of his Spanish subjects gradually, over the years, with his undisputed diligence, his obvious religious sincerity, and his equally obvious respect for Spanish culture and Spanish power. Yet, as emperor, he had obligations to his many disconnected territories, and during his nearly forty years of kingship, he spent more than twenty-four years outside Spain; indeed, from 1543 to his abdication in 1556, he was steadily occupied elsewhere.[18] Spain, though ostensibly central in Charles' mind, was no more than a good place to visit.

Philip II, on the other hand (apart from the years 1556 to 1559, which he spent in Flanders), lived in Spain as though it were one vast protective citadel. This long physical presence in Spain—he died there, after a long reign, in 1598—did not merely reflect his sense of himself as a Spaniard. Nor did it reflect sedentary habits. Rather, Philip II conceived his task as king to be one of assiduous application to paper work, for the sake of his subjects. Almost two centuries before Frederick II of Prussia spoke of himself, in a famous phrase, as "the first servant of his people," Philip II thought of himself as such a servant and acted accordingly. The heroic age of Spanish kingship was over; the time for bureaucratic regularity had come. In 1561, Philip moved his court from Toledo to Madrid, which was in the mathematical center of his Iberian realm, and after some years, Madrid gained ascendancy over other cities to become the capital of Spain.[19] It was near Madrid that Philip built his enormous retreat, the Escorial, which with its immense walls, its austere gridiron shape, and its symmetrical, uninviting facades, symbolized and guaranteed the king's isolation from the subjects he strove to serve.

Whatever later historians—many of them Protestant—may have said, most Spaniards thought Philip II served them well. Yet his successes were never easy: they were hard-won victories, wrested from continual travail. Philip's life was marred by a succession of private tragedies—the deaths of wives and children, and the bizarre episode of his strange wild son, Don Carlos, whom his father felt compelled to arrest and who died in detention. If Philip seemed aloof, a stranger to emotions, a victim of self-imposed courtly ritual, these characteristics point not to an absence of feelings but to a desperate and iron-willed search for control over feelings.

At home and abroad, enemies loomed large. At home, with the aid of the Inquisition, Philip II routed the small minority of Protestants, silenced Catholic cosmopolitans attracted by the urbane, tolerant philosophy of Erasmus, encouraged the growth of fanatical racist doctrines demanding pure blood—*limpieza de sangre*—directed against Catholic Spaniards of Jewish ancestry (see

---

[18] See Elliott, *Imperial Spain*, 154.
[19] The best treatment of this development is in Elliott, *Imperial Spain*, 242–251.

p. 104),[20] and ended what he regarded as a continuing source of infection and possible treason by moving decisively against the Moriscos.[21] For decades, no one had troubled to take these poor and insignificant "new Christians" of Muslim antecedents seriously. But in 1566, in the midst of his campaign to continue the purification of Spain, Philip II issued a "pragmatic," or decree, that reiterated standing prohibitions against the Moriscos' traditional dress, custom, and Arabic language.[22] The Moriscos protested: they had evaded these regulations before, but they were good Christians, and loyal Spaniards. Philip's officials, decree in hand, zealously chose to enforce what their predecessors had wisely ignored, and by 1568 the Moriscos had been goaded into revolt. After fierce and ugly fighting, the rebellion was crushed, and Philip (in this as in so many other things anticipating twentieth-century practices) ordered the wholesale removal of Moriscos from Andalusia to all parts of Castile. This ended a concentration of a population separatist in habits and perhaps in loyalty, which threatened a possible Morisco-Turkish alliance. At the same time, while Philip's drastic policy lessened the intensity of the Morisco problem, it widened its impact. The problem was finally solved by Philip III with a ruthlessness worthy of his father: in 1609, he ordered all Moriscos expelled from Spain, and by 1614 the process was reported complete. Crusades are rarely the work of one king, or one generation.

Abroad, too, the Spaniards triumphed over the Infidel and in spectacular fashion. The year was 1571. It was a tense moment in the history of international Catholicism: France was in the midst of civil war (see p. 178). England, under Queen Elizabeth, if not quite at war with itself, was torn among Anglicans, Puritans, and Catholics; besides, the pope had excommunicated Elizabeth in 1570 and thus declared her, to her Roman Catholic subjects, an outlaw (see p. 185). The Protestant movement, notably its Calvinist wing, proved as international in scope and busy in correspondence as its Roman adversary. The Infidel—as defined by Rome—was distinctly on the defensive. Then came the Spanish confrontation with the Ottomans, and the victory that had so long eluded Philip II's father now fell into his hands: in May 1571, Pope Pius V, the very pontiff who had recently excommunicated the queen of England, organized a Holy League—a naval coalition of Western powers, chiefly Venice and Spain—to expel the Turks from the eastern Mediterranean, where they had just taken Cyprus. On October 7, 1571, the opposing forces, vaster than any within memory, drew up at Lepanto, in the Gulf of Corinth. It was the battle of the century, and when the day was over, the victory of the

[20] This unsavory development to which we, after Hitler, have become particularly sensitive, deserves more attention than historians have hitherto given it. Once again, Elliott has given the matter lucid treatment; see his *Imperial Spain*, 213–217.

[21] This was the name applied to Spanish subjects of Moorish ancestry who, after the *reconquista* of the peninsula, had chosen to stay in Spain at the price of conversion to Roman Catholicism. They kept their own communities, practically all in the south, in the province of Andalusia around the city of Granada.

[22] The decree was actually published on January 1, 1567, and this is generally known as its official date.

century: Ottoman ships were dispersed, captured, and destroyed in impressive numbers. Don John of Austria, natural son of Charles V and half-brother of Philip II, who had commanded the Spanish troops against the Moriscos, now commanded the allied navy against the Moriscos' cousins. Among the Spaniards who fought at Lepanto was Miguel de Cervantes. [23]

While the Ottoman fleet had been routed in the battle, the response of Catholics all over Europe and the reputation that Spain reaped, or confirmed, through her victory were the triumph of appearance over reality. Cervantes himself later proudly described the battle as "the noblest occasion that past or present ages have seen or future ones may hope to see," [24] but the long-range advantages to Spain or to Christendom were slim indeed. Unable to agree on a future course of action, the allies dissipated their immediate advantage; the Ottomans repaired their losses with impressive speed; and the Spanish-Turkish confrontation ended in most unspectacular fashion in 1578, when the two powers entered a truce. But before then, Lepanto became a symbol and a legend: it was proof that the formidable Ottomans were not invincible, proof that Spain was foremost in Europe, proof above all that the Catholic crusade might be more than brave talk. In 1580, while Spain was still enjoying its reputation, Philip II claimed the throne of Portugal, which had just fallen empty and was subject to confused and multiple claims, and successfully reinforced his claim by invading the country and defeating its defending army. In the same year, he annexed Portugal and made himself, as Philip I, its king.

Yet in the midst of all these signs of prosperity, at the height of his glory, Philip II could look about him and discern threatening signs: France in the midst of civil war was of doubtful help in his Catholic crusade; England under Elizabeth was proving a determined adversary; the Spanish dependencies in the Netherlands were in open revolt; and the economy was showing signs of strain. Philip's proverbial gloom was a reflection not merely of his temperament or his dour piety, but of reality.

LIMITS ON SPAIN'S POWER: FRANCE AND ENGLAND

France: The Age of Fanatics

For most of Philip II's long reign, France was too near anarchy to be either a dependable ally for Spain's Catholic crusade or an effective challenger to Spain's hegemony. From the early 1560s to the early 1590s France was torn apart by civil wars, the Wars of Religion. Some historians have called these

---

[23] For the glorious days of Spanish culture, see p. 220.
[24] *Don Quixote,* introduction, part II; see Reginald Trevor Davies, *The Golden Century of Spain* (1965), 174.

decades "the age of fanatics." [25] It is an apt name, for while these mutual massacres were also class and regional and political and even family wars, Frenchmen killed Frenchmen with that special pleasure, that peculiar sense of righteousness associated with religious war. Others have called these decades the "age of Catherine de' Medici." [26] This, too, is an apt name, for Catherine, that wily, often cruel Florentine politician, dominated the French scene for thirty years, practically to the day of her death in 1589.

In her earlier years, as wife to King Henri II of France, Catherine had displayed mainly her talent for self-control and self-abasement: she was all too aware of her "low" mercantile origins. Thus she countenanced her husband's lasting infatuation with Diane de Poitiers, a grasping, aging beauty who was twenty years older than her royal lover. Then a grotesque accident precipitated Catherine from the wings of affairs into the center: in June 1559, at a tournament celebrating the dynastic marriages agreed upon at Cateau-Cambrésis (see p. 163), Henri II entered the lists in person; a few days later he was dead, mortally wounded by one of his great nobles. Francis II, the eldest of Catherine's surviving sons, aged fifteen and sickly, took the throne, while his mother took the power. When Francis died the next year, his younger brother succeeded him as Charles IX; he reigned for fourteen years, until 1574, but he did not rule—his mother ruled in his place. She could hardly do anything else: Charles was only ten when he assumed the throne and proved neither stable nor competent. The last of her surviving brood, Henri III, was far more intelligent than his brothers; but his fifteen-year reign, to 1589, proved him, too, incapable of ruling: a striking combination of self-denying penitent and self-indulgent homosexual, half flagellant and half debauchee, he furnishes material more interesting to the psychoanalyst than to the student of monarchy.

Seeking to rule the country as she ruled her sons, Catherine faced a formidable task. France was financially bankrupt, politically fragmented, and religiously divided. It had barely emerged from feudalism and was hesitantly constructing the rudiments of a national government against the stubborn resistance of local privilege—against cities, provinces, nobles, each with some special right to defend, some special tax exemption to protect. In this volatile situation, court intrigues acquired general political significance, and the court of Catherine was a snake pit of intrigues.

Three superb families, each with considerable territories at its disposal and each a great aristocratic clan, struggled for preeminence. The feebleness of Catherine's sons made the greatest prize of all—the crown of France, or at the least, control over the king of France—appear not too remote. None of these miserable kings seemed capable of, or interested in, producing heirs, and if the

[25] See Georges Duby and Robert Mandrou, *A History of French Civilization from the Year 1000 to the Present* (tr. 1964), 284.
[26] See J. E. Neale, *The Age of Catherine de' Medici* (1943).

house of Valois died out, who should succeed? The extensive Guise clan, from Lorraine, enormously rich and solidly entrenched in high positions in church and state, was one powerful court party. The Montmorency clan, tied to the French crown through distinguished public service, was a second. The Bourbons, ostensibly headed by Anthony, king of Navarre, but actually headed by his younger brother, the prince of Condé, of royal blood and with the most authentic claim to the succession, was the third—it would, in the end, prove the first.

Family rivalries were exacerbated by religious hatreds. True, not all Frenchmen were equally firm in their religious beliefs—Henri Bourbon of Navarre, who was to become the great King Henri IV of France, changed his confession several times. But often religious loyalties were powerful and fiercely held. Religious convictions sometimes even took precedence over family solidarity: the head of the Montmorency clan, Anne de Montmorency, constable of France, remained faithful to the Roman Catholic confession, but the constable's three nephews, including Gaspard de Coligny, admiral of France, became sincere converts to Protestantism. Regions, cities, families were torn apart in this painful way.

Calvinism—a sect, after all, with a French father—exercised a strong appeal among wide circles. As elsewhere, so in France, this appeal was a mixture of revulsion against Catholic practice and attraction to Calvinist piety. The concordat that Francis I had concluded with Rome in 1516 had been, in Neale's vivid phrase, "a deal in the spoils of the Gallican Church." By giving the French crown the power to nominate (which meant, in practice, to appoint) clerics to practically all posts, it gave the crown a splendid instrument of patronage. Courtiers, dependents of influential nobles, friends of the king's mistress, even foreigners, were made abbots and bishops: "Not a single French bishop," as Neale summarizes it, "obtained his post because of religious zeal or spiritual worthiness."[27] Pluralists, absentee holders of great sees, indifferent, ignorant (and it was said, in some districts, illiterate) clerics were in charge of French souls; as the scandals continued to grow, the influence of the reformers grew with them. At first, there had been Lutherans around Francis I; later, with the rise of militant French Calvinism, indulgence toward Protestants in high quarters gave way to impatience; by the 1550s, impatience had given way to persecution. The Calvinists, with their tight congregational, local, regional, and eventually national organization, with their firm beliefs and obvious popularity, constituted a real danger to central authority. The more energetic and more learned among the lower clergy, professors and lawyers, a considerable sprinkling of merchants, and with the passage of years, a growing number of the lesser nobility, made up the army of Huguenots.[28] And the nobles among

---

[27] Ibid., 11.

[28] This name, first applied to the French Calvinists around 1562, is of uncertain origins; it may come from the Swiss-German *Eidgenoss*, a confederate bound to his fellows with an oath.

them were armed, imbued with notions of feudal obligation and with resentment against authority centered in Paris. While they always remained in a minority, the Huguenots made up for their limited numbers with energy, fervor, intelligence, and a collection of grievances—part religious, part social, part economic—that forged them into a formidable political force. And they were not quite that insignificant numerically; by the 1560s perhaps one out of every two French nobles was a declared Calvinist, and by 1561 there were over two thousand Huguenot congregations in France. [29]

In 1559, the year of Francis'—or, rather, Catherine's—accession, the Huguenots convened their first national synod in Paris. Hundreds of their sympathizers had fled to Geneva, and while Calvin himself still frowned on armed resistance against authority, his Geneva was headquarters of the French Protestant movement. The scores of French printers who had fled to Calvin's City of the Saints poured out pamphlets, and Calvin poured out directions. In 1560 and 1561, after the accession of Charles IX, the Huguenots came out into the open. All across France, Calvinist preachers, protected by faithful body-guards, expelled Catholic priests and preached the Word, in French, according to the German dispensation. The younger Montmorencys, and the Bourbons, were on their side. The tinderbox was ready to explode.

Two conspiracies served as prologue to the Wars of Religion; both were led by Condé from a safe, protected position and directed against Guise influence at court. Both were beaten back. Then, in 1562, the Huguenots, emboldened but not appeased by Catherine's conciliatory policies, responded to the bloody Massacre of Vassy with a general call to arms. [30] From then on, a series of sometimes large-scale, often fitful, always brutal encounters—nine in all—punctuated by truces, kept France in a turmoil from which it emerged only in the 1590s, with the triumph of Henri of Navarre.

For several years, Catherine veered among the parties. She offered the Huguenots a measure of toleration—not enough to suit them, too much to suit the Catholics. She toyed with dynastic marital arrangements including Protestant houses, and even, for a time, with war against Spain. The Catholic party was strong and united: in 1561, before open violence had erupted, the leaders of the Montmorency and the Guise clans had joined to form what was to become the Catholic League; it would play a formidable part for over thirty years. But the Huguenots were quite as determined. Catherine cared chiefly for the perpetuation of the French monarchy, and threatened by one party, she would approach the other. Her statesmanship, marred at this point not by its aims but by its vacillations, found support among a small but articulate group of Catholic moderates, the *politiques,* who included such distinguished figures

[29] See Neale, *Age of Catherine de' Medici,* 29.

[30] On March 1, 1562, a group of the duke de Guise's men fell on Protestant worshipers at Vassy, in Champagne, slaughtering more than seventy of them, and wounding more than a hundred. The duke did not object.

as Catherine's chancellor de l'Hôpital, the political theorist Jean Bodin, and that imperishable explorer of the self, the essayist Michel de Montaigne. The *politiques* preferred peace to salvation; in a time of fanaticism, they raised the improbable standard of reason and decency.

The influence of the *politiques* was short-lived; in 1572, Catherine abruptly abandoned conciliation and tried a new policy: murder. Looking back, Huguenots later asserted that she had long planned her moves. They recalled a meeting at Bayonne, in 1565, at which Catherine had discussed—who knew what?—with the Spaniards. In fact, Catherine's shift was quite impulsive. After 1570, with the close of the third War of Religion, the Huguenots had been in the ascendancy, and their most prominent leader, Coligny, was energetically pushing for war with Spain.[31] To everyone's surprise, young King Charles IX, charmed by Coligny, and without consulting his mother, agreed to support Coligny's policy. Wounded maternal pride and shrewd political calculation moved Catherine to sabotage Coligny's plans. Ironically, she chose an occasion of reconciliation, the wedding of her daughter Margaret to Henri of Navarre, to have Coligny murdered. Paris was full of Huguenot nobles come to help their favorite celebrate his marriage. On August 22, 1572, an agent of the duke of Guise tried to kill Coligny and failed; faced with exposure, Catherine decided to cover her guilt by converting a single murder into a general slaughter. By the evening of August 23, she had won over her feeble son; early the next morning, the St. Bartholomew's Day massacre began. A few days later, after the provinces had loyally followed the example of Paris, many thousands of Huguenots were dead—perhaps four thousand had been killed in Paris alone. Coligny was among the victims; Henri of Navarre one of the few Huguenot leaders who escaped.

Like all major incidents in the French Wars of Religion, the St. Bartholomew's Day massacre was an international event. All over Europe, Catholics rejoiced and celebrated. The pope announced the news to his cardinals and had a Te Deum chanted in honor of the event; Catholic powers sent their congratulations to France; Philip II told Catherine that the "punishment" she had meted out to Coligny and his "sect" was "of such value and prudence and of such service, glory, and honor to God and universal benefit to all Christendom that to hear of it was for me the best and most cheerful news which at present could come to me."[32] Protestants for their part excoriated the massacre as a characteristic expression of Catholic fanaticism. They forgot that they had earlier hailed one of their own number for murdering the duke of Guise, and that their troops had murdered women and children without mercy or compunction, violated truces, and invented bestial tortures for hapless

---

[31] Here, as everywhere, the international situation must be taken into account. In 1572, the Dutch rebels had scored a great success against Spanish troops, and news of their victory suggested an opportunity for breaking the grip of a power that surrounded France on practically all sides.

[32] Neale, *Age of Catherine de' Medici*, 80.

priests. The St. Bartholomew's Day massacre was unusual only in the number of its victims. During the Wars of Religion, the Christian virtue of charity was in short supply on both sides.

As the impenitent Catherine de' Medici soon discovered, the massacre had been, to paraphrase a famous modern epigram, both a crime and a blunder.[33] It solved nothing and exacerbated everything. War resumed and went on, getting more atrocious and involving more and more foreign troops. The reign of Henri III was in this respect no better than the reigns of his brothers. In other respects it was worse; the king disfigured it with extravagant and ostentatious pleasures, enjoyed in the company of his young men, his *mignons,* who were his partners in piety, politics, and debauchery alike. The house of Valois was dying, not with a bang, but a whimper. Henri's end was strangely apt: in 1588, the current duke of Guise had taken over the city of Paris in defiance of his king. The Catholic League seemed to be master of France. Henri III, defying his ailing, aging mother, took revenge. In December 1588, he had the duke of Guise and his powerful brother, the cardinal of Lorraine, murdered. He did not enjoy his new-found independence long. Early in 1589, his mother died, and on August 2, Henri III himself was murdered by a fanatical Dominican. The way for Henri of Navarre was now open, in law if not yet in fact.

France: The Age of Henri IV

Henri IV, the first Bourbon king of France, is a striking and enigmatic figure. A compulsive womanizer, a man of impressive charm effective with proud nobles, substantial burghers, and ordinary people alike, Henri was above all a consummate politician and a statesman who shared the *politiques'* vision for France: peace, prosperity, religious forbearance. His task in 1589 was far from easy. The dying Henri III had recognized him as his rightful heir, provided he turn Catholic—which remained, after all, the religion of most Frenchmen. But Henri of Navarre could not simply shift his confession once again. His earlier shifts had been too opportune not to be opportunistic, and a timely conversion now, in 1589, would only have aroused unanimous skepticism. He had been born a Catholic, but his mother, a powerful and intelligent woman, had taught him the Calvinism he adopted in his youth; then, in 1572, in semicaptivity after the St. Bartholomew's Day massacre, he had announced his reconversion to Rome, a return he annulled in 1576, when he placed himself at the head of Huguenot forces.

Henri faced other claimants to the throne, with dubious legal standing but with the appropriate religion; besides, in 1589 much of France, including devout

---

[33] "This is worse than a crime, it is a blunder," is what Talleyrand is quoted as saying in 1804, when he learned of Napoleon's execution of the duke of Enghien (see p. 511).

Catholic Paris, was in the hand of League troops and Spain was intervening in the League's behalf: domestic and international politics were once again wholly intertwined. As a true *politique,* Henri made religion serve his politics. In July 1593, after a prudent wait, he turned Catholic, for the sake of France. In February 1594 he was crowned at Chartres, and in March he entered Paris in triumph; in 1595 Pope Clement VIII gave the old heretic absolution, and the League dissolved, and with it all serious resistance. Paris had been worth a mass.[34]

Henri governed as he had fought: with a realistic sense of his France, with an eye to reconstruction. His treatment of even the most prominent Leaguers was clement in the extreme. Henri would rather bribe men than kill them, and all but his most fanatical Huguenot followers agreed with him: there had been too much killing already. His first task as king of a united France was the elimination of a Spanish threat, which took Henri three years to accomplish. In 1595 he declared war on Spain, and by 1598, with English and Dutch help, he had fought that greatest of European powers to a standstill. The Peace of Vervins guaranteed France Brittany, Calais, and the strips of northern France that the Spaniards had occupied. It was Cateau-Cambrésis all over again, but with the meaning reversed. Cateau-Cambrésis had marked France's defeat and the end of its Italian adventures; Vervins marked Spain's defeat and the end of its French adventures.

In the same year, 1598, Henri IV issued his edict of toleration, the Edict of Nantes, which is his claim to immortality. Like other men who rise from being party chiefs to a position of national leadership, Henri IV found himself compelled to be more generous with his enemies than with his friends. The Huguenots, whose leader he had been and without whose loyalty he would never have become king, grumbled at Henri's "apostasy" and feared for their future in a land officially, overwhelmingly, and in many quarters intolerantly, Catholic. After more than a year of tense discussions, Henri devised an edict of concord, a truce that would last, with certain modifications, for ninety years.[35] While it excluded the Huguenots from Paris and episcopal seats, the edict granted them the right to worship in the households of nobles who were professing Calvinists, and in designated towns. And it recognized that the Huguenots were a minority, scattered all across the land, in need of some protection. It guaranteed them their own *places fortes*—perhaps a hundred fortified towns under their control—and gave them special courts of justice

---

[34] Henri's most celebrated saying, "Paris is well worth a mass," the staple of all textbooks and biographies, has been attributed to him since the early seventeenth century but is unfortunately not satisfactorily documented. It is a remark, though, he might well have made.

[35] For the revocation of the Edict of Nantes, see p. 307; for an interpretation, see Elliott, *Europe Divided,* 363.

staffed by Huguenots and Catholics to protect their interests. Finally, the edict provided that the Huguenots had the same right as Catholics to hold public office or to attend university.

It was a measure of its evenhandedness that all parties should receive the Edict of Nantes with disclaimers and detestation. The Huguenots wanted more toleration, but, having shrunk to perhaps a tenth of the population, they could scarcely ask anyone, not even their old leader, to give them more. The Catholics wanted one religion, but Henri was determined to have the *politiques'* conception of the state prevail. It was a new idea, pregnant with possibilities for the future of a Europe that must remain religiously divided not only among, but within nations. And it worked better than its original reception might have led anyone to believe; after a time of protest, especially by the powerful *parlements*,[36] Henri forced the edict on his reluctant country.

Once Spain had been turned back and religious turmoil quieted, Henri IV could concentrate on domestic reconstruction. He was determined, he said, to serve *l'utilité publicq*—the public good.[37] After more than thirty years of ferocious slaughter, royal indifference, and general incompetence, France was in disrepair, almost in dissolution. Houses, cities, roads, rivers, the government, the very economy bore the marks of strife, hatred, and neglect. During the Wars of Religion, the town of Vienne had changed hands twenty times, and whoever took it pillaged what was left; three times during these years, as if war had not been enough, it had been attacked by the plague. When it finally surrendered to Henri IV in 1595 it was "a mass of ruins and half deserted."[38] In the reign of Henri IV there were many Viennes in France. Henri IV knew this. He was ubiquitous: in depending on his ministers and his emissaries instead of appealing to local estates or the Estates General, Henri IV was one of the first of modern kings, a true predecessor of Louis XIV. But he did not rule in obedience to some abstract theoretical principle; he governed as he did, by himself and through his agents, because no one else was capable of bringing a devastated country back to a semblance of order and a government in disarray

---

[36] The identity of the English word "parliament" with the French word "parlement" discloses the identity of their origins. England's Parliament, now the supreme legislature, began as a court; the French parlements, wiped out during the French Revolution, never lost their original character, though in the seventeenth and eighteenth centuries the judges who sat in them claimed the right to participate in the making of laws. As we shall see, much of the political history of France during these centuries was dominated by rival interpretations of the French past, notably the position of the parlements in the state. The first of the parlements was that of Paris, which emerged in the thirteenth century. It was soon joined by other, provincial parlements; by the seventeenth century, the number had risen to a dozen. But the parlement of Paris retained its central position; it had the highest prestige, the largest jurisdiction, and the most articulate spokesmen. The judges who sat in these parlements were ennobled, forming the "nobility of the robe." With its caste pride, the robe nobility sought marital alliances with other, older nobles, especially among the ancient "nobility of the sword."

[37] See Orest Ranum, *Paris in the Age of Absolutism* (1968), 59.

[38] Karl F. Helleiner, "The Population of Europe from the Black Death to the Eve of the Vital Revolution," in *Cambridge Economic History of Europe*, vol. IV (1967), 33.

back into working effectiveness. In his feverish but purposeful and consistent activity, Henri placed the stamp of the state on manufactures, trades, and the arts.

Capable of arousing fervent loyalties, Henri IV found intelligent and outspoken public servants, many of them, significantly enough, Huguenots. The duke de Sully, soldier and economist, became superintendent of finances before 1600 and carried through a far-reaching program of fiscal reform. It was one thing to demand taxes; it was another to collect them and keep the hands of officials off the revenues. Within the limits imposed by early seventeenth-century communications, Sully did all that. An ancestor of the eighteenth-century Physiocrats (see p. 363), Sully was a fanatical supporter of agriculture and did all he could to encourage farmers by clearing land, draining marshes, and securing property from marauders or greedy creditors. After 1599, he turned to the rebuilding of roads and waterways and bridges: he took his mission to reconstruct France quite literally.

His associate, Barthélemy de Laffemas, seconded Sully's efforts. Like all economists of the time a mercantilist (see p. 300), he strove for a surplus of exports over imports, encouraged new luxury industries that would make the importation of silk unnecessary, and sponsored French expansion into the New World, notably Quebec. Whatever the disadvantages of such authoritarian interventions into economic life, whatever the inevitable disparity between glorious dreams and harsher realities, Henri's interference with the economy and restoration of governmental efficiency had rapid and remarkable success. The public debt was converted into a surplus; a second-rate economic power turned into a first-rate one; for the first time in many decades French population markedly increased, and prosperity was widespread.

But Henri's work was cut short: in May 1610, he was stabbed to death by François Ravaillac, a pious paranoiac who heard voices and felt it necessary to kill a king who, he feared, would lead the Huguenots in a mass slaughter of Roman Catholics. A century and a half later, reflecting on the untimely end of his favorite French king, Voltaire, who detested the death penalty, wrote that he would make Ravaillac the one exception to his humane convictions.

England: Elizabethan Policies

Henri IV's most impressive, if inconstant, ally against the menace of Spain was Elizabeth I of England. The two monarchs in fact had much in common beyond an enemy. Both were courageous, shrewd, exceptionally humane for their age; both believed in a kind of practical toleration. Both used their sexuality in politics; Henri his undisputable virility to offer himself to fellow Frenchmen as a model of kingly strength, Elizabeth her celebrated virginity to dangle the throne of England before the hungry suitors of Europe as a prize too valuable to give up despite repeated rebuffs. Elizabeth, one might say, reversed the marital diplomacy of the Hapsburgs: she achieved her political and diplomatic aims not by marrying, but by not marrying. Both, in short, were *politiques;* both, great statesmen. But they were also very different: Henri was the activist, Elizabeth the scholar who had mastered several languages and liked nothing so much as a theological disputation. And where Henri was profligate, Elizabeth was parsimonious—from need as much as from inclination. Besides, her overriding problems, though much like Henri's, were not identical with his: she had, not to heal the wounds of civil war, but to prevent one.

The first five years after her accession in 1558 were frantic with activity, not all of it conclusive. Elizabeth had to find a husband that she might give her country an heir, but she postponed and postponed her decision, carrying on for over a year an unpromising and still obscure affair with Lord Robert Dudley, and later listening to proposals without accepting any of them. The queen's need for a husband, and her reluctance to acquire one, furnished her reign with suspense and surrounded her throne with danger. In economic matters these early years were more productive. In 1563, as part of a series of parliamentary enactments, a statute of apprentices set long terms of apprenticeship, encouraged (or rather, enforced) the entry of the young and able-bodied into agriculture (economically the most useful, if not, among laborers, the favorite kind of work), and made local justices of the peace responsible for setting decent wage scales adjusted to the locality and the season.[39] And in these years, as all through her reign, Elizabeth found the religious passions that divided her country a formidable obstacle to social peace: the so-called Elizabethan Settlement (see p. 159) turned out to be a patchwork of compromises that few liked and many tried to undo.

Quite like Henri IV, Elizabeth I treated religion as a political question. She had her own convictions, but after a brief time of candor, she kept those convictions to herself and tried instead to impose rules that would make the state the master of the church and guarantee public order. But religious peace was as scarce as international peace. The exiles Bloody Mary had made had come back from the Continent accustomed to speaking their minds and filled with the Calvinist's confidence that theirs was the only true way. In characteristic sixteenth-century fashion, the toleration they demanded for themselves they were wholly unwilling to grant others, on the perfectly logical ground that their doctrine was the truth while the doctrines of their rivals were abysses of error. A few of the most intransigent of the Puritans sought to separate themselves from the Church of England, but most of them refused to become Separatists and worked for reform with the Church of England; these "moderate" Puritans found that church "but halfly reformed"[40]—neither pure enough to be acceptable without serious amendment, nor wicked enough to

---

[39] This enactment, which later came to be called the Statute of Artificers, was a codification of a mass of traditional and regional regulations and customs.

[40] See Patrick Collinson, *The Elizabethan Puritan Movement* (1967), 29 ff.

call for its eradication. The Puritans' grievances were real and extensive; their demands were far-reaching. They were hostile to episcopacy, the "Romish" Anglican hierarchy with its bishops and archbishops, though they were far from unanimous about the shape of the purified church they wanted. The religious "parties," whose debates would enliven and embitter the political life of England in the early seventeenth century, were present under Elizabeth in rudimentary form, though without the names they would later acquire. Some Puritans were tending toward Presbyterianism, a form of church government by elders and with a certain centralized structure, the synods, that held the congregations together. Other Puritans were tending toward Independency, or Congregationalism, which (as the names make clear) demanded the self-government of each congregation. On matters other than organization, however, the Elizabethan Puritans were at one. They wanted a clergy less corrupt, less ignorant, less inarticulate; they wanted a further simplification—"purification"—of doctrine and preaching. Elizabeth's parliaments, which she hoped to call more rarely than her steady need for money and support compelled her to do, became sounding boards for Puritan demands. At first she handled the vigorous protest with forbearance; only later, when Puritan spokesmen remained persistent and became even more offensive, did she grow severe.

Elizabeth's Catholic policy had a similar career. In the 1560s, the hostility English Catholics encountered was mainly rhetorical; the crown and in general the country allowed them to exist in peace, demanding only some superficial marks of conformity to the established religion. "There was no mention then of factions in religion," one Catholic later recalled, "neither was any man much noted or rejected for that cause; so otherwise his conversations were civil and courteous." [41] Then foreign aggressiveness and domestic anxiety forced the queen's hand. In 1570, by excommunicating Elizabeth, Pius V invited her Roman Catholic subjects to see her as a rebellious heretic who deserved no obedience and might deserve assassination. While most English Catholics rejected the sinister implications of the Papal Bull of Excommunication, a number of them left the country, some to found Catholic seminaries to prepare for an eventual recapture of England for the Church of Rome, others to plot against the queen's life. In the 1570s, there were several such plots—all real enough, none of them trumped up for public consumption—and in 1580 the most militant of Catholics, the Jesuits, sent missionaries to England. And the queen was still unmarried, still without an heir. The danger of a Catholic succession, produced either by natural death or (since by and large Elizabeth was in excellent health) by assassination, worried the country greatly. Then in the early 1580s, relations with Spain, already strained, worsened. Parliament, which loved the queen better than she loved it, pressed legislation on Elizabeth; her advisors urged action, her dependable Sir William Cecil (later Lord Burghley) at their head. In 1581, Edmund Campion, the head of the Jesuit

---

[41] S. T. Bindoff, *Tudor England* (1950), 234.

<u>mission</u>, was executed, and other executions followed. The realm was in
<u>danger,</u> both from war abroad and subversion at home.

England: Confrontation with Catholicism

The long encounter of Elizabeth Tudor and Mary Stuart gains its significance
from this concatenation of threatening circumstances. It has been dramatized
by playwrights and novelists—beyond need; the reality was dramatic enough.
Mary Stuart, for a time queen of the Scots, was in all respects the opposite of
her great adversary: Catholic, irresponsible, cruel, and anything but virginal. As
a granddaughter of one of Henry VIII's sisters, she had an undisputed claim to
the English throne upon Elizabeth's death; when she arrived in England in 1568,
she had already occupied and lost two thrones, one through misfortune, the
other through misconduct. As the young wife of Francis II, she had been briefly
queen of France, from 1559 to 1560; as the daughter of James V of Scotland, she
assumed the Scottish crown in 1561. Charming and clever, she held her place
for some time, a Catholic queen in a Protestant country, but a series of
unsavory adventures which included the murder of her second husband
presumably with her connivance and her marriage to the man who had been
in charge of the murder, aroused the Scots against her. She was compelled to
abdicate in favor of her son, James VI,[42] and to flee the country. Her arrival in
England made her a nuisance to Elizabeth; her stay, which gradually changed
into semi-imprisonment, made her a danger. Swearing by all that was holy that
she was innocent, she was involved in nearly every foreign machination against
England and nearly every plot against Elizabeth's life. Elizabeth's advisors and
parliaments grew frantic, but for years Elizabeth temporized; she was reluctant
to execute a royal personage who had been twice a queen, and might be queen
yet a third time, no matter how guilty or duplicitous she might be. In the end,
Mary's involvement in still another assassination plot broke down Elizabeth's
resistance, and she agreed to have Mary tried. In February 1587, Mary was
decapitated. Queen Elizabeth, whether from grief or from policy no one can
say, mourned her dead rival and berated her rash officials. But England,
delivered, rejoiced.

Deliverance was brief. The execution of Mary moved Philip II of Spain,
who had been deeply engaged in Mary's plans, to go forward with his
Enterprise of England. For years the English had been as provocative as Spain
was powerful. The Spanish annexation of Portugal in 1580, which added
Portuguese ports and Portuguese colonies to the Spanish arsenal, only
increased the Spanish menace to English eyes, and the English, who had for
years harassed Spain, mainly through privateers, stepped up their aggressive
activities on sea and land alike. In 1584, the English government expelled the

[42] He was to succeed Elizabeth I in 1603 as James I; see p. 262.

Spanish ambassador for his part in a plot to murder Queen Elizabeth. In 1585 England concluded a treaty with the Dutch, who had been in rebellion against their Spanish masters since the 1560s (see p. 190). This was a drastic step, for while the rebels were Protestants and natural allies for England, they were rebels, and Elizabeth was as reluctant to support rebels, no matter how sympathetic, as she was reluctant to cause the death of a queen, no matter how dangerous. In 1587—the year of Mary Stuart's execution—Sir Francis Drake, slave trader and flamboyant sailor, made a brilliant raid on Spanish territory. He swooped down on Cadiz, destroying more than thirty vessels and invaluable cargo; later, cruising near the Azores, he took a Portuguese ship, the *San Felipe,* laden with spices, ivory, silk, gold, silver, and jewels, worth over £100,000: "All the barrel staves and all the fishing-boats in Spain could not have been sold for such a figure."[43]

Philip II retorted by pushing his plans for an invasion of England. But the greatest of all armadas suffered the greatest of all disasters. It sailed in late spring of 1588, under rigid and incomplete instructions to meet Spanish troops stationed in Flanders and protect their invasion. The Armada was huge, totaling one hundred thirty ships, of which only forty were proper men-of-war; it was an awkward procession vulnerable to accidents in timing, to intelligent opposition, and to bad weather. Much as in 1812 the Russians would let Napoleon reach Moscow, only to destroy his army on its retreat, the English navy, brilliantly led and bravely joined by private vessels, allowed the Armada to pass through the English Channel. Then, the English fleet fell on the Spaniards, burned some of their vessels, sank others, disabled and scattered the rest. What they did not do on that day, the winds and English harassment did in following days, as the surviving Spanish vessels struggled northward, through hostile waters and against stormy seas. The invaders who did not drown were slaughtered in remote isles off Scotland or in Ireland, and many of those who reached safety in Spain died at home of typhus and of exhaustion. English losses were insignificant. The Enterprise of England was over.

England: A Good Queen in Hard Times

Once again, as after the death of Mary Stuart, England rejoiced, but the breathing space that the shattering of the Armada gave Elizabeth in foreign affairs only called attention to domestic problems. Elizabeth's reign would end, as it had begun, amid widespread distress. The queen's trusted counselors died one by one—Burghley in 1598—and among their potential successors there was strident, often undignified competition for the queen's attention. The Elizabethan religious settlement was more threatened than it had been in decades, with Puritan Separatists noisier than ever—after 1590 a number of Puritan

[43] Garrett Mattingly, *The Armada* (1959), 120.

leaders were jailed and a few extremists were executed—and with Catholics, especially in remote Ireland, restless and rebellious. The rise of commercial monopolies under royal approval—over foreign trade and domestic manufacture—stimulated commercial activity, but led to fraud, influence-peddling, intimidation of independent merchants, and widespread public complaints. Bad harvests brought high prices for bread, and in the late 1590s there were bread riots of a violence that England had not seen for fifty years. First in 1597 and then, more comprehensively in 1601, earlier legislation was supplemented by the Elizabethan Poor Law, a law which, as S. T. Bindoff has said, "was as much the offspring of fear as of pity, of hatred as of charity." [44] It provided local relief for those who could not work, and local compulsion—work houses or whippings—for those who could, but would not, work.

And with the queen's person quite as much as with her realm, the last decade of her reign echoed its first. In the late 1590s, as long before in the 1560s, Elizabeth found her affections engaged, much to the distress of her realm. Her early infatuation with Robert Dudley had almost led to a disastrous marriage; it had ended happily in mutual indifference and in Dudley's service (as earl of Leicester) in the Netherlands. Her late infatuation, with the earl of Essex, ended less happily. Essex, handsome, undisciplined, inordinately ambitious, rapidly rose in the aging queen's favor and, wielding patronage, soon exercised great influence in the realm. He wanted more. Sent to subdue rebellious Ireland, he played with treasonous plots, possibly designed to oust his rivals from the court, possibly to impose his will on the queen. Elizabeth had loved Essex, but she could not save him from the end that his rashness and the standards of the time dictated. In 1601 he was executed. Two years later Elizabeth, too, died, melancholy and alone. The Tudor line died with her.

The pathos of her end is the kind of shadow the Elizabethans would have taken as a reminder of human frailty in the midst of splendor. In poetry, in music, in architecture (see p. 216), as in politics and, despite all the endemic distress, in economic affairs, the age of Elizabeth was a memorable age— vigorous, expansive, the stuff from which legends are made. And the queen herself was the cause and center of that legend. Behind all the great impersonal and often invisible forces of social and economic change there stands her figure, a queen who loved her subjects as much as her subjects loved her, and who spent many hours wooing her subjects as though she needed their votes. In one of her many stately progresses through her realm, when the city fathers of Coventry handed her the customary cup with the customary donation in it, Elizabeth thanked the lords of the city: "It was a good gift, £100 in gold; I have but few such gifts." The mayor replied, "If it please your Grace, there is a great deal more in it." "What is that?" she asked. "It is," he told her, "the hearts of all your loving subjects." To which the queen, consummate politician that she was, gave answer: "We thank you, Mr. Mayor; it is a great deal more indeed." [45]

[44] *Tudor England*, 293.
[45] See J. E. Neale, *Queen Elizabeth I* (rev. ed., 1966), 205.

SPAIN IN DIFFICULTIES

The Birth of the Dutch Republic

During the decades that Spain disastrously failed to subdue England by marriage, diplomacy, or invasion, it suffered another failure, in the north, equally disastrous. After prolonged, confused fighting, some of the lands that had come into Hapsburg hands a century before detached themselves from Spanish overlordship and secured their independence. Both the war itself and the eventual loss proved expensive to Spain.

The Netherlands was a conglomerate of seventeen provinces divided by particularism, economic interest, and language; they were united, or at least drawn together, by geography, common experiences with their Burgundian masters, and later, military accident. The southern, Walloon population spoke French; northerners spoke a Germanic language that was assuming, in these years, the lineaments of Dutch. But this was not a divisive force in an age that was still a stranger to nationalism. The Reformation further complicated matters: there were for many years more Protestants in the south than in the north, and during the revolt, the great city of Amsterdam, in Holland, stubbornly remained a Catholic island in a Calvinist sea. It was a prosperous region fiercely concentrated on perpetuating that prosperity, a region of commercial cities, grown fat on fishing, shipping, small manufacture, banking. It lived by, and from, the sea. Its old aristocratic families were influential but not dominant. The culture and the politics of the region were urban, and the decisive power was exercised by commercial oligarchies reigning unchallenged in the cities which, in turn, controlled the provincial estates. The favorite political slogan of the Netherlands was "liberty," which they defined in good medieval fashion as freedom from interference by central authorities or outside powers. It was another name for local custom, local law, local privileges. There were two possible rallying points for common action, the States General and that rather peculiar institution, the Stadholderate. The first was simply an assembly of delegates from each province, shackled by instructions from home; it could act only if it could obtain unanimity, and thus reflected, with its relative impotence, the centrifugal nature of power in the Netherlands. The role of the second depended on the vagaries of history. The king of Spain had stadholders—lieutenants, representatives—in each of his Netherlands provinces; in the sixteenth century, the house of Orange had been granted the stadholderate of several provinces and was to keep its hold through the rebellion into the republic. But the stadholder was not (and after the revolt only sometimes became) the chief executive of the state. Thus "liberty" was preserved, and liberty meant that each merchant oligarch, in his own city, could grow rich in his own way.

With the accession of Philip II, this liberty was in danger. "Turk like," wrote Sir Walter Raleigh with more passion than justice, Philip II was seeking "to tread under his feet all their national and fundamental laws, privileges, and ancient rights." [46] In the course of the fourteenth and fifteenth centuries, parts of the Netherlands had been acquired by the dukes of Burgundy, and upon the death of Charles the Rash in 1477, his daughter Mary had brought to her husband, Maximilian of Hapsburg, most of the region as dowry (see p. 113). Her grandson, Charles I of Spain—Emperor Charles V—eventually inherited and rounded out his Netherlands possessions, and in 1548, he gathered the seventeen provinces into the Burgundian circle of his empire. But while the emperor's policies were dictated mainly by his imperial and his Spanish concerns, he governed these provinces with a relatively light hand. When, in October 1555, in Brussels, Charles handed over his northern domains to his son, Philip II, the delegates of the seventeen provinces, witnessing the solemn occasion, broke into tears. They would soon know they had been right to weep.

The revolt of the Netherlands, with its dashing raiders, its savage Spanish oppressors, its dramatic battles, and its patient leader, William the Silent, has often been simplified and sentimentalized as a struggle between Protestants and Catholics, or (which for many historians has been the same thing) between good and evil. In fact, especially in the early years, there were as many Catholics among the rebels as there were Protestants, and progress lay probably more with the policies of Philip II than with those who resisted them. "The rebellion against the Spanish authorities," Johan Huizinga has noted, "was a conservative revolution and could not have been otherwise—in those days, it was not the rebels but the lawful governments who were the reformers and innovators." [47] Nor was the revolt a nationalistic struggle against foreign oppression: the sentiment of Dutch nationality was the consequence, not the cause, of the rebellion. Nor, finally, was the outcome predestined by political or ethnic or religious realities; it was the result of military fortunes.

Philip II alienated his northern subjects first of all by what he was, not by what he did. He was as unmistakably Spanish as his father had been Burgundian, as ignorant of Dutch as Charles V had been, at the outset, of Spanish (see p. 172). But he soon added the irritant of policy to the accident of birth. Operating through his half-sister, Margaret of Parma, as regent, and through Cardinal Granvelle, Philip sought to introduce some administrative centralization. In 1559, he ordered a massive reorganization of the churches which would place the nomination to bishoprics into the hands of the crown,

[46] Quoted by Sir George Clark, "The Birth of the Dutch Republic" (1946), in Lucy S. Sutherland, ed., *Studies in History* (1966), 121.

[47] "Dutch Civilisation in the Seventeenth Century," in Huizinga, *Dutch Civilisation in the Seventeenth Century and Other Essays* (Torchbook ed., 1968), 26.

increase the number of bishops, insist on proper qualifications for high church officials, and rationalize the boundaries of the dioceses. It was, as one Dutch historian has put it, "a very great measure; its bold logic and symmetry and its vigorous attack on historic development and ancient rights were thoroughly characteristic of the spirit of the monarchy and its rationalistic lawyer servants"; altogether it was a "striking instance of what the monarchy could do in the way of state building." [48] The measure was utterly reasonable, thoroughly progressive, and vastly unpopular. It offended Catholics and Calvinists alike, for it constituted an invasion of cherished rights over patronage, and it was an ominous sign that Philip would enforce the uncompromising decrees of the Council of Trent against his "heretical" subjects in the north (see p. 169).

Unrest grew. At first, protests against the Spanish policy were the work of prominent nobles—of the vain, vacillating, self-deluded count of Egmont, who was stadholder of Flanders; of the count of Hoorne, who was a Knight of the Golden Fleece and admiral-general; and of that puzzling statesman, William of Nassau, who was prince of Orange, the most influential and clear-sighted statesman the rebellion was to produce. He came later to be called William the Silent, not because he was taciturn but because he had shown himself a wily diplomat from his youth. [49] It is a sign of the deep feelings stirred by the new policy that William of Orange should participate in the movement at all. He was a prince imbued with dynastic loyalty, an aristocrat of immense wealth, a prominent servant of Philip II, and stadholder of Holland, Zeeland, and Utrecht since 1559.

By 1564, the Protestants had won their first victory: Philip had abandoned his plan and sent Granvelle into exile. A year later, riding the crest of this precarious triumph, more than four hundred nobles from practically all of the Netherlands joined to form the "compromise," a league of the nobility led by Protestants but open to Catholics.

The league's first step was to plead with the government to mitigate the edicts against heresy. Representatives went to Spain, and in April 1566, a group of about two hundred nobles appeared in Brussels to present their petition to Margaret of Parma. The occasion gave the rebellion its most enduring slogan: looking at the petitioners, the count of Berlaymont, one of Margaret's closest advisors, derisively referred to them as *gueux*—beggars. As is so often true of party names, so here: the name *beggar*, bestowed in contempt, was soon flaunted with pride.

---

[48] Pieter Geyl, *The Revolt of the Netherlands, 1555–1609* (rev. ed., 1958), 71, 74.

[49] Perhaps, as more than one historian has suggested, the epithet "silent" is apt because William's private religious convictions and some of his aspirations remained unclear to those who knew him, as they have remained unclear to historians since. Yet, writes H. G. Koenigsberger, who makes this point, "it was always clear what he fought against: despotic government and religious persecution" ("Western Europe and the Power of Spain," in *The New Cambridge Modern History*, vol. III [1968], 281). A cosmopolitan among patriots, an urbane believer in toleration among religious fanatics, such reserve was perhaps not only useful, but essential.

The nobles could not contain what they had begun; in the summer of 1566, the lower orders took the rebellion into their own hands. They were impatient with passivity, harassed by widespread unemployment and high prices, and thus ripe for provocative Calvinist preachers. The Calvinists were still a small minority of the population, but unlike other Protestant sects, they were energetic, bellicose, and well organized; since 1560, their ranks had been strengthened and their passions inflamed by Huguenot refugees from France. They had begun to hold public services, and in August 1566 they indulged themselves in an orgy of iconoclasm. In city after city—the contagion spread like a wave—Calvinist mobs invaded Catholic churches to "purge" houses of the Lord of all symbols of hateful image worship. They toppled statues and broke windows. "It is a small matter, or revenge," wrote one Calvinist apologist at the time, "thus to have destroyed the images, which are only a species of idolatry, since the ecclesiastics have done us a thousand times more hurt and hindrance through their persecutions which broke those statues which God Himself had made and for which He once shed His precious blood, namely, our dearest friends, fathers and mothers, sisters and brothers." [50] To justify one's own violence by blaming others for starting it is special pleading common among those who are perhaps a little ashamed of their actions, but truculence was the attitude of a militant and powerful minority in the Netherlands. The outlook for compromise was dark.

Philip II responded to these Calvinist outrages with uncharacteristic speed and rare determination. Some of the leading nobles, helpless to check a movement whose fanaticism they detested, had left the country; William of Orange was stripped of his posts under the crown. Now Philip, in effect superseding Margaret, reinforced the Spanish garrisons with crack troops drawn from his Italian possessions. They were commanded by the duke of Alva, who had long deplored his sovereign's indulgence with the northern heretics. Indifferent to local customs and contemptuous of time-honored rights, Alva speedily instituted a reign of terror. *"Non curamus privilegios vestros,"* he coldly told delegates from the University of Louvain who had come to protest his arbitrary proceedings: "We don't care about your privileges." [51] By the fall of 1567, only a few months after his arrival, Alva had arrested dozens of leading nobles; by the following summer, he had executed hundreds of them, Egmont and Hoorne among them. Alva's tribunal, the Council of Troubles—quickly labeled the Council of Blood—terrorized the population and thus minimized the possibility of revolt. [52] Then, after death, taxes: in 1569, Alva demanded that

---

[50] Quoted in Geyl, *Revolt of the Netherlands,* 93.

[51] Ibid., 102.

[52] The actual figures are less terrible than the reputation of the council: in six years, between 1567 and 1573, it convicted around nine thousand persons out of the twelve thousand who came before it, but only one thousand were actually executed. The number of those, however, who avoided the executioner's axe by emigration—about sixty thousand—may explain this relatively moderate figure. For the precise figures, see A. L. E. Verheyden, *Le Conseil des Troubles: Liste des condamnés, 1567-1573* (1961).

the States General approve a 10 percent impost on all goods sold—the notorious "tenth penny." The Netherlanders were outraged. It was a thoroughly Spanish tax, reminding them, once again, that they were in the hands of Spaniards; besides, it struck directly at their commercial prosperity. Unrest spread further. Undeterred, Alva continued his executions and his exactions and confiscated the properties of wealthy rebels, including William of Orange.

The result was disaster—for Spain. The rebels were by no means united: William of Orange never gave up his dream of unity and toleration, while the Calvinists, determined to win the right to practice their religion, had no intention of extending the same right to others. But before Alva retired from his post in November 1573, he had managed to arouse in aristocrats and merchants, Calvinists and Catholics, one fierce desire: to be rid of the Spaniards. In April 1572, a bold band of sea-Beggars had captured the strategic port of The Brill, which made them masters of the lower Rhine; the two northern provinces of Holland and Zeeland now took the lead in the rebellion. But it was in no way a purely Protestant cause: there were many Catholics in Brabant and Flanders quite as determined as the Protestants to do without Spanish troops, Spanish governors, and Spanish taxes.

In 1576, this determination acquired new firmness. Late in the previous year, the Spanish government had gone bankrupt, an event fatal for a war in which most soldiers, "mercenaries" in the literal sense, died only for money. Alva's successor, Requesens, had fought ably in the field, but after his death in March 1576, his lieutenants could no longer restrain their impatient and irritable troops. They mutinied, and in November, they vented their "Spanish fury" on Antwerp, in a week of pillage, murder, and wanton cruelty. Calvinists had committed atrocities against priests, but their ferocity was mildness compared with this systematic, unrestrained savagery. The response was an agreement among the seventeen provinces, the Pacification of Ghent, published in November 1576. It was an alliance concluded to drive out the Spaniard, and it foresaw an eventual settlement of that most troublesome of questions, the religious question, which threatened to undermine the precarious understanding almost as soon as it had been reached.

But, as elsewhere in Europe in these years, in the emerging Netherlands the religious question could not be settled simply because most of the disputants did not want to settle it. They wanted not to tolerate error, but destroy it. William the Silent was a *politique*, but like his French counterparts (see p. 178) he found his ideals unpopular and his vision premature. While he cast about for some foreign sovereign who would take the united provinces under his protection, intransigent Calvinists entered city after city, expelled Catholic officials, and drove out priests and monks. Don John of Austria, Requesens' successor, agreed to make peace with the States General on condition that the Catholic religion be everywhere restored, but the Beggar-dominated provinces, Holland and Zeeland, with their Calvinist allies elsewhere, frustrated this possible compromise. When the intelligent and able

Alexander Farnese, duke of Parma, was made governor-general over the rebellious regions in 1578, he found it possible to divide by diplomacy and the judicious application of military pressure what his predecessors had united with their rashness, cruelty, and lack of realism.

The decisive year was 1579. In that year, the southern provinces joined in the Union of Arras, and proclaimed their continued loyalty to the Spanish crown, while the seven northern provinces formed their own alliance, the Union of Utrecht, the germ of the modern Dutch state. Neither side precisely foresaw, or intended to produce, the future. "The treaty of union," Huizinga reminds us, "was not expressly concerned with political freedom and independence, nor was it intended to be the constitution of a free state." Rather, "the Union of Utrecht was, in principle, no more than an *ad hoc* military alliance."[53] Indeed, the future was to be determined by the fortunes of war. When two years later, in 1581, the States General abjured its allegiance to the Spanish crown and called its members the United Provinces of the Netherlands, a number of cities now in Belgium—Antwerp, Bruges, Brussels, Ghent—still formed part of the newly born state. The three provinces, Holland, Zeeland, and Utrecht, over which William of Orange had been stadholder, now honored him, once again, with that title and made it hereditary. But Farnese vigorously and patiently reconquered the major centers in the south by winning strategic sieges and making strategic concessions. By 1585, Brussels and Antwerp had surrendered to him, and the shape of the Dutch Republic was, in all essentials, final. William the Silent, the leader of the republic, had been assassinated the year before, in July 1584, shot down at Delft by a fanatic encouraged, no doubt, by the outlawry Philip II had proclaimed four years before. The States General, mourning William's loss, called him the father of the fatherland. It was a tribute to his aims and his eventual influence. The manner of his death, the legends surrounding his life and end, were no substitute for his diplomacy and his skill, but they remained a force in Dutch affairs. His son, Maurice, who succeeded him, inherited his father's titles and much of his father's authority.

Now definitively divided, the Spanish Netherlands and the United Provinces began to sort themselves out religiously, with Catholics migrating southward and Protestants northward. By 1585, when Queen Elizabeth, after maddening hesitations, finally committed some troops to the rebels' cause (see p. 187), a Protestant front against the Spanish crusade had taken shape. The English intervention in the revolt of the Netherlands, led by Elizabeth's favorite, the earl of Leicester, was more a burden on the Dutch than a help, and Parma for some years extended Spanish military gains. But by the 1590s, after the defeat of the Spanish Armada, and in the declining years of Philip II, the Spaniards found themselves unable to reconquer the lost territories. Thus, in 1609, after extended and tedious negotiations, the belligerents concluded a

[53] "Dutch Civilisation," 28.

twelve-year truce which, in effect, recognized the existence of a new Dutch state. [54]

It was inevitable that the young Dutch Republic should undergo strains. The truce with Spain gave abundant room for internal dissension: nothing is so productive of domestic quarrels as international peace. Doctrinaire Calvinists, who never ceased reminding themselves and others of the noble part they had played in winning independence, found themselves beleaguered far less by Catholic or nonconformist Protestant minorities than by theological currents within the Calvinist persuasion itself. Soon religious quarrels, exacerbated by new opportunities for settling old political scores and by bitter differences over economic policy, brought the United Provinces to the edge of civil war.

The ascendancy of strict Calvinism had never gone wholly unchallenged. William the Silent himself, and Jan van Oldenbarneveldt, William's closest associate in the rebellion and, after William's death, the undisputed political leader of the United Provinces, both believed in toleration and obviously had their doubts about the stark Calvinist doctrine of predestination. In 1602, with the appointment of Jacobus Arminius to a chair at Leyden, this explosive theological issue assumed new prominence, for while Arminius stressed man's original sin, he insisted that man at least participated in shaping his eternal destiny. After his death in 1609, his partisans among the professors, the commercial oligarchy, and the ministry kept his teachings very much alive. They had distinguished support, including the brilliant scholar Hugo Grotius (see p. 230) and Oldenbarneveldt himself. The orthodox charged the Arminians with denigrating God's majesty and with wishing to reintroduce the noxious doctrine of free will—in a word, with secretly favoring popery. The Arminians charged the orthodox with insulting God's goodness by making Him the father of sin.

In a society as small and as intensely engrossed in religious matters as the seventeenth-century Dutch Republic, the state could hardly allow this theological squabble to go on unchecked. In 1610, a group of Arminian ministers addressed a Remonstrance to the States of Holland, in which they stated their side of the theological issue and asked for protection. Oldenbarneveldt was only too ready to give it. As advocate of the Province of Holland, as spokesman for its delegation to the States General, as one of the architects of independence, simply by the force of his person, Oldenbarneveldt exercised enormous political authority. And he was certain—he had insisted on it as early as 1586— that the state must not be ruled by the church, even by the most godly of ministers.

Sound as Oldenbarneveldt's policy was, his position progressively weakened. He had been at the head of affairs too long not to make enemies. The war party detested him for concluding a truce with Spain; there were merchants

---

[54] The official recognition had to await the general European settlement that followed the Thirty Years' War in 1648 (see p. 254).

who disliked his championship of the East India Company (see p. 211); the Contra-Remonstrants tried to ruin his reputation by spreading slanders and resorting to the lowest demagogy, while Oldenbarneveldt, in retaliation, only alienated wider circles by aiding the Remonstrants in high-handed ways. Then, in 1617, Maurice of Nassau, with whom he had clashed before, openly joined the orthodox Calvinists. Nibbling away at Oldenbarneveldt's basis of support, Maurice filled clerical and governmental posts all across the country with extreme Calvinists; in 1618, with a show of force, he took over Holland and had Oldenbarneveldt arrested. After interminable and humiliating questioning before a court illegally constituted and packed with men lusting to revenge themselves on the aging statesman, Oldenbarneveldt was condemned to death and executed in May 1619. He went to his death resigned but uncomprehending, after a lifetime of brilliant service. He was seventy-two years old.

Maurice's coup d'état brought a time of decreased influence of the provinces on Dutch affairs, and a time of persecution of Arminians, censoring of intellectuals, and a new harshness of life in the Genevan fashion. The packed Synod of Dort, held in 1619, confirmed the hold of the Contra-Remonstrants on the ministry and the universities. But not for long. When Maurice died in 1625, his younger brother and successor, Frederick Henry, rapidly moved to suspend the persecutions, and by 1630 Remonstrants found themselves once again in pulpits and in city governments. These years were years of real troubles, and they issued in real crimes, but Dutch prosperity soon dimmed memory of them.

There are Dutch historians who deplore to this day the settlement that produced a truncated republic, small in population, poor in resources, incapable in the long run of competing with the great powers of Europe. They have called it a disaster. [55] If it was a disaster, the naval prowess, imperial acquisitions, commercial profits, and cultural glories of the seventeenth-century Dutch Republic managed to conceal it well. The Spanish Netherlands bore the scars of the conflict far more visibly: far more than remote Holland, southern provinces like Flanders and Brabant had been theaters of war for years; their cities had been despoiled by Calvinists, by Spanish troops obeying the orders of their general or—which was far more devastating—by Spanish troops disobeying the orders of their general. Antwerp, once the most splendid commercial metropolis of the north, lost half its population and all its splendor during the Dutch wars, undergoing, first the Spanish fury, later Parma's siege which led to massive emigration of Calvinists, and finally, loss of access to the sea (see p. 210). The implacable Dutch throttled Antwerp in 1585 by blockading the mouth of the Scheldt and kept the river closed to ocean-going shipping during the truce and after; when peace was concluded in 1648, they wrote the economic death sentence of Antwerp into the treaty. It was the enemies of the

[55] See Geyl, *Revolt of the Netherlands,* 256–259.

Dutch, the Spanish Netherlands and Spain itself, that seemed to have suffered the disaster.

The Erosion of Spanish Power

Despite all its setbacks, Spain remained a power to be reckoned with. Its vast empire in Europe and America, the flow of precious metals from its mines overseas, the sheer resiliency of what had once been the arbiter of European affairs, combined with the troubles that continued to beset its rivals, sustained the strength, or the reputation, of Spain for some decades. True, by the time Philip II died in 1598, some Spaniards had noticed symptoms of decay, yet the country could still muster considerable energy in the 1620s and 1630s, in the reign of Philip IV, under the leadership of the count-duke Olivares. But in 1640, Spain's decay was palpable and, as it were, official, with the outbreak of a long-drawn-out rebellion in Catalonia, and the short, successful revolt, in the same year, of Portugal, which recaptured the independence it had lost in 1580 (see p. 175).

The decline of Spain in the early seventeenth century is often taken as a salutary lesson; it is cited as proof that intolerant crusading zeal, excessive political ambition, and disdain for the humble virtues of work and thrift must bring punishment in their train. The moralizing is beside the point, but there is some merit in the diagnosis. Spain was by no means alone in keeping up its intolerance, overextending itself abroad, and rewarding the holy idleness of the priest and the secular idleness of the courtier. It is only that Spain could afford such policies and such ideals less than other states, and pursued them more vigorously. As the events of 1640 were to prove, Spain was far from united; in 1591–1592 there had been a brief, bizarre rebellion in Aragon, and Spaniards outside Castile resented its dominance in Spanish affairs. Castile, which had over six million of Spain's eight millions, was undergoing plague, famine, and an untoward shift of population from the countryside to the towns—a sign not of urban prosperity, but of the intolerable exactions to which the peasants were subject. By 1600, Castile was importing grain and its industries were stagnant. "The nature of the economic system was such," writes J. H. Elliott, who has convincingly suggested that the decline of Spain was first a decline of Castile, "that one became a student or a monk, a beggar or a bureaucrat. There was nothing else to be." [56] The Spanish crown offered an equally depressing picture. The kings of Spain were inordinately expensive; what Philip II had spent on war (the Invincible Armada had cost a fortune), his successor, Philip III, spent on the court. The bankruptcy of the first, in 1596, was followed by the bankruptcy of the second, in 1607.

[56] "The Decline of Spain," in Trevor Aston, ed., *Crisis in Europe* (1965), 183.

But Spain was bankrupt in more than funds. Philip III, passive and patient, let himself be duped by a grasping, smooth aristocrat, whom he created duke of Lerma and made master in his house. The result was that the gap between the privileged and the unprivileged grew wider, that pressing problems went unsolved, and that a host of desirable offices were filled with Lerma's relatives. The most memorable policy of Lerma's reign was the expulsion of the Moriscos (see p. 174) which, by removing nearly three hundred thousand people from a population already stationary or perhaps declining, only weakened an already shaky economy. The enormous amounts of silver that flowed through the port of Seville into Spain actually reached their maximum around 1600, but they did not remain in the country to support industry despite all official efforts to keep silver at home (see p. 208). While there were more who strove for advancement in the church or at court or in the army than in other countries, their chances for mercantile ventures or industrial investment were correspondingly smaller. What was missing, more than in France or the Dutch Republic or in England, was an urban middle class. This was apparent as early as 1600: in that year a perceptive public official, Gonzalez de Cellorigo, invidiously compared the Spain of 1492, with its harmonious balance among the classes, with the Spain of 1600, which had come, he wrote, "to be an extreme contrast of rich and poor," with "no means of adjusting them to one another." The condition of Spain, he added, "is one in which we have rich who loll at ease, or poor who beg, and we lack people of the middling sort, whom neither wealth nor poverty prevents from pursuing the rightful kind of business enjoined by natural law" [57]—by which he meant the kind of productive effort that was making the Dutch so rich.

Beneath all this was a fatal loss in morale. The terrible tragedy of the Armada and the humiliating spectacle of a truce with the Dutch contrasted bitterly with the glorious legend of the *reconquista;* the concentration on further military adventures in the early seventeenth century was less a commitment to glory than a final admission of incompetence and a failure of will, a confession of inability to use the breathing space of peace. If more and more Spaniards sought courtier's jobs or clerical benefices, this was less from conviction than from despair, not a gratification but a refuge. The age that was dawning was the age in which the inglorious—the merchant, the scientist, the engineer—would achieve glory. It was an age in which the Spain of the Counter-Reformation, despite its great painters and writers, would have no place.

SELECTED READINGS
For sixteenth- and early seventeenth-century Spain, see, J. H. Elliott, *Imperial Spain, 1469–1716* (1963); H. Mariéjol, *The Spain of Ferdinand and Isabella* (tr. 1961); and J. Lynch, *Spain Under the Hapsburgs,* vol. I, *Empire and Absolutism, 1516–1598* (1964).

[57] Quoted in Elliott, *Imperial Spain,* 305.

Lynch's second volume, *Spain and America, 1598-1700* (1969), continues his lucid account. The standard biography of Charles V remains Karl Brandi, *The Emperor Charles V* (tr. 1939). Reginald Trevor Davies, *The Golden Century of Spain, 1501-1621* (rev. ed., 1965), remains useful for this period.

For the age of the Counter-Reformation, see J. H. Elliott, *Europe Divided, 1559-1598* (1969); R. B. Wernham, ed., *The Counter Reformation and Price Revolution, 1559-1610* (1958), a volume in *The New Cambridge Modern History;* and H. O. Evennett, *The Spirit of the Counter Reformation* (1968). See also the magisterial account by Hubert Jedin, *The Council of Trent* (1957-1961). A. G. Dickens, *The Counter Reformation* (1969), is popular and accurate. Amidst a controversial literature on the Jesuits, one may single out René Fülöp-Miller, *The Power and the Secret of the Jesuits* (1930), and Christopher Hollis, *The Jesuits* (1968). Hollis has also written a biography of Loyola (1931), which may be read in conjunction with James Brodrick, *The Origin of the Jesuits* (1956).

For Spain overseas, see in addition to the books on Spain just cited, J. H. Parry, *The Spanish Seaborne Empire* (1966), to be supplemented by Parry's earlier monograph, *The Spanish Theory of Empire in the Sixteenth Century* (1940); Lewis Hanke's, *The Spanish Struggle for Justice in the Conquest of America* (1949) and his *Aristotle and the American Indian* (1959), which ably sums up the moral and theological problems of conquest. Charles Gibson, *Spain in America* (1966), is a dependable synthesis. For the economic impact of Spanish expansion, see the pioneering, still controverted E. J. Hamilton, *American Treasure and the Price Revolution in Spain, 1501-1650* (1934); on this point see J. Vincent Vives, *An Economic History of Spain from the Earliest Times to the End of the Nineteenth Century* (tr. 1969).

J. E. Neale, *The Age of Catherine de' Medici* (1943), is a clear but very short history of France in the second half of the sixteenth century; it should be supplemented with the old yet still useful study by James Westfall Thompson, *Wars of Religion in France, 1559-1576* (1909); Jean Héritier's biography, *Catherine de Medici* (tr. 1963); and A. J. Grant's *The Huguenots* (1934). Among many biographies of Henri IV none is wholly satisfactory; the best in English is perhaps Hesketh Pearson, *Henry of Navarre, The King Who Dared* (1963). See also Davis Bitton, *The French Nobility in Crisis, 1560-1640* (1969). David Buissert, *Sully and the Growth of Centralized Government in France, 1598-1610* (1968), ably deals with Henri's great minister, while Raymond F. Kierstead, *Pomponne de Bellièvre: A Study of the King's Men in the Age of Henry IV* (1968), ably deals with another. See also the opening chapters of Orest Ranum, *Paris in the Age of Absolutism* (1968).

The Elizabethan reign is best approached through J. E. Neale, *Queen Elizabeth I* (rev. ed., 1966); see also the judicious survey by J. B. Black, *The Reign of Queen Elizabeth, 1558-1603* (1936). The politics in the early part of her reign are lucidly examined in Wallace MacCaffrey, *The Shaping of the Elizabethan Regime* (1968). Joel Hurstfield, *Elizabeth I and the Unity of England* (1966), is short and clear. For Elizabeth's ministers there are the splendid volumes by Conyers Read: *Mr. Secretary Walsingham,* 3 vols. (1925), *Mr. Secretary Cecil* (1955), and *Lord Burghley and Queen Elizabeth* (1960); for her parliaments there are the equally splendid volumes by J. E. Neale: *Elizabeth I and Her Parliaments, 1559-1581* (1953), and *Elizabeth I and Her Parliaments, 1584-1601* (1957). For the Elizabethan Settlement, see J. V. P. Thompson, *Supreme Governor* (1940). Lawrence Stone, *The Crisis of the Aristocracy, 1558-1641* (1965, abridged ed., 1967), profoundly analyzes the social history of England's peerage. Louis B. Wright analyzes a lower social stratum in *Middle Class Culture in Elizabethan England* (1935). The failure of the attempt of Philip II to overthrow Queen Elizabeth is told in Garrett Mattingly's superb narrative and analysis, *The Armada* (1959).

On English religious history, see Patrick Collinson, *The Elizabethan Puritan Movement* (1967); see also Marshall Moon Knappen, *Tudor Puritanism* (1939); William Haller, *The Rise of Puritanism* (1938); and J. F. H. New, *Anglican and Puritan: The Basis of Their Opposition, 1558-1640* (1964). Christopher Hill, *Economic Problems of the Church: From Archbishop Whitgift to the Long Parliament* (1956), is an excellent survey of a neglected subject. J. H. Pollen, *The English Catholics in the Reign of Queen Elizabeth* (1920), and Wilbur K. Jordan, *The Development of Religious Toleration in England to the Death of Queen Elizabeth* (1931), are both very useful.

For English commercial enterprise in those decades, see J. A. Williamson, *The Ocean in English History* (1941); Williamson's biography, *Sir Francis Drake* (1951); G. D. Ramsay, *English Overseas Trade During the Centuries of the Emergence* (1957); and the modern, technical essay by Theodore W. Rabb, *Enterprise and Empire: Merchant and Gentry Investment in the Expansion of England, 1575-1630* (1967). D. B. Quinn, *Raleigh* (1947), is a good biography.

The best known work on the birth of the Dutch Republic is Pieter Geyl, *The Revolt of the Netherlands, 1555-1609* (rev. ed., 1958), which revises earlier views of the revolt as a purely Protestant rebellion against Catholics. Geyl continued his history with *The Netherlands in the Seventeenth Century,* Part One (tr. 1961). Johan Huizinga, "Dutch Civilisation in the Seventeenth Century," in Huizinga, *Dutch Civilisation in the Seventeenth Century and Other Essays* (tr. 1968), is suggestive. *William the Silent,* by C. V. Wedgwood (1944), is the best biography in English. The early chapters of Charles Wilson, *The Dutch Republic and the Civilisation of the Seventeenth Century* (1968), are short and authoritative. See also Book I of G. J. Renier, *The Dutch Nation: An Historical Study* (1944), which draws extensively on pamphlet literature.

5

Commerce
and Culture

COMMERCE: THE EXPANSION OF THE
EUROPEAN ECONOMY

Commercial Capitalism

In 1721, in his speech from the throne at the opening of Parliament, George I
of England observed that it was the nation's commerce upon which "the riches
and grandeur of this nation chiefly depend."[1] A quarter of a century later,
David Hume praised merchants as "one of the most useful races of men."[2]
Neither of these remarks was startling, nor were they intended to be. The
benefits of commerce and the value of commercial men had long been

---

[1] Quoted in C. H. Wilson, "Trade, Society and the State," in *Cambridge Economic History of
Europe,* vol. IV (1967), 516. The author of this speech, of course, was not the king but his chief
minister, Sir Robert Walpole.

[2] "Of Interest," *Philosophical Works,* III, 324.

recognized, certainly since the middle of the fifteenth century—such matters are impossible to date with any precision—when the more advanced sectors of the European economy had entered the era of commercial capitalism.[3]

Historians seeking to define capitalism normally throw up their hands in despair and then bravely list some characteristics they hope may point the reader in the right direction. Certainly trade and greed—two of its indispensable ingredients—are as old as civilization itself. And the medieval centuries that directly precede the capitalist era displayed many of its qualities; they too had known far-flung commercial activities like international fairs and the long-range hauling of goods. What distinguishes early modern capitalism from previous phases is that it vastly extended the range and intensity of economic relations, gave them a complex organization, eased them with a series of novel techniques, and made a revolution in credit. And these changes were accompanied and rationalized by a change in attitude: "Capitalism," the influential German sociologist Max Weber wrote half a century ago, "is identical with the pursuit of profit, and forever renewed profit, by means of continuous, rationalistic, capitalistic enterprise."[4] Medieval economic life was severely circumscribed; goods were produced principally for direct use or local sale and, if sold, paid for generally in kind; in commercial capitalism goods came to be produced primarily for exchange and were paid for in currency. What had been parochial, occasional, difficult, dangerous, and primitive became international, customary, easy, safe, and complicated.

While the coming of capitalism was anything but a sudden irruption, its eventual triumph remade the face of Europe so decisively that its origins, its "causes," have held considerable fascination for historians. One ingenious and comprehensive interpretation that long captured historians' imagination and continues to have its adherents is associated with Max Weber. Impressed by the extraordinary share of Protestants, and especially Calvinists, in capitalist enterprise, Weber postulated a direct relationship between the Calvinist idea of "calling" and the "spirit of capitalism." Calvinism, Weber suggested, propagated a "worldly asceticism," which prized sobriety, thrift, and upright conduct in secular affairs as part of the Christian's duty. Calvinists therefore, far more than other Christians, would be inclined to postpone gratification, save money, and see worldly success as one of the signs of election.[5] Surely, someone who

---

[3] The very name "capitalism" had and in many quarters continues to have, tendentious overtones; similarly, the various adjectives that describe its "stages"—commercial, industrial, financial—have been part of the long debate over the role of capitalism as a necessary stage on the road to socialism. None of them wholly fits, since in the stage with which we are here concerned finance played a very significant part, as did private small-scale industry. Yet the adjectives are not wholly without value; they tell us which aspect of capitalist enterprise was dominant.

[4] *The Protestant Ethic and the Spirit of Capitalism* (1904-1905, tr. 1930), 17.

[5] It will be recalled that Calvin offered his sectaries no guarantees; God had chosen or rejected them before they had ever been born, and their fortunes in life were at best a sign of election, never a means to it. Still, far from inducing apathy, the Calvinist doctrine of predestination produced a race of responsible and hard-working men (see p. 151).

would work rather than play, and invest rather than spend, was precisely the kind of person useful for capitalist accumulation.

The difficulty with the Weber thesis, attractive as it appears, is twofold, and ultimately it must be rejected as an explanation. Many capitalists, both before and during the reign of capitalism, were not Calvinists; and many Calvinists were not capitalists. In fact, on the crucial moral issue on which Roman Catholic teaching can be said to have been anticapitalist—its insistence on the "just price" and its associated condemnation of "usury"—Christians of all persuasians were of the same mind. Medieval theologians had thought it evident and right that a product should be sold for what it cost to produce, a cost calculated to include the wage of the producer. They thought it just as evident, and just as right, that since money was "sterile," merely a medium of exchange, lending should be without profit. Thomas Aquinas formulated and reinforced this hostility to interest-taking by associating the word of Aristotle to the explicit text from Scriptures. The prohibition entered the canon law and was occasionally enforced by secular courts; in 1179 the Third Lateran Council denied "usurers" access to communion. But Luther was quite as scathing against the Fuggers and their money-lending, Calvin himself took little interest in the question, and Calvinist divines in the commercial Dutch Republic down to the seventeenth century inveighed against usurers with the same aversion, and even the same arguments, that St. Thomas Aquinas had expended upon them four centuries earlier. What made interest-taking finally acceptable was not the Calvinist spirit but the practical necessity of extending credit, the recognition that the lender should be compensated for his risks, the drop in the interest rate, and the rise of dependable and respectable banks.

This much seems clear: the capitalist style was above all urban, cosmopolitan, impatient with traditional constraints. A remarkable early capitalist was Francesco Di Marco Datini, a fourteenth-century merchant from the city of Prato, near Florence, who pyramided a minute inheritance into a vast fortune. Datini made money at anything from which money could be made: spices and wool, slaves and lead, oranges and wine. His ledgers (all of them, with his memoranda and his enormous business correspondence meticulously preserved for posterity) bear the telling motto: "In the name of God and profit." He lived, his modern biographer tells us, in a "small, busy earthy society" and was strangely like a modern capitalist: "In the extent and variety of his ventures, in his powers of organization, in his international outlook, in his swift adaptability to the changes of a society in turmoil, as in his own ambition, shrewdness, tenacity, anxiety, and greed, he is a forerunner of the businessman of today."[6] In the 1360s, in Avignon, he sold arms both to the pope and to his enemies. The Dutch merchants who, in the midst of their desperate struggle for independence, sold goods to Spain, and later, during the Dutch war with England, munitions to the English, were Datini's spiritual offspring.

---

[6] Iris Origo, The Merchant of Prato, Francesco Di Marco Datini, 1335-1410 (1957), introduction, passim.

This striking freedom from patriotic, religious, and ethical shackles has long given socialists and other critics of capitalism rich material for derision. But these vices were virtues essential to the system. Medieval thought was dominated by ruminations about the just price, by conservative legal and professional institutions, which all stood in the way of the massive accumulation of capital without which capitalism would have been unthinkable. It is therefore anything but surprising that capitalism in recognizable form should first have taken shape in the Italian city-states, and that Italians should have retained a strong grip on trading and banking firms all across Europe for centuries, even after Flemings and Englishmen had risen to compete with them. The Italian cities were schools of cosmopolitans, freer than their counterparts elsewhere from feudal habits; while, by the sixteenth century, their gilds obstructed necessary innovation and healthy competition, the early gilds were machines of economic progress. Italians invented all the techniques that were to mark commercial capitalism, including double-entry bookkeeping, a rationalistic device on which Luca Pacioli published a classic treatise in 1494, soon imitated in other countries. Similarly, the Italians were the first to develop maritime insurance, which spread the risks of expensive trading voyages among large numbers of investors, and the first, or at least the most active, in transforming themselves from money-lenders into commercial bankers—organizers of usury. The bankers from Milan became proverbial; it is a reminiscence of these early itinerant Italians from Lombardy that the financial district in London should be centered in Lombard Street. Flanders, the second center of capitalist enterprise, was crowded with, and dominated by, representatives of Florentine, Genoese, and Venetian firms. As rapidly and as aptly as they could, northerners acknowledged Italian superiority and copied Italian techniques for their own profit: when the Augsburg banking house of Fugger wanted to expand its operations, it sent one of its family to Venice to live there and study the Italian methods. And the Italians also excelled in manufacture: Florence in particular was preeminent in the weaving and finishing of cloth.

Capitalism, of course, was not simply a matter of the "capitalist spirit." It was a conjunction of mentality with opportunity. The Italian cities, notably Venice, profited enormously from the commercial stimulation the Crusaders had given them on their way to and from the Holy Land; and the Italian republics were splendidly situated to participate in the Mediterranean grain trade and the trade in luxury goods with the Orient. Flanders, which came to rival Italy in the fifteenth century, followed the Italian lead: its commercial cities served as entrepots, transhipping grain and lumber from the Baltic and spices and textiles from the Mediterranean. And, also on the Italian model, the Flemish cities developed their own cloth industries.

While it is of the essence of capitalism that private traders and private manufacturers enter the market for the sake of private gain, competition among capitalists was not confined to rivalry among individuals or houses. In order to raise capital for large-scale ventures and to secure protection for representatives abroad, capitalists often leagued together. Competition then simply reappeared on a larger and more vicious scale, among cities or regions. The history of the Hanseatic League is a vivid instance of this sort of collective capitalism. Formed in the fourteenth century by an association of German merchants from trading cities like Hamburg, Leipzig, Bremen, Danzig, Stettin, and Lübeck, it achieved official standing as a league in 1370 and henceforth acted as a political and military entity, flying its own flag and concluding its own treaties. The Hanse established "factories," settlements in foreign cities which served as protected enclaves where Hanse merchants settled or visited and lived by their own regulations. In the fifteenth and sixteenth centuries the Hanse was a powerful force, dominating trade in the Baltic region, and spreading its factories from the Norwegian town of Bergen to the Russian town of Novgorod, participating in the Netherlands trade with its factory in Bruges and the English trade with its factory, the "Steelyard," in London. Then, with the rise of the political power of the English and the Dutch, the Hanse found formidable and in the long run fatal rivals. The Dutch, with their incomparable ships, began to interfere with the Hanse monopoly in the Baltic Sea; Dutch fishermen began to outstrip their Hanseatic competitors; the English, in search of independence, established their own small Hanse, the Merchant Adventurers. In 1611, this English association set up its factory at Hamburg, a sign that the great days of the Hanse were over.

The drastic decline of the Hanse, however, was not merely the consequence of economic warfare among rival traders; it was symptomatic of a more general and more fundamental shift in the patterns of trade and centers of economic power that took place in the late sixteenth century. Much went into that shift: the fortunes of war, the recovery of population, and above all the belated effects of the expeditions of Columbus, Vasco da Gama, and Magellan. The discoveries made their economic impact slowly, but when it came, it was stunning.

Commerce and Prices: Two Revolutions

Historians are coming to be as embarrassed with the word "revolution" as they have long been with the word "capitalism," and with justice. Surely the French Revolution and the Russian Revolution, with their explosive speed, bloody action, and drastic and permanent overturn of authority, are authentic specimens; to call the enlargement of trade and the inflation of the early modern period "revolutions," as historians have normally done, is to lend an aura of rapidity and violence to developments that were slow, devious, and so complicated that their contemporaries often could hardly describe them. Yet the changes in commerce and prices were so vast and so irreversible that we may perhaps, if we are duly cautious, speak of the "commercial revolution" and the "price revolution."

By 1600, long-distance trade was an old story. As early as the second half of the thirteenth century, the Polos, a Venetian family, among whom Marco Polo is only the most famous, had reached China on several expeditions, and thereafter the European market had enjoyed highly coveted spices from the East. Later, toward the end of the fifteenth century, Portuguese explorers sought and found a direct route to India by sea, around the Cape of Good Hope, and the Spaniards explored America, bringing back its sugar, tobacco, and silver (see p. 84).

Yet the obvious did not happen, certainly not immediately and not simply. Portuguese and Spanish ports—Lisbon and Seville above all—were the direct beneficiaries of the empires their governments were establishing in India and in Central and South America. For a few heady decades, Lisbon became the dominant port for the Oriental spice trade—pepper, cinnamon, nutmeg—and Seville the receiving center for bullion from the seemingly inexhaustible American mines. But the pouring in of unknown commodities or of unprecedented quantities of precious metals was beyond the capacity of the Portuguese and Spanish governments to cope with. The commercial potential uncovered by the voyages seemed more frightening than exhilarating. In any event, the Spanish and Portuguese way of managing them—royal protection and close state supervision—turned out to be unfortunate. With the rise of the early modern state, simultaneous and associated with the age of discovery and commercial revolution, every government took a consuming interest in economic affairs.[7] But the Iberian governments depended on control almost entirely, at the expense of private investment and commercial independence. The Portuguese monarchy granted some monopoly rights to favored individuals, but kept monopolies over bullion and over the most desirable of commodities, the spice imports; and it owned, or tightly controlled, Portuguese merchant fleets. The Spanish government, far from avoiding Portugal's mistakes, simply repeated them: it organized commerce under royal officials, arbitrarily granted away monopolies, and engaged in trade directly. The short-run consequence was the rapid amassing of wealth; the long-range consequence, the conquest of trade by more flexible nations.

The inability of Portugal and Spain to convert their discoveries and their conquests into lasting economic advantage supports the dictum of the English historian, Charles Wilson, that it was "not merely coincidence" that trade after 1500 should flourish above all in the northern Italian and in the Flemish cities. These were "areas where the tradesmen of the cities had been most successful in emancipating themselves from feudal interference and in keeping at bay the newer threat of more centralized political control offered by the new monarchies," and where men "glimpsed the material advance that was possible when tradesmen were left in peace unflattered by the attentions of strategists who regarded their activities as sinews of war."[8] The Italian cities, therefore, never

---

[7] For a discussion of mercantilism, see p. 300.
[8] Wilson, "Trade, Society, and the State," 492.

had to fear their Iberian rivals as their gravest threat. The Venetian spice trade, though it dropped briefly early in the sixteenth century, revived later. Plainly the economic decay so evident in Italian life in the seventeenth century, resulted mainly from the ossification of Italian economic institutions, unwise governmental policies, and the ruthless competition offered by areas in the north—England and the Dutch Republic—that had once been so dependent on their Mediterranean teacher.

The decline of Italian manufacturing, shipping, and trade was only one consequence of the commercial revolution. That revolution changed the face of Europe. Along with political power, economic power gradually but decisively shifted northward. As the volume of trade grew, commodities that had been rare became common, and new commodities, hitherto wholly unknown, changed habits of consumption. By the middle of the seventeenth century, thousands of Europeans were drinking tea and coffee and smoking tobacco. Other exotic items, like china, remained luxuries, while such strange new products as quinine and opium gave European physicians new opportunities for experimenting with their patients. A new world, quite literally, had opened for European culture, supplying it with materials for unheard-of profits, new myths, and troublesome reflections—what *was* one to make of a highly civilized country like China which was obviously living so well without the blessings of Christianity?

One unmistakable characteristic of the commercial revolution, there for all to see, was the rise of large cities. While in 1500, only four European cities— Paris, Milan, Venice, and Naples—had over one hundred thousand inhabitants, by 1600, the number had risen to twelve and had come to include, in addition, Palermo and Messina, Lisbon and Seville, Rome and London, Antwerp and Amsterdam. Smaller cities like Florence and Hamburg and Danzig were not far behind.[9] This urbanization both followed and caused new manufactures and larger consumption, radical ideas and social problems. The city, a microcosm of the economic changes then overtaking Europe, was proof of the mixed quality of "progress": life in the city was more colorful, but also shorter; men were as open to new notions there as they were vulnerable to the plague.

The other economic upheaval of the time, the price revolution, was inextricably tied to the growth of European commerce. With our present state of historical information, it remains, despite diligent research, hard to assess the significance of the inflation that engulfed Europe in the sixteenth century, especially from the 1560s on. We still know too little about real wage rates; prices rose differently in different areas and for different commodities. This much we may say with confidence: the inflation Europe had been experiencing since the late fifteenth century was greatly intensified as precious metals, first gold and then silver, began to pour into Europe after the conquests of Mexico and Peru. While there was widespread puzzlement over the phenomenon,

---

[9] See maps in *The New Cambridge Modern History,* vol. III (1968), 35. Paris and Naples actually had over two hundred thousand inhabitants.

some writers acutely diagnosed it on the spot. In the late 1560s, Jean Bodin (see p. 179) attributed inflation to several minor causes but chiefly to the influx of precious metals from overseas. And it *was* an overwhelming experience. In Spain, the first recipient of the metals, prices trebled in a century; in France and England they more than doubled. Nor do these figures tell the whole story: the price of grain was far more subject to inflation than that of other commodities. By around 1600, wholesale grain prices (a sensitive indicator for the price of food) were roughly five times what they had been a century before, while in France in the same period they had increased about seven times.

Spain, to be sure, had not intended to produce this effect. Officially, the gold and silver received at Seville were to stay in the country in obedience to the generally accepted notion that the possession of precious metals was equivalent to the possession of wealth. But, while prohibiting the export of bullion, the Spanish government made its export unavoidable. There was smuggling, which the Spaniards did little to prevent. Worse than that, there was Spain's unfavorable balance of trade: while the country exported salt and oil, it needed large infusions of wheat and cloth, for consumption both at home and in Spanish America. All this had to be paid for mainly in silver. Worst of all, Spain insisted on its ruinously expensive foreign policy, which meant the shipment of bullion, mainly to Antwerp, to pay for troops and war supplies. Thus gold and silver spread, became commodities for speculators, and fed manufacturing and trade alike.

Bodin's explanation for the impressive inflation of his day has much plausibility, but it does not seem to be the whole truth. The rapid rise or, rather, recovery of population also played its part. Precise population estimates are impossible in the absence of reliable statistics, but the fairly well-documented growth of towns in this period is only one of several strong indications of a remarkable rise: by no means all the new city dwellers were migrants from the land. Population increase (like so much else in social history) was both a blessing and a curse: it showed that the plague was receding and health improving; it gave the prosperous farmer the manpower he needed, and the merchant new customers. But increased population also exercised pressure on scarce food resources, which did not grow as rapidly as the number of people, and helped to depress wages, which did not rise as rapidly as did prices. The result was that peasants found themselves subdividing land among their children, laborers found themselves working longer hours for less real income, and all the poor (which is to say, the bulk of Europe's population) found themselves closer to sheer hunger through the rise in food prices. Thus the pressure of population—that is, increased demand—is likely to have been an element in the great inflation of the sixteenth century.

The consequences of these far-reaching and fundamental economic changes are as hard to assess as their causes; they remain the subject of intense investigation and vociferous controversy. The continuing debate among English historians over the rise (or decline) of the English gentry in the seventeenth

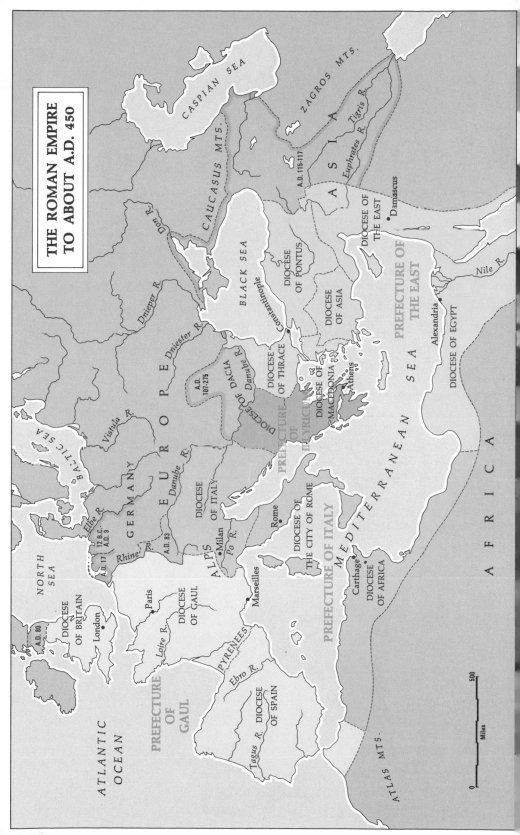

THE ROMAN EMPIRE
TO ABOUT A.D. 450

ATLANTIC OCEAN

NORTH SEA

BALTIC SEA

CASPIAN SEA

DIOCESE OF BRITAIN

A.D. 80

London

DIOCESE OF GAUL

PREFECTURE OF GAUL

Paris

Loire R.

PYRENEES

Ebro R.

Tagus R. DIOCESE OF SPAIN

Marseilles

ALPS

Milan

Po R.

Rome

DIOCESE OF ITALY

DIOCESE OF THE CITY OF ROME

PREFECTURE OF ITALY

Carthage

DIOCESE OF AFRICA

MEDITERRANEAN SEA

ATLAS MTS.

AFRICA

Rhine R.

A.D. 17

12 B.C. A.D. 9

Elbe R.

GERMANY

Vistula R.

A.D. 83

Danube R.

EUROPE

Dnieper R.

Dniester R.

Danube R.

A.D. 107–275

DIOCESE OF DACIA

DIOCESE OF ILLYRICUM

PREFECTURE OF ILLYRICUM

DIOCESE OF THRACE

Constantinople

DIOCESE OF MACEDONIA

Athens

BLACK SEA

Don R.

CAUCASUS MTS.

DIOCESE OF PONTUS

DIOCESE OF ASIA

A.D. 115–117

ZAGROS MTS.

Tigris R.

Euphrates R.

A S I A

DIOCESE OF THE EAST

Damascus

PREFECTURE OF THE EAST

Alexandria

DIOCESE OF EGYPT

Nile R.

AFRICA

500

Miles

0

Plate 1

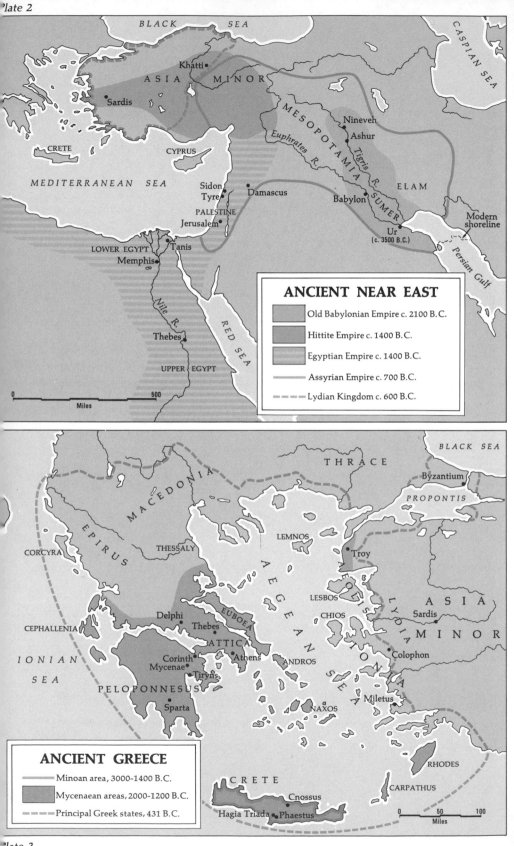

Plate 2

ANCIENT NEAR EAST

- Old Babylonian Empire c. 2100 B.C.
- Hittite Empire c. 1400 B.C.
- Egyptian Empire c. 1400 B.C.
- Assyrian Empire c. 700 B.C.
- Lydian Kingdom c. 600 B.C.

BLACK SEA

CASPIAN SEA

Khatti

ASIA MINOR

Sardis

MESOPOTAMIA

Euphrates R.

Nineveh

Ashur

Tigris R.

ELAM

SUMER

Babylon

Ur
(c. 3500 B.C.)

Modern shoreline

Persian Gulf

CRETE

CYPRUS

MEDITERRANEAN SEA

Sidon

Tyre

Damascus

PALESTINE

Jerusalem

LOWER EGYPT

Tanis

Memphis

Nile R.

RED SEA

Thebes

UPPER EGYPT

0   500
Miles

ANCIENT GREECE

- Minoan area, 3000–1400 B.C.
- Mycenaean areas, 2000–1200 B.C.
- Principal Greek states, 431 B.C.

BLACK SEA

THRACE

Byzantium

MACEDONIA

PROPONTIS

EPIRUS

THESSALY

LEMNOS

Troy

CORCYRA

A E G E A N   S E A

LESBOS

CHIOS

ASIA MINOR

LYDIA

Sardis

Delphi

EUBOEA

Colophon

CEPHALLENIA

Thebes

ATTICA

IONIA

IONIAN SEA

Corinth

Mycenae

Athens

ANDROS

Tiryns

Miletus

PELOPONNESUS

NAXOS

Sparta

RHODES

CRETE

CARPATHUS

Cnossus

Hagia Triada

Phaestus

0   50   100
Miles

Plate 3

Ancient Near East

Sumer. The first Mesopotamian civilizations emerged at Sumer c. 4000 B.C. City-states developed theocracies with a rich culture and ceremonial religion; writing appeared c. 3000. Akkadians from north of Sumer led by Sargon I conquered Sumer c. 2300. His dynasty, which lasted until 2150 when the Sumerians regained independence, was followed by a succession of kings who ruled until c. 2000 when Elamite invaders captured the capital, Ur.

Assyria. In the third millennium the city of Ashur was ruled by Sumer and shared its culture. As Sumer waned, Assyria rose and in 1380 Ashur-uballit I became the first great king of Assyria. Under a series of aggressive rulers, Assyria conquered most of Mesopotamia and dominated it until defeated in 612.

Babylonia. Rival to Assyria and Sumer, Babylonia developed an independent theocracy c. 2000. While the Gilgamesh epic reveals a despairing religion, materially Babylonia's centralized irrigation system made it the breadbasket of Mesopotamia. In the 1700s Hammurabi, Babylon's great lawgiver, took Sumer and Akkad, but c. 1000 Babylon was overrun by Bedouins and declined. After subjection to Assyria, Babylon joined Persia to destroy Assyria in 612 but in 538 fell to the Persians.

Egypt. About 3000 B.C. King Menes of Upper Egypt conquered the delta kingdom of Lower Egypt and founded an empire that lasted to 332 B.C., though the Hyksos invaded and held Egypt briefly from c. 1700 to 1570. The pharaohs consolidated their power under Amenhotep III (c. 1411) and extended their empire around the Mediterranean. Later, Egypt was defeated by the Hittites and lost its Syrian cities. Rameses II (1299–1232) tried to win back the cities and hold the Hittites off by signing a treaty of friendship with them. After his death invaders appeared; wars with Libya, Canaan, and raiders from Asia Minor sapped Egypt's strength. From c. 1100 the country declined further as weak kings poured wealth into sterile religious ceremonials and neglected the needs of the state.

Ancient Greece

Crete. The island was occupied in 4000 B.C. and by 2000 developed a rich civilization sustained by Mediterranean trade. Farmers, artisans, and traders were prominent in Crete's economy while at Cnossus, Phaestus, and Hagia Triada the architecture of the palaces suggest a relatively egalitarian society. This brilliant Minoan civilization came to an end when sea raiders destroyed Cnossus and Phaestus in 1400.

Mycenae. On the mainland c. 2000 B.C., Greek-speaking invaders began to establish settlements, of which Mycenae was the most prominent. In the 1600s they traded extensively across the Mediterranean and built impressive palaces at Mycenae. Mycenean civilization lasted until the city fell to the Dorians in 1200. Four centuries of barbarism followed, yet later Greeks regarded the Myceneans as their ancestors.

Greece. In the 700s Greek life began to develop as trading increased and the city-states evolved more organized forms of government. Contacts with Asia Minor introduced writing, new religions, and new forms of art. Sparta and Athens emerged as the most powerful Greek states and bore the brunt of the Persian War. After the Greek victory at Plataea in 479, Athens led the other states, except Sparta, into a permanent defensive alliance. When, in 468 several states tried to withdraw from it, Athens attacked and made vassals of its former allies. At its height, the Athenian empire extended over 200 cities. By 450 Pericles presided over Athens' greatest development, following twin policies of imperialism and peace, but by 431 Athens and Sparta were at war. This Peloponnesian War lasted until 404 ending in the total defeat of Athens. The city never regained its political and cultural supremacy.

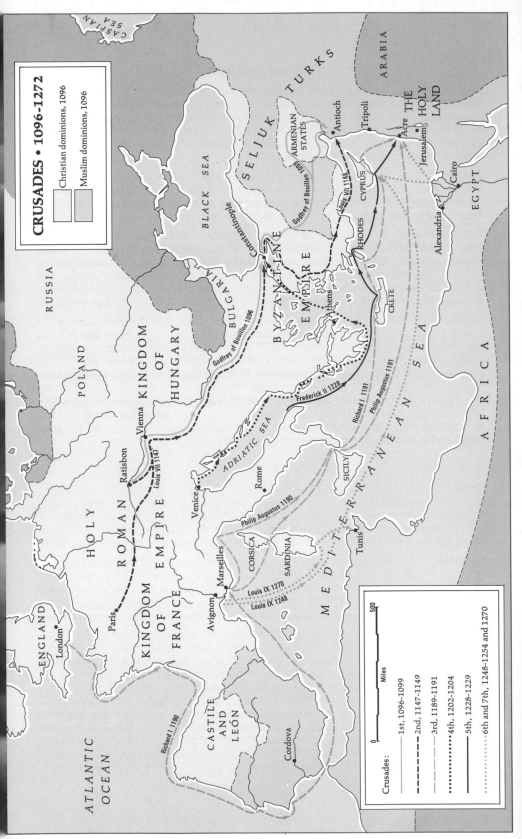

Plate 4

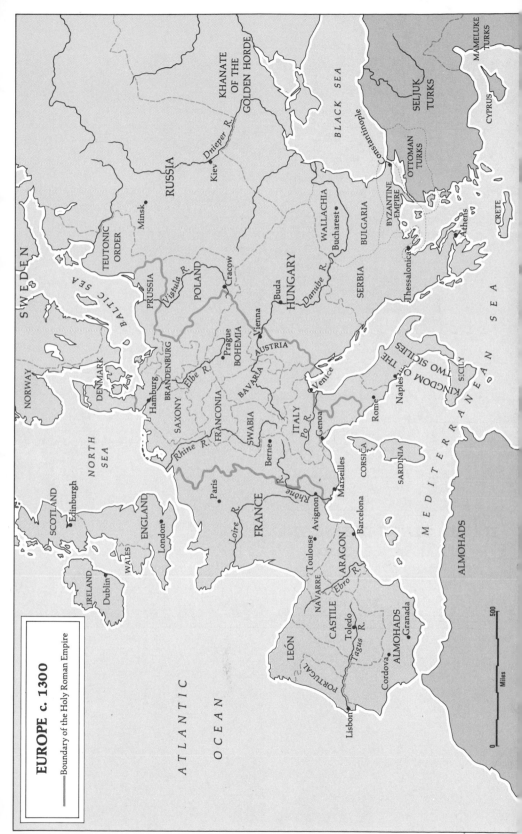

EUROPE c. 1300

—— Boundary of the Holy Roman Empire

ATLANTIC OCEAN

SCOTLAND
Edinburgh

IRELAND
Dublin

ENGLAND
London

WALES

NORTH SEA

NORWAY

SWEDEN

DENMARK
Hamburg

BALTIC SEA

TEUTONIC ORDER

Minsk

RUSSIA

Dnieper R.

Kiev

KHANATE OF THE GOLDEN HORDE

PRUSSIA

Vistula R.

POLAND
Cracow

BRANDENBURG

SAXONY
Elbe R.

Prague
BOHEMIA

Buda
Vienna
AUSTRIA
HUNGARY

Danube R.

WALLACHIA
Bucharest

BULGARIA

SERBIA

BLACK SEA

Constantinople
BYZANTINE EMPIRE

Thessalonica

Athens

SELJUK TURKS

OTTOMAN TURKS

MAMELUKE TURKS

CYPRUS

CRETE

FRANCONIA

BAVARIA

SWABIA

Berne

Rhine R.

Paris

FRANCE

Loire R.

Toulouse

Avignon

Rhône R.

Marseilles

Barcelona

ARAGON

NAVARRE

Ebro R.

CASTILE
Toledo

Tagus R.

LEÓN

PORTUGAL

Lisbon

Cordova

ALMOHADS
Granada

ALMOHADS

CORSICA

SARDINIA

ITALY
Po R.
Genoa

Venice

Rome

Naples

KINGDOM OF THE TWO SICILIES

SICILY

MEDITERRANEAN SEA

500
Miles
0

Plate 5

SWISS
CONFEDERATION

Geneva

HUNGARY

Sava R.

Danube R.

DUCHY

OF

Milan

Aosta

MILAN

REPUBLIC OF VENICE

Verona

Trieste

Po R.

M. OF
MANTUA

Padua

Venice

OTTOMAN

DUCHY

Turin

ISTRIA
(Venice)

EMPIRE

FRANCE

OF

M. OF
MONTFERRAT

Piacenza

Modena

D. OF
FERRARA

M. OF
SALUZZO

SAVOY

REP. OF GENOA

D. OF
MODENA

Bologna

Ravenna

DALMATIA
(Venice)

Genoa

MONACO

REP. OF LUCCA

REP. OF SAN MARINO

Nice

Pisa

Arno R.

Florence

Ragusa

REP. OF FLORENCE

A
D
R
I
A
T
I
C

S
E
A

Siena

Assisi

ELBA

REP. OF
SIENA

PAPAL
STATES

D. OF
PIOMBINO

Tiber R.

CORSICA
(To Genoa 1284)

Rome

KINGDOM
OF NAPLES
(To Spain 1504)

Brindisi

SARDINIA
(To Spain 1478)

Naples

T Y R R H E N I A N

S E A

Palermo

Reggio

SICILY
(To Spain 1504)

ITALIAN STATES DURING THE
RENAISSANCE c. 1500

Claimed by the Pope

D.—Duchy   M.—Marquisate

0   100   200

Miles

Plate 6

BURGUNDIAN LANDS • 1363-1477

Lands of Philip the Bold, 1363-1404

Partition of 1404 (collateral branch of Nevers-Rethel)

Acquired by Philip the Good, 1419-1467

Acquired by Charles the Rash, 1467-1477

Areas under Burgundian influence or protection

Boundary of the Holy Roman Empire, 1056-1493

1474 × Battle site with date   1475 Date of acquisition

NORTH SEA

Hambur

●Bremen

ENGLAND

HOLLAND
1428-1433

Amsterdam

GELDERLAND
1475

UTRECHT
●Utrecht

HOLY

Rotterdam

Rhine R.

ZEELAND
1433

BRABANT
1430

Antwerp

Bruges
Ghent●

LIÈGE

Neuss
1474

Cologne

ROMAN

Calais

FLANDERS
1383

Brussels

LIMBURG
1430

BOULOGNE
1435

Lille

Brussels●

Liège

Namur

ARTOIS
1384

HAINAUT
1428-1433

CAMBRAI

Meuse R.

LUXEMBURG
1443

Mosel R.

Frankfurt●

EU

PICARDY
1435

Amiens●

VERMANDOIS
1435

Luxemburg

EMPIRE

E

RETHEL

VERDUN

Seine R.

Oise R.

Marne R.

BAR

METZ

LOWER
ALSACE

Rhine R.

Paris●

TOUL

Nancy
1477

Strasbourg●

FRANCE

LORRAINE
1475

UPPER
ALSACE

BREISGAU

ILES

BAR-S.-
SEINE

SUNDGAU

Loire R.

AUXERRE
1435

Héricourt
1474 ×

Basle

Dijon●

FREE
BURGUNDY

Creuse R.

NEVERS
1384-1404,
1465

BURGUNDY
1363

Saône R.

●Besançon

Murten
1476

SWISS

●Berne

(FRANCHE-
COMTÉ)
1384

Grandson
1476

CONFEDERATION

CHAROLAIS
1360

MÂCON
1435

Allier R.

Rhône R.

Lyons●

0   50   100
Miles

Plate 7

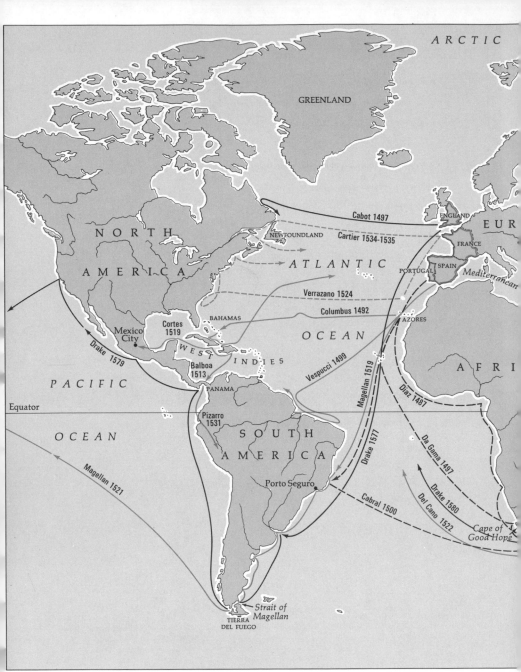

ARCTIC

GREENLAND

NORTH
AMERICA

Cabot 1497

ENGLAND

EUR

Cartier 1534-1535

FRANCE

NEWFOUNDLAND

ATLANTIC

PORTUGAL SPAIN

Mediterranean

Verrazano 1524

OCEAN

AZORES

Columbus 1492

BAHAMAS

Cortes
1519

Mexico
City

WEST

INDIES

Drake 1579

AFRI

Vespucci 1499

Balboa
1513

Magellan 1519

PACIFIC

PANAMA

Diaz 1487

Equator

Pizarro
1531

OCEAN

SOUTH
AMERICA

Da Gema 1497

Drake 1577

Magellan 1521

Porto Seguro

Drake 1580

Cabral 1500

Del Cano 1522

Cape of
Good Hope

Strait of
Magellan

TIERRA
DEL FUEGO

Plate 8

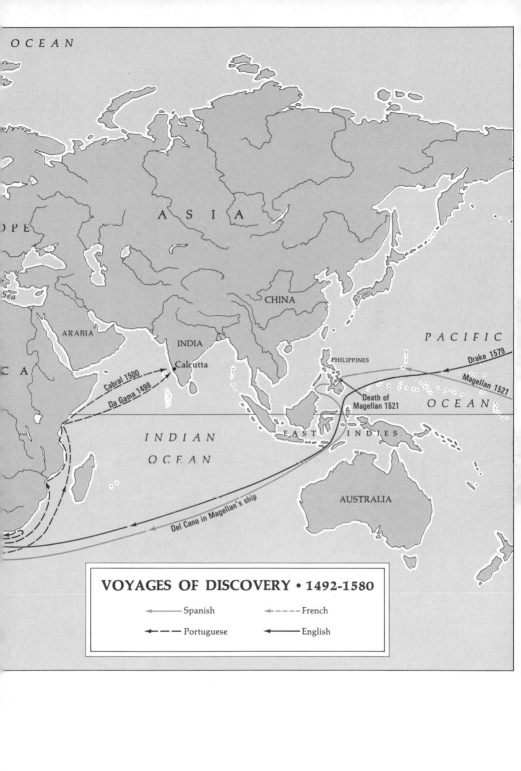

OCEAN

ASIA

CHINA

ARABIA

INDIA

Calcutta

PACIFIC

PHILIPPINES

Drake 1579

Cabral 1500

Da Gama 1498

Magellan 1521

Death of
Magellan 1521

OCEAN

INDIAN

EAST   INDIES

OCEAN

Del Cano in Magellan's ship

AUSTRALIA

Sea

OPE

CA

VOYAGES OF DISCOVERY • 1492–1580

Spanish   French

Portuguese   English

THE CHRISTIAN RECONQUEST OF THE IBERIAN PENINSULA

Dates of Christian conquest of Moorish territory shown thus: 1083

Christian states prior to 910

Acquired, 910 to 1037

Acquired, 1037 to 1150

Acquired, 1150 to 1492

Acquired in 1492

Spain, united in 1516

FRANCE

Marseilles

Narbonne
Toulouse

MEDITERRANEAN SEA

MINORCA

MAJORCA

IVIZA

BALEARIC ISLANDS
1229-1233

Barcelona

KINGDOM OF ARAGON

Adour R.

Saragossa
1118

K. OF
NAVARRE
(To Spain
1516)

Pamplona

Ebro R.

Valencia
1238

KINGDOM OF CASTILE

Madrid
1083

Valladolid

Toledo
1085

Duero R.

LEÓN

Guadalquivir R.

Cordova
1236

Granada
GRANADA

Málaga
1487

Seville
1242

Gibraltar
1309

ISLAMIC DOMINIONS

Tagus R.

Guadiana R.

Badajoz

KINGDOM OF PORTUGAL

Lisbon
1147

Miño R.

La Coruña

ATLANTIC OCEAN

Strait of Gibraltar

Tangier
(Port.)

0   100   200
Miles

Plate 9

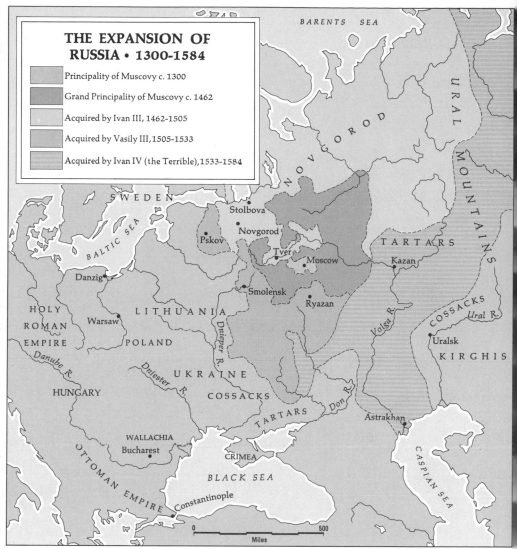

THE EXPANSION OF RUSSIA · 1300-1584

- Principality of Muscovy c. 1300
- Grand Principality of Muscovy c. 1462
- Acquired by Ivan III, 1462-1505
- Acquired by Vasily III, 1505-1533
- Acquired by Ivan IV (the Terrible), 1533-1584

BARENTS SEA

URAL MOUNTAINS

SWEDEN

Stolbova

Novgorod

NOVGOROD

Pskov

BALTIC SEA

Tver

Moscow

TARTARS

Kazan

Danzig

Smolensk

Ryazan

Volga R.

COSSACKS

Ural R.

Uralsk

KIRGHIS

HOLY ROMAN EMPIRE

Warsaw

LITHUANIA

POLAND

Dnieper R.

Danube R.

Dniester R.

UKRAINE

COSSACKS

Don R.

TARTARS

Astrakhan

HUNGARY

WALLACHIA

Bucharest

CRIMEA

BLACK SEA

CASPIAN SEA

OTTOMAN EMPIRE

Constantinople

0   500
Miles

Plate 10

In the 1400s Russia was changed by strong rulers from a land of independent princes into a powerful central monarchy. Ivan the Great (1462-1505) began the process by victories over foreign powers and by subordinating other Russian princes; he annexed Novgorod, Tver, and most of Ryazin. In 1480 he repulsed a Tartar advance on Moscow and established an armed truce and partial alliance with them. His marriage to Sophia in 1472 brought Byzantine manners to Russia. Ivan established a formal court, emphasizing his position as a monarch above his nobles. To show his supremacy, Ivan adopted the titles Tsar and Sovereign of All Russia and stressed his sense of divine mission by referring to his conquests not as new land but as his "patrimony of old," now regained. His son, Vasily (Basil) III (1505–1533) continued the expansion.

On Vasily's death in 1533, his 3-year-old son Ivan IV succeeded. His bloody regime of 50 years (earning him the epithet the Terrible) was marked by a policy of internal subjection: he weakened the power of provincial rulers and checked the noble families who had tried to regain their old strength. Ivan organized a personal arm of government, the *oprichnina*, whose original 1000 members were settled on lands taken by Ivan from their hereditary owners. With the conquest of Kazan and Astrakhan, Ivan pushed his borders further south and east, beyond the Volga River. He successfully invaded Siberia, but defeats in wars with Poland and Sweden meant the loss of territory and important ports in the Baltic.

The expansion of Russia gave the peasants room to move; and as wars, famine, and plague were rife in the 1570s and 1580s, many peasants fled east and south. By the 1580s the lords forced the passage of laws binding the peasant to the land: he became a serf—a chattel unable to move and subject to sale with the estate to which he belonged. When Ivan died in 1584, a series of weak rulers or aspirants with unclear titles brought the old aristocratic families back to power.

EUROPE c. 1500

Boundary of the Holy Roman Empire
Church lands

NORWAY AND DENMARK

NORTH SEA

SCOTLAND
Edinburgh

IRELAND
Dublin

ENGLAND
London

ATLANTIC OCEAN

NETHERLANDS
Amsterdam
Antwerp
Brussels
Cleves
Rhine R.
Hamburg
BRANDENBUR
Berlin
SAXONY

LUXEMBURG
Paris
Frankfurt
Worms

Augsburg
BAVARIA
Munich

BURGUNDY
Berne
SWISS CONFEDERATION
Geneva

FRANCE

SAVOY
MILAN
VENICE
Venice

NAVARRE
Toulouse
Rhône R.
AVIGNON
Genoa
GENOA
FLORENCE
PAPAL STATES

Marseilles
Barcelona
CORSICA
Rome
Naple

PORTUGAL
Lisbon
SPAIN
Madrid
Toledo
CASTILE
ARAGON

Granada
SARDINIA

SICIL

MEDITERRAN

0   500
Miles

Plate 11

SWEDEN

BALTIC SEA

TEUTONIC
ORDER

Danzig

TEUTONIC
ORDER

PRUSSIA

LITHUANIA

RUSSIA

POLAND

SILESIA

Prague

BOHEMIA

Cracow

Dnieper R.

Vienna

AUSTRIA

Buda

HUNGARY

MOLDAVIA

CRIMEA

BLACK SEA

WALLACHIA

BOSNIA

OTTOMAN

BULGARIA

Constantinople

NAPLES

EMPIRE

Athens

CRETE

CYPRUS

EAN

SEA

1560

Spanish
Hapsburgs

Austrian
Hapsburgs

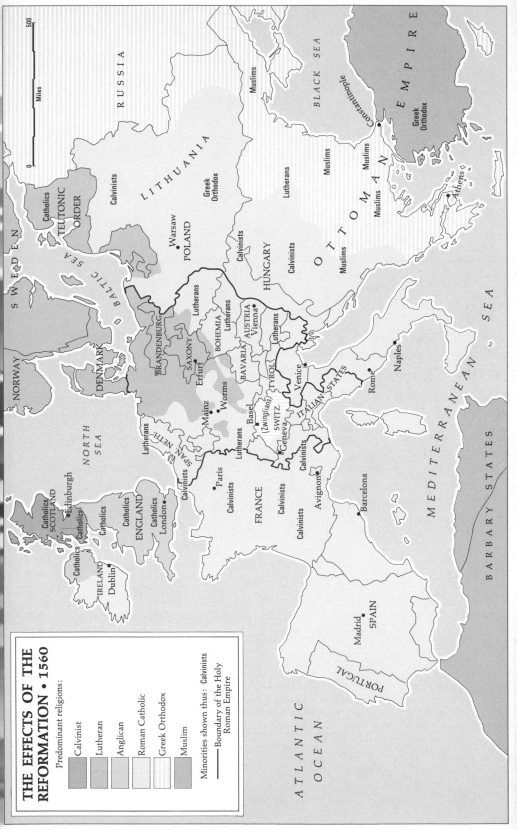

THE EFFECTS OF THE
REFORMATION · 1560

Predominant religions:

Calvinist

Lutheran

Anglican

Roman Catholic

Greek Orthodox

Muslim

Minorities shown thus: Calvinists

—— Boundary of the Holy
Roman Empire

ATLANTIC
OCEAN

PORTUGAL

SPAIN
Madrid

BARBARY STATES

MEDITERRANEAN SEA

FRANCE
Calvinists
Calvinists
Calvinists
Calvinists
Avignon

Paris

Barcelona

IRELAND
Dublin
Catholics

SCOTLAND
Catholics
Edinburgh
Catholics

ENGLAND
London
Catholics
Catholics

NORTH
SEA

Lutherans
Lutherans
SPAN. NETH.
Calvinists

NORWAY

SWEDEN

DENMARK

BALTIC SEA

Lutherans

Mainz
Worms
Basel
(Zwinglians)
SWITZ.
Geneva
Calvinists

BRANDENBURG
SAXONY
Erfurt
Lutherans
Lutherans

BOHEMIA
Lutherans
BAVARIA
AUSTRIA
Vienna
TYROL
Venice

ITALIAN
STATES
Rome
Naples

Lutherans
Lutherans

TEUTONIC
ORDER
Catholics

Calvinists

LITHUANIA

RUSSIA

POLAND
Warsaw

Calvinists

HUNGARY
Calvinists

Greek
Orthodox

Lutherans

Muslims

Muslims

OTTOMAN

Muslims

Muslims
Muslims

Muslims

BLACK SEA

Constantinople

EMPIRE

Greek
Orthodox

Athens

500

Miles

0

Plate 12

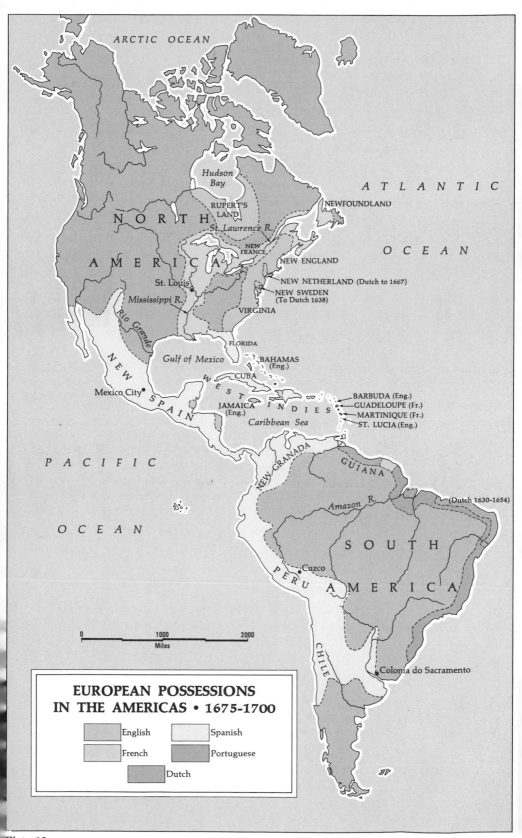

ARCTIC OCEAN

Hudson Bay

RUPERT'S LAND

St. Lawrence R.

NORTH

AMERICA

NEW FRANCE

NEW ENGLAND

NEWFOUNDLAND

ATLANTIC

OCEAN

St. Louis•

NEW NETHERLAND (Dutch to 1667)

NEW SWEDEN
(To Dutch 1638)

Mississippi R.

VIRGINIA

Rio Grande

FLORIDA

Gulf of Mexico

BAHAMAS
(Eng.)

NEW

CUBA

W E S T

Mexico City•

SPAIN

JAMAICA
(Eng.)

I N D I E S

Caribbean Sea

BARBUDA (Eng.)
GUADELOUPE (Fr.)
MARTINIQUE (Fr.)
ST. LUCIA (Eng.)

PACIFIC

NEW GRANADA

GUIANA

(Dutch 1630-1654)

OCEAN

Amazon R.

SOUTH

AMERICA

PERU

•Cuzco

CHILE

Colonia do Sacramento

0   1000   2000
Miles

EUROPEAN POSSESSIONS
IN THE AMERICAS • 1675-1700

English
French
Dutch
Spanish
Portuguese

Plate 13

NETHERLANDS · 1555–1609

Union of Arras, 1579

Lands under Spanish control, 1607

United Provinces, formed 1581

- - - Approximate linguistic boundary

NORTH SEA

GRONINGEN

Leeuwarden

FRIESLAND

DRENTHE

ZUIDER ZEE

Amsterdam

OVERYSSEL

Leyden

The Hague

Utrecht

GELDERLAND

HOLLAND

Rotterdam

Brill

UPPER GELDERLAND

ZEELAND

Rhine R.

Bruges

Antwerp

Ghent

Scheldt R.

FLANDERS

BRABANT

LIÈGE

LIMBURG

Lys R.

Brussels

Flemish

Flemish

Walloons

Walloons

Lille

Liège

ARTOIS

Arras

HAINAUT

NAMUR

CAMBRAI

LUXEMBURG

Somme R.

FRANCE

Luxemburg

Aisne R.

Meuse R.

Moselle R.

0   50   100
Miles

Plate 14

century should warn us against rash generalizations. This much we can say: those, like much of the French lower nobility, whose income was in fixed rents, found their income cut in half and were compelled, for the most part, to seek employment in the army or at court. Those landlords who could force their tenants off the land and farm it with servile labor, profited from the inflation; so did most merchants, whose investments in goods and equipment rose with rising prices, and who could hedge against losses by diversifying their activities and speculating in economic fluctuations. Normally, especially where governments were too feeble to repress the exploiters, the real sufferers were the peasants; especially in eastern Europe, the growing distance between lord and serf, and the increasing dependency of the serf, dates from these years (see p. 259). But everywhere, the revolution in economic affairs brought increased social mobility, with some rising and many falling in the scale. And the poor on the whole got poorer; even the skilled laborers discovered that their wages rose more slowly than prices—there were many self-respecting journeymen in those years who fed the endemic revolutionary mood with their discontent. Hardship and misery were general. The West has never been free of them, but the late sixteenth century, it seems, was a time conspicuous for beggars. In the midst of wealth and luxury, thousands starved, millions hungered.

Two Commercial Giants: Antwerp and Amsterdam

The expansion and shifting fortunes of the European economy in the sixteenth century are lucidly reflected in the history of two of its leading commercial cities, Antwerp and Amsterdam.[10] The spectacle of Brabant's chief city, Antwerp, aroused the admiration, almost the awe, of visitors. In the 1560s, the Florentine traveler Ludovico Guicciardini noted: "Many goodly buildings there are in Andwerp, as well private as publike, but the publike especiallie are very sumptuous," including "the Butchery, the Waighhouse, the English house," as well as the "newe lodging for the discharging of marchandise that commeth to the towne by land," yet all of these, and others, are "farre surmounted by the townhouse, the building whereof cost almost 100,000 crowns." Antwerp, he added, "is marvelouslie wel furnished both out of their own countrey and out of forren countreyes, of all kinde of victuals and dainties, both for the necessary use of man, and also for wantonnesse."[11] Active in banking, manufacture, and trade, Antwerp was supreme in northern commerce, the center through which activity flowed both north and south. Bruges, in Flanders, had been the first commercial city in the Netherlands in the fifteenth century, only to be overtaken, early in the sixteenth century, by Antwerp. A fine harbor (equipped,

[10] We are indebted, for the former, to S. T. Bindoff, "The Greatness of Antwerp," in *The New Cambridge Modern History*, vol. II (1958), 50–69; for the latter, to Violet Barbour, *Capitalism in Amsterdam in the 17th Century* (1950).

[11] Lodovico Guicciardini, *The Description of the Low Countryes and of the Provinces thereof, gathered into an Epitome out of the Historie of L. G.* (1593), 26r, 26v.

Guicciardini wrote, with "eight principall chanels within the towne,"[12] the biggest of which could accommodate a hundred ships) and a sensibly liberal policy toward merchants and bankers gave the city a splendid position for rapid growth. Perhaps the chief single impulse for its rise came with the decision of the Portuguese crown to make Antwerp its spice staple. In 1499, the royal factor, the official representative of the king, settled in Antwerp, and two years later the first shipment of goods, including precious pepper, reached the city from Lisbon. By 1504, Antwerp was receiving Portuguese consignments regularly, in increasing number and volume. In return, Antwerp supplied the royal factor with commodities that Portugal needed, notably metal goods and cloth. Even before the Portuguese had favored Antwerp with their business, traders from other nations, mainly England and southern Germany, had established themselves in Antwerp to enliven the scene and enrich the city. In its far-flung international markets, Antwerp traded in an impressive range of commodities: cloth from England and Italy and Germany, wines from Germany and France and Spain, spices from Portugal, salt from France, wheat from the Baltic. The city was more than an entrepot. With its sizable and growing population, it was a large-scale customer for food, textiles, and luxury goods. With its skilled labor force, it was a significant center for the processing of raw materials: the making of soap, the curing of fish, the refining of sugar, and above all, the finishing of cloth were flourishing local industries. Banking—including the extending of large loans to the Netherlands government—and speculation flourished side by side with the carrying trade and the processing industry.

Appropriately enough for a capitalist center, Antwerp was a cosmopolitan city. While domestic traders and manufacturers kept a hand in all profitable affairs, German and Italian financiers, Portuguese and English merchants, visited or settled there, encouraged by Antwerp's marked and unusual hospitality toward foreigners. When the great Antwerp bourse was founded in 1531, an inscription proudly proclaimed it to be open "to the merchants of all nations."[13]

But decline came, far more precipitously than anyone might have guessed. The Portuguese factor, as though sensing trouble, left the city in 1549, and the spice trade took other routes; the English cloth industry sought independence from its continental entrepot. Beginning in 1557, a series of bankruptcies—of Spain and France, and then of Portugal—were so many blows against the financial houses of the city. The disasters that were to strike the city during the revolt of the Netherlands (see p. 196) only confirmed and hastened the decline that had begun in the 1550s. Antwerp did not collapse, but it abdicated its part as master of northern commerce.

---

[12] Ibid., 22r.
[13] Henri Sée, *Modern Capitalism: Its Origin and Evolution* (tr. 1928), 30.

By the turn of the century, Amsterdam had inherited the glory of Antwerp, and its profits. The exclamations of mingled astonishment and envy that foreign visitors had expended on the one they now expended on the other. In 1601 an English visitor characterized Amsterdam as one of the "new upstarte townes in Holland,"[14] and it is true that while Amsterdam had long been a trading town, its rise to a position of European dominance came swiftly, in the course and partly by the agency of the rebellion against Spain. All the institutions that mark a great commercial center came into being within a few years: a "chamber of assurance" which regulated marine insurance policies in 1598; the East India Company in 1602; the bourse—designed, of course, in the Italian style—in 1608; an exchange bank in 1609; a lending bank in 1614. By that year, or a little later, Amsterdam joined the handful of European cities with over one hundred thousand inhabitants; it had more than trebled its population in the course of fifty years. With its bustling traffic, its aura of steady activity, and its network of canals, Amsterdam reminded everyone of Venice; it was an epithet of praise.

Much like Antwerp before it, Amsterdam's greatness sprang from its versatility. It was an impressive center of shipping, harboring large numbers of vessels of all nations and supplying ships to all with its burgeoning ship-building industry. It was an equally impressive center of trade, superintending an unceasing flow of merchandise of all kinds; the city's merchants and (which was much the same thing) the city's government did their best to make Amsterdam into the inescapable marketplace of northern Europe: its ware-houses, its wholesale dealers, its insurance agents, its brokerage houses, its official lists of prices were proverbial for efficiency and reliability. In addition, Amsterdam grew into the industrial capital of the Dutch Republic; trade brought capital for local investment, and imported raw materials gave oppor-tunities to processing industries. Thus, like Antwerp, Amsterdam developed plants for finishing silk, leather, wool, sugar, wood, tobacco, metal. Amster-dam's printing presses, gun foundries, and lens grinders had customers across the Western world. Finally, and not surprisingly in view of all this intense activity, Amsterdam became a financial capital. Its banks were the depositories, and the causes, of immense wealth; its bourses the centers of large-scale, often anxious speculation. The fortunes of war, or of a trading expedition, were reflected on the faces of the traders milling about its stock exchanges.

Inevitably, most of these activities made themselves felt all across Europe. The exchange bank of Amsterdam was, for many decades, a model for all other banks; none could duplicate the cool rationality of its operations and its exemplary trustworthiness; princes and merchant princes alike deposited their fortunes in it. Moreover, its dependable coins and credit operations helped to simplify and stabilize the money markets of commercial cities everywhere. Similarly, Amsterdam merchants and financiers took dominant roles in the

[14] Quoted in Barbour, *Capitalism in Amsterdam,* 17n.

economic ventures that made the Dutch Republic rich and formidable. When in 1602 a number of Dutch merchants founded the United East India Company, more than half its starting capital of 6.5 million florins came from Amsterdam. The importance of that company, and with it of Amsterdam, for enlarging and maintaining Dutch prosperity and power can hardly be overestimated.

From its formation on, the East India Company, founded just two years after its English counterpart, was partly public and partly private, at once an engine for economic and for military operations. It organized the exploits of armed Dutch merchants in areas that had traditionally "belonged" to the Portuguese, especially India and the Spice Islands in the East Indies. It insinuated itself into the confidence of local potentates, destroyed the old Portuguese monopoly and set up its own. Whenever necessary, it reinforced economic pressure with military force, capturing Portuguese trading posts, founding fortified cities, massacring people suspected of favoring the "enemy," building an empire—at the expense, of course, of the local populations, whom the Dutch treated with unrelieved contempt and cruelty. The avidity for total monopoly even brought into conflict in the East powers that were at peace in Europe: while the Dutch government for political reasons explicitly forbade the East India Company to use force against English settlers and traders in the Spice Islands, the Dutch commanders on the spot resented and defied these orders. In 1623, officials of the company came to suspect that English settlers on the island of Amboyna were planning "treason" against them. They confirmed their suspicions, mainly by torturing the suspects, and then executed ten English traders and, with them, ten Japanese soldiers presumably implicated in the affair. There is no evidence that the "massacre of Amboyna" troubled any consciences back home. The Amsterdammers who invested in the company, lent it money, and solicitously watched over its profits, cared little about Asiatics or even about Englishmen.

The Amsterdam merchant who emerges from this brief portrait is much like other merchants, only more intensely so: a trading animal, calculating, greedy, tight-fisted, and implacable. If the Weber thesis has any validity, it might be demonstrated here: "Their common Riches," said Sir William Temple of the seventeenth-century Dutch, "lye in every Man's having more than he spends; or, to say it properly, In every Man's spending less than he has coming in, be that what it will."[15] Such a man, ready to furnish munitions to all sides, ready to forego immediate for the sake of remote pleasure, ready to forget all teachings of religion if profit is at stake, was, in Violet Barbour's words, an "international capitalist," and "where business was concerned, a Man without a Country." The seventeenth-century Amsterdammer, though by no means a man without a city, was strikingly uninhibited by abstract considerations of patriotism or by theories of economic nationalism."[16]

[15] Ibid., 29.
[16] Ibid., 130.

But there is another, more positive way of expressing the same thing: one may call the capitalist a cosmopolitan. And this is of great importance, in the career of Amsterdam as in the career of capitalism in general. Rumors to the contrary, economic behavior is by no means always rational. Over and over again, history shows that traditional ways of conducting business often prevail over demonstrably more profitable new ways, that religious injunctions against profitable activities often act to inhibit them, and that an anxious and hidebound preoccupation with immediate returns and cosy security, as in the gild system, often delays or prevents the kind of innovation that purely economic rationality would call for. It is for this reason that capitalism, which demands contempt for tradition and security above all, has depended to such a great extent on outsiders. For the outsider—the religious pariah, the political refugee, the ambitious climber—has played a central role in capitalism. He has done jobs that were necessary but unpalatable to traditional society—like taking usury—and he has brought much-needed skills to his new home. In Amsterdam, the first to do serious money lending were Lombards, and when the exchange bank was founded in 1609, over half of its biggest depositors were refugees from the southern provinces, now in Spanish hands. Besides this, Jews from Spain and Portugal brought trading skills and financial resources, Walloons and Flemings brought new or improved techniques for the processing industries. None of this would have been to Amsterdam's economic benefit if its leading circles, with all their rigidity and conservatism, has not seen the good sense of tolerance. It was this good sense, after all, that was to move Karl Marx, in the *Communist Manifesto,* to his much-quoted tribute to the capitalist bourgeoisie: "The bourgeoisie . . ." he wrote, "has created enormous cities, has greatly increased the urban population as compared with the rural, and has thus rescued a considerable part of the population from the idiocy of rural life." [17]

Marx's ambiguous tribute suitably complicates matters. To generalize easily about the bourgeoisie, or about merchants, or even about Amsterdam merchants may be a tempting, but it is a perilous, exercise. There were many kinds of Amsterdam merchants, divided by occupation, wealth, and personal predilection. And there is abundant evidence that wealth-getting was by no means their only activity. Certainly by the 1620s and 1630s, when their wealth and their state were relatively secure, they spent a good deal of time and money on culture. When John Evelyn came to Rotterdam in 1641, he observed that Dutchmen bought pictures because they did not have land to invest in, and then sold them "at their Kermas'es to very great gains." But the year before another English visitor, Peter Mundy, was less cynical about the burghers of Amsterdam. "As for the art of painting and the affection of the people for pictures, I think no other goes beyond them, there having been in this country many excellent men in that faculty, some at present, as Rimbrantt, etc., all in

[17] Karl Marx and Friedrich Engels, *Communist Manifesto* (tr. 1964), 9.

general striving to adorn their houses, especially the outer or streetroom, with costly pieces, butchers and bakers not much inferior in their shops, which are fairly set forth; yea, many times blacksmiths, cobblers, etc., will have some picture or other notion, inclination and delight that the natives of this country have to paintings."[18] Inclination and delight—these bourgeois took to art not for investment but for pleasure.

CULTURE: AN AGE OF GOLDEN AGES

If Dutch burghers, and their counterparts elsewhere, bought a great deal of art, there was a great deal of art to buy. The century beginning before 1550 and ending after 1650 was an age that produced giants worthy to stand beside Leonardo da Vinci or Michelangelo, an age of golden ages in literature and art alike. In a rough way, these renaissances coincided with economic and political power. But only in a rough way, for there was also cultural splendor in the midst of decline. Thus, by the 1520s the Italian states had become mere puppets on the stage of European politics, but Italy continued to generate artists and ideas to export for another century and more. Italians originated, or played a leading part in, all the dominant styles that followed upon the High Renaissance. When Bernini, the greatest, most versatile of Baroque artists, came to Paris in 1665 to serve Louis XIV, he found nothing in France he liked, except the paintings of Poussin, who had, of course, lived in Italy; with superb self-assurance he advised French painters to study in Rome before they ruined their style by staying at home.[19] Cultivation may be a substitute for power, as much as its expression.

Mannerism: An International Italian Style

Mannerism, the first of the post-Renaissance styles, was largely an Italian style—but not wholly, for the early Mannerists greatly admired the "primitivism" of Dürer. Born in Rome and Florence around 1520, Mannerism rapidly spread across Italy and then the rest of Europe, where its evolution and convolutions were followed, more or less faithfully.

It is tempting but inaccurate to see Mannerism simply as a reaction against the Renaissance. Actually, the Mannerists worked out the implications of the High Renaissance to their logical (and sometimes their illogical) conclusions.

---

[18] Both quotations from Jakob Rosenberg, Seymour Slive, and E. H. Ter Kuile, *Dutch Art and Architecture, 1600–1800* (1966), 9; modernized.

[19] Howard Hibbard, *Bernini* (1965), 171, and see p. 227. For a definition of Baroque, see p. 225.

The founders of Mannerism in painting—Pontormo, Rosso, and Parmigianino—and the leading Mannerist sculptors—Benvenuto Cellini and Giovanni Bologna—took the giants of the High Renaissance not as adversaries to be overcome but as inspirations to be exploited. They emphasized elegance, virtuosity, artificiality, all in the best senses of these now ambiguous words: "mannered" and "artificial" had not yet become pejorative terms. They called attention to their technical facility with sinuous lines, distorted bodies, and crowded, nervous, deliberately unharmonious compositions. They replaced the Renaissance goal of the figure that follows nature, or the figure that purifies nature, by the artist's free vision. [20] Mannerist paintings seem restless; Mannerist buildings, strained: Michelangelo's oddly ungraceful anteroom to the Laurentian Library in Florence or the violent activity in Rosso's *Deposition* reject the serenity of the High Renaissance. Mannerism was a civilized style, and it held the interest of European artists for a long time—El Greco, in many respects a Mannerist, painted his finest canvases in the 1580s and after. But the exaltation of style over content, which makes Mannerism interesting, also made its decline inevitable.

Half a century ago, Mannerism as a distinct style was unknown. Today there is a tendency to describe European art from 1520 to 1590 simply as Mannerist. This excess is as regrettable as the earlier neglect: anti-Mannerist artists continued to flourish, especially in Venice, where painters of genius made their own adaptation of the High Renaissance style. The father of the sixteenth-century Venetian school was Giovanni Bellini, in whom the characteristic Venetian qualities—sensuality, the free disposition of figures on canvas, and an almost self-indulgent love of color—found brilliant expression. His pupils, Titian and Giorgione, brought the Venetian style to perfection. But the love of life in no way excluded deep piety: Bellini chose subjects mainly from the New Testament, and Titian, that long-lived master who died in 1576 (some say at the age of ninety-nine), painted voluptuous Venuses, virile portraits, classical allegories, but also powerful Assumptions of the Virgin and affecting Pietàs. And Titian's tragically short-lived contemporary, Giorgione, who died in 1510 in his early thirties of the plague, painted an altarpiece and a Virgin, along with his dream-like genre scenes. Giorgione is the most mysterious great painter in the history of painting: canvases in many styles have been attributed to him; canvases probably from his hand have been attributed to Titian. The very subject matter of his most famous paintings remains unexplained: his *Fête champêtre* shows four principal figures in a landscape—two young Venetian gallants, elegantly attired and most impolitely inattentive to two young women, one about to play music, the other getting water from a well, and both entirely nude. His *Tempesta* portrays similar detachment: the center of the painting is taken up with a bizarre landscape with unexplained and useless architectural detail; a bolt of lightning strikes in the distance; at the right a young woman,

---

[20] See Walter Friedlaender, *Mannerism and Anti-Mannerism in Italian Painting* (ed. 1965), 8.

naked, nurses a child, while at the left a young man, dressed, stands rigid, barely looking on. Whatever these pictures mean—and they mean, probably, just themselves, conveying a mood, no more and no less—they have nothing in common with Mannerism. The same was true of architecture: Palladio, the greatest Italian architect of the second half of the cinquecento, who has been called, with justice, "the most imitated architect in history,"[21] built his exemplary villas and churches almost in defiance of the Mannerist activity around him. What made Palladio great and so influential was his ability to learn from ancient Roman architecture and to apply his lessons freely to a new, lucid, beautifully proportioned classicism.

Yet, since Mannerism was dominant, it was against Mannerism that artists explicitly rebelled before 1600. The most imitated of the early Baroque painters, another striking instance of Italy's continuing cultural vitality, was Michelangelo Merisi, called Caravaggio after his native town, the Palladio of painting. Born in 1573, his career was short and violent; it included charges of manslaughter, flights from the police, and feverish creative activity, and ended abruptly in 1610, with his early death from malaria. His choice of religious subjects (Christ at Emmaus and The Conversion of St. Paul) was traditional; his genre paintings, showing a fat, pampered, effeminate youth lolling at his ease as Bacchus, or a young man gulled by a gypsy fortune teller, were new. But whatever his subject, his technique was revolutionary. Caravaggio broke with Mannerist contortions and distortions and rendered his figures in what appeared to be massive realism. But the realism—and this is the real secret of his power—was only apparent. Caravaggio modeled his figures with great ingenuity, gave them emphatic gestures to enhance their emotional impact, and placed them into sharp light contrasted with deep shadows—his famous *tenebroso*. Caravaggio was a master of the technique of chiaroscuro, the play of light and dark in the service of pictorial drama. The impact of his paintings was enormous and unmeasurable: practically all Italian painters of the early Baroque, even those who never met him and responded only to his pictures, became his disciples, and the school of Caravaggisti spread all across Europe. No one, not even Rembrandt, wholly escaped him.

The Elizabethan Renaissance

The diversity of artistic styles that marks the age reflected not merely resistance to, or rebellions against, Mannerism, but also the burgeoning of national styles in the midst of international currents. The Elizabethan Renaissance is a brilliant instance of this emergent cultural independence, and, as well, of the coincidence of culture with power. During the reign of Elizabeth, England acquired unprecedented prominence in international politics, and Englishmen respond-

---

[21] James S. Ackerman, *Palladio* (1966), 19.

ed with a new self-confidence—some would say, self-satisfaction—that was nurtured by the nation's writers. In ancient Rome, Vergil and Horace had sung the glory of Caesar Augustus; they had helped his reign by praising it. In Elizabethan England, playwrights, historians, and poets sang the glory of the Tudors, the humiliations that doughty English sailors had inflicted on the Spaniards, and the astonishing efflorescence of "civility"; and they too hoped to perpetuate what they praised, by praising it. "Plays arc writ with this aim," the dramatist and essayist Thomas Haywood said around 1608, "to teach their subjects obedience to their king, to show the people the untimely ends of such as have moved . . . insurrections, to present them with the flourishing estate of such as live in obedience, exhorting them to allegiance, dehorting them from all traitorous and felonious stratagems." [22] When Haywood wrote these candid words, James I was already on the throne; the momentum that had been gained in Elizabeth's glorious decades, in the 1570s and 1580s, had survived the troubles of her last years and her death in 1603. Petrarch's poems, Palladio's writings and sketches, Castiglione's *Courtier,* were admirable models, but especially in literature, England was developing her own classics, second to none—not even to the Italians.

The giant looming over this literary Renaissance is, of course, William Shakespeare. Indeed, Shakespeare's place in the history of literature, and in our consciousness, is so secure and so exalted that it seems impertinent even to praise him. But it is worth remembering that while he was, in Ben Jonson's words, "for all time," he was also very much of his time, an Elizabethan among Elizabethans. Considering how much we admire, quote, and even read him, it is tantalizing how little we know of his life. He was born in 1564, at Stratford-on-Avon, of prosperous yeoman stock; he seems to have had adequate schooling—adequate surely to read Plutarch, and Hakluyt's *Voyages,* and his other sources, and to write his own plays. The old remark, "The plays of William Shakespeare were written by an actor named William Shakespeare," is certainly apt. Sometime in the mid-1580s he went to London as an actor, and by about 1589 he had begun to write. Judging from his dedications and other scanty evidence, he moved in noble circles and enjoyed distinguished patronage. The theatrical companies in which he was prominent—the Lord Chamberlain's Men in the Globe Theater and later the King's Men in the Blackfriars Theater—were fashionable and profitable ventures. Around 1610, evidently comfortably off, he retired to Stratford, where he died in 1616, already something of a legend.

It is impossible to date his work with precision, but it may be roughly divided into four periods: The first five years of his production, beginning around 1589, were years of apprenticeship, in which he wrote comedies like

[22] *An Apology for Actors* (ca. 1608); quoted in L. G. Salingar, "The Elizabethan Literary Renaissance," in Boris Ford, ed., *The Age of Shakespeare,* vol. II of *The Pelican Guide to English Literature* (1956), 65.

The Taming of the Shrew and history chronicles like his trilogy on King Henry VI. Then, from around 1594 to 1600, the time of his sonnets and other poems, he perfected the dramatic genres he had explored earlier: the late 1590s saw such mature comedies as *Twelfth Night* and such historical dramas as *Henry V* and *Julius Caesar.* The third period, dating down to about 1609, established his claim to immortality; it is the period of his incomparable tragedies—*Hamlet, King Lear, Othello, Macbeth, Antony and Cleopatra*—and of those strange dramas, the "dark comedies" *Troilus and Cressida* and *Measure for Measure,* that have strained his interpreters to the utmost. His last plays are distinctly autumnal; Prospero's farewell in *The Tempest* reads like Shakespeare's own valedictory:

> I'll break my staff,
> Bury it certain fathoms in the earth,
> And deeper than did ever plummet sound
> I'll drown my book.

It is perilous to discover Shakespeare's "philosophy" in his plays and vulgar to reduce them to some scheme of thought. They are poems, works of the imagination, in which the personality of the poet disappears behind his creations. The shifting assessments of Shakespeare through three centuries are tributes to the wealth and profundity of his invention. *Hamlet* (1601) is only the most puzzling of his many puzzling creations; it can be read as a revenge tragedy derived from an earlier version by Thomas Kyd; or as a psychological drama of a young man who could not make up his mind; or as a metaphysical exploration of a world unhinged by unnatural crime; or as all of these, and more, together. *Hamlet* was instantly popular, but it is new for each reader or spectator. *King Lear,* probably Shakespeare's most overpowering creation, is quite as multifaceted; while we may trace its sources and explore its world view, as a total poem it remains elusive, awesome, and unique. Yet there are some things we may say with some confidence. Like his fellow writers, Shakespeare borrowed from his contemporaries, expressed current attitudes toward life, and made political propaganda. His chronicle plays are part of a larger literature which includes John Stow's patriotic chronicles of London and of England, and Edmund Spenser's vast allegorical *Faerie Queene,* a modernized version of the Arthurian legend in which Queen Elizabeth I appears transmuted into Queen Gloriana. *Richard III,* one of Shakespeare's earliest plays, echoes the official Tudor version by making Richard into a melodramatic and murderous villain (see p. 107). *Henry V* invidiously contrasts the snobbishness, cowardice, and treachery of foreigners with the geniality, courage, and straightforwardness of Englishmen. Such plays are more than propagandistic exercises; they are memorable because they contain memorable poetry and memorable characters, but they fit perfectly into the Elizabethan scheme, in which the "Tudor myth"[23] and general self-congratulation played a significant part. Moreover,

---

[23] The term is E. M. W. Tillyard's; see his *Shakespeare's History Plays* (ed. 1962), 39–42.

Shakespeare, whatever his private feelings, beautifully articulated fundamental Elizabethan ideas about order: the old medieval vision of a hierarchical universe in which each star and each man obeys and governs according to his proper place had survived into the sixteenth century with few modifications. Hamlet returns to Denmark to find the time "out of joint" and laments, and yet accepts, his obligation "to set it right." A famous speech, which Shakespeare puts into the mouth of Ulysses in his *Troilus and Cressida,* sums up this Renaissance view to perfection:

> The heavens themselves, the planets, and
>   this centre
> Observe degree, priority, and place
> Insisture, course, proportion, season, form
> Office, and custom, in all line of order;

This heavenly arrangement is mirrored in human institutions, in orders of rank or "degree."

> But when the planets
> In evil mixture to disorder wander,
> What plagues and what portents, what mutiny,
> What raging of the sea, shaking of earth . . .
> Take but degree away, untune that string,
> And hark what discord follows.

The political implications of such cosmic doctrine were inescapable.

Yet, it is worth repeating, Shakespeare's plays are above all great literature, and as his London audiences were the first to recognize, great theater. In fact, Shakespeare's contemporaries were particularly fortunate in their theater, for while poets and historians and translators were publishing impressive work, it was on the stage that the Elizabethans shone most brightly. It was there that the culture of the people and the humanism of the educated clashed and coalesced: Shakespeare was not alone in marrying low comedy to high tragedy, and in pleasing groundlings and courtiers at the same time. The profusion of dramatists was so great, indeed, that such fine playwrights as Tourneur and Webster and Middleton, who would have stood out in any age but this, recede before the immortal trio, Shakespeare, Marlowe, and Jonson.

Christopher Marlowe, born like Shakespeare in 1564, was, unlike Shakespeare, a university man. A master of blank verse, which he domesticated in England with his powerful dramas, he compressed his output into a few years: *Tamburlaine the Great, The Jew of Malta,* and the greatest of them all, *Doctor Faustus,* were written between 1587 and 1589 or perhaps 1591. He did not have much longer to live: in 1593 Marlowe was stabbed to death in a drunken tavern brawl. His plays are filled with blood and destruction, with boast and rant and sonorous speeches, but their precise nature remains a matter of dispute: T. S. Eliot provocatively called *The Jew of Malta,* with its "savage comic humour," a "farce." Yet the speeches of Marlowe's gigantic figures wrestling with their ambitions and their fate continue to resound in the ear of those who love the

English language. Like Marlowe, Ben Jonson was an educated man: he professed to despise the mob, and he dedicated his *Volpone* to Oxford and Cambridge, "the most noble and most equal sisters." He was scholar and wit, educator and entertainer, classicist and Englishman, and he fused these disparate elements into that vigorous and pure diction that is perhaps the most impressive contribution of the Elizabethan Renaissance to world literature. Yet, while the particular and permanent attractiveness of Jonson seems Elizabethan, he lived into a new world, with new literary luminaries. Born in 1572, he had Shakespeare acting in his *Every Man in His Humor* in 1598, but his most enduring comedies, *Volpone* and *The Alchemist,* date from the reign of James I, and he lived on to 1637, well into the reign of Charles I. This was already the time of the metaphysicals: of John Donne and his fellow Baroque poets, and of John Milton's early verse. England's cultural efflorescence did not abate, it only changed expression.

Spain and the Dutch Republic: Two Golden Ages

Even more than England, both Spain and the Dutch Republic derived impulses for their cultural flowering from Italy. The Spanish *Siglo de Oro* began in the 1540s, in the reign of Charles V, with a volume of poems by two Spanish writers, Juan Boscán and Garcilaso de la Vega, who brought Italian verse forms to Spanish literature, and thus liberated Spanish poetry from timeworn shackles. Similarly, Spanish painting enormously profited from Italian Mannerists either imported into Spain by royal patrons or studied on the spot: El Greco, the greatest of them, was a Greek, born Domenicos Theotocopulos in 1541, who, before he settled in Spain around 1576, spent profitable years in Venice and Rome.

Like Italy, Spain enjoyed a cultural flowering during the years of its decline; its finest writers did their best work after the failure of the Armada. Lope de Vega, poet and playwright, has been called "the greatest literary improviser ever seen."[24] In his long lifetime (he was born in 1562 and died in 1635) he wrote innumerable poems and over fifteen hundred plays, many of them dashed off in two or three days. His fluency made much of his work trivial and trite, but his best plays are full of brilliance, wit, naturalness, and a fresh dramatic sense. Calderón belongs to a later generation and to a later style, the Baroque. Born in 1600, he lived to 1681, almost to the nadir of Spanish power. He borrowed ideas and incidents from Lope de Vega, and he wrote worldly comedies and melodramas, but his strength lay in aristocratic tragedies depicting the clash of love and honor, and in religious allegory. To read the latter, with their deep feeling and their disdain for all secular virtues, is to be

[24] Gerald Brenan, *The Literature of the Spanish People* (2nd ed., 1962), 204.

back in the world of the Counter-Reformation, a world Spain had never left—except perhaps for Cervantes.

Don Quixote breathes a freer spirit. Cervantes took to writing after an adventurous career, which included service at the battle of Lepanto and five years of slavery in a Moorish prison. Impecunious and neglected, Cervantes wrote romances, plays, and poems, but his first success came with Part One of *Don Quixote,* published in 1605, when he was fifty-eight. Part Two, which takes Don Quixote to disenchantment and death, came out in 1615, a year before Cervantes' own death. *Don Quixote* is the *Hamlet* of novels: it invites, and has survived, many interpretations. Cervantes himself insisted that he had written the book to expose popular novels of chivalry, and its first claim to fame was its humor. The mad don was irresistible: riding out on his nag Rozinante, accompanied by his squire Sancho Panza, to restore true chivalry to the country, tilting at windmills, and taking inns for castles. But the novel is far subtler than that: Quixote and Sancho Panza are not merely polar opposites but, in many respects, parallels; as their adventures proceed, they learn from one another, and sometimes exchange roles. The don is mad only on the subject of chivalry; he is sane, kind, observant in all other respects. And when he discards his fantasy at the end, he dies. In our own century, it has been tempting to take the don as the sane critic of a mad world and the common sense of Sancho Panza as complacency or resignation in the face of horror and evil. This is a permissible reading. But it is likely that Cervantes himself did not have such polemical intentions. Only the greatness of his masterpiece remains beyond question.

In painting as in literature, the Spanish seventeenth century is more interesting than the sixteenth. El Greco, it is true, had mastered his characteristic style as early as the 1570s, but his celebrated *View of Toledo,* and his religious compositions, angular, harsh in color, distorted in their figures—the work of a religious visionary, subjective and fervent—date from the decade before his death in 1614. And the other major Spanish painters belong wholly to the age of decline: Ribera was born around 1590, Zurbarán in 1598, Murillo in 1617. All these, the first two quite directly, the last through his Spanish masters, learned much from Caravaggio. Their Madonnas and beggars, spiritual, colorful, perhaps a little cheap in their search for effects, hang in many museums and retain some of their luster; only Velázquez (born in 1599, a year after Zurbarán) retains it all. Like Rubens, whom he met, Velázquez associated with princes, popes, and nobles, and wasted much valuable time in official tasks for the kings of Spain. While his debt to Caravaggio is clear, his portraits have a controlled realism, his still lifes a palpable vitality, that are quite distinctive: labels like "poetic realist" and "religious realist," which betray the helplessness of words in the face of great art, do capture something of his particular quality. Velázquez' best known paintings—the portraits of Philip IV of Spain and of Pope Innocent X, the candid and touching depictions of Spanish court fools, the celebrated *Venus and Cupid,* lovely and chaste at the same time—are obviously masterly in their control. But there is something more in them—a kind of democratic openness to experience and a search for meanings behind surfaces. In Velázquez' century, only Rembrandt saw deeper into his subjects than this.

The Dutch Golden Age, more than the others, was concentrated on the visual arts, especially on painting, drawing, and etching.[25] All the Dutch painters, including Hals, Rembrandt, and Vermeer, were attuned to the international Baroque style; there was a whole school of painters called the Haarlem Mannerists; early seventeenth-century artists closely followed Caravaggio with their anecdotal subjects and their experiments in chiaroscuro— witness Gerrit van Honthorst's *Supper Party* and Dirck van Baburen's *The Procuress*. And down to midcentury, Italianate painters like Nicholas Berchem were immensely popular, and in consequence prosperous, with scenes of Italian peasants riding on their mules past antique ruins, bathed in a golden sunlight the Dutch knew only from travel or from such pictures as these.

Yet there is also an unmistakable Dutch style, as there are unmistakable Dutch interests. Everyone likes to have his face immortalized; the Dutch, it seems, liked it even more than others. It is not an accident that Dutch painters were among the most accomplished and most prolific of portrait painters: Jan van Miereveldt, almost legendary among his contemporaries, did nothing but face painting after a short, shaky start as a history painter, and is reported to have turned out over ten thousand portraits. Military companies, syndics of gilds, regents of old men's homes had themselves portrayed in groups, and the most famous among Dutch artists sought the substantial fees and enjoyed the technical problems that these vast pictorial machines brought them. In addition, as avid consumers of paintings, prosperous Dutch burghers called for landscapes, still lifes, and genre scenes, and in all these subjects their painters reached true distinction. Jacob van Ruisdael and Jan van Goyen painted waterfalls shadowed by majestic trees, canals dominated by old castles, windmills in a field under the vast cloudy Dutch sky—the first with vigorous, dense brushwork of greens and browns; the second with a delicate touch and harmonious palette. The humblest objects served the purposes of art: Pieter Claesz posed a glass of wine and a loaf of bread (not forgetting the crumbs) on a white tablecloth; Willem Kalf beautifully composed combinations of silver vessels, Delft bowls, and fruit. Aert van der Neer specialized in nocturnal landscapes bathed in moonlight; Hendrick Avercamp in cheerful, brilliantly painted snow scenes showing Dutch villagers disporting themselves on the ice.

[25] The Dutch produced important theologians and philosophers, and one poet of distinction, Joost van den Vondel, a prolific and versatile translator, a political poet who lent his pen to the Remonstrant cause, and a Baroque, often verbose dramatist. But he is strictly a local classic. "We Dutchmen know," Johan Huizinga sadly observes, "that Vondel must be counted among the finest writers of all time. We also realise, and are resigned to the fact, that the world neither knows him nor is ever likely to do so." Nor is this, Huizinga concedes, because he wrote in Dutch—other writers, like Cervantes, have enjoyed and survived translation. See *Dutch Civilisation in the Seventeenth Century* (1968), 69.

A considerable number of painters, of whom Willem van de Velde the Younger was only the most accomplished, painted Dutch ships under full sail, becalmed at sea, or in the midst of battle. Jan Steen and Adriaen van Ostade reproduced the simple charm of domestic and the rowdy vigor of tavern life with their carousing peasants, playing children, reflective pipe smokers. Gerard ter Borch lovingly recaptured interior scenes in which elegant ladies dressed in satin read love letters. And Pieter de Hooch painted luminous Dutch interiors, with the light streaming through the window onto those obsessively clean Dutch tiles. This catalogue seems long, but it offers only a selection of names and subjects. Never in history has one country—and so small a country!—produced so many painters of such high caliber in such a short time.

Amid this wealth of talents, Frans Hals, Rembrandt van Rijn, and Jan Vermeer tower as painters of genius. Hals was one of many benefits the northern Netherlands received from its southern neighbors during the great migration. Born in Antwerp around 1580, Hals came to Haarlem with his parents after the fall of his native city to the Spaniards (see p. 194). He lived to a ripe age—to 1666—and tried his hand at a variety of subjects. But he early recognized that his true talent lay in portraiture, individual and collective; as he grew older, and his mood more subdued, he gave up genre painting altogether. He brought radical, almost revolutionary techniques to a traditional genre. His life-size portraits of militia companies and other respectable groups—he did nine of them, more than any of his competitors—completely loosened up the old, stiff, soldiers-all-in-a-row kind of portrait. Hals' companies are informal, animated, wholly individualized, yet so beautifully composed that the eye may calmly travel from one figure to another, or rest with pleasure on the painting as a whole. Even more perhaps than these group portraits, Hals' portraits of individuals display his gift for life-like rendering, for capturing the animation and the unique quality of his subject. In his attempt to give a convincing representation of fleeting emotion he is very much the Baroque artist; in his darting, casual-looking but wholly deliberate brushwork, he seems like an Impressionist.[26] Hals was very much a man of his time, and of the future.

Rembrandt, like Shakespeare, is "for all time." A true genius, he converted the elements around him—late Mannerism, the Baroque, the Dutch predilection for landscape—into a profoundly personal expression. Like other Dutch painters, Rembrandt loved to do portraits; unlike most of them, he constantly returned to biblical subjects: some of his greatest etchings show scenes from the life of Christ. We know much about him, and yet not enough: he did more than a hundred self-portraits, a moving record of his development from confident youth to tragic old age, rendered with an unsurpassed eye and no sentimentality whatever. We know also that in the 1630s, in Amsterdam, he grew rich and famous, that gradually he became unfashionable, went bankrupt in 1656, and was compelled to auction off a fine and varied art collection. But most

[26] See Rosenberg et al., *Dutch Art and Architecture,* 37–38.

conjecture about his spiritual life is sheer speculation, prompted by his somber masterpieces.

Rembrandt was born in 1606 at Leyden, the son of a comfortably situated miller. By 1625, he had set up on his own. From his earliest paintings onward, Rembrandt showed himself master of chiaroscuro, and his particular use of it became his signature. Caravaggio and the Caravaggisti had used alternations of light and dark in sharply delimited regions, achieving drama by stark contrast. Rembrandt, on the other hand, graduated his tones to create a single, highly expressive atmosphere.[27] With the Caravaggisti, a single look establishes the configuration of the painting; with Rembrandt, long and repeated viewing yields surprising dividends, as figures emerge from the darkness. In his Leyden years, Rembrandt became not merely an accomplished painter, but a prolific etcher—etching, indeed, was an art in which he was to become supreme.

In 1632, he moved to Amsterdam, where he spent the rest of his life, down to 1669. He married, moved in cosmopolitan circles, enjoyed his fame. Gradually he discarded the shock techniques of the early Baroque and participated in the current fashion of landscape painting. But it is as a portrait painter that he gained his fame; indeed, the picture that made his reputation, The Anatomy Lesson of Dr. Tulp (1632), is one of the most active, most brilliantly composed group portraits ever painted: it shows Dr. Tulp lecturing to an intent group of seven observers and dissecting a corpse which lies, brightly lit, in full view.

Fashions changed in the 1640s, and Rembrandt changed too, though, to his cost, in his own way. The tale of Rembrandt's sudden fall from favor is a legend; gradually, as his vision grew more private and his canvases darker, many of the most desirable commissions went elsewhere. Yet he continued to have customers: Rembrandt executed the Night Watch[28] and the Syndics of the Cloth Drapers' Guild, the two most famous group portraits ever painted, in 1642 and 1661–1662, respectively. They are, of course, wholly different pictures, solving wholly different problems: the first shows an animated group striding out in the open, with brilliant light falling on the captain and his lieutenant; the second depicts a composed smaller group of five syndics and one servant, unified by the table at which they are seated and by their alert looking at the same point, perhaps at a person just entering the room. These last decades of Rembrandt's life are also the years of his most powerful self-portraits and some of his finest religious etchings. He never gave up portraiture; late and early, he liked to dress up his subjects in extravagant finery, to create a harmony, or a contrast, between accessory and face—witness his late The Man in the Gilt Helmet, in which a somber, strong elderly man, his fact deeply lined and his mouth tightly

---

[27] Ibid., 51–52.
[28] The name is a complete misreading of the painting, but it has stuck. Its proper, though admittedly clumsier, title is The Company of Captain Frans Banning Cocq and Lieutenant Willem van Ruytenburch.

drawn, grimly poses with a shining, plumed helmet on his head. And, just as he had liked to paint his wife Saskia until her death in 1642, so he later painted Hendrickje Stoffels, who came to live with him, and his one surviving child, his son Titus. He painted wrinkled old women, elderly philosophic-looking Jews, Jesus at Emmaus—his output, though increasingly concentrated on portraits and religious subjects, remained varied. And his achievement is universal, for his gifts were not confined to the play of light and shadow. "Throughout his career," Rudolf Wittkower has noted, "chiaroscuro remained his most power-ful means of expression." But there were also "other important features of his art: his colouristic treatment, his draughtsmanship, his brushwork, his compo-sitional devices."[29] It was Rembrandt's genius to unite these gifts in the paintings and etchings we know so well.

If the mystery of Rembrandt is his internal development, the mystery of Vermeer is his external career. He was born at Delft in 1632, became prominent in the painters' gild at Delft, and died at Delft in 1675; little else is known about him. Not surprisingly, his greatest landscape, one of the greatest landscapes ever painted, depicts his city serenely stretched out by its river under the typical Dutch sky—part sunny, largely cloudy. Like all painters, Vermeer incurred his debts: his early *Procuress* is an essay in the Caravaggisti tradition, a restatement of Baburen's earlier treatment of the same theme. He learned much from Carel Fabritius, Rembrandt's most talented pupil, who settled in Delft after 1650. But his later paintings, of the 1660s and early 1670s, could only have been painted by one man. They are nearly all genre paintings, mainly indoor scenes with one or two figures—a woman reading a letter, a servant pouring out milk, a man and woman drinking and talking—all of them bathed in Vermeer's unique light, organized with supreme clarity, and painted with blues and yellows that remain unsurpassed in their luminous beauty. Vermeer's art has been called simple and accessible, and we respond to it today with sheer pleasure. Yet Vermeer, whose output was small, was nearly forgotten and was rescued from obscurity only about a century ago. And nothing in his color or his composition is accidental: the simplicity of his mature work is the result of supreme artistic intelligence, the work of an individualist to whom the extravagance of Baroque meant nothing.

Two Baroque Masters: Rubens and Bernini

The term Baroque, which has already appeared on these pages, is a vexed and vexing name; it is easier to point to Baroque works of art than to define the Baroque itself, partly because it differed in different hands and different arts, partly because it underwent a distinct internal development, normally distin-guished as Early, High, and Late Baroque. The Baroque style, which grew out

[29] *Art and Architecture in Italy, 1600–1750* (1958), 52.

of, and in response to, an enfeebled Mannerism at the end of the sixteenth century, was in part a return to the Renaissance ideal of order, rendered with verve and through a magnificent massiveness. Baroque artists sought to control and portray emotions, especially religious emotions; the tricks for which they are famous—the false perspective in architecture, the gesture that attacks the viewer out of the canvas, the general air of theatricality—are not tricks for their own sake, but attempts at making these emotions palpable and, if possible, overwhelming.

Yet inspection is superior to definition. A refined portrait painter like Anthony van Dyck, who could make peasants look like gentlemen, and a boisterous religious painter like Jacob Jordaens, who could make gentlemen look like peasants, both belong to the Baroque. So, in his way, does the great neoclassical painter Nicolas Poussin (see p. 297). But the enormous vitality of the Baroque is most distinctly embodied in two universal men, Peter Paul Rubens and Gian Lorenzo Bernini. Both were men of the world, consorting with dukes and popes. Both were supremely energetic. Both possessed an uncanny versatility: Rubens was a good classical scholar, an accomplished linguist, a professional diplomat, a remarkable letter writer, and a shrewd businessman, who liked to display his multiple talents by painting while he was dictating a letter, conducting a conversation, or listening to a reader. Bernini for his part could do anything; as John Evelyn noted: Bernini "gave a public opera wherein he painted the scenes, cut the statues, invented the engines, composed the music, writ the comedy, and built the theatre."[30] It is in their art that they diverge: Rubens was exclusively a draftsman and painter; Bernini a sculptor and architect who could have been, had he wanted to be, a remarkable painter.

Though a Brabanter in origin, Rubens was born in Germany in 1577 and raised in Cologne. As an adolescent he moved to Antwerp, his parents' city, and despite prolonged absences on diplomatic missions and painter's commissions, the Spanish Netherlands were his home. His legendary facility and his characteristic style (despite some change and some growth) evidenced them-selves early. He was a vigorous draftsman, a natural colorist, and a genius at crowded large-scale compositions that obeyed, with all their movement, the ideal of Baroque order. He made power palatable, even graceful. Prosperity came early, and commissions poured down on him from across Europe; Rubens soon found himself compelled to open a large workshop. Many "Rubenses" are so largely by courtesy: planned by Rubens in a quick sketch, perhaps touched up by the master at the end. But only his most discriminating patrons ever knew the difference: he surrounded himself with talented young men and seems to have been an inspiring teacher who imparted some of his touch to his assistants.

It is impossible to single out any one work from an output which has been estimated at over two thousand paintings. Rubens did everything: portraits,

[30] Quoted in Hibbard, *Bernini*, 19.

landscapes, hunting scenes, religious subjects, allegories. In the late 1620s he did a series of twenty-four huge allegorical paintings for Marie de' Medici, widow of Henri IV and queen mother of France. Some of his smaller paintings are the best known: the elegant wedding picture showing himself and his first wife Isabella Brant, the exuberant *Italian Straw Hat* showing his lovely young second wife Helena Fourment, and for obvious reasons, a number of canvases depicting classical legends concerning buxom nude young women being abducted by virile young men—Rubens rivaled Titian in his flesh tones. Our own time perhaps responds most readily, less to his elaborate productions than to his preparatory essays—to his quick oil sketches (called *bozzetti*) and to his drawings, which demonstrate his daring and his unsurpassed eye with their bold foreshortening, esoteric subjects, and complicated postures, and with their triumphant sense not of difficulty felt, but of difficulty overcome. Nor was his art simply an outpouring of spontaneity. As the French critic Roger de Piles put it some thirty years after Rubens' death: Rubens' works are "full of a beautiful imaginative fire, profound erudition, and intelligence in painting."[31]

Bernini was, if anything, even more prodigious than Rubens. He was born in Naples in 1598, the son of a Florentine sculptor who mercilessly drove his son, as Leopold Mozart was to drive *his* son a century and a half later, and with the same remarkable results. Only, unlike Wolfgang Amadeus Mozart, Bernini lived on to a ripe and productive old age: when he died in 1680 he had just ceased sculpting. His virtuosity emerged early; long before he was twenty, he was a famous sculptor. His early Mannerist works are still a little forced, as though the sculptor is trying to squeeze drama out of his marble. By the 1620s, his style was ripe and his aim clear: he sought to connect the piece of sculpture to its environment, and make the whole a single experience, so cunningly devised that the spectator would be compelled to see the total precisely as the designer had planned it. His *Ecstasy of St. Teresa,* which is the centerpiece of the Cornaro chapel in the Roman church of Santa Maria della Vittoria, dates from the late 1640s, but everything he had done before then leads up to this celebrated work. The saint lies swooning back as a smiling angel, who has stabbed her before, is about to stab her once more with his arrow. The whole composition is crowned by golden rods representing the rays of the sun, and light actually comes from behind and above the niche; the niche itself, with its tense curves and crowded columns, seems like a door forced open; the side walls of the chapel are populated by lively representations of the Cornaro family. The composition is a single whole, a *Gesamtkunstwerk.*[32] Much play has been made with the expression on St. Teresa's face, and to profane eyes she indeed appears to be in the throes of orgasm. But in fact Bernini was seeking

---

[31] Quoted in H. Gerson, and E. H. Ter Kuile, *Art and Architecture in Belgium, 1600–1800* (1960), 71–72.

[32] This notion of the "total work of art" in which several arts collaborate to create a single experience, is an idea attributed to Richard Wagner, but Bernini had some such idea, without the word, two hundred years before Wagner.

to reproduce as faithfully as he could St. Teresa's graphic report of her religious experiences; besides, we know that Bernini was a devout Catholic, and whatever his worldly connections, anything but a worldling in religious matters. His Cornaro chapel is theatrical Christianity at its most theatrical, but there is no reason to doubt that it is Christian.

A sculptor with Bernini's gift of expression and passion for environment could be supposed to excel in portraiture and in architecture. Bernini in fact did both superbly well. His busts, mainly but not exclusively of popes and cardinals, are among the supreme achievements of portrait sculpture: convincing, vivid, and penetrating. His achievement as an architect is no less distinguished; among his many works, probably the best known is the piazza before St. Peter's, a cunning embrace inviting the masses of worshipers to receive the papal blessing. Nor is this all. No one who has been to Rome can forget those among Bernini's works that combine sculpture and architecture: his many charming fountains and that eloquent monument to Catholic piety, the canopy over St. Peter's grave under the dome of St. Peter's. The *baldacchino* consists of four twisted columns topped by four curving volutes meeting high in the center—a splendid invention, but a reminder, too, that Bernini stood at the end of an age, looking back to Christian glories that had passed rather than the modern world to come.

CULTURE: ANCIENT DOCTRINES AND NEW PHILOSOPHY

The Revival of Classical Philosophy

This age of artistic creativity was also an age of extraordinary intellectual vitality. The impulse of the Renaissance was by no means exhausted; the currents of thought set in motion by Erasmian humanism and fed by the turbulent torrent of the Reformation continued to work in the minds of Europeans, to confuse and trouble, but also to liberate them. Medieval conceptions of life were slowly eroding, although the temper of the times then emerging can scarcely be called secular. These were Christian times, as their predecessors had been. But the process of widening the intellectual horizons of Christendom, begun in the twelfth century with the rediscovery of Aristotle and the influx of Arab philosophy and greatly advanced in the Renaissance, now reached new intensity. Ancient doctrines, dusted off and purged by the Humanists of centuries of pious misreadings, found learned modern supporters and, disseminated by printed books and skillful popularizers, a wide public. This was the age of Christian Humanists, Christian Stoics, even Christian Epicureans.

It was Michel de Montaigne, *politique* and essayist, who demonstrated in his famous essays the variety and vitality of antique thought and its relevance to the sixteenth century. Born in 1533 in a merchant family and rising to property, office, and noble status, Montaigne made garrulity into an art and self-absorption into the foundations of modern individuality. Like a pedant, Montaigne filled his essays with frequent, often interminable quotations from the classics; like a bore, he dwelled lovingly on anecdotes. But he was neither a pedant nor a bore; he was an explorer of the meaning of man, the inventor of introspection. His radical innovation was to use himself as his favorite witness. When he looked inward he did not pray or seek mystical union with God, he recorded his feelings candidly and clearly; with the aid of ancient pagan writers—Epictetus, Cicero, Seneca, Plutarch—he thought his way to a ripe philosophy of man. Montaigne is best known as a skeptic; his query, *"Que sais-je?,"* suggests that he knows nothing and that by acknowledging his ignorance he has demonstrated, as Socrates had demonstrated long before him, the greater ignorance of other men. But there is more to Montaigne than this. As a young man he had been much taken with Roman Stoics like Seneca and Marcus Aurelius; his essay entitled "To Philosophize Is To Learn How To Die" was characteristic of this early mood. Then his Stoic detachment gave way gradually to explorations in skepticism, and this, in turn, to the humane, almost relaxed thought of his last years, which holds that "our great and glorious masterpiece is to live appropriately." When he died in 1592, he died, as he had been born, a Catholic; but (as a good *politique*) he hated fanaticism and preferred living in peace with error to exterminating heretics. Thus—and this was his meaning to his readers—he was not a sectarian theologian but a cosmopolitan moralist, not so much a pagan as an urbane Christian offering, in his copious essays, a splendidly usable anthology of classical philosophy.

Montaigne's popularity was instantaneous and his following wide. John Florio translated the *Essais* into florid English in 1603, but even before then, such cultivated Englishmen as Sir William Cornwallis had borrowed from Montaigne. In his own essays, published two years before the Florio translation appeared, Cornwallis examined himself much in Montaigne's fashion; his observation, "Montania and my selfe . . . doe sometimes mention our selves,"[33] is a charming understatement. Critical introspection had come to stay.

Yet, influential as Montaigne's catalogue of humanism proved to be, another current of thought, nourished like Montaigne by antiquity, was even more influential: Stoicism. The church fathers had found much that was admirable in Stoicism, especially Roman Stoicism. Its natural piety, its insistence on social service, its praise of such virtues as patience in adversity, had tempted the most classically trained among the early Christians to welcome

[33] Quoted in Douglas Bush, *English Literature in the Earlier Seventeenth Century, 1600–1660* (1945), 188.

Stoicism as a groping anticipation of Christian truth. In the Renaissance, as the writings of Roman Stoics and their allies—Cicero and Seneca—became once more widely available, Stoicism exercised wide appeal: Epictetus' noble manual was rendered from its original Greek into Latin and, in 1567, into French. Gradually, scholars disentangled Stoic doctrine from Christian admixtures and presented it not as a rival but an auxiliary to Christian philosophy, an elevating guide to life. The Renaissance Stoics insisted that Stoicism was no danger to the sacred truth—*that* was the ultimate monopoly of Christianity. As the Flemish scholar Justus Lipsius, the leading popularizer of Christian Stoicism, wrote around 1600, in his book *On Constancy*, and elsewhere: it was a rare thing for Stoicism and Christianity to conflict, but when they did, as with the Stoics' defense of suicide and the idea of fate, Stoicism was in error and Christianity was in the right. Yet, despite such occasional clashes of doctrine, Stoicism was the best philosophy the best of pagan philosophers had been able to devise. In the late sixteenth century, a time of warring fanaticisms and destructive civil conflict, the reasonableness and cosmopolitanism of Stoic teachings seemed a possible way out of turmoil.

The assertions of modern Stoics that Stoicism was no danger to Christianity must be taken more or less at face value; it was not until later, in the eighteenth century, that pagan reason became a direct threat to Christian revelation. But the classicizing tendencies of seventeenth-century thinkers were hardly innocuous; consider the writings of Hugo Grotius, diplomat, theologian, patriotic Hollander, and by general consent, the founder of modern international law. Grotius was prominent among the Dutch Arminians (see p. 195) and, late in life, found Roman Catholicism, with its universality and its vision of comprehensive peace, most appealing. In his epoch-making *De jure belli ac pacis* of 1625, Grotius, the declared disciple of Seneca and Cicero, sought to derive the rules of international law not from man's dependence on God but from his nature and his place in the natural universe. Even assuming that God does not exist, he wrote, the rules of natural law would remain valid, and again: "Natural law is so unalterable that God himself cannot change it." Seeking to give substance and authority to the law of nations, Grotius returned to the ideas of classical philosophy and liberated natural law from its subordination to theology. This was not secularism, but it helped to widen the road to secularism that was being constructed, slowly and largely unintentionally, by the philosophers and scientists of the seventeenth century.

"New Philosophy Calls All in Doubt"

The return to antiquity took many forms: Romans and Greeks—especially Greeks—had, after all, speculated on all aspects of nature and man. And one antique current, Epicureanism, entered into the rising tide of scientific inquiry, which had been quickening since mid-sixteenth century. Unlike Stoicism,

Epicureanism was almost impossible to reconcile with Christianity; even in antiquity, their shocked opponents had stigmatized the Epicureans as atheists for teaching that the world is essentially composed of material atoms and for denying that the gods, remote and serene spectators, had any power over man. Yet, perhaps partly from caution, certainly largely from conviction, the leading modern Epicurean, Pierre Gassendi, earnestly proclaimed his piety: he was, like the ancient Epicureans, an atomist, but as a priest he found it both politic and persuasive to argue that God had made the atoms. Friend and correspondent to most of the leading scientists and philosophers of his day, Gassendi lived at a time critical for the scientific revolution. He was born in 1592 and died in 1655, which makes him the contemporary of Bacon, Galileo, and Descartes; his writings and his letters are a bridge between ancient doctrines of materialism and the distinctly modern enterprise of the seventeenth century—the making of a scientific universe—an enterprise we have come to call the "scientific revolution." Among Gassendi's distinguished admirers, the most distinguished was Isaac Newton: Gassendi, Newton thought, had been entirely right about the critically important questions of God, space, and time. [34]

The scientific revolution was a long and slow process. But once it had taken final shape in the work of Newton, man's way of looking at the world and man's relation to nature had changed forever, beyond recognition. Newton would bring the worlds of the heavens and of the earth under a single rubric, a single set of natural laws; Newton himself would hint that what he had done for physics and astronomy might be done for chemistry, and even for what the eighteenth century would call the sciences of man. The old dream that man might gain dominion over nature now seemed near realization. And yet, the revolution took place within a Christian context: John Donne's much-quoted— too much quoted—lament of 1612, that "new philosophy calls all in doubt," mirrored the dismay of a small minority. For most seventeenth-century natural philosophers—pious Christians, nearly all of them—the study of nature was the devout tracing of God's handiwork. It is not an accident that Newton should have spent as much time and effort on establishing biblical chronologies as he did on finding equations for gravity. In 1692, five years after he had published his epoch-making *Principia* (see p. 341), he wrote to the classicist Richard Bentley, who had used arguments from Newton to defend the Christian dispensation: "When I wrote my treatise about our system, I had an eye upon such principles as might work with considering men for the belief of a Deity, and nothing can rejoice me more than to find it useful for that purpose." This was the voice of the majority. The scientific revolution was a revolution, but its anti-Christian and, beyond that, antireligious implications troubled only a few theologians and philosophers in the seventeenth century and became the mainstay of Enlightenment propaganda only in the eighteenth century. They did not really pervade European culture until the nineteenth century.

[34] This is what Voltaire reports in his well-informed study of Newton, published in 1738.

While the religious consequences of the scientific revolution manifested themselves slowly, its roots were deep. To dismiss medieval civilization as simply antiscientific would be to oversimplify a complicated story. The twelfth-century revival of philosophy had given room for speculation on the phenomena of nature; especially in optics and biology, medieval scientists did respectable work. Much like the seventeenth-century scientists, these medieval scientists were devoutly certain that their studies could only confirm and enhance man's awe for God's truly marvelous creation. They did much: in the thirteenth century two English Franciscans, Robert Grosseteste and Roger Bacon, spread Greek and Roman scientific thought among learned circles with their voluminous writings and laid down canons of scientific procedure that read like passages from a modern textbook. Bacon prophetically argued for the use of mathematics, defended experimentation, called for the classification of the various sciences by their objects of study, and sounding much like his seventeenth-century namesake, Francis Bacon, proclaimed the aim of science to be power over nature. [35]

Despite all this, the scientific revolution remains just that—a revolution: Roger Bacon might speak highly of experiments, but neither he nor any of his admiring readers performed them; he might advocate the classification of the sciences, but for centuries after him, astrology and astronomy, alchemy and chemistry, magic and mathematics cheerfully coexisted. The very motive for studying nature in the Middle Ages inescapably limited the conclusions such study might reach: Christian theology laid down rigid boundaries beyond which the most brilliant medieval mind did not dare go—quite literally could not think of going. Since the only aim of science was to serve religious purposes—to settle the precise dates of holidays or to confirm once again the glory of God—it was not science that benefited or progressed. Methodological pronouncements remained empty; reliance on authority remained practically universal. And then, with the decline of fresh thinking in the fourteenth and fifteenth centuries, with the logic-chopping and sublime irrelevance of late Scholastic philosophy, whatever energies Grosseteste and Bacon might have generated dissipated themselves. Not even the Renaissance markedly changed this. While the philosophical preoccupations of the Humanists had some indirect effect on the temper of inquiry, and while their scholarly efforts restored indispensable scientific texts, the Humanists themselves were more interested in philology and literature, and in purely speculative natural theology, than in science proper. Leonardo da Vinci, as we have noted (see p. 78) was a remarkably fertile and precise scientific observer, experimenter, and discoverer, but his achievements were uncharacteristic of his age and in

---

[35] Grosseteste (ca. 1168–1253) became a bishop, Bacon (ca. 1214–1292) was Grosseteste's student. It is worth adding that only lack of space prevents a longer discussion: these two Franciscans were by no means alone in their passion for God's handiwork in the natural world.

any event, hidden as they were in his notebooks, remained unknown. It took a drastic shift in the intellectual temper of Europe before Roger Bacon's bold prophecies could become realities.

Sixteenth-Century Revolutionaries

The first evidence, and indispensable cause, of this shift came in the year 1543, with two books: Copernicus' *Concerning the Revolutions of the Celestial Spheres* and Vesalius' *On the Fabric of the Human Body*. Two years later, the French physician Jean Fernel hailed the dawn of a new age: "The world sailed round, the largest of the Earth's continents discovered, the compass invented, the printing-press sowing knowledge, gun-powder revolutionizing the art of war, ancient manuscripts rescued and the restoration of scholarship, all witness to the triumph of our New Age." [36] Fernel was a follower of Vesalius and could appreciate his master's work. But the epoch-making discovery of his day, the one that marked the first real breach in the medieval conception of the world— the Copernican revolution—he passed by in silence. That was only natural: it took some years to disseminate Copernicus' theory and many more years before it was generally accepted.

Nicholas Copernicus, a Polish mathematician and astronomer, was born in 1473, studied first at Cracow and then at Bologna, and spent his life pondering his subversive ideas. For decades he kept his convictions to himself—too long for worldly glory, for his book came out in the year of, but after, his death. Like many revolutionaries, Copernicus was a conservative, a careful student of the scientific tradition, respectful of its teachings. What drove him to dissent was the mathematical difficulties surrounding the prevailing view of the world, the "uncertainty," as he put it, "of the mathematical tradition in establishing the motions of the systems of the spheres." [37] That mathematical tradition was the legacy of the Greek-Egyptian mathematician and astronomer Ptolemy, who had collated and summarized one school of ancient astronomy early in the second century after Christ in his *Almagest*, which was eagerly studied in manuscript and printed in the sixteenth century. Ptolemy's central assertion, that the earth is the stationary center of the universe, was not the unanimous view of ancient astronomers, but Ptolemy's authority choked off debate for over a millennium; it was, of course, a welcome theory for Christians who could hardly be expected to believe that God would place man, made in His image (or that Jesus Christ, God's only begotten son, would take the trouble to be incarnated) on a relatively minor planet. One half of this theory, that the earth is stationary, had not gone unchallenged: a few medieval scholars had tried to reduce the difficulties in Ptolemy's theory by suggesting that the earth, though

[36] Quoted in Marie Boas, *The Scientific Renaissance, 1450–1630* (1962), 17.
[37] Ibid., 69.

the center of the universe, rotated on its axis. Copernicus took the next and far more important step: he argued that the earth indeed revolves on its axis but, in addition, revolves around the sun, in a circular orbit.

Like all astronomers of his day, Copernicus began with Ptolemy, but, precisely like Ptolemy a mathematician, Copernicus could not rest content with him. He found Ptolemy's account of planetary motion too clumsy and ultimately unconvincing. The observed paths of the planets are maddeningly irregular, and the better the observation of the planets became, the more maddening the irregularities. For mathematicians since Plato and Pythagoras, the ideal had been lucidity and simplicity, but Ptolemaic astronomers found themselves compelled to be at once obscure and complex: to give a persuasive explanation of planetary motion, they developed an extremely involved system of epicycles—little circles which together make up a large circle in which the planets travel around the earth. The center of all this planetary motion—this was another desperate attempt to "save the appearances"—was not precisely at the earth, but near it. While Copernicus did not wholly give up the epicycles, and while his heliocentric hypothesis had obscurities and complexities of its own, he explained some of the more embarrassing eccentricities of the planetary orbits. Copernicus himself, in any event, was convinced of his theory largely on rationalistic and mathematical grounds. To reduce irregularities to mere apparent motion, and to place the sun into the center of the universe, were to serve the ideals of simplicity, harmony, reason, and beauty. "In the middle of all," he wrote, almost ecstatically, "sits the Sun enthroned. How could we place this luminary in any better position in this most beautiful temple from which to illuminate the whole at once? He is rightly called the Lamp, the Mind, the Ruler of the Universe." [38]

Copernicus' heliocentric astronomy was a scientific accomplishment of the first order, even if his argumentation for it has an antique aura. His proposal required enormous daring and imagination: it was nearly impossible even for advanced spirits of the sixteenth century to conceive an earth that moved, and the psychological and religious consequences (though they were not immediately perceived by anyone) were bound to be enormously troubling. As Sigmund Freud was to observe almost four centuries later, here was the first of three scientific discoveries to humble man's pride: Copernicus expelled man from the center of the universe, Darwin would deprive man of his unique privileged place in creation, while Freud would show the frailty of human reason by demonstrating the power of the unconscious. [39]

Such penetrating interpretations of Copernicus' work were still far off, though its theological implications began to worry thoughtful natural philoso-

[38] Ibid., 81.
[39] There had been three blows that science had dealt man's narcissism, Freud wrote, the first cosmological, the second biological, the third psychological. The first of these, normally associated with Copernicus, had actually been hinted at before by the ancient Greeks. See "A Difficulty in the Path of Psycho-Analysis," in *Standard Edition of the Complete Psychological Works of Sigmund Freud*, vol. XVII (1953), 137-144.

phers in the generation after his death. The great controversy over the possibly subversive character of the Copernican system did not break out until the time of Galileo, early in the seventeenth century (see p. 238), but it already figured in the thought of the Danish astronomer Tycho Brahe, indisputably the greatest student of the stars in the late sixteenth century. Brahe, who spent his life observing planets and comets, constructing calculations and charts, and vastly improving man's knowledge of the heavens, admired Copernicus as a great man and a powerful mathematician; he wholeheartedly accepted Copernicus' criticism of the Ptolemaic system. That system, Brahe said, is hopelessly inelegant and accounts for far too little of celestial motion. However, both on physical and theological grounds, Brahe rejected the notion of an earth in motion; this, he argued, ran counter to what we know of the "sluggishness" of our earth and counter to explicit passages in Scriptures. His own substitute system was perhaps less offensive than Copernicus', but no more elegant and far less convincing.

Johannes Kepler, on the other hand, briefly Brahe's assistant, accepted Copernicus' revolution and, in his own astronomical work, confirmed and extended it. Characteristically, and wholly in tune with Copernicus' own aesthetic, classical, and philosophical preoccupations, Kepler assented to Copernicus' views because he found them more imposing, more beautiful, than those of his rivals: "I have confessed to the truth of the Copernican view, and contemplate its harmonies with incredible rapture." In general, Kepler went through life in a condition of religious excitement. He sought, and found, mystical correspondences between the heavenly bodies and the Holy Trinity; like a modern Pythagoras, he saw enchanting harmonies in the laws of the universe. At the same time, he respected Tycho Brahe, the observer, and made meticulous calculations; at the dawn of the scientific era, mysticism and precision were not yet enemies.

Kepler was born in Germany in 1571, and was among the first to be thoroughly trained in both the Ptolemaic and the Copernican astronomy. After some years of teaching mathematics in the Austrian town of Graz, he moved to Prague in 1600, where Tycho Brahe was installed as imperial mathematician. Kepler became Brahe's assistant and, after Brahe's death in the following year, his successor. He had already published a defense of the Copernican system. Indeed, despite his private musings and subjective insights, Kepler distinctly belonged to a scientific tradition then developing: he proclaimed he had taken most of his ideas from others—"I have built all Astronomy on the Copernican Hypothesis of the World; the Observations of Tycho Brahe; and the Magnetic Philosophy of the Englishman William Gilbert."[40] Such collaboration was becoming a widespread experience: William Gilbert, whom Kepler here singles out, exercised considerable influence on Kepler with his *De Magnete* of 1600, which gave Kepler the idea that the sun emits a magnetic force as it emits light

---

[40] Quoted in Boas, *Scientific Renaissance*, 301.

and thus animates the planets in their orbits; Gilbert in turn singled out Copernicus as the restorer of true astronomy.

Fame came to Kepler after Brahe's death, with his famous three laws of celestial motion. These laws are a triumph of science over aesthetics: reluctantly, and after many attempts at rescuing Copernicus' circular orbits, Kepler came to the conclusion that in fact the planets move not in circles, but in ellipses. Fortunately for him, the ellipsis too was a harmonious figure, testifying to the mathematical loveliness of God's creation. He published the first two of his laws in 1609. They held, first, that planets travel around the sun in elliptical orbits, with the sun in one focus; and second, that the speed of the planets varies with their distance from the sun so that the planet's path sweeps out equal areas in equal times. But ten years later, in 1619, in a work significantly entitled *The Harmony of the World*, Kepler announced his third law: the squares of the revolution of any two planets are proportional to the cubes of their mean distance from the sun. And it was this third law that made his astronomy complete, and harmonious, and thus satisfying almost beyond Kepler's power to express. He himself testified to his ecstasy: "Eighteen months ago the first dawn rose for me, a very few days ago the sun, most wonderful to see, burst upon me." And he spoke of his "divine rage"—which is to say his overpowering pleasure—at his discovery. Kepler, this frenzied mathematical philosopher, was saying that Aristotle was dead; he had been put to rest forever by Plato, that divine mathematician. It is a mistake to think of the scientific revolution as a rebellion of the new against the old: it was the creation of the new by means of the rebellion of one ancient philosophy against another.

Galileo: The Making of Modern Dynamics

The most extraordinary of these modern Platonists was Galileo Galilei, but he was not simply that: Galileo was also supremely endowed with the curiosity that is the true scientific spirit. Sometime in May or June 1609, he heard of a Flemish "spyglass" which, it was reported, brought distant objects near. To hear of the device was enough: Galileo instantly set about constructing a telescope, and then trained it on the heavens. The radical reconstruction in method that Francis Bacon was calling for in England (see p. 240) was about to take place in Italy. What Galileo saw in his telescope, and what he deduced from it, enormously enriched scientific knowledge and prepared the way for Newton.

Early in 1610, Galileo reported his discoveries in the *Sidereal Messenger*: the mountains of the moon, the starry composition of the Milky Way, four moons of Jupiter, the phases of Venus, and spots on the sun. His report made him famous overnight. Born in Pisa in 1564, he had displayed his talents and, more than that, his intellectual independence, early; at twenty-five he secured the chair of mathematics in Pisa, and soon after he moved to Padua. When he made his astronomical discoveries, he was forty-five, the correspondent of Kepler and other scientific pioneers; he had long before satisfied himself that dominant Aristotelian theories of motion were wholly wrong. But few knew of his work. Now he became embroiled in controversy which he would have been wise, but loved too much, to avoid.

Many scientists accepted Galileo's observations, and, about this time, Copernicus' heliocentric theory enjoyed wide support. But in 1616 the Holy Office condemned that theory as absurd, false, and heretical. Galileo was in a dangerous position; his experiments reinforced his early support of Copernicus. Then, in 1623, his old acquaintance, Cardinal Barberini, a humane, civilized intellectual, was elected Pope Urban VIII. Galileo therefore felt safe in pursuing his path. His *Dialogue of the Two Chief Systems of the World*, published after long delays in 1632, gave Galileo's convictions clear—all too clear—expression. What followed was a personal quarrel raised to historic importance by the stature of the participants and the stakes of the controversy. Urban had encouraged Galileo to proceed with his investigations, but warned him to stay clear of theological questions and to present the Copernican view as nothing more than a plausible hypothesis: the intellectual freedom Barberini could permit himself and his friends as cardinal was unavoidably circumscribed by the obligations he had accepted as pope. Galileo supplied his *Dialogues* with disclaimers, but they were obviously disingenuous; no one could read his delightful exposition without recognizing that the Copernican had all the good lines. The sequel is known to everyone: Urban VIII felt betrayed and was furious. In June 1633, the Inquisitors found Galileo guilty of disobedience and condemned him to abjure his errors, confess his rebelliousness, and go to prison. His *Dialogue* was placed on the Index, but his judges commuted the prison sentence to house arrest. In house arrest Galileo remained until his death in 1642; he published only one more book, the *Discourses on Two New Sciences*. Hearing of Galileo's fate, Descartes decided to withhold a treatise on cosmology from publication.

To place the trial of Galileo into proper perspective is important but difficult; it is easy to overestimate or, by reaction, to slight its effects on scientific inquiry. In Italy certainly, and in other countries in which the Counter-Reformation and, more specifically, the Inquisition were influential, science languished. It was not wholly stifled: Galileo abjured his heresies and went on holding them, and other Catholic scientists were converted to his views. But by and large scientific activity moved northward, to Protestant countries. The trial of Galileo suggests a dawning realization that the scientific revolution might bring a religious and intellectual revolution in its train. But these attendant revolutions were still far in the future; what matters most about Galileo is not the implications of his trial, but the implications of his work. It amounted to a revolution in dynamics—the science of motion—which was to find its culmination in Newton's laws half a century later. It was on the matter of motion that the authority of Aristotle would be finally overthrown.

Controversies over motion go back to the earliest Greek philosophers, and not all Greeks reasoned like Aristotle. But with the Roman Catholics' adoption of Aristotle as their official classical ancestor, Aristotle's authority over science was absolute. Now, Aristotle had postulated two qualitatively different kinds of motion: celestial motion proper to the perfect beings of the heavens, and terrestrial motion proper to the imperfect beings here on earth. This was not the only myth the slavish reading of Aristotle had fastened on scientific thought: Aristotle had held that the "natural" condition of bodies is rest, so that they will persist in motion only as long as they are being pushed. Finally, Aristotle taught that "light" bodies tend upward while "heavy" bodies tend downward, so that bodies must fall at a speed proportionate to their weights.

The point about such thinking was not simply that its ultimate conclusions were wrong, but that its underlying methods were unscientific, for what persuaded Aristotle to hold these views, and his followers to perpetuate them, were philosophical, religious, and aesthetic considerations—considerations, that is to say, important in themselves but irrelevant to scientific inquiry. Kepler had already drawn some of this kind of thinking into question by discovering that the orbits of the planets around the sun were not "perfect" circles but ellipses—a mathematical figure universally considered to be inferior to the circle in beauty and perfection, though also harmonious. Kepler was a mystic and an enthusiast, but he allowed his discoveries to override his preferences.

This was the road to scientific thinking, and Galileo continued on it. Proceeding with care, Galileo formulated the principle of inertia, which holds that a body at rest, or in motion at a constant speed on a straight line, will persist either at rest or in its course without alteration. Aristotle was wrong: a force was required not to keep a body in motion, but to stop it or to change its speed or its course. This formulation was the critically important distinction between velocity and acceleration. Galileo also refuted Aristotle with his discovery that bodies will drop at speeds proportionate to their time of fall, not to their weight. It is true that Galileo, like his predecessors, was prompted in his discoveries by philosophical convictions: his rejection of Aristotle led him to Plato, to the view that the universe is governed by uniform, universal laws that can be expressed in the lovely and precise language of mathematics. But, at least in Galileo's hands, Plato was a far more dependable guide to science than Aristotle had ever been.

Galileo's scientific work—his astronomical discoveries, his formulation of the laws of inertia, his empirical and mathematical proofs for Copernicus' heliocentric theories—is of the most far-reaching significance. But the importance of Galileo's discoveries is overshadowed by that of his method. He was observer, experimenter, mathematician together, and he taught that true science is possible only through the conjunction of observation, experiment, and mathematics. By ridiculing those doctrinaires who would not look through his telescope, he exalted the open-minded inquirer who is willing to learn from experience over the dogmatic traditionalist who persists in deriving his knowledge from ancient authoritative books. And by showing, finally, that theological or aesthetic considerations have no place in scientific findings, Galileo widened the domain of scientific thinking and made way for the reign of quantity and objectivity, on which all real science must depend. When he died in 1642, the year Newton was born, Galileo had delineated the possibility of a unified physical science that would explain the orbit of a planet and the fall of an apple by the same overarching law. It was Isaac Newton who would turn the possibility into reality (see p. 340).

The Emergence of Scientific Philosophy

Copernicus and Kepler had been revolutionaries in their discoveries, but not in their method or their rhetoric; Galileo was a revolutionary in what he found, how he found it, and the way he defended his findings. He was not alone. The subversive potential of early modern science emerged with fair clarity in the antiauthoritarianism of physiologists like Vesalius and William Harvey, and in the codification of the new mentality by philosophers like Francis Bacon and Descartes.

Like astronomy, the science of the human body had been mired for many centuries in the adoration of the past. Galen, a Greek scholar like Ptolemy active in the second century after Christ, had left behind a large number of treatises on anatomy, physiology, and medicine, and Renaissance scientists treated these documents as Holy Writ, as the Scriptures of physiology, devoutly to be followed and never to be questioned. The difficulty for science was not Galen's errors, but Galen's authority; the habit of "proving" a point by appealing to ancient texts, which was the method of theology, remained prevalent in the natural sciences as well. It was notorious that when these scientists performed dissections and their findings differed from the received text, they made light of their own observations and kept the authority of the text intact. Down to the sixteenth century, medical students would attend dissections and look at the cadaver while a standard work—Galen, or perhaps a treatise by the fourteenth-century anatomist, Mondino—would be read aloud to them. How heavily this kind of thinking weighed on scientists appears plainly enough in the career of the great sixteenth-century physiologist Andreas Vesalius. Born in 1514 in Flanders, trained at Louvain, Paris, and— most significantly—Padua, Vesalius was enormously ambitious and insatiably curious: unlike his predecessors, he insisted on seeing for himself and on drawing his own conclusions. His masterpiece of 1543, *On the Fabric of the Human Body,* and associated writings of the same period were spirited attacks on his teachers; they marked a revolutionary advance over man's previous knowledge of the human skeleton, muscles, arteries, veins, nerves, inner organs including the brain, and the relation of the part to the whole. The splendid illustrations that accompanied Vesalius' work remain striking evidence of how much the method of strenuous and uninhibited empiricism could discover. Yet not even Vesalius could wholly free himself from the past; the organization of his book was a deliberate restatement of Galen's main concerns, and much of what Vesalius found he found with an eye to the master he sought to replace: he advertised some of his discoveries as insights the great Galen had missed, and on many fundamental principles of physiology he simply followed that ancient authority who had been dead for fourteen centuries.

In the seventeenth century, the English anatomist William Harvey laid down what had become a commonplace among scientists, thanks in large part to Vesalius: "I profess to learn and teach anatomy not from books but from dissections, not from the tenets of philosophers but from the fabric of nature."[41] Yet not even Harvey wholly dispensed with books or even with Galen. Trained in Padua and practicing in London as a prosperous physician, Harvey carefully stored up what he had learned from his professors in Italy, piously quoted Galen, but also patiently experimented in the laboratory for many years. Finally, in 1628, he published his *On the Movement of the Heart and Blood*, which established firmly what some Italian physiologists had already partly understood: the circulation of the blood. However imperfect Harvey's empiricism, however adroit his obeisances to established authority, his work proved how far the scientific method had advanced in the course of less than a hundred years, and how much it produced in the way of tangible and permanent results.

Ironically, the man who drew out all the implication of the new philosophy and the new method, Francis Bacon, was curiously insensitive to the magnificent scientific work that was being done around him. Bacon rejected Copernicus, underestimated Harvey, misread Galileo, and slighted the importance of mathematics in scientific inquiry. He has been called, with much justice, the prophet and the poet, of science; essayist, lawyer, statesman, utopian philosopher, Bacon understood the meaning of science without understanding science itself. While this anomaly resists explanation, his role in the scientific revolution is clear and was central; he was right to think of himself as a pioneer, the first to see with total clarity a new vision of man's ways of thinking and of his ultimate possibilities: Bacon was, as he said, with that vivid lucidity of his unsurpassed English style, "a bellringer which is first up to call others to church."

He did his bell-ringing in the midst of feverish political activity. Bacon was born in 1561 and entered Parliament in 1584, but despite his obvious brilliance rose slowly and rather tortuously into higher government circles. His associ-

[41] Ibid., 280.

ation with the unfortunate Essex (see p. 188) and later, his opportunistic repudiation of Essex on trial, held him back. It was not until the reign of James I that his political talents found an appropriate outlet. James knighted Bacon in 1603, the year of his accession, named him attorney general in 1613, Baron Verulam and lord chancellor in 1618, and Viscount St. Albans in 1621. Yet in the same year, he was indicted for taking bribes (which meant probably doing what everyone else was doing, but that his enemies were powerful); he was convicted and disgraced. In his last five years—he died in 1626—Bacon wrote a history of Henry VII, his scientific utopia, the *New Atlantis,* and recast and expanded what he regarded as his life's work, the *Instauratio Magna*—The Great Renewal, which he left incomplete. The first part of that ambitious project designed to lay out a wholly new way of studying and mastering the world, *The Advancement of Learning,* had already appeared in 1605; the second part, the *Novum Organum,* in 1620. While historians have tended to belittle these efforts as naive in method and vulgar in aim, their influence proved enormous, and their merit is perhaps greater than is commonly recognized.

· Bacon's case must be understood as part of a great polemic against the survivals of Aristotelianism and what was generally called "Scholasticism" in scientific inquiry. "The knowledge whereof the world is now possessed," he argued, "especially that of nature, extendeth not to magnitude and certainty of works. The Physician pronounceth many diseases incurable and faileth oft in the rest. The Alchemists wax old and die in hopes. The Magicians perform nothing that is permanent and profitable. The mechanics take small light from natural philosophy, and do but spin on their own little threads." What was needed, therefore, was a complete housecleaning; mankind, Bacon said in his ringing tones, must "commence a total reconstruction of sciences, arts, and all human knowledge, raised upon proper foundations." Bacon's central effort was to discover, and to disseminate knowledge of, these foundations. What he sought to do, then, was to find knowledge that all reasonable men could accept and use: "I am labouring to lay the foundation, not of any sect or doctrine, but of human utility and power." The much-debated Baconian method was simply the spelling out of this labor.

The method meant, first of all, the diagnosis and cure of the kinds of judgments that confuse and mislead men, the so-called "idols"—the loose language, entrenched prejudices, unfounded judgments, that keep man from true knowledge. The "Idols of the Tribe" have "their foundation in human nature itself"; the "Idols of the Cave" are "the idols of the individual man"; the "Idols of the Market-place" are "formed by the intercourse and association of men with each other"; and the "Idols of the Theatre" are "received into the mind from the playbooks of philosophical systems." All must be exposed before the reconstruction of rational inquiry and social policy can begin. Second, the Baconian method stressed induction, the painstaking collection and skeptical sifting of facts, which give rise to preliminary hypotheses which in turn can be expanded into general theories. [42] Associated with this method was, in the third place, experimentation, the deliberate construction of situations in which notions could be tested and could serve as confirmations of, and guides to, observation. Bacon did not stop there; perhaps his most significant contribution to scientific procedure—the one that had the most immediate and most visible results—was his clearheaded view of inquiry. He, more than most, saw the complexity of scientific investigation, and he insisted that henceforth natural philosophers must agree to divide their labors that they may know well the subjects in which they specialize. And it followed also that this division of labor must be organized: the new learning should be public, cooperative, and cumulative—cooperation was the clue to scientific progress. It was out of this insistence, largely, that the Royal Society of London for Improving Natural Knowledge was to grow (see p. 341).

Bacon never wearied of insisting that the new method he was advocating was above all practical—knowledge, as he said in a celebrated aphorism, is power. He hoped to lay down the grounds of a science that would produce "a line and race of inventions that may in some degree subdue and overcome the necessities and miseries of humanity." He was eager to make man the architect of his fortune. With all its obvious limitations, then, Bacon's thought points to a new civilization in which men would be masters rather than victims of their world.

Descartes essentially had the same program in view. Beginning in the eighteenth century, later generations would pit Bacon against Descartes as though their philosophies were wholly irreconcilable. In the seventeenth century, their convergence was far more important than their differences. Like Bacon, Descartes developed a thoroughgoing and systematic impatience with all earlier modes of inquiry: the quibbling logic of Scholastic philosophers, the far-flung speculations of ancient thinkers, and the pretentious claims of theologians had perpetuated ignorance and sowed confusion. "As for the other sciences," Descartes added, "since after all they borrow their principles from philosophy, I decided that nothing solid could have been built on such unstable foundations." From this dissatisfaction Descartes derived his program: to construct solid knowledge on solid foundations. Like Bacon he was convinced that one could do this only by beginning at the beginning.

---

[42] It is at this point that the charge of naivete is most commonly leveled. A scientist, it is often and rightly pointed out, does not arrive at his discoveries by piling up facts one by one; he has insights, hunches, wild guesses, which he then substantiates or drops in the course of systematic testing. And much scientific discovery has significant irrational components: aesthetic appreciation, say, or the need for applause. Certainly Bacon's insistence on induction and practicality slight the playfulness of much scientific thinking. But Bacon was not a dogmatic advocate of induction. He hoped, rather, for a "true and lawful marriage between the empirical and the rational faculty." Mere reasoners, he suggested, are spiders "who make cobwebs out of their own substance," but mere experimenters are ants, who "only collect and use." The ideal natural philosopher is like the bee, which gathers its material and then digests it "by a power of its own." If Baconian is mere vulgar empiricism, then Bacon was not a Baconian.

Descartes was more than a mere methodologist or a utopian dreamer. Born in 1596 at La Haye, in Touraine, he spent much of his life in retirement, almost seclusion, abroad; when he died in 1650, he was, significantly enough, in Sweden as Queen Christina's guest. Descartes wrote widely on philosophical and psychological subjects, and was the first to apply algebra to geometry. His invention of analytical geometry has been immortalized by what are still called, after him, "Cartesian coordinates." But his most celebrated and most influential contribution to the reconstruction of inquiry and the spread of the scientific method was his *Discourse on Method,* all the more influential for being written in lucid French. It was published in 1637 and explicitly designed as a guide for "correctly conducting the reason and seeking truth in the sciences." Precisely like Bacon, Descartes offered his method full of optimism about the new learning, and of irritation against the old: "It is possible to obtain knowledge highly useful in life. . . . Instead of the speculative philosophy taught in the Schools we can have a practical philosophy with which . . . we may make ourselves the masters and possessors of nature." All that men know, Descartes insisted, "is almost nothing compared to what remains to be known; we could be freed from innumerable maladies, of body and mind alike, and perhaps even from the infirmities of old age, if we had sufficient knowledge of their causes and of all the remedies with which nature has provided us."

Descartes made his revolution in method by turning to himself; since no previous way of inquiry had brought certain truth or reliable information, introspection was all that was left. It is not an accident that the *Discourse* should be largely an autobiography detailing Descartes' early confusion, growing restlessness, and decisive intellectual discoveries. Whatever Descartes' debt to medieval schools of thought, this self-reliance was a radical step, a triumph of self-confident rationalism. Seeking to avoid the old traps in the way of reasoning, Descartes devised a set of four rules that would clear all obstacles and produce dependable knowledge. These rules were, first, to accept only clear, distinct, self-evidently true ideas; second, to divide each difficulty into "as many parts as may be necessary for its adequate solution"—that is, to analyze; third, to arrange each acceptable idea in a sequence beginning with the simplest and moving on to the more complicated ones, and thus to propel human reason forward cautiously but surely, step by step; and four, to make the enumeration of instances and the review of one's way of thinking as complete as they could be.

By rigorously following this program and by looking into himself, determined to trust nothing that was not wholly trustworthy, Descartes established his famous first truth: "*Cogito, ergo sum*—I think, therefore I am." It was a slender foundation, and later thinkers would question its adequacy, but for Descartes it was enough to construct a world. Nothing else was certain, but even the most radical doubt required a doubter: thinking, therefore, implied the existence of a thinker. Moving forward from this first step, with the caution he had prescribed, Descartes proved the existence of God, of matter, and of motion. His proof for the existence of God infuriated such devout thinkers as Pascal who suspected (rightly enough, it turned out in the eighteenth century) that Descartes' conception of a remote God, coupled as it was with his rigidly mechanistic philosophy, was first cousin to sheer materialism. Descartes said that animals are machines—how far was this from the atheist's assertion that men, too, are machines? But for Descartes this chain of reasoning was ground for true philosophical piety: since man can conceive of something higher, more perfect, than himself, something higher, more perfect, must have inspired this conception—and that is God.

Reasoning in this way, from clear ideas to clear ideas, Descartes constructed a mental and physical world that contained a number of indefensible notions: since space, in the Cartesian system, means extension, and extension presupposes matter, there can be no void; consequently, the universe must be filled with impalpable matter. Newton was to refute this view half a century later. But while Descartes' scientific ideas were to come under decisive attack before long, his *Principles of Philosophy* (1644), which outlined them, seemed to his many admirers a powerful and coherent account of the universe. Much of Descartes' power lay, doubtless, in his eclecticism: in his willingness to move from deductive reasoning to an appeal to experience, and from mathematics to experimentation. It lay, also, in his rationalism: no one before Descartes had so effectively assailed authoritarian ways of thinking and so elegantly asserted the autonomy of the rational self. For a hundred and fifty years or more, even his severest critics were to some degree his disciples (see p. 340n). But it lay, above all, in his vision. Descartes, much like Bacon, offered a hope that was as grandiose as it was—or was proclaimed to be—realistic: man could lengthen life, abolish the terrors of old age, improve health, and do away with onerous labor. Yet one thing was clear, even to those who read these scientific prophets with excitement and sought to put their ideas into practice: the realities of their time were quite different—they were, as they had always been, and perhaps even more so, the old realities of war, pestilence, and hunger.

SELECTED READINGS

In two long essays of 1904-1905, *The Protestant Ethic and the Spirit of Capitalism* (tr. 1930), the great German sociologist Max Weber argued that Calvinist "worldly asceticism" was a powerful agent in the creation of a capitalist "spirit." In his *Religion and the Rise of Capitalism* (1926), the English economic historian R. H. Tawney takes up and modifies Weber's argument. Amid a considerable controversial literature, the outstanding recent polemic, which seeks to disprove the "Weber thesis" root and branch, Kurt Samuelsson, *Religion and Economic Action: A Critique of Max Weber* (tr. 1961), is the most persuasive; it contains a survey of the literature. H. M. Robertson, *Aspects of the Rise of Economic Individualism: A Criticism of Max Weber and His School* (1933), is an earlier, less incisive critique.

For the rise of capitalism and the "commercial revolution," see Henri Sée, *Modern Capitalism: Its Origin and Evolution* (1928); John U. Nef, *Industry and Government in*

France and England, 1540–1640 (1940); and many excellent articles in E. E. Rich and C. H. Wilson, eds., *The Economy of Expanding Europe in the Sixteenth and Seventeenth Centuries,* vol. IV, *Cambridge Economic History of Europe* (1967), notably Wilson's own long essay, "Trade, Society and the State," pp. 487–575. Among monographs, Bernard Bailyn, *The New England Merchants in the 17th Century* (1955); Stella Kramer, *The English Craft Gilds: Studies in Their Progress and Decline* (1927); and Louis B. Wright, *Religion and Empire: The Alliance Between Piety and Commerce in English Expansion, 1558–1625* (1943), are particularly useful. For Antwerp, see S. T. Bindoff, "The Greatness of Antwerp," in G. R. Elton, ed., *New Cambridge Modern History,* vol. II (1958), 50–69; H. Van Der Wee, *The Growth of the Antwerp Market and the European Economy,* 3 vols. (1963). For Amsterdam, see especially Violet Barbour, *Capitalism in Amsterdam in the 17th Century* (1950); John J. Murray, *Amsterdam in the Age of Rembrandt* (1967); and C. R. Boxer, *The Dutch Seaborne Empire, 1600–1800* (1965).

For Mannerism, see the intelligent recent essay by John Shearman, *Mannerism* (1967); see also Guiliano Briganti, *Italian Mannerism* (1962), and the civilized study by Walter Friedlaender, *Mannerism and Anti-Mannerism in Italian Painting* (ed. 1965). For the most influential architect of the age, see James S. Ackerman, *Palladio* (1966). And for Titian, see the splendid study by Erwin Panofsky, *Problems in Titian, Mostly Iconographic* (1969).

Boris Ford, ed., *The Age of Shakespeare* (1956), vol. II of *The Pelican Guide to English Literature,* is a handy introduction to the Elizabethan Renaissance. Douglas Bush, *English Literature in the Earlier Seventeenth Century, 1600–1660* (1945), moves into the Jacobean period and beyond. Amid a vast literature on Shakespeare, Mark Van Doren, *Shakespeare* (1939); E. E. Stoll, *Art and Artifice in Shakespeare* (1935); and Henri Fluchère, *Shakespeare* (tr. 1953), may be mentioned. For Ben Jonson, see L. C. Knights, *Drama and Society in the Age of Jonson* (1937); for Christopher Marlowe, Harry Levin, *The Overreacher* (1952). T. S. Eliot has some remarkable essays on Shakespeare, Jonson, Marlowe, and other Elizabethan dramatists brought together in *Selected Essays* (1932).

The Golden Age of Spain is lucidly discussed in Gerald Brenan, *The Literature of the Spanish People* (2nd ed., 1962), and George Kubler and Martin Soria, *Art and Architecture in Spain and Portugal and Their American Dominions, 1500–1800* (1959). For the greatest of Spanish writers, see W. J. Entwistle, *Cervantes* (1940), and the essay by Salvadore de Madariaga, *Don Quixote* (1934). For Velázquez, José López-Rey, *Velázquez: A Catalogue Raisonné of his Oeuvre with an Introductory Study* (1963), is essential.

The best introduction to the Dutch Golden Age is Jakob Rosenberg, Seymour Slive, and E. H. Ter Kuile, *Dutch Art and Architecture, 1600–1800* (1966). H. E. Van Gelder, *Guide to Dutch Art* (1952), is very useful. Ingvar Bergström, *Dutch Still-Life Painting in the Seventeenth Century* (1956), and Wolfgang Stechow, *Dutch Landscape Painting of the Seventeenth Century* (1966), add much of use. For Rembrandt, see Jakob Rosenberg, *Rembrandt,* 2 vols. (1948); Seymour Slive, *Rembrandt and His Critics: 1630–1730* (1953); and Ludwig Goldscheider, *Rembrandt: Paintings, Drawings, and Etchings* (1960), which reprints three early biographies and has excellent notes. The best monograph on Vermeer is P. T. A. Swillens, *Johannes Vermeer, Painter of Delft* (1950).

For the Baroque, see the authoritative surveys by Rudolf Wittkower, *Art and Architecture in Italy, 1600–1750* (2nd ed., 1965); H. Gerson and E. H. Ter Kuile, *Art and Architecture in Belgium, 1600–1800* (1960); and Anthony Blunt, *Art and Architecture in France, 1500–1700* (1954). To this should be added John Pope-Hennessy, *Italian High*

Renaissance and Baroque Sculpture (1963), which sketches the transition between styles; Ellis Waterhouse, *Italian Baroque Painting* (1962); Walter Friedlaender, *Caravaggio Studies* (1955); R. A. M. Stevenson, *Peter Paul Rubens* (1939); and Howard Hibbard, *Bernini* (1965), a brilliant essay to be read in conjunction with Rudolf Wittkower, *Gian Lorenzo Bernini, The Sculptor of the Roman Baroque* (1955).

The best work on the revival of ancient philosophy, by Wilhelm Dilthey, "Weltanschauung und Analyse des Menschen seit Renaissance und Reformation," in *Gesammelte Schriften,* vol. II (5th ed., 1957), has not been translated; we can refer the reader to Chapter 5 of Peter Gay, *The Enlightenment: An Interpretation,* vol. I, *The Rise of Modern Paganism* (1966). And see Chapter 13 of Ernst Cassirer, *The Myth of the State* (1946); Jason Lewis Saunders, *Justus Lipsius: The Philosophy of Renaissance Stoicism* (1956); Donald M. Frame, *Montaigne's Discovery of Man: The Humanization of a Humanist* (1955); and Johan Huizinga, "Grotius and His Time" (1925) reprinted in his *Men and Ideas* (1959). See also William S. M. Knight, *The Life and Works of Hugo Grotius* (1925).

A judicious survey of the early scientific revolution is Marie Boas, *The Scientific Renaissance, 1450–1630* (1962). The early chapters of A. R. Hall, *The Scientific Revolution, 1500–1800: The Formation of the Modern Scientific Attitude* (1954), are also very useful. See also Herbert Butterfield, *The Origins of Modern Science, 1300–1800* (2nd ed., 1966), and the more technical I. Bernard Cohen, *The Birth of a New Physics* (1960). For the evolution of the new cosmology, see Thomas S. Kuhn, *The Copernican Revolution: Planetary Astronomy in the Development of Western Thought* (1957). E. M. W. Tillyard, *The Elizabethan World Picture* (1943), and Theodore Spencer, *Shakespeare and the Nature of Man* (2nd ed., 1955), deal with the mental world in the span between Kepler and Galileo. For the latter, see Giorgio di Santillana, *The Crime of Galileo* (1955). Bacon's relation to the scientific revolution remains controversial. Especially recommended are F. H. Anderson, *The Philosophy of Francis Bacon* (1948), and R. F. Jones, *Ancients and Moderns: A Study of the Background of the Battle of the Books* (1936). Catherine Drinker Bowen, *Francis Bacon* (1963), is less searching but still informative. For Bacon's legacy—the organization of science—see Martha Ornstein, *The Role of Scientific Societies in the Seventeenth Century* (3d ed., 1938). Descartes' "modernity" is also subject to debate. See Norman Kemp Smith, *New Studies in the Philosophy of Descartes: Descartes as Pioneer* (1952), and T. F. Scott, *The Scientific Work of René Descartes* (1952).

6

Times of Troubles: Europe at Mid-Seventeenth Century

Most times in history are times of troubles, but in the middle of the seventeenth century, economic, social, intellectual, religious, and political upheavals were so devastating and so general that historians have come to call this period "the crisis of the seventeenth century." In their love for labels, they may have overstressed the uniqueness and intensity of this particular time of troubles— the middle of the sixteenth century, after all, appeared as a crisis to *its* contemporaries[1]—but there can be no question that the mid-seventeenth century was a difficult time. "These days are days of shaking," an English preacher declared in 1643, "and this shaking is universal: the Palatinate, Bohemia, Germania, Catalonia, Portugal, Ireland, England." The days of shaking were recorded on battlefields, in starving villages, on scaffolds, and in men's minds. Their most striking expression, perhaps, was Thomas Hobbes' *Leviathan*, published in the time of Cromwell's republic, in 1651. The *Leviathan* cannot be summarized in a phrase: it is a masterpiece in the history of political

---

[1] See J. H. Elliott, "Revolution and Continuity in Early Modern Europe," *Past and Present,* 42 (Feb. 1969).

theory, an icily logical effort to discover how man, the animal that seeks power, can be effectively governed. But it was also a response to its own somber time. Civil war, Hobbes tells his readers, is the worst of times, worse than tyranny, bad though that may be: "The state of man can never be without some incommodity or other," but "the greatest, that in any form of government can possibly happen to the people in general, is scarce sensible in respect of the miseries, and horrible calamities, that accompany a civil war, or that dissolute condition of masterless men, without subjection to laws, and a coercive power to tie their hands from rapine and revenge." Without a civil power strong enough to overawe the boldest, man's condition is a "war of every man against every man" and his life "solitary, poor, nasty, brutish, and short." When Hobbes was writing, many thought this dismal series of adjectives a fitting description, not for some imaginary state of nature, but for their own day (see p. 346). [2]

THE THIRTY YEARS' WAR

The Opening Phases

The earliest manifestation, and in many respects an aggravating cause, of the general crisis was the Thirty Years' War.

The name is somewhat arbitrary: much of the fighting ended well before the peace of 1648, while other fighting broke out, in different constellations, well after 1648; and the events of 1618 that are customarily taken as the beginning of the war were actually the culmination of long-growing religious and political tensions. Nor was it a single war; it was, rather, a series of intermittent and interlocking wars. Still, its traditional name and the traditional subdivisions on which the textbooks are virtually unanimous adequately stress its salient features. The opening years (1618 to 1625) are known as the Bohemian phase after the first theater of war. Between 1625 and 1629 the war was widened by the entry of the Danes, and this second phase was followed (1630 to 1635) by the spectacular intervention of Sweden; finally, the entry of France brought the war to its last and most general phase (1635 to 1648). Other complexities abound. The war began as a relatively local conflict but spread

---

[2] Among the first historians to call attention to the general crisis was Roger B. Merriman in a lecture delivered in 1937; it was expanded into a book in 1938: *Six Contemporaneous Revolutions.* Since then a whole group of historians has considerably advanced and refined the idea and has come up with far more than six revolutions. The fundamental papers have been collected in Trevor Aston, ed., *Crisis in Europe, 1560–1660* (1965), which contains, among others, articles by E. J. Hobsbawm, H. R. Trevor-Roper, J. H. Elliott, Michael Roberts, and Roland Mousnier. The quotation from the English preacher in the text is drawn from Trevor-Roper, "The General Crisis of the Seventeenth Century," in Aston, *Crisis in Europe,* 59.

across nearly all of Europe; the main place of the action, and the main sufferer, was Germany, but far more than Germany's destiny was involved; while the official participants were states and their armies, private military adventurers, *condottieri* of the north, entered and further confused the lineup of forces; the original confessional division of sides—Catholics versus Protestants—gave way to divisions based on sheer considerations of foreign policy. A largely religious war became primarily a power struggle.

The event that precipitated war in 1618 was the Defenestration of Prague. In May, a crowd of Czechs, Protestants all, invaded a council chamber in the Hradschin Castle and threw two imperial officials and their secretary, Catholics all, out of the window. The victims landed safely, bruised but alive, and made their escape through the vast throng that had assembled to witness the incident. "A pile of mouldering filth" had broken their fall: "A holy miracle or a comic accident according to the religion of the beholder."[3] But whether the one or the other, it was signal for revolt in Bohemia and for wider war.

The Bohemian revolt achieved its larger significance through Bohemia's peculiar position. It was a kingdom which took pride in its religious spiritedness—was it not the land of Hus?—and in its right to elect its own king. But in fact the first meant strenuous infighting among Protestant sects—Utraquists, Lutherans, and Calvinists were steadily at one another's throats—and led to effective domination of Hapsburg, that is to say, Catholic, officialdom. And the second amounted to little more than the dubious privilege of endorsing a Hapsburg prince, who was, in addition to being king of Bohemia, ruler of the neighboring Austrian lands, an imperial elector, and Holy Roman Emperor. In 1617, Emperor Matthias, childless, had designated Archduke Ferdinand as king of Bohemia and as his successor in the imperial seat, a succession that, in view of Matthias' advancing age, could not be long delayed. Ferdinand's religious fervor, his energy, and his eagerness to stamp out the Protestant heresy were well known; the victims of the Defenestration of Prague, Ferdinand's representatives, could hardly be popular with the Bohemians. The materials for trouble were therefore gathered well before Ferdinand's "governors'" lives were saved by a pile of dung.

Events moved with uncommon swiftness. The Bohemian rebels purged officials, expelled the Jesuits, and appealed to Protestant Europe for help; Archduke Ferdinand, king-elect of Bohemia, prepared for a crusade. By June of 1618, the Bohemians had enlisted the support of Frederick, imperial elector of the Palatinate, in the German Rhineland. Frederick was young—twenty-two in 1618—charming and optimistic. For reasons of simple arithmetic, he had long had his eyes on the kingdom of Bohemia: there were seven imperial electors— three of them Roman Catholic bishops, three of them Protestant rulers including himself, while the decisive seventh vote was held by the king of Bohemia. In the hands of a Hapsburg the imperial election must fall to a

[3] C. V. Wedgwood, *The Thirty Years' War* (ed. 1944), 79–80.

Catholic; in the hands of a Protestant, a Protestant would become emperor, and part of Hapsburg power would be whittled away. In addition to holding his electoral office, young Frederick was son-in-law to King James I of England and president of the Protestant Union, a loose defensive confederation of German Protestant princes and cities, most of them Calvinist, that had been formed in 1608.

While the Protestant Union timidly rejected Frederick's aggressive plans for aiding the Bohemian rebels, Frederick himself, with the support of the duke of Savoy, equipped an army and placed it under the command of a distinguished general, Ernst von Mansfeld. At first the war went well for the Protestants. When Matthias died in March 1619, Ferdinand seemed ready to recognize new realities: he offered the rebels a compromise. But the moderates were not in control at Prague. In August 1619, confident—or desperate—the Bohemians declared Ferdinand deposed and, to no one's surprise, elected the elector palatine, Frederick, king of Bohemia. Independently, and at the same time, the imperial electors met at Frankfurt and chose Ferdinand as the new emperor. When news reached the electors that the Bohemians had deposed Ferdinand, all possibility of accommodation vanished.

Ferdinand was in serious difficulties; he was helpless in Bohemia and beset by dissidence elsewhere in his sprawling dominions. And Frederick, though reluctantly and prayerfully, accepted the Bohemian crown in September 1619, and was solemnly crowned King Frederick V. He was faced with an implacable enemy, tepid friends, and the ominous prediction of the Jesuits that he would be nothing more than a "winter king." He was: he got little help from his fellow Protestants; they recognized his reign and scanted their aid. Not even his own family thought it wise to commit themselves to his precarious cause: James I from the first had deplored his son-in-law's rashness. Ferdinand, on the other hand, mustered the military and financial resources of Catholic Europe: Maximilian of Bavaria and his Catholic League, Pope Paul V, and Spain sent troops and money. By the middle of 1620, the Spaniards, using troops gathering in the Netherlands, invaded Frederick's own Rhenish domains, and finally, on November 8, 1620, Ferdinand's army decisively won the battle of the White Mountain, outside Prague. The Winter King's short pathetic reign was over.

The emperor's triumph was so complete that Bohemia lay at his mercy; speedily Ferdinand took advantage of his position. He did more than execute leading rebels, expel Protestant officials, or let his troops sack Prague; he confiscated the estates of Bohemian nobles and used the vast domains now in his gift to reward reliable servants and to found monasteries and convents. Many thousands—burghers, scholars, aristocrats—fled into exile, while Jesuits brought their forceful Catholic message to those compelled to stay and listen. The Counter-Reformation triumphed in a largely Protestant land through religious example, economic pressure, and physical compulsion. And while Ferdinand restored Bohemia to the True Catholic Faith, and destroyed

Bohemia's old social structure with his "new nobility," he crushed rebellion elsewhere in his lands.

But the war was not over. The Protestant Union was dead. Frederick had lost his territory and his post as elector; his intrigues, conducted from exile at The Hague, were scarcely important. But in 1625 another Protestant ruler, Christian IV of Denmark, decided to challenge Ferdinand in Germany. Christian's motives were largely dynastic and only incidentally religious: he was anxious to provide new territories for a son. As duke of Holstein, Christian was an imperial prince, and until 1625 he proclaimed his continued loyalty to his emperor, Ferdinand. Then he acted. His prospects were promising: the English, the Dutch, the French were all deeply concerned over Spain's presence in Germany and what appeared to be Spain's formidable power. But while Christian got large promises, he got little help. At the same time, his adversary, Emperor Ferdinand, was fortunate in his generals: he had Tilly, the victor of the White Mountain, and Wallenstein, with his own army.

Albrecht von Wallenstein remains a mysterious figure, a military magnate who took the moderate legacy his wife left him and converted it into one of the greatest fortunes in Europe. A man of violent temper and unpredictable moods, he had been born a Lutheran in 1583 and converted to Catholicism as a young man, but he believed, it seems, only in the stars and in himself. In 1625, when King Christian of Denmark entered the conflict, Wallenstein had acquired vast holdings in Bohemia and elsewhere in the empire, and the emperor was deeply in his debt. Ferdinand had created him prince of Friedland the year before, and now Wallenstein offered to raise an army of fifty thousand men. With some misgivings, Ferdinand accepted, and Wallenstein moved northward. Four years later, his work against Christian was done: collaborating with Tilly at Lutter, he defeated the Danish troops in 1626; in the same year, he defeated Mansfeld at Dessau. And in 1627, marauding through central and northern Germany, Wallenstein effectively put an end to both General Mansfeld's and King Christian's armies. By 1629, Wallenstein's men were in Danish territory, and Wallenstein had taken the duchy of Mecklenburg for himself. In the same year, Christian IV, soundly beaten, agreed in the Treaty of Lübeck to evacuate Germany and stop interfering in imperial (which is to say, Ferdinand's) affairs.

But, as the emperor's Edict of Restitution suggests, victory was dangerous for the victor. The edict was an act of unmeasured self-confidence, when measured self-restraint would have been wiser. The Bohemian incident of 1618 had blown up into a European-wide war partly because the settlement of Germany, attempted in 1555 at the Peace of Augsburg, had settled very little. The fragmentation of the German lands and the principle that the religion of the ruler was the religion of his subjects converted each prince's death into a scramble for territorial gain. Moreover, the Calvinists, who had found no place in the provisions of the Peace of Augsburg, had managed to secure adherents in a number of states. There were numerous incidents, small wars, harbingers of greater wars to come. The formation of the Evangelical League in 1608 and the response of the German Catholics with their own league in the following year, were further signals of turmoil ahead. Now, in 1629, Emperor Ferdinand, master of Germany, sought almost literally to turn back the clock to a time before Augsburg: his edict bluntly declared almost a century of tentative religious and political accommodation null and void. It invalidated Protestant purchases of church lands and grants of church lands to Protestant princes. It held that Calvinism had no legal standing at all. The stakes were high: if the edict were enforced, so contemporaries reckoned, many free cities, including the great Lutheran center of Augsburg, many former bishoprics and other territories would be compelled to return to Catholicism; princes like the duke of Wolfenbüttel in northern Germany would have to surrender the lands once owned by thirteen convents and most of the old bishopric of Hildesheim.[4] It would restore Catholicism in the very heart of Protestant Germany.

In addition, as an imperial edict, Ferdinand's action was the assertion of independent Hapsburg power, an assertion that even Catholic princes like Maximilian of Bavaria greatly resented. Ferdinand could rationalize his edict as a supreme expression of piety, a late fruit of the Counter-Reformation; Ferdinand's victims, Catholics as well as Protestants, could only see it as a typical Hapsburg maneuver, a cynical grab for hegemony in the name of a spiritual cause. Whatever Ferdinand's motives—and they were probably even more complex than he himself knew—the Edict of Restitution revived Protestant energies and dampened the eagerness of Catholic powers to continue service in a religious crusade that appeared more and more like a Hapsburg war. Ferdinand posed a particular threat through Wallenstein, the great general who laid waste territories wherever he went and who obeyed, if he obeyed anyone, the emperor alone. While the debate over the edict raged, Wallenstein's many enemies, fearful—with reason—of his vast and cloudy ambitions, compelled his dismissal. And then, in 1630, the Thirty Years' War entered a new and, for Ferdinand, perilous, phase with the intervention of Sweden.

Competition for Power: The Intervention of Sweden and France

Gustavus II (Gustavus Adolphus) of Sweden could hardly remain indifferent to the threat of an all-powerful Hapsburg empire, the territorial ambitions concealed (or revealed) in the Edict of Restitution, and the implications of Wallenstein's recent title, "Admiral of the Oceanic and Baltic Seas." King since 1611, Gustavus Adolphus had secured overwhelming popularity with all segments of his people, including the nobility, by his friendly bearing, his soldierly courage, his impressive learning, his administrative skills, and his domestic policies. He had encouraged commerce, built schools, improved

[4] Ibid., 243 ff.

justice, pacified the aristocracy, vastly modernized his army. Moreover, he made progress in the seemingly endless war against the Poles. "The lion of the north" is only the best known of the many admiring epithets his astonished contemporaries bestowed on this brilliant statesman and charismatic leader. He got the advisors he deserved, above all his chancellor, Axel Oxenstierna, intellectual, cool, devoted to his master, though independent enough to offer criticism. Nearly from the beginning of his reign, Gustavus Adolphus had been diplomatically and militarily involved in the Baltic shores of Germany; in 1628 he had promised to aid King Christian IV of Denmark; in 1629, after Christian's defeat, he intensified his negotiations with France, which, although a Catholic power, opposed the extension of Hapsburg dominion (whether Spanish or Austrian) across the German lands.[5] In June 1630, Gustavus Adolphus was ready: he invaded Pomerania with his superbly disciplined army. His ulterior motives were, and remain, unclear; there were even rumors that he wished to become emperor. But it is too easy to say that he masked territorial ambitions behind his championship of Lutheranism. Gustavus Adolphus was at once a devout Lutheran and an aggressive statesman, and he obviously had no difficulty in identifying the expansion of Swedish power on North German soil with the interest of German Protestants.

All went as he expected at first. With the financial help of France, officially settled by treaty in 1631, and with the military support of Saxony and Brandenburg, Gustavus Adolphus defeated the imperial army under Tilly at Breitenfeld, near Leipzig, in September 1631. Alarmed, Ferdinand recalled Wallenstein, who, after canny negotiations, agreed to fight once again for the emperor. Gustavus Adolphus, in control of central Germany and ambitious to march to Vienna, now had a worthy adversary. The two confronted one another, indecisively at first, then decisively in mid-November 1632, at Lützen, just west of Leipzig. Gustavus Adolphus, as always in the midst of the fighting, was killed. It was an incalculable loss, but the Protestant cause, in any event, had been saved by his brief and brilliant intervention. The central aim of the Counter-Reformation, to wipe out the Protestant heresy, had been frustrated. But the war went on, mainly because the French wanted it to go on. While the Swedes continued their German campaign under Oxenstierna's leadership, the Saxons made peace with the emperor in 1635. By that time Wallenstein, the emperor's most formidable and least dependable aide, was dead. Pursuing his own devious designs, Wallenstein had privately and treacherously negotiated with the Swedes and probably with other heretics, conducted himself in the field and in territory under his control as a merciless and brutal ruler, and made ready to take his army over to the Protestant side. His plans failed; in January 1634, the emperor dismissed him, and in the following month Wallenstein and his fellow conspirators fell to the swords of assassins. Ferdinand, immensely relieved, rewarded the murderers. It was that kind of war.

---

[5] Cardinal Richelieu, in fact, helped Gustavus Adolphus to win a favorable truce with Poland in 1629, which gave the Swedes Livonia.

The Great Settlement of 1648

From the mid-1630s, hostilities were punctuated by truces and separate treaties. Emperor Ferdinand II died in 1637 and was succeeded by his relatively pacific son Ferdinand III, but the Spaniards, the Swedes, and the French were bent on further adventures. General negotiations began tentatively in 1641 and then seriously in 1644, at the Westphalian towns of Münster and Osnabrück. Yet even during the negotiations, there was more fighting, more marauding, more destruction; as late as 1648 a French-Swedish army devastated Bavaria. The main antagonists, France and Spain, both Catholic powers, continued their bloody struggle, and in the late 1630s, in a last assertion of her once majestic authority, Spain dealt heavy military blows to the French and brought the war to French territory. But this situation could not, and did not, last: in 1640, the French could take advantage of the revolts of Catalonia and Portugal against Spain (see p. 257), aid the rebels, and briefly invade Spanish soil. Once the French forces were under the generalship of the young prince of Condé and of Marshal Turenne, Spain's eventual defeat was only a matter of time—though the Spaniards did not give up until 1659, when they signed the Peace of the Pyrenees with France. The lineup of forces became positively bizarre: for a brief period (1643-1645) the Swedes even became embroiled in a war with their fellow Lutherans, direct neighbors, and old allies, the Danes. Religion became a minor consideration: the alliance of Catholic France and Lutheran Sweden which, more than anything else kept the war going, continued in force until peace was made.

But peace finally came. In October 1648, after tedious negotiations, the negotiators affixed their signatures, and bells rang in churches of all denominations. There were grown men and women all across central Europe who now saw peace for the first time. The precise toll of despair, devastation, and death will never be known. Their incidence has been exaggerated, and their long-range effects are hard to measure: some areas, such as northwestern Germany, saw little action; others, such as central and southern Germany, sustained repeated sieges and the surging of marauding armies in both directions, and thus suffered far more heavily; some cities, like Magdeburg, and some regions, like Bavaria, may have lost half their population. But not all, perhaps not even most, of these losses were the results of massacres. The indirect effects of war—famine produced by dislocation and migration and an unusual incidence of diseases—were probably worse than the spectacular looting and killing by undisciplined soldiers. [6] But whatever the truth, the Peace of Westphalia, which did not settle everything, at least put an end to most of the fighting.

It did much more. The Peace of Westphalia set the pattern for the

---

[6] See D. C. Coleman, "Economic Problems and Policies," in *The New Cambridge Modern History,* vol. V (1961), 19-21.

emerging state system of early modern Europe. It exalted the sovereign state at the expense of universal empire, and this meant, before long, the dominance of large powers over small. Few of the provisions of the peace were new; they were important more for what they confirmed than for what they created. The peace confirmed, first of all, the disintegration of Germany, a reality since the early sixteenth century, now officially recognized and thus harder than ever to reverse. At the insistence of the chief victors, Sweden and France, the three hundred or more German states participated in the peacemaking as individual sovereign powers, and the peace itself granted them all the sovereignty they had demanded. Sovereignty meant self-determination in foreign and domestic affairs—the peace specified that the Reichstag, in which all these hundreds of sovereign units participated as equals, alone could levy taxes, raise armies, make treaties. This official recognition of the old "German liberties" reduced the emperor to little more than a ceremonial head of a quarrelsome collection of independent entities.

One of the most highly desired consequences of sovereignty was self-determination in religious matters. The principle of the Peace of Augsburg, now almost a century old, giving each prince the right to dictate the faith of his subjects, was now written into the peace settlement; in addition, the peace recognized the Calvinists and granted the Protestants all the conquests they had made since 1624. This meant that Germany was to be long divided among small free cities, vest-pocket states, and a few larger and voracious units—each Lutheran, Calvinist, Catholic as its master chose. The old principle of *cuius regio, eius religio* benefited not merely the Lutherans and the Calvinists: it meant also that the Protestants promised not to interfere in the vigorous Hapsburg campaign to convert all the subjects in its scattered territories into obedient Catholics. Both the Reformation and the Counter-Reformation had failed in their common aim—the only thing they had in common: their hope of cleansing Europe of heretics.

Since no single German state was powerful enough to overawe and control the others, the assault on the remaining powers of the empire amounted to the elimination of Germany from international politics for a long time to come. This obviously pleased the French, who wanted Germany weak, but it also pleased the German princelings, who wanted to be, or at least appear to be, independent rulers. Since the peace named Sweden and France as guarantors, for more than a century France (for Sweden soon dropped out of the great-power game) happily meddled in German affairs on the excuse of safeguarding the settlement of 1648. And that settlement enfeebled the empire not merely by confirming the sovereignty of German states, but also by recognizing the independence of the Dutch Republic and of the Swiss Cantons (another pair of old realities now signed and sealed) and removing them from the empire. The peace further reduced the empire's territory by giving the French three bishoprics in Lorraine—Metz, Toul, and Verdun—which they had held for almost a hundred years.[7] Sweden, too, was paid off: no victor went empty-handed. While the territories granted to Sweden—the bishopric of Bremen and most of Pomerania—remained within the empire, these acquisitions gave the Swedes control over the mouths of several important German rivers, including the Oder and the Elbe. Since Westphalia also confirmed the Dutch hold over the mouth of the Scheldt (see p. 196), and since the Dutch already held that of the Rhine, the settlement of 1648 left the outlets of all major German rivers in the hands of foreign powers.

The Peace of Westphalia thus exacerbated Germany's weakness and imposed recognition of religious coexistence and of the state system. It also loosened the hold of the Hapsburgs over Europe by weakening each of its branches—the Spanish and the Austrian—and by weakening the bonds between the two. Spain turned inward, Austria turned toward eastern Europe. Thus 1648 brought to the forefront, more than ever before, the states of northwestern Europe: France, England, and to a lesser degree, the Dutch Republic. Yet not even these states escaped the times of troubles that plagued Europe in these decades.

TIMES OF TROUBLES

The Travail of Spain

From a later perspective, Spain's travail in and after the 1640s seemed foreordained. But contemporaries did not see it quite that way. True: Spain was far from prosperous, far from displaying the formidable power it had displayed in the sixteenth century, but the reign of Philip IV began in 1621 with some signs of recovery. The king's chief minister, the count-duke Olivares, vigorously addressed himself to domestic reform. Besides, the presence of Spanish troops in Germany and, for a time, in France itself, forcefully suggested that Spain was still a great power to be feared. Yet what had been true in the sixteenth century was true now: the show of strength abroad revealed, and produced, the reality of weakness at home; one of the causes of Spain's time of troubles was a foreign policy the country could not afford. In 1640, the impression of power proved an illusion.

The first evidence of the real state of affairs came from Catalonia. This northeastern province of Spain, with its indigenous tradition and proud culture, had long viewed its subjection to Madrid with resentment, and Catalans had

---

[7] In the imperial province of Alsace, the French were handed the governance of cities and territories on conditions so unclear that Louis XIV later built claims to absolute control on them (see p. 305).

long asserted a measure of independence. When, in 1639, Richelieu's troops invaded Spain by taking the Catalonian fortress of Salces, the Catalans found themselves in an odd position: they vehemently defended their own territory and asked Madrid for additional help. But it seemed to the Catalans, with much justice, that Olivares was interested more in securing the submission of Catalonia to the central monarchy than in driving out the French. Philip's viceroy, the count of Santa Coloma, though Catalan in origin, found himself compelled to carry out policies that his fellow Catalans found intolerably humiliating: he billeted Castilian troops on Catalonia, disregarded Catalan advice, had distinguished Catalans arrested. In March 1640 there were riots in the streets; in May Catalans forcibly freed their imprisoned leaders; in June there were serious and bloody clashes and Santa Coloma himself was murdered. Civil war began. It did not end until 1659, with a substantial victory for the Catalans. While Spanish troops had taken Barcelona in 1652, this proved a hollow victory for Madrid: the city surrendered on condition that provincial autonomy be respected, and the crown was too weak to disregard its promises. Spain's territorial integrity was preserved, at a price.

In the early stages of the Catalan uprising one great piece of news sustained the rebels: in December 1640 there was a revolt in Portugal, itself stimulated by the events in Catalonia. As in Barcelona, so in Lisbon, Richelieu encouraged unrest; the duke of Braganza was persuaded by his family and his advisors to advance his claim to the Portuguese throne, and on December 1, 1640, with Portugal practically empty of Spanish troops, the rebellion began. It was quick and almost bloodless. Acclaimed as King John IV early in the same month, Braganza officially took the throne in January 1641, and Spain's tepid, conspiratorial efforts to nullify the results of the revolt came to nothing. France and the Protestant powers recognized John as king of Portugal; in 1644, at the battle of Montijo, Portuguese troops decisively defeated a Spanish army, and Portugal's independence was secure.

Even in the distant dependency of Naples, Spain reasserted its authority only at the cost of some concessions. Naples was governed by viceroys with extensive powers and dominated by a narrow oligarchy of local, landowning barons; it was a colony of Spain, existing mainly to support Spain's adventures elsewhere; it suffered, as Merriman put it, "from all the bad consequences of an antiquated feudal system and of modern absolutism" without enjoying any "of the compensating advantages of either."[8] Resentment of Castilian domination and of ever-intensifying exploitation was general, but the revolt that broke out in 1647 was essentially a class war, and thus fatally divided the Neapolitans. It began in early June in consequence of a new and stringent tax on fruit; it was the most regressive impost possible, hard on the poor and insignificant for the rich. The revolt was led by a fisherman, Tommaso Aniello, known as Masaniello, a charismatic leader—young, inexperienced, eloquent, and violent.

[8] *Six Contemporaneous Revolutions,* 19.

In a week of confused fighting, widespread pillaging, and large-scale executions, Masaniello and his irregular troops terrorized the viceroy and wholly alienated the aristocracy. Masaniello himself was murdered after a few days of heady, absolute power, but the popular rebellion continued; in October, the rebels proclaimed a republic and once again (as they had done all summer) begged the French for aid. But French policy was too hesitant, and French affairs were too confused, for French assistance to be effective, and by early 1648, the rebellion had flickered out after some conciliatory gestures on the part of Spain. It stands in history as little more than a dramatic episode in the long history of man's exploitation of other men.

Russia: A Century of Turmoil

Between the death of Ivan the Terrible in 1584 (for the period preceding and following, see p. 323) and the accession of Peter the Great in 1689, Russia was in a state of endemic political and social turmoil. The very name "time of troubles" was first coined for the melodramatic years 1604 to 1613, when the power of the boyars—the Russian aristocracy—was at its height. But it can be generalized for the century as a whole. The struggle for the throne bore a certain resemblance to the political struggles elsewhere in Europe: the feudal nobility sought to perpetuate its privileges in the face of timid attempts at assertion of state power. But the uncertainty of the succession and the social consequences for the vast majority of Russians, poor peasants, made the Russian experience particularly bitter.

The dynastic situation may be quickly summarized. Ivan IV was the first Russian ruler to take the title of tsar. His sustained ferocity, notorious even in a country where life was hard and cruelty common, was a deliberate policy to establish some form of central control. But such a policy required time and a succession of effective rulers. These Russia did not enjoy: Ivan's son and successor, Feodor I (1584–1598), allowed power to revert into hands from which Ivan had striven to wrest it: the boyars. The effective ruler, even during Feodor's reign, was his brother-in-law Boris Godunov, whom an assembly of nobles elected tsar upon Feodor's death. Once in power (1598–1605) Boris attempted to secure Ivan's aims, with the same shrewdness and the same ferocity, but his efforts were frustrated a year before his death by the appearance of the "false Dmitri," a pretender claiming to be the son of Ivan IV, who had presumably been murdered on orders of Boris in 1591. A year later, Boris died, and for nine confused and terrible years, the succession to the throne was regulated by assassination: Boris' son Feodor was tsar briefly, until he was murdered; he was succeeded by the false Dmitri, who was murdered in turn; and so it went, amid popular rebellions and Polish invasions. Finally, in February 1613, a national assembly elected as tsar Michael Romanov, Ivan the Terrible's great-nephew; from then on at least the succession was clear: Michael (1613–1645) established a dynasty that was to end only with the Russian Revolution in 1917.

Yet, though Romanov was to follow Romanov, social unrest continued and burst into the open in several memorable rebellions. While boyars plotted and murdered, Russian peasants sank deeper and deeper into dependence, and Russia bled; as the fool says in his moving song in Mussorgski's magnificent opera, *Boris Godunov:*

> Cry, faithful heart,
> cry in deep anguish:
> soon the foe will come—
> and the dark will fall—
> night will blind us all
> and no hope of dawn
> is great Russia's sorrow—
> cry—cry—
> Russian land—
> hungry people—
> cry. [9]

The triumph of serfdom in Russia was the triumph of a vicious circle: rich, noble landlords needed peasants to cultivate their vast and underpopulated lands; miserable overworked peasants often chose to flee their exploiters to the border lands, an outward movement of population that landlords sought to prevent by tightening legal control over "their" peasants; this in turn led to renewed flights, which naturally produced efforts at even tighter controls. The flight of the peasant beyond the borders of Muscovy's effective control—into permanent vagrancy, to Siberia, or to the military bands of the Cossacks in the south or southwest—reached its climax late in the sixteenth century: "Many villages and townes of halfe a mile and a mile long, stande all unhabited," a contemporary English visitor noted, "the people being fled all into other places, by reason of the extreme usage and exactions done upon them." [10] By the seventeenth century, economic pressure and legal enactments had reduced such movement to a minimum. Down to the fifteenth and in many areas the sixteenth centuries, Russian peasants had by and large met their tax, labor, and military obligations as free men; now, in a series of laws passed at the insistence of landlords and as rigorously enforced as was humanly possible, Russian peasants became serfs, practically slaves. They were bound to the land; they had few legal rights against their masters, who in contrast, had almost complete jurisdiction over them; by the end of the seventeenth century, peasants could be bought and sold like so much merchandise. The landlord was employer, father, judge, tsar to the peasant, all in one, and the peasant's lot depended wholly on his master's character and caprice.

This degradation of the vast majority of Russians, exacerbated by continuous warfare, political disorder, and ever-increasing taxation, was fuel for unrest and rebellion. In 1648, there was a merchant-led uprising in Moscow

---

[9] Act IV, scene 3, tr. by John Gutman (1953).
[10] Quoted in Geroid Tanqueray Robinson, *Rural Russia Under the Old Regime* (1932), 16-17.

to protest the harsh imposition and arbitrary collection of a salt tax; in 1662, the debasement of the coinage provoked another urban rebellion. But it was the Cossack-led peasant uprisings that seemed most threatening to the state bureaucracy. Such uprisings were a recurrent theme in Russian history; in the seventeenth century they were only more frequent and more desperate than at other times. In 1668, the Don Cossacks, led by Stenka Razin, started a campaign of terror in the region near the Caspian Sea and along the lower Volga; they resented what they considered the encroachment of Russian landlords on their own free land. As their rebellion spread they appealed to all the nostalgia burgeoning in a time of drastic social change: the longing for the old days when tsars had been good fathers and when *boyars* had been servants not masters. In 1670, Stenka Razin's motley but energetic army, reinforced by runaway serfs, resentful tribesmen, restless nobles, and disaffected government troops, turned northward and took some fortified cities. Yet his reign of terror against the state and against the landlords was short-lived; in September 1670, Stenka Razin, a figure of almost legendary stature, suffered his first defeat, and in April 1671, he was betrayed, captured, and taken to Moscow. In June he was executed with a barbarity still widespread in Europe but particularly characteristic for the Russia of his day: he was tortured, drawn, and quartered. The ferocity with which the Russian state suppressed all these rebellions has been taken as a sign of weakness and fear; that may be so, but its consequence was the confirmation and strengthening of serfdom in Russian society. [11]

Troubles for the Victors

The crisis of the seventeenth century left its mark even on those countries that had profited from the Thirty Years' War. When Gustavus Adolphus of Sweden fell at Lützen in 1632 (see p. 253), his daughter, Christina, was a girl of six; the early years of her reign were therefore years of regency under the governance of Gustavus' trusted chancellor, Axel Oxenstierna. But even after she took command in 1644, Christina proved less interested in ruling than in art, philosophy, and display. Yet it was not her indifference, it was her consistent policy of favoring the nobility, that caused seditious murmurs. In 1650, the Swedish Diet, which had won considerable freedom of action in preceding decades, found its three unprivileged estates—peasants, burghers, and priests—pitted against the nobility; the queen herself lamented that "neither king nor *parlement* have their proper power, but the common man, the *canaille,* rules according to his fancy." [12] It was hardly a just complaint: since before her

---

[11] For cultural and political developments leading to the reign of Peter the Great, see p. 324.
[12] Quoted in Michael Roberts, "Queen Christina and the General Crisis of the Seventeenth Century," in Roberts, *Essays in Swedish History* (1962), 112.

accession, and in greatly increased tempo after 1648, the crown had alienated, by sale and donation, much of its land to the nobility, in part to simplify the Swedish tax structure, in part to reward loyal officers, in part to gratify aristocrats who pleased the queen. In consequence, an exclusive group grew even richer than before and threatened the lower estates, particularly the peasants on their land, with their powers to exploit and tax their dependents. It was against this that the Riksdag protested, demanding that the crown take back some of its lands. The queen was already toying with conversion to Roman Catholicism and was bent on having her cousin, Charles, declared her successor and hereditary prince of Sweden. In 1649 she persuaded the Diet to grant the first; in 1650, offering concessions to the lower orders, she obtained the second. When she abdicated and emigrated in 1654, leaving the country in the hands of Charles X, the crisis was over, and only a pair of victims, executed for sedition, testified to its potentially explosive quality.

In the Dutch Republic, the crisis was less bloody and more consequential. Since its inception, the republic had witnessed a struggle between the centralizing forces led by the house of Orange, and the decentralizing forces represented in the States General. The defeat of Oldenbarneveldt by Prince Maurice (see p. 196) had given the Orangists the ascendancy; Maurice's successor, Frederick Henry, though less militant, was quite as insistent on his authority: stadholder in six of the seven provinces, and addressed after 1637 as Your Highness, he wielded great power. In 1647 he died; his son, William II, succeeded to his father's titles. William was young, headstrong, bellicose, and inordinately ambitious: that he was the husband of Mary Stuart, daughter of Charles I of England, did not help him to recognize his limitations or those of his country. The States were looking toward peace and final recognition of the independence of the Dutch Republic; the stadholder, in secret conversations with France, sought to continue the war against Spain. The States wanted to muster out most of the Dutch army—which was, of course, under the stadholder's command—but William II resisted. Conflict grew sharper month by month; neither of the two greatest powers in the United Provinces was willing to yield more than a few steps. But in late October 1650, William II was stricken with the smallpox; early in November 1650, he died, just in time to avoid civil war. Mary Stuart was pregnant, but she was delivered too late; her son, the future King William III of England, was born after his father's death, and in any event, the Orangist party was leaderless. Province after province decided to forego electing a stadholder, and for twenty-two years, until William III of Orange resumed the office, the provinces looked to their own affairs. But they did not fall into anarchy: in 1653, Jan de Witt became grand pensionary of Holland and, in effect, chief statesman of the Dutch Republic. In this one country, at least, the crisis took a mild, even beneficent form. With the Netherlands' neighbor and rival across the channel, it was to be a far more sanguinary affair.

ENGLAND: FROM RESENTMENT TO REVOLUTION

James I: The Road to Confrontation

In the course of the eighteenth century, Great Britain acquired an enviable reputation for political stability; in the seventeenth, Britain was a byword for turmoil. Its dubious record included one king executed, another king exiled; the monarchical succession interrupted by a republic; the state church torn apart, deposed, reinstated; the nobility discredited, disfranchised, restored; Parliament enlarging its power at the expense of the crown. Fittingly enough, when James VI of Scotland came south in 1603 to assume the English throne as James I, he was greeted by a short, devastating outbreak of the plague in London. But affairs in general seemed prosperous and promising. Two days before her death, Elizabeth I had emphatically silenced all speculation about her successor: "A King," she said, "should succeed me; and who should that be but our cousin of Scotland?" What was more, England was pleased by her choice, and Elizabeth's able advisor, Robert Cecil, the son of her old mentor, Lord Burghley, was ready to serve his new monarch, the first of the Stuart line. Cheered by his reception, James reciprocated the loyal acclaim of his English subjects by diluting the estate of knighthood: in the first four months of his reign, he dubbed 906 knights, thus trebling the size of the order. [13]

Early Stuart England was still a minor power: counting Wales, its population amounted to little more than four million, and as an island protected from invasion, it had a sizable navy but no army. Yet the signs of growth were everywhere. English traders roamed the seas: the Baltic, the Mediterranean, the Atlantic, the rich spice islands of Asia lay open to its adventurous sailors. While most of England's towns were small—Norwich, its second city, had thirty thousand inhabitants—bustling, bursting London, with its cluster of suburbs, boasted (though visitors complained of) its two hundred thousand inhabitants. When James I first saw it, the city controlled seven eighths of England's trade. The yeoman estate was flourishing. The English coal industry could barely satisfy the rapidly growing demand; at the accession of Elizabeth I in 1558, total production had amounted to two hundred thousand tons a year; at the accession of James I, it had risen to 1.5 million, and by the time of the Glorious Revolution, to nearly three million tons.

> England's a perfect world! has Indies too!
> Correct your maps: Newcastle is Peru—

[13] Lawrence Stone, *The Crisis of the Aristocracy, 1558–1641* (1965), 74.

exclaimed the poet John Cleveland in 1651.[14] The woollen industry continued to be, as it had been for a century, England's principal manufacture and England's principal exporter. Though rudimentary in organization and small in size, there were industries in James' reign capitalized at £10,000 and more. Spain and France might disdain England as a second-class power, but its emergence as a first-class power could not be long delayed.

Yet James I had scarcely settled into his office when he confronted a set of problems he was to hand on, unsolved, to his successor: problems above all of religion and finance, exacerbated by England's unsettled foreign relations and by his own awkward personality. And all these problems brought James into conflict with Parliament.

The Elizabethan religious settlement had been not so much a permanent solution as a screen behind which conflicts of conscience might play themselves out in veiled decency. The studied ambiguities of Anglicanism, adroitly captured in the formulas of its Thirty-Nine Articles, had permitted large segments of the English people to live in peace with themselves and their state. But Puritan discontent, both with the organization of the Anglican church and with its doctrine, was endemic and unappeasable—matters of religious principle are notoriously hard to compromise.[15] The Church of England was burdened at the top with wealthy, relatively worldly pluralists, and crowded at the bottom with unlettered and impecunious clerics. And the whole panoply of Anglican ceremonial and discipline remained offensive to Puritan souls intent on confronting their God without intermediaries.

In Scotland, James had been humiliated by the dominant and domineering Presbyterians, but he was not wholly unsympathetic to the complaints that English Puritans now addressed to him. The so-called Millenary Petition[16] that Puritan clerics had presented to James on his way to London seemed to him worth investigating. Puritan grievances, which this petition summarized, were fivefold: Anglican ceremonies were reminiscent of the old popish faith discarded at the Reformation; preaching was perfunctory; Anglican bishops were "pluralists," holding too many livings at once, thus scanting their pastoral duties; the Anglican church was omnipresent and too severe, using its power of excommunication to excess; finally, the Anglicans' neglect of the Sabbath urgently called for correction.

In 1604, James I met at Hampton Court Palace with delegations of churchmen and granted the Puritans some of their demands: he promised to check pluralism and to see to better preaching. He agreed also to secure a "uniform translation" of the Bible—this was the germ of the celebrated, irreplaceable Authorized Version, the "King James Version," of 1611. But the

---

[14] Charles Wilson, *England's Apprenticeship, 1603–1763* (1965), 80.

[15] English "Puritans," it must be remembered, were loyal members of the Anglican church and sought to reshape it from within.

[16] It is called this because its drafters claimed a thousand signatures, a dubious figure.

king had no intention of reorganizing the Anglican church on Presbyterian principles. "A Scottish Presbytery," he said caustically, "agreeth as well with a monarchy as God and the Devil. Then Jack and Tom and Will and Dick shall meet, and at their pleasures censure me and my Council." And in a testy outburst, he warned the Puritans to conform: otherwise he would "harry them out of the land." Every student of American history knows that this is what James actually was to do: some three hundred clergymen who would not accept the Book of Common Prayer were stripped of their livings, and it was a group of Puritan Separatists from Nottinghamshire who, tired of ridicule and harassment, left England for the Dutch Republic in 1607 and finally landed in America in 1620, where they formed Plymouth Colony. There had been English colonists in Virginia since 1607, but the founding legend of the United States— the voyage of the *Mayflower* and the travails of the Pilgrim fathers—had its origins in the Anglican policy of James I. Religion was not a trivial issue for seventeenth-century Englishmen: religion, and the church, impinged on their lives literally every day. James' Anglican policy, which became more stiff-necked with the passage of years, was a touchy political issue. And it incensed many members of Parliament, already in a bellicose mood, for Parliament was filled with men of Puritan sympathies.

It was only James' desperate need for money—"this eating canker of want," he called it—that made this confrontation so consequential. James had inherited a debt of £400,000 from Elizabeth I, a debt that had risen to over £700,000 only three years later; in subsequent years the king, who was nothing if not prodigal, would spend on the average £200,000 a year more than he took in. The medieval principle that the king must live on his own income, often breached before, now was wholly inapplicable: the sources of revenue on which James I could draw were simply inadequate. He had at his disposal anachronistic feudal privileges, like wardships, which brought some income and much irritation; he increased customs duties; like his predecessor, he sold crown lands, a technique that secured immediate but reduced long-term revenues; he sold monopolies to merchants and honors to anyone who could buy them. In 1611 the crown marketed—it is the only word—the new hereditary title of baronet for £1095, with the promise that it would name no more than two hundred, a promise that James kept and his successor would break. All these desperate fiscal expedients brought in less than the king needed, and so James had to go to Parliament for supplies. Thus the epic struggle began.

Liberal historians, imbued with detestation for absolutism and admiration for parliamentary government, have often portrayed this struggle as a virtuous assertion of parliamentary rights endangered by swollen royal pretensions. But this is anachronistic: however much we may wish to applaud the outcome of the struggle, in the Stuart period Parliament was, in fact, the aggressor. Elizabeth had kept her parliaments under tight control, shrewdly exploiting the length and successes of her reign and converting the liability of her sex into an asset. She too had insisted on the royal "prerogative." It was not so much what James I claimed, as when and how he claimed it, that aroused parliamentary opposition.

James' most formidable adversary was his chief justice, Sir Edward Coke, grown into a rigid defender of the common law and Parliament as the source of legislation. The king, Coke insisted, cannot create law, and he angered his royal master by arguing that however great the king's "natural reason," the law must rest on "artificial reason," that is, the judgment of those who were, as the king was not, "learned in the laws of his realm of England." It was against the assertion that the courts must be independent of royal pressure and Parliament the sole source of legislation that the king pitted his claim to absolute authority. It did not help his cause that he should so often and so tactlessly reiterate it. As early as 1598 James had anonymously published a treatise, *The True Law of Free Monarchies,* in which he had committed himself to what was known as the divine right of kings. The theory, for all its formidable name, was merely an extreme statement of a widely accepted idea: that the king is the source of legislation. In 1616, James restated it in a particularly offensive way: "That which concerns the mystery of the King's power is not lawful to be disputed," for to argue about it is "to take away the mystical reverence that belongs unto them that sit in the throne of God."

Obviously the conflict between James I and his parliaments was more than a clash of individuals: it sprang from, and expressed, the growing wealth, power, and self-confidence of the Commons, and it reflected, ironically enough, the increasing safety of England from foreign invasion. But it was also a matter of personalities. True, his popularity was reinforced by the extravagant Catholic Gunpowder Plot of 1605, which aimed at blowing up the king along with Parliament. But James I was a learned man [17] who showed his learning, something few men can tolerate. And he was a homosexual addicted to favorites for qualities irrelevant to statesmanship. The most damaging and most lasting of his attachments was to George Villiers, whom in his infatuation he created duke of Buckingham, and who vastly enriched himself and his family. Greedy and corrupt almost beyond belief, Buckingham shamelessly sold monopolies and honors and pushed his relatives into profitable and conspicuous posts. Buckingham's visibility was as high as his influence was pernicious, and his ascendancy did little to support James' pretensions to more than human stature.

Charles I: The Confrontation

James' son Charles, who succeeded in 1625, was neither learned nor homosexual; but his liabilities were, if anything, more crippling. For one thing, he retained Buckingham as his chief advisor, and between them, the two rapidly plunged the country into political and military folly. Charles was not enough of a statesman to find his way through the maze of international events, not enough of a politician to come to terms with Parliament. He was stubborn,

---

[17] The disdainful epithet of "pedant" is a late and inaccurate invention.

devious, wholly undependable. His father had made peace with Spain in 1604, a peace many Englishmen had resented for economic as much as religious reasons; when in 1623, James had sent Charles, accompanied by Buckingham, to Spain to woo the Spanish infanta, protests were loud. But Charles had come back without a bride, insulted by the treatment he had received and anxious for war with Spain. After his accession, Charles made ready for that war. Like his father he was in need of money and called Parliament. Like his father, he found Parliament intractable.

James had called four parliaments in all and each had gathered strength and experience from its predecessors. His first parliament had sat from 1604 to 1611, accomplishing little but to define the opposing positions; the second sat for two months in 1614 and accomplished nothing except to train new parliamentary leaders including Sir John Eliot and Sir Thomas Wentworth [18] in the art of frustrating royal designs—it is known, from its inaction, as the Addled Parliament. The third sat for a year, from early 1621 to early 1622, and is noted for the Great Protestation of December 1621, which declared "that the liberties, franchises, privileges, and jurisdictions of Parliament are the ancient and undoubted birthright and inheritance of the subjects of England; and that the arduous and urgent affairs concerning the King, State, and defense of the realm, and of the Church of England, and the maintenance and making of laws, and redress of mischiefs and grievances which daily happen within this realm, are proper subjects and matter of counsel and debate in Parliament; and that in the handling and proceeding of those businesses every member of the House of Parliament hath, and of right ought to have, freedom of speech to propound, treat, reason, and bring to conclusion the same." James I, in a fury, tore this offensive declaration from the journal of the House with his own hands. Yet his last parliament, which sat from early 1624 to early 1625, secured a right that English kings had always reserved to themselves: to advise on foreign policy. And this parliament, like its immediate predecessor, used its privilege of impeachment against royal servants to weaken the royal power and enhance its own.

Royal weakness quickly became apparent with Charles I's first parliament, a short affair lasting from June to August 1625. Spain was vastly unpopular, but Buckingham's oily assurances of loyalty to Protestant principles and of his readiness to take advice on policy were so obviously mendacious that the Commons took an unprecedented step. It had been normal practice for centuries to grant a new monarch the revenues from customs duties ("tonnage and poundage") for life; Commons now proposed to grant them for one year. Before it could enact this rebellious measure, Charles I had dissolved Parliament and collected the customs revenues on his own authority. But from the outset his war with Spain (complicated after early 1627 by a rash war with France) went badly: disasters befell the British navy with almost comical

[18] In 1639 Charles I would create Wentworth earl of Strafford.

repetitiousness, and most of these were the direct responsibility of Buckingham who was, after all, lord high admiral. When Charles called his second parliament in February 1626, it had a naval fiasco off Cadiz to brood about. Sir John Eliot, once a supporter but now a resolute enemy of Buckingham, an independent country gentleman and an eloquent orator, moved to impeach him: "In reference to the King," Eliot said, Buckingham "must be styled the canker in his treasure; in reference to the State, the moth of all goodness." The king briefly imprisoned Eliot, then released him, and dissolved Parliament in June, continuing to raise revenues without parliamentary assent, largely by collecting forced loans. The expedient, vigorously resented and widely resisted, produced less than Charles needed; when Buckingham once more disgraced his policy, his king, and himself by an incredibly incompetent effort to relieve the French Huguenots, then under siege by Richelieu at La Rochelle (see p. 284), the old tragicomedy repeated itself: in March 1628, Charles I called his third parliament.

Predictably, its members were in an unyielding mood. To appease tempers all around, the government had released seventy-six men imprisoned for refusing to pay the forced loan. But twenty-seven of these, including Sir Thomas Wentworth, sat in the third parliament, and they did their best not to calm, but to inflame the temper of both houses.[19] They refused to vote supplies before the redress of grievances, and upon Coke's suggestion, drew up a Petition of Right, which was agreed upon, after much debate, in May. This concerted attack on the prerogative is a great constitutional document. It declared that forced gifts, benevolences, or loans must not be levied without Parliament's assent; that no one must be arbitrarily imprisoned; and that the billeting of soldiers on private subjects without their consent must henceforth cease. Protesting that the petition would "dissolve the foundation and frame of our monarchy," Charles I nevertheless signed it in June, and obtained, in return, some of the funds he had asked for. But his troubles were not at an end. The Commons, more and more inclined to take the lead in parliamentary business, demanded Buckingham's dismissal: "I think the Duke of Bucking-ham," said Coke, speaking for them all, "is the cause of all our miseries. . . . That man is the grievance of grievances." Charles, rather than heed the outcry, prorogued Parliament, but indirectly Parliament had its revenge on the hated minister: in August 1628, John Felton, a naval lieutenant, brooding on a fancied failure to receive adequate recognition and adequate pay, and further disori-ented by the Commons' denunciations of the royal favorite, stabbed Bucking-ham to death.

Ironically, the assassination, far from smoothing Charles' relations with Parliament, only exacerbated them; the general outlines of his policy were set in his mind, and Buckingham's abrupt death compelled him to find new men.

[19] See Joseph Robson Tanner, *English Constitutional Conflicts of the Seventeenth Century, 1603-1689* (1962), 61.

These proved more competent, and also more determined, than the friend he had lost. When Charles I confronted a new session of Parliament in January 1629, he had as his chief advisors Thomas Wentworth, now Viscount Wentworth, who, alarmed by the course of events he had helped to shape, had joined the royal service in 1628, and William Laud, bishop of London since the same year. Both were strong and effective men; both have remained controversial. Their policy was vigorous, even merciless, and wholly consistent: to strengthen royal authority by finding revenues if necessary without the aid and against the wishes of Parliament and the interests represented there, and to subject the country to firm Anglican rule. It is from the amicable correspondence of the two statesmen that their policy derives its name of Thorough. It meant resolute government by the king and his ministers and the crushing of opposition.

The first sign of the policy of Thorough came in March 1629, after some rousing sessions in the House of Commons in which three truculent resolutions of Sir John Eliot had been read out, while two strong members of Commons held the Speaker in the chair to prevent adjournment at the king's command. Eliot and other leaders of the opposition were arrested and imprisoned, and Parliament was dissolved. Charles I, it was said, acted as if a weight had been taken from his shoulders. It was, for eleven years: from 1629 to 1640, a time known dramatically and rather inaccurately as the Eleven Years' Tyranny, Charles I and his ministers governed England without benefit of parliamentary advice or consent. And they did so, it must be added, with fair success. By 1630, Charles had made peace with France and Spain, and while he continued a foreign policy of drift, at least two costly ventures were over. And at home, while the rule of Wentworth and Laud was scarcely millennium for the poor, the government did make some effort at efficient administration, caring for the indigent, and controlling greedy monopolists and enclosers of land. The great royalist historian Clarendon was exaggerating when he said later that in 1639 "England enjoyed the greatest measure of felicity it had ever known," [20] but it remains true that the English people did not groan under unprecedented tyranny and did not stage demonstrations for the return of parliamentary government. The forces dominating the House of Commons—self-respecting country squires and lawyers with pronounced leanings toward Puritanism— were prosperous, angry, and articulate, and it was these groups, and their followers, whom Charles I mortally affronted.

For some years the king had things his own way. Eliot, growing feeble and denied leave from the Tower to recover, died in prison in November 1632. As Charles had held Eliot responsible for the death of Buckingham, the parliamentary party now held Charles responsible for the death of Eliot. And in August 1633, Charles named Laud archbishop of Canterbury, thus endorsing, with as much emphasis as he could muster, Laud's ferocious Anglicanism. Laud was

---

[20] Quoted in Maurice Ashley, *England in the Seventeenth Century* (1960), 71.

honest and courageous, but his undisputable virtues came perilously close to being vices: His gravity amounted to humorlessness, his candor to tactlessness, his clarity to imperiousness, his energy to ruthlessness. Besides, he was unlucky, perhaps inescapably so, in being tarred with the papist brush: the king he served so well was married to Henrietta Maria, sister of Louis XIII of France, a Roman Catholic who enjoyed a notorious ascendancy over her husband. Charles was surrounded by Catholic ministers and allowed ambassadors from Roman Catholic countries access to him. Of humble origins but with an excellent Oxford education, Laud was determined to secure uniformity of Anglican observances throughout his domains and obedience of all to the state; James I's celebrated aphorism "no bishop, no king," expressed Laud's ecclesiastical politics to perfection. Laud protected the High Church service from contamination; he assiduously visited churches to see that their furnishings and their preaching accorded with High Church principles and that no unlicensed lecturers—Puritans all—could seduce Anglican flocks from true principles. As chief advisor to the king and as archbishop of Canterbury, Laud had free recourse to the Star Chamber and the ecclesiastical court of High Commission to harass and silence Puritans. He was anything but a papist; he was an Arminian (see p. 195 for the origins of the term), but to his Puritan enemies this was a distinction without a difference: "An Arminian is the spawn of a Papist," one member of Parliament said in 1629, ". . . if you mark it well, you shall see an Arminian reaching out his hand to a Papist, a Papist to a Jesuit, a Jesuit gives one hand to the Pope and the other to the King of Spain."[21]

Charles' campaign for religious conformity struck at the Puritans; his search for fiscal solvency without Parliament systematically offended merchants, gentry, and nobles. Against often courageous resistance, the king continued to levy tonnage and poundage on his own authority and revived a series of obsolete laws as excuses for extorting money from men of wealth and property. He fined gentlemen who refused knighthoods and the expenses that came with them; he forced property owners with land once held as royal forests to pay for the right of continued ownership; he discovered new and obnoxious possibilities for that old abuse, the monopoly. But his most offensive and most profitable expedient was ship money, a tax originally imposed on seaports to supply ships or, failing that, funds to the navy. In 1634, Charles issued a traditional writ for ship money; in 1635, he extended it to inland counties; in 1636, in a third writ, he abandoned all pretense of raising emergency funds for the navy: ship money stood revealed, quite plainly, as a tax, levied, moreover, without parliamentary consent. In the following year, John Hampden, country squire, member of Parliament, and cousin to Oliver Cromwell, challenged the

---

[21] Quoted in Tanner, *Constitutional Conflicts*, 68n. It is worth noting that what James' Anglican policy began, Laud's policy of Thorough continued: in the 1630s and early 1640s, some sixteen thousand Englishmen, nearly all of them unhappy Puritans, swelled the colony of Massachusetts Bay, which had begun so inconspicuously as Plymouth Colony in 1620.

legality of ship money; by the narrow vote of seven to five, the judges in the Court of the Exchequer found for the crown, in an alarming extension of the royal prerogative. "I never read nor heard, that lex was rex;" one of the judges wrote, "but it is common and most true, that rex is lex, for he is 'lex loquens,' a living, a speaking, an acting law." [22] This meant that in emergencies, the king could do as he pleased, and what was an emergency was defined by the king. It was a great victory for Charles I, but he had soon cause to regret it. Resistance to collection of ship money stiffened, and in the same year, in 1637, rebellion broke out—not over money but over religion, and not in England, but in Scotland.

Charles I: Into Civil War

In 1603, a union of crowns began a process that was completed in 1707 with a union of parliaments; in the intervening century, Scotland played a peculiarly disturbing part in English affairs. [23] Early in his reign, in 1606 and 1607, James I had broached the possibility of a closer union between the two countries, but his plans had collapsed under the concerted prejudice of his English subjects. James still had the support of the Scottish nobility; his son Charles, though born in Scotland, alienated that nobility with an act of revocation by which, at a single stroke, he took back lands his predecessors had handed out for nearly a century. More ominous, he aroused the hatred of the dominant Calvinists with his effort to impose Anglicanism on Scotland. Laud had been making efforts in this direction since 1633, but real riots erupted only in July 1637, when a clergyman in St. Giles Cathedral in Edinburgh read the service from the new prayer book, adapted from the Anglican Book of Common Prayer. "The mass is entered amongst us!" Jenny Geddes shouted, threw her stool at the minister's head, and started a melee which grew into countrywide resistance. Charles, backed by Laud, refused to yield or compromise, and in February 1638, thousands of Scots subscribed to the National Covenant, a vehement repudiation of Laud's attempts to fasten "the Popish religion and tyranny" on Scotland, and a solemn pledge to "recover the purity and liberty of the Gospel." The uncompromising policy of Thorough had produced an uncompromising response. The Scots were the first to arm; the bloodless First Bishops' War proved an embarrassing setback for the royal forces. In June 1639, Charles was compelled to conclude the Treaty of Berwick which gave the Scots the right to call a new assembly of the church. When that assembly insisted on the abolition of episcopacy—a decision Charles could under no circumstances accept—full-scale war was inevitable. But such war was expensive, and so Laud

----

[22] Ibid., 83.
[23] See H. R. Trevor-Roper, "Scotland and the Puritan Revolution" (1963), in his *Crisis of the Seventeenth Century: Religion, the Reformation, and Social Change* (1968).

and Wentworth persuaded Charles to convoke Parliament. What Englishmen anxious about their liberties or their pocketbooks had been unable to do with speeches, lawsuits, or tax evasion, Scottish Calvinists, zealously attached to their beliefs and their ceremonies, did with a show of force. In mid-April 1640, Charles I called his fourth parliament.

It is not called the Short Parliament for nothing: Charles dissolved it after three weeks. The Short Parliament was dominated by an experienced member of the Commons, John Pym, a sensible speaker and skillful parliamentarian. In long and memorable speeches, Pym urged the House to put the redress of grievances before the granting of supplies, and reinforced his position by patiently listing the wrongs to which the country had been subjected in the last fifteen years. Pym carried the House with him; Charles, infuriated, had to find his funds elsewhere. The subservient Irish Parliament and an equally pliant Convocation (the legislative body of the church) had already granted him £300,000; Wentworth (now earl of Strafford) advised the king to appeal to the wealthy merchants of the City of London. But the City refused, and English officers faced the Scots in the field with scant supplies and mutinous troops. In late October, Charles ended the Second Bishops' War, on terms as humiliating as the Treaty of Berwick. He left the Scots in possession of northern England and undertook to pay the Scottish army still under arms. Only a new parliament could fulfill the promises a humiliated king had been compelled to make.

In November, Charles' fifth and last parliament met at Westminster; it was as long as its predecessor had been short. The most dramatic parliament in English history, it was not officially dissolved until 1660. The men who had been masters in its predecessor were masters in the Long Parliament as well. Under Pym's able and implacable leadership, the House of Commons, far from voting supplies, addressed itself to redressing grievances. On its orders, Puritan leaders now in prison were released; then it impeached the king's chief ministers for breaking "fundamental laws"—Strafford in November, Laud in December of 1640. The king himself was still beyond the reach of his rebellious subjects. When it became clear that Strafford would be acquitted in his trial before the House of Lords, the Commons abandoned the impeachment and secured his conviction on a bill of attainder instead; if his guilt could not be adjudicated, it could be legislated. The Lords and Charles, under pressure from conveniently engineered mobs, gave their consent, and Strafford died bravely in May 1641; Laud, harmless in prison, was attainted later and executed in January 1645. Other royal ministers fled.

Having eliminated the agents of absolutism, Pym and his associates now wrecked its machinery. As early as February 1641, Parliament had underscored its new-found power with the Triennial Act, which specified that Parliament must be called into session every three years. Late in the spring and through the summer of 1641, in a burst of frantic activity, the Commons continued on its revolutionary course. In May Parliament declared that it could not be dissolved without its own consent. In June it insisted that taxes could be levied only with parliamentary assent. In July it abolished the Star Chamber, the Court of High Commission, and other prerogative courts, those lethal instruments of the royal will—once beneficent but now perverted. In August it declared the hated ship money unlawful. And also in August it deprived the king of his last fiscal expedients by undoing his manipulations of royal forests and knighthoods. [24] Never before in English history, and never since, has so much power been shifted so easily.

Pym had managed to keep his forces united by concentrating on grievances they all shared and avoiding an issue on which they differed: religion. As religious matters had brought rebellion in 1637, so were they to bring disunity to the parliamentary forces in 1641. Early in the year there had been rumblings among radical Puritans, the "root and branch" men, intent on abolishing episcopacy and drastically revising the Book of Common Prayer. In November 1641, when Parliament addressed a Grand Remonstrance to the king, the principles of root and branch found vivid expression. Much of the Remonstrance, to be sure, was a plain appeal to the public; it catalogued what Charles I had done wrong and what Parliament had already done, and must still do, to set it right. But its demand for a "reformation" in the church caused exhausting debates and sharp divisions, and the Remonstrance carried by only a small majority—159 to 148. It was a great moment in the history of the great events then unrolling, and those present at the debate knew it. "If the Remonstrance had been rejected," Oliver Cromwell said about himself, "he would have sold all he had the next morning, and never have seen England more; and he knew there were many other honest men of the same resolution." [25]

Commons was divided on another issue as well. Late in October a revolt had broken out in Ireland, an unhappy country long colonized—that is to say, systematically exploited—by Englishmen. Strafford, lord deputy of Ireland since 1632, had kept Ireland under firm control; his absence brought relief and rebellion. Charles asked Parliament for troops to suppress the Irish rebels, but Pym, suspicious of a king he thought capable of using troops intended for Ireland against the Parliament, insisted that funds should be granted only if Parliament approved the king's ministers. This was a revolutionary assertion of parliamentary supremacy, and it passed by only 151 to 110.

Charles now made a characteristic mistake: instead of playing on the divisions in Parliament, he united it with a foolish act of force. In January 1642, he tried to have five members of Commons arrested, including Pym and Hampden. The House refused to turn them over to his men, and when the king appeared in person, the five members were gone. When Charles asked the Speaker of the House, once a royal appointee and mere messenger boy, if any of the members were present, Speaker Lenthall fell on his knees and humbly,

[24] For these laws, see Tanner, *Constitutional Conflicts*, 96–99.
[25] Ibid., 111.

but firmly replied: "May it please your Majesty, I have neither eyes to see nor tongue to speak in this place but as this House is pleased to direct me, whose servant I am here."[26] The City of London gave the five members, and Parliament, protection, and Charles I, aware that civil war had become inevitable, left London.

The rebels did not throw off their obedience lightly. Unpopular as a king might be, kingship was still dressed in grave majesty, and there was anguished searching of heart and shedding of tears among those about to take arms against their lawful sovereign. Through the spring and early summer of 1642, king and Parliament continued their negotiations, but Parliament's claims had become the claims of men who wanted nothing less than a parliamentary monarchy, with the making of laws, the levying of taxes, the affairs of the church and the army in the hands of the old High Court of Parliament that had come to see itself as a supreme legislature. Out of harm's reach, Charles I refused, and gathered about him his family and sympathizers frightened by the Puritan rigidity and the rebelliousness of the parliamentary aggressors. Pym's party responded by raising an army. In August 1642, at Nottingham, Charles I raised the standard of war. Few had thought things would go this far. They would go much further.

ENGLAND: FROM REVOLUTION TO RESTORATION

The Great Civil War

The civil war divided the country more sharply than anything else had ever divided it before. Yet, after centuries of historical inquiry, historians have not reached agreement on patterns of partisanship. While, by and large, the south and east of England were parliamentarian, and the west and north royalist, this map of support was dotted with exceptions. The war itself created parties. As the lines of battles shifted and both sides levied troops in the territories under their control, the majority of Englishmen who had hoped to stay remote from civil strife found themselves compelled to take sides. Differences in religion were doubtless of central importance, but it was not simply that a Puritan was a man of the opposition: often a man in opposition for nonreligious reasons found himself being called a Puritan. The aristocracy, the gentry, merchants, cities, even families, were split. The City of London, headquarters and mainstay of the parliamentary rebels, was royalist in sympathies and remained so until Pym's supporters in early 1642 expelled the old loyalists.[27] The familiar names of the adversaries—Cavaliers and Roundheads—derive from, and imply, social

[26] Ibid., 114.
[27] See Wilson, *England's Apprenticeship*, 116.

distinctions,[2] ind social distinctions were among the causes of the conflict. At the same time, like the name Puritan, the name Roundhead was often applied as a partisan epithet, and sometimes to men of the "better sort."[29] Even the House of Commons split down the middle. Nearly half of its members committed themselves to the king's side and an exhaustive study of the Long Parliament has shown that the only marked differentiation was not wealth or status or regional origins or religious affiliation, but age: the rebels in Parliament, trained in the first years of Charles I, embittered by the Eleven Years' Tyranny, and nurtured in Puritan severity, were on the average some years older than the royalists.[30] In 1642, men took the sword for many reasons.

The war began with deliberate speed, as both sides raised troops and carried on desultory negotiations. In a series of indecisive engagements, Charles I improved his position; by late 1643, Parliament and its forces were mainly clustered around London and the southeast of England. Cavaliers seemed to be getting the advantage of Roundheads. Thoroughly alarmed, Parliament imposed new and unpopular taxes, took steps to reorganize its armed forces and adopted (as it had so often before) a policy long advocated by Pym. In September 1643, only three months before Pym's death, it reluctantly concluded a solemn league and convenant with the Scots, pledging both signatories to extirpate "popery and prelacy" and to establish the reformed religion "according to the Word of God." Subsequently, the parties to the pact were to interpret these words in widely differing ways; many Englishmen, even Puritans, were appalled by the dour clerical discipline of the Scottish Presbyterians. But the parliamentary cause was in peril, and a Scottish army might be useful. It was: in January 1644, a Scottish force crossed the border into England; Charles was now held in a pincer from which he could not extricate himself.

The first tangible reward for these policies came on June 2, 1644, with the parliamentarians' victory of Marston Moor, where the Scots were joined by detachments from England. What mattered about this battle was less its clear outcome than its dubious aftermath. Lacking decisiveness of aim and unity of command, the parliamentarians bickered over the conduct of the war and dissipated their advantage in the summer and fall of 1644; by early winter the need for a thoroughgoing constitution of their armies had become the first order of business. Parliament compelled its generals to lay down their command by passing a self-denying ordinance, and equipped the New Model Army with new leaders: Sir Thomas Fairfax was named commander in chief; Oliver Cromwell, whose cavalry had distinguished itself at Marston Moor, became Fairfax's lieutenant general.

[28] The partisans of Parliament, a contemporary wrote, "were, most of them, men of mean or a middle quality . . . modest in their apparel but not in language. They had the hair of their heads very few of them longer than their ears, whereupon it came to pass that those who usually with their cries attended Westminster were by a nickname called *Roundheads*. The courtiers, again, wearing long hair and locks and always sworded, at last were called by these men *Cavaliers*" (quoted in Christopher Hill and Edmund Dell, eds., *The Good Old Cause* [1949], 245–246).

[29] See Wilson, *England's Apprenticeship*, 110.

[30] See D. Brunton and D. H. Pennington, *Members of the Long Parliament* (1954).

In early 1645, Oliver Cromwell was already a widely known and highly respected figure. Born in 1599 in Huntingdon, he was a landed gentleman of middling rank, a solemn, sober Puritan who had undergone a prolonged and exhausting religious conversion and did nothing without devout appeals to his God. He had sat both in the parliament that preceded and the parliaments that ended King Charles' Eleven Years' Tyranny and proved himself an articulate champion of poor farmers threatened by enclosures and an equally articulate enemy to Laud's Anglicanism. In 1642 he displayed a new talent organizing and leading troops; he had learned much from studying the cavalry tactics of Gustavus Adolphus. His "ironsides"[31] became the model for the New Model Army: composed of "honest, godly men, thoroughly trained, thoughtfully looked after,"[32] firmly disciplined, devoted to their officers, courageous and above all, determined to see the cause of true religion prevail. On June 14, 1645, at the battle of Naseby, the parliamentary troops displayed these qualities, decisively routing the king's troops. By fall, even Charles' hopes for Scotland, pinned insecurely on the brilliant military sallies of the royalist earl of Montrose, were dashed by Montrose's defeat. In June 1646, Oxford, Charles' headquarters since early in the war, surrendered, and the king fled to Scotland. The New Model Army had proved a superb instrument.

But it was not content to remain an instrument, and here Charles, untiring in intrigue, saw his opportunity. Though trained to iron discipline, Cromwell's troops steadily engaged in discussions among themselves and with their officers, and their vision of the future differed markedly from the vision held by the parliament to which they owed their allegiance. Many of the troops were Independents, strongly in favor of a Congregationalist church organization free from the heavy hand of central control, free even from Presbyters. The great poet and pamphleteer John Milton, the most eloquent recruit the Independent cause could boast during the Civil War, bitterly commented on the compromises now in the air: "New Presbyter," he said, "is but old Priest writ large."[33]

---

[31] The name was first bestowed on Cromwell himself by Prince Rupert, commander of the royalist troops at Marston Moor, and then extended to the troops under Cromwell's command. See Charles Firth, *Oliver Cromwell and the Rule of the Puritans in England* (ed. 1953), 106.

[32] Ibid., 89.

[33] While Milton is remembered as one of the great poets in the English language, his long life included much vigorous political pamphleteering. In the middle of the nineteenth century, the English liberal statesman John Bright told a working-class audience that Milton was "the greatest name in English political history" (quoted in John Gross, *The Rise And Fall of the Man of Letters* [1969], 121). Born in 1608 in London, educated at St. Paul's School and Cambridge, Milton gave up his early intention to join a church he increasingly disliked and devoted himself to poetry. In 1640, returning from an Italian journey, he joined the Presbyterian cause of church reform, but by the middle of the Civil War he had moved to Independency, and wrote brilliant polemics in its behalf. His *Areopagitica* of 1644, which voices his discontent with parliamentary censorship, remains one of the most powerful defenses of a free press ever written; his *The Tenure of Kings and Magistrates* of 1649, which grew out of his commitment to the Cromwellian cause, was an almost equally powerful defense of popular sovereignty taken to its logical conclusion: the right to dispose of the tyrant. Appointed Cromwell's secretary for foreign tongues in 1649, he went completely blind in 1652; his most celebrated poetry, including his finest English sonnets and the epic *Paradise Lost* (published in 1667), date from his last years. When he died in 1674, he was a famous poet.

The epigram reflects the aspiration of solemn seekers intent on forming and governing their own congregations that they might find their own way to God, and the rancor of left-wing Puritans against their more conservative brethren in control of Parliament. After 1646, too, radical political ideas were percolating through the army; there were demands for manhood suffrage, a republic, and annual parliaments. The spokesmen for these new ideas were nicknamed "Levellers," disdainfully and misleadingly, by their enemies. In an animated debate held in October 1647, and attended by Cromwell and his son-in-law General Henry Ireton, a Colonel Rainborough laid down the Leveller principles in a moving speech: "For really I think that the poorest he that is in England hath a life to live, as the greatest he; and therefore truly, sir, I think it's clear, that every man that is to live under a government ought first by his own consent to put himself under that government; and I do think that the poorest man in England is not at all bound in a strict sense to that government that he hath not had a voice to put himself under." [34] Actually, neither Rainborough nor John Lilburne, the leading Leveller publicist, meant "the poorest he" literally; they did not wish to extend the franchise to paupers or servants, but rather to the respectable lower orders, to those who had given up all they had to fight in a righteous cause. But while Cromwell keenly appreciated the part that independent Protestant sectarians had played in his New Model Army, while he pleaded for freedom of conscience and was himself strongly sympathetic to Independency, he had no intention of enlarging the political nation to include those who owned no property—to those who, as a long-popular phrase had it, had no stake in the country.

The struggle within the army was secondary to the struggle between army and Parliament. The Levellers did not prevail, but the effervescence of religious and political ideas they helped to produce radicalized the troops and, to some degree, the generals. In February 1647, after undignified squabbles, the Scots had turned over Charles I to the English Parliament, for a promised payment of £400,000. But what to do with him could hardly be resolved while Parliament and its military arm were at one another's throats. The parliamentary leaders sought to weaken the army by partially demobilizing it and by sending some of it to Ireland, but they only brought its distrust to a new pitch, and its generals shared the rage and the suspicions of their men. In the midst of these verbal skirmishes, Charles I escaped from detention in November 1647 and made a new agreement with the Scots giving them what they wanted; early in 1648, the second Civil War began. It did not last long. Despite political and social strains, the New Model Army continued to fight brilliantly, and by August 1648, Cromwell had put down scattered risings and beaten the royalist forces mustered by the Scots.

The army was now determined to put the king out of the way; Charles I had converted rebellious monarchists into vindictive republicans. Cromwell

---

[34] "The Putney Debates," in A. S. P. Woodhouse, ed., *Puritanism and Liberty* (2nd ed., 1950), 53. In the late 1640s George Fox founded the sect contemporaries unkindly called Quakers.

had long hesitated, but late in 1647 he had made up his mind: Charles, "that man of blood," had subverted the constitution and proved himself slippery, mendacious, and dangerous. But Parliament clearly would not accept the radical implications of the army's program. A show of force resolved the impasse: on December 2, 1648, the army was in London; on December 6 a detachment of troops led by Colonel Pride turned away or arrested most of the members of Parliament; Pride's Purge left a small Rump of presumably dependable men. But when it was moved to try the king for treason and other heinous crimes, the vote was only twenty-six to twenty. Old attachments, and old taboos, die hard.

The trial of Charles I began in mid-January 1649. Of the 135 commissioners named to try their king, only 68 appeared, and not all these could bring themselves to condemn their sovereign to death. Charles steadfastly refused to recognize the jurisdiction of the court, there were disturbances in the hall, and disapproval of the proceedings was widespread. When the expected verdict was given, on January 27, Cromwell had to exercise considerable pressure to obtain 58 signatures. His own was among them. On January 30, 1649, Charles died on the block, bravely, better than he had lived, and with his last words defending the idea of a personal monarch ruling in a balanced constitution.

Cromwell's Republic

The execution of Charles I had solved one problem but it created many others—institutional, political, diplomatic. The government was in the hands of the minority of a minority: of army leaders and of the Rump,[35] an unrepresentative fragment, ranging from fifty to eighty, of a House of Commons which had considerably diminished in size during the course of the Civil War. As Cromwell recognized more clearly than anyone, the new state sorely needed a framework of legality. Rapidly, the Rump set about providing it. In February 1649 Parliament, now sovereign, abolished the monarchy and the House of Lords, and established a Council of State which was essentially an agent of Commons: it numbered forty-one and was chosen for one year; thirty-one of its members were members of Parliament. In May, the Rump declared England to be a "Commonwealth and Free State," and in a gesture foreshadowing the French Revolution, ordered a new great seal bearing the inscription, "In the first year of freedom by God's blessing restored." These were words, symbols, but as Gibbon said two hundred years ago, mankind is governed by names.

---

[35] The difficulties of classifying the actors in this historic drama are underlined by the composition of the Rump. Presumably, Pride's Purge had eliminated the Presbyterians and left only Independents. But many of these so-called Independents were in fact elders in the Presbyterian church: clearly, the motives of men in history are more complicated than historians are often willing to recognize. See J. H. Hexter, "The Problem of the Presbyterian Independents" (1938), in Hexter, *Reappraisals in History* (1961).

Words were not enough: difficulties multiplied on all sides. The execution of the king had caused horror abroad, even among Protestant powers. At home, mourning royalists, unappeased Presbyterians, discontented soldiers, rebellious Scots and Irishmen plunged England into the semblance of a new civil war. For two years Cromwell, who bore most of the burden, had little time for constructive statesmanship. He performed his tasks with his characteristic and prayerful realism: Cromwell was a Puritan zealot who justified his actions and his arbitrariness by claiming divine guidance, but he was also a statesman, eager to found a republic in law, and at peace, with a degree of toleration narrow perhaps by modern, but generous by seventeenth-century, standards. The Leveller mutiny in the army (complicated by the emergence of the "True Levellers," or Diggers, a small communist sect) was easiest to deal with: Cromwell could understand the grievances, even if he could not honor the demands, of his soldiers. "Freeborn John" Lilburne was confined to the Tower, three leading mutineers were shot, and the rest sent to Ireland.

The Irish and Scottish rebellions demanded more severe action and brought out Puritan self-righteousness in its most repellent form. The Irish, Catholics and Presbyterians alike, proclaimed Charles I's eldest son as King Charles II; so did the Scots, who had veered from hatred of Anglicanism toward devotion to a dynasty that was, after all, Scottish, and toward a young prince who seemed ready to grant them the Presbyterian order they craved. Cromwell took command of the English expedition to Ireland and soundly beat the rebels in August, 1649. In September, he besieged the port of Drogheda; when the defenders refused to surrender, he took the city by storm and had the survivors cut down. In October, his troops took Wexford, and a second massacre ensued. Cromwell was anything but an indiscriminate killer of men, but he thought the Irish massacres authorized not merely by the laws of war, but by the laws of revenge as well. What had happened at Drogheda, he told the Speaker of the House, was "a righteous judgment of God upon these barbarous wretches, who have imbrued their hands in so much innocent blood"—an unmistakable allusion to the Ulster massacre of 1641, when rebellious Irishmen had killed new Protestant settlers wholesale. Thus, as so often, murder begot murder. By spring 1650, Cromwell was back in England; his lieutenants spent two years mopping up the Irish rebels, cruelly starving out the resisters. Cromwell's program for settling Ireland with Protestants was rapidly carried out; all across the land, miserable Irish Catholic peasants confronted substantial Protestant English landlords, nourishing mutual hatreds that have not died down to this day. The Scottish situation was, if anything, more delicate: young Prince Charles was among the Scots, negotiating, promising to uphold their cherished covenant. It was not until September 1651, with the battle of Worcester, that Scotland was subdued and pacified: Worcester was probably Cromwell's most brilliant victory in a career studded with brilliant victories. Charles II, whom the Scots had solemnly crowned at the beginning of the year, made a melodramatic escape; in October, he was in France, to resume his intrigues and wait for a call to take his rightful throne.

In 1651, such a call seemed a remote possibility; the Rump and the generals were in firm control. There was much dissension, but also much able government: "Not only are they powerful by sea and land," one of Mazarin's agents reported back to France, "but they live without ostentation, without pomp, and without mutual rivalry. They are economical in their private affairs, for which each man toils as if for his private interest. They handle large sums of money, which they administer honestly, observing a strict discipline. They reward well and punish severely." [36] The forcible pacification of the British Isles was the first success of the new regime; Cromwell's foreign policy and conduct of war abroad was the second. Late in 1651, Parliament enacted the first Navigation Act, England's most ambitious venture into mercantilist policy so far (see p. 300). It provided that goods imported into England must be carried only in English ships or in ships of the exporting country, a measure directed, more than against any other power, against the Dutch—Protestants, but also the princes of the carrying trade. Trade rivalry between the two countries, already keen and burdened with bitter memories, [37] soon degenerated into war, and from July 1652 on, able English commanders confronted able Dutch admirals in a series of naval engagements. Two years later, when the two countries made peace, the English had won a significant share of Dutch trade, and Cromwell could begin to think of the Dutch Republic less as a rival than as a potential ally.

But by 1654, the Commonwealth had given way to a new experiment in republicanism: the Protectorate. Cromwell did not take this step irresponsibly; his earlier reluctance to put Charles I to death was now repeated in his reluctance to tear apart the flimsy legal fabric of the young English republic. Parliament forced his hand. There was widespread sentiment for new elections, but in 1651 the Commons resolved to stay in being for three more years. There was urgent demand for "reform of the law," and Cromwell strongly supported it: "Relieve the oppressed," he wrote from Scotland in 1650, after he had beaten the Scots at Dunbar, "reform the abuses of all professions, and if there be any one that makes many poor to make a few rich, that suits not a commonwealth." [38] But (as Cromwell realistically noted) the entrenched legal profession and equally entrenched property owners made reform impossible.

There was, finally, growing need for a religious settlement; English religious life was in a state of anarchy, since the abolition of the Anglican church had not been followed by an establishment of a Presbyterian or any other kind of order. Cromwell wanted an established church that would

---

[36] Quoted in Firth, *Cromwell*, 241–242.
[37] For the Dutch massacre of English traders in Amboyna in 1623, see p. 212.
[38] Quoted in Firth, *Cromwell*, 298.

tolerate other Protestant sects, but Parliament, deeply split, remained indecisive. True, in February 1652 Cromwell had induced the Commons to pass an Act of Oblivion for earlier treasons, but it had few practical results. As reforms were stalled and the promised dissolution of Parliament was about to be compromised by parliamentary chicanery, the army pressed Cromwell to act. Finally, on April 20, 1653, in a dramatic scene, Cromwell came to the House of Commons, and after listening to the debate, rose and accused his fellow members present of all sorts of crimes and misdemeanors. "Come, come," he exclaimed, "I will put an end to your prating. You are no parliament, I say you are no parliament." Then he called his musketeers and had the house cleared. If not officially, at least in effect, the Long Parliament was over.

His decisive intervention depressed Cromwell deeply: "It's you that have forced me to this," he shouted after the departing members, "for I have sought the Lord night and day, that he would rather slay me than put me upon the doing of this work." [39] The next five years, the last of Cromwell's life, were years of institutional improvisation. A new council of state was formed, and in the summer of 1653, a small parliament was called together, not elected but appointed by Independent congregations. [40] Respectable, serious, but immobilized by the plethora of reforming projects its members poured forth, it lasted only until December, 1653, when it handed its authority back to Cromwell, who became Lord Protector of the Commonwealth of England, Scotland, and Ireland, under the Instrument of Government, England's first written constitution. It could not provide stability. Two more parliaments came, were purged, and dissolved; Cromwell, offered the crown, refused it in May 1657. While a war with Spain, begun in 1656, went exceedingly well, [41] at home discontent was general: Cromwell was beset by religious fanatics who preached that the end of worldly government had come; by principled republicans who distrusted him, particularly after he accepted the right to name his own successor; by rigid Puritans who detested his tolerance; by monarchists who longed for the day of Charles II's return. Against the continuing pressure of political radicals, Cromwell had moved toward the right, more concerned at the end with the privileges of the propertied than with protection of the poor against the propertied. When he died in September 1658, only a handful mourned, and Cromwell's son, Richard, named Lord Protector, could not hold his father's structure together.

In February 1660, General Monck put an end to the chaos. He marched his army from Scotland into London. Without political ambitions of his own, eager only to restore stability, Monck called together a "free parliament"—the Long

[39] Wilbur Cortez Abbott, ed., *The Writings and Speeches of Oliver Cromwell,* vol. II (1939), 643.

[40] This parliament is known as the Little Parliament (for it had only 140 members) or Barebones Parliament, after Praise-God Barbon, member for the City of London.

[41] The great prize was Jamaica.

Parliament as it had been before Pride's Purge in December 1648. Restoration was in the air; Charles II made it a certainty with his statesmanlike Declaration of Breda, issued, he said, to bind up old wounds. It undertook to restore "King, Peers and people to their just, ancient and fundamental rights"; it offered a general pardon, excepting only those whom Parliament itself would single out for punishment; it promised "liberty to tender consciences" in matters of religion; and it reassured those who had acquired land during the upheavals that disposition of their property rights, too, would be determined by Parliament. A freely chosen Convention Parliament voted to accept the declaration and invited the exile home. On May 29, 1660, Charles II entered London: "This day came in his majesty Charles the Second to London," the diarist John Evelyn recorded, "after a sad and long exile and calamitous suffering both of the King and Church, being seventeen years. This was also his birthday, and with a Triumph of about 20,000 horse and foot, brandishing their swords and shouting with unexpressable joy. The ways strewn with flowers, the bells ringing, the streets hung with tapestry, fountains running with wine. The Mayor, aldermen, all the companies in their liveries, chains of gold, banners. Lords and nobles, cloth of silver, gold and velvet everybody clad in; the windows and balconies all set with ladies, trumpets, music; and myriads of people flocking the streets and ways as far as Rochester, so as they were seven hours in passing the city, even from two in the afternoon 'til nine at night. I stood in the Strand and beheld it and blessed God. And all this without one drop of blood, and by that very army which rebelled against him. But it was the Lord's doing, and wonderful to our eyes, for such a Restoration was never seen in the mention of any history ancient or modern, since the return from the Babylonian Capitivity, nor so joyful a day and so bright ever seen in this nation."

In the light of such sentiments, and of Charles' subsequent actions, England's travail over the past decades seems at first glance like so much waste motion. Charles II kept the promises he made at Breda: only some of the surviving regicides, thirteen of them, were executed for their vote to condemn Charles II's father to death. A royalist parliament turned the king's promises to advantage: it returned to royalists the land they had lost by confiscation, though not the land that royalists—a far larger number—had felt compelled to sell during the Civil War. It restored the monarchy, the House of Lords, the Church of England, and drove the nonconformists out of the Anglican communion. But the Puritan Revolution and the regime of Cromwell left a permanent mark on England and on the British Isles. Parliament retained much of the power it had won; the crown surrendered much of its prerogative. Neither the prerogative courts nor the royal claim to a right of taxation without parliamentary consent returned to haunt and divide Englishmen. While France solved the problems of political anarchy by turning to absolutism, England solved these problems by devising a parliamentary monarchy. Nor was Cromwell forgotten. He had made

England into a great power; when Charles II degraded England into a mere client of France (see p. 308), Englishmen began to recall the great days of Cromwell with some nostalgia. "It is strange," Samuel Pepys noted in his diary in July 1667, how "everybody do now-a-days reflect upon Oliver and commend him, what brave things he did, and made all the neighbour princes fear him; while here a prince, come in with all the love and prayers and good liking of his people, who have given greater signs of loyalty and willingness to serve him with their estates than ever was done by any people, hath lost all so soon."

FRANCE: THE REIGNS OF TWO MINISTERS

In the half century between the murder of Henri IV in 1610 and the onset of Louis XIV's personal rule in 1661, France was successively governed by two great statesmen: Richelieu and Mazarin. Yet their statesmanship could not keep France from the ravages of peasant uprisings, political divisions, religious troubles, and civil war. The awesome splendor of Louis XIV, whose power loomed over Europe in the second half of the seventeenth century, was in part a response to the disturbances that marked the first half. But it was also the heir of those years, for it was in the reigns of Richelieu and Mazarin that France achieved enough stability to survive its internal troubles and rise to commanding stature in Europe.

Louis XIII: The Reign of Richelieu

When Louis XIII ascended the throne in 1610 after Henri IV's premature death (see p. 183), he was a boy of nine; this meant a regent, a post held during the next four years with stunning incompetence by Louis' mother, Marie de' Medici. The king's conduct after 1614, when he proclaimed himself officially of age and ended his tutelage, suggests that dependency was a lifelong habit, or necessity, with him: Louis XIII was alert, hard-working, even persistent, but he was moody, spiteful, and perpetually in need of advice. Luckily for him, he had Richelieu to govern him for most of his reign. At the same time, though neurotic and indecisive, Louis was not incapable of action; he even instigated an important political assassination. The queen mother had induced the valued Sully to hand in his resignation early in 1611 and, instead of trusting Henri IV's able ministers, surrounded herself with a camarilla of court favorites. Most conspicuous and most obnoxious among these were Leonora Galigai, Marie's lady-in-waiting and Leonora's husband, Concini, Italians both. The pair were grasping and ostentatious, if intelligent, adventurers, who were not above snubbing the adolescent king. After years of enduring such treatment, Louis induced some of his entourage to murder Concini. The queen mother went into exile, while the young king, weeping with joy, exclaimed: "I am your king. I was king before, but now I am and, God willing, will be king more than ever." [42]

It was harder to be king than Louis fondly believed. The death of his great father had revived the ambitions and quarrels of the feudal princes; rumors that Henri IV's murderer, Ravaillac, was in the pay of the Jesuits raised the tempers of the restless Gallican clergy; French Huguenots organized for the defense of their Protestant faith and of the political privileges secured for them in the Edict of Nantes (see p. 181) which they believed to be in jeopardy. In 1614 the regent convoked an Estates General. It wrangled for half a year and dissolved, leaving tensions as high as before. Its only visible result was the public demonstration of its incapacity to govern. [43] Nor was Marie's departure from the center of power permanent: in 1619, the queen mother made peace with her rebellious son with the aid of a superbly skillful negotiator, Richelieu. Concini's death had brought into prominence young Louis' favorite, the duke de Luynes, advocate of an implacable Catholic policy; Luynes' own death in 1621 gave the queen mother renewed and undue influence. It was not until 1624 that Louis XIII was persuaded to make Richelieu his chief minister. Unrest did not cease, but the French state now had a formidable, purposeful advocate.

Armand Jean du Plessis, Cardinal Richelieu, is a fascinating figure and something of an enigma. He felicitously combined passion and self-control, personal ambition and public service, efficiency in religion and a vocation for politics; he awed others by his very presence and clawed his way to power by a superiority of intellect and a toughness of will that would not be denied. His early path was smoothed by his ancient lineage: born in 1585, he was a bishop by 1608. Once his abilities had brought him to the attention of the queen mother, he had to contend with jealous courtiers; that is why it was not until 1624 that Richelieu held power in his hands. Despite intrigues against his post and his life, he did not relinquish that power until his death in 1642.

Richelieu was at once the characteristic product and the supreme promoter of the early modern state. He subordinated everything to a single purpose: *raison d'état*—reason of state, the securing of the French monarchy against its internal and external rivals. This meant the ordering of the French government for effective action in peace and war and the improvement of the French position in the councils of Europe. Richelieu was not an irreligious man, but he, a cardinal of the Church of Rome since 1622, serenely concluded treaties with Protestant powers when his conception of French interests demanded it. Richelieu had no intention of subverting a society built on rank and status, but

---

[42] Quoted in Jean H. Mariéjol, *Henri IV et Louis XIII (1598–1643)* (1911), 193.

[43] Its failure, coupled with the rise of the absolute monarchy, led to its long sleep; the next Estates General was not called until 175 years later, in the fateful year of 1789 (see p. 463).

he mercilessly repressed French aristocrats who set themselves against the authority of the crown. Richelieu was not a fanatic—his foreign policy proved that—but since, in his judgment, the semiautonomy of French Huguenots was a danger to the state, he found it necessary to curtail their power. All his moves, both in foreign and in domestic policy, were intertwined: that is why Richelieu and *raison d'état* are practically synonymous.

The Huguenots were the first to test Richelieu's view of *raison d'état*. Early in 1625, Protestant nobles staged an uprising, limited in scope but embarrassing to Richelieu, who was occupied elsewhere; a truce gave him time to prepare his forces against possible repetition. When in 1627 there was a Huguenot rebellion centered on La Rochelle, Richelieu took personal charge of the expedition against that western port. For a year the Huguenots held out, encouraged and misled by sporadic help from England; they were to discover that to have the duke of Buckingham as one's ally was as bad as having Richelieu as one's enemy. In late October 1628, a starving La Rochelle surrendered to its determined besieger; the other Huguenot strongholds surrendered soon after. In June 1629, the Peace of Alais brought the first major modification of Henri IV's Edict of Nantes: the Huguenots lost their special towns, their ports and fortresses, and their legal privileges; they retained the right to practice what French Catholics liked to call "the so-called reformed religion." At a stroke, Richelieu had broken the Huguenots' power and guaranteed their docility; a mixture of ruthlessness and leniency, with ruthlessness dominant, was always his favorite technique.

The Huguenot rebellions had been led by the dukes de Soubise and Rohan; other nobles, with their vast estates, small private armies, political independence, and ceaseless intrigues, prevented Louis XIII from playing the role that Richelieu insisted a king of France must play: master in his own house. To that end, Richelieu did not scruple to have rebellious nobles executed— Henri IV would have paid them off instead—or to have their fortified castles razed to the ground. The feudal sport of dueling, a romantic reminder of the old aristocratic privilege of avenging insults, real or fancied, against one's honor, was one of Richelieu's first targets in his campaign to reduce the French nobility into decorative and docile servants of the state. In 1626 he induced his king to outlaw the duel; in the following year, to everyone's surprise, he enforced the law against the count de Montmorency-Bouteville, a notorious offender who had defied Richelieu by fighting a duel under Richelieu's very eyes: "On 22nd June 1627, the indignant and astonished young man mounted the scaffold." [44] Dueling did not cease but it began to go underground. More constructively, Richelieu undertook to domesticate the nobility by increasing the administrative authority of the central government—a difficult task in those days of provincial autonomy, lumbering transport, and slow communications.

[44] C. V. Wedgwood, *Richelieu and the French Monarchy* (1949), 62.

Richelieu strengthened the royal hand in the provinces by charging commissioners, intendants, with superintending royal policy and enforcing royal orders. With the intendants as with his other administrative measures, like his reorganization of royal councils, Richelieu showed himself an effective and sensible reformer: he took old offices and fashioned them into instruments of royal policy. Not surprisingly, the intendants came into conflict with local grandees, who had hitherto exercised so much unchecked power, and with the provincial parlements which found their old privileges as courts of final instance and as leviers of taxes greatly reduced. In France, as elsewhere, the growth of the modern state amounted to a transfer of power from nobility to crown.

The administrative reforms brought some changes in the status of the old aristocracy: Richelieu chose many of the king's chief ministers, and many of his counselors, from relatively obscure, sometimes from nonnoble, families, thus securing "creatures" who usefully combined competence in their work with gratitude to their master. [45] But these innovations did not penetrate into French society as a whole. Richelieu had some fairly rudimentary notions about commercial policy; he improved communications, built canals, supervised the silk industry, protected domestic commerce with a simple (and wholly unenforceable) anticipation of the English navigation acts (see p. 279), and launched trading and colonial companies. But his ideas were too ambitious for his means of realizing them. Moreover, his foreign policy, a policy of intervention in the European wars to the greater glory of France, was, like all such policies, extremely burdensome on the French people. New adventures abroad meant new taxes at home, and these brought rebellions. In 1630 there were riots at Dijon; in 1631, at Paris; in 1632, at Lyons, all against the introduction of new, or the raising of old, taxes. In the countryside, there were sporadic but extremely violent peasant uprisings. Bands of rebels, usually driven by hunger and normally encouraged by their landlords, tore royal officials to pieces. These are the famous revolts of the nu-pieds—revolt was the only language the "shoeless" had for their protest and the only language the powerful could understand. Most of these rebellions were put down with unmitigated ferocity; on rare occasions, the government would appease the rebels by withdrawing some obnoxious tax.

Yet from Richelieu's own point of view—power politics—his policies, so burdensome at home, were supremely successful. Power—on this Richelieu agreed with Machiavelli—must increase, lest it decline and the power of one state can increase only at the expense of another. The Hapsburgs were the greatest power in Europe, hence it was against the Hapsburgs that Richelieu directed his most sustained efforts. That is why the Thirty Years' War offered such splendid opportunities for the French; that is why Richelieu did not scruple to ally himself with Protestant Sweden on the principle that the enemy

[45] See Orest A. Ranum, *Richelieu and the Councillors of Louis XIII* (1963).

of your enemy is your friend; that is why, in 1635, when general peace threatened to break out, Richelieu intervened to keep the pot of power politics bubbling. When Richelieu died in December 1642, his aims—to "ruin the Huguenot party," to secure the state against the nobility, and to wrest European hegemony from Spain—had been only partly realized. But his legacy was plain. "The torment and the ornament of his age," an English writer called him upon his death. "France he subdued, Italy he terrified, Germany he shook, Spain he afflicted, Portugal he crowned, Lorraine he took, Catalonia he received, Swethland he fostered, Flanders he mangled, England he troubled, Europe he beguiled." [46] Cardinal Mazarin would find it hard to follow such a man in office.

Young Louis XIV: The Reign of Mazarin

Louis XIII survived his minister and master by five months, and when he died in May 1643, events had a curious familiarity about them. Like Louis XIII, his son, Louis XIV, was a child at his accession—not yet five. Consequently, the reign of Louis XIV, like that of his father before him, began under a regency, and like his father, Louis XIV found his widowed mother in charge. Moreover, Louis XIII and Marie de' Medici had governed with the aid of a wily cardinal-statesman; Louis XIV and Anne of Austria had *their* statesman-cardinal to guide the business of France: Jules Mazarin, who retained his influence unbroken until his death in 1661. In their policies, if not in their characters, the two cardinals were much alike: where Richelieu was pitiless, Mazarin was diplomatic; where Richelieu employed the weapon of fear, Mazarin relied on the persuasiveness of devotion. Anne of Austria, at least, and her young royal son, found him lovable. Louis XIV, indeed would always remember Mazarin with filial fondness.

The country at large did not share this affection. It was bad enough that Mazarin should be a foreigner—he was a Neapolitan, naturalized in 1639; to make things worse, he was obsessively preoccupied with the welfare of his family, including himself: loyalty to his private fortune and to his five nieces was second only to his loyalty to France, and there were times when he had trouble keeping the two apart. And his loyalty to France was, like Richelieu's before him, expensive and unpopular: Mazarin preached absolutism to his king and followed an aggressive anti-Spanish policy abroad; he raised taxes and offended old families with his appointments.

The Frondes,[47] those riots, treacheries, and civil wars that intermittently

---

[46] Quoted in Wedgwood, *Richelieu*, 191.

[47] "The word *fronde* means a child's sling. The police had tried to prevent the *gamins* of Paris from disporting themselves with these playthings in the time of Richelieu, but had conspicuously failed. When the Paris populace successfully defied the government in 1648, men said: 'Ils font comme leurs enfants: ils jouent à la fronde'" (Merriman, *Six Contemporaneous Revolutions,* 61n). This view of the Frondes as a set of irresponsible games overstresses the comical aspects of these events and fails to do justice to their long-range consequences, which became palpable only after 1661, when Louis XIV began his personal reign (see p. 293).

plagued France between 1648 and 1653, were in part responses to Mazarin's policies and Mazarin's conduct. Imitating Richelieu in substance though not in style, Mazarin increased taxes through the 1640s, had them collected by shameless profiteers, and kept France in the war—the cause of, or excuse for, the heaviest exactions. Mazarin's rapacity was real enough, even by the lax standards of his day; rumors that he was exploiting his powerful position to bleed France to death for the sake of his own family made his rapacity appear even worse than it was. But in large part, the Frondes were a delayed response to Richelieu's disappearance from the scene. Since the reign of Louis XI in the late fifteenth century, feudalism had appeared moribund (see p. 101), and Richelieu had done his utmost to unify France and reduce the remaining power of the nobility and the parlements. His death offered an opportunity to undo his work. In the summer of 1648, rural uprisings coalesced with aristocratic dissatisfaction and parlementary rebellions to make the first Fronde, the *Fronde parlementaire.* Failing other spokesmen, the forces arrayed against the regent and her favorite relied upon the Parlement of Paris to speak, and act, for them all. The oldest of the twelve supreme courts of France, the Parlement of Paris, was also the most aggressive. Through the early part of 1648, it had showered remonstrances on the queen mother, demanding the recall of royal intendants and the right to pass on proposed taxes. The parlementary cause was popular, yet it was anything but disinterested: the call for reform meant, in substance, the call for increased authority for itself at the expense of the crown. By March 1649, the first Fronde was over; the parlement secured most of its demands, and Mazarin kept away from the court, in voluntary exile.

But in early 1650 the second Fronde, the *Fronde princière,* took up where the first had left off. It was plain that the crown had no intention of keeping its promises; moreover, the great nobles wanted more power than they had or could reasonably expect. The second Fronde offered a strange spectacle, explicable only by the incomplete unification of France: here were Condé, a royal prince, Turenne, a brilliant general, and the cardinal de Retz, a courtier and prominent churchman, terrorizing the French countryside, battling against other French troops, and making alliances with Spain, even permitting Spanish troops to enter French soil, at a time when France was still officially at war with Spain. Amid this confusion of heedless, wholly self-centered, and conflicting ambitions, Mazarin constructed a loyalist coalition, raised an army to fight the rebels and the Spaniards, and finally carried the day. By September 1653 all rebels were out of commission and all rebellious cities under royal control. Concessions offered under pressure were withdrawn, and the Parlement of Paris remained silent. Nothing seemed to have happened—nothing except more devastation of the countryside, looting, and unpunished murder. But appearances were deceptive. In the years that remained to him, Mazarin kept his control undiminished and triumphantly concluded the war with Spain in 1659, at the Peace of the Pyrenees, which extended French territory in the north and south alike, at Spain's expense. Then in 1661, with Mazarin's death, the real consequences of the Fronde became clear to all. As a young boy, silent and bewildered, Louis XIV had witnessed the disloyalty of the great, of the parlements, and of Paris, and experienced a brief but uncomfortable exile. When he took power into his own hands to begin a long, glorious, and terrible reign, he acted like a man who remembered and like a ruler determined to make all further Frondes impossible.

SELECTED READINGS

The question of the nature and extent of the mid-seventeenth-century crisis remains controversial. The essays that began the debate—mainly by E. J. Hobsbawm and H. R. Trevor-Roper—some responses and criticisms, are in Trevor Aston, ed., *Crisis in Europe, 1560-1660* (1965); Roger B. Merriman, *Six Contemporaneous Revolutions* (1938), anticipated much of the discussion.

The most useful general discussion of the military upheaval is C. V. Wedgwood, *The Thirty Years' War* (ed. 1944), to be supplemented by S. H. Steinberg, *The Thirty Years' War* (1967), and Georges Pagès, *The Thirty Years' War, 1618-1648* (tr. 1971). For three central actors on the European stage at the time, see Francis Watson, *Wallenstein: Soldier Under Saturn* (1938)—though a modern analysis remains desirable; Michael Roberts, *Gustavus Adolphus, A History of Sweden, 1611-1632,* 2 vols. (1953, 1958), to be read with several of Roberts' shorter essays, collected in *Essays in Swedish History* (1966); and, amid a sizable literature, Carl J. Burckhardt, *Richelieu: His Rise to Power* (tr., rev. ed., 1964), and *Assertion of Power and Cold War* (1970). C. V. Wedgwood, *Richelieu and the French Monarchy* (1949), is clear and reasonable. See also, on Richelieu's style of governing men, Orest A. Ranum, *Richelieu and the Councillors of Louis XIII* (1963). For the decline of Spain, see J. Lynch, *Spain and America, 1598-1700* (1969), already cited. To this should be added J. H. Elliott, *The Revolt of the Catalans: A Study in the Decline of Spain, 1598-1640* (1963), a brilliant book, and H. G. Koenigsberger, *The Government of Sicily Under Philip II of Spain* (1952), which shows the seeds of decay under the cover of grandeur.

For the Russia of the time, see the relevant chapters in Michael T. Florinsky, *Russia: A History and an Interpretation,* 2 vols. (1953); Jerome Blum, *Lord and Peasant in Russia from the Ninth to the Nineteenth Century* (1961); the opening chapter of Geroid Tanqueray Robinson, *Rural Russia Under the Old Regime* (1932); and Ian Grey, *Ivan the Terrible* (1964). The travail of the Dutch Republic at midcentury is traced in Pieter Geyl, *The Netherlands in the Seventeenth Century,* 2 vols. (2nd. ed., 1961, 1964).

A good survey of English history from the death of Elizabeth to the Restoration is Godfrey Davies, *The Early Stuarts, 1603-1660* (1937); the first half of Maurice Ashley, *England in the Seventeenth Century (1603-1714)* (3rd ed., 1961), is introductory and clear. See also the early chapters in J. P. Kenyon, *The Stuarts* (1958). Wallace Notestein, *The English People on the Eve of Colonization: 1603-1630* (1954), ably surveys English society; it may be supplemented with Carl W. Bridenbaugh, *Vexed and Troubled Englishmen, 1590-1642* (1968). David Willson, *King James VI and I* (1956), is a scholarly and dependable biography of the first Stuart king. For his successor, see Christopher Hibbert, *Charles I* (1968).

The great "storm over the gentry"—rising or falling?—has been ably anatomized in J. H. Hexter's article of that title, now in Hexter, *Reappraisals in History* (1961). One immensely valuable contribution, to this debate and to English history of the period in general, is Lawrence Stone, *The Crisis of the Aristocracy, 1558-1641* (1965), abridged by the author (1967). For the economic history of these decades, see the appropriate chapters in Charles Wilson, *England's Apprenticeship, 1603-1763* (1965). For the civil war there are the eloquent narratives by C. V. Wedgwood, *The King's Peace, 1637-1641* (1959) and *The King's War, 1641-1647* (1959); her biography, *Oliver Cromwell* (1956), is equally readable. These narratives need to be supplemented by analytical and interpretative works like J. H. Hexter, *The Reign of King Pym* (1941); D. Brunton and D. H. Pennington, *Members of the Long Parliament* (1954); A. S. P. Woodhouse, ed., *Puritanism and Liberty* (2nd ed., 1950), which prefaces Leveller documents with a long informative introduction; Joseph Frank, *The Levellers* (1955); William Haller, *Liberty and Reformation in the Puritan Revolution* (1955); George Yule, *The Independents in the English Civil War* (1958); Christopher Hill, *Society and Puritanism in Pre-Revolutionary England* (1964); and Michael Walzer, *The Revolution of the Saints: A Study in the Origins of Radical Politics* (1965), whose thesis is revealed in its subtitle. Cromwell remains enigmatic; in addition to Wedgwood's biography, see Charles Firth, *Oliver Cromwell and the Rule of the Puritans in England* (ed. 1953), and G. M. Young, *Charles I and Cromwell* (1935), which, though of an earlier vintage, retain their interest.

For France, in addition to the biographies of Richelieu mentioned, see Ernst H. Kossmann, *La Fronde* (1954), which partially supersedes the earlier Paul R. Doolin, *The Fronde* (1935). Davis Bitton, *The French Nobility in Crisis, 1560-1640* (1969), is a study in politics and ideology. A. D. Lublinskaya, *French Absolutism: The Crucial Phase, 1620-1629* (tr. 1968), is a Marxist interpretation by a Soviet historian.

7

The Age
of Louis XIV

In 1751, Voltaire published *Le siècle de Louis XIV,* a masterpiece of historical literature. The title is significant: Voltaire characterized an age with the name of a man. As this chapter will show, Voltaire's historical instincts were sound. Louis XIV was not all of Europe; there were developments in England, in Brandenburg-Prussia, in the Hapsburg domains, in Sweden and Russia that owed little to Louis' plans and were relatively immune to his interventions. Yet Louis XIV dominated half a century of European history. It is in this sense that the years stretching from 1661 to 1715 were what Voltaire called them: "The age of Louis XIV."

31535

5.35

440

2.2
1.79
1.77

5.39

November 6, 19

Hi Maureen

The investment certificate you and [...]
have with Cosco has matured and must [...]
redeemed.

Enclosed investment certifi[...]

THE MAKING OF A MYTH

The Costs of Splendor

The reign of Louis XIV is synonymous with glory, splendor, magnificence. The flattery courtiers lavished on the Sun King was not merely the forced tribute of hirelings greedy for preferment, protection, and pay; it was, for many, the spontaneous expression of awe for a ruler who seemed more than human. The hostility of foreign princes was only another kind of tribute. All across Europe, Louis XIV was specter and model, whom lesser rulers feared and imitated. At the same time, for the vast majority of Frenchmen, Louis XIV was a remote and shadowy being; the golden rays that scattered from his presence did not warm them. Their realities were starvation, pestilence, war, the yield of the harvest, the price of bread. Louis XIV might smile or frown on his courtiers and fight battles in distant lands; most Frenchmen fought their wars with nature and with the tax collector. Out of twenty million Frenchmen over fifteen million were peasants, ranging from the miserable squatter to the small farmer to a small minority of substantial proprietors. Even among the more fortunate minority of the peasants, many lived perilously near the edge of misery and, in bad years, of outright starvation. In the cities, over a million Frenchmen formed a starving proletariat, conscious not of class but of their destitution, dependence, and incurable insecurity. A million more, perhaps, made up a lower middle class of more or less independent craftsmen and small shopkeepers. The rest—around two million—were substantial bourgeois, nobles, and priests. Clerics, like others, showed considerable differences in wealth and status. Few clerics were really poor; many were rich and noble; all were influential whether in their parishes in the provinces or among politicians in Paris; all enjoyed tax exemptions. Finally, at the top of the social and economic pyramid clustered the courtiers; they strove upward toward the king yet took care to keep their distance, for the king insisted on presiding over "his" people in splendor made all the more splendid by his remoteness and uniqueness. "Nine out of ten of King Louis' subjects worked hard and thanklessly with their hands"—so the French historian Pierre Goubert sums it up—"in order to permit the tenth to devote himself comfortably to the life of bourgeois, nobleman or mere idler." [1] A king's splendor—court ritual, mistresses, châteaux, hunts, wars—bore down heavily on those least able to resist and least able to spare what an omnivorous

[1] *Louis XIV and Twenty Million Frenchmen* (tr. 1970), 46.

and insatiable state demanded of them. Generalizations are hard to make, for imposts varied greatly from province to province, even from village to village; but everywhere the peasant found himself paying a good share of his crop, every year, to the local seigneur as feudal dues, to the local church as tithes, and to the local representative of the king as taxes. The overwhelming mass of the peasantry were dependent on good harvests, sturdy laborers in the family, and a fortunate absence of pestilence. But such conjunctions were all too rare. Contrary to the widespread belief, peasant families in the Old Regime were by no means very large. Birth control was infrequent, and women conceived as often as nature permitted them to conceive, but they married late, and the number of children stillborn and dying in infancy was enormous—so enormous, indeed, that it seemed a daily event, "of less moment than a bad storm, a freak tempest, or the death of a horse."[2] The average life expectancy was perhaps twenty-five years; of one hundred children, one fourth died before they were a year old, another fourth before they reached twenty. It took very little—the black death, which periodically recurred in France, as elsewhere, throughout the seventeenth century; a marauding foreign army; a plague of one's own troops; or a disastrous harvest—to carry off ten or fifteen out of a hundred villagers.

Let one case stand for many. There was a family in Beauvais, named Cocu: Jean Cocu, weaver, his wife, and three daughters working for him as spinners of wool—the youngest being nine. Between them, the five ate seventy pounds of bread a week, a diet they could easily afford when bread cost one half sol a pound. But in bad years the price of bread would rise, markedly. In 1693, there was a bad harvest and a shortage of work—two crises that normally came together. The price of bread went up, first to one sol, then to two, then to more than three sols a pound. The Cocu family ate up their meager savings and pawned what they had; then started to eat unwholesome food, moldy cereals, cooked nettles, the entrails of animals. They fell ill, suffering from undernourishment and the diseases attendant upon such a regimen. In December 1693, the Cocus registered at the Office of the Poor—too late; in March 1694 the youngest daughter died, to be followed in May by the eldest daughter and the father. They were fortunate, the Cocus, for the two who survived—the mother and the middle daughter—worked, and they doubtless survived because they worked. All this "because of the price of bread."[3] At Versailles, in the midst of stately court ritual, religious ceremonies, and the making of high policy, Louis XIV heard rare, isolated voices lamenting the lot of his people, but there is no evidence that he listened.

---

[2] Ibid., 21.

[3] Pierre Goubert, *Beauvais et le Beauvaisis de 1600 à 1730,* vol. I (1960), 76–77. This passage has also been sympathetically noted by Peter Laslett, *The World We Have Lost* (2nd ed., 1971), 112–113.

The Beginning of the Reign

The young Louis XIV of France loved Cardinal Mazarin as a father, but when he had his opportunity, he showed himself more eager to govern than to mourn. On March 9, 1661, Mazarin died; on March 10, Louis entered upon the task which, he said, he had "so longed for, and so feared." He summoned his ministers and advisors and told them, one by one, that he, Louis, was now in charge. "You will assist me with your counsels when I ask for them." He would take advice, but he himself would govern. Until his death in 1715, Louis XIV held to his resolve. For nearly half a century before, France had been governed by two great prime ministers in succession. During the half century of Louis' reign, there was to be no third.

Clearly, Louis XIV enjoyed being king: he often spoke, then and later, of the grandeur and glory that are the lot of kings. Ruling, he confessed, brought out gifts he did not know he had. He was short, but this only made him stand up straight; his famous high heels and high wig were the external supports of an inner sense of command and a need to control, sharpened, no doubt, by his untoward experience in the Frondes with disloyal nobles and rebellious cities. He was superbly healthy, active, and despite his great sexual appetite, eager to master all the details of government; he was, in an age of great courtiers, the greatest courtier of them all, the faultless chief and first member of a dazzling aristocracy.

Assiduous, suspicious, intent on controlling everything, Louis XIV sought to extend his influence into all reaches of French society. Everything became part of his policy—the performance of plays or the building of châteaux no less than the gathering of armies or the supervision of merchants. It was an understandable exaggeration for Bishop Bossuet, the official political theorist of the reign, to say: "The whole state is in him; the will of the whole nation is contained in his." Bossuet's theory that kings rule by divine right—a traditional Christian doctrine brought up to date—seemed realized in this omnipresent young ruler. Certainly it was the impression the king did his best to cultivate. He enjoyed and exploited the mysteries of power. When he was born he was called—in gratitude that his father should have been able to beget him at all—"the God-given," *Louis, Dieu-donné.* That was an assertion of piety. But when panegyrists placed him above Alexander and Caesar, when he took the sun as his device and consciously acted the part of the *roi soleil,* the cult of the king reached, perhaps breached, the bounds of blasphemy. It is probable that Louis XIV never said, "L'état c'est moi," the most famous words attributed to him. But they epitomize his view of himself.

Yet *l'état c'est moi,* whether actual or fictitious, conceals a trap of which the historian should beware. Louis' boundless vanity and extravagant fantasies have induced historians to interpret his reign as the apogee of absolutism. But this view mistakes aspirations for realities. It is possible that Louis XIV wanted to exercise as close a supervision, and as tight a control, over France as

Napoleon I was to exercise a century later—his recorded utterances certainly sound that way. But true absolutism required the kind of administrative machinery, the kind of transportation and communication, and the kind of legal uniformity that seventeenth-century France simply did not provide: "France" was a geographical expression far more than a political or legal, let alone a national, entity. Louis XIV was king of all Frenchmen, but while lawyers fondly dwelled on the loyalty that all his subjects owed him, millions of peasants and thousands of nobles in effect felt their chief loyalty to their immediate, visible lords; if feudalism in the strict sense had long been moribund, local obligations of peasant to landlord, retainer to seigneur, took precedence over obligations to the crown. All across provincial France, the king and his bureaucrats appeared mainly as an intermittent threat to their independence and their income. The civil wars of the late sixteenth and the Frondes of the mid-seventeenth centuries had brought local particularism into some disrepute and had, in the general bloodletting, eliminated some competitors for royal authority. But the country remained a bewildering, almost incomprehensible patchwork of overlapping and conflicting jurisdictions. Understandably, royal authority was at its most effective near the center of the kingdom: in the Ile-de-France around Paris or in the Loire valley to the south. But the "new" acquisitions, Brittany and Provence (which had been French for two centuries) and even Normandy (which had come into the hands of the Capetian dynasty as far back as the thirteenth century), had their own parlements and their own local estates, their own sets of laws, their "liberties," and they clung to them with a tenacity normal for men defending their cherished interests. Every professional corporation and ecclesiastical establishment had its own *coutume,* its set of laws, and its privileges, as though they were so many cities or provinces. There were as many dialects as there were local or provincial tariff barriers; there were competing systems of weights and measures and coinage; there were literally hundreds of *coutumes.* The intendants and other royal agents whom Richelieu had sent into the provinces and the lawyers who had sought to codify this mass of custom, legislation, and privilege had made no more than a beginning when Louis XIV assumed the burden he had wanted and feared. When he began his personal government in March 1661, he found that "disorder reigned throughout the land."

From the outset, Louis acted energetically, often brutally, to reduce that disorder. One plausible instrument of centralizing the government—the Estates General—was hardly suitable for a king determined to bend the traditional order rather than to govern through it. Louis wanted a system responsible—and responsive—directly to him. To that end he acted as his own prime minister and radically reconstituted the royal council; with pitiless consistency, he excluded from the High Council, the *Conseil d'en haut,* the princes of the blood, the princes of the church, the great generals, the great nobles, his younger brother, called Monsieur, and even his mother, Anne of Austria, who had once acted as his regent—all those who had taken their right to advise the king as practically

God-given. Instead, Louis began his reign by retaining three of Mazarin's creatures: Le Tellier, secretary of state for war and later chancellor; Lionne, a well-trained and experienced diplomat for foreign affairs; and Fouquet, superintendent of finances. All were "new men," all belonged to relatively obscure families of bourgeois or unimpressive aristocratic origins. This was what the proud duke de Saint-Simon would call "the reign of the vile bourgeoisie": Louis systematically relied on men who owed their prominence and their power not to ancient lineage but to their master alone. "I had no intention of sharing my authority with them," Louis wrote about his advisors. "It was important that they should not entertain hopes higher than those it pleased me to give them." Before his first year as king–prime minister was over, Louis had shown his intention not merely of humbling the old grandees, but also of keeping the new men in their place. Fouquet, who had grown immensely rich in the 1650s and had built up a personal empire of loyal followers, aspired to the place his old master Mazarin had left vacant. But he built his empire and displayed his wealth too lavishly not to arouse the ire of a young king determined to lead rather than to be led. Too eager to rise, Fouquet had to fall: in September, Louis had him arrested and imprisoned. Fouquet's enemy, Colbert, another new man, entered the king's council in his place (see p. 299).

One by one, French institutions felt the sting of Louis' intentions. The once influential assembly of the clergy found itself under the king's watchful eye; disobedient cities were saddled with rapacious garrisons; old aristocratic army commanders were replaced by obedient professional officers. Above all, Louis XIV reduced the parlements to their judicial functions and, in effect, to silence. "It was necessary," he wrote later, "to humble them less for the wrongs they had done than for the wrongs they could do in the future." The truth was a little different: Louis bitterly remembered what they had done in his youth and wished to keep them from doing it in his reign. A series of decrees culminating in the edict of 1673 commanded the parlements to register all royal decrees without delay; this deprived the parlements' remonstrances of all political importance. Louis neither destroyed institutions nor invented them: he shaped them to his will. He enlarged and disciplined the army, widened the powers of his intendants, and improved his bureaucracy. All France felt the king's rule—but the nobility most of all.

The Politics of Culture

Nothing escaped the king; everything could be converted into a servant or symbol of his dominance. Versailles, probably the most famous royal palace ever built, reflects its builder's purposiveness: it was even more a political than an architectural masterpiece. Yet Versailles, and the social system that Louis XIV perfected there, were of slow growth. In the first years of his reign, the king's court was peripatetic, as all medieval courts had been; it moved with all its gear from château to château, setting up theaters, fireworks, hunts, gambling casinos. While he did not like Paris or the Parisians, Louis did not forget the old palace in the heart of his capital. He imported Bernini to redesign the Louvre, and Bernini made drawings, perfect for a sun king, placing the royal apartments squarely into the center, noisy and uncomfortable but symbolic. Eventually, nothing came of Bernini's plan, and Perrault's classical facade was adopted instead.

In any case, by 1667, the king had another idea: he would convert the simple hunting lodge of Versailles into a complex that would mirror by its magnificence his own. With his sure taste and his customary disregard of cost, Louis enlisted France's leading architects, landscape artists, painters, and sculptors, and by 1686, Versailles was ready for him and his entourage: a microcosm of the great world that Louis XIV adorned and governed. It was at Versailles that the king converted his aristocracy from semi-independent princes into adoring and decorative satellites. The duke de Saint-Simon, whose brilliant and malicious memoirs can still be read with great pleasure although they must be used with some care, records the solemn, unvarying charade on page after page: the king, with his fine sense of discrimination, knew just how to indicate, by the degree of his bow or the width of his smile, the precise rank of the courtier before him, the precise degree of favor he enjoyed. Louis insisted that his nobility attend him at Versailles, a policy that was ruinously expensive for the nobles and politically profitable for the king; it removed the noble from his local base, his landed property, and set him adrift to live by the fickle favor of his master. The most trivial detail of the king's daily existence was invested with dignity; great magnates struggled for the privilege of handing the king his shirt, or at night, his candle. His *lever,* his *souper,* his *coucher* were like so many sacred rituals, minutely subdivided to permit the largest possible number of courtiers to serve the king as he rose, ate, and went to bed. To obtain favor, or favors, required a constant presence—of body and mind alike. If (Saint-Simon reports) a courtier spoke in behalf of a noble who rarely or never appeared at Versailles, the king would say, "I do not know him," or, "He is a man I never see." These were more than comments; they were condemnations. In such an atmosphere, obsequiousness plumbed new depths of servility; intrigues surrounded all acts and pervaded conversation. The court was indispensable for advancement, but its frozen routine became, after a while, infinitely monotonous; the moralist La Bruyère described it as a place where "the joys are visible but false, and the sufferings are hidden but real." The whole seemed like an absurd game, but it worked; by the middle of Louis' reign the old nobility of the sword was domesticated.

Like the nobility, the arts too felt Louis's presence. The king made himself into a munificent patron, distributing pensions, handing out commissions, expressing authoritative opinions. "Without being a scholar," the Prussian ambassador Spanheim said of him, "Louis XIV writes well. He loves the arts and protects them; he knows his way about, especially in music, painting, and architecture."[4] His chief instruments for reducing the arts to order were the academies. In 1672 he became the official protector of the Académie Française, established in 1635 by Richelieu; other academies—of painting and sculpture, of science, of music, of architecture—flourished under his (or Colbert's) benign yet severe eye. The academies had several well-delineated tasks: the Académie Française, with its forty members, honored the great or harbored the well connected of literature and guarded the French language by prescribing what was and was not acceptable. All the academies were busy finding new ways of praising their king and of serving him by submitting ideas and designs for his approval. But most important of all, they trained the younger generation in the accepted style and set standards on which men of taste were supposed to agree. At the same time, as Louis XIV well knew, masterpieces did not arise by command. His reign was a time of great talents, and he had the good judgment to encourage them. It was an age, Voltaire wrote later, "worthy of the attention of ages to come," dominated by "the heroes of Corneille and Racine, the characters of Molière, the symphonies of Lully," the pulpit eloquence of Bourdaloue and of Bishop Bossuet, the greatest rhetorician of his age: "The time will not come again when a duke de La Rochefoucauld, author of the *Maxims,* upon leaving a conversation with Pascal or Arnauld, would go to the theater of Corneille." Voltaire might have added the fables of La Fontaine, the architecture of François and Jules-Hardouin Mansart, and the paintings of Claude Lorrain and Nicolas Poussin.

The dazzling productions of these artists were part of Louis' system; they brought his name and the name of France greater glory, at less cost, than the stratagems of his diplomats and the strategies of his generals. But Louis did not achieve absolute control over the arts; after all, he never achieved that in politics either. Under Louis XIV artists worked under the constraint of the officially approved style: neoclassicism. But its rules were shackles only for the second-rate, or the epigones, who painted or versified according to prescription only because that was all they could do. The masters of the seventeenth century treated neoclassicism as a call to discipline, not as an obstacle to invention. Essentially, neoclassicism[5] was a system of appropriateness; its rules were designed to prescribe what each art can do and how it must do it. Neoclassicists taught that art is a science, capable of discovering objective standards of beauty; that it is moral, designed to improve, as it entertains, the public; that it is dignified, eschewing the vulgar; that it is natural, striving for verisimilitude. This last demand, for the natural, introduced complications. Like the ancients, seventeenth-century critics held that art is mimesis—imitation—but this did

[4] Quoted in Peter France and Margaret McGowan, "Louis XIV and the Arts," in John Cruickshank, ed., *French Literature and Its Background,* vol. II, *The Seventeenth Century* (1969), 85.

[5] It took its name from its origins: its precepts went back to the aesthetic writings of Aristotle and Horace.

not mean plain realism. It meant an idealization and purification of nature—not as we see it around us in individual, imperfect specimens, but as we can glimpse it by long practice and the contemplation of the most beautiful objects we can find. That had been the way, the neoclassicists said, of the ancient Greek sculptors and playwrights; modern men could do no better than to follow them. The whole machinery of neoclassical rules was a logical consequence of these fundamental precepts. Playwrights must observe the three unities of time, place, and action because this lends the play verisimilitude. Paintings have their place in a hierarchy of dignity: historical paintings, with their depiction of heroic postures and exemplary actions, are at the top of that hierarchy; still lifes, with their humble subject matter, are at the bottom; portraits rise in stature as they aspire to universality. Playwrights and poets must work within a single genre: to introduce comic scenes into tragedies (as Shakespeare had done with the gravedigger's scene in *Hamlet*) or common speech into elevated dramas (as Shakespeare had done in play after play) was to fall into barbarism. From this point of view, the paintings of Poussin, with their crowded but orderly scenes from classical mythology or sacred history, calmly posed, their postures copied from antique sculptures, were neoclassicism to perfection.

Not all neoclassicists avoided controversy: Pierre Corneille established his reputation and started a famous quarrel with *Le Cid* in 1637; as his critics pointed out, the play was far too crowded to stay within the "proper" span— one day—and permitted more vehement action on stage than neoclassical doctrine countenanced. In the great tragedies that followed in rapid succession—*Horace, Cinna,* and *Polyeucte*—Corneille accordingly worked more closely within the accepted canon. In these early plays, and in the plays he wrote during the reign of Louis XIV, Corneille populated the stage with outsized heroes who defy, or seek to remake, their world, and who fail, if they fail, with superb nobility. Corneille was not simply an aristocratic moralist anatomizing the trials of ambition; he was above all a dramatist whose announced purpose was to astound and dazzle his audience with the tension of his action and the virtuosity of his language. Jean Racine, Corneille's successor and only rival in the tragic genre, pursued the same ends with similar means. Worldling, courtier, royal historian, and in his last years, devout Jansenist,[6] Racine, like Corneille before him, drew his themes from ancient history, classical myths, and the Old Testament. Like Corneille, too, Racine explicitly aimed to please his audience and to move them, but he achieved these dramatic aims by strictly obeying the canons of neoclassicism. The plots of his plays are notable for their simplicity; all is subordinated to the clash of great passions among, and within, his magnificent personages. His language is elevated: it is rare that a speaker will break away from the measured rhythms of his alexandrines. The emotions Racine portrays—love, ambition, conflict between inclination and duty—are at once elemental and universal, but the elevation of his dramatic style makes his tragedies more than simply psychological dramas;

[6] For the Jansenists, see p. 305.

they are, as critics have often noted, ritual occasions. Yet the tensions are there, all the greater for being concealed under decorous speech. To portray the stirring of passionate, almost unbearably intense life beneath a formal rational surface was the contribution of neoclassicism to literature and the arts. In his *Phèdre* of 1677, among Racine's most famous plays, he follows the doomed guilty love of the queen, Phèdre, for her stepson, Hippolyte, through to its terrible end—an end that has been implicit from the opening scene. Like Corneille, Racine was interested less in surprising his audiences than in making them witness the gradual unfolding of a human destiny.

Racine lived on to 1699, through the grim middle years of Louis' reign. Molière, the comic genius of the age, died young, in 1673, when the reputation of the king for whom he poured out his productions was still untarnished. Molière's plays are a rogue's gallery that portray, not merely types he saw around him, but universal human foibles: miserliness, hypocrisy, snobbery, hypochondria. Not unexpectedly, his victims—or those who chose to see themselves victimized—were furious. At least one of his plays, *Tartuffe* (first version, 1664), in which a religious impostor nearly ruins a credulous family, precipitated him into a quarrel that went beyond the theater; the young Louis XIV, intent on asserting his ascendancy over the church in France, defended Molière against the charge of blasphemy. Molière's genius made him more than the scourge of obvious targets; his plays are brilliantly developed dramatic entities, and his language—the quick turns of phrase, and above all, the repetitions he used to immense comic effect—remains unsurpassed. And Molière's vision, though comic, is complex: many have read his *Misanthrope* as pouring ridicule on a young nobleman who seeks sincerity and, failing to find it in high society, decides to flee to a desert island. Actually, the play is a debate among three incompatible points of view: demanding honesty, pliant sociability, and mature, if lax, common sense. Molière leaves the solution open. Even under Louis XIV, the arts did not teach a single message.

Jean Baptiste Colbert: The Perfect Mercantilist

It was different, of course, in the economic sphere. There, Louis XIV's grand design was perfectly obvious. Fortunately for himself, he had the services of Colbert. Born in 1619 into a merchant family, Jean Baptiste Colbert had entered the royal service early, had impressed Mazarin and been bequeathed to Louis XIV, who rapidly gave him post after post. In 1661, he took Fouquet's post but not his title; in 1664, he became superintendent of buildings; in 1665, he was officially named controller general of finance; in 1668, secretary of state for the navy—critical offices all. French finances were in grave disarray: a quarter century of war and the ruinous financial policies of Mazarin had left their toll. The king's building program, far from a mere private hobby, was central to his search for glory and reputation—and fabulously expensive. And the French navy needed to be increased enormously and improved if France was to compete with her greatest rivals, the seafaring Dutch and English. Colbert set about his many tasks with obsessive, almost legendary energy. But he was not an innovator. His fiscal expedients for raising ever more money from a restive populace and a spoiled aristocracy; his founding of monopolistic companies to exploit the West and East Indies and the Baltic Sea; his attempts to control the quality of manufactured goods and encourage the output of new industries; his programs for improving communications by building roads and canals, went back to Richelieu and beyond him, into the sixteenth century. The "isms" that have been foisted onto Colbert—"mercantilism" and "Colbertism"—are post-humous, undeserved honors. True, Colbert was the most consistent and systematic mercantilist in history; he has been called "perhaps the only true 'mercantilist' who ever lived."[7] But even for Colbert, mercantilism was little more than a loose collection of economic policies, tied together, if at all, by certain fundamental assumptions about economic life in a system of competing states and in a condition of scarcity. The assumptions were that growth in one state required decline in other states and that economic activity was, therefore (like diplomacy), war carried on by peaceful means. Indeed, Colbert said so explicitly, as did other students of economic affairs in his time: "All trade," Colbert's English contemporary, Sir Josiah Child, declared, "is a kind of warfare."[8] This warfare drove states to strive for what was significantly called "a favorable balance of trade"—an excess of exports over imports—by giving bounties to the former, by placing crippling tariffs on the latter, and by hoarding bullion; to put restrictions on the emigration of skilled craftsmen; to superintend the quality of goods and the training of those who made them; to encourage the growth of population; to foster domestic shipping. One implication of these policies was that while prosperity is desirable partly for its own sake, its fundamental importance—at least from the statesman's point of view—is that it serves and enhances political power. As long as profits and power coincided, there was no difficulty; when they clashed, profits must give way. Another implication, more elusive, is this: the policies that go under the names of Colbertism or mercantilism are a search for strength, not its expression. They betoken weakness and recession.[9]

For a decade or so, Colbertism was a success. Like his king and master, Colbert was everywhere. He read, he planned, he composed endless memoranda, for himself and for Louis XIV. He began by saving money: he abolished sinecures, tightened the collection of taxes, investigated false claims to nobility and thus tax exemption, improved the management of the royal estates, and

---

[7] By D. C. Coleman, "Economic Problems and Policies," in *The New Cambridge Modern History,* vol. V (1961), 46.

[8] Quoted in William Letwin, *The Origins of Scientific Economics* (1963), 44.

[9] For this point, see F. J. Fisher, "16th–17th Centuries: The Dark Age in English Economic History?" *Economica,* new series, 24 (Feb. 1957), 2–18.

squeezed more money out of the privileged provinces and the clergy by inducing them to increase their "voluntary donations." Partly for purely economic reasons (to decrease the need for imports), partly for reasons of state (to increase the show of royal magnificence), he founded new luxury industries and new trading companies. And he moved rapidly: in 1664, he was instrumental in the establishment of the royal tapestry works at Beauvais, founded the East and West India companies, and began simplification of the immensely complex internal tariff structure of France. In 1665, he laid plans for a great canal, the *canal des deux mers,* to link the Mediterranean with the Atlantic. In 1666 he set down new regulations concerning manufactures. In 1667, he converted the Gobelin tapestry works, which he had taken over five years before, into a royal factory; showing what he meant by saying that trade was a species of war, he imposed new high tariffs directed mainly against English and Dutch cloth merchants. He brought in Venetian glassmakers and Flemish clothmakers; he protected the silk industry at Lyons and encouraged iron foundries; he set the port cities of Brest and Toulon humming with activity, building docks and shipyards.

If one judges simply by intentions, this was a decade of unparalleled economic achievement, based on a program of unmatched rationality. But intentions count for little in history. Colbert could decree regulations, establish monopolies, and multiply formulas for apprenticeship or workmanship, but the temper of the country was not on his side. His attempts to rationalize the tax structure, even though they would strike a modern reader as mild indeed, offended powerful vested interests; his tariffs benefited some and hurt others; his regulations were strange to many and, despite all the efforts of his officials, relatively easy to evade. Besides, his policies had a severely restricted goal: to make his king more magnificent and more powerful than any other king anywhere in Europe or, perhaps, in history. Such a policy could wholly delight only a few men—the king himself and those of his subjects, like Colbert, who identified their interests and their welfare with those of Louis XIV. Still, Colbert's achievement in these years was impressive, if only as an effort to counteract the depression that was gripping the country. Then, in 1672, with the great French assault on Holland and the beginning of decades of war, Colbert's policy was wrecked completely. He had formulated it at least in part to make war possible; he had, indeed, enthusiastically supported Louis' early military ventures in 1667. But when war became large-scale and long-lasting, as it did from 1672 on, the paradox built into Colbertism emerged into the light of day: the aggressive policies for whose sake it had been devised were also its nemesis.

LOUIS XIV AT WAR: 1667-1685

War Abroad: The Rectification of Frontiers

Louis' unremitting search for glory was a psychological need with military consequences. It was not that he was ambitious; every self-respecting prince longed to increase his prestige and enlarge his domains. But Louis XIV wanted hegemony over Europe, an aspiration that did not lend itself readily to compromise. It was the unmeasured quality of his desires that brought into being those great coalitions against France—coalitions even he could not defeat. Louis XIV enjoyed humbling foreign ambassadors, compelling smaller powers to send envoys to France and apologize for "insults." That was easy enough. But Louis XIV was after larger game than the Genoese Republic or the Papal States. He hoped to grab Spanish possessions, taking advantage of Spain's obvious military weakness. There has been an inconclusive debate among historians whether the French king and his advisors had a consistent vision of French "natural frontiers" on the Rhine, the Atlantic, and the Pyrenees. But even if his policy did not have the clarity of a vision, as soon as he had mastered the administrative apparatus and had unmistakably taken power, Louis XIV strove to extend French borders by all means at his command.

The diplomatic and the military situations were favorable. England under Charles II was in France's pay. The German princes, including Brandenburg, were France's dependents. And in September 1665, King Philip IV of Spain died, leaving a sickly four-year-old heir and a sprawling, tempting heritage on France's frontiers. From 1662, Louis' lawyers had been busy finding plausible reasons why the king of France was the true heir to most of these territories. In May 1667, Louis was ready; his troops moved east into Franche-Comté and north into the Spanish Netherlands. The War of Devolution had begun. [10]

For a while, it went well, Louis' fine commanders—Turenne in the Netherlands, the great Condé in Franche-Comté—swept all before them. But Louis was frustrated by the joint effort of the Dutch, the English, and the Swedes. To his fury, the Dutch, a mere nation of shopkeepers and simple

---

[10] The war takes its name from the efforts of Louis' lawyers. Seeking to substantiate his flimsy claim to Spanish territory, these lawyers managed to dredge up the "right of devolution," according to which the private possessions of the Spanish crown, which included the territories Louis XIV had invaded, could be passed on only through the children of a first marriage. While Maria Theresa had renounced her inheritance upon marrying the young king of France, Louis' lawyers argued that this renunciation was invalid since the Spaniards had never paid Maria Theresa's dowry. The whole business shows the anxiety with which the greediest of rulers tried to find at least shreds of legal justification for naked aggression.

republicans, had laid aside a war with England to protect their southern borders by engineering this Triple Alliance. In May 1668, at Aix-la-Chapelle, the belligerents made peace. Louis XIV obtained twelve strongholds on the frontiers of the Spanish Netherlands, including Lille, but he restored Franche-Comté to its Spanish owners. Everyone knew the peace was only a truce. The Sun King would not rest content with such meager rewards.

Louis XIV's second war lasted longer, from 1672 to 1678, and had more serious consequences both abroad and at home. Again private motives shaped public policy. Louis XIV could not forgive the Dutch for their role in the War of Devolution. The Dutch War was to be their chastisement. But Louis was not governed by emotion alone; he had meticulously laid the ground for war by breaking up the Triple Alliance. He bribed the Swedes, "senator by senator," [11] to desert their allies. He made secret arrangements with King Charles II of England at the Treaty of Dover in May 1670. He bought support and troops from German princes. In late March 1672, Charles II of England declared war on the Dutch; in early April, French troops moved into Dutch territory. For a time, domestic discord kept the Dutch from countering the danger, and in June they sent an embassy to Louis XIV offering peace at the expense of the terrain they had already lost and of heavy indemnities. Louis, self-confident to the point of megalomania, made counterdemands so vast and so insulting that the Dutch could only break off negotiations. Beaten as they felt themselves to be, and despite some counsels of despair, they would not give up half their lands, grant the French exorbitant commercial privileges, permit Catholics freedom of worship, and annually humble themselves in solemn ceremonies at Paris. True, the United Provinces were deeply disunited. In August 1672, an excited crowd murdered Jan de Witt, the grand pensionary of Holland, and his brother Cornelius, both firm advocates of resistance to France. The consequence of this mob action was to bring to undisputed command William III, prince of Orange, the most implacable enemy Louis XIV was to face. William gathered authority in his hands and continued the de Witt policy. By 1674, he had made peace with England and cemented the First Coalition, which included the emperor, Brandenburg, Spain, and the duke of Lorraine. One fruit of his policy, which was to be of transcendent importance later, was his arrangement with Charles II to marry the English king's niece, Mary.

For some years the fortunes of war seesawed. In 1675, Turenne was killed in battle; the French navy acquitted itself remarkably well—Colbert's preparatory labors had not been in vain. But by 1678 it was clear that no side could hope for a decisive victory, and negotiations began. They resulted in the Treaties of Nimwegen, signed by the separate belligerents in 1678 and 1679. Dutch territory was integrally preserved, but Franche-Comté, so much coveted by France, finally fell to Louis XIV. In other complicated arrangements, France and Spain exchanged strongholds, but France got the better of the bargain. By

---

[11] Goubert, *Louis XIV*, 112.

1679, French territory to the north and east was rounded out and strengthened by the addition of fortified towns.

The high point of Louis XIV's reign had been reached and passed, but there were no indications that he, or anyone else, knew it. French expansion continued, and once again legal subterfuge assisted territorial greed. Nimwegen had shown Louis to be less than omnipotent, but at the same time, Spain and the empire were proved almost wholly impotent. The provinces of Alsace and Lorraine, strategically located on France's frontiers to the east and providing access to the Rhine, were ideal subjects for obfuscation and victimization. They consisted of numerous towns and small regions, all standing in complicated feudal relationships to the emperor and to various monarchs. The Treaties of Westphalia, which had settled the Thirty Years' War (see p. 255), only compounded the confusion. Louis perceived the possibilities, and in 1679 he set up four special courts, the *chambres de réunion,* which examined French claims to these desirable lands and, not unexpectedly, found them valid in case after case. Armed with this feeble excuse, French troops through the next four years peacefully annexed Alsace, Lorraine, and some surrounding territories. In 1681, Louis made the most important of these conquests—he moved into the free city of Strasbourg. While German princes and the emperor, either bribed or powerless, were silent as the king of France rounded out his northeastern frontiers, the capture of Protestant Strasbourg, to which he had no right at all, aroused widespread and outraged protests. In vain. In 1684, Louis XIV and the emperor concluded a Twenty Years' Truce at Regensburg, which confirmed French acquisitions, including that of Strasbourg. The truce opened prospects of peace, but meanwhile, at home, Louis XIV was engaging in policies that could only end in renewed war.

War at Home: The Imposition of Religious Uniformity

Like all rulers, Louis XIV found domestic and foreign policy inextricably intertwined. Colbert, as we have seen, discovered that war ruined his most carefully laid plans to rescue the finances of the state. In turn, domestic uprisings diverted troops from duty at the front to duty against French subjects: in 1675, in the midst of the Dutch War, "some of the king's troops had to be spared to carry murder and pillage to the inhabitants of lower Brittany and Rennes who were in violent rebellion against taxes and nobility alike." It took a winter to restore order. Then, "having hanged a few thousands of his subjects, the king was able to send back his troops to face the members of the coalition."[12] Precisely in the same way, foreign policy would both affect, and be affected by, Louis' religious policy. The king's own religious convictions remain somewhat obscure; it seems likely that, as he grew older, he retreated from a

12 Ibid., 135.

certain measure of libertinism to a certain measure of piety. After he moved to Versailles in 1682, the elaborate festivities of his younger years gave way to a more solemn and more boring routine, and he increasingly surrounded himself with *dévots*. The favorite royal mistress of his later years, the widow Scarron, whom he created Madame de Maintenon and probably married in secret after the death of Maria Theresa, was both extremely pious and extremely influential. But whatever his private persuasion might have been, through all his reign he fully intended to be master over all spheres of public life, and that included religion. This intention brought him into intermittent, embittered conflict with the Jansenists, the papacy, the Huguenots—and Europe.

In essence, the Jansenists were Augustinians—serious Catholics who derived their theology from St. Augustine's pessimistic appraisal of man's nature and possibilities. The derisive epithet their enemies applied to them— "Calvinists who go to mass"—though harshly denying them the status of loyal Catholics, aptly captures their severity. The Jesuits and other "relaxed" Catholics of the day were preaching that man plays an active part in securing his salvation; this was not merely far more cheerful than Augustine's doctrine of human corruption and powerlessness, but it also implied what the Jansenists strenuously denied: that all men might be saved. Cornelis Jansen, after whom this French movement was named, was an unimpeachably orthodox Catholic theologian, a professor at Louvain who had died in 1638, as bishop of Ypres. Two years after his death, his lifework, *Augustinus,* appeared, and it restated Augustine's austere position on grace without any mitigation. In the following year, in 1641, the book appeared in Paris, to be taken up by Jansen's friend, Jean Duvergier de Hauranne, abbé of Saint Cyran (he is known as Saint Cyran) and Antoine Arnauld, head of a large and distinguished clan of theologians and ecclesiastical administrators. Saint Cyran went to the convent of Port Royal des Champs, outside Paris, as confessor and found a ready supporter there in Angélique Arnauld, the mother superior, Antoine Arnauld's sister. It was Antoine who precipitated the great controversy in 1643, with his *Concerning Frequent Communion;* the Jesuits, quite rightly, thought this highly offensive polemic aimed at them. The book excoriated priests who winked at worldliness as long as lapses were confessed and "purified" by frequent communion.

The Jesuits had the ear of the papacy, and in 1653 Pope Innocent X condemned in detail five propositions of the Jansenists. They were indeed imprudent in the extreme: the Jansenists argued that it was heretical to assert that man cooperates in achieving grace and that Christ died for all men. But these assertions, the pope countered, were perfectly orthodox. His condemnation placed the Jansenists in a terrifying quandary. Whatever their enemies might say, they were not Calvinists; they wanted to continue enjoying the right to go to mass. So they prevaricated: they humbly agreed with the pope that the five propositions he found objectionable and heretical were indeed both, but they submitted, just as humbly, that *Augustinus* actually did not contain them. This was sheer sophistry, but it was the sophistry of troubled, even desperate men.

In January 1656, Antoine Arnauld was expelled from the faculty of theology at the Sorbonne, and the Jansenists moved from defense to attack. In the same year the brilliant mathematician Blaise Pascal, who had come to Port Royal the year before, published his *Provincial Letters* in Arnauld's defense. They are a savage, telling, and at the same time, amusing attack on Jesuit beliefs and practices—they still make good reading today. But they are not a wholly candid performance: Pascal took the Jesuits' casuistry as expressing their true convictions. Casuistry is a legalistic game, the setting up of hypothetical situations for the sake of examining all eventualities, thus to clarify the muddy region between honest error and mortal sin. True, the Jesuits were sometimes guilty of abusing casuistry in behalf of their highly placed penitents, but Pascal's charge that the Jesuits condoned lying, adultery, and murder, and degraded religion into the observance of empty forms, was hardly justified.

This was the position in 1661, when Louis XIV assumed personal power. The Jansenists were not prospering. Angélique Arnauld died that year, Pascal died in 1662, and the young king was hostile to Jansenism in spite of, and partly because of, its influential supporters. The nuns at Port Royal were subjected to harassment. But other countervailing forces were at work. Eager to assert his authority not merely over France but over all Europe, Louis XIV found himself in a pronounced antipapal mood for over twenty years. And the Jansenists, being anti-Jesuit and thus hostile to ultramontane tendencies, found themselves taken up by the robe nobility of the French parlements. It was as part of this Gallican phase that the Jansenists survived. Jansenist writings appeared in rapid succession: Pascal had compiled voluminous notes for a comprehensive "apology" for Christianity; he had never completed his work, but in 1670 the first edition of his *Pensées* appeared; they explore in lucid, memorable aphorisms man's lost condition after his fall from grace. Then came the writings of Saint Cyran, of Antoine Arnauld, and others, all serious, all Augustinian in doctrine, all, it seemed, superior in style and argumentation to the more relaxed view of their opponents. Louis, meanwhile, left the Jansenists alone while he perfected his version of Gallicanism—that old doctrine (see p. 100) of royal independence from Rome, especially in the appointing power. In the 1670s, the king claimed the right to nominate to certain benefices and certain convents, as well as the right to collect the income from vacant sees all across France, without regard to ancient exemptions. In 1678, Pope Innocent XI, as courageous as his redoubtable adversary, vigorously censured Louis' policies, and in the years that followed he threatened the Sun King with reprisals. This was too much. Employing subservient bishops for the purpose, Louis XIV in 1682 countered the papal threat with four articles, which asserted the king's freedom from ecclesiastical (even papal) jurisdiction in secular matters; the supremacy of general councils over the papacy; the superiority of French law in regulating relations between the Holy See at Rome and the French state; and the need to obtain universal assent to make papal decrees binding. This was strong language, and schism seemed a possibility. But neither the pope nor the French king had any intention of bringing matters to a breach. Innocent XI died in

1689, and his successors found ways to settle the matter peaceably; by 1693, the Gallican articles had been withdrawn, Louis XIV had declared his sympathies with Rome, and the persecution of the Jansenists resumed. [13]

Like the Jansenists, the Huguenots found their fate bound up with events abroad. Louis, in search of uniformity, had little use for the Protestants in his realm. At first he had forsworn the use of violence and instead offered to reward converts to the true faith, but by 1669 there were signs that he was getting ready to revoke the Edict of Nantes (see p. 181) under whose protection the Huguenots continued to shelter. Only his alliances with Protestant princes induced him to wait. Then, beginning around 1679-1680, a combination of circumstances (still incompletely unraveled) allowed him to wait no longer. Colbert, who valued the industrial and commercial skills of the Protestant minority, and especially the Huguenot bankers, found himself increasingly bypassed, as Louis XIV listened more and more to Louvois, [14] who was far more militant at home, and far more aggressive abroad, than Colbert had ever been. Then, in 1683, Colbert died, and this too helped to loose the dogs of persecution in France. These were the years when the king grew more solemn in his religious observances and listened to Madame de Maintenon and to his Jesuit confessors. And abroad all was going well, if not quite so well as Louis had privately hoped. The motives that had held him back, then, no longer operated.

The campaign to eradicate Protestantism from French soil began in all seriousness in 1679 and gained further momentum in 1681. More forceful methods than paid conversions gained in favor. The chief means of pressure were the so-called *dragonnades*—the quartering of dragoons on unwilling Huguenot families, an inconvenience (to put it mildly) that procured thousands of hasty conversions. By 1684, nearly six hundred out of about eight hundred Huguenot churches were closed. Then, in October 1685, the king officially revoked the Edict of Nantes and forbade Huguenots to exercise their faith, to educate their children as Protestants, and to leave the country. The repression was effective, backed up as it was by the demolition of churches, the kidnapping of children, and the expulsion of Huguenots from strategic cities like Paris. The prohibition on emigration failed: of the more than one million Huguenots in France, many went underground at home, but over two hundred thousand left the country to find shelter in hospitable places elsewhere— mainly in England, in the Dutch Republic, and in Brandenburg. The émigrés took with them rare skills and a great anger. The revocation was one of Louis' greatest mistakes. It strengthened France's enemies at its direct expense, united

[13] To anticipate: in a series of bulls, notably *Unigenitus* of 1713, the papacy continued its campaign against Jansenist teachings; in France itself, Louis XIV attacked the Jansenists directly. In 1708, Port Royal des Champs was officially suppressed; in 1709, the remaining nuns were expelled; in 1710, the buildings were razed and the graves of distinguished Jansenists desecrated. The Paris foundation suffered the same fate.

[14] François-Michel le Tellier, marquis de Louvois, son of the trusted Le Tellier on whom Louis XIV had relied at the beginning of his reign.

Europe against Louis XIV, and helped to precipitate a revolution in England and turn England into a formidable adversary.

ENGLAND: THE UNEXPECTED ENEMY

From Restoration to Revolution

The transformation of England from a dependent into an enemy was a disconcerting turn of events for Louis XIV. England under Charles II was once more a second-rate power. The rousing mobilization of national energies that had animated the country under Cromwell had come to an abrupt end with the Restoration; the austerity imposed by the Puritans was relaxed. Charles II was ideally suited to lead the country in this cheerful direction: he was witty, charming, tolerant, given to science, mistresses, and bawdy plays. The sonorous Milton was famous, but in retirement. Restoration comedies, with their cynicism, their polish, and their sensuality, accurately reflected both the royal taste and a widespread thirst for a less strenuous mode of living. One victim of the new style was Cromwell's vigorous foreign policy. To make doubly sure of English subservience, Louis XIV did his utmost to put, and keep, Charles II in France's pocket with subsidies and promises. Several times during his reign, Charles was bribed to countenance and even to support Louis' quest for hegemony. But kings, like other blackmailers, do not stay bought: Charles II proved an expensive and not wholly trustworthy ally. After all, he had to reckon with powerful anti-Catholic, anti-French sentiments in his own country. Still, he was more of a help to Louis XIV than an obstacle. Then, in 1685, when Charles II was succeeded by his Roman Catholic brother, James II, the new king immediately asked Louis XIV for money. It looked as if the cordial arrangement between France and England would continue.

But other forces were at work within English society. The Puritan legacy could not be liquidated and would not be denied. The Restoration, as we have seen (p. 281), did not restore the old monarchy, but gave Parliament a continuous, influential voice in public affairs, and by converting the source of the king's income from traditional feudal dues to modern forms of taxation, took yet another step toward the modern state, away from the old conception of the king as the country's greatest feudal landlord. Even more important, the Puritan religious impulse remained a vital force in the country, even in the restored Church of England. The conflicts that marked Charles' long reign mainly erupted over religious issues. Charles II was not only not a Puritan—that was scandalously evident to all—he was, if he was anything at all, a crypto-Catholic. And he was surrounded by Catholics: His brother James, duke of York, converted to the Roman persuasion around 1668; his queen, Catherine of

Braganza, whom he married in 1662, had been born into it. His foreign policy (though the Dutch Wars were largely wars over trade) certainly showed no hostility to Catholic powers. And his religious policy, though devious, appeared calculated to strengthen Catholicism in a country that by and large had hated and feared Catholics for a century.

Charles' divergence from dominant ways of English thinking impelled him into some adroit political maneuverings. The king had spent his youth in exile and, as he later said to his impetuous younger brother, the duke of York: "I am too old to go again to my travels: you may, if you choose it." The elections of 1661 gave Charles a loyal but not wholly pliant parliament; it was filled with staunch Anglicans and equally staunch royalists—its nickname, Cavalier Parliament, was not undeserved. [15] But Parliament's loyalty to the restored monarchy was aggressive, almost embarrassing, and its Anglicanism was accompanied by vindictiveness against Puritans. For four years, this Cavalier Parliament enacted stringent legislation against the Puritan sectaries. Proposals to establish a comprehensive English Protestant church that would at least include Presbyterians were shunted aside with impatience. The Corporation Act of 1661 excluded from municipal office all who did not belong to the Anglican communion or refused to swear an oath of nonresistance to the king. In 1662 an Act of Uniformity drove from their livings all those clergymen who would not use the newly revised Book of Common Prayer. In 1664, the Conventicle Act prohibited religious meetings of more than five persons. Finally, the Five Mile Act of 1665 imposed on all preachers who had not sworn to the Act of Uniformity a new oath of nonresistance and loyalty, and prohibited those who refused to come within five miles of any incorporated town. With this legislation—known, somewhat inaccurately, as the Clarendon Code [16]—the Cavalier Parliament made the split between Anglicans and Puritan Dissenters official and created English Nonconformity. In abandoning the old idea of "comprehension" in a single, truly national church, it at once legalized and disfranchised Dissent and drove a wedge between Englishmen that would shape English history for two centuries.

Charles had other ideas, and the emergence of Nonconformity gave him an opportunity to seek toleration for Catholics by linking their cause to that of the Dissenters. He failed. In 1662, he tried to suspend the Act of Uniformity and issued a Declaration of Indulgence offering to suspend the operation of the laws against Dissenters. Bishops and Parliament together persuaded him to desist. In 1672, he tried again; in his second Declaration of Indulgence, he declared the suspension of "all and all manner of penal laws in matters ecclesiastical against

---

[15] It also has another nickname: Pension Parliament. Under the management of the earl of Danby, parliamentary corruption became a standard procedure: the crown influenced parliamentary decisions by bribery and the free use of influence.

[16] Edward Hyde, first earl of Clarendon, a distinguished historian and statesman, followed Charles into exile in 1646 and returned in 1660, with the Restoration. For seven years, down to 1667, he was King Charles II's lord chancellor. While Clarendon disliked the stringencies of the laws named after him, he did little to prevent their enactment and loyally enforced them.

whatsoever sort of nonconformists and recusants." But then, early in 1673, Parliament induced him to drop the declaration by offering, in return, a grant of money for the Dutch War then under way. To drive its meaning home, Parliament then passed the Test Act, which specified that Anglicans alone— only those, that is, who took the sacraments according to the rites prescribed by the Church of England—could hold military or civil office. The king's brother James, duke of York, who had been a capable lord high admiral, had to hand in his resignation. This parliamentary victory in no way appeased the religious troubles; victories rarely make the victors content. In September 1673, the duke of York married Mary of Modena, like him a Catholic. Here was a terrible danger to Reformed England. James' first wife had given him two daughters, Mary and Anne. Both were raised as Protestants, both were destined to be queens of England. But in 1673, no one could foresee that: all that seemed obvious, and ominous, was that King Charles II and his queen were not going to have an heir, and that James and his new wife were likely to produce Charles' successor. Englishmen—Nonconformists as much as Anglicans—shuddered at the thought. Charles' evident capacity to govern without parliamentary subventions, at least in times of peace, only fueled the general suspicion. In 1678, suspicion was turned into hysteria by the bizarre Popish Plot. It was completely imaginary, the brainchild of an utterly convincing and utterly unprincipled Anglican cleric named Titus Oates. According to Oates and his associate, Israel Tonge, the Jesuits planned to assassinate King Charles, murder leading Protestants, and put Catholic James on the throne of England. Fortunately for their fiction, a London magistrate named Godfrey, who had heard the charges, was found dead under melodramatic circumstances. To heated imaginations nothing could be more clear-cut: the Jesuits had murdered Godfrey to silence him. Hysteria now burst all bounds. Parliament met in October 1678. This was to be the last session of Charles' Long Parliament—still loyal, but more loyal to the principle of the Protestant succession than to the whims of Charles and his dangerous brother. It unanimously passed a resolution declaring that "there hath been, and still is, a damnable and hellish Plot, contrived and carried on by the Popish recusants for the assassinating and murdering the King, and for subverting the government, and rooting out and destroying the Protestant religion." [17] It impeached Danby, the king's chief minister, for his secret correspondence with the French, and forced his dismissal and imprisonment. It passed an act excluding all papists from both Houses—the duke of York alone excepted. It consigned five Catholic peers to the Tower. It created and exacerbated an atmosphere in which perhaps two score innocent or merely indiscreet persons were executed for "treason."

Persuasive charlatans can do much; their role in history is impressive. Parliament acted entirely under the impress of Oates' impudent charges. And Oates did more. By embittering the already serious divisions within the English

[17] Quoted in J. R. Tanner, *English Constitutional Conflicts of the Seventeenth Century, 1603-1689* (1962), 239.

political public, Oates and his Popish Plot spurred the growth of English parties. The Whigs, speaking broadly, were intent on securing a Protestant succession; they were opposed to what they called "the French interest," and harped much on the English constitution. The Tories, for their part, were diehard loyalists, ready to swallow a pro-French policy, and even a Catholic on the throne, for the sake of stability. [18]

In 1679, the Whigs, under the able leadership of the earl of Shaftesbury, brought in an Exclusion Bill that explicitly denied the succession to the duke of York. This became the great goal of the opposition and the leading theme of parliamentary rhetoric in the two years that followed. To save the throne for his brother, Charles II dissolved Parliament early in 1679. Three parliaments followed in rapid succession; each brought up the Exclusion Bill, and each was accordingly dissolved. From March 1681 on, Charles II ruled without Parliament. He had subsidies from France, and beginning in 1682, a royalist reaction on his side. In that year a confused medley of plots, mainly invented but some real enough, gave the king his opportunity. He had some potential rebels sent to the block; his brother, who had gone into exile, returned; leading exclusionists found it prudent to leave the country. Among the exiles was the philosopher John Locke. But Charles did not have long to enjoy his triumphs; he had the pleasure of seeing Oates exposed and in prison, but in February 1685, he died, a Catholic on his deathbed. James succeeded him, fulfilling, indeed exceeding, the worst premonitions of his worst enemies.

At first all went well for the king. James freed the imprisoned peers and took further revenge on Oates and his friends. His Parliament was royalist, patient, and generous. Events helped: in May 1685, the earl of Argyll invaded Scotland; in June, the duke of Monmouth, an illegitimate son of Charles II and a great favorite with the Protestant opposition, landed in western England. This double rebellion rallied the political leadership around James. Argyll was easily beaten in June, taken, and executed. Monmouth was beaten, just as easily, at Sedgmoor, in July. His royal parentage did not save him—he too was executed, and his followers were decimated in the following months with signal brutality by the notorious Jeffreys, lord chief justice, in the Bloody Assizes. James' throne seemed beyond challenge.

But the king rapidly wasted the capital of good will on which an English monarch—*any* monarch—could draw after the unsettling decades of civil war and commonwealth. And Louis XIV powerfully aided the opposition to James with his increasingly ruthless persecution of the French Huguenots. When he officially revoked the Edict of Nantes in October 1685, he gave troubled

---

[18] Like most party names, these were first words of abuse. "Whig" meant a Scottish Presbyterian outlaw; "Tory" an Irish Catholic bandit. More important than these etymologies is the recognition that these "parties" had almost nothing in common with the modern English party system. They were not disciplined; they were shifting alliances, often rather strange, and their class base was far from clear. While on the whole the Whigs were hospitable to Dissenters and urban merchants, the Tories drew heavily on country squires and Anglican clergymen. But this division was neither firm nor final (see p. 383).

Englishmen much to think about. James' ostentatious piety was annoying, but what mattered more was his public policy. For three years, continuously, impatiently, he did everything he could to remind his subjects that they were not far from Continental despotism, that even the old religious settlement going back to Queen Elizabeth was not safe. He called for repeal of the Clarendon Code to relieve the Dissenters and of the Test Acts to relieve the Catholics. He packed the army, the navy, the public service, and the universities with Roman Catholics, in open and repeated defiance of the law. He was clearly dominated by Roman Catholic advisors. In the face of parliamentary uneasiness, he kept troops stationed around London. In April 1687, he issued his first Declaration of Indulgence, much like his brother's declaration of 1672. A year later, he returned with a second declaration and ordered it read in all churches. Most Anglican clerics, though used to obedience, disobeyed. In addition, Sancroft, the archbishop of Canterbury, and six other bishops remonstrated with him and were sent to the Tower. Late in June, they were tried for seditious libel. It was a decisive trial in English history. On June 30, the seven bishops were acquitted. Revolution was now only a matter of time and of detail.

From the Glorious Revolution to the Grand Coalition

The causes of the Glorious Revolution are transparent. James' policies were tactlessness carried to the point of self-destructive mania. In three years the king had managed to offend and frighten nearly all Englishmen; the Catholics alone were grateful for his attentions. The Dissenters did not value what he planned to do for them. The Whigs saw him as a despot on the model of Louis XIV or Bloody Mary. Even the Tories and the High Anglicans, who were among the most patient of Englishmen, turned against this high-handed autocrat. But the immediate cause of the Glorious Revolution was, quite simply, the birth of a child. In June 1688 Mary of Modena finally had a son. "In the seventeenth century," G. N. Clark comments, "people would believe anything. The Catholics thought it was a miracle and the Protestants said it was an imposture. It was neither." [19] Whatever it was, it was too much. In July, seven distinguished Englishmen, including the old royal servant Danby, calmly invited William of Orange to invade England. William quickly accepted. Late in the summer, James II suddenly veered about; he restored some suspended officials, clerics, and university fellows, promised to call Parliament, and made other concessions—too late. In November, with a favorable wind, William landed at Torbay on the south coast and found the country with him. James II, his queen, and their baby escaped to France.

It was a bloodless invasion; the only victims were the king, his family and friends, and the four hundred or so "nonjurors"—Anglican clerics who refused to swear allegiance to the usurper. But these victims lost only their posts, not

[19] The Later Stuarts, 1660–1714 (1934), 121.

their lives. In January 1689, a Convention Parliament legalized this Glorious Revolution; it found James guilty of having tried to subvert the constitution "by breaking the original contract between king and people," and, in violation of all constitutional logic, it declared the throne vacant. By February, William and Mary were installed jointly as king and queen of England. Mary died not long after, in 1694, and Dutch William reigned alone until his death in 1702. But in their relatively brief reign a political and religious settlement was patched together that set the stage for the rule of the English oligarchy, with all its grave flaws the most progressive and most widely admired regime of eighteenth-century Europe (see p. 348). In early 1689, Parliament issued the Declaration of Rights and tied it to its offer of joint kingship. The declaration insisted on the right of Parliament to make and unmake all laws. This meant that the royal power to suspend laws or to dispense with their penalties for favorite individuals was unconstitutional and that all money must be raised with the approval of Parliament. To put teeth into this declaration, Parliament provided that standing armies could be raised only with parliamentary consent, enforced by requiring annual renewal of an act authorizing military discipline; that Parliament had the right to petition the crown; that its elections and debates must be free; and that a new parliament must be elected every three years. (In 1701, the Act of Settlement further spelled out the meaning of the Glorious Revolution; it settled the succession specifically in a Hanoverian princess, Sophia, the Protestant granddaughter of James I, and her descendants, and it generally held Roman Catholics ineligible to take the English crown.) A Toleration Act of 1689 granted the Nonconformists relief from the penalties specified in earlier laws for failure to take the Anglican sacraments—a large step in an atmosphere inflamed by the revocation of the Edict of Nantes, but still far short of the comprehension some Englishmen had hoped for and far short of the civil equality Dissenters wanted.

The intervention of a Dutch prince in the affairs of England underscores the Europe-wide view that dominated William's mind. To be sure, William of Orange had dynastic interests in England: he was the grandson of King Charles I and the son-in-law of King James II. But what mattered most to him was to stop Louis XIV, and he was doubtful just what England under James II might do once France moved its superb war machine into the field. William for years had been in a delicate position and conducted himself circumspectly. From 1687 on, however, he became increasingly anxious to secure English resources in the struggle against Louis' unending search for "reputation." It was a sound calculation. In 1686, William had constructed the League of Augsburg—a coalition against France adhered to by Sweden, the emperor, Spain, the Palatinate (to which Louis XIV, in his usual fashion, was laying claim), and the electors of Bavaria and Saxony. Savoy joined in 1687. Then, in October 1688, while William was making ready to invade England and dethrone his father-in-law, Louis XIV attacked the Rhenish Palatinate, laying it waste, not for the first time. And he declared war on the Dutch. In March 1689, the exiled James

II invaded Ireland, whence he was not expelled until July 1690, after the bloody battle of the Boyne. James' move, which would have been impossible without substantial French support, practically guaranteed English adherence to the League of Augsburg. All Europe was now joined against Louis XIV.

The War of the League of Augsburg raged for eight years, bringing financial troubles to the leading allies, devastation to the invaded territories, and depression, unemployment and famine to France; the years 1693–1694 especially were years of drastically declining births and mounting deaths. Many Frenchmen starved (see p. 292). By 1696 the Grand Coalition had broken up with the defection of Savoy, but general peace was not made until late 1697, at Ryswick. Few were wholly happy with it, but William III had achieved most of his objectives. Louis XIV had been checked. He was compelled to recognize William III as king of England, to promise to cease supporting James II and the Jacobites,[20] and to give up most of the conquests gained from the "reunions," with the exception of territory in Alsace, Strasbourg, and Saarlouis.

Louis XIV's armies had been checked; his appetite had not. One prize had long haunted him, and he had no intention of abandoning it: the crown and the domains of Spain. Spain's Hapsburg king, Charles II, had ascended the throne in 1665, but childless and in perpetual ill health, his endlessly imminent death had been arousing the greedy hopes of several European princes for decades. His putative heirs could hardly wait, although contrary to all expectations, Charles II lived until 1700. Louis XIV had a certain claim to the Spanish inheritance, both as the husband of Charles II's older sister and as the grandson of Philip III. Another claimant was Emperor Leopold I, the Austrian Hapsburg, as husband of Charles II's younger sister and as another grandson of Philip III. A third claimant, the young prince-elector of Bavaria, had a much weaker claim, but he became the beneficiary of a partition treaty, signed in 1698, which divided the Spanish inheritance. Barely alive but alive enough to be piqued at not being consulted, Charles II offered Spain and its empire to the prince-elector, but in 1699 the boy suddenly died, and another, more complex, partition treaty was arranged. At last, on November 1, 1700, Charles II died; his will, insisting that the Spanish dominions be left undivided, made Philip of Anjou, second grandson of Louis XIV, sole heir provided he renounce his claim to the throne of France. After serious consideration, Louis XIV accepted in his adolescent grandson's name.

While Frenchmen boasted that there were no more Pyrenees, others were determined to prevent this destruction of the European balance of power. Louis XIV made the Grand Alliance against him a certainty in 1701; he violated his own pledges by asserting that Spain's new Bourbon king, Philip V, had a right

[20] The Jacobites—so called from Jacobus, the Latin form of James—were partisans of the house of Stuart. Down to James II's death in 1701, they conspired to have him restored; after that, they pinned their hopes on his son, James Edward Stuart, the Old Pretender. And after *his* death, they pressed the claim of his son, Charles Edward Stuart—Bonnie Prince Charlie, the Young Pretender—to the English throne. In vain, as we shall see below.

to both the Spanish and the French thrones, and he violated the Peace of Ryswick by attacking the barrier forts in the Spanish Netherlands. These actions silenced the peace party in England and brought together an alliance too formidable even for Louis XIV. William III died in early March 1702, to be succeeded by his wife's younger sister, Anne, but not before he had forged a great coalition against France. By May 1702, the allies were in the field, and the War of the Spanish Succession had begun. The allies were brilliantly led by John Churchill, duke of Marlborough; Prince Eugene of Savoy; and Anthony Heinsius, grand pensionary of Holland—an impressive trio of generals and statesmen. Spain, a puppet of France, and Bavaria, the inveterate adversary of Hapsburg Austria, were Louis' only allies. For some years, the war went badly for France. In a series of memorable battles, the allies repeatedly defeated Louis' forces: in August 1704, Marlborough routed the joint Bavarian-French army at Blenheim; in May 1706, Marlborough reconquered the Spanish Netherlands with a victory at Ramillies; in the same year, Prince Eugene drove the French from Italy with a victory at Turin. In July 1708 at Oudenarde, and again in September 1709 at Malplaquet, Marlborough and Eugene together set back the French. But both battles, especially Malplaquet, were bloodbaths, and by 1710 the bellicose Whigs were out of office in England, and a Tory ministry tried to make peace. Louis XIV, gravely hurt, had offered to negotiate as early as 1708, but the allies, blinded by success, demanded such humiliating terms that Louis felt compelled to withdraw from the talks. He was ready to give up a great deal of territory and to recognize the Hanoverian succession in England, but he could not bring himself to expel his own grandson from Spain. The war resumed, with better fortune for France in the last years. Peace finally came in a series of treaties concluded in 1713 at Utrecht and in 1714 at Rastatt and Baden.

The Peace of Utrecht, as this collection of agreements is summarily called, was a settlement of decisive importance. Whatever the disgruntled Whigs might say, it was a triumph for England. Cromwell's aspiration to make his country into a great power had finally become reality. In 1704, the British navy had captured Gibraltar; Utrecht guaranteed its possession. In addition, Britain gained firm footholds in America, at France's expense: Newfoundland, the Hudson's Bay territory, and Nova Scotia. While the Bourbon king of Spain, Philip V, was confirmed on the throne, the separation of the Spanish and French crowns was written into the peace, and Spanish possessions in the Mediterranean and the Netherlands were handed to the Austrian Hapsburgs and other members of the coalition. The Dutch, too, profited, not so much in territory as in military security. England's triumph was France's defeat. It was not Cromwell's dream alone that was realized; Utrecht was a posthumous vindication of William III. France remained a great power, but Louis' fantasy of hegemony was frustrated, it would seem forever. Even eastern Europe entered into the settlement. Prussia obtained new territories, and the title of "king in Prussia," which the elector Frederick had taken in 1701, was officially confirmed (see p. 323). The Peace of Utrecht reads like a definitive, final judgment on the reign of Louis XIV. The old king died on September 1, 1715, after long suffering, the power of his country diminished, many of his promises unfulfilled, his children and grandchildren dead before him, his lust for conquest and passion for "reputation" a source of bitter regret and self-reproach at the end. But the comprehensive provisions of Utrecht also suggest that the age of Louis XIV cast its shadow wide and far, even into eastern Europe.

EASTERN EUROPE IN THE AGE OF LOUIS XIV

The struggles that convulsed western Europe for the century between the outbreak of the Thirty Years War in 1618 and the death of Louis XIV in 1715 resulted in significant shifts of power—in the weakening of Spain, the containment of France, the flourishing of the Dutch, the emergence of England. But the physical outlines of these states had been, roughly speaking, fixed, and remained relatively stable. In eastern Europe on the other hand, these years saw fundamental changes on the map. Poland, once a sizable empire, shrank into insignificance—first a universal joke, later the hapless victim of its neighbors (see p. 435). The Ottoman Turks, a persistent threat, reached a final paroxysm of aggressiveness and then receded to become "the sick man of Europe" (see Ch. 13). The Austrian Hapsburgs, an old and declining dynasty, regained their position. Brandenburg-Prussia and Russia, both marginal to the West, became great powers and henceforth played a role in all diplomatic calculations and in every major European war.

The Austrian Hapsburgs

The seventeenth century was a time of trial for the Austrian Hapsburgs—a trial they overcame, though at great cost. Relations with Hapsburg Spain grew more distant and, in any event, less rewarding as Spain sank into torpor and political insignificance. And the Peace of Westphalia in 1648 made the imperial crown, traditionally in Hapsburg hands, an ambiguous honor by turning the Holy Roman Empire into a patchwork of hundreds of small sovereign states, hard to rule, impossible to unite (see p. 255). The Thirty Years' War had raised havoc in the Hapsburg domains; many of them had been theaters of battle and objects of pillage. Impoverished and depopulated, they showed the scars of war for many years. The persistent and pitiless Catholicizing policies of the Hapsburgs left other scars: the utter neglect of local culture in Bohemia and the large-scale emigration of Protestants unwilling to convert to the Roman church. By 1660, the Hapsburg monarchy was a disparate collection of inheritances, the uneasy home of several languages: German, Czech, Magyar, and others. In the west and south, there were the "hereditary provinces" of the Austrian house, subject to the ruler in Vienna who united within one person a confusing but, for the age, perfectly typical number of titles. He was duke of Upper and Lower Austria, of Carinthia and Carniola; he was margrave of Styria, and lord of lands in Swabia—the only noncontiguous territories in the Austrian domains. After 1665, he became Landesfürst of the Tyrol as well. In the north, the Hapsburg wore the crown of St. Wenceslas: he was king of Bohemia, margrave of Moravia, and duke of Upper and Lower Silesia. In the east, he was king of Hungary, endowed with the crown of St. Stephen, which had fallen into Hapsburg hands in 1526. It supposedly gave him sovereignty over Hungary, Transylvania, Croatia, Dalmatia, and Slavonia. In actuality, the Austrians held only the northwest quarter of Hungary, and even there, what with the stubborn pride of the local Magyar aristocrats, their control was more nominal than real. They had little influence over the principality of Transylvania in central Hungary, ably led in the first half of the seventeenth century by Bethlen Gabor and George I Rakoczy. Amid the decay of Ottomans to their east and the preoccupations of Hapsburg to their west, these Transylvanian princes had secured virtual autonomy from both and had carved out a Calvinist enclave surrounded by Catholics and Muslims. The eastern parts of Hungary, finally, were firmly in Ottoman hands. Thus, estranged from Spain, enfeebled in Germany, impotent in most of Hungary, Austria in 1660 was both troubled and compact.

Yet the Austrian Hapsburgs turned both their troubles and their compactness to good account. They set about solving manageable tasks: extirpating the Protestant heresy from their lands, concentrating administration in Vienna, and surrendering hopes of a great Germanic empire, creating instead an empire in eastern and southeastern Europe. A succession of competent Hapsburg rulers did all this. When Ferdinand II died in 1637, Bohemia was a pitiful Hapsburg dependency (see p. 250). His son, Ferdinand III, who ruled from 1637 to 1657, participated in the making of general peace in 1648, and in the nine years that remained to him, did something to repair the damages of war and devastation, intensified the Catholicizing of his Bohemian subjects, and worried about the imperial succession. When his second son succeeded him in 1658 as Leopold I, the basis for economic recovery and territorial reconquest seemed secure. Leopold I was an unlikely warrior-king. He had not been expected to succeed to the Hapsburg dominions, but when his older brother Ferdinand died in 1654, Leopold had to give up his study of theology to enter into his heritage. He did so unwillingly; he never lost his religiosity and his shyness. But, unlikely as he was in the role of warrior-king, he filled it, and well, until his death in 1705.

Leopold I faced two enemies: Louis XIV in the west and the Ottoman Turks in the east. These two enemies were not unconnected. Louis XIV resented the king of Spain's parading the title "Catholic majesty" and liked to think of himself as the "most Christian king," the scourge of heretics. Indeed, when he revoked the Edict of Nantes in 1685, the delighted Bishop Bossuet apostrophized him as a "new Constantine." But the exigencies of policy overrode the demands of piety, and in the Turkish wars the French king tacitly supported, or openly encouraged, the Turks (France's traditional ally) against Austria (France's traditional enemy).

Leopold I was put to the test not long after his accession. Since 1648, the prince of Transylvania had been George II Rakoczy, a man with visions of empire. By the mid-1650s, he had concluded an alliance with Sweden and invaded Poland. But his plan for an eastern European domain was ruined, first by the desertion of his Swedish allies and then from an unexpected source: the revitalized Turks. In 1656, a new grand vizier, Mohammed Kuprili, had taken control. Brutal and energetic, he purged his opposition, reorganized economic affairs, and refurbished his army. In July 1657, he defeated George II Rakoczy at Tremblowa and forced Rakoczy's deposition. In defeat, Rakoczy turned to the Hapsburgs for aid, and before his early death in 1660, Austrian and Turkish troops were engaged, though still fitfully.

Sporadic fighting turned into large-scale war soon after. The fall of Transylvania to the Turks brought them perilously close to Austria's hereditary provinces. In 1661, Ahmed Kuprili succeeded his father and extended his father's expansionist policies; in April 1663, he moved his army up the Danube, toward the prize—Vienna. But not yet; in August 1664, at the battle of St. Gotthard in western Hungary, a European, mainly Hapsburg, army defeated the grand vizier and imposed on him a twenty-year truce. Foiled, the Turks attacked elsewhere. They raided Poland and, in the 1670s, Russia, but their aggression bore indifferent fruit: while the Turks took Ukrainian territory from the Poles in 1676, they were obliged to disgorge it to the Russians in 1681. And in any event, Vienna was their real target.

By mid-July 1683, the Turks had closed in on it. They surrounded the city and heavily bombarded its walls. While Emperor Leopold I took himself and his family to safety, the garrison, vastly outnumbered, bravely refused to surrender and waited for relief. Relief finally came, in the shape of a motley army—Austrians, Saxons, Bavarians, Poles—under the leadership of John III (John Sobieski), king of Poland. Here was a critical moment in European affairs: the effects of the heathens conquering Vienna would have been momentous. Louis XIV, the most Christian king, was conspicuously absent; in fact, his emissaries had done their best to dissuade Sobieski from relieving the city. Yet, in mid-September, the allied forces routed the Turks, and the danger was over.

Their defeat ended the Turkish threat to Austria and created an opportunity for a latter-day crusade to expel the infidel from Europe. Financed largely by the pope, a European army of Austrians, Poles, Venetians, and later, Russians, under the command of Prince Eugene, conducted a successful counterattack, the War of the Holy League. [21] It came to an end in January 1699,

---

[21] One casualty of the war was the Parthenon in Athens. Used as a powder magazine by the Turks, in 1687 it was shelled by the Venetian navy and an unlucky hit severely damaged the structure.

with the Treaty of Karlowitz. Prince Eugene had decisively defeated the Turks at Senta, in September 1697, and the peace reflected the military situation. Austria's allies, Venice and Poland, obtained some territory at the Turk's expense, but the Austrians took the prizes: Hungary, Transylvania, Croatia, and Slavonia. The Austrian Empire in southeastern Europe was taking shape.

Leopold and his successors did not disdain the old imperial game in the west. Leopold I died in 1705, to be succeeded by the short-lived Joseph I (1705–1711), and by Joseph's brother, Charles VI (see p. 389). Under Leopold Austria participated in the Grand Alliance against Louis XIV; under Charles it reaped its reward for its work in the War of the Spanish Succession: The Treaty of Rastatt in 1714 converted the old Spanish Netherlands into the Austrian Netherlands and confirmed Austrian occupation of Spanish dominions—Naples, Sardinia, and Milan—in Italy. Between the Peace of Karlowitz and the Peace of Rastatt Austria's glory and might had been restored, but this was not a time for complacency. The Turks remained a threat, though they increasingly tended to turn their attentions northward, against the Russians. And the Hungarians were restive. They resented the increasing interference of Viennese officials in their affairs, the obvious subjugation of Hungarian to Austrian interests, and the settlement of Catholic Austrians in their territory. In 1703, led by Francis II Rakoczy, they rebelled, but the rebels were defeated and in 1711 they agreed to a settlement. Significantly, the Peace of Szatmar was a compromise which reaffirmed Austrian sovereignty over Hungary but granted a general amnesty and promised to respect Hungarian constitutional rights and redress Hungarian grievances. Hapsburg power depended on holding together a motley assortment of peoples and aristocracies, and on making these subjects, to some degree at least, partners in this fragile empire. For the eighteenth century this proved a workable arrangement. But the same century also provided the Hapsburgs with a new and unlooked-for rival in the north, in Prussia.

From Brandenburg to Prussia

The emergence of Prussia as a great power was the triumph of will over nature. Since the establishment of the Hohenzollern dynasty in 1415, Brandenburg had extended its territories with policies reminiscent of the Hapsburgs: the Hohenzollerns negotiated cleverly and married well. They needed to: Brandenburg's soil was sandy, its climate was raw, and its natural resources were scanty; its possessions, moreover, were scattered across the low-lying tableland of northern Germany, vulnerable to invasion.

When Louis XIV ascended to personal power in 1661, Frederick William had been elector of Brandenburg for twenty-one years, decisive years for Brandenburg's growth. Both at Westphalia in 1648 and at Oliva in 1660, Frederick William had acquired important dominions in west and east alike. He had also determined to stake his future on a standing army. This was a momentous decision in Prussian history, indeed for world history. All the proverbial meanings that cluster around the word "Prussian," all the caricatures of snobbish, cruel, bemedaled Junkers, all the widespread fears of Prussian militarism have their roots in that decision. As Freiherr von Schrotter, ex-soldier and liberal minister, would ruefully say around 1800: "Prussia was not a country with an army, but an army with a country which served as headquarters and food magazine."[22] Yet until 1740 (see p. 389) this army was rarely in the field; Frederick William and his successors increased its size, improved its equipment, and maintained its reputation by husbanding its strength. Prussian militarism is the offspring of this irony: it grew formidable by not fighting.

Three aspects of Prussian militarism deserve particular attention: its financial resources, its social base, and its cultural consequences. Both the old dominions of Brandenburg and those it acquired in the seventeenth century had estates jealous of their prerogatives, particularly of their right to vote taxes. But Frederick William, eager to participate in the European power game and to build an effective and loyal armed force, wanted more money and more international involvements than the estates were ready to grant. In his early years, the elector compromised; when the Baltic War[23] erupted in 1655, he rapidly overthrew the constituted order. Illegally, he raised money without the estates' consent, and when the war was over, kept his standing army in being. Soon all power was in his hands and in the hands of his chosen bureaucrats. The estates were broken; while they retained certain privileges, their capacity to resist the elector or sabotage his plans had vanished. Even in the western provinces of Cleves and Mark, where the estates had once been strong, participation in the making of public policy meant little more than solemn ratification of what the elector had dictated. What opposition remained, Frederick William crushed by cajolery and, more often, by brute force. On a scale far smaller than Louis XIV, but in a far more thoroughgoing manner, the elector of Brandenburg welded his disparate territories into a unified country subject to a ruler with absolute power. It has often been noted that in these years, and for long thereafter, the Brandenburg-Prussian state did not even have a name. But it had substance: a full treasury, an impressive army, an efficient bureaucracy, and an obedient populace.

Frederick William's chief instrument of government was, or rather became, the *Generalkriegskommissariat*. As its name suggests, this "general war commissariat" was established during the Northern War of 1655–1660. Its first duties were directly connected with that conflict: it had to raise money for the

---

[22] Quoted in Hans Rosenberg, *Bureaucracy, Aristocracy, and Autocracy: The Prussian Experience, 1660–1815* (1958), 40.

[23] This conflict is sometimes called the Northern War; it should not be confused with the Great Northern War, which began in 1700 (see p. 328).

army and see to its training, equipment, victualling, and all other aspects of supply. During the decade of peace its role was reduced, but in 1672, when Brandenburg joined the Dutch Republic in the war against France, the *Generalkriegskommissariat* grew into the vital center of Brandenburg's bureaucracy. It served as the central treasury and, gradually, without any theoretical pronouncements about "mercantilism," entered the general domain of economic superintendence. It collected the new excise tax in the towns. It supervised the establishment of new industries and commercial ventures. It inspected Brandenburg's gilds and participated in foreign affairs by controlling Frederick William's tentative ventures in navy-building and colonial entrepreneurship. In 1685, after the revocation of the Edict of Nantes, when fourteen thousand Huguenots streamed into Brandenburg, it was the *Generalkriegskommissariat* that was in charge of settling the new immigrants. Directly responsible to the elector, aware of their importance, these new bureaucrats interfered with the estates and were as arrogant with the general public as they were loyal to their chief. It is almost unnecessary to add that practically all higher officials in this body were members of Prussia's rural aristocracy—Junkers. [24]

Though not confined to it, the essential task of the *Generalkriegskommissariat* was to maintain the army, that instrument of policy that became the center of a national cult. After the 1660s, with a population of little over a million, the Brandenburg army stood at twenty-five thousand to forty thousand—an imposing number to be sustained by so small and so poor a population. It has been estimated that Prussians bore more than twice as much in taxes as did contemporary Frenchmen, even though Prussia was poor and France rich. Prussia's poverty, indeed, was the center of a vicious circle: the poverty ostensibly required an expansionist militarist foreign policy; the expansionist militarist foreign policy kept Prussia poor. True, Brandenburg-Prussia's revenues increased threefold in the reign of Frederick William, [25] but for many years the state had no money to squander on luxuries like civilization. Yet Prussians bore these burdens with few murmurs—and when murmurs were heard, they were quickly stilled with methods more familiar in eastern than in western Europe. The most burdened, and the quietest, subject of these exactions was, of course, the Prussian peasant. Like his Russian counterpart, he had sunk into servitude in the sixteenth century and his servile status had been legally confirmed early in the seventeenth century (see p. 259). Here, too, the Brandenburg dominions were moving in the direction of their eastern rather than their western neighbors.

In the army, as in the bureaucracy, leadership was the preserve of the Junker. Practically all officer posts were reserved to Junkers, though there were some branches, notably army engineering, where talent might prevail over birth. The place of the Junkers in the Prussian state was essentially the fruit of

[24] The name derives from the Middle High German *junc herre,* young lord.
[25] See F. L. Carsten, *The Origins of Prussia* (1954), 270.

a tacit bargain. In return for surrendering independent political power, the landed aristocracy was granted a monopoly over the higher posts; in return for blind obedience to the dynasty,[26] the Junkers might exact the same obedience from "their" peasants on the land, "their" subordinates in the bureaucracy, or "their" recruits in the army. "Many of these experts in local tyranny," as the historian Hans Rosenberg has put it, "were experienced in whipping the backs, hitting the faces, and breaking the bones of 'disrespectful' and 'disobedient' peasant serfs. Thus they were eminently fitted to be the drillmasters of common Prussian soldiers who, as Frederick II envisaged their proper status, should 'fear their officers more than any danger to which they might be exposed.'"[27] Contrary to their reputation, many Junker landowners had amassed considerable wealth through shrewd estate management and commercial dealings in the sixteenth century. But the dislocations of the Thirty Years' War and the unsettled conditions that followed it left many of them stranded on backward farmlands, with no provision for their numerous progeny. The state made entry into the aristocracy nearly impossible by stringent legislation against the alienation of Junker lands to commoners, and at the same time reserved jobs and prestige for Junkers alone. This was a bargain from which both sides profited.

There were no classes or institutions to challenge or bend this authoritarian structure. The soil was barren not for agriculture alone: Brandenburg-Prussia was no place for intellectuals, journalists, or poets. Nor could the urban bourgeoisie offer any competition. Brandenburg's cities were small, and their local autonomy was ruined during the reign of Frederick William by the ever-present bureaucracy. The Huguenots who populated Berlin after 1685 gave it some color and imported some new trades, but on the whole, burghers were trained to work and obey. The efflorescence of commercial enterprise that had made the Dutch great in the seventeenth century and would make the English great in the eighteenth passed Brandenburg by. Those naive diagrams that would distort and other social system of the time have some application to Brandenburg-Prussia: the ruler ruled, the aristocrats gave orders, the burghers worked, the peasants toiled.

As generations passed, and as King Frederick William I early in the eighteenth century elaborated that pattern his grandfather had laid down (see p. 320), the social structure necessity had created was rationalized into an ideal. This is a delicate matter, and historians today, after the Nazi experience, are still seeking to define a "Germanic" political style and to trace its divergence from a Western style. That style consisted of talk of "service," an exaltation of military over civilian ideas, a bureaucratic temper with its characteristic mixture of probity, efficiency, obsessiveness, and authoritarian arrogance, a contempt for politicians and for "mere" commercial values. Whatever its precise

---

[26] The characteristic German word is *Kadavergehorsam*, that is, the obedience of a corpse.
[27] *Bureaucracy, Aristocracy, and Autocracy,* 60.

contours, it originated well before 1700, in the long reign of Frederick William, whom German historians would soon call the Great Elector.

Frederick William died in 1688, leaving behind an anti-French foreign policy, a legacy of accepting generous subsidies from other countries, and a relatively unified state. His son could hardly be expected to compete with so overwhelming a father. In fact, there was something of a reaction against the Great Elector's austerities. Frederick III built palaces in and near Berlin and an opera house. In 1694 he opened a university at Halle; in 1696 he founded an academy of arts and, four years later, upon Leibniz's plan, an academy of sciences. He spent money on food and festivals, on precious jewelry and magnificent gardens. Contemptuous historians, thinking of his powerful father and equally powerful son, have dubbed Frederick's twenty-five-year reign an "interregnum." But this is hardly accurate. The civilizing amenities he introduced would prove to have more than decorative value in the eighteenth century. And the temporary relaxation of strenuousness had its own salutary effect, though the vastly rising expenditures on baubles and buildings, accompanied by continuing expenditures for the army, led to some uncomfortable, though temporary, deficits.

Besides, in his own way, Frederick did his part to increase his patrimony. Keeping the army in being proved eminently useful in 1700, when Emperor Leopold prepared to enter the War of the Spanish Succession against France. Frederick undertook to support the Hapsburgs in return for a substantial subsidy and—a long-cherished dream—a royal title. Accordingly, in 1701, Frederick III of Brandenburg-Prussia was granted the right to style himself Frederick I, king in Prussia.[28] In 1713, when Frederick I was succeeded by his son, Frederick William I, one of the new king's first acts was to have his royal title confirmed at the settlement that followed the War of the Spanish Succession. Prussia was on its way to greatness.

From Muscovy to Russia

Like Prussia, Russia emerged from remoteness and isolation late in the seventeenth century and, like Prussia, Russia secured great-power status under the driving knout of a single ruler—Peter I. In 1721, a grateful Russian Senate acknowledged the tsar's labors by calling him emperor, father of his country, and "the Great." Peter, the senators declared, had led his subjects "from the darkness of ignorance on to the theatre of glory before the whole world and, so to speak, from non-existence to existence."[29] The label has stuck, but its

---

[28] The "in" of this title was a compromise, agreed upon to pacify Frederick Augustus of Saxony, who had become king of Poland and held western Prussia. It was not until the reign of Frederick the Great that the preposition was changed to "of."

[29] Quoted in B. H. Sumner, *Peter the Great and the Emergence of Russia* (1951), 121.

justification must be modified: it is true that Peter was exigent, inexorable, passionately devoted to bringing his backward country to military, economic, and administrative modernity. But, just as the problems he faced were inherited from his predecessors, so were most of his proposed solutions. What Peter did was to speed up a process already under way with an unprecedented ruthlessness that sometimes achieved its purpose, more often defeated it. An inveterate borrower, Peter was by no means blind to the difficulties of transplanting ideas and institutions from one cultural climate to another. He hounded his advisors to adapt to Russian conditions what they had learned abroad. But in a long and stormy reign, he would discover what all reformers have to discover: styles of thinking—and even more, styles of feeling—have an extraordinary tenacity and resist the most rational refutation. Peter's most effective adversaries were not the Swedes or the Turks, but his own obstinate, conservative people.

Peter was born in 1672. The famous rebel Stenka Razin had been captured and executed the year before (see p. 260). In the West, Muscovy had made significant gains: in 1667, in the Treaty of Andrussavo, Tsar Alexis had acquired large parts of the Ukraine, including the towns of Kiev and Smolensk, from the Poles. But at home there was unrest; the rebellion that Stenka Razin led after 1670 was only one virulent symptom among many. Perhaps most damaging, certainly most persistent, was the schism that divided the Russian Orthodox church and, with it, the Russian people. Ignorance and illiteracy were more widespread in Russia than in the West, but beyond accepting these conditions with perfect complacency, many Russians viewed them with undisguised pride. The intellectual storms that had agitated the West since the Renaissance had passed Russia by, and there was much boasting about Russian resistance to Greek or "German" innovations.[30] This pride in Muscovite uniqueness was a perfectly understandable response to Russia's situation; it translated a defect into a virtue. But it confirmed and worsened a cultural isolation that was to give Peter the Great much trouble. Among the defenders of this cultural chauvinism, the Russian Orthodox church was the most articulate. Since 1589, when the Greek Orthodox patriarch at Constantinople had established a patriarch in Moscow, the Russian Orthodox church had been virtually independent of its Greek mother-church. This led to large claims. Moscow had become the Third Rome, the true center of orthodoxy, and since Constantinople had been in heathen hands since 1453, the only sovereign power to harbor and espouse the faith. But the Russian Orthodox church also produced the antidote to this isolationism. When Alexis came to the throne in 1645, he surrounded himself with Graecophiles intent upon reforming the church and bringing it closer to Greek traditions. The church needed reform: the clergy were ignorant, often illiterate, and mired in casual corruption. To introduce stringent tests of

---

[30] The word "German," it appears, came to be used for any Western invention or idea that such eager reformers as Peter brought back with them from their travels.

performance was to threaten their accustomed ways, and so "Greek innova-tions" came to be contrasted invidiously with "Muscovite traditions." In 1652, Nikon, an energetic and vastly ambitious man, became patriarch and set about revising the ritual of the Russian Orthodox church; in 1655 he introduced a new liturgy. His changes left dogma intact; most of them, in fact, were trivial: Nikon insisted, for instance, that the proper way to make the sign of the cross was with three fingers instead of two, as the Moscow Council had prescribed in 1551. But to simple religious minds, ritual has vast significance, and every gesture tremendous implications. Nikon had his way: while he was deposed for his secular ambitions, two councils in 1666 and 1667 confirmed his reforms and excommunicated those who persisted in their accustomed ritual. The resulting schism was a defeat for the church and a tragedy for Russia. It showed the church incapable of blending Muscovite traditions with Western innovations. [31] And it divided Russia, more deeply than ever before, along class—or rather, caste—lines. A large and growing number of clerics and laymen, many of them peasants, refused to adopt Nikon's "reforms." These were the Old Believers. They split into sectarian groups, wrestled with their souls, bravely resisted pressure, and suffered persecution. Thousands of them burned themselves to death; thousands of others were saved that exertion by the state. When Peter was born, the schism had assumed violent forms. Old Believers had denounced Peter's father, Tsar Alexis, as Anti-Christ in person; Peter's own persistent efforts to bring his people closer to the West would face the same rhetoric and be resisted on the most unyielding of grounds—religion.

All this was unpromising enough. Peter's personal situation was even more menacing. Peter was a Romanov, and the dynasty itself was secure. But he was the son of Alexis' second wife, and for some time the supporters of the tsar's first wife had the upper hand. When Alexis died in 1676, he was succeeded by Peter's ailing half-brother, Feodor III, who reigned for six years. When he in turn died in 1682, he left no sons. The result was confusion and a bloody struggle for power, issuing in a compromise: Ivan V, Feodor's younger brother, and Peter were proclaimed co-tsars under the regency of Ivan's older sister, Sophia. The terrible scenes in which the *streltsi*[32] rioted murderously in the Kremlin left a permanent mark on Peter, quite similar to that which the Frondes had left on Louis XIV—an abiding hatred of the *streltsi*, an aversion to the Kremlin, and a thirst for sole rule.

Peter had his first opportunity in 1689, though he did not fully seize it for some years. In a brief and sanguinary court revolution, Peter took power, sent the regent Sophia to a convent, and had her advisors exiled or executed. But he left the government to his mother and persisted in his strange self-education:

---

[31] See Werner Philipp, "Russia: The Beginning of Westernization," in *The New Cambridge Modern History,* vol. V (1961), 589–591.

[32] The *streltsi* were a kind of palace guard, but more sizable and more independent than most such guards. Organized into twenty-two regiments of a thousand men each, they regarded themselves as a privileged force, and their political support was considered of vital importance.

in Moscow he continued to hang about the "German suburb," a quarter in the city populated by foreign Protestants, including Dutchmen and Scots, who brought him news of Western ways. And in the country he continued to play his "war games," exercises with his soldiers which, as he grew to manhood, developed into full-fledged maneuvers. But then Peter's mother died in 1694 followed by his inoffensive co-ruler Ivan in 1696, and the responsibilities of rule could no longer be evaded. Nor did he evade them. But he did not cease his education. In 1697 he went West, on his "great embassy," complete with court chaplains and court dwarfs. The trip has been much romanticized, but it was extraordinary enough. It was, in itself, an unprecedented gesture for a Russian tsar, and while abroad, Peter behaved less like a ruler than like an apprentice. In Amsterdam, he worked in the shipyards of the East India Company; early in 1698, after nearly half a year among the Dutch, he sailed to England. Wherever he went, he asked questions. He looked everywhere: in hospitals, naval installations, carpenters' shops. His thirst for knowledge, above all mechanical knowledge, was insatiable. A tall, powerfully built man, he was coarse in his tastes, brutal in his pleasures, and sadistic in his practical jokes. At the same time, he was capable of simple family affection; Peter was a strange mixture endowed with an incongruous collection of traits, all distorted to gigantic size. He was a dreaded guest: rude in manners, drunken, and destructive. Yet his trip had practical results: he imported over seven hundred Westerners—shipwrights, mathematicians, engineers—and, quite as useful, an ineradicable impression of Russia's need for instruction in all practical things. He saw his country mired in superstitions and ignorant of modern military tactics, naval skills, commercial enterprise. Culture meant nothing to him, but he was certain that he must modernize his Russia in order to give it the formidable army and navy it needed. Charles XII, the observant king of Sweden, plainly saw the meaning of Europe for this Russian tsar: Moscow's power, he said, had "risen so high thanks to the introduction of foreign military discipline." [33]

It was in foreign affairs that Peter's education paid its earliest dividends. But there was one score he needed to settle first. His European tour was cut short in the spring of 1698, when news came that the *streltsi* had revolted in his absence. Peter rushed back to Moscow and put down the rebellion in an orgy of public torture and executions. It was on this occasion, too, that Peter enacted that celebrated scene of shaving off his court nobles' beards with his own hands. Sumptuary laws prescribing European dress and taxing those who kept their beards quickly followed. Peter, it was clear, would tolerate no disloyalty and no delay in bringing Russia into Europe by bringing Europe into Russia. For the nobles, many of them already half Westernized, this was scarcely painful; for the peasants, especially the Old Believers among them, this assault on time-honored dress and appearance was, quite literally, blasphemy.

[33] Quoted in Sumner, *Peter the Great*, 64.

But war was foremost on Peter's mind. Here, too, Peter followed a policy laid down by a predecessor: through most of his short reign, Feodor III had battled the Turks for the territories that lie on the north of the Black Sea; in 1681, he had acquired the Turkish Ukraine. Now, in 1695, just before he went on his "great embassy" to the West, Peter extended Feodor's gains by assaulting the port of Azov, which commands the entrance to the Black Sea. He took it in 1696 and turned it into Russia's first naval stronghold. But the Swedes offered Peter his strongest challenge and provided him with his greatest triumphs.

Sweden's times of troubles had passed with the abdication of Queen Christina in 1654 (see p. 261). Her successor, Charles X, reestablished domestic order, and for the six years of his reign successfully fought in the War of the North. At the peace of Oliva, in 1660, the Poles definitively abandoned all claims to the Swedish throne and ceded the province of Livonia. And by the Treaty of Copenhagen of the same year, the Danes surrendered what is today the southern tip of Sweden. But Sweden's new king, Charles XI, was a boy of four at his accession and his regents proved incompetent. Territorially a satisfied power, Sweden's foreign policy was, quite simply, to keep her gains intact.[34] But isolation was impossible, and Sweden's participation in the wars of the seventies proved a waste of resources. War with Brandenburg brought a resounding defeat at the battle of Fehrbellin in June 1675; and in 1679, when Sweden returned to general peace, the Treaty of St. Germain-en-Laye restored the status quo. Happy to have lost nothing, Sweden also gained nothing. But peace gave Charles XI, who had attained his majority in 1672, the opportunity to assert royal supremacy. In the seventeen years that remained to him— between 1680 and 1697—Charles XI broke the independent power of the Swedish nobility. He did so with a simple device: reversing Queen Christina's openhanded alienation of crown lands, Charles XI energetically resumed those lands, as well as the royal revenues that his prececessors had granted away. This was the famous *reduktion;* it reduced the influence of the Swedish nobility by depriving it of its economic base. Rebuilding the army, improving the navy, reforming the finances, constructing a bureaucracy, subduing the Riksdag and the church, Charles XI built an absolute regime remarkable for its control over the country. He was a pallid man, and shy, and his work seemed plodding labor after the military exploits of Gustavus Adolphus and Charles X. But, as Michael Roberts has rightly noted, Charles XI "was of critical importance in the history of his country: the hinge upon which the whole of modern Swedish history swings."[35] That he had labored well appeared plainly enough in 1697, when his fifteen-year-old son succeeded to the throne as Charles XII and drew on the resources his father had amassed.

---

[34] For this paragraph, see Michael Roberts, "Charles XI," in Roberts, *Essays in Swedish History* (1966), 226–268.

[35] Ibid., 227.

Charles XII was a strange man, much resembling his great adversary, Peter the Great, in his brute strength and his contradictions. Voltaire, one of his first biographers, called him half Don Quixote, half Alexander the Great, and the epigram captures Charles—his quixotic ambitions, his brilliant generalship, his sublime impatience with common sense. He displayed his gifts shortly after his accession. In the summer of 1700, as soon as Peter had freed his hands by making peace with the Turks, Russia, supported by Poland and Denmark, declared war on Sweden. Charles XII moved swiftly; late in November 1700, his small but disciplined force of eight thousand soldiers routed a Russian army of forty thousand at Narva. The Great Northern War was under way. [36] While the great powers were struggling to redraw the map of western Europe in the War of the Spanish Succession, lesser powers struggled for similar stakes in the north and east.

The defeat at Narva proved a disguised blessing for Peter the Great. It was, as he candidly admitted, a "terrible setback," but at the same time, a vital lesson: he must reconstruct his army completely, in every way. He acted with his customary ruthlessness, drawing, as he always did, on the West, by importing officers and military tactics. And Charles helped him, through his obstinacy. Instead of following up his victory over the Russians—which would have deprived Peter of the time he so badly needed—Charles wasted valuable years fighting an inconclusive war in Poland. Retribution came in 1709, in southern Russia. Charles XII, with his highly trained army, disregarding the length of his lines and the scorched earth that greeted him everywhere, followed Peter deep into Russia. There, in July 1709, at the battle of Poltava, Peter had his revenge. Swedish troops fled and capitulated in droves, and Charles sought refuge in Turkish territory. For Peter, Poltava had special meaning. In 1703, in the frozen north and in the teeth of Swedish forces, he had founded a new city, St. Petersburg, on which he lavished all his organizational energies, enormous amounts of money, and that most expendable material of all—his peasants. Victory over Sweden made his city secure. "Now," with Poltava, Peter said, "the final stone has been laid of the foundation of St. Petersburg." [37]

The Great Northern War dragged on until 1721, but the threat of Charles XII was broken at Poltava. When Charles finally returned to Sweden from Turkey in 1714, he found that the Russians had taken a wide swath of territory to the north: Estonia, Livonia, Finland, Karelia. Stettin had been turned over to Prussia in 1713. Then, in December 1718, while on a military campaign in Norway, Charles XII was shot to death under mysterious circumstances. But he had lived long enough to see Russia beginning negotiations for peace. Finally, in 1721, at the Peace of Nystadt, Russia retained all her northern gains except

[36] It is important to distinguish this war from an earlier, less decisive conflict, the Northern War (1655–1660), involving Sweden, Poland, and Prussia (see p. 320).
[37] Quoted in Sumner, *Peter the Great*, 73.

Finland—a minimal concession. It was on the occasion of Nystadt that the Russian Senate endowed Peter with the epithet, "the Great." Russia was now a European power. Nor is this observation mere hindsight: Peter deliberately aimed at this end. In 1717, on a diplomatic mission to Paris, he had explicitly told the French that the European system had changed and that Russia should now take the place of Sweden.

Peter the Great was not a systematic thinker, but this single aim—to make Muscovy into Russia and Russia into a European empire—animated him in all he did, in domestic as much as in foreign policy. The cost of greatness was enormous, but Peter cheerfully imposed it on his country. The building of St. Petersburg alone claimed thousands of lives. The workmen there perished in floods and from fevers; they were overwhelmed by fires and eaten by wolves. "The wretched peasants, soldiers and prisoners—Finns, Swedes, Esthonians, Karelians, Cossacks, Tartars, Kalmucks—who were brought to the Neva in their thousands to build a city of which every foot had to be made on piles, had most of them to sleep in the open air among the marshes. Their labour was inhuman—for long they had no tools and were forced to dig with sticks or with their nails and carry the earth in their coats or in the tails of their shirts; and they were kept perpetually short of food and drank foul water. In consequence they died like flies." One of Peter's jesters gloomily described the position of the new city in these words: "On one side the sea, on the other sorrow, on the third moss, on the fourth a sigh." [38]

War meant conscription, endless military service, further extension of serfdom and intensification of demands on serfs, extortionate taxes (borne, as usual, by those least able to afford it), and a system of informers to report tax evasion. The Old Believers had other grievances: Peter was Satan, who shaved off the beards that God had given man, he was Anti-Christ. There were rebellions, among the volatile Cossacks on the Don, the people of Astrakhan, the Ukrainians. Peter disposed of these revolts with his usual ferocity. His conduct on such occasions was part of his character, but Peter rationalized his predilections into a policy: cruelty, he said, was all this rabble could understand. Even his son, the heir-apparent, felt the full force of Peter's barbarity. Alexis, Peter's oldest son, had been a grievous disappointment to his father from the start: sympathetic to the Old Believers, indifferent to administration and hostile to military affairs, lazy and incompetent, a focus for all opposition to Peter's reform program, Alexis seemed a most improbable heir to all his father's enormous efforts. After renouncing the succession at his father's request, in 1716 Alexis fled to Vienna, but was lured back late in 1717 by Peter's promise of pardon. His suspicions of treason unallayed by his son's protestations, Peter had Alexis interrogated and tortured. Some of Alexis' supporters were

[38] Christopher Marsden, *Palmyra of the North: The First Days of St. Petersburg* (1942), 47–48, 51.

executed, and Alexis himself died in prison in July 1718. The coroner's verdict was apoplexy; the popular verdict was murder—certainly instigated, probably witnessed, and some said, personally committed by Peter himself.[39] In October 1721, Peter assumed the title, Emperor of all the Russias.[40] In 1722, he reiterated that he was absolute autocrat by issuing the law of succession, which claimed his right to name his successor. It was a pathetic move: all the sons by his second wife, Catherine, died in infancy, and when Peter himself lay on his deathbed, he scribbled a fragmentary note that read: "I leave all . . ." But to whom he left his Russia was not left for him to say.

Peter the Great died in 1725, at the age of fifty-two. Much of his work was rapidly undone in the aristocratic reaction that normally follows upon the death of an absolute ruler who has destroyed the regular channels of authority.[41] But then much of his work was of doubtful value: the price of transforming a backward Asiatic country into a modern European power was, as we have said, enormous. Yet some of his work, whatever its cost, lasted through the turmoil that followed his disappearance from the scene. To govern his vast empire, Peter in 1711 instituted a senate to make decisions in his absence; during the last years of his reign, when its ineffectiveness became apparent, Peter borrowed from the West the institution of "colleges," boards of bureaucrats charged with specific tasks—the navy or foreign affairs. Western, too, was Peter's administrative division of Russia—at first, in 1708, into eight *gubernii*, and then, in 1719, after these proved too unwieldy, into fifty provinces. His aim was to create a "police state"—a term that has acquired sinister connotations in our time, but which meant in the eighteenth century a rational administrative machinery that would diligently supervise public affairs, deal out justice, and govern under law. In 1721, a law creating the college for municipal affairs ambitiously defined the kind of police state to which Peter was aspiring: police, it said, is "the soul of citizenship and of all good order and the fundamental support of civil security and propriety." It superintends justice, creates good morals, thwarts thieves, prevents disease, keeps the streets clean, helps the poor and the sick, protects widows and orphans.[42] Of course, Peter failed in all this. No rule of law could emerge from a system based on compulsion, forced labor, and arbitrary decision-making by the tsar or his trusted army officers. Yet he did much. He raised much-needed funds by adopting Western mercantilist policies, protecting old or founding new industries, constructing a large navy, and exploiting rich domestic resources like the iron mines in the Urals. He levied new taxes, mainly a poll tax, to finance his endless wars: Peter was at war without interruption for twenty-eight years, between 1695 and 1723, and in

[39] For a strikingly similar story about Frederick William I of Prussia and his son, see p. 391.
[40] For the sake of convenience, we have used the traditional term, "tsar," throughout.
[41] For this general, Europe-wide phenomenon, see p. 376.
[42] See Sumner, *Peter the Great,* 132.

some years his armed forces, including his expensive navy, took as much as four fifths of the entire revenue. His exactions required several censuses of the population, each more stringent than the earlier one, and backed up with the threat of the death penalty for "concealment."

The clergy and the aristocracy were enlisted in Peter's inexorable search for military might. After the patriarch of the Russian Orthodox church died in 1700, Peter managed church affairs with acting patriarchs wholly beholden to him. Then, in 1721, Peter made the political impotence of the church official and permanent by abolishing the patriarchate and establishing in its place the holy governing synod, headed by a procurator, which tied the church into Peter's autocracy. And the nobility was mobilized by the doctrine of "state service," an old device that Peter employed with new vigor. He attempted to force the boyars to send their children to school—a command the Russian aristocracy resisted so fiercely that even Peter moderated it. But while he could not make the young nobles read, he could make them perform in the army or the civil service. In 1722, Peter imposed an elaborate table of ranks which listed the hierarchy of positions both in the military and the civilian service through which all must pass regardless of their birth or their wealth. Thus service to the state, rather than traditional aristocratic status, became the way to prestige and power. Whatever he failed to do, Peter made a social revolution, substituting a new service nobility for the old landed warrior class of boyars.

Our final verdict on Peter the Great's autocracy must be dotted with question marks. Everything, including education, stood under the sign of war and glorification of the tsar. Reforms were hasty and profoundly inorganic. Thus the so-called Westernization of the Russian mind remains a dubious enterprise. Peter set up a printing press to increase the circulation of books in his country and to add to the production of religious tracts already being produced by a theological "publishing house." But the publications of Peter's press were hardly impressive: the bulk was devotional literature, with a liberal sprinkling of technical manuals on such subjects as shipbuilding. The single true work of literature to be published in Peter's reign was a Russian translation of Aesop's fables. [43] Despite all Peter's intentions and declarations, the great movement of enlightenment that was sweeping western Europe made little impact on him and less on his country.

SELECTED READINGS

For the Sun King, see the expansive scholarly biography by John B. Wolf, *Louis XIV* (1968). Pierre Goubert, *Louis XIV and Twenty Million Frenchmen* (tr. 1970), relates the man to his age and his people. Maurice Ashley, *Louis XIV and the Greatness of France* (1953), is an introductory survey; Laurence B. Packard, *The Age of Louis XIV*

---

[43] See L. R. Lewitter, "Peter the Great, Poland, and the Westernization of Russia," *Journal of the History of Ideas*, 19 (Oct. 1958), 493–506.

(1938), is even briefer. W. H. Lewis, The Splendid Century (1953), is chatty but helpful. See also the opening chapters of E. N. Williams, The Ancien Régime in Europe: Government and Society in the Major States, 1648-1789 (1970). For Louis' dictatorship over French culture, Peter France and Margaret McGowan, "Louis XIV and the Arts," in John Cruickshank, ed., French Literature and Its Background, vol. II, The Seventeenth Century (1969), is economical but informative. Anthony Blunt, Art and Architecture in France, 1500-1700 (1954), is valuable on this point. See James E. King, Science and Rationalism in the Government of Louis XIV, 1661-1683 (1949). Among interpretations of French literature in the age, especially recommended are Martin Turnell, The Classical Moment: Studies of Corneille, Molière and Racine (1947); E. B. O. Borgerhoff, The Freedom of French Classicism, (1950); and Paul Bénichou's sophisticated social analysis, Man and Ethics: Studies in French Classicism (tr. 1971).

Charles W. Cole, Colbert and a Century of French Mercantilism, 2 vols. (1939), and its sequel, French Mercantilism, 1683-1700 (1943), are standard for Louis' great minister. For mercantilism in general, see the great treatise by Eli Heckscher, Mercantilism, 2 vols. (2nd ed., 1955), which should be contrasted with Jacob Viner, "Power versus Plenty as Objectives of Foreign Policy in the Seventeenth and Eighteenth Centuries," in Viner, The Long View and the Short: Studies in Economic Theory and Policy (1958), and Charles Wilson, Profit and Power (1957). See also Paul W. Bamford, Forests and French Sea-Power, 1660-1789 (1956). On the growth of economic thought, see Edgar A. J. Johnson, Predecessors of Adam Smith: The Growth of British Economic Thought (1937), to be read in conjunction with William Letwin, The Origins of Scientific Economics (1963). On the Huguenots, see Warren C. Scoville, The Persecution of the Huguenots and French Economic Development, 1680-1720 (1960), as well as the older study by A. J. Grant, The Huguenots (1934), and Guy H. Dodge, The Political Theories of the Huguenots of the Dispersion (1947). For the Jansenists, see Nigel Abercrombie, The Origins of Jansenism (1936). Two important monographs on French foreign policy are G. N. Clark, The Dutch Alliance and the War Against French Trade, 1688-1697 (1923), and N. M. Crouse, The French Struggle for the West Indies, 1665-1713 (1943).

For England after the Restoration, see the later chapters of Maurice Ashley, England in the Seventeenth Century (1603-1714) (3rd ed., 1961), and J. P. Kenyon, The Stuarts (1958); see also the more detailed G. N. Clark, The Later Stuarts, 1660-1714 (1934). David Ogg's detailed volumes, England in the Reign of Charles II, 2 vols. (1934), and England in the Reigns of James II and William III (1955), are very valuable. On William III see the biography by Steven B. Baxter by that title (1966). G. M. Trevelyan's The English Revolution, 1688-1689 (1939), though brief and Whiggish, says the essential. Trevelyan has also given a detailed account of England Under Queen Anne, 3 vols. (1930-1934), distinguished by his usual narrative lucidity. Harry G. Plum, Restoration Puritanism (1943), Gerald R. Cragg, Puritanism in the Age of the Great Persecution (1957), and R. S. Bosher, The Making of the Restoration Settlement (1951), adequately cover religious events. Peter Laslett, The World We Have Lost (2nd ed., 1971), is interesting social history.

Eastern Europe in this period is well surveyed in numerous chapters of J. S. Bromley, ed., The Rise of Great Britain and Russia, 1688-1725 (1970), which is volume VI of The New Cambridge Modern History. For the Hapsburgs, see in addition to general histories of Europe, Paul Frischauer, The Imperial Crown: The Rise and Fall of the Holy Roman and the Austrian Empires (1939), to be read in conjunction with Adam

Wandruszka, *The House of Hapsburg* (tr. 1964), an authoritative account; L. S. Stavrianos, *The Balkans Since 1453* (1958), disentangles a complex story. For Hungary (in this and other periods), see the magisterial history by C. A. Macartney, *Hungary* (1934).

On the emergence of Prussia, Sidney B. Fay, *The Rise of Brandenburg-Prussia to 1786* (rev. by Klaus Epstein, 1964), is a brief essay; J. A. R. Marriott and C. G. Robertson, *The Evolution of Prussia* (ed. 1946), is longer if superficial. Hajo Holborn, *A History of Modern Germany,* vol. II, *1648-1840* (1964), has already been cited. For Frederick William, see Ferdinand Schevill, *The Great Elector* (1947); for the father of Frederick the Great, see Robert Ergang, *The Potsdam Führer: Frederick William I, Father of Prussian Militarism* (1941), which is rather better than its tendentious title indicates. It should be supplemented with the careful analysis by Reinhold A. Dorwart, *The Administrative Reforms of Frederick William I of Prussia* (1953). The early chapters of Hans Rosenberg's brilliant study of the rise of "bureaucratic absolutism," *Bureaucracy, Aristocracy, and Autocracy: The Prussian Experience, 1660-1815* (1958), are relevant here, as are the equally brilliant chapters in Gordon A. Craig, *The Politics of the Prussian Army, 1640-1945* (2nd ed., 1964). So, finally, is F. L. Carsten, *The Origins of Prussia* (1954).

On Russian developments see, in addition to the general studies by Florinsky, Blum, and Robinson cited in Chapter 6, B. H. Sumner, *Peter the Great and the Emergence of Russia* (1951), brief but informative; it should be supplemented with Vasiliu Kliuchevsky, *Peter the Great* (tr. 1958). For Peter's great enemy to the north, see R. M. Hatton, *Charles XII of Sweden* (1969), and some of Michael Roberts' *Essays in Swedish History* (1967).

8

An Age of Science and Enlightenment

The Enlightenment was a time of hope. The intellectuals who spoke for the movement, the philosophes, looked to the future as a realm in which many possibilities would be realized. And, in the eighteenth century, their many allies—reasonable, humane Christians—used the word "innovation," an old term of abuse, less with fear than with approval. Progress was an expectation, a program, and a reality. It became almost a fad. "The age," Samuel Johnson said in 1783 with some acerbity, "is running mad after innovation; all the business of the world is to be done in a new way; men are to be hanged in a new way; Tyburn itself is not safe from the fury of innovation." The year after Johnson made this caustic observation, Immanuel Kant defined the Enlightenment as "man's emergence from his self-imposed tutelage," and offered as its motto, "*sapere aude*—dare to know."

The philosophes were anything but alienated from their culture. They were subversive on the important matter of religion: whether they were deists, skeptics, or atheists they were certainly not Christians. But they were surrounded by educated Christians who, like them, deplored superstition, idealized science, and aimed at reasonableness and humaneness. Kant thought he discerned a general "revolt against superstition"; many Frenchmen who were not philosophes liked to call their century the *siècle des lumières*. And just as the philosophes were not isolated from their time, they were not cut off from the past. They were radicals, but they were not rootless. Their most admired intellectual ancestors were the philosophers of pagan antiquity, the critical scholars and disenchanted historians of the Renaissance, and the revolutionary political, religious, and scientific thinkers of the seventeenth century. Without them the Enlightenment would have been impossible.

ROADS TO ENLIGHTENMENT: THE SEVENTEENTH CENTURY

Modern Christianity

The world of educated men in the late seventeenth century had changed out of all recognition since the Renaissance and the Reformation. Neither had aimed at the dissolution of religious authority; quite the contrary. But, as we know, the venturesome diligence of Renaissance Humanists and the quarrels of theologians that marked the Reformation inevitably produced a certain degree of independent judgment; where dogmatic authorities conflict, there is room for skepticism. Few even of the boldest spirits stepped beyond the sacred domain of Christian belief, but many insisted on the need to simplify it and to strip it of inessential admixtures.

Seventeenth-century Europe offered many incentives to skepticism. Not that skepticism was rampant or a serious threat to established religions; most scientists did their work, much as medieval scientists had done theirs, to testify to the splendor of God's handiwork. The great chemist Robert Boyle (see p. 341) wrote tracts designed to prove the religious utility of his scientific researches, and left £350 in his will to endow lectures demonstrating the truth of Christianity. But Boyle's very concern was a sign that science was emerging as a threat to religion: one does not bother to defend what is not under attack. The churches themselves showed signs of a changing spirit. Late in the seventeenth century, partially in reaction to the austerity of the Puritans, now overthrown, the Anglican church embraced Latitudinarianism—a mild, rationalistic Christianity purged of emotionalism and improbable beliefs. "Enthusiasm" and "superstition" were decried and proscribed. Anglicanism consequently lost much genuine religious feeling. In France, "modern" Catholics, most strikingly represented by the Jesuits, toned down their sermons on sin, hell, and damnation; cheerfully they concentrated on men's chances of realizing Christian ideals in this life and of obtaining bliss in the next. Catholics and Protestants alike were moving toward a civilized, relatively worldly faith.

The growth of this new spirit has often been called a crisis, but it was too imperceptible, too long-drawn-out, and in a sense too pleasant to be really a crisis. It was the slow readjustment of educated men and women of their world view to new knowledge which led most of them, not to unbelief, but to tepid belief. Many of them pushed religion, once the center of everyone's concern, to the margins of their existence. [1]

Knowledge and Change

Among the many agents of intellectual change culminating in the Enlightenment, three assumed special prominence: travel reports, historical scholarship, and biblical criticism. Travelers—the ancestors of the cultural anthropologists—showed the world to be larger and far stranger than earlier ages had even suspected. Their discoveries in America and, later, in the Far East had made Europeans acquainted with civilizations that were highly developed and functioned well, and all without the blessings of Christianity. This discovery, as the French anthropologist Claude Lévi-Strauss has observed, was profoundly demoralizing: "Never had the human race been faced with such a terrible ordeal." [2] Yet it was also exhilarating; for every pious believer unsettled by the spectacle of civilized pagans, there was a venturesome European ready to treat them as fascinating specimens in the museum of man. But whether demoralizing or exhilarating, advanced Chinese and Indian civilizations compelled Europeans to weigh their own culture against others and relate it to a worldwide spectrum. Travel became an antidote to parochial isolation and a spur to cultural relativism: the discovery that Christianity was not the only "valid" culture led to the further discovery that there was much wrong with Christian culture. And behind cultural relativism there stood religious skepticism. While most of the travelers were unimpeachable Christian missionaries, the consequence of their work was to throw at least some doubt on the received religious wisdom: Christianity was, it seemed, only one of several religions, one story among many.

As travel made the world larger and stranger than it had been, history made it older and richer. The dominant view of history remained scrupulously devout. In 1681, Bishop Bossuet published a *Discours sur l'histoire universelle* which took as its central events the dispersal of Noah's offspring and the coming of Christ, and as the central cause of historical change the will of God. But there were other currents in the widening stream. There was the school of historical Pyrrhonists who, appealing to the ancient skeptic Pyrrho, held all knowledge of the past to be uncertain and rejected most writing about it as a

---

[1] While the materials for the struggle between science and religion were amassed in the eighteenth century, the struggle itself was fought out largely in the nineteenth.

[2] *Tristes Tropiques* (ed. 1964), 78.

set of fables. This view of the past—or rather, assault on the past—had a hint of impiety about it; but even priests sharpened the instruments of historical research and thus, however unwittingly, prepared the way for the Enlightenment. In 1681, the Benedictine monk Jean Mabillon, member of the distinguished scholarly congregation of Saint Maur in Paris, published a Latin treatise that few men have ever read, but that transformed the discipline of history. *De Re Diplomatica—Concerning Charters*—originated as an attempt to vindicate the authenticity of documents in the possession of the Benedictines which their malicious rivals, the Jesuits, had called into question. Mabillon succeeded, and in the process he established the science of diplomatics—the science of reading historical documents, of establishing their authenticity or spuriousness, of detecting emendations and layers of editions.[3] Other scholars, armed with such instruments, weeded out forgeries, extended the scientific examination of documents to coins, wrote dictionaries: Charles Du Cange published a "glossary" of "late" Latin that vastly improved men's grasp on medieval literature. Knowledge multiplied, with bewildering speed.

In this atmosphere, the critical reading of the Bible touched a particularly sensitive spot. In his *Leviathan,* Thomas Hobbes coolly divided religion from superstition with criteria drawn from politics: "Publicly allowed [tales are called] Religion; not allowed, Superstition."[4] And he suggested that the most fruitful way of understanding Scriptures was by means of the higher criticism. Such a reading, he thought, would prove, among other things, that the books of Kings, Chronicles, and Judges had been written later than tradition asserted. Baruch[5] Spinoza took the higher criticism to new heights in his *Tractatus Theologico-Politicus* of 1670, in which he treated the Bible as a book like any other: "The method of interpreting Scripture does not differ greatly from the method of interpreting Nature—in fact, it is almost the same." Spinoza found the ethical teachings of Scriptures to be parochial—written for, and principally applicable to, one people in one age. Moreover, since the natural order is unalterable and the Bible recounts many tales in which divine intervention interferes with that order, Scripture must be full of later interpolations. Finally, Spinoza argued, the Pentateuch, with its duplicate set of narratives and irreconcilable chronologies, must be a conflation of many manuscripts. The intemperate controversialist Richard Simon, a French priest who flaunted his orthodoxy as he undermined it, added to Spinoza's philosophical penetration a sensitive discrimination of styles. If we carefully read the Old Testament,

---

[3] Renaissance erudition, of which the Humanist Lorenzo Valla's exposure of the Donation of Constantine is a fine example, was an ancestor to this scholarly enterprise.

[4] Renaissance scholarship devoted to establishing a reliable and definitive text of the Bible—textual criticism—was called "lower criticism." Historical criticism, which seeks to settle the meaning of biblical passages by reference to the historical context and general probability, was called "higher criticism." It emerged in the Reformation but required many decades of cautious work before it was generally accepted.

[5] Or, after his expulsion from the synagogue, Benedict.

Simon wrote, we can detect the interpolations of medieval scribes and glaring inconsistencies, like the purported claim of Moses to have written the whole Pentateuch, even though these first five books of the Old Testament include an account of his own death.

These secular readings of sacred texts were offensive to religious authorities, but they remained isolated events; specialized, abstruse, technical, they were read in the main only by a few theologians and by the censors who condemned them. Only the deists in England and Pierre Bayle on the Continent won a wide public with their controversial writings, and thus seriously widened the public for secularism. There were deists on the Continent as well, but the headquarters for this philosophical faith was England. One of its most prominent spokesmen was John Locke's self-proclaimed disciple John Toland, who published *Christianity Not Mysterious* in 1696, a year after Locke's *Reasonableness of Christianity*.[6] The two titles are similar, but they enshrine a decisive difference: Locke had wanted to defend the essence of Christianity by reducing its content; Toland wanted to discard its essence by proving that in its origins Christianity had been quite simply a reasonable belief. Mystery-mongering priests, he argued, had tampered with the primitive Christian doctrine. Without the "pretense" of mystery, "we should never hear of the Transubstantiation, and other ridiculous Fables of the Church of Rome; nor of any of the Eastern Ordures, almost all received into the Western sink." Down to the 1730s or so, the small but loquacious tribe of English deists made a good deal of noise. It has been customary to separate them into "critical" and "constructive" deists, but actually each of them was both one and the other. In their criticism, the deists threw doubt on the authenticity of biblical texts; pointed out contradictions, absurdities, and unpalatable doctrines in both the Old and New Testaments; assailed established churches and ecclesiastical authority. In their constructive work, they portrayed God as a blessed watchmaker who had made the world in all its magnificent variety, with unbreakable physical and self-evident moral laws, and then had withdrawn to allow men to work out their own destiny.[7]

Pierre Bayle

Pierre Bayle appealed to the Enlightenment on other grounds; whatever crisis there was in the mind of the seventeenth century is epitomized in his work. Born in 1647, the son of a Huguenot minister and briefly a Catholic convert, he ended up a Pyrrhonist. After the French government began to persecute the Huguenots seriously, Bayle fled to Holland. There, in 1682, he published his *Miscellaneous Thoughts on the Comet of 1680,* a brilliant assault on the

[6] For Locke, see p. 344.
[7] For later applications of this argument, see p. 354.

superstitious fears that had clustered around the appearance of Halley's comet and a proof that superstition, which converts a natural event into a sign of divine wrath, is more dangerous to civilization than atheism. After the revocation of the Edict of Nantes, Bayle continued these polemics with a moving, powerful appeal for toleration. His *Philosophical Commentary on the Words of Jesus Christ, "Compel Them To Come In,"* is a scathing critique of Catholics' persecuting their Protestant brothers. As a consistent skeptic, Bayle argued that persecutors are not merely vicious but unreasonable for they are certain that their faith is correct and that all other faiths are wicked error. Yet all we know is that we are forever ignorant. And to compel belief is the antithesis of, not the road to, religion—it makes men into victims or hypocrites.

Bayle's masterpiece was the *Historical and Critical Dictionary,* first published in 1697. While it parades as a biographical compendium chastely arranged in alphabetical order, it is actually a shrewd, laboriously disguised statement of Bayle's convictions. It luxuriates in footnotes and sidenotes and interminable cross-references which lead the reader to an article denying what an earlier article had asserted, in unexpected criticisms of traditional heroes like King David, and in occasional salacious anecdotes that pique the reader's interest. The *Dictionary* is a full-throated assault on everything Bayle hated: intolerance, dogmatism, superstition, gullibility, persecution. It is an immensely erudite book, but the erudition is in the service of a new vision of man and society: a vision of brothers, ignorant and comradely, who acknowledge their imperfections and live in peace. Bayle's innermost religious convictions vanish before his passionate propaganda in behalf of toleration, but it is clear that his principled modesty, his Socrates-like insistence that all men are utterly ignorant, is far from incompatible with a certain kind of Protestant belief, and may well have had its roots in such belief.[8] Whatever the elusive truth of the matter, the philosophes treated Bayle quite simply as a skeptic: he was the most welcome and most eloquent ally against "superstition" they could find anywhere.

ROADS TO ENLIGHTENMENT: NEWTON AND LOCKE

While the philosophes quoted Bayle, they deified Newton. All the philosophes—Voltaire and d'Alembert, Hume and Jefferson—treated Bacon, Locke, and Newton as a trinity of great minds, and one of these, Newton, as the

---

[8] It has recently become the subject of scholarly controversy; Howard Robinson's standard *Bayle the Skeptic* (1931) has been countered by writers ready to discover a "positive," and positively religious, philosophy in Bayle. See especially W. H. Barber, "Pierre Bayle: Faith and Reason," in Will Moore et al., eds., *The French Mind: Studies in Honour of Gustave Rudler* (1952), 109–125.

greatest man who ever lived. We must examine Newton's work and, to a lesser degree, the work of Locke to understand how the philosophes employed the heritage they claimed.[9]

Newton's World

Isaac Newton was a legendary figure even in his lifetime, and most of the legends about him are true. The adulation the world showered on him was the tribute appropriate to an achievement unmatched in the history of thought. David Hume called him, in his *History of England,* "the greatest and rarest genius that ever rose for the ornament and instruction of the species," and no one accused Hume of flattery or hyperbole. He had stated a simple truth on which every educated man could agree, and not in England alone.

With his well-known eccentricities and his self-imposed isolation, Newton lent plausibility to the stories about the solitary genius, "voyaging," as Wordsworth would put it, "through strange seas of thought alone." It is in no way to disparage his originality to say that while Newton was voyaging through strange seas, he was not alone. He was part, and culmination, of a philosophical and scientific tradition; he was the heir of the ancient Epicureans, the beneficiary of Bacon's distrust of metaphysics, of Galileo's gift for experimentation, of Descartes' inventions in mathematics. When Newton entered the fraternity of natural philosophers, there was vigorous scientific activity in most European capitals. The eighteenth, and even more the twentieth, century would celebrate Blaise Pascal as the lucid, brooding Christian existentialist who, in his fragmentary *Pensées,* confronted man with his fallen and desolate condition; but his contemporaries knew Pascal as a brilliant mathematician who put the theory of probability on a sound footing, and as an equally brilliant physicist who did research on atmospheric pressure and the behavior of fluids. In biology, a group of scientists used that splendid invention, the microscope, to confirm and extend Harvey's discoveries about the circulation of the blood (see p. 240). One of these was Marcello Malpighi, an Italian anatomist, who published his pioneering treatise on the lung, *De Pulmonibus,* in 1661, in which he described the movement of the blood through capillaries. Another was the Dutch naturalist Jan Swammerdam, who discovered red blood corpuscles in 1658 and the valves of the lymphatics in 1664; he greatly improved scientific knowledge of that mysterious progression—caterpillar into butterfly—which he studied with minute attention and faultless precision. Two other great

[9] For strict accuracy we must also understand the heritage they did not claim. The French philosophes in particular were much in debt to Descartes, especially to his doctrine of clear ideas and his analytical energies. His physiology could also be used—and was so used—as a basis for downright materialism. But Descartes had been "captured" by the forces of respectable piety late in the seventeenth century, his physics had been disproved by Newton, and his methodology seemed excessively rationalistic. Thus it seemed more profitable for the philosophes to disown and attack Descartes than to acknowledge fully how much they owed him.

scientists, Robert Hooke in England and Antony van Leeuwenhoek in Amsterdam, refined the microscope they used so effectively: in 1665, in his *Micrographia,* Hooke described both his new design and some of his discoveries, including the cells of plant tissues. And Leeuwenhoek, diligent correspondent to the Royal Society of London, astonished his contemporaries with his meticulously designed microscopes and with the minute objects he was the first to see and describe: red blood cells, protozoa, bacteria. Chemistry, too, was gradually being transformed from alchemy into a true science. Robert Boyle, ingenious experimenter, bold theorist, and indefatigable writer, applied mechanical philosophy to fluids and gases; he saw the chemist as a physicist dealing with small material particles. His famous *Skeptical Chymist* of 1661 was a critique of traditional procedure and a program for treating substances as composites which the chemist must resolve into their elements—minute particles. The fruits of his work were many and varied; the best known was Boyle's law, which holds that, if temperature is held constant, the volume of a confined gas will decrease in proportion as the pressure is increased.[10]

Newton, then, did his work in a congenial, even fostering, environment. As in other countries, so in England, serious gentlemen, the *virtuosi,* studied natural philosophy in obedience to Bacon's advice to cooperate in the search for knowledge. They clustered in scientific societies that enabled them to exchange ideas, share instruments, and publish experiments. The first of these ambitious associations to survive infancy was the group of scientific amateurs who gathered at Gresham College in London from the mid-1640s on, not long after Newton was born; they met weekly to discuss "experimental Philosophy." In 1662, shortly after the Restoration of Charles II, the Royal Society of London for Improving Natural Knowledge received its charter.[11] Newton's connection with the Royal Society was intimate if rather intermittent. Averse to the squabbling that invigorated and impeded the gatherings of these pioneers, he joined in 1672 but did not play a major part in its deliberations for some years. Then, in 1687, when he published his greatest work, the *Philosophiae Naturalis Principia Mathematica,* he dedicated it to the Royal Society. This is a symbol of the great collaboration that science had become. The *Principia,* for all its lonely eminence, is the top of a pyramid of thought which had been under construction for a century and a half.

Newton's Principia

Like other scientific geniuses, Newton worked out most of his fundamental ideas early. He was born at Woolsthorpe in Lincolnshire, on Christmas Day, 1642; when he succeeded his Cambridge teacher, Isaac Barrow, as Lucasian

[10] On Boyle's religion, see p. 335.
[11] Its French counterpart, the Académie Royale des Sciences de Paris, protected by Louis XIV and Colbert, was chartered in 1666; it, too, emerged from the gatherings of leading scientific theorists and practitioners.

professor of mathematics in 1669, he was already far advanced on the calculus, had discovered the binomial theorem, had performed path-breaking optical experiments that brought him to his theory of colors, and had settled the fundamentals of his greatest discovery, the theory of gravitation. "All this," he recalled much later, "was in the two plague years of 1665 and 1666, for in those years I was in the prime of my age for invention, and minded Mathematicks and Philosophy more than at any time since." Late in 1665 an outbreak of the plague in Cambridge had driven him to retreat at his mother's house at Woolsthorpe, and it was there, in 1666, that he "began to think of Gravity extending to ye orb of the Moon, & (having found out how to estimate the force with which a globe revolving within a sphere presses the surface of the sphere), from Kepler's rule . . . I deduced that the forces which keep the Planets in the Orbs must [be] reciprocally as the squares of their distances from the centers about which they revolve." The essential idea of gravitation, he remembered, had come into his mind as he watched an apple fall. This is the most famous anecdote about him, and it may even be true. But true or not, Newton withheld his discoveries for years, in part because his calculations were at variance with his postulates for the power of the gravitational force. He kept quietly to himself at Trinity College, Cambridge. Then, stung by the astronomical calculations of Robert Hooke (which came perilously close to the truth as Newton divined it) and encouraged by Edmund Halley, astronomer royal and prominent Fellow of the Royal Society, he emerged from his isolation. By 1684, Newton had begun work on the *Principia;* in 1687, he published it to an astonished world.

It is customary to call the *Principia* the greatest scientific work ever written, and custom is right. It is customary also to call Newton's work a synthesis, and once again custom is right. Newton's *Principia* synthesized the scattered discoveries of the pioneers into a single, comprehensive science of mechanics. It suggested solutions to a number of puzzling phenomena like the precession of the equinoxes and the rhythm of the tides. It united such seemingly diverse theories as Galileo's laws of falling bodies and Kepler's laws of planetary motion. And it demonstrated, once and for all, the mutual service that mathematics and the physical sciences can, indeed must, perform for each other. Not the least remarkable aspect of the Newtonian synthesis was that Newton had to invent a language—called "fluxions" then, differential calculus now—before he could construct his system. [12]

The controversial idea that held Newton's system together was gravitation. The *nature* of this astounding force was a mystery Newton did not pretend to unravel. But this much was clear: his theory contradicted Descartes' theory of

[12] The question of priority on the calculus caused one of the celebrated quarrels of the scientific revolution. Newton was doubtless first with the calculus: he wrote of "fluxions" in 1671 and described his method even earlier. Leibniz published his first essay on calculus in 1684. Newton's English admirers then charged Leibniz with plagiarism—a charge of doubtful validity. The ugly controversy simmered for decades.

vortices, which holds that the planets are propelled in their orbits by an impalpable ether in which they rest as they circle around the sun. When the idea of gravitation came to him in 1666, Newton had noted that though the apple was very small and the earth very large, their action must be mutual: "The apple draws the earth, as well as the earth draws the apple." It was precisely this peculiar, almost incredible interaction that permitted Newton to think of gravitation as a universal and uniform force. Every body, every particle, in the universe attracts all other bodies and particles with a power inversely proportional to the square of their distance and proportional to the product of the masses of the bodies involved. These laws of motion show the gravitational pull of the earth on the moon and on an apple to be the same. Bodies terrestrial or celestial, large or small, familiar like planets or rare like comets, moving through an unresisting void or a resisting medium all obey the same law. While the *Principia* was an inordinately inaccessible book, with its Latin and its archaic geometric formulas, its teachings won an instantaneous and complete triumph—at least in England. In France, dominated by the physics and astronomy of Descartes, the conquest took a little longer, but by the 1750s every respectable scientist was a disciple of Newton. What Bacon had hoped for, and scientific societies were advocating, Newton realized with his *Principia:* he made science an international, contentious but cooperative discipline, capable of vast explanatory power.

Newton's Opticks

Once in the public eye, Newton remained there; much of the rest of his life was a diversion from the pursuits that interested him most: theology, chemistry, optics. In 1689, in the midst of the Glorious Revolution, Cambridge elected him to Parliament; in 1693, he suffered a severe breakdown, from which he recovered only gradually; in 1696, he was named warden of the mint; in 1703, he was appointed president of the Royal Society. Two years later, he was knighted—the first scientist to be so honored for his scientific achievement. When he died on March 20, 1727, he was buried in Westminster Abbey with a pomp due a giant among men and hitherto reserved for such dubious benefactors of mankind as princes and generals—"like a king," Voltaire wrote, "who has been good to his subjects."

His many distractions—for fame and fortune are distractions to a speculative mind—did not prevent Newton from completing his early researches on light. The *Opticks: Or a Treatise on the Reflections, Refractions, Inflexions and Colours of Light* appeared in 1704; written in English and attractively argued, it was a relief after the austere complexities of the *Principia*. The *Opticks* gave a precise account of Newton's experiments with the prism and proved the composite nature of colors from the pure colors of the spectrum. While other scientists had known something of the properties of the prism, Newton established the theory of optics on a firm basis and brought it into the range of physics. The results were enormously fruitful. Newton fully explained the color of the rainbow and of soap bubbles and a host of other optical phenomena; his speculative queries opened the tantalizing possibility that light might be both wave and particle; and he successfully demonstrated his incredible contention that white is not a simple color, but a composite of all pure spectral colors.

This in itself was a very great deal. But Newton did more. His historic importance lay in his capacity to move from the substance of science to its method—or rather, to move to its method *through* substance. The theory of gravitation led to a strange paradox: since the nature of gravitation was admittedly unknown, Newton's critics accused him—him, the master empiricist!—of reintroducing into science the "occult qualities" of the Scholastics. Gravitation, after all, supposedly acted across vast distances, through empty space, and how was such a mystery to be accounted for? Newton did not find these difficulties daunting; he denied that his principles were occult in any way. The idea of gravity worked, and the effects of gravitation were clear and measurable; now if the cause of a phenomenon is not known, the scientist must remain content with studying its effects. This disclaimer was a giant step in the emancipation of science from metaphysics. "*Hypotheses non fingo*—I feign no hypotheses," he insisted; this meant not that the "experimental philosopher" can do without imaginative leaps, but that he is always guided by the phenomena, always returns to experience, always checks his results through experimentation. "Whatever is not deduced from the phenomena is to be called a hypothesis; and hypotheses, whether metaphysical or physical, whether of occult qualities or mechanical, have no place in experimental philosophy." It was under the pleasing name of "philosophical modesty" that these methodological principles would become the battle cry and the announced, if not always the actual, method of Newton's self-proclaimed disciples in the eighteenth century (see p. 349).

Newton's Ally: John Locke

From the perspective of the philosophes, the only rival to the immortal Newton was John Locke, the philosopher who, they thought, took the methods of Newton and opened the way to science where there had been nothing but fancy before. Locke himself enormously admired Newton. Although he was born in 1632, and was thus ten years older than Newton, Locke talked of him as a guide, almost a master. Next to "the incomparable Mr. Newton" he wrote in his *Essay Concerning Human Understanding,* he himself was but "an underlabourer in clearing the ground a little and removing some of the rubbish that lies in the way to knowledge."

As a characteristic model for the Enlightenment, John Locke was proficient in many fields and wrote with authority on many matters. He was trained at

Oxford, lectured there on philosophy, studied the sciences, and briefly practiced medicine. He moved all his life among the Whig magnates whose convictions and political fortunes he shared; late in 1683, when the Whig leaders were under suspicion or in exile, he took ship to the Dutch Republic and did not return until early in 1689, in the train of the successful revolutionaries, Dutch William and his queen, Mary (see p. 313). He brought with him the manuscripts of books he had been working on for a number of years: a *Letter Concerning Toleration*, published in the year of his return, *Two Treatises of Government* and the *Essay Concerning Human Understanding*, both published in 1690, all three landmarks in their spheres. Locke's *Some Thoughts Concerning Education* (1693) would be scarcely less epoch-making for the history of pedagogical theory.

John Locke has been called a conservative revolutionary, but in some respects his political ideas reached beyond the boundaries that his own associates, the architects of the Glorious Revolution, set for England. In his *Letter Concerning Toleration*, he argued against religious persecution on both moral and practical grounds. A church is a "voluntary society" with no right to use force against its members; a state may use such force, but not in religious matters. Persecution, whether by the religious or the secular arm, is unlawful. It is also foolish: dissenting sects become seditious and conspiratorial only when they are being persecuted, not otherwise. Locke wanted to exclude only two groups from toleration: Roman Catholics, because their loyalty was to a foreign power, the papacy; and atheists, because they are without a firm foundation for moral conduct, belief in God. Locke's arguments for broad toleration are practical, political, secular. Yet, while Locke's ideas would echo in the writings of the philosophes, his England of the 1690s was not yet ready for them. The toleration Locke desired was what English politicians called "comprehension" and rejected in behalf of a narrower policy—a state church of Anglicans that excluded the dissenting sects from higher education and political participation (see p. 313).

The ideas of Locke's *Two Treatises*, on the other hand, fitted the new conditions to perfection. The accident of their publication after the expulsion of James II, and Locke's own claim in the preface that they were designed "to establish the throne of our great restorer, our present King William; to make good his title, in the consent of the people," gave them the appearance of apologies written for the Glorious Revolution. They could be so used, and Locke, as we have seen, was glad to see them so used. But he had actually written them earlier, as a contribution to the exclusion campaign aimed at keeping the Catholic duke of York from succeeding to the throne.[13] That political tracts written for one occasion could be cited for another is a tribute to their reach for general application.

Actually, the first of these treatises, little read today, is highly specialized. It is a contemptuous refutation of Sir Robert Filmer's posthumous *Patriarcha*.

---

[13] See the critical edition of the *Two Treatises* by Peter Laslett (2nd ed. 1967).

Filmer, an extreme royalist, had died in 1653, in Cromwell's reign, but his pamphlet conveniently—or inconveniently—appeared in the midst of the exclusion crisis, in 1680. Filmer had argued in behalf of the divine right of kings from the absolute right of fathers over their children. Locke demolished the theory by demolishing the analogy. He pictured man's original condition not as one of natural subjection, but of natural equality and freedom given to all men by God. This is the meaning of Locke's "state of nature." While this portrait seems at first glance cheerful enough, actually Locke's view of man's prepolitical condition was little more cheerful than Hobbes'—with its war of all against all and its vision of the life of man as "solitary, poor, nasty, brutish, and short." Locke suggested that while men might live in peace without any public authority, the absence of impartial judges and the endemic threat of war made the state of nature at best an inconvenience and at worst a hell on earth. Man, Locke reasoned, is driven by these realities into making a social contract, which establishes a society, which in turn establishes an authority to govern. He insisted that this grant of power was conditional: it must rest, no matter how indirectly, on the consent of the governed and act in their interest. While with his characteristic moderation Locke circumscribed the right of revolution, he explicitly recognized conditions when the state invites disobedience and thus makes revolution lawful. The state, Locke wrote in a famous chapter, exists principally to protect the subjects' "property"—an ambiguous term that Locke himself broadly interpreted to include man's physical possessions and his liberty and life as well. When a monarch deprives his subjects of their property without their consent or interferes with the proper functions of the legislature, he has broken the social contract, and the people may form a new state. "The community," Locke insisted, "perpetually retains a supreme power."

In the Enlightenment, these ideas were generalized beyond the English political scene to the Western world. They became principles underlying the demands for constitutional government, for the rule of law, for protected rights—for liberalism. Locke as a liberal did not maintain, "the fewer laws the better"; Locke took care to argue that the executive must be endowed with adequate powers to carry out his duties. He even envisaged occasions when the executive acts outside the laws: "This power to act according to discretion for the public good, without the prescription of the law and sometimes even against it, is that which is called prerogative." But the dominant direction of his thought was in behalf of individual freedom and the rule of law, and this is how his ideas were taken in the eighteenth century.

Influential as Locke's political ideas proved to be, his ideas on philosophical method and the theory of knowledge proved even more influential. Arguing against Descartes and the Cartesians, Locke held in his *Essay* that man has no innate knowledge at birth, but acquires all the materials for knowledge through the senses and then gives his acquisitions shape through reflection. Thus Locke became the patron of modern empiricism—the philosophy that derives all knowledge ultimately from experience and continually sends the inquirer back to experience. This view placed enormous stress on the power of environment over ideas and thus opened the way for an optimistic appraisal of the possibilities for reforming man and society. In his pedagogic treatise, *Some Thoughts Concerning Education,* Locke drew these consequences with perfect consistency: "Of all the men we meet with," he wrote, "nine parts of ten are what they are, good or evil, useful or not, by their education." In his analysis of knowledge, Locke, following Galileo and Newton, divided the qualities of the things we experience into primary and secondary. The primary qualities—extension, shape, motion—inhere in the things themselves; they exist in the outside world independently of the observer. The secondary qualities—smell, color, taste—are supplied by the observer. Thus Locke denied knowledge to be a mere copy of the outside world; it was instead a correspondence established by clear perceptions and careful discriminations. Locke implicitly argued what the philosophes would make explicit: philosophy is scientific method. This, in essence, was the meaning of Locke—and Newton—for the Enlightenment.

THE ENLIGHTENMENT: MAP OF A MOVEMENT

An International Family

The accepted name for the men of the Enlightenment, "philosophe," is French. But there were philosophes in Scotland, England, Geneva, Milan, Prussia, and the British colonies in America as well; while the French representatives of the movement were the most celebrated and the most conspicuous, the type was truly international. [14] The philosophes did not form a disciplined party or a tight school. They were a loose, generally cordial coalition of literary men, academics, public servants, scattered all over the Western world—Voltaire and Lessing were men of letters, Adam Smith and Immanuel Kant were professors, Turgot and Jefferson were statesmen. They were friends, correspondents, members of informal coteries. They might argue, even quarrel, with one another, but they were allies, self-conscious and self-selected, in a great cause. They were an international family. Paris was the headquarters, and French the favored language of these radical intellectuals all across the Western world, but other countries too played their part in the shaping of the Enlightenment. Its first inspiration came, as we have seen, from seventeenth-century England. Until the romance began to fade in the 1760s, the men of the Continental Enlightenment admired, even envied England as the home of philosophy, freedom, and decency, and held up English institutions for imitation. Voltaire, who came to England in 1726 and stayed for over two years, and Montesquieu, who arrived for a long visit in 1729, were indefatigable propagandists for England. They were "Anglomaniacs" and proud of it. Voltaire's sprightly,

---

[14] That is why, instead of italicizing "philosophe," we have naturalized it here.

much-read report on his love affair with England, the *Lettres philosophiques*,[15] is a cardinal document of the Enlightenment. It affectionately surveys English religious diversity, English political freedom, and English cultural wealth. England, Voltaire told his readers, is tolerant, free, and prosperous, and prosperous precisely because it is tolerant and free. "The commerce which has enriched the citizens of England, has contributed to making them free; from this has sprung the greatness of the state." Here was a country that respected merchants, idolized scientists, and rewarded literary men with good incomes, influential positions, and social prestige. This enviable situation of writers was of particular interest to Voltaire, that ambitious and self-respecting man of letters; it was, he wrote, still another consequence of England's political structure. In England, "literature is more highly honored than in France. This advantage is a necessary consequence of their form of government."

While French philosophes were the receptive disciples of English writers and delighted observers of English institutions, they in turn influenced the rest of the Western Enlightenment. The Neapolitan legal reformer Gaetano Filangieri acknowledged that the impetus for his treatise on legislation had come from Montesquieu; Hume in Scotland, Gibbon in England, Madison in America were all deeply in Montesquieu's debt. One of the two best known German *Aufklärer*, Gotthold Ephraim Lessing, learned a great deal from Diderot's aesthetic writings and bourgeois dramas; the other, Immanuel Kant, declared that he owed his respect for the common man to his reading of Rousseau.[16] And while the French Enlightenment imported ideas, it also exported them, through the whole eighteenth century. Cesare Beccaria, the great Milanese legal theorist, traced what he called his "conversion to philosophy" to Montesquieu, d'Alembert, Diderot, Helvétius, Buffon, and Hume—all but the last of these Frenchmen. But his celebrated treatise on legal reform, the essay *On Crimes and Punishments* (1764), had considerable influence in France, especially on Voltaire. The collaboration among the philosophic family was intense and reciprocal.

The terms of that collaboration differed from country to country, and depended on local political realities. England had had its revolution, and the voices of Enlightenment in that country were least demanding, most closely associated with respectable circles. France was on its way to revolution; conservative forces were just tenacious enough to place the philosophes into opposition and to unite them through harassment, but not strong enough to prevent them from disseminating their often subversive views. Further east, in the authoritarian regimes of the German states and beyond, *Aufklärer* for the most part timidly worked within the system as much as they could, as advisors to the ruling house.

---

[15] It was first published, incomplete, in English, in 1733, as *Letters Concerning the English Nation*, and complete, in French, in the following year.

[16] Rousseau was a Genevan, but French in language and largely in culture. In thinking of him, though, we must never forget that he was, first and foremost, a Genevan.

The philosophes, then, differed in their temperament, their tactics, and their hopes. But they were united by a common set of convictions and a common style of thinking. What characterized them all, in the face of their differences, was an aggressive secularism and its accompaniment, a commitment to the critical spirit. Everything—including politics and religion, those two sacrosanct subjects—was open to criticism; everything, including the very methods of inquiry, was open to inquiry. "Facts," Denis Diderot wrote in his *Encyclopédie* (see p. 356), "may be distributed into three classes: the acts of divinity, the phenomena of nature, and the actions of men. The first belong to theology, the second to philosophy, and the last to history properly speaking. All are equally subject to criticism." It was in this spirit that David Hume could write a long essay entitled *The Natural History of Religion:* for the men of the Enlightenment, religion was a psychological disposition and a social institution like any other. The universal criticism of the philosophes led away from piety and to a determined critique of Christianity.

On this crucial issue, of course, men of the Enlightenment repudiated Newton, for Newton had been a devoutly religious man. He had spent a great deal of effort seeking to establish biblical chronologies, and he was piously certain that God actively and continuously governed the universe. The deists' conception of God as the divine watchmaker struck Newton as blasphemous. God supplements and corrects the laws of nature by direct intervention; he had done his scientific work, Newton said in 1692, to establish "such principles as might work with considering men for the belief of a Deity" (see p. 231). The philosophes labored in precisely the opposite direction. Polemics against superstition and fanaticism in general, and Christianity in particular, invaded all their work and compromised some of it: one need only read Voltaire's or Hume's historical writings on the Middle Ages to see that irreligiosity may, in addition to enlarging men's horizons, narrow their sympathies and color their judgment. Not even Locke was an acceptable guide in this touchy field. Locke's little treatise, *The Reasonableness of Christianity,* had proposed that revelation is only an exalted form of reason and that a good Christian must accept only one dogma: the divinity of Christ. But these large concessions to the secular spirit were not enough for the philosophes: "Mr. Lock's reasonableness of christian relligion," Voltaire wrote in one of his notebooks, in English, "is really a new relligion." And if there was anything the philosophes wanted, it was surely not the making of a new religion but an end to the old.

The meaning of Newton for the Enlightenment, to reiterate, lay not in what he believed, but in how he went about his work.[17] Newton—and to a degree his precursor, Bacon, and his ally, Locke—had been an empiricist.

---

[17] It lay also in what he was—and what Bacon and Locke were. This trinity is interesting not merely in whom it includes, but in whom it excludes. None of these three was a king, a conqueror, a visionary, or a saint. The philosophes greatly preferred merchants to politicians, scientists to generals, secular to religious men, as they preferred pleasure to austerity, prosperity to glory, reasonableness to exaltation. What Nietzsche undertook late in the nineteenth century—a transvaluation of values—was also a significant aspect of the philosophes' work.

Bacon, Voltaire emphatically told his readers, was the "father of experimental philosophy," builder of "the scaffolding with which we have built the new philosophy," a thinker who, if he himself did not know nature, "knew and showed all the paths that led to it." Locke, the sage and practical thinker had refused to write "the romance of the soul," and "modestly wrote its history" instead. And Newton, as Voltaire often reiterated, taught mankind to "examine, weigh, calculate, and measure, and never to conjecture." He had refused to construct futile systems: "He saw and he made people see, but he did not put his fantasies in place of truth." This modesty in the face of impenetrable mysteries, this confession of partial ignorance, was a strategic weapon in the conquest of knowledge; it protected intelligent men from wasting their lives quibbling about mere words and instead helped them to concentrate their energies on what can be known and must be done. The unprecedented triumphs of Newton—on this Voltaire and the other philosophes endlessly insisted—were not simply the unduplicable work of a unique genius. They were the triumphs of a method that lesser men, too, could acquire and apply.

Reason, Passion, and Hope

Since the early nineteenth century, when a number of Romantic critics charged the philosophes with "shallow rationalism" and "facile optimism," these two labels have clung to the Enlightenment. But, as the philosophes' devotion to Newton's "philosophical modesty" should make clear, both are largely unjust. Their Newtonianism pointed the philosophes toward practicality. Somewhat narrowly, they defined philosophy as effective criticism; a century before Marx said it, they held that the task of the philosopher is not merely to understand the world but to change it. The philosophes have been called irresponsible coffeehouse politicians and wide-eyed utopians, but these charges, too, will not stand examination. While few of them held public office, most of them derived their criticisms, proposals, and expectations from the world in which they lived. They were neither isolated nor sheltered. If they were men of good hope, the world pressed such hope upon them. In fact, while optimism was the spreading mood of the age, the philosophes fenced in their hopes with skepticism and pessimism. The theory of progress, which sees improvement inherent in the world's way and inescapable, was not widespread among them. The philosophe Condorcet, whose celebrated *Essay on the Progress of the Human Spirit* has often been treated as a typical expression of the Enlightenment's view of life, actually stood at the rosiest end of the philosophic spectrum. And even he saw most of the world still plunged into darkness, ignorance, suffering, and superstition and pinned his hopes mainly on "the sweet hopes" of the future. For Condorcet, belief in progress was a form of therapy. Most of the other philosophes asserted, with the historian Gibbon, that for much of the past, progress had in fact taken place, but they did not commit themselves to the continuation of such advance. It was pleasing to note, that, in Gibbon's words, "every age of the world has increased, and still increases, the real wealth, the happiness, the knowledge, and perhaps the virtue of the human race." But most philosophes agreed that progress was slow and highly selective: it might take place in the sciences and in the standard of living, but it was improbable in morals and unthinkable in the arts. Besides, many philosophes were convinced that human affairs undergo a certain cycle of growth and decay. "Empires, like men," d'Alembert argued, "must grow, decay, and die." David Hume put it even more strongly: "When the arts and sciences come to perfection in any state, from that moment they naturally, or rather necessarily decline, and seldom or never revive in that nation, where they formerly flourished." In addition, most of the philosophes held the uncomfortable conviction that all progress must be paid for. A civilization that achieves the benefits of politeness acquires the vice of artificiality; improvements in trade and industry often increase the chances of despotic rule. This was not merely the kind of paradox for which Jean Jacques Rousseau was to become notorious; it was the general view of the Enlightenment. "No advantages in this world are pure and unmixed"—it was not Rousseau who wrote these words, but Hume.

The philosophes' attitude toward reason was as nuanced as their optimism. Their commitment to practicality, in fact, led them to repudiate the rationalist philosophies of seventeenth-century thinkers—those grandiose, ambitious systems of thought which, they charged, were derived not from experience but from rumination, and which undertook to explain what sensible men renounced as forever inexplicable. In this sense, the philosophes' philosophy was a revolt against rationalism. The Enlightenment is often called an Age of Reason, but these two names are not contradictory. It is worth repeating that to the philosophes reason meant scientific method: it meant reasonableness and a constant appeal to experience. Voltaire's motto, au fait!—to the facts!—was the motto of the Enlightenment. The methods of theology and metaphysics, which had traditionally dominated men's thinking, had only produced endless squabbles and unresolved contradictions. The new philosophy—science—was showing a way of breaking away from this scandal and promised to produce knowledge that men could agree upon and use.

The philosophes did not merely limit the competence of reason by insisting that there was a great deal man could never know. They also rehabilitated the great competitor of reason in insisting on the power and defending the effects of the passions. Hume's much-quoted remark, "Reason is, and ought only to be the slave of the passions," is less a critique of the Enlightenment's philosophy from within the camp than an expression of confidence in the passions that most of the philosophes shared. "People ceaselessly proclaim against the passions," Diderot wrote, "people impute to the passions all of men's pains, and forget that they are also the source of all his pleasures. It is an element of man's constitution of which we can say neither too many favorable, nor too many unfavorable things. . . . It is only the passions, and the great passions, that can raise the soul to great things." The philosophes recognized the significance of dreams, the driving force of unacknowledged emotions, and even the Oedipus complex[18] because they seriously respected, and scientifically studied, the passions.

It has often been noted, rightly enough, that the Enlightenment assailed Christianity for its supposed hostility to reason. In fact, as the philosophes saw it, Christianity offended against reason in two ways: by harboring superstitions no reasonable man could accept and by constructing ambitious systems (as in Scholasticism) that violated reasonableness in the opposite direction—by excess. But in addition, the philosophes assailed Christianity for what they thought its hostility to innocent or beneficent passions, especially pride and sensuality. They acknowledged that pride, in the form of conceit or snobbery or love of power, had its harmful aspects. But, rejecting the Christian doctrine of original sin in all its forms, they cherished man's proud self-reliance: "One should say to every individual," Voltaire wrote, "'Remember your dignity as a man.'" For the same reason, they offered a sympathetic view of man's sensual nature; to denounce sexual desire as "lust" and to demand "evangelical perfection" was, quite simply, to stifle an essential part of man's nature and to lead him into confusion, misery, and crime. In his Supplement to Bougainville's Voyage, part book review, part imaginary dialogue, Diderot pitted reasonable Tahitians, who copulate freely and have no incest taboo, against the hypocritical and immensely damaging doctrine of Christian shame and chastity. Indeed, Christian notions about sensuality irreparably corrupt the mind: "People will no longer know what they must do or not do; guilty in the state of innocence, tranquil in the midst of crime, they will have lost the north star that should guide their course." Diderot's little extravaganza states the Enlightenment's case rather strongly, but his defense of sensuality was characteristic. Enlightened man, who was the philosophes' ideal, would be both more freely reasonable and more freely passionate than the Christian man. The philosophes' program for social, legal, political improvement for which they are best known—their cosmopolitanism, their call for tolerance and humanity—logically followed not merely from their hopes, but from this analysis of reason and the passions.

Three Generations of Philosophes

This definition of the philosophes and summary of their philosophy gives a misleading impression of immobility. In fact, the Enlightenment had its own

---

[18] In his dialogue, Rameau's Nephew, Diderot has one of the two speakers say to the other about his child: "If your little savage were left to himself, keeping all his childish foolishness and joining the bit of rationality of the infant in the cradle to the violent passions of the man of thirty, he would strangle his father and sleep with his mother." A hundred and fifty years later, Sigmund Freud delightedly quoted this passage.

internal history; each generation of philosophes confidently built on the work of its predecessors, each could take for granted the critical achievements of its elders and thus be more radical than they.

Broadly speaking, the Enlightenment unfolded within the hundred-year span between the Glorious Revolution and the French Revolution. These dates are, to be sure, only approximate, but they are convenient and evocative: Montesquieu was born in 1689 and Holbach died in 1789. Within this period, we may distinguish three overlapping generations of philosophes. The first of these was dominated by Montesquieu and Voltaire, those two Anglomaniacs who formed their thought while Locke and Newton were still alive. Montesquieu was born into a noble family near Bordeaux; he briefly served in the local parlement in a seat he had inherited from his uncle and was active in the local academy, where he read his earliest philosophical papers. His first important work, the *Lettres persanes,* was published in 1721 during the Regency (see p. 379). It was a witty, sly collection of disenchanted reflections on love, religion, and freedom, with some daring hits at French society and the Christian religion. With its sympathy for slaves, its contempt for persecutors, its impatience with humbug, and its literate way of saying serious things in a light-hearted manner, the *Lettres persanes* set the tone for nearly a century of Enlightenment propaganda. It gave Montesquieu first some notoriety and then, in 1728, a seat in that exclusive club, the Académie Française. After an extended time of travel, Montesquieu sat down in his splendid library at La Brède, and translated his copious notes and omnivorous reading into *De l'esprit des lois,* a vast, disheveled masterpiece, the pioneer of modern sociology.[19] It appeared in 1748, and achieved international influence by the 1750s. When Montesquieu died in 1755, his only rival in the world of wit and intellect was Voltaire.

Voltaire—really François Marie Arouet—was born at Paris in 1694, the son of prosperous bourgeois parents. He was intended for the law, but chose literature instead; in his fashionable Jesuit school, Louis-le-Grand, and in equally fashionable salons which welcomed him as a very young man, he acquired a reputation for his literary gifts and his unmatched wit. His facility with words was almost proverbial, but he disciplined his talents to serve the one virtue he prized above all others—clarity. The wide popularity of the Enlightenment owes as much to his style as to its teachings. His irreverence and his associations soon got him into trouble. In 1717-1718 he spent eleven months in the Bastille (for scurrilous verses against the regent); he emerged with a new name, "de Voltaire," and his first tragedy, *Œdipe.* The name stuck, and the tragedy was an immense success: the public, parched for talent, hailed him as the successor to Corneille and Racine. Buoyed by his triumph, Voltaire tried his hand at a new genre—the epic. He aspired to being the Vergil of France. During the 1720s, he published various versions of the *Henriade,* an overlong and relatively uninspired—though at the time much praised—paean to his favorite

[19] For an appraisal of the book, see p. 361.

French king, Henri IV. The *Henriade,* with its sallies against fanatical priests and praise of the tolerant Henri, suggested certain intellectual and political interests. Events were to force these interests to the fore. In the winter of 1725, Voltaire became involved in a petty quarrel with a dissolute aristocrat, the chevalier de Rohan, who treated his non-noble adversary with superb disdain; early in 1726, Rohan watched from a cab as his footmen gave Voltaire a humiliating beating. The consequence—for Voltaire—was arrest; after some weeks of comfortable imprisonment in the Bastille, Voltaire went to England, where he breathed the air of a free society, nourished his resentments, and strengthened his political and philosophical convictions. When he returned, he had new language for ideas he had held before. The first result was the *Lettres philosophiques* (see p. 348); another was a lucid popularization of Newtonianism, published in 1738. The *Eléments de la philosophie de Newton* was written at Cirey, the château of his mistress, Madame du Châtelet, a scientifically inclined bluestocking. There, at Cirey, conveniently remote from Paris, Voltaire studied science and theology. But his subversive investigations into Scriptures long remained private; instead he published poetry and philosophical tales and campaigned for a seat in the Académie Française. Famous as he was, and assiduously as he flattered his influential friends, he did not achieve that goal until 1746: despite his caution, he could not repress his irreverence. The long Cirey episode ended in 1749, when his mistress died in childbirth, bearing someone else's child. A year later, the disconsolate, displaced Voltaire finally yielded to the entreaties of Frederick II and went to Prussia. By this time the second generation of philosophes was active and had moved, in some respects, beyond its masters.

Midcentury: A Turning Point

Like most of the early philosophes, Voltaire was and always remained a deist. He repudiated the cruel and vengeful God of the Old Testament and the fabulous tales of the New Testament, and instead pictured the divine watchmaker, who had made the world perfectly, giving it unalterable physical and moral laws. Some of the second generation were in sympathy with these doctrines—they certainly permitted a great deal of vocal anticlericalism. And all the philosophes welcomed Voltaire's advocacy of toleration. But some of them went toward skepticism or into outright materialism.

This was a generation rich in talent. Benjamin Franklin, who would later serve as a model for philosophes in search of the enlightened statesman, was born in 1706. Buffon, the greatest natural scientist of the century (the Newton of geology and biology), was born in 1707. La Mettrie, the most amusing of the materialists, was born in 1709. Others followed in a cluster: David Hume was born in 1711, Rousseau in 1712, Diderot in 1713, Condillac and Helvétius in 1715, d'Alembert in 1717. At midcentury, these men had done some striking work. Actually, the most remarkable among all these remarkable men, David Hume, had published his first book, the *Treatise of Human Nature*, a decade before, in 1739–1740. Unlike many of the philosophes, Hume was a technical philosopher: his *Treatise*, and his more accessible revisions of it, developed what he himself called a moderate skepticism—a devastating critique of Christian, deist, and metaphysical dogmatism, and a psychological analysis that traced the roots of human actions and the firmest of convictions to habit. At the same time, like the other philosophes, Hume was a versatile man of letters, polished in manner and persuasive in argumentation. In an impressive burst of creativity, he wrote epoch-making essays on demography, political economy, cultural history, religious sociology (see p. 360). By 1751, when he published the *Enquiry Concerning the Principles of Morals*, his philosophy was familiar to the literate public, though few adopted it; Hume's skepticism, for all its moderation, was an uncomfortable guide even to the enlightened.

In contrast, Jean Jacques Rousseau, born the year after Hume, championed a kind of philosophical faith—an emotional, sentimental deism—all his life. Unlike Hume, who was edgy in his philosophy and amiable in his conduct, Rousseau breathed warmth in his writings and alienated everyone. The son of a watchmaker who abandoned him, Rousseau never shed his Genevan Calvinist background (it marks all his thinking) and never overcame his neurotic dependence. He longed for friendship and he made enemies; yet he was so obviously perceptive, so clearly a man of unprecedented vision, that many men of great talent—Diderot, Voltaire, Hume—were his friends for a time. He broke with them all; indeed, late in life his sense of isolation and fear of persecution overwhelmed him. But in his troubled, wandering life he produced cultural criticism and social theory of great penetration and enduring influence.

In 1750, still Diderot's friend and living in Paris, Rousseau became famous overnight with an essay that won a prize offered by the Academy of Dijon. In this extravagant and eloquent *Discourse on the Arts and Sciences*, Rousseau argued that man, innately good, had been corrupted by the advances of culture. The essay, stronger in rhetoric than in logic or history, gave him a reputation he strenuously repudiated but never quite outgrew—that of a primitivist. Rousseau insisted that one fundamental principle informed all his writings: man is born good and society has depraved him; he can never return to his prepolitical condition, but must rise to a higher civilization. While Rousseau's second discourse, *On the Origin of Inequality*, published in 1754, was far more nuanced than the first, it did not rescue him from the charge of primitivism. In fact, the phrase, "the noble savage," which is often identified with him, does not appear in his writings. In this second discourse, he developed a hypothetical history of civilization in which the invention of private property appears as the clue to most social evils. In these early diagnostic works, Rousseau noted in passing that civilization had brought man suffering, but also inestimable benefits like the rule of law. In the early 1760s he would move from criticism to construction, diagnosis to prescription (see p. 358).

His old friend Denis Diderot, meanwhile, had launched an *Encyclopédie,* an enterprise that marked the increasing radicalism of the Enlightenment and the increasing tension between the philosophes and the Old Regime. The son of a prosperous provincial craftsman, Diderot had at first thought of entering the church, but had lost his faith and drifted to Paris, where he made a precarious living doing translations from the English and occasional writing. He moved from orthodox Catholicism to a vague philosophical religion to materialism, and in the summer of 1749, his philosophical opinions landed him in the dungeon of Vincennes. A place of detention near Paris, it proved far less comfortable than the Bastille. He was released after making an abject apology, and on the insistence of his employers, a consortium of publishers for whom he had been editing an encyclopedia since 1747.

A ponderous, multivolume enterprise like an encyclopedia seems a most unsuitable weapon in an intellectual crusade, but this is what Diderot's *Encyclopédie* in fact became. It was a piece of drudgery as well, and a mine of politically innocuous information; Diderot, who wrote hundreds of the articles himself and supervised a stable of contributors, took care to include informative articles on crafts and the sciences. But his chief associate, the brilliant mathematician Jean le Rond d'Alembert, was a philosophe like himself, and the two brought such philosophes as Montesquieu and Voltaire, Holbach and Rousseau, and others, to write pieces that ridiculed superstition, advocated toleration, and more or less candidly supported the new philosophy of the Enlightenment. A good encyclopedia, Diderot ambitiously announced, should "change the general way of thinking." His *Encyclopédie,* with its thousands of subscribers and thousands of additional readers in public libraries, did nothing less.

At first all went relatively smoothly. The first volume was published in 1751; it aroused some adverse comment and widespread enthusiasm. The turning point—it proved a turning point not merely for the *Encyclopédie* but for the Enlightenment in general—came in 1757, with the seventh volume. It included a long, highly tendentious article on Geneva by d'Alembert: he had praised the Genevan Calvinist clergy for their modernity and freedom from superstition and insinuated that they were practically all deists. This, for a philosophe, was high praise, but the Genevan pastors treated it as an insult or a grave indiscretion. There was a storm, first by Genevans against d'Alembert, then by pious Frenchmen against the *Encyclopédie.* Early in 1758, d'Alembert prudently withdrew from the enterprise and Diderot, though shaken, went on alone. But then, in July of that year, Helvétius published *De l'esprit,* a treatise on psychology and morals that analyzed man as a purely selfish animal. It caused a scandal far greater than d'Alembert's article on Geneva, and the two were linked in the minds of alarmed Christians. *De l'esprit* is hardly a first-rate book, but its frank hedonism suggested how subversive the philosophes had already become. The censor who had approved the book for publication was fired, Helvétius was dismissed from his post at court, and in the general swarm of charges of impiety the *Encyclopédie* was victimized as well. In 1759 it was officially suppressed, and Diderot continued to publish it—underground.

The Mature Enlightenment: The 1760s and Beyond

The suppression of the *Encyclopédie* was a symptom and a sign. Except for Montesquieu, the philosophes of the first two generations were still active—in new fields, with new intensity. And a third generation of philosophes had joined them to add new talents and new lands to the domain of philosophy. After midcentury, the German states could boast a modest but growing Enlightenment. A small, intrepid band of *Aufklärer*, frustrated by the domination of French culture, handicapped by the small size of the reading public, and shackled by stringent censorship, sought to bring the new ideas to a new audience. They, too, were part of the international family of philosophes. The eldest of these, though not the first to distinguish himself, was Immanuel Kant. Born in 1724, a lifelong resident and professor at Königsberg, Kant developed a philosophical system of striking coherence and originality. The problem he posed to himself was a characteristic Enlightenment problem: how are knowledge and morality possible? Nor is it an accident that his three great works were entitled "critiques." All of them—*Critique of Pure Reason, Critique of Practical Reason*, and *Critique of Judgment*, published between 1781 and 1790—sought to establish the possibility of knowledge and morality on grounds that Newton had prepared and in response to problems that Hume and Rousseau had raised. Kant's decisive insight, which he likened to the Copernican revolution, was to reverse the accepted view that the structure of men's knowledge reflects the structure of the outside world. He held instead that the structure of the outside world conforms to the structure of men's minds: we can only know what we know because we, as men, are made as we are. Original though his answer was, his way of asking questions, and his general philosophical orientation, belongs squarely to the Western Enlightenment. It was Kant who gave the aim of the Enlightenment its most comprehensive formulation: it was, he said, human autonomy (see p. 334).

The other *Aufklärer* resembled their Western counterparts perhaps even more closely. Gotthold Ephraim Lessing and his Jewish friend, Moses Mendelssohn, both born in 1729, were men of letters with a most versatile range. Lessing wrote poems; essays on the theater, aesthetics, religion, and freemasonry; and plays advocating reconciliation and toleration. His most famous drama, *Nathan the Wise*, a sermon on brotherhood, took Mendelssohn—a religious thinker, epistemologist, translator, poet, and aesthetician—as its model. A third *Aufklärer*, Christoph Martin Wieland, born in 1733, moved to freethinking on the Voltairian model after a pious youth, and proliferated tales,

novels, essays, poems, and satires. His writings breathe a modern Epicureanism; they preach (if such elegant writings may be said to preach) reasonableness
and responsibility, urbanity and tolerance, worldliness and civilization.

In France, too, younger men entered the field. There was Anne Robert
Jacques Turgot, born in 1727, famous for his youthful discourse on progress, an
economist and public servant who became intendant of Limoges in 1761, and
in 1774, after the accession of Louis XVI, was appointed to the cabinet (see
p. 461). There was the gifted mathematician Condorcet, born in 1743, the
disciple of Turgot, d'Alembert, and Voltaire. There was Baron Holbach, born
earlier, in 1723, but achieving prominence late, in the combat-ridden 1760s. A
rich German nobleman resident in Paris, Holbach copiously entertained the
advanced spirits of the day; at his table men praised materialism, assailed
superstition, and collaborated in their diatribes against God and the godly. His
"factory" produced most of the anticlerical and antireligious literature of the
1760s and 1770s; his own *Système de la nature,* an earnest, wholly uncompromising treatise, summed up the materialism from which most of the older
philosophes vehemently dissented, and which only Diderot found possible to
accept.

Most remarkable of all, perhaps, was the continued vigor of the older men.
Diderot, now nearing fifty, turned to pioneering essays in art theory and art
criticism, and wrote experimental dialogues like *Rameau's Nephew* and novels
like *Jacques le fataliste.* The 1760s also was the decade in which Rousseau,
though increasingly estranged from the other philosophes, produced in rapid
succession his trio of masterpieces—*La nouvelle Héloïse, Emile,* and *Contrat
social.* The first is a sentimental epistolary novel in the style Richardson had
made famous; the second is a philosophical romance on education; the third is
a treatise on political theory in the classical vein. But Rousseau thought of them
together, and they elucidate one another. Civilization, as he saw it around him,
had not merely stifled the passions—or rather, substituted artificial passions
like snobbery for elemental passions like family feeling and candor—it had also
perverted reason. The problem was to rescue both. Far as man had fallen,
Rousseau argued, the possibility for regeneration lies in his hands. The gravest
social evil, doubtless, was the atrophy of the simple emotions—the cooling of
friendship and the fading glow of honesty. When the emotions are starved, cold
calculation, which is only an excuse for reason, must take over, and men
become hypocrites. It is true that Rousseau indulged himself—and invited
countless others to indulge themselves—in sentimental effusions about the
outdoors and about simplicity. At the same time, Rousseau found room for
reason. In his novel, the heroine, who has "sinned" with her lover makes a
rational marriage and substitutes virtue for inclination; in *Emile,* that most
influential of Rousseau's writings, he takes a solitary pupil through a "nega-
tive" and "natural" education that avoids the pitfalls of artifice and cultivates
the emotions first and reason last. This sequence, Rousseau argued, displays
not hostility to reason but respect for nature: "Of all man's faculties, reason . . .

is the one that develops last and with the greatest difficulty." If a man is ever to be treated like a man, the child must first have been treated like a child. It is an educational idea stunning in its simplicity.

Emile, in which a single boy is entrusted to a single tutor, was a brilliant thought experiment. The *Contrat social* displays Rousseau's originality in another way. It attempts to answer the ancient question of political obligation— Why should men obey authority?—in a new way, not by delimiting the relative spheres of individual freedom and social power, but by dissolving the two. The citizen of the *Contrat social* is ruler and ruled at once; he obeys willingly because the laws he obeys are the laws he himself has made. The good society is governed by the "general will," a complex notion which Rousseau himself did not do enough to clarify. Essentially, it is the public good, arrived at by a community of rational, public-spirited men. Rousseau was not a blind believer in the multitude; the will of all may contradict the general will. But in the good society, which dominates its agent, the government, through frequent assemblies, the will of all and the general will *are* the same. The relation of the *Contrat social* and *Emile* should now be obvious: only a community of Emiles can make the good society a reality.

While thousands wept over *La nouvelle Héloïse* and reformed their educational practices after reading *Emile,* the *Contrat social* had little immediate influence. Its real impact came later, in the nineteenth century, when its arguments were used to support many political positions, but one position above all: popular sovereignty. And Rousseau himself grew ever more suspicious of his erstwhile friends; the late 1760s and the 1770s were times of deep distress and paranoid episodes. He was lucid enough to write three autobiographies of which one, the *Confessions,* is a psychological masterpiece in its own right. But when he died in 1778, many, even his former friends, thought him little better than a gifted madman.

Voltaire, who died in the same year, left the world with quite a different reputation. The old Voltaire is an astonishing sight. His visit to Frederick of Prussia had ended disastrously in 1752, with a quarrel and Voltaire's departure. He did not settle down until in the late 1750s, first at Les Délices in Geneva, then at Ferney nearby, on French territory. He was rich and famous, but he grew more radical with the years. His aggressive deist tracts, some first noted down at Cirey, now found their way into print, and his fierce slogan, "*écrasez l'infâme!*—crush the infamous one," began to dot his vast correspondence. More and more, Voltaire used his fertile pen to propagate toleration and to pillory persecution. He was a one-man propaganda factory. In essays, stories, dialogues, poems, even plays, he reiterated the same message: work hard, criticize nonsense, tolerate your brothers, hate persecutors, unmask the tellers of religious lies. His passions entered all his work and dominated much of it— his immortal philosophical tale, *Candide,* of 1759, little less than his influential philosophical handbook, the *Dictionnaire philosophique,* of 1764. The infamous thing he exhorted his friends to crush was not simply superstition, or

Catholicism; it was all supernatural religion, for such religion, no matter how bland, contained the germs of infection—rampant fanaticism.

In 1762, Voltaire tied his antireligious to his humanitarian views in the celebrated Calas case. Late in 1761, in Toulouse, a Huguenot cloth merchant named Jean Calas was accused of murdering his son, who had been found hanged in his father's shop. The ostensible motive was that young Calas was supposedly contemplating conversion to Catholicism. While it was likely that the moody young man had actually committed suicide, the father was tortured, convicted, and in March 1762, executed. Voltaire was at first wryly amused at this spectacle of fanaticism: if he was guilty, Jean Calas showed how far Huguenots would go in their hatred of the popish religion; if he was innocent, the case showed how credulous Catholics were willing to be about Protestants. But his amusement gave way to generous rage, and he inundated Europe with tales of the case, pleas for an end to such judicial murder and for general toleration. Jean Calas' good name was in fact rehabilitated three years after his execution, and the effect of Voltaire's campaign—and similar campaigns in behalf of similar victims of French justice—helped to shift the climate of public opinion toward the philosophes. When Voltaire came home to his native Paris in 1778, to be deified and to die, he was hailed not merely as the poet of the century but also as *"l'homme aux Calas."*[20]

THE ENLIGHTENMENT: THE SCIENCE OF MAN

In his *Traité des systêmes* of 1749, a devastating critique of seventeenth-century system-makers, the French psychologist Condillac expressed a hope widespread among the philosophes. "Today," he wrote, "a few physical scientists, above all the chemists, are concentrating on collecting phenomena, for they have recognized that one must possess the effects of nature, and discover their mutual dependence, before one poses principles that explain them. The example of their predecessors has been a good lesson to them; they at least wish to avoid the errors that the mania for systems has brought in its train. If only all the other philosophers would imitate them!" Thus Condillac, like his fellows, expected that Newton's methods might be extended beyond the exact natural sciences to disciplines that had been hitherto mere collections of observations and aphorisms. Newton himself had hinted at this tantalizing possibility in the *Opticks:* "If natural Philosophy, in all its parts, by pursuing this method, shall at length be perfected, the bounds of moral philosophy will also be enlarged." The prospect haunted the philosophes and exhilarated them. David Hume subtitled his *Treatise of Human Nature,* "An Attempt To Introduce

---

[20] For the persistence and revival of religious ideas, see p. 402.

the Experimental Method of Reasoning into Moral Subjects." And in the introduction he expressed his firm conviction that once men had understood human nature, they could construct on that knowledge "a science, which will not be inferior in certainty, and will be much superior in utility, to any other of human comprehension." Hume had no illusions: the science of man would be difficult, but he thought it possible at least in principle. Hence, the Enlightenment was crowded with students of man and society who aspired to Newton's mantle. They did not wholly succeed; there could be only one Newton. Still, the social scientists of the eighteenth century—philosophes, nearly all of them—placed their disciplines on a rational, if not precisely scientific, basis. Condillac and Hartley developed a psychology using what they considered to be Newton's methods, and even using such Newtonian terms as "attraction." David Hume, in a brilliant and learned essay, *Of the Populousness of Ancient Nations,* laid the foundation for modern demography. But the chief of these new sciences were sociology, history, and economics.

Sociology: From Facts to Freedom

While playing their part of social scientists, the philosophes did not abandon their favorite role of educator and—which was the same thing—reformer. They wanted the truth, but for the sake of humanity. "I should think myself the happiest of mortals," Montesquieu wrote, "if I could help men to cure themselves of their prejudices." These words are from the preface to his *De l'esprit des lois.* The book is disorganized, seemingly without direction. It begins with political sociology—the nature and forms of government and the "principles" that underlie them. It goes on to a celebrated if now dated analysis of the relation of environment to politics—the power of climate over government. It concludes with a collection of topics that Montesquieu was interested in, the historical origins of the French state and political economy. Voltaire, who like everyone else learned immensely from the book, called it "a labyrinth without a clue."

Yet it was more than that. Montesquieu argued that "physical causes," like climate, soil, size of country, interact with "moral causes" like religion or form of government. Here was a significant instrument for the understanding of society. In addition, Montesquieu recognized that each formal set of political institutions is underpinned by a set of convictions, a style of public and private life. By emphasizing these subterranean "principles," Montesquieu transformed the study of governments from a formal catalogue into a substantive and critical analysis. The principle of democratic republics, he wrote, is public spirit; the principle of aristocratic republics is the self-restraint of the governing aristocratic clans; the spirit of monarchies is what Montesquieu calls "honor"—an awareness of status and competition for places. The principle of despotism (a government which, to Montesquieu, is always bad) is fear. As long as the appropriate principle rules a given state, its form of government is secure; when other principles invade it, social change or outright revolution are inevitable. It is true that Montesquieu was far from being wholly neutral. In his famous admiring survey of the English constitution, he portrayed king, Parliament, and the courts as each endowed with its distinctive sphere—executive, legislative, and judicial—each separate and each checking the others. The realities were by no means so neat; still, we can grasp Montesquieu's intentions by a look not at England but at France. Montesquieu's insistence on the separation of powers was in actuality a contribution to a great political debate that pervaded his country. He meant to support the claims of the French aristocracy to political power: "No monarch, no nobility," Montesquieu argued, "no nobility, no monarch." Montesquieu was saying that without a strong aristocracy, a king would turn into a despot. This was partisanship in the name of analysis. But Montesquieu's model of the good government went beyond the pretensions of his social group. Simply to call Montesquieu a conservative, or a partisan of the French nobility, is vastly to underestimate him. With all his biases, he was the first political sociologist.

Montesquieu's numerous disciples took his ideas into new fields. Hume's sociological essays aimed destructive criticisms at the myth of the social contract and proposed instead an empirical treatment of social origins and social cohesion. Hume's friend and fellow Scot, Adam Ferguson, published in 1767 an admirable *Essay on the History of Civil Society* that explicitly tried to abandon speculative system-making in favor of an account based on careful observation and careful comparisons. Like Montesquieu, Ferguson argued that "man is born in society" and that it is only through society, including social conflicts, that his nature and his possibilities can be understood. Ferguson's originality lies in his comprehension of the social function of conflict. "He who has never struggled with his fellow-creatures, is a stranger to half the sentiments of mankind." This cool view of human nature, which characterized the social scientists who followed Montesquieu, coupled with the equally characteristic hope that science can be used for progress, also animates the *Federalist* papers, the greatest political tract produced in the eighteenth century. It is worth mentioning here for its symbolic value quite as much as for its intrinsic merits. America was a model for the European philosophes and a great hope; a place where men, free of feudalism and open to new ideas, would arrange things better. And documents like the *Federalist* papers suggested not only how well founded these hopes might be, but how much the Americans had learned from the European Enlightenment.

In the *Federalist,* a reasoned polemic in behalf of the proposed constitution of the United States, Madison, Hamilton, and Jay argued that power must check power because men are men. While men have sociable passions, their dominant passions—"ambition, avarice, personal animosity"—lead to anti-social thoughts and actions. Hence men need government, a bridle they would not need if they were angels. But hence, also, governments need to be controlled, for the rulers are as fallible as the ruled. Arguments like these, like all the arguments of enlightened social science, were attempts to place knowledge in the service of happiness and progress. "An extension of Knowledge," Ferguson wrote, in impeccably Baconian fashion, "is an extension of power."

Political Economy: From Power to Prosperity

What held true for enlightened sociology also held true for enlightened political economy: it was intended to be scientific for the sake of welfare. The mercantilist writers of the seventeenth and early eighteenth centuries had not neglected prosperity, but if the wealth of the subject and the power of the state came into conflict, wealth must give way. In the course of the Enlightenment, mercantilist ideas—and ideals too—were first refined, then overturned. In France the Physiocrats, in Scotland David Hume and his younger friend, the economist Adam Smith, abandoned the protectionist notions of "political arithmetic"; they visualized the world as a single market of peacefully competing traders and set the stage for a scientific political economy.

The Physiocrats were a small band of devoted followers of François Quesnay, physician at the court of Louis XV: the sect included the elder Mirabeau, Pierre Samuel Du Pont, Mercier de la Rivière, and—with some misgivings—the philosophe and statesman Turgot. Quesnay was the master, the "Confucius of Europe"; his famous *Tableau économique,* first circulated in 1758–1759, offered a rather mysterious diagrammatic representation of his views. His most abject admirers admitted that they did not wholly understand the *Tableau,* but Quesnay's basic ideas and those of his disciples are anything but opaque. The economy is a single system composed of the productive class (agricultural laborers and entrepreneurs), the sterile class (merchants, professionals, nonagricultural laborers and entrepreneurs), and the proprietors' class (the owners of land who make income from the land, chiefly through rents). The point of economic policy is to aid the productive class by taxing the proprietors' class, thus improving the lot of those who work the land, and through them, the country as a whole. The notion that taxes can be reduced to one was typical of the Physiocrats' systematizing and reforming spirit. That spirit finds expression in their famous slogan, *laissez faire, laissez passer.*[21] This was a call to the state to reject and repeal that host of crippling survivals from earlier, more primitive times—of regulations, taxes, tariffs, monopolies perhaps appropriate to a medieval economy but crippling to enterprise, initiative, and investment in the new day. Many ridiculed the Physiocrats, but while their claims were extravagant and their language was often pompous, their ideas

---

[21] The probable author of this phrase was Vincent de Gournay, who anticipated many of the Physiocrats' ideas, but died in 1759, before the school became really influential.

were rational and sensible—not mysticism parading as science, but science dressed up as mysticism.

Adam Smith, who spent some time in France during the early 1760s, has been called the disciple of the Physiocrats. But while he was indebted to them, his essential ideas date back to early lectures he delivered at Glasgow and to the pioneering essays of David Hume. Hume argued for relative economic equality, for high standards of living among the laboring classes, and in the face of prevailing prejudices, for free trade: "I shall therefore venture to acknowledge," he wrote, "that, not only as a man, but as a British subject, I pray for the flourishing commerce of Germany, Spain, Italy, and even France itself." These ideas, brilliantly enunciated but still informal, were ranged into a system in Adam Smith's *An Inquiry into the Nature and Causes of the Wealth of Nations* (1776), a masterpiece of political economy and of the Enlightenment.

Adam Smith was a philosopher; his *Wealth of Nations* does not offer his complete view of human nature, but concentrates on man in one special, though important role, that of the trader. As its title makes clear, the book is primarily a study in economics, but it is economics in a social setting. It begins with a celebrated analysis of the division of labor. Writing at the very dawn of the industrial age, Adam Smith shrewdly perceived that this institution enormously increases "the productive powers of labor" through specialization. But as a philosophe, Smith was alert to the social cost of progress, and his analysis includes a somber portrayal of what happens to workers "confined to a few very simple operations." Such operatives become "as stupid and ignorant as it is possible for a human creature to become." They become "incapable of relishing or bearing a part in any rational conversation" and of "conceiving any generous, noble, or tender sentiment, and consequently of forming any just judgment concerning many even of the ordinary duties of private life."

This mixture of scientific spirit and enlightened compassion characterizes the *Wealth of Nations* as a whole. Smith's chief target was "the mercantile system," and his sarcasms against the mercantilists are biting and, indeed, conclusive. But while he speaks highly of the virtues of private enterprise and lauds the unintended social benefits of self-centered economic behavior, he insists at the same time on the need for regulation. As things are now, he writes almost cynically, "Civil government, so far as it is instituted for the security of property, is in reality instituted for the defence of the rich against the poor, or of those who have some property against those who have none at all." This is not as it should be. The role of government in the economy should be a restricted one—after all, Adam Smith wrote his book to get the state out of regulation, rather than into it—but it should prevent or at least mitigate the antisocial activities, especially the secret conspiracies, of merchants and industrialists. For Adam Smith, it was a point of humanity and of good economic sense to have wages high, and rising: "No society can surely be flourishing and happy, of which the far greater part of the members are poor and miserable" (see also p. 407). However dismal a science political economy might become in the nineteenth century, in the age of the Enlightenment it sought to enlist rational policy in the cause of the population as a whole.

History: The Secularization of Time

The search for science and the urge for reform also pervaded the historical writings of the age of Enlightenment. But here this combination proved something of a problem: the philosophes' passion for polemics invaded their portrait of the past, somewhat to its detriment. They could see, more clearly than their pious predecessors, the failings of the Christian past; they could not see its virtues. The philosophes' historical writings on the Middle Ages are less one-sided than their reputation might suggest, but they can hardly claim to be exercises in historical sympathy. Still, the Enlightenment produced great historians—Voltaire, William Robertson, David Hume, and Edward Gibbon. If their secularism limited their vision, it was also an asset of inestimable value. While these philosophe-historians did little, if anything, to advance scholarly research, they were formidable readers in their own right. Gibbon devoured books in the classical and modern languages like a man starving; Voltaire skeptically examined documents and aspired to make history into a science; Robertson wrote all across Europe for documents; and Hume, in preparing his essay on the populousness of ancient nations, "read over all the classics, both Greek and Latin." Voltaire's two finest histories, the *Siècle de Louis XIV* and the *Essai sur les mœurs*, David Hume's *History of England*, Robertson's *History of America*, and above all, Gibbon's *History of the Decline and Fall of the Roman Empire* were regarded as monumental achievements in their own day and remain splendid reading in ours. Despite their admixture of anticlerical propaganda, they substantiate Hume's claim that his was "the historical Age."

In fact, far from being unhistorical, the philosophe-historians made a revolution in the discipline of history, and they did so because they were philosophes. They secularized the idea of historical causation, they stretched the canvas of history in time, and they broadened its scope from court annals or saints' lives to the history of culture. This freed the historian to study economic, social, geographic, and psychological factors to explain the course of events; by eliminating God as a cause, the philosophes could focus on the events themselves, rather than seek their explanation in theology. It meant, further, that the historian, instead of concentrating on Christianity, its fortunes and its ancestors, could examine the course of non-Western civilizations—appreciatively if not always knowledgeably. It meant, finally, that history-writing gained in depth by abandoning trivia. If the philosophe-historians did not supply all the right answers, they asked most of the right questions: Voltaire, whose history of the reign of Louis XIV included informative chapters on the arts and literature, put it programmatically: "A lock on the canal that joins the two seas, a painting by Poussin, a fine tragedy, are things a thousand times more precious than all the court annals and all the campaign reports put together." The whole modern ideal of social history is contained in these words.

The masterpiece that sums up the achievement of enlightened history-writing is Gibbon's *Decline and Fall of the Roman Empire.* Born in 1737 to a prosperous family, Edward Gibbon spent most of his life as a private scholar in Lausanne, publishing in French before he published in English. Brilliant in style, masterly in detail, malicious in temper, his *Decline and Fall* traces the gradual decay of the Roman Empire from its pinnacle of order and splendor in the second century, through its gradual dissolution, and its later career into the early modern period. As he remembered it, the inspiration to treat this majestic theme came to him on his Italian journey: "It was at Rome, on the 15th of October 1764, as I sat musing among the ruins of the Capitol, while the barefooted friars were singing vespers in the temple of Jupiter, that the idea of writing the decline and fall of the city first started to my mind." It was, almost literally, a life's work: the first volume appeared in 1776, the last in 1788, and Gibbon himself died in 1794. His undertaking was vastly ambitious and wholly successful in execution. The irony of his first discovery—the Christian friars amidst the pagan ruins—sets its tone. Penetrating in his perception, Gibbon presents an all-too-human picture of the past: men with mixed motives—the lower usually predominating—struggling with their ambitions and with one another. His chilly irony was perfectly calculated to offend Christian sensibilities; his two chapters on the rise of Christianity roused much adverse comment among the pious. Yet Gibbon, his reputation to the contrary, did not simply blame the fall of Rome on the enervating effect of Christianity, coupled with the barbarian incursions. He was too good a historian, too much the disciple of Montesquieu, for that. He thought that this long, tragic decline had many causes—the long peace, the unwieldy size of the empire, economic exploitation. But if Gibbon remains worth reading today, it is not simply for his historical sophistication; it is, above all, for his intelligence and his wit. With Gibbon, as with all the philosophes, the most solemn pronouncement somehow turned into literature.

THE CIVILIZED EIGHTEENTH CENTURY

The Power of the Word

The reputation of the eighteenth century as a civilized century is thoroughly deserved. The philosophes were self-conscious and indefatigable pedagogues; it is not an accident that one of their masters, Locke, and one of their luminaries, Rousseau, should have written pioneering tracts on education. Voltaire's pamphlets on deism and legal reform, Diderot's long hard labor on the *Encyclopédie,* Lessing's diatribes on the German theater, were all characteristic expressions of the Enlightenment's passion to civilize its age. There was nothing new in this: the attempt to marry the instructive to the entertaining was a classical ideal, and the classics, especially of ancient Rome, dominated the minds of the philosophes, as they dominated those of other educated persons in their century.

The thirst to teach was matched by the thirst to learn. The eighteenth century saw a marked widening of the reading public; this was the age when municipalities founded public libraries, when publishing became a fairly large-scale industry, when practical works like popular encyclopedias, almanacs, and grammars sold by the hundreds of thousands. In 1762, the German *Aufklärer* Wieland optimistically noted that "the number of readers is growing steadily"; in 1781, Samuel Johnson called the English "a nation of readers." It is notoriously difficult to measure the size of the reading public and the quality of its reading. And it is certain that most readers devoured sentimental novels or religious tracts; the best seller of the eighteenth century in England was probably Bishop Sherlock's *Letter from the Lord Bishop of London to the Clergy and People of London on the Occasion of the Late Earthquakes,* published in the spring of 1750, when London was repeatedly shaken by slight tremors. More than a hundred thousand copies of the Bishop's *Letter* were sold or given away, recommending (in Hume's caustic summary) "fasting, prayer, repentance, mortification, and other drugs, which are entirely to come from his own shop." But the didactic streak of the age took diverse forms; at the other end of the scale were the new periodicals that flourished, first in Britain, then, by imitation, on the Continent. The best known, and the best, of these periodicals were the *Tatler* and the *Spectator,* edited and largely written by Joseph Addison and Richard Steele between 1709 and 1714. Both these journals inculcated decency, good manners, courtesy, urbanity, industry, and humanity. And they did so by following the classical recipe: "I shall spare no pains," Mr. Spectator said of his readers, "to make their instruction agreeable, and their diversion useful. For which reasons I shall endeavor to enliven morality with wit, and to temper wit with morality." His ambition, he wrote, was to follow Socrates, who brought philosophy down from heaven, and to bring "philosophy out of closets and libraries, schools and colleges, to dwell in clubs and assemblies, at tea-tables and in coffee-houses." To judge from their circulation of several thousand and a far larger readership, Mr. Spectator succeeded in leaving his mark on his age.

The best writers of the century were as happy to instruct as they were eager to please. Jonathan Swift, prominent Tory in the last years of Queen Anne and distinguished Anglican cleric, expended his wit on the foibles of his fellowmen—he lampooned religious enthusiasts and empty-headed scientists with impartial spleen. His greatest and most famous book, *Gulliver's Travels* (1726), which every child knows, remains controversial; especially Gulliver's last voyage among the rational horses, the Houyhnhnms, has been variously interpreted. But there can be no question that it is a didactic work castigating man's parochialism, pretentiousness, and pride, his false science and his real vices. Similarly, Swift's friend, Alexander Pope, an elegant satirist whose ear was unsurpassed and whose diction was unrivaled, did not disdain the part of educator. Some of his most famous poems are lessons in verse: his *Essay on Criticism* (1711) is a sprightly yet organized treatise on aesthetic theory and the rules of taste; his *Essay on Man* (1733-1734) is a philosophical survey of man's station in the universal chain of created beings, and a sermon on resignation. The novelists, too, joined the ranks of the educators. The novel, which grew out of medieval romances and picaresque tales like *Don Quixote,* is essentially an eighteenth-century invention, or rather, development. It is impossible to say which was the "first" novel—Daniel Defoe's *Robinson Crusoe* of 1719 or Samuel Richardson's *Pamela* of 1740. But both these works of fiction were addressed to that new and wider reading public, and qualify as literary works designed to instruct as they please. *Robinson Crusoe* taught self-reliance; *Pamela* praised virtue and condemned vice. Indeed, Richardson's many admirers thought him a profound moralist. Henry Fielding, dramatist and magistrate as well as novelist, lampooned sentimentality in *Joseph Andrews* (1742), and his vigorous *Tom Jones* (1749) aspired to portray human nature in all its variety.

It will not do to be too solemn about these works of the imagination. Pope wrote charming poems with no didactic purpose whatever; Fielding enjoyed telling a tale quite as much as teaching a lesson. In fact, lightness of touch, calmness of voice, ease of manner were in themselves educational. Many Englishmen and Frenchmen looked back on the seventeenth century as a time of gravity, solemn theological debates, and competing religious fanaticisms, and thought that the time for urbanity had come. That is why the eighteenth century was such a great age of conversation. It is significant that one of the favorite literary forms of the age should have been the dialogue. The philosophes talked to each other at Holbach's dinner table or through their entertaining and strenuous correspondence; they met the influential at urbane salons in Paris. Others talked at coffeehouses, at scientific societies, in clubs. One of the most famous of these last was The Club, founded in London in 1764; it included among its prominent members such distinguished artists and literary men as Sir Joshua Reynolds, Edward Gibbon, Adam Smith, James Boswell, Edmund Burke, Oliver Goldsmith, and that greatest talker of them all, Samuel Johnson. Born in 1709 at Lichfield, the son of an impecunious bookseller, and for most of his life impecunious himself, Samuel Johnson was an ornament of the civilized eighteenth century. He was a sound classicist, an elegant stylist, an earnest moralist. By profession he was a literary man: his *Dictionary of the English Language,* first published in 1755, was a monument of comprehensiveness, unprecedented in its scope; his edition of Shakespeare (1765) displayed his uncommon common sense; his monumental *Lives of the Poets* (1779-1781) combined criticism and biography and was marked, as was all of Johnson's work, by his sturdy independence. But by avocation Johnson was a talker. He was fortunate in meeting James Boswell in 1763; the younger man, a good friend and a better listener, recorded Johnson's sayings—

combative, witty, profound—for posterity. When Johnson died in 1784, he was a familiar figure on the English literary scene; when Boswell's *Life of Samuel Johnson* appeared in 1791, he became an immortal.

The Arts

Clearly, the age of the Enlightenment was crowded with talent, but there were many, including Voltaire, who thought it a mere "silver age" after the "golden age" of the seventeenth century. And it is true that the eighteenth century produced no Rembrandts, no Berninis. Its characteristic painters were François Boucher, a specialist in female flesh; or Jean Honoré Fragonard, a charming recorder of frivolous high society. But their Rococo grace did not exhaust the painterly productivity of the century. They had after all, been preceded by a master like Antoine Watteau, whose canvases of country festivals or Italian clowns go beyond the surface to capture something deeper: the fragility of life and pleasure. And it could boast a whole school of English painters, trained in the styles of Italy and Flanders but solidly English in their independence: William Hogarth, with his lively portraits and his moralizing series of engravings depicting the London poor or the decline and fall of a rake; Thomas Gainsborough, who raised portraiture and landscape-painting to a high art; and Sir Joshua Reynolds, more monumental in his style than Gainsborough, but a skillful, fertile—and prosperous—portrait artist in his own right. A century that could boast Jean Baptiste Chardin, who turned humble still lifes into luminous and moving works of art with his mastery of color, or Giovanni Battista Tiepolo, who endowed his small wash drawings and gigantic ceilings with dramatic life, can scarcely be dismissed as second-rate.

Indeed, in painting and in the other arts, the age of the Enlightenment was a time of profusion and of rapid change. In their writings on aesthetics, the philosophes powerfully contributed to this change. The official doctrine ruling the arts—and for a time ruling the writing of Diderot and Lessing as well—was neoclassicism (see p. 297). But gradually there was a move toward freedom. Addison had already celebrated the imagination in his *Spectator,* and as the century progressed, aestheticians more and more came to give precedence to the artist's imagination and the audience's taste, and to play down the importance of the rules. By stressing the power and the value of subjectivity, the aestheticians of the eighteenth century were not calling for chaos; they continued to argue that an artist and his public should be calm and well informed in their judgment. They thought to create stability of style and continuity of taste by appealing to the consensus of cultivated men. But the tendency was away from the search for objective laws of beauty toward a psychology of artistic creation and appreciation. Neoclassicism retained its charms: in architecture, notably in England, the model of Palladio (see p. 216) continued to exercise a great fascination over architects and patrons alike; late in the eighteenth century there was to be another wave of neoclassicism, seeking grandeur and powerful spatial organization, and concentrating on themes from Roman antiquity. But other styles jostled for attention, including chinoiserie and bourgeois sentimentality. It was an age richer than many of its participants understood.

It was particularly rich in music. The modern listener is apt to think of the century crowned by Bach and Mozart as a single entity—the age of "classical music." But the composers and listeners of the time thought of their century as a time of movement, reform, even of revolution. Like other eighteenth-century revolutions, the one in music had been prepared in earlier centuries—by the triumph of harmony over polyphony. From the ninth century onward, and with increasing subtlety through the Middle Ages, composers had woven melodic lines into long, complex horizontal patterns, normally for the unaccompanied voice. In the sixteenth-century compositions of Giovanni Pierluigi da Palestrina and Orlando di Lasso, harmonies emerged from the polyphonic interplay of the melodic line. Then harmony gradually became an aim musicians sought for its own sake. In the seventeenth century, the long-lived Claudio Monteverdi, "the first modern composer," wrote operas, cantatas, madrigals, on the new principles. He depicted character by descriptive instrumental accompaniment—agitation by tremolos, serenity by quiet long lines—and gave new prominence to vertical harmonic combinations. At the end of the Baroque era, the keynote of the musical scene was variety, indeed confusion. The fine composers of the late seventeenth and early eighteenth century—Scarlatti and Vivaldi, Telemann and Buxtehude, Couperin and Corelli—composed in a number of genres and loosely employed general names like "concerto" and "sinfonia" without giving them any fixed meaning: a "sonata" could be a composition for a small orchestra or for a single instrument. Bach and Handel, the two giants of the early eighteenth century, were not so much innovators as clarifiers. Their genius has obscured how much they owed to the past.

Johann Sebastian Bach was born in 1685; many of his twenty children became gifted performers and well-known composers in their own right. He began, as most composers did, by listening and copying and by training himself as a versatile instrumentalist. All his life he lived with, and for, music; after holding several positions, he settled at St. Thomas' church in Leipzig and stayed there until his death in 1750. He composed for a wide variety of purposes and a wide variety of instruments: finger exercises for his students (including his children), humorous secular cantatas, religious cantatas, concertos, pieces for the unaccompanied violin, cello, organ; he wrote light-hearted orchestral suites and sonorous masses. His didactic music—his *Well-Tempered Clavier* and his *Art of the Fugue*—are rescued from tedium by his genius; the former stabilized the tempered keyboard, then still new;[22] the latter explored the unsuspected

---

[22] The system of "equal temperament," now standard, still experimental in Bach's day, takes the octave as the stable basis, and divides it equally into twelve semitones. This permits keyboard instruments to play compositions in all keys.

possibilities of counterpoint. His religious music, among which the St. Matthew Passion and the B Minor Mass remain the most famous, reflect his seriousness and his intense, pious desire to make "well ordered music in the honor of God."

George Frideric Handel, born like Bach in 1685, and like him in Saxony, was in contrast a secular-minded composer. After acquiring a thorough grounding in Italy, he began his own abundant musical production with operas in the Italian style. In 1712 he moved to England and remained there until his death in 1759, thoroughly acclimated to his chosen home. Appropriately enough, he was buried in Westminster Abbey among the great of England. His taste ran to gigantic performances, with large orchestras making unprecedented noise. He composed suites like the Firework Music for outdoor performances; his familiar Water Music was designed for a procession of royal barges making their stately progress down the Thames. Much of his music lies unperformed, though his operas, when revived, show remarkable vitality despite their stylistic conservatism. And his suites and concertos have never lost their popularity. Yet for most listeners his fame rests on the sacred oratorio, Messiah, first performed in 1742. A worldling, a businessman, a robust figure who was, if he was anything, a deist, Handel survives mainly as a religious composer on the strength of one of his rare religious works. It is one of history's minor ironies.

While Bach and Handel perfected what they had received, Gluck, Haydn, and Mozart broke new ground. Christoph Willibald von Gluck was almost a philosophe in his earnest reforming passion. The object of his ardor was opera, which had reached depths of absurdity by midcentury. Ordinary operas, ground out by the hundreds, mainly in Italy, were mere display pieces for vocal dexterity, and their librettos, generally stilted and ridiculous tales, bore no relation to the music. This is one reason why John Gay's Beggar's Opera of 1728 was such a resounding success in London: in addition to portraying recognizable local types and lampooning well-known political figures, it satirized the arid artificiality of Italian opera with so much gusto that the audience cheered, and the Royal Academy of Opera, headquarters for Italian opera, went bankrupt. In France, at midcentury, the philosophes became involved in the battle for reasonable music. French opera was wholly Italianate; when Pergolesi's refreshing, simple, and melodious comic opera, La Serva Padrone, came to Paris in 1752, a number of leading philosophes, including Rousseau and Diderot, spoke in its defense. It was this new temper, this search for the natural in opera, that Gluck discovered and satisfied in 1762 with his Orfeo ed Euridice.

Gluck, born in Bavaria in 1714, had made a considerable reputation with operas in the old Italian manner. But then, in association with a new librettist, Raniero de' Calzabigi, Gluck put this style behind him. His Orfeo, deliberately modeled on a classical Greek myth, explicitly sought naturalness and simplicity. Its music matches the words; its chorus remains in character and forms part of the action; traditional florid declamations give way to simple (and therefore truly eloquent) expressions of feeling. In 1767, when Gluck and Calzabigi collaborated on another masterpiece, Alceste, Gluck signed (but Calzabigi probably wrote) a manifesto: "It was my design to divest the music entirely of all those abuses with which the vanity of singers, or the excessive complacency of composers, has so long disfigured Italian opera." Any modern performance will testify that he succeeded.

Gluck specialized in opera; Franz Josef Haydn wrote music in a wide variety of forms, in quantities so large that even today his total output remains uncounted. His symphonies alone number one hundred four. These symphonies and his late string quartets greatly influenced the development of both forms, but while Haydn was an innovator in music, he was a hired hand practically all his life. Born in 1732, he became musical director to two immensely rich Hungarian aristocrats, the brothers Esterhazy, in 1761. He stayed in their service, docile and content, most of his life; it was only a pair of visits to London in 1790 and 1794, that gave him a taste of freedom. He liked it, and he was enormously productive during his English stay. But habit was too strong to be conquered: he returned to his comfortable servitude and died in it, a cheerful old man, in 1809.

The only composer to exceed Haydn's versatility was Wolfgang Amadeus Mozart. It is impossible to guess what Mozart might have done had he lived as long as Haydn, but his life was tragically short—he was born in 1756 and died in 1791. Trained and driven by his gifted martinet of a father, Leopold, young Mozart showed himself a child prodigy. When he was six, he concertized on the harpsichord; when he was twelve, he wrote his first opera. Despite his gifts and his fame, he never held a post he deserved and was pathetically short of commissions. The archbishop of Salzburg, whom Mozart served intermittently as court musician between 1772 and 1781, treated him like a menial servant, almost like a serf. Yet his music belies his poverty and his ill fortune; it sounds, at least at first hearing, easy, light, serene. It is impossible, and happily unnecessary, to choose among his works: the compositions of the last ten years of his life remain, quite simply, unsurpassed. He wrote six fine string quartets dedicated to Haydn between 1782 and 1785; he wrote his last and greatest three symphonies within three months in 1788; he wrote four of his operas, transcendent masterpieces all—*The Marriage of Figaro, Don Giovanni, Così fan tutte,* and *The Magic Flute*—between 1786 and 1791. It was in this last year of his life that he wrote the last of his splendid piano concertos and nearly all of his mysterious Requiem. This was a commission from an unidentified aristocrat, but Mozart, feeling low and ill, saw it as his own requiem. He was right; he did not live to finish it.

When Mozart died, he was buried in a pauper's grave; it was unmarked, and no one knows where he lies. Mozart, no less than these other great makers of music of his century, lived in a world of patronage and intrigue, of courts and concert promoters. Some, like Handel, were its masters; others, like Mozart, were its victims. But there was another world in which their part was marginal—the world of war and peace, diplomats and statesmen. It was a wider, if not exactly a better world.

SELECTED READINGS

For a general survey of seventeenth-century intellectual tendencies, see the first volume of Preserved Smith's *A History of Modern Culture* (1930). Franklin L. Baumer's *Religion and the Rise of Skepticism* (1960), keeps the promise of its title. The rise of scientific presuppositions is lucidly traced by E. A. Burtt, *The Metaphysical Foundations of Modern Physical Science* (2nd ed., 1932). Alexandre Koyré, *From the Closed World to the Infinite Universe* (1957), is a sophisticated analysis. E. J. Dijksterhuis, *The Mechanization of the World Picture* (tr. 1961), takes the rise of scientific ideas down to Newton. Richard S. Westfall, *Science and Religion in Seventeenth-Century England* (1958), reports on the emerging divergence between the religious and the scientific world views. Charles C. Gillispie, *The Edge of Objectivity: An Essay in the History of Scientific Ideas* (1960), is important for the scientific revolution and eighteenth-century thought alike. General histories of science in this period include Herbert Butterfield, *The Origins of Modern Science, 1300–1800* (2nd ed., 1966), and A. R. Hall, *The Scientific Revolution, 1500–1800: The Formation of the Modern Scientific Attitude* (1954). See also the splendid summary in Hall, *From Galileo to Newton, 1630–1730* (1963), and the English version of G. Taton, ed., *A General History of the Sciences*, vol. II, *The Beginnings of Modern Science from 1450 to 1899* (tr. 1966).

For Newton, see L. T. More, *Isaac Newton: A Biography* (1934), which is likely to be superseded once the edition of Newton's correspondence by H. W. Turnbull and others, now in progress, is completed. E. N. da C. Andrade, *Sir Isaac Newton* (1954), is very brief. Frank E. Manuel has explored Newton's historical-biblical researches in *Isaac Newton Historian* (1963) and Newton's unconscious in *A Portrait of Isaac Newton* (1968). H. G. Alexander, ed., *The Leibniz-Clarke Correspondence: Together with Extracts from Newton's "Principia" and "Opticks"* (1956), throws much light on Newton's thought. I. Bernard Cohen, *Franklin and Newton: An Inquiry into Speculative Newtonian Experimental Science and Franklin's Work in Electricity as an Example Thereof* (1956), illuminates Newton's use of hypotheses. Marjorie Nicolson's *Newton Demands the Muse* (1946), proves that the Newtonian world view did not ruin the poets' appreciation of nature; Marie Boas lucidly analyzes Newton's great contemporary in *Robert Boyle and Seventeenth-Century Chemistry* (1958). See also A. E. Bell, *Christian Huygens and the Development of Science in the Seventeenth Century* (1947).

H. R. Fox-Bourne's ancient *Life of John Locke*, 2 vols. (1876), has not yet been superseded; Maurice Cranston, *John Locke, a Biography* (1957), effectively uses some recently opened papers but is weak on Locke's ideas. For these one may go to Richard I. Aaron, *John Locke* (2nd ed., 1955), and D. J. O'Connor's brief, introductory *John Locke* (1952). Peter Laslett's critical edition of Locke's *Two Treatises of Government* (2nd ed., 1967), is indispensable; it corrects many misreadings.

The interpretation of the Enlightenment followed in this chapter is drawn from Peter Gay, *The Enlightenment: An Interpretation*, vol. I, *The Rise of Modern Paganism* (1966), which analyzes the philosophes' debts to antiquity and rebellion against Christianity, and vol. II, *The Science of Freedom* (1969). Both volumes have extensive polemical bibliographical essays. In addition, see Gay's *The Party of Humanity: Essays in the French Enlightenment* (1964). Ernst Cassirer, *The Philosophy of the Enlightenment* (tr. 1951), concentrates, as its title indicates, on the philosophy. Other general interpretations are Alfred Cobban, *In Search of Enlightenment: The Role of the Enlightenment in Modern History* (1960), and the economical essay by Norman

Hampson, *A Cultural History of the Enlightenment* (1969). Paul Hazard's *The European Mind: The Critical Years, 1680–1715* (tr. 1953), though brilliant, sees intellectual changes too abruptly and too much in isolation from culture as a whole; Hazard's *European Thought in the Eighteenth Century: From Montesquieu to Lessing* (tr. 1954), has many insights. The second volume of Preserved Smith, *A History of Modern Culture, The Enlightenment, 1687–1776* (1934), is conventional but intelligent. Carl Becker's brilliant and influential essay, *The Heavenly City of the Eighteenth Century Philosophers* (1932), is no longer tenable; it should be read in conjunction with R. O. Rockwood, ed., *Carl Becker's Heavenly City Revisited* (1958).

On the philosophes' presumed "rationalism" and "optimism," see in addition to Gay's books cited above, R. V. Sampson, *Progress in the Age of Reason: The Seventeenth Century to the Present Day* (1956), and, especially, Henry Vyverberg, *Historical Pessimism in the French Enlightenment* (1958). There is a lucid analysis of a celebrated legal case by David D. Bien, *The Calas Affair: Persecution, Toleration and Heresy in Eighteenth Century Toulouse* (1960).

There is a vast literature on individual philosophes; the following selection indicates the range. For Voltaire, see Gustave Lanson, *Voltaire,* now old (it was published in 1906 and translated in 1966) but still remarkably fresh; Theodore Besterman's *Voltaire* (1969) is large-scale, shallow on ideas, but dependable on details. Peter Gay, *Voltaire's Politics: The Poet as Realist* (1959), seeks to rescue Voltaire from his reputation as an abstract and superficial thinker. See also Norman L. Torrey, *The Spirit of Voltaire* (1938). For Diderot, see Arthur M. Wilson's definitive biography *Diderot* (1972). Rousseau has been brilliantly studied in Jean Guéhenno, *Jean Jacques Rousseau,* 2 vols. (tr. 1966). Ernst Cassirer, *The Question of Jean Jacques Rousseau* (tr. 1954), is a splendid brief analysis that connects Rousseau's life with his times; Ronald Grimsley, *Jean Jacques Rousseau: A Study in Self-Awareness* (1961), is a fine psychological (though not psychoanalytical) study, while Grimsley's *Rousseau and the Religious Quest* (1968), dependably surveys Rousseau's complicated religious ideas. And see Charles W. Hendel, *Jean Jacques Rousseau, Moralist,* 2 vols. (1934). For Montesquieu there is Robert Shackleton, *Montesquieu: A Critical Biography* (1961), judicious and comprehensive; it can be supplemented by Franz Neumann's "Introduction" to Montesquieu's *Spirit of the Laws* (ed. 1945). For Holbach, see W. H. Wickwar, *Baron d'Holbach: A Prelude to the French Revolution* (1935); the pivotal philosophe and psychologist Helvétius has been well surveyed in D. W. Smith, *Helvétius: A Study in Persecution* (1965). J. Salvwyn Shapiro, *Cordorcet and the Rise of Liberalism* (1934), is well meaning but too adoring. Douglas Dakin does justice to Turgot in *Turgot and the Ancien Régime in France* (1939). Ronald Grimsley's recent biography, *Jean d'Alembert, 1717–83* (1962), is the best in English.

There are few good titles on the German Enlightenment in English. See the relevant pages in Hajo Holborn, *A History of Modern Germany,* vol. II, *1648–1840* (1964); W. H. Bruford, *Germany in the Eighteenth Century: The Social Background of the Literary Revival* (1935), along with Bruford's more recent study, *Culture and Society in Classical Weimar, 1775–1806* (1961). The best biography of Lessing in English is H. B. Garland, *Lessing: The Founder of Modern German Literature* (1937). For Kant, see the useful intelligent biography by A. D. Lindsay, *Kant* (1934), and the brief recent analysis by S. Körner, *Kant* (1955). One other German *Aufklärer* has been fortunate in English: see J. P. Stern's fine long study, *Lichtenberg: A Doctrine of Scattered Occasions* (1959).

For English thought, the old volumes by Leslie Stephen, *English Thought in the*

Eighteenth Century, 2 vols. (1876), and *English Literature and Society in the XVIIIth Century* (1907), though partly dated, retain much of value. See also chapters VI and VII of J. M. Saunders, *The Profession of English Letters* (1964). Among analytical biographies see Mary P. Mack, *Jeremy Bentham: An Odyssey of Ideas* (1963), highly sympathetic to its controversial subject. The most comprehensive biography of Gibbon remains David M. Low, *Edward Gibbon, 1737-1794* (1937); it can be read in conjunction with G. M. Young's brilliant, brief *Gibbon* (1932). Hume, the greatest of the Scots, has an adoring, accurate, and dry biography by E. C. Mossner, *The Life of David Hume* (1954). See also Norman Kemp Smith, *The Philosophy of David Hume: A Critical Study of Its Origins and Central Doctrines* (1941), and J. A. Passmore, *Hume's Intentions* (1952).

On the science of man see, in general, Gladys Bryson, *Man and Society: The Scottish Inquiry in the Eighteenth Century* (1945), and in particular, David Kettler, *The Social and Political Thought of Adam Ferguson* (1965), William C. Lehmann, *Adam Ferguson and the Beginnings of Modern Sociology* (1930), and the same author's *John Millar of Glasgow, 1735-1801* (1960), Glenn R. Morrow, *The Ethical and Economic Theories of Adam Smith: A Study in the Social Philosophy of the Eighteenth Century* (1923), and C. R. Fay, *Adam Smith and the Scotland of His Day* (1956). For history, see the civilized essay by J. B. Black, *The Art of History: A Study of Four Great Historians in the Eighteenth Century* (1926), to be read in conjunction with Nellie N. Schargo, *History in the Encyclopédie* (1947), and J. B. Brumfitt's brief *Voltaire Historian* (1958). For economic thought see, in addition to the titles on Adam Smith, Ronald L. Meek, *The Economics of Physiocracy* (1962), the old but still useful *The Cameralists: The Pioneers of German Social Polity* (1909) by Albion Small, and William Letwin, *The Origins of Scientific Economics: English Economic Thought, 1660-1776* (1963).

For the group around the *Spectator,* see Peter Smithers, *The Life of Joseph Addison* (1954), and Calhoun Winton, *Captain Steele: The Early Years of Richard Steele* (1964).

For the history of eighteenth-century music see the later chapters in Manfred F. Bukofzer, *Music in the Baroque Era from Monteverdi to Bach* (1947); Adam Carse, *The Orchestra in the XVIIIth Century* (1950); and the relevant chapters in Paul Henry Lang, *Music in Western Civilization* (1941). Biographies of leading composers include E. M. and S. Grew, *Bach* (1949); Paul Henry Lang, *George Frideric Handel* (1966); Percy M. Young, *Handel* (1947); Alfred Einstein, *Gluck* (tr. 1936); Karl Geiringer, *Haydn: A Creative Life in Music* (1946); and, among a vast literature on Mozart, W. J. Turner, *Mozart: The Man and His Works* (1938), and the often penetrating if speculative study by Alfred Einstein, *Mozart: His Character, His Work* (tr. 1945).

9

Europe in the Eighteenth Century: 1713-1763

A TIME OF WAITING: EUROPE TO 1740

In 1713 and 1714, after decades of making war, the European powers made peace. The one serious eruption was the War of the Polish Succession, which brought most of Europe into the field in 1733—another episode in the drawn-out, inexorable decline of the Polish kingdom, once so impressive (see p. 435). In the main, however, country after country had time to absorb domestic developments—the change of rulers, the opportunities and ravages of economic change. In 1711, Charles VI acceded to the Hapsburg throne; in 1713, the year of Utrecht, Frederick William I to that of Prussia. In 1714, the year of the supplemental peace treaties at Rastatt and Baden, Queen Anne, the last Stuart ruler of England, gave way to George I, the first Hanoverian; in 1715, Louis XIV finally died, and, while his dynasty survived him, his threatening posture toward Europe did not. In 1718, after the death of Charles XII, Sweden became, in effect, an oligarchic republic with a crowned figurehead; in 1725, Peter the Great left a stage he had so long monopolized, to be followed by a succession of bizarre and inadequate rulers. Indeed, the signature of the quarter-century now beginning was the reaffirmation of aristocratic against autocratic claims—in France, in Sweden, in Russia, as well as in the Dutch Republic and in Spain under Philip V. The most conspicuous exceptions were Prussia, where the aristocracy obeyed, and England, where it shared power with the squirearchy. But in general, all across Europe, "absolutism" was under siege.

The Travail of Authority: Northern Europe

While most of Europe experienced this travail of authority, each country experienced it in its own way. In the emerging age of great powers, the Dutch Republic was in decline. Its international economic position in shipping, manufacturing, and banking remained impressive, but receded from the heights it had reached in the seventeenth century, when the Dutch had routed naval powers like England and defied military giants like France. Its international decline was matched by the triumph of particularism. Dutch history, we know, is a pendulum perpetually swinging between the centralizing tendencies of the house of Orange and the decentralizing tendencies represented chiefly by the richest of the seven provinces, Holland. When the stadholder William III died in 1702, he left no successor, and for over forty years the regent patriciate governed the republic without a stadholder. Republicans everywhere hailed this regime as a model of freedom—a view encouraged by the regents' paid partisans who were bitter about the house of Orange: "Our own prince," one of these propagandists wrote, "made us suffer worse oppression than had the enemy."[1] Others, watching the commercial decline and the obvious military impotence of the Dutch, were not so sure.

As in the Dutch Republic, so in Sweden, the restoration of an aristocratic oligarchy had to await the disappearance of a strong ruler: the effective regime that Charles XI had constructed and Charles XII exploited, collapsed with the latter's sudden death in 1718 (see p. 328). The social and political fissures these two kings had done their utmost to paper over reemerged to plague the kingdom and delight its neighbors. In 1720, the Swedish nobility, cowed into silence for half a century, imposed a constitution on Queen Ulrika Eleonora—Charles XII's sister—which in effect turned power over to the Riksdag and, within that, to the nobility. Until young King Gustavus III boldly seized power in 1772, the Swedish nobility governed the state for well or ill, in its own interest. Like the Dutch, the Swedes had a name for this oligarchic interlude: they called it *Frihetstiden*—the age of freedom. Like other ages so named, it meant freedom for a few, and freedom to indulge in factional infighting. For

[1] Quoted in Pieter Geyl, *The Netherlands in the Seventeenth Century*, part II, *1648–1715* (1964), 306.

half a century, Sweden was prey to the acrimonious debates of two parties: the Caps, who favored a cautious, pacific foreign policy, and the Hats, who sought glory through war. [2] For nearly twenty years, while affairs were in the hands of a responsible minister, Count Arvid Horn, the age of freedom was in fact an age of peace and healing for Sweden. But Horn was overthrown in 1738 by the Hats, and after that the irresponsibility of the Swedish oligarchy became truly apparent.

The Russians watched developments in Sweden with keen interest and undisguised pleasure; they firmly supported the new Swedish constitution which they rightly saw as an instrument that would weaken Sweden abroad by dividing it at home. But within a few years, Russia was in danger of going the way of Sweden. Only the size of the country, the extent of its resources, and the surprising competence of some of its ministers preserved it as a great power. There was little talk here about ages of freedom; the single attempt to hedge monarchical authority with a revived Senate and constitutional "conditions" came in 1730, at the accession of the Tsarina Anna. It failed immediately. At the same time, while the Russian nobility did not impose itself on the state with such complete authority as its Swedish counterpart had done, its position in the Russian system grew more and more favorable. Taking advantage of Peter's successors, Russian aristocrats progressively reduced their obligations to the state. In 1736, under Anna, they managed to fix compulsory service at twenty-five years; in practice, this meant that noble families would "inscribe" in service their children at birth, so that young men reached exalted rank and freedom from state service at the same time. And in 1762, Tsar Peter III freed the nobility from service altogether. Thus, the noble landowner gained after, and by, the death of Peter the Great.

In the succession, as in so much else, Peter the Great left an ambiguous legacy. By having his son Alexis murdered and by reserving to the tsar the right to name the successor, he ensured a series of palace intrigues, military interventions by privileged troops, and recourse to assassination as an instrument of policy. It was not until 1762 that Russia would see a monarch worthy of Peter the Great; Catherine II would prove as shrewd, as energetic, as single-minded, and as unscrupulous as he. In contrast, those who reigned between Peter the Great and Catherine the Great were memorable mainly for their vices and their eccentricities. Peter was succeeded by his widow, Catherine I, who, in her two years of authority, proved a tsarina as intelligent as she was uneducated. Unlike Peter the Great, who had died before naming his successor, Catherine lived to name hers: Peter II, the twelve-year-old son of Peter the Great's hapless son Alexis. His was a short reign—from 1727 to 1730—marked

---

[2] The origin of these party names is amusing. The bellicose party called themselves "Hats" to evoke the image of military headgear and gave their adversaries the nickname "Caps" to recall the notion of unheroic men in unheroic nightcaps.

by the court rivalries of two great Russian families. He was followed by Anna, daughter of that Ivan V who had been Peter the Great's complaisant co-ruler for some years (see p. 325). The decade of her rule (1730–1740) was a decade of favorites who withstood all efforts at bridling her authority in the interest of the great magnates. Anna acted, in fact, as a true autocrat: she moved the court back to St. Petersburg, resorted to the secret police and to widespread arbitrary arrests. Her lover, the Courland baron Ernst Johann Bühren, exercised his enormous influence through her good will alone. Bühren brought in his friends, Germans all, and while they were on the whole active and capable men, his rule and that of his friends came to stand for all that was baneful about a regime dominated by foreign favorites. During the short reign of her successor, the infant Ivan VI, Anna's pro-German policies were faithfully followed by Ivan's mother, a duchess of Courland. But then, late in 1741, a palace revolution brought to the throne Elizabeth, daughter of Peter the Great and Catherine I, and she held the throne for twenty-one years, until 1762. Exceedingly ignorant, inordinately vain, she was an attractive, even seductive figure who amused herself and scandalized Western observers by arranging transvestite parties. But her erotic preoccupations did not keep her from throwing her weight into the scales of European diplomacy. With her aggressiveness and her inconsistencies, she was too formidable to be ignored, too erratic to be respected. In 1759, the *Universal Magazine,* an English journal, expressed Western opinion with curt contempt: "The crown of Russia may now be deemed elective, and of the worst kind of elective monarchies."[3]

The Travail of Authority: France

The assault on autocratic pretensions was most dramatic where they had been most far-reaching—in France. Their dismantling took precisely as long as their first assertion—twenty-four hours. Louis XIV had laid claim to full royal authority the day after the death of Mazarin (see p. 293). The symbol of that authority—his will—was broken the day after his own death.

Louis XIV died on September 1, 1715. His successor was Louis XV, his great-grandson, who was then five. The unavoidable regent was Louis' nephew, Philippe, duke of Orléans, an intelligent and debauched worldling. But since Louis XIV did not trust Orléans, he fenced him in with a regency council and assigned to the duke of Maine, one of his bastards, the guardianship of the young king. The Parlement of Paris had the royal testament in its care; Orléans found it easy to persuade the magistrates to break it and to hand sole authority to him. On September 2, in a famous session, the parlement declared portions of the late king's will invalid. In return, the parlement resumed the right it had

---

[3] Quoted in M. S. Anderson, *Europe in the Eighteenth Century, 1713–1783* (1961), 180.

lost under Louis XIV—to remonstrate, which is to say, to obstruct legislation. Thus the nobility of the robe reasserted its power. The nobility of the sword, reduced to sheer decorativeness in the great reign, also reappeared as a political power under the regency. Orléans set up the Polysynodie, a set of six councils, with ten members each, which for a time shouldered aside the secretaries of state. These councils were a haven and a power base for the old nobility.

The regent's experiment in government failed. As Franklin L. Ford has said, "The results, in administrative terms," of calling into service the most assertive of the nobles, "were about what could be expected from a group of barely literate soldiers and pompous courtiers."[4] By 1718, the councils had been replaced by the old ministers. But the social and political consequences of Orléans' bid for power remained after the Polysynodie had gone the way of other ill-founded ventures in administration. Both segments of the French nobility, robe and sword, were to become centers of power in the French state and sources of resistance to royal policies of reform, notably in finance. The crucial political issue for France, raised in spectacular fashion on September 2, 1715, and kept alive right down to 1789, was this reassertion of noble power, especially of the parlements' right to participate in the making of legislation.

The regent's most intractable problem was, of course, the need for money. Decades of war had saddled France with a vast public debt. Taxes were in time-honored disarray: the two privileged estates, clergy and nobility, were exempt from the most onerous imposts, many towns and well-situated bourgeois managed to make special arrangements, which meant, in practice, evading most if not all taxes. The rolls from which taxes were levied were out of date, and so inequity was piled on inequity. For a time, Orléans permitted a partial repudiation of the public debt, but this halfway bankruptcy rightly struck him as an inadequate solution to France's financial plight. It was his desperate search for remedies that put him into the hands of John Law, a Scottish adventurer and financial wizard, whom he had met in earlier, less responsible days, at the gaming table. What happened now can be understood only if we understand the rudimentary and chaotic condition of public finance in early modern Europe. The line between private and public finance was thin and faint: in many states, France included, the collecting of taxes was "farmed" to private entrepreneurs who contracted to supply the state with a fixed sum. Profiteering, collusive arrangements, and savage treatment of the helpless were almost guaranteed by such a system; nor was tax farming calculated to produce adequate sums for the state's treasury—too much stuck to the fingers of the tax farmer. The balance sheets that ministers of finance occasionally prepared bore little resemblance to the carefully detailed and scrupulously audited budgets of modern states; they were, for the most part, fantasies with figures. Law was by no means a crook or a fool; he was manipulating a complex financial system

---

[4] *Robe and Sword: The Regrouping of the French Aristocracy After Louis XIV* (1953), 176.

with inadequate means and discovering the mysterious power of credit. "Unfortunately," as Alfred Cobban has put it, these "early experiments with its magic were only to be performed by apprentice sorcerers."[5]

In 1716, Law persuaded the regent to set up a central bank, a device that worked well and increased public confidence in his schemes. In 1717, Law established the Company of the Occident holding the monopoly on trade with Louisiana. Two years later, in 1719, this "Mississippi Company" became the Company of the Indies; it superseded all other overseas trading companies and expanded its operations to the whole of France's colonial trade. Armed with public authority, Law's company undertook to underwrite the public debt: all holders of government certificates could trade them in for shares in the company. Nor was this all: in 1718 and 1719, Law took charge of indirect and direct taxes and issued paper money. Law was an entrepreneur, a reformer, and one of the first of modern economists; he was trying to simplify and rationalize a structure long marked by incredible complexity and confusion. In January 1720, the regent signalized his satisfaction with Law by appointing him controller general.[6] But Law's phenomenal success became the cause of his catastrophic failure. The circulation of paper money, the accessibility of shares in the Mississippi Company, and Law's evidently infallible touch, induced the French, normally so prudent, to indulge in a riot of speculation. Speculation brought inflation, inflation the smile of prosperity.

It was a painted smile. No amount of overseas trade could sustain the prices to which the universal hunger for quick profits had driven his shares. Issued at a face value of 500 livres and promising a dividend of 12 percent, they were soon traded at 12,000 livres and above. A few shrewd investors recognized that this could not last, and gradually speculation decreased in intensity. The price of shares dropped. In the course of 1720, the Mississippi Bubble burst.[7] Thousands who had borrowed heavily or mortgaged everything, lost everything. In December 1720, John Law went into exile. His legacy was ruin, shaken confidence in the French state, increased suspicion of credit, some newly rich speculators, and some lasting, if largely invisible, benefits to the French economy.[8]

While the bursting of the Mississippi Bubble appeared at the time as sheer disaster, in his international ventures the regent, ably seconded by Cardinal Dubois, did far better. When he died in December 1723, he left behind a fragile

[5] "The Decline of Divine-Right Monarchy in France," in *The New Cambridge Modern History,* vol. VII (1957), 223.

[6] Like other French statesmen later, Orléans was to find France's restrictive religious policy a burden; only Roman Catholics could hold official posts. Indeed, this would be an issue as late as the reign of Louis XVI, with the Swiss Protestant, Necker (see p. 462). But Law made things easy for the regent: he converted to Catholicism and became a naturalized French citizen.

[7] It was an international bubble; for its impact on England, see p. 384.

[8] ". . . the stimulus given to economic life by the System was not entirely lost. Commerce and industry profited, and the great roads and canals planned by Law were not all abandoned" (Cobban, "Decline of Divine-Right Monarchy," in *The New Cambridge Modern History,* vol. VII [1957], 223).

alliance with France's old enemy, England, and a pacific foreign policy. In the following two decades, France gradually abandoned the first and generally sustained the second.

Orléans' successor was the duke of Bourbon, hag-ridden and demonstrably incompetent. Therefore in 1726, Cardinal Fleury, Louis XV's tutor, found it easy to encompass Bourbon's dismissal and to become, in effect, first minister. Fleury was an old man of seventy-three at his accession; he was moderate and diplomatic. He knew what he wanted or rather, what he did not want. And he had the full confidence of his former charge who, despite intermittent attacks of responsibility and religiosity, preferred hunting and whoring to governing. Married in 1725 to Marie Leszczynska, daughter of Stanislaw, the deposed king of Poland, Louis XV soon plunged into a series of highly public love affairs and left the conduct of government business to Fleury.

Both at home and abroad, Fleury aimed at a policy of pacification for the sake of financial stability and economic progress. He was fortunate in his associates and largely successful in his intentions. He could not wholly silence the religious controversies centering around a revived Jansenism; the lower clergy were in a rebellious mood against the bishops, and popular agitation issued in an irrepressible series of hysterical outbursts and unauthorized, embarrassing miracles in public places. And in foreign affairs, Fleury, much against his will, found himself dragged into the War of the Polish Succession in 1733. But until 1740, three years before his death, when the aged cardinal was finally shunted aside by new favorites, France prospered under his benign hand. Then, with Europe engaged in the War of the Austrian Succession (see p. 389), France, too, joined the general scramble for position and power. Its time for a great duel with England was at hand.

A TIME OF WAITING: BRITAIN TO 1740

1714-1722: A Confusion of Whigs

What France virtually experienced in 1715, Britain had experienced in full force the year before—a change in dynasty. In accord with the Act of Settlement (see p. 313), Queen Anne was succeeded in 1714 by George I, the elector of Hanover. Like the Glorious Revolution, the shift from Stuarts to Hanoverians was bloodless and, for the standards of the time, remarkably easy. Obviously, most Englishmen passionately preferred a Prostestant monarch, even a foreigner and a mediocrity, to a Catholic, no matter how eligible. The most conspicuous victims of the accession of George I were the Tories. A Tory ministry had precariously governed the country since 1710; Viscount Bolingbroke and Robert Harley (later earl of Oxford), its two dominant personalities, had quarreled, and their quarrel paralyzed the Tory leadership. Still, in the face of strident war propaganda by the Whigs, the Tories had managed to make peace with France.[9] It was a good peace: the Whigs' cry of treason at Utrecht was pure demagogy. But while the accusation was unjust, it was telling. When George I came over to England in September 1714, the Tory party was ejected from power. Bolingbroke fled the country to serve the pretender—"James III," as his supporters called him. Oxford was sent to the Tower. Jacobite[10] mobs roamed the London streets, and in September 1715, the earl of Mar raised the standard of revolt in Scotland. By December, the pretender had joined the rebels. The rebellion was easily contained early in 1716, and Oxford was acquitted of treason in 1717. But the fear of a Stuart restoration remained to poison party politics. The abortive "'15," coupled with Bolingbroke's defection, seemed to lend substance to the Whig charge that the Tories were all secret Jacobites.

Both political parties were loose and unstable alliances; the notion of party discipline was far in the future. Whatever the Whigs might say, many Tories were aghast at the thought of a James on the English throne; whatever the Tories might say, not all Whigs were money-grabbing parvenus. Yet, while the party labels were becoming increasingly meaningless, in these years they still designated more than the struggle between ins and outs, or between court and country; they stood for real divisions on matters of principle and of policy.

The Whig rule initiated by the change of dynasty was far from easy. For over seven years—from the accession of George I in 1714 to the accession of Walpole in 1722—there was vehement, often bitter debate among the ruling Whig factions. This internal division, like the larger division between Whig and Tory, was not simply a naked struggle for power: "The groups," J. H. Plumb writes, "differed on how to make the world safe for Whigs and on how far to undo the work of the last Tory ministry. This was their battle-ground."[11] On one side were Lord Stanhope and Marlborough's son-in-law, the earl of Sunderland—aggressive men, eager to play a large role in the councils of Europe. The death of Louis XIV permitted Stanhope, in charge of foreign affairs, to reverse the old Whig anti-Bourbon policy by an alliance with France. By 1718, England was part of a Quadruple Alliance that also included the Dutch and the empire. It was directed against Spain and the machinations of the pretender, and was designed to defend Hanover, whose interests George I never

---

[9] Since these party labels are used a great deal and formed the staple of political talk at the time, it is worth noting that the groups designated by these names changed policies and character in the reign of Queen Anne. At the time of the Glorious Revolution, the Whigs were critical of monarchical power, anticourt, and depending on Parliament to defend their interests; by 1700, they had countered Tory influence at court by cultivating the crown, and they had become deeply skeptical of parliamentary power in an age when members of Parliament depended so heavily on royal patronage. So by 1700 the roles of Whig and Tory were reversed.

[10] For this term, see p. 314n.

[11] *England in the Eighteenth Century (1714–1815)* (1950), 55.

neglected. But, despite the French alliance, Stanhope was a true Whig: he worked to remove the disabilities placed on English Dissenters during the Restoration and retained after the Glorious Revolution. His success was only partial; resistance to repeal of the Test Act and the Corporation Act (see p. 309) was too tenacious to be overcome. Some disabling acts were dropped, and though the Dissenters remained second-class subjects, they gradually, often surreptitiously, began to rejoin the political nation. The methods of reunion were characteristically English compromises; some Dissenters practiced "occasional conformity," taking the Anglican communion once a year; after 1727, many Dissenters were saved the legal penalties for violating anti-Nonconformist laws by the provisions of an indemnity act.

Sunderland, meanwhile, was in charge of repairing the finances disorganized by the long wars, and finance gave the leaders of the opposing faction, Sir Robert Walpole and his brother-in-law, Charles, second Viscount Townshend, their opportunity. They, too, wanted Whig rule, but not Stanhope's or Sunderland's. As good Whigs they supported the Septennial Act of 1716, which prolonged the life of the sitting Parliament and prescribed general elections every seven instead of every three years. But they wanted a less expensive foreign policy, and they wanted power. As in France, so in England, overseas commerce offered irresistible temptations to get rich. In 1710, a South Sea Company had been formed to trade in South America and the Pacific; in 1717, it proposed to assume a large part of the national debt and sell shares to the general public. Early in 1720, Parliament approved the scheme. The new mood of confidence, encouraged by peace, prosperity, reports of Law's triumphs in France, and the government's low interest policy, produced an orgy of speculation. Everyone was in it, including the king's mistresses. In May 1720, Oxford's brother, Auditor Harley, wrote: "The madness of stock-jobbing is inconceivable. This wildness was beyond my thought." [12] Late in June, shares with a par value of £100 traded at £1050; in July they still stood at over £940. [13] The speculative wildness spawned numerous other companies, each advertising huge dividends and promising huge profits. The capital of new companies floated in a single week in June added up to £224 million. [14] But, as in France, commercial realities could not sustain such inflated prices, and the shares began to drop. By September, they stood at £180; ruin was widespread and scandal loud. Walpole, a well-known critic of the South Sea Company, took charge of rescuing what could be rescued. His task was complicated but not insuperable: the country, including its trade and its bank, was sound. But the bursting of the South Sea Bubble drove the Stanhope-Sunderland faction from office. In April 1721, Walpole became chancellor of the exchequer and first lord of the treasury; his old ally, Townshend, and, after some maneuvering, a new ally, the

[12] Quoted in J. H. Plumb, *Sir Robert Walpole: The Making of a Statesman* (1956), 293.
[13] Ibid., 299.
[14] See Charles Wilson, *England's Apprenticeship (1603–1763)* (1965), 316.

duke of Newcastle, were appointed secretaries of state. Sunderland, though out of office was still dangerous, but then, in April 1722, he suddenly died. The road to Walpole's primacy lay open.

1722-1733: Walpole in Command

"I am no Saint, no Spartan, no Reformer"—thus Sir Robert Walpole on Sir Robert Walpole. The self-appraisal is shrewd; it underscores not merely his liabilities, but his assets. And it explains why Alexander Pope and other literary lights of the Augustan Age who flourished under his hand despised Walpole the man and Walpole the statesman even more. They detested his passion for commercial values. Peace, trade, prosperity—these were Walpole's aims. But the motto first attributed to him by his son—*quieta non movere*—is apt to mislead: Walpole was anything but passive. He had a great appetite for life, great energy for work, great capacity for detail; and he was never content "to let sleeping dogs lie"—he was a manager of men. He needed to be: his enemies were influential and his power rested on two props—the favor of the crown and the support of the House of Commons. He strove mightily to secure both.

The House of Commons that Walpole led with such consummate skill was a microcosm of the minority that dominated Great Britain. After the union with Scotland in 1707, it totaled 558 members—513 for England and Wales, 45 for Scotland. The franchise under which electors sent members to Parliament varied enormously; sizable towns like Birmingham were badly underrepresented, tiny hamlets grossly overrepresented. Many boroughs were owned more or less outright by immensely rich and politically influential peers; some, like Westminster, enjoyed practically manhood suffrage. There were more than six million people in England, Scotland, and Wales; of these perhaps a quarter of a million had the franchise—and many of these voted as they were told to vote. Elections were expensive and avoided whenever possible. Thus, the House of Commons was a tiny oligarchy speaking for a larger oligarchy. The country squires in the Commons boasted of relative independence; they gave Walpole some bad moments. But Walpole remained in control through his personality, his program, and his skillful manipulation of pensions and government jobs—"places"—for obedient members.

Most of the members of the House of Commons knew one another intimately; many were related to one another and to members of the House of Lords. That upper house, too, could be managed by an alert politician who had the ear of the crown. Peerages were, of course, hereditary, and most peers were rich landowners, but, as courtiers or as lord lieutenants of their districts, they too were part of the political machinery. And, especially under Walpole, the twenty-six bishops of the Church of England, who sat in the House of Lords, docilely voted at government orders; they saved Walpole more than once. Parliament was a large, often irritable and intractable family with a common vocabulary, and, by and large, common aims. This made management manageable.

For a dozen years Walpole's control of the political machinery was so complete that he has often been called Britain's first prime minister. The title is an anachronism, but it reflects his mastery. Walpole took care to keep that mastery intact; while he did not resort to violent methods, he purged all opposition and even competition; in 1730, even Townshend had to leave the government. But power was not an aim in itself; Walpole's vision was limited but sensible. He had a passion for stability. In retrospect the threat of a Stuart restoration seems remote. But Walpole did not enjoy hindsight: the Jacobites were active intriguers, and the possibility of foreign aid to their cause was ever present. Walpole therefore feared the Jacobites and frantically worked to keep the Hanoverian settlement secure. When George I died in 1727, to be succeeded by George II, Walpole passed his first test on this score: there was no move to dislodge the dynasty and (which was almost as gratifying) no move to dislodge him. In fact his relation to Queen Caroline approached that of friendship. Until she died in 1737, Walpole might suffer occasional defeats in Parliament, but he need fear no rival.

Walpole enlisted his talent for finance in this search for stability. The bursting of the South Sea Bubble had fastened on England, as it fastened on France, a lasting suspicion of joint stock companies; the Bubble Act, passed at the height of the speculative fever, carefully controlled the activities of joint stock companies and thus continued to channel investment into partnerships. But, while this served as a long-range check on large-scale investment, it did not compromise the prosperity Walpole was determined to impose upon the country. He succeeded splendidly. He rationalized customs rates, abolished export duties, imposed protective tariffs in behalf of domestic industry, and aided the port of London by instituting bonded warehouses that permitted storage of goods to be transshipped. He refused to raise taxes. Since 1717, a sinking fund—Walpole's idea—had served as a permanent reserve to back up the national debt; its reassuring presence guaranteed to the public that the state would meet its obligations. This, too, raised general confidence and brought the interest rate down: by 1727, it stood at 4 percent, and an even lower rate of 3 percent was in the offing.

Walpole was certain these gains could be preserved only if Britain followed a pacific (which is to say, cheap) foreign policy. Townshend had more bellicose ideas; supported by vehemently anti-Spanish sentiments in England, he negotiated expensive alliances and conducted what amounted to an undeclared war against Spain. Walpole superseded his brother-in-law; in 1729 he joined France and Spain in the Treaty of Seville, and in 1731, after he had forced Townshend from the government, he concluded the Treaty of Vienna with the emperor, both leading to general pacification. Thus Britain saved money, and kept Gibraltar, first taken in 1704, into the bargain.

Paradoxically, finance, which had given Walpole his undisputed ascendancy, also gave him his first intimations of fallibility. Part of Walpole's eminently successful warehouse scheme had been the provision of an excise tax to be imposed on such colonial products as coffee, chocolate, and tea, if they were not transshipped but consumed in Britain. It was a workable system, and it raised much-desired revenue. In 1732, seeking to keep taxes low and perhaps abolish the land tax, Walpole announced his intention to extend the excise first to tobacco, then to wine. It was an immensely unpopular move, tailor-made for the opposition in search of an opening against the invulnerable minister. Bolingbroke, who had been permitted to return home in 1723, was too brilliant to miss his opportunity. Joined by an equally brilliant and equally disgruntled Whig, William Pulteney, Bolingbroke, in an unscrupulous propaganda campaign, represented Walpole's new excise as an invasion of the rights of Englishmen and the prelude to new imposts. Undeterred, Walpole introduced his tobacco excise into Parliament in March 1733, but in April, finally aware of the extent and determination of his opposition, he dropped the scheme. It was his first great defeat. Others would follow.

1733-1742: Walpole in Eclipse

Walpole was too formidable to crumble quickly. All the best writers and all the leading politicians were arrayed against him; theirs was a coalition of Tories whom he had kept from office and dissident Whigs whom he had driven from office. What Gibbon said of the Roman Empire, we may say of Walpole's ministry: the very length of his tenure provided the precondition for his fall. Very few of the opposition were principled: they wanted, quite simply, to be where Walpole was. Practically all of them accepted the Glorious Revolution; the Jacobites, who rejected it, were weak and isolated. Talking points against Walpole's supposed subservience to the crown's Hanoverian interests or his resort to corruption carried little conviction; it was obvious that his most vociferous enemies, once in power, would assiduously obey the Hanoverian crown. And their cry for purity in politics was the old story of the sour grapes. Besides, Walpole spoke for much of England. The country could be swayed by chauvinistic appeals, but it was, at the same time, weary of instability at home and ruinous adventures abroad. This was the heart of Walpole's strength with the public and the House of Commons: he gave them something better than glory.

Yet in the end it was glory, shrewdly linked to trade by a rising young politician, William Pitt, that would bring Walpole down. In 1733, Walpole managed to keep Britain out of the War of the Polish Succession, and he boasted of it with some self-satisfaction: in 1734 he told Queen Caroline that of the fifty thousand men killed in Europe that year, not one was an Englishman. The War of the Polish Succession was a short war, but Europe would not remain pacified, and in the general maneuvering, Britain found itself more and more isolated. Walpole's efforts to stay in office and on top of events grew more and more strenuous. In 1734, he barely squeaked through a general election, though he used the financial and influence-peddling talents of Newcastle as unsparingly as he could. The clamor for war—especially for war against Spain—grew in intensity: "When Trade is at stake it is your last Retrenchment," Pitt told the country, "you must defend it, or perish." Pitt was not a greedy man; he thought war part of a nation's destiny. But he did not hesitate to play on the greed of his rapt listeners: "Spain knows the consequences of a war in America. Whoever gains, it must prove fatal to her." Walpole was anything but indifferent to trade, but he judged that war in the interest of a segment of the commercial community—the traders in slaves, in sugar, and in smuggled goods—would be a calamity for the country as a whole. But even timid, neurotic Newcastle was for war, and so, in October 1739, to Walpole's open chagrin, Britain was drawn into the War of Jenkins' Ear against Spain. [15]

"It is your war," Walpole told Newcastle, "and I wish you joy of it." It was the end of Walpole's system. The general elections of 1741 showed that the country was no longer with him, and in February 1742, Walpole resigned and was elevated to the House of Lords as the first earl of Orford. His end is a commentary on the changing locus of political power in Britain and on his own peculiar capacities. Thirty years before, the House of Lords had been so powerful that passage of the unpopular Peace of Utrecht could be secured only be creating twelve Tory peers to swamp the upper chamber. But in mid-eighteenth century, the center of power moved to the Commons. Walpole, whose natural habitat had always been the House of Commons, of course knew this; he took his elevation not as a promotion but as an interment. Meeting his old adversary Pulteney, just created earl of Bath, Walpole told him: "You and I, my lord, are now two as insignificant men as any in England." [16] Three years later Walpole was dead. It was perhaps just as well: his pacific system had grown inappropriate not to Britain alone, but to Europe as well. For by 1740, the time of waiting was over and had given way to a quarter century of war.

[15] The war takes its bizarre name from a Captain Robert Jenkins, who testified before the House of Commons in 1738 that the Spaniards had captured his ship, pillaged it, tied him to a mast, and cut off an ear—which he carried about with him in a little box. Asked what he did then, he said that he "committed his soul to God and his cause to the country." The war party could not ask for a better, more inflammatory slogan than this.

[16] Basil Williams, *The Whig Supremacy, 1714-1760* (1939), 201.

A TIME OF WAR: 1740–1763

The War of the Austrian Succession: Rewards of Militarism

In October 1740, Charles VI, the Hapsburg emperor died, leaving his young daughter, Maria Theresa, as his heir. Two months later, in December, Frederick II of Prussia invaded the prosperous Hapsburg province of Silesia. His aggression set off a general conflict that moved across three continents and did not subside until 1763, with the Peace of Paris.

Frederick's action was ungallant but perfectly comprehensible: never before had Prussia, still small, still poor, been given a chance to acquire such desirable loot—and so cheaply. Maria Theresa was married to Francis Stephen of Lorraine, an insignificant and unpopular figure. She was expected to have difficulties with her Bohemian and Hungarian subjects. She was known to be unprepared for the burden her father's death imposed upon her. True, he had attempted to secure the succession. In 1713, he announced a pragmatic sanction [17] regulating that succession; by 1720, when it became evident that his issue would consist of two daughters, no more, Charles VI began to induce all his domains and all of Europe to recognize the succession rights of his eldest daughter. By 1732, the Hapsburg dominions had given their assent; other European powers followed suit after protracted negotiations, usually for a price. But for the powers the pragmatic sanction was a bargaining point and a scrap of paper. When Charles VI died, there were influential voices around Louis XV asking that France tear up the agreement and seize part of the rich Hapsburg territory. To make her plight even more acute, Maria Theresa was confronted with rivals to her inheritance. Philip V, king of Spain, Frederick Augustus II, elector of Saxony, and Charles Albert, elector of Bavaria, related by blood, marriage, or treaty to the Austrian Hapsburgs, hastened to present their claims. But it was the invasion of Silesia that precipitated the general War of the Austrian Succession.

For a ruler, Frederick of Prussia's action was not surprising; for the man he claimed to be, it was nothing less than shocking. After all, Frederick II was a philosophe, whom Voltaire and other assiduous literary flatterers of the time had hailed as the incarnation of the modern philosopher-king. Just before his accession, while he was still crown prince, he had written a relatively high-minded treatise entitled *Anti-Machiavel* with Voltaire's editorial assistance. In December 1740, he coolly disregarded his own precepts. It was this contradic-

---

[17] For the meaning of the term, see p. 100.

tion that Voltaire had in mind when he noted a little sourly in his *Memoirs* of 1759 that if Machiavelli had tutored a prince, he would have begun by advising him to write against Machiavellianism.

Frederick II came by his ambivalence honestly: as a child, at home. His father, Frederick William I, was everything that popular legend and unsympathetic historians have called him: a boor, a tyrant, a drill sergeant as king. A vicious caricature of the Protestant ethic, he thought himself a divine instrument chosen to administer his legacy, Prussia; everyone must serve him blindly, just as he served God. Ostentatiously he saved money by dismantling his father's costly court and by living simply; everything—almost everything— went for his military forces. His only extravagance was his "giants," those tall recruits whom his roving, ruthless agents found in his domains (and, on illegal raids, even in neighboring countries) and "enlisted" in the Prussian army. Frederick William I might have been merely a comic figure, but in his single-minded devotion to Prussia he was, instead, a ruler to be reckoned with. An alert, energetic, and intelligent manager of his country, he beat down the last lingering resistance of the Junkers to royal authority, founded domestic industries like textile and powder factories (significantly related to military requirements), and persistently pursued his ideal of a large, well-manned, well-trained army. With careful attention to detail, he reorganized the financial administration of his state and rationalized the civil service; even as crown prince he had insisted on the need for a central treasury, and as king he brought the reforms of his grandfather, the Great Elector, to their logical conclusion by establishing a general finance directory in charge of all domestic revenues. Finally, in 1723, Frederick William rationalized his administration by creating a single administrative body, the General-Ober-Finanz-Kriegs- und Do-mainen-Direktorium. With justice, he has been called "the father of Prussian bureaucracy."[18]

Frederick William I worked himself unsparingly, but he did not spare his ministers or his people either. The results were gratifying, even astounding: a certain economic independence, a trebling of revenues, a reserve fund of eight million thalers, and an army doubled in strength, from forty thousand men at his accession to eighty thousand at his death. And Frederick William I husbanded his resources by a cautious foreign policy. His armies and his financial resources were a counter, a threat, more effective in reserve than in use. His successor, Frederick II, would deploy this legacy to great advantage and reap the rewards of militarism.

But Frederick William I left his son another legacy as well—a miserable youth and ineradicable inner conflicts. Just as Frederick William I had rejected the civilized ways of his father, his son rejected the barbaric ways of *his* father. Born in 1712, brought up by a cultivated tutor and under the influence of his mother, young Frederick early showed a talent for the flute and an inclination

[18] By Hajo Holborn, in *A History of Modern Germany*, vol. II, *1648–1840* (1964), 196.

for gambling and reading. Like Crown Prince Alexis of Russia, Frederick detested the military drill the king loved above all else and sought to force on him. Conflict between such a father and such a son was foreordained. Like Peter the Great, Frederick William I found it particularly galling to reflect that this shameless creature would some day inherit the realm that he, the hard-working king, was safeguarding with such paternal care. Relations deteriorated; there were violent scenes with the violence all on one side; Frederick William did not hesitate to humiliate or beat his son in public. When the sixteen-year-old boy sent a submissive message to his father, the king curtly replied that he had no use for a "self-willed" child who does not love his father, an "effeminate chap" without "manly leanings," a boy incapable of riding and shooting, who is, at the same time, "personally unclean, wears his hair long and curled like a fool." At eighteen, Frederick could stand it no longer; in 1730, he tried to escape abroad. Easily overtaken and brought back, the king compelled him to watch the execution of his friend, Katte, his confederate in the escapade. This was a gratuitous bit of sadism, but it was also a specimen of *Kabinettsjustiz*—arbitrary justice: a court martial had sentenced Katte to life imprisonment, but Frederick William I tore up the verdict and substituted decapitation. For some time the crown prince himself was in danger of execution, but at length the king relented and instead imposed a long, hard penance of work. Helpless, Frederick submitted and buried his private tastes more deeply than ever. After his accession, however, it became clear that he had not escaped the training his father had willed for him—he became something of a drill sergeant himself, addicted to cruel practical jokes and punishing work, and possessed by a fierce sense of devotion to his post. He would express that sense in a famous phrase: the king, Frederick II said, is the first servant of the state. But his other side, more civilized and more feminine, never wholly disappeared. Beneath the cold, cynical, hard-driving and hard-driven administrator there smoldered an ambitious poet and incurable worldling, a German barbarian who never quite forgave fate for not letting him be born a Frenchman.

In 1740, Frederick II acted as his father's son, only more rashly. He committed the troops and the funds his father had so diligently amassed to a gamble for big-power status. His friends the philosophes were appalled at him. Frederick had no illusions about his legal rights; he knew perfectly well that his claims to Silesia did not bear a moment's candid examination. But he told his lawyers to find good reasons and gave marching orders. To his surprise, Maria Theresa proved a doughty opponent. She fought gallantly to keep what she rightly thought was hers and indignantly rejected Frederick's offer of compromise. Frederick himself was lucky in this war: his first major engagement, at Mollwitz in April 1741, was only narrowly won. But this victory was the signal for the French to enter the war on the Prussian side. In June, France and Prussia concluded an alliance; Saxony and Spain also ranged themselves on the anti-Austrian side. But Maria Theresa persevered. In the summer of 1741 she bravely went to Hungary to claim the crown of St. Stephen and to enlist the loyalty of her wavering subjects. Her youth, her gallantry, her carefully staged emotional scenes won the day and secured substantial military support. Yet Frederick had occupied Silesia, and reluctantly Maria Theresa decided to treat with him. In October 1741, with the secret Convention of Klein-Schnellendorf (soon repudiated), and in July 1742, at Berlin, Hohenzollern and Hapsburg made a separate peace: Prussia was to keep practically all of Silesia. Frederick's negotiations were a clear violation of Prussia's treaty with France. The king of Prussia was acquiring a bad reputation not merely among idealistic philosophes but among hardened diplomats.

Meanwhile Frederick of Prussia had Silesia—a splendid addition to his poor territories. Yet the last months of 1742 and the year 1743 brought Maria Theresa successes that early 1742 had withheld. The English were now active in the war, and the "pragmatic army," consisting of English, Hanoverian, and Hessian troops, defeated the French in June, at Dettingen, while the Austrians took Bavaria and invaded Alsace. By the end of the year, Frederick's hold on Silesia was in jeopardy.

Frederick II had started the First Silesian War in the winter of 1740 to take that rich province. He started the Second Silesian War in the summer of 1744 to keep it. All went as appointed; Frederick's troops took Prague. But once again Maria Theresa proved resourceful: in January 1745, she had constructed an alliance with England, Saxony, and the Dutch Republic. And she was lucky as well; in 1742, after her defeat, she had been unable to prevent the imperial crown from going, for the first time in centuries, out of Hapsburg hands: Charles Albert of Bavaria had become emperor as Charles VII. But now, in January 1745, the emperor died, and his son, the Bavarian elector Maximilian Joseph, was anxious for accommodation. It came in April: Austria agreed to restore her Bavarian conquests while Bavaria promised to vote for Maria Theresa's husband, Francis Stephen, at the forthcoming imperial election. But Frederick II, too, had resources to draw upon. While his French allies defeated the pragmatic army at Fontenoy in May 1745, Frederick scored some notable victories over an Austrian-Saxon army at Hohenfriedberg in June and over an Austrian army at Soor in September. The drill sergeant's son was proving himself to be a tenacious, inspiring, even brilliant general. His protests against the election of Francis Stephen as Emperor Francis I were unavailing, but he drove the Saxons from the war by routing their troops at Kesseldorf in December. On Christmas Day 1745, the Second Silesian War was settled with the Peace of Dresden. It left Silesia in Frederick's hands, gave Prussia indemnities from Saxony, and guaranteed Frederick's acceptance of Francis' coronation. His people were beginning to call Frederick "the Great." The other belligerents fought on, but the sides were too evenly matched to make continuation of hostilities anything but an absurdity.

In October 1748 the Peace of Aix-la-Chapelle offered a general settlement which had something for everyone and satisfied no one, except Prussia. Its occupation of Silesia was generally recognized; certain Italian possessions of

Austria, notably Parma and Piacenza, were handed over to Spain; England and France, the originators of Aix-la-Chapelle, agreed to keep things as they had been before the outbreak of hostilities (see p. 382). One result of Aix-la-Chapelle cast its shadow far forward, into the mid-nineteenth century: there were now two major German powers—Prussia, still vulnerable and anxious but infinitely more powerful than before 1740, and Austria, wounded and reduced, but after years of battering largely intact.

The Diplomatic Revolution

The Peace of Aix-la-Chapelle was not a peace but a truce. It could not be anything else. Maria Theresa was in no position to retake Silesia, but she was wholly unwilling to cease planning for its eventual reconquest. Britain and France had fought to a standoff, but the wars had brought their colonial rivalries into the forefront. For almost a decade there was a deceptive calm that deceived no one. Rulers exploited the breathing space to undertake domestic reforms for the sake of a stronger military posture next time; diplomats, working feverishly, took up where generals had left off.

It was in Hapsburg Austria that these reforms had their strongest impetus. Maria Theresa, the Catholic empress, supreme housewife, loving spouse, and fertile mother,[19] has often been contrasted with her son and successor, Joseph II, enlightened ruler, cool administrator, radical innovator. The contrast should not be overdrawn. Even in matters of government, Joseph was the son of his mother.[20] Maria Theresa's father, Charles VI, had presided over a glittering and cultivated court and turned high government posts over to the magnates of the realm. His administrative machinery was clumsy and in need of clear directives; state intervention in the economy was half-hearted and unimpressive; the army, despite all Prince Eugene's brave efforts, suffered from poor organization, inadequate provisions, and low morale; the state's debt was astronomical and the treasury almost literally empty. What is more, the ill-assorted lands gathered under the Hapsburg crowns enjoyed a good deal of freedom, which only increased the general sense of laxity and made the collection of adequate taxes a near impossibility. If Maria Theresa wanted to take back Silesia, she needed a stronger bureaucratic, economic, and military base than this. With an energy that secured her the reluctant admiration of Frederick II, she set about constructing it. Her reforms took time—many of them were far from complete in 1763—but she began them early.[21] She decided to leave the relative independence of Hungary untouched, and to obtain troops,

---

[19] Her well-known "good heart" did not extend to the Jews in her realm; they were subject to repeated pogroms and, in 1745, they were expelled from Prague.

[20] For Joseph, see p. 426.

[21] For the late reforms including that of serfdom, see p. 426.

money, and general compliance through persuasion; but she deprived the Austrian and Bohemian diets of their right to vote on taxes and abolished the old separate chanceries that had dealt with their respective realms. Instead, in 1749, she established the Directorium in Publicis et Cameralibus, which handled the regions in common. Administrators with instructions from Vienna replaced the old officials, who had taken orders from, and owed their loyalties to, local estates. In a memorandum intended for her children, Maria Theresa shrewdly recognized the main evil in her realm to be that "various *ministri* only regarded each his own land. It was also a great abuse, which weakened the service, that the Capi and Presidents were paid by the Estates and remunerated by them at their pleasure." [22] This she was determined to cure, though slowly and with her customary good sense: distance did not permit the Viennese bureaucracy to dominate the Italian and Netherlands possessions completely. But in the center, chaos gave way to a certain measure of order. Results became visible after 1748, when Vienna took over the collection of taxes from local estates. Maria Theresa invaded the exemptions of the privileged estates and made nobles and clerics pay substantial taxes. The Hapsburg army could now be strengthened. The empress tightened up the recruiting system and founded a military academy in Vienna. In as many ways as possible, Maria Theresa was diligently imitating Frederick of Prussia in order to defeat him.

For the realization of her ambitious if unsystematic program, the empress found the ministers she deserved. The officials left her at her father's death were well-meaning, elderly, and ineffective; she did not have the heart to dismiss them and instead waited for them to die. They did, in rapid succession, and she replaced them with a group of men who, with her active assistance, reshaped the Hapsburg monarchy. One of these was Count Ludwig Haugwitz, a Silesian aristocrat, who proposed many of the early tax measures and became president of the Directorium upon its establishment. Another was Count Rudolph Chotek, a Czech aristocrat, who succeeded Haugwitz in 1761 and devised the tax laws which drew the whole population into the net of contribution. A third and the most remarkable of these public servants was Prince Wenzel Anton von Kaunitz. He had come to Maria Theresa's attention early in her reign as a skillful diplomat; in 1748 he participated in the settlement at Aix-la-Chapelle; in 1750 he went to Paris as ambassador; and in 1753 his ascendancy was confirmed with his appointment as court and state chancellor. An unbeliever and a rationalist in politics who trusted the power of systematic thinking, he was unhampered by traditional preconceptions. This made him a rather dangerous councillor in domestic, and especially in religious affairs. But in foreign affairs his perception was unsurpassed. The Diplomatic Revolution, which forms the prelude to the Seven Years' War, was largely his work.

From 1748 on, Kaunitz consistently argued that old diplomatic alignments no longer corresponded to realities. England, Austria's ally, had proved worse

---

[22] Quoted in C. A. Macartney, "The Hapsburg Dominions," in *The New Cambridge Modern History*, vol. VII (1957), 411. For Prussian administration, see p. 423.

than worthless; it had pushed Hapsburg negotiators into unfavorable treaties and was clearly interested in Austria simply as a makeweight against France. On the other hand, France, Austria's enemy from time immemorial, no longer had any real reason for its hostility. The Austrian Netherlands were in any case indefensible if France should decide to take them. The true, indeed the sole enemy of Austria, Kaunitz continued, was that new power, Prussia. Consequently, the single aim of Austrian foreign policy must be to isolate Prussia and to secure allies who (unlike Britain) would assist Austria in regaining Silesia. France must be won over so that, recognizing Prussia as a threat to the balance of Europe, France would ally itself with Austria. The idea was so simple that most thought it fantastic. Maria Theresa, encouraged by her wily minister to regard the reconquest of Silesia as a religious crusade, rightly thought it brilliant.

When Kaunitz went to Paris in 1750, he found the French-Prussian alliance firm, and for some time his proposals fell on unsympathetic ears. But then circumstances altered the calculations of France and made it more receptive to Kaunitz's idea for a reversal of alliances. One of these was the game Russia was playing on the diplomatic chessboard. Despite weak and mediocre monarchs, Russia retained the active interest in European affairs that Peter the Great had manifested and fostered. Like Austria, Russia saw Prussia as the enemy—or rather, as the friend of its enemies: the Ottoman Empire, Sweden, and Poland. Austria, on the other hand, was a close ally, formally so after 1726. Russian expansionist drives, toward the Black Sea in the south and the Baltic in the northwest, continued. Prussia was thus, in Russian eyes, a potential obstruction. After Elizabeth was proclaimed tsarina in late 1741, Russia grew even more active in foreign policy, and wholly unreliable. Kaunitz, though, thought he could count on Elizabeth to be consistently anti-Prussian and handled her with great tact. He wanted Russian *and* French aid in the reconquest of Silesia, and the forging of such a combination would take time and subtlety. To complicate matters further, the British concluded a subsidy treaty with Russia in September 1755; it stipulated that the Russians would keep a British-paid army of fifty-five thousand men in their northwestern province of Livonia. This open show of hostility alarmed Frederick of Prussia and precipitated him into a miscalculation. Convinced that he could appease the British if he promised to leave Hanover alone, he approached them and, in January 1756, Britain and Prussia signed what is known as the Convention of Westminster.

It seemed harmless enough; all it provided for was peace in Germany. But the French took a grave view of Frederick's diplomatic initiative: the British, they argued, had been fighting an offensive war against French possessions overseas, and for Prussia, France's ally, to come to terms with Britain, France's enemy, was nothing less than treachery. Whatever it was, the Convention of Westminster did reflect Frederick's low opinion of France and his conviction that if Prussia were attacked, France would be of no real assistance. What Kaunitz's words had not achieved, Frederick's actions did: on May 1, 1756,

France and Austria signed the First Treaty of Versailles. It involved a declaration of Austrian neutrality in the Franco-British war and a defensive alliance. But Kaunitz's triumph was only partial. The agreement was a surprise to Europe, but it did not commit France to the destruction of Prussia. The Russians, on the other hand, were ready. Kaunitz had assiduously kept St. Petersburg informed of the Austro-French negotiations; while the Russians were quizzical about close association with France, Kaunitz had maneuvered them into a position where they could hardly retreat. Elizabeth, in fact, became impatient, and Kaunitz had to hold her back: "The Russians," he wrote in some alarm, "are behaving too precipitately." [23] Elizabeth wanted to move against Prussia in 1756; Kaunitz wanted to prepare more carefully and start war in 1757.

The Colonial Stakes

Elizabeth's irresponsible aggressiveness and Frederick's blundering anxiety were two ingredients in the Diplomatic Revolution; the undeclared war that raged between France and Britain overseas was the third. Much eighteenth-century European history was made in Asia and America; in return, valuable colonies in remote areas were prizes for which European armies battled in the field and diplomats haggled at the conference table. By the time of Walpole and Fleury, Europe's political and economic systems were worldwide. William Pitt's celebrated remark, "America was conquered in Germany," captures this development to perfection. And Pitt was not the only European statesman to recognize that colonial trade was worth a war. Colonial possessions were prized as strategic outposts and commercial centers: Voltaire contemptuously dismissed the Anglo-French struggle over Canada as a quarrel over "a few acres of snow," but this was a rare instance when his judgment was obtuse. In fact, the stakes of the colonial system were high; as consumption of luxury goods and exotic raw materials increased in the eighteenth century, they were raised higher still. To the extent that mercantilism was a system of ideas at all, it was in the doctrine of colonies that the system emerged most clearly. Colonies furnished their mother country with rare materials impossible to raise, mine, or capture in Europe—sugar from the West Indies, fur from Canada, tobacco from Virginia, spices from India—and, in return, a protected market for finished goods. This early imperialism aimed not at the conquest of large territories, but at strategic spots that could be used as ports, trading stations, and gathering depots for slaves and other goods. As one French minister put it in 1765, writing to the governor of the French possession of Martinique: "It would be making a great mistake to think of our colonies as French provinces separated only by the sea from the mother-country. They are absolutely nothing but commercial establishments." [24] By the eighteenth century, Euro-

---

[23] Quoted in Herbert Butterfield, *Man on His Past* (1955), 168.
[24] Quoted in Anderson, *Europe in the Eighteenth Century*, 267.

pean colonies stretched across the known world, but they were tiny dots on the map, normally on the sea, and often widely scattered.

As the earliest colonial powers, Spain and Portugal, lost overseas territories and commercial privileges to upstart rivals, two of these upstarts, France and England, engaged all across the world in a titanic struggle for empire. Wherever Englishmen and Frenchmen sailed and settled—in India, the West Indian islands, the North American continent—they competed with one another, sometimes peacefully, often with force of arms. It was possible for rival companies overseas to be in a state of war while the mother countries in Europe enjoyed peaceful relations. At times it was even possible for the colonists to be at peace while the home countries were at war. But both situations were rare: by the eighteenth century the two realms, Europe and the world, could no longer be kept separate.

India, with its vast resources, half-unexplored domains, and political weakness, had been an inviting hunting ground for venturesome European traders since the early sixteenth century, when the Portuguese seized the port of Goa on India's western coast. The great Mogul Empire, with its capital at Delhi in the north, had established Muslim hegemony over most of India's millions; but its ascendancy of the sixteenth century crumbled in the seventeenth. The tolerant and civilized rule of Akbar set high standards of administrative effectiveness and of diplomatic forbearance with the large number of Hindu sects that his successors could not match. When Akbar died in 1605, his empire underwent a period of slow decline: the Taj Mahal, that star of tourist attractions, was built between 1632 and 1653 by Shah Jehan, one of Akbar's successors, as a tomb for his beloved wife—symbol if not of artistic, then of political decadence. It was in Shah Jehan's time, in 1639, that the site of Madras on the east coast was granted to the English East India Company. Aurangzeb, Akbar's last notable successor, devoted much of his long reign— 1659 to 1707—to a reversal of Akbar's policies. He prohibited the exercise of Hindu worship and destroyed Hindu temples, and thus invited widespread Hindu uprisings, led by the militant Sikhs. These uprisings, coupled with incursions across the frontier by Afghan tribes, produced growing disorder and, after Aurangzeb's death, open anarchy. Princes once subservient to the Moguls declared their independence, and India became a mere geographic expression— a patchwork of small and large kingdoms.

While this chaotic, fluid situation held its dangers for the colonial settlements on the coast, it also offered an unprecedented opportunity. Bold officials of the French and English East India companies alike bargained for privileges with local potentates and meddled in local politics. It was this meddling that proved the undoing of the marquis Dupleix, commandant general of the French East India Company. The French had come to India fairly late, in the time of Louis XIV, and had established several prosperous "factories"—commercial settlements—chiefly at Surat, Pondicherry, and Mahé. Part commercial agent, part military commander, part empire-builder, Dupleix, ambitious and sanguine, repeatedly exceeded his instructions. In 1746, while England and France were at war in Europe, he took Madras, but his conquest was annulled in 1748, in the settlement at Aix-la-Chapelle. Peace in Europe did not bring peace in Asia; the idea of a French empire, including an array of native puppet rulers, seems to have grown in Dupleix's inventive mind, and when the rulerships of the Carnatic and the Deccan fell vacant, he intervened. Ably seconded by the generalship of the marquis de Bussy, Dupleix for a time in effect ruled both regions. His first setback came in September 1751 when Robert Clive, Dupleix's English counterpart, took Arcot and, later, other towns in Madras. This held the French troops in check. In 1754, Dupleix was recalled, but the hostilities between French and English forces did not abate. With the coming of general war in 1756, the battles between the French and English East India companies merged into the wider conflict.

Similar confrontations marked the encounter of the British and French in America. At the Peace of Utrecht the British had acquired some valuable French possessions that strengthened their hold on the east coast of the American continent and in the West Indies. They won access to the rich cod fisheries; Hudson Bay, with its share of the Canadian fur trade; Acadia (Nova Scotia), a strategic base for operations against the French; and St. Kitts, another toehold on the rich sugar islands of the West Indies. In the Caribbean the British held several islands, in addition to St. Kitts, Jamaica, Antigua, and Barbados. The French, for their part, despite their losses at Utrecht, were well placed for economic exploitation and military adventure. They built the fortress of Louisbourg in Nova Scotia to counteract a possible threat from the British in the north; they founded New Orleans to gain access to the Mississippi from the sea; they consolidated their alliances with Indian tribes whom they managed with a suppleness and a real understanding that eluded the British.

There was trouble all along this extended frontier. In June 1745, New England militiamen supported by an English naval squadron, took Louisbourg, but, just as Madras in India reverted to the British at Aix-la-Chapelle, so did Louisbourg to the French in the same settlement, to the outrage of the colonists. In the West Indies, there was a similar standoff; British vessels vigorously harassed and successfully disrupted French trade for a time, but Aix-la-Chapelle temporarily restored calm in the islands. On the American mainland the conflict was more extensive and more virulent. The French treated the Ohio valley as private preserve, but British land speculators were eager to challenge this monopoly. Virginians formed the Ohio Company, and British colonists started ambitious settlements in the "French" region. The French quickly responded by strengthening their old forts and building new ones. The core of their military position was Fort Duquesne on the site of what is now Pittsburgh. "It was their absolute Design to take Possession of the *Ohio*," they told the young British officer George Washington, "and by G— they would do it."[25] In

[25] Quoted in John A. Garraty, *The American Nation: A History of the United States to 1877* (2nd ed., 1971), 108.

1753, they sent a detachment of troops. In June 1754, the British Board of Trade called a conference at Albany, attended by representatives of the Iroquois and of seven colonies. Here, Benjamin Franklin proposed a statesmanlike plan of union, but the colonial legislatures, too parochial for concerted action, had no intention of ratifying it. Military action alone was left. It was a disaster—for the British: in July 1755, the British commander, General Braddock, allowed himself to be surprised near Fort Duquesne. Braddock was killed, his troops fled, and the plan against the French forts was dropped, for a time. American historians like to remember that one officer who distinguished himself in this dismal campaign was Colonel George Washington. Both sides skirmished and constructed fortified places for future use. Action was not long in coming.

The Climax of the Anglo-French Struggle Overseas

After 1756, the continuing Anglo-French struggle was part of a general war, the Seven Years' War. [26] As we know, we cannot separate the action in India and America from that in Europe. At the same time, while the outbreak of the Seven Years' War in Europe was marked by distinct acts of aggression and followed a period of intense diplomacy, overseas the war was simply the continuation of a war that had been going on intermittently for some time. In India, Britain's declaration of war on France simply lent a sheen of legality to Clive's military operations and encouraged him to broaden his activities. In a series of encounters, Clive took Calcutta back from its Indian ruler, conquered the French fort of Chandernagor, and in June 1757, routed the French and their native allies at the decisive battle of Plassey. A brilliant and brooding man, Clive was laying the foundation for British supremacy over the large Bengal region in the northeast and the Carnatic in the south, and for extensive British dominion over most of the Indian subcontinent. Native rulers were puppets moving to Clive's orders. England watched, amazed, impressed, but also a little uneasy: Clive had opened the way to vast power, vast profits, and their inevitable shadow, vast corruption. But these problems were still in the future. When the powers made peace at Paris in 1763, the French retained a few stations in India, including Pondicherry and Chandernagor, but in substance, India became a British dependency. It was to bring Britain profits beyond the dreams of Clive.

In America, the profits were to prove more problematical. The war, after unpromising beginnings, was a series of heady triumphs for Pitt, his army and even more, his navy. By supplying his Prussian ally with generous subsidies, Pitt freed his hand for wide-ranging military action. The British navy concentrated on harassing the French fleet, capturing and sinking as many vessels as it could and bottling up the others in their ports. The British armies, too, fought

[26] In America, this war is known as the French and Indian War.

bravely and, by and large, intelligently. In July 1758, General Wolfe took Louisbourg; in November, General Forbes took Fort Duquesne and promptly renamed it Fort Pitt. Early in 1759, the British captured the rich sugar island of Guadeloupe; in November, Hawke permanently disabled the French navy in America with a splendid victory in Quiberon Bay. Meanwhile, in September, the British had taken Quebec, after the romantic battle of the Plains of Abraham, celebrated by historians, poets, and painters. Quebec was a strongly defended citadel, ably manned by French troops under Montcalm. After feints and explorations, Wolfe discovered access to Quebec across the Plains of Abraham just outside the fortifications, and after a pitched battle, took the fortress itself. Both Wolfe and Montcalm died in combat, but victory went to the British. In September 1760, Montreal, too, surrendered to them, and Canada was in their hands. Then, in 1762, the British took Grenada, Martinique, and the other French islands in the West Indies. As we shall soon see, they did not keep them long; but the general settlement of 1763 gave Britain a far larger and far more secure hold on America than it had had before (see p. 401).

War and Peace in Europe

As in 1740, so in 1756, it was Frederick II of Prussia who brought war to Europe. In August he marched into Saxony; early in September he took Dresden, and in October, after he defeated the Austrian army at Lobositz, the Saxon army surrendered. As in 1740, so now, Frederick's move was an act of aggression, but in 1756 he had a real, in place of a trumped-up, excuse: while he did not fully recognize the extent of Tsarina Elizabeth's designs, he knew that his enemies planned to attack and eventually to dismember Prussia. His assault on Saxony was a preventive war; his plan was to win a quick victory campaign of surprise.

But while his early successes gave Frederick significant advantages, victory eluded him and he was forced into the very kind of war he had feared—long-drawn-out and on several fronts. Frederick had a thoroughly trained military machine, a handful of minor allies, and enormous subsidies from Pitt; the allies had vast armies, superior resources, and a thirst for revenge. Frederick fought bravely and brilliantly, driving his troops, and himself, to exertions excessive even for him—Frederick veered during these years between elation and depression, confident predictions and suicidal fantasies. His victories became proverbial; every German schoolchild for two centuries after could rattle off such resounding names as Prague, Rossbach, Leuthen—three personal triumphs for the Prussian king, all scored in 1757 over the Austrian and French armies. The defeats at Kolin (June 1757), which compelled Frederick to leave Bohemia to the allies, and at Kunersdorf (August 1759), which gave them Saxony, were less familiar. For all his brilliance, Frederick could do little to stem the allied advance: in October 1760, the Russians succeeded in entering Berlin

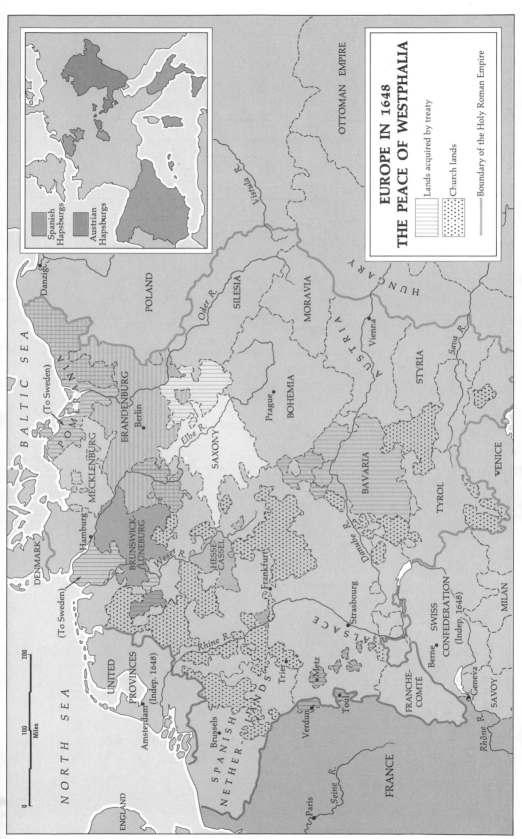

EUROPE IN 1648
THE PEACE OF WESTPHALIA

Lands acquired by treaty
Church lands
Boundary of the Holy Roman Empire

Spanish Hapsburgs
Austrian Hapsburgs

NORTH SEA

BALTIC SEA

Danzig

POLAND

SILESIA

MORAVIA

OTTOMAN EMPIRE

HUNGARY

(To Sweden)

POMERANIA

MECKLENBURG

BRANDENBURG

Berlin

Prague

BOHEMIA

AUSTRIA

Vienna

STYRIA

Sava R.

VENICE

Oder R.

Vistula R.

Elbe R.

SAXONY

DENMARK

Hamburg

BRUNSWICK-LÜNEBURG

(To Sweden)

Weser R.

HESSE-CASSEL

Frankfurt

BAVARIA

Danube R.

TYROL

MILAN

SAVOY

UNITED PROVINCES
(Indep. 1648)

Amsterdam

Brussels

SPANISH NETHER-LANDS

Trier

Rhine R.

Metz

Toul

Verdun

Strasbourg

ALSACE

FRANCHE-COMTÉ

Berne

SWISS CONFEDERATION
(Indep. 1648)

Geneva

Rhône R.

ENGLAND

Paris

Seine R.

FRANCE

Miles
0   100   200

Plate 15

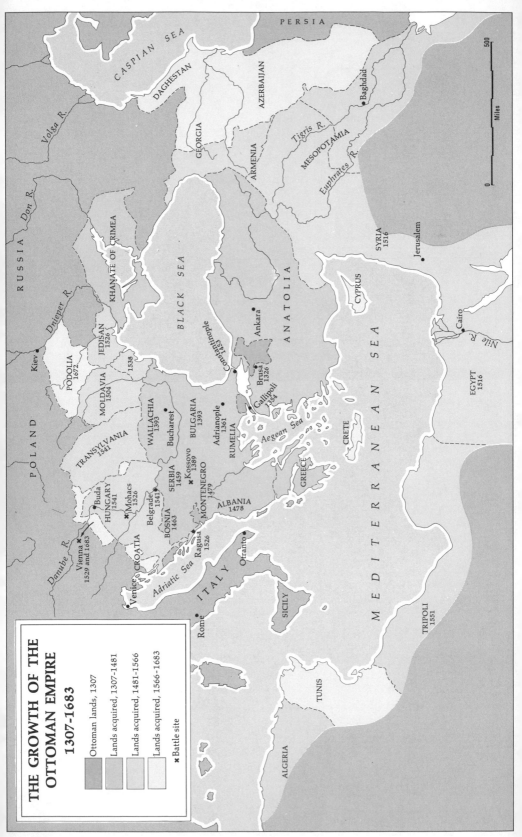

THE GROWTH OF THE OTTOMAN EMPIRE
1307–1683

- Ottoman lands, 1307
- Lands acquired, 1307–1481
- Lands acquired, 1481–1566
- Lands acquired, 1566–1683
- ✕ Battle site

PERSIA

CASPIAN SEA

DAGHESTAN

AZERBAIJAN

GEORGIA

ARMENIA

Volga R.

Don R.

RUSSIA

Dnieper R.

KHANATE OF CRIMEA

JEDISAN 1526

1538

PODOLIA 1672

Kiev

MOLDAVIA 1504

POLAND

TRANSYLVANIA 1541

WALLACHIA 1393

Bucharest

BLACK SEA

Constantinople 1453

Ankara

ANATOLIA

Brusa 1326

Gallipoli 1354

BULGARIA 1393

Adrianople 1361

RUMELIA

Aegean Sea

CYPRUS

Tigris R.

MESOPOTAMIA

Euphrates R.

Baghdad

SYRIA 1516

Jerusalem

Cairo

Nile R.

EGYPT 1516

SERBIA 1459

✕ Kossovo 1389

MONTENEGRO 1479

ALBANIA 1478

GREECE

CRETE

MEDITERRANEAN SEA

Buda

HUNGARY 1541

✕ Mohacs 1526

Belgrade 1541

BOSNIA 1463

CROATIA

Danube R.

Vienna ✕ 1529 and 1683

Venice

Adriatic Sea

Ragusa 1526

Otranto

ITALY

Rome

SICILY

TUNIS

TRIPOLI 1551

ALGERIA

500

Miles

0

Plate 16

The Growth of the Ottoman Empire • 1307–1683

The Ottomans came out of Central Asia where they had roamed since the sixth century as a subgroup of the Turks, dispersed from Mongolia to the Near East. Although many tribes were called "Turk," they were joined by no ethnic ties but related as a linguistic family. In the ninth and tenth centuries, the Ottomans were converted to Islam. As nomads, they moved westward; by the eleventh century they had conquered their way to lands close to Constantinople and set themselves up in warlike posture at the borders of the Byzantine Empire.

The Ottomans, or Osmanlis, took their name from their first dynastic ruler Osman I who, between 1290 and 1326, chipped away at the Byzantine Empire reaching as far west as Brusa, which fell in 1326. Orkhan I, Osman's successor, consolidated the empire into a self-conscious entity, striking coins and taking the title Sultan of the Ghazis—warrior of the faith. Wars of conquest took on the quality of crusades. In 1354 Orkhan established the first permanent Turkish settlement in Europe at Gallipoli. In 1366, having taken Adrianople, the Turks moved their capital from Asia Minor and continued their pressure into Europe. In a string of victories in Bulgaria, Serbia, and Bosnia during the next century, they subdued the entire Balkan peninsula.

Under Mohammed II, the Ottomans captured Constantinople in May 1453, ending a thousand years of Christian rule in Asia Minor. Mohammed made Constantinople into a flourishing capital; its population grew from 10,000 in 1453 to 70,000 by the end of his reign in 1481. Not content with Constantinople, the Turks continued to push westward, and in a war with Venice, 1463–1479, won most of Albania and Venetian tribute. In 1480, the year before his death, Mohammed took Otranto on the Adriatic.

The legendary brutality of the Turks was not confined to foreigners. It was a long-standing, drastic practice for new rulers to consummate their accession by killing all contenders, that is, their brothers and sons. Mohammed made this practice into law and did, indeed, stabilize the succession. The height of Ottoman power and culture was reached under Suleiman the Magnificent (1520–1566) who penetrated farther into Europe than his predecessors. In 1526 he defeated the Hungarians at Mohacz, and in 1529 he reached and besieged Vienna. But a month of bad weather and determined resistance by the Viennese led him to withdraw. He maintained a foothold in the west, waging war with Venice over the straits of Otranto and with Charles V over Tunis. Within five years after his retreat from Vienna, he conquered Baghdad and Mesopotamia and reached Tabriz.

The fear inspired by Suleiman's Empire, more powerful than any in Europe, led in 1538 to the Holy League which included Charles V, the Pope, and Venice. In 1571, under Selim II (Suleiman's son), Pius V organized a second Holy League, which backed its intentions with an allied fleet under Don John of Austria. The allied victory at Lepanto, October 1571, was thrown away when Spain and Venice fell out, which permitted the Turks to rebuild their fleet. The Turkish Empire began to suffer from the internal weakness produced by its system of succession, which led to puppet emperors; real power was divided between competing vizirs and a professional military corps, the Janissaries. It took another century before the Turks once again mustered the strength to mount a last unsuccessful attack on Europe.

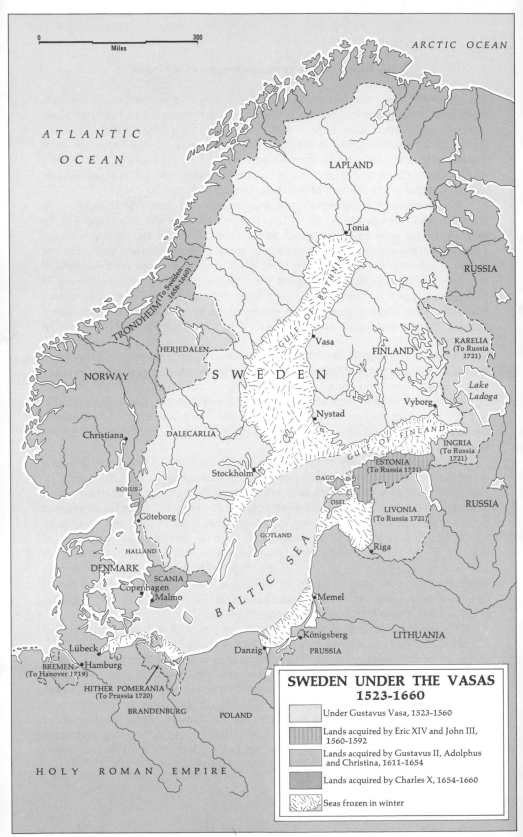

ARCTIC OCEAN

ATLANTIC
OCEAN

LAPLAND

Tonia

RUSSIA

TRONDHEIM (To Sweden 1658–1660)

HERJEDALEN

Vasa

FINLAND

KARELIA
(To Russia
1721)

NORWAY

SWEDEN

*Lake
Ladoga*

Vyborg

Christiana

DALECARLIA

Nystad

GULF OF FINLAND

INGRIA
(To Russia
1721)

Stockholm

DAGO

ESTONIA
(To Russia 1721)

RUSSIA

BOHUS

ÖSEL

Göteborg

GOTLAND

LIVONIA
(To Russia 1721)

Riga

HALLAND

BALTIC SEA

DENMARK

SCANIA

Copenhagen
Malmo

Memel

LITHUANIA

Königsberg

Lübeck

Danzig

PRUSSIA

BREMEN
(To Hanover 1719)

Hamburg

HITHER POMERANIA
(To Prussia 1720)

BRANDENBURG

POLAND

HOLY   ROMAN   EMPIRE

0   300
Miles

GULF OF BOTHNIA

SWEDEN UNDER THE VASAS
1523–1660

Under Gustavus Vasa, 1523–1560

Lands acquired by Eric XIV and John III,
1560–1592

Lands acquired by Gustavus II, Adolphus
and Christina, 1611–1654

Lands acquired by Charles X, 1654–1660

Seas frozen in winter

Plate 17

Sweden Under the Vasas • 1523–1660

In 1397 the three major countries of Scandinavia—Sweden, Norway, and Denmark—formed the Kalmar Union under the leadership of Queen Margaret of Sweden and accepted her nephew, Eric of Pomerania, as their joint king. The Union proved unstable, lasting only until Margaret's death in 1412. The ensuing years were bloody struggles as Eric tried to weld his territories into one kingdom and to push his Danish border south. Popular opposition to a powerful monarch led to his deposition in 1439 by Denmark and Sweden and in 1442 by Norway. In Sweden the state council (later the *Riksdag* or parliament) seized power and reverted to the system of electing a king. Denmark, too, elected its own king, Christian I, who succeeded in establishing a dynasty, while Norway became the vassal of Denmark and remained its subordinate until 1815.

In the sixteenth century, a complex struggle between Sweden and Denmark ensued; it included a period of temporary union, a revolt by Sweden, and a battle in which the regent of Sweden, Sten Sture, was killed. After the Danes' victory, the Danish king, Christian II, grandson of Christian I, was made king of Sweden in 1520. He marked his coronation several months later by a massacre of the nobles attached to the late regent's party, an event known in Swedish history as the Stockholm Bloodbath.

One of those who escaped, Gustavus Eriksson, whose father had been killed in the massacre, continued the struggle for independence. He enlisted the support of the city of Lübeck and the Hanseatic League, whose merchants had a strong interest in Swedish trade. By 1523, having led a peasant army against the Danes, he was elected king of Sweden by the *Riksdag* and took the name of Gustavus I Vasa.

During his long reign from 1523 to 1560 Gustavus presided over the emergence of Sweden as a great Baltic power and its conversion to Lutheranism. In 1526 the New Testament was published in a Swedish translation. In 1527 the state took actions that markedly weakened Catholic power in Sweden: the *Riksdag* made the appointment of bishops the prerogative of the king rather than the church, and simultaneously ceased to send its annual tribute to Rome. Meanwhile, church holdings were confiscated, an action caused in part by the government's need to raise funds for its Lübeck creditors. In 1529 church services were reformed to follow the Protestant order. It was not until 1537, however, following a war with Lübeck that Sweden freed itself from the economic domination of the Hanseatic League.

In addition to winning political and spiritual independence for Sweden, Gustavus persuaded the *Riksdag* to declare his family hereditary monarchs of Sweden, and on his death his crown passed without dispute to his son Eric XIV. Despite the expansion of Swedish territory to include Reval and Estonia under Eric, his reign was clouded by insanity which led to the elevation of his brother John III to the kingship in 1568. John's son, Sigismund, who succeeded him in 1593, was also king of Poland, and attempted to reimpose Catholicism on Sweden. An ensuing rebellion in 1599 led to the regency of Charles IX, Gustavus' youngest son, who took immediate action to have the *Riksdag* declare Lutheranism the state religion. Charles became king in 1604 and during his seven-year reign entered two wars that outlasted his lifetime. A war with Denmark over Lapland ended in defeat in 1613; another with Poland endured until the Peace of Oliva in 1660. On his death in 1611, he was succeeded by his son, Gustavus II Adolphus.

THE ENGLISH CIVIL WAR
1642-1646

Land controlled by Royalists,
Aug. 1642

Land controlled by Parliamentarians,
Aug. 1642

Land controlled by Royalists,
end of 1645

Land controlled by Parliamentarians,
end of 1645

× Battles

SCOTLAND

Glasgow

Edinburgh

Philipaugh
1645

Newburn
1640

Newcastle

NORTH
SEA

ISLE OF MAN

IRISH

SEA

Marston
Moor
1644

Hull
1643

Preston
1643

ENGLAND

Trent R.

Naseby
1645

Nen R.

IRELAND

Lichfield
1643

Severn R.

WALES

Edge Hill
1642

Ouse R.

Cambridge

Monmouth

Pembroke

Thames R.

Turnham
Green
1643

London

Newbury
1643 and 1644

Dover

Langport
1645

ISLE OF WIGHT

Bradock Down
1643

ENGLISH   CHANNEL

FRANCE

0   50   100
Miles

Plate 18

WARS OF LOUIS XIV
1667-1697

Treaty of Aix-la-Chapelle, 1668:

To France

Treaty of Nimwegen, 1678-1679:

To France

To Spain

Treaty of Ryswick, 1697:

To France

Boundary of France, 1648

William's invasion of England, 1688

DENMARK

ENGLAND

Amsterdam • UNITED

The Hague • PROVINCES

HOLY

ROMAN

EMPIRE

London

Tor Bay

ENGLISH CHANNEL

Rhine R.

FLANDERS

Brussels • Liège

SPANISH NETHERLANDS • Aix-la-Chapelle

LILLE

ARTOIS

LUXEMBURG

RHENISH

PALATINATE

Philippsburg

Seine R.

Paris •

LORRAINE

ALSACE

Strasbourg

Loire R.

Nantes •

FRANCE

FRANCHE-COMTÉ

SWITZERLAND

ATLANTIC

OCEAN

Geneva

Bordeaux •

SAVOY

MILAN

Rhône R.

Garonne R.

AVIGNON

Marseilles •

ROUSSILLON
(To France 1659)

SPAIN

0   100   200
Miles

Members of the League of Augsburg:

Austria

Brandenburg

England

Holy Roman Empire

Hungary

Savoy

Spain

Sweden

United
Provinces

Plate 19

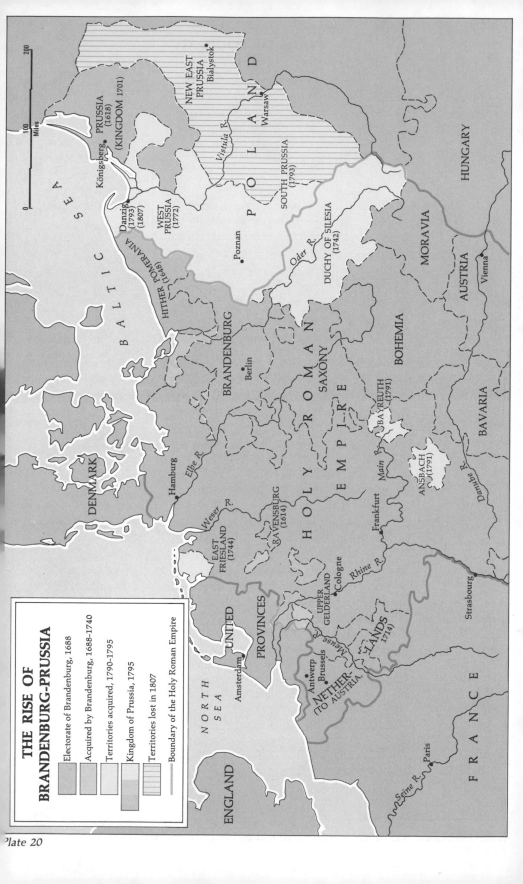

THE RISE OF
BRANDENBURG-PRUSSIA

Electorate of Brandenburg, 1688

Acquired by Brandenburg, 1688–1740

Territories acquired, 1790–1795

Kingdom of Prussia, 1795

Territories lost in 1807

Boundary of the Holy Roman Empire

ENGLAND

NORTH
SEA

DENMARK

BALTIC SEA

Königsberg

PRUSSIA
(1618)
(KINGDOM 1701)

NEW EAST
PRUSSIA

Białystok

Danzig
(1793)
(1807)

WEST
PRUSSIA
(1772)

HITHER POMERANIA
(1648)

Poznan

Vistula R.

P O L A N D

Warsaw

SOUTH PRUSSIA
(1793)

BRANDENBURG

Berlin

Oder

DUCHY OF SILESIA
(1742)

MORAVIA

AUSTRIA

Vienna

HUNGARY

Hamburg

Elbe R.

S A X O N Y

BOHEMIA

Weser R.

RAVENSBURG
(1614)

EAST
FRIESLAND
(1744)

H O L Y   R O M A N   E M P I R E

Frankfurt

Main R.

BAYREUTH
(1791)

ANSBACH
(1791)

Danube R.

BAVARIA

UNITED
PROVINCES

Amsterdam

UPPER
GELDERLAND

Cologne

Rhine R.

LANDS
1714)

Antwerp
Brussels

Meuse R.

NETHER-
(TO AUSTRIA)

Strasbourg

F R A N C E

Paris

Seine R.

Miles
0   100   200

Plate 20

The Rise of Brandenburg-Prussia

Medieval Brandenburg had a mixed population of Slavs and Teutons whose languages showed their mutual distaste. The German word for Slavs referred to their earlier status as slaves, while the Slavic word for Teutons, *Niemtsi,* nonspeaking, reflected on their "barbarism." The Germans prevailed, steadily pushing eastward, overcoming and absorbing the Slavs and converting them to Christianity. The borders of Brandenburg had been roughly set in the tenth century as a diocese between the Elbe and the Oder and widened in succeeding centuries by the Ascanian ruling house to the valley of the Vistula. Here they were repulsed by the Teutonic knights, a militant religious order that was carving a new state out of the lands east of the Vistula in the name of a crusade to convert the Slavs. By the fourteenth century their relentless warfare had won them the districts that make up Prussia.

As the Margraves of Brandenburg, the Ascanian house became one of the seven electors of the Holy Roman Empire in the thirteenth century. When their line died out, the Hohenzollerns succeeded them in 1415; by diplomacy and marriage they built a powerful state out of an unpromising principality. By 1618 the Hohenzollerns straddled northern Europe with territories scattered from the Rhine to the Niemen.

A claim to Pomerania, which did not materialize until 1637, was based on a treaty of 1529 which names the Margraves of Brandenburg as successors to the ruling house should that line fail. Earlier, a marriage in 1591 of John Sigismund of Brandenburg to Princess Anne, eldest daughter of the duke of Prussia, advanced some of the Hohenzollerns' greatest ambitions. In 1609 on the death of Anne's uncle, duke of Cleves and Jülich, both were claimed and won by her husband because the duke had left no heir.

When Anne's father died in 1618, also without male heir, John Sigismund became duke of Prussia; he survived by only two years and was succeeded by his son Georg William. But Georg William's power over his territories was sharply limited by the local Estates, and further weakened during the Thirty Years' War when Imperial troops invaded Brandenburg in 1627 and Swedish troops took Berlin in 1631. Even when he fell heir to Pomerania in 1637 under the terms of the old agreement, he was unable to take it from the Swedes. Paradoxically, during this time the Elector's chief minister tightened his control over the Estates of Brandenburg and Prussia by levying taxes.

On Georg William's death in 1640 his son Frederick William, then 20, succeeded and used his power of taxation so effectively that within several decades he had laid the foundations for an absolutist regime. He expelled the Swedes from Brandenburg; at the Peace of Westphalia in 1648 he received eastern Pomerania and three bishoprics in western Germany. In the Northern War between Sweden and Poland (1655 to 1660), Frederick William fought first with Sweden and then with Poland and managed at the Peace of Oliva to gain general European recognition of Brandenburg's sovereignty over Prussia. By this judicious combination of diplomacy and arms, the Great Elector assembled a territory of 40,000 square miles, second in the Holy Roman Empire only to Austria.

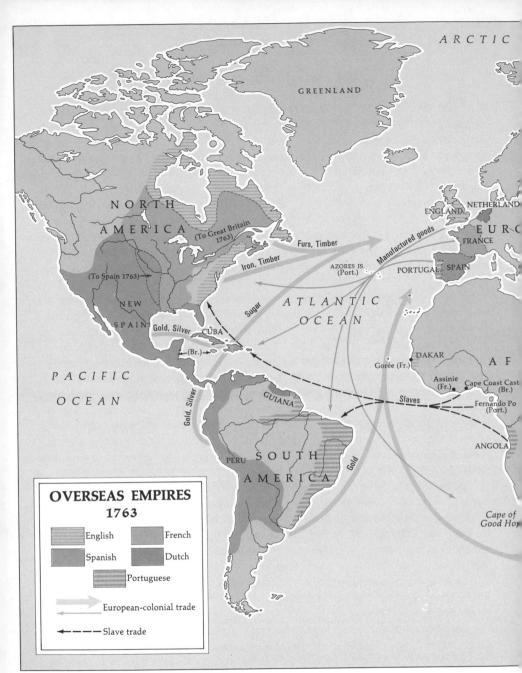

ARCTIC

GREENLAND

NORTH
AMERICA

(To Great Britain 1763)

Furs, Timber

Manufactured goods

ENGLAND   NETHERLAND

EUROP

FRANCE

Iron, Timber

(To Spain 1763)

AZORES IS.
(Port.)

PORTUGAL   SPAIN

NEW

SPAIN

Sugar

ATLANTIC

OCEAN

Gold, Silver   CUBA

(Br.)

A F

PACIFIC

OCEAN

DAKAR

Gorée (Fr.)

Assinie
(Fr.)   Cape Coast Cast
(Br.)

Fernando Po
(Port.)

Gold, Silver

GUIANA

Slaves

PERU   SOUTH

AMERICA

Gold

ANGOLA

Cape of
Good Ho

OVERSEAS EMPIRES
1763

English   French

Spanish   Dutch

Portuguese

European-colonial trade

Slave trade

Plate 21

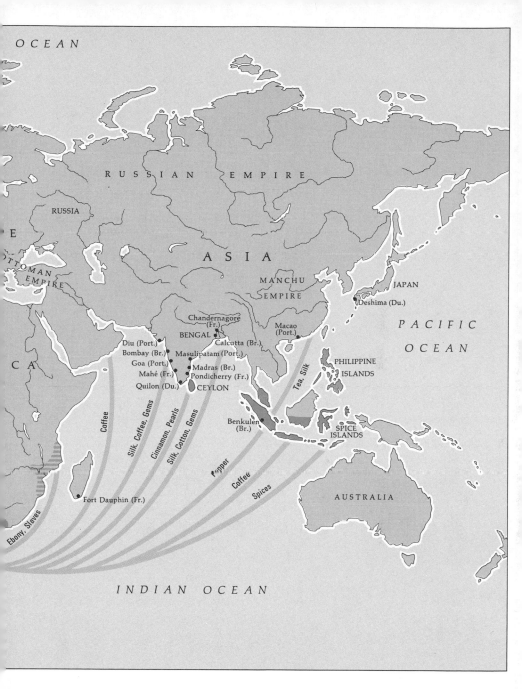

OCEAN

RUSSIAN EMPIRE

RUSSIA

ASIA

MANCHU
EMPIRE

JAPAN

Deshima (Du.)

PACIFIC

OCEAN

OTTOMAN
EMPIRE

E

CA

Chandernagore
(Fr.)

BENGAL

Macao
(Port.)

Diu (Port.)

Calcutta (Br.)

Bombay (Br.)

Masulipatam (Port.)

PHILIPPINE
ISLANDS

Goa (Port.)

Madras (Br.)

Mahé (Fr.)

Pondicherry (Fr.)

Quilon (Du.)

CEYLON

Tea, Silk

Coffee

Benkulen
(Br.)

SPICE
ISLANDS

Silk, Coffee, Gems

Cinnamon, Pearls

Silk, Cotton, Gems

Pepper

Fort Dauphin (Fr.)

Coffee

Spices

AUSTRALIA

Ebony, Slaves

INDIAN OCEAN

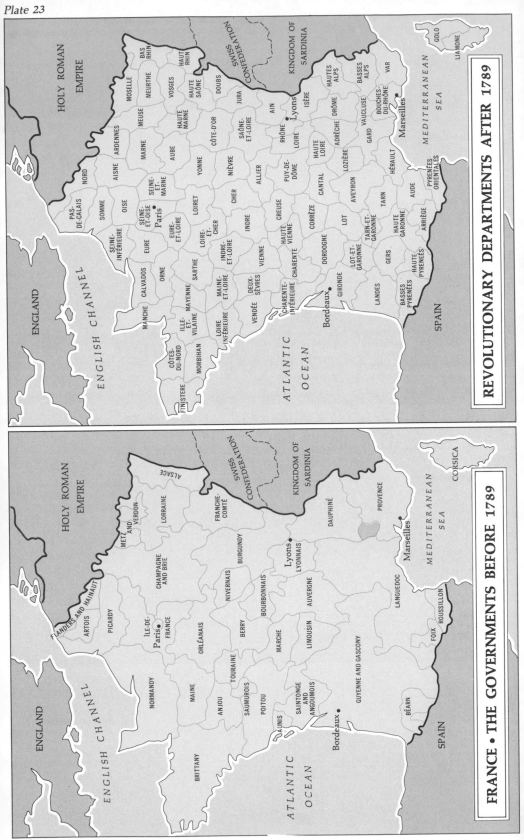

Plate 23

REVOLUTIONARY DEPARTMENTS AFTER 1789

HOLY ROMAN EMPIRE

SWISS CONFEDERATION

KINGDOM OF SARDINIA

GOLO

LIAMONE

MOSELLE
BAS RHIN
HAUT RHIN
MEURTHE
VOSGES
HAUTE SAÔNE
DOUBS
MEUSE
HAUTE MARNE
JURA
AIN
HAUTES ALPS
BASSES ALPS
VAR
ARDENNES
MARNE
AUBE
CÔTE-D'OR
SAÔNE-ET-LOIRE
Lyons
RHÔNE
ISÈRE
DRÔME
VAUCLUSE
BOUCHES-DU-RHÔNE
Marseilles
NORD
AISNE
YONNE
NIÈVRE
ALLIER
LOIRE
HAUTE LOIRE
ARDÈCHE
GARD
HÉRAULT
PAS-DE-CALAIS
SOMME
OISE
SEINE-ET-MARNE
Paris
LOIRET
CHER
INDRE
CREUSE
PUY-DE-DÔME
CANTAL
LOZÈRE
AVEYRON
TARN
AUDE
PYRÉNÉES ORIENTALES
SEINE-INFÉRIEURE
SEINE-ET-OISE
EURE
EURE-ET-LOIR
LOIR-ET-CHER
INDRE-ET-LOIRE
VIENNE
HAUTE VIENNE
CORRÈZE
LOT
TARN-ET-GARONNE
HAUTE GARONNE
ARIÈGE
MANCHE
CALVADOS
ORNE
SARTHE
MAINE-ET-LOIRE
DEUX-SÈVRES
CHARENTE
DORDOGNE
LOT-ET-GARONNE
GERS
HAUTE PYRÉNÉES
CÔTES-DU-NORD
ILLE-ET-VILAINE
MAYENNE
LOIRE-INFÉRIEURE
VENDÉE
CHARENTE-INFÉRIEURE
GIRONDE
Bordeaux
LANDES
BASSES PYRÉNÉES
FINISTÈRE
MORBIHAN

ENGLAND
ENGLISH CHANNEL
ATLANTIC OCEAN
MEDITERRANEAN SEA
SPAIN

Plate 22

FRANCE · THE GOVERNMENTS BEFORE 1789

HOLY ROMAN EMPIRE

SWISS CONFEDERATION

KINGDOM OF SARDINIA

CORSICA

ALSACE
METZ AND VERDUN
LORRAINE
FRANCHE-COMTÉ
DAUPHINÉ
PROVENCE
FLANDERS AND HAINAUT
ARTOIS
PICARDY
CHAMPAGNE AND BRIE
BURGUNDY
NIVERNAIS
BOURBONNAIS
Lyons
LYONNAIS
LANGUEDOC
ROUSSILLON
ÎLE-DE-FRANCE
Paris
ORLÉANAIS
BERRY
MARCHE
AUVERGNE
LIMOUSIN
FOIX
NORMANDY
MAINE
TOURAINE
ANJOU
SAUMUROIS
POITOU
AUNIS
SAINTONGE AND ANGOUMOIS
GUYENNE AND GASCONY
BÉARN
BRITTANY
Bordeaux

ENGLAND
ENGLISH CHANNEL
ATLANTIC OCEAN
MEDITERRANEAN SEA
Marseilles
SPAIN

ARCTIC
OCEAN

ATLANTIC
OCEAN

NORWAY

SWEDEN

FINLAND

St. Petersburg

BALTIC SEA

Riga   NOVGOROD

W. Dvina R.

Danzig

P R U S S I A

Moscow

R U S S I A

POLAND

Warsaw

HOLY

ROMAN

EMPIRE   Danube R.

Vistula R.

AUSTRIA

Kiev

HUNGARY

(Boundary of Poland before
the 1st partition 1772)

CRIMEA

BLACK SEA

Constantinople

O T T O M A N   E M P I R E

N. Dvina R.

U R A L   M O U N T A I N S

SIBERIA

Volga R.

Ural R.

Don R.

Astrakhan

C A U C A S U S   M T S.

CASPIAN SEA

I T A L Y

M E D I T E R R A N E A N   S E A

THE GROWTH OF RUSSIA

Russia in 1682

Acquired, 1682-1762

Acquired, 1762-1796

0   500
Miles

THE PARTITIONS OF POLAND

BALTIC SEA

LITHUANIA

(To Russia)

(To Prussia)

(To Prussia)

(To Prussia)

(To Russia)

(To Russia)

PODELIA

(To Austria)

(To Austria)

1st partition,
1772

2nd partition,
1793

3rd partition,
1795

0   200
Miles

Plate 24

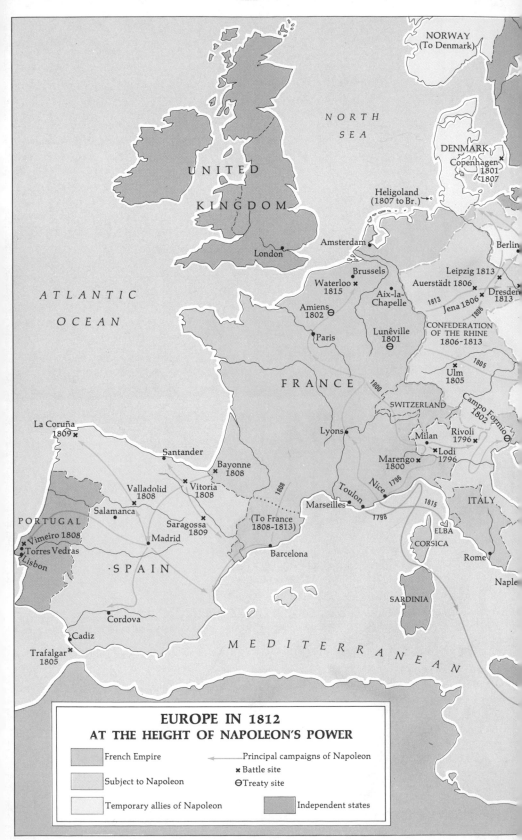

NORWAY
(To Denmark)

NORTH
SEA

DENMARK
Copenhagen
1801
1807

Heligoland
(1807 to Br.)

Berlin

UNITED

KINGDOM

Amsterdam

London

Leipzig 1813

Waterloo
1815

Brussels

Auerstädt 1806

Dresden
1813

ATLANTIC

OCEAN

Aix-la-
Chapelle

1813

Jena 1806

Amiens
1802

1806

CONFEDERATION
OF THE RHINE
1806-1813

Paris

Lunéville
1801

F R A N C E

1800

1805

SWITZERLAND

Ulm
1805

Campo Formio
1802

La Coruña
1809

Lyons

Milan

Rivoli
1796

Santander

Bayonne
1808

Marengo
1800

Lodi
1796

Valladolid
1808

Vitoria
1808

1808

Toulon

Nice

1796

ITALY

Salamanca

PORTUGAL

Saragossa
1809

Madrid

(To France
1808-1813)

Marseilles

1798

1815

ELBA

Vimeiro 1808

CORSICA

Torres Vedras

Rome

Lisbon

S P A I N

Barcelona

Naple

Cordova

SARDINIA

Cadiz

Trafalgar
1805

M E D I T E R R A N E A N

EUROPE IN 1812
AT THE HEIGHT OF NAPOLEON'S POWER

French Empire

Principal campaigns of Napoleon

✕ Battle site

Subject to Napoleon

⊖ Treaty site

Temporary allies of Napoleon

Independent states

Plate 25

SWEDEN

BALTIC SEA

Tilsit 1807
1812
Danzig
Vilna
Friedland 1807
Eylau 1807

PRUSSIA

DUCHY OF
1806
WARSAW
Warsaw

Austerlitz 1805
Vienna
Wagram 1809
Pressburg 1805
AUSTRIA
Leoben
HUNGARY

RUSSIA

Borodino
1812
Moscow

Smolensk
1812

BLACK SEA

ILLYRIAN PROVINCES

ADRIATIC SEA

APLES

OTTOMAN

EMPIRE

Constantinople

AEGEAN SEA

SICILY

SEA

IONIAN ISLANDS
(To Venice to 1797;
to France 1797-1799
and 1807-1815; to
Russia 1799-1807)

CRETE

CYPRUS

Acre

0   500
Miles

Alexandria
1798
Cairo

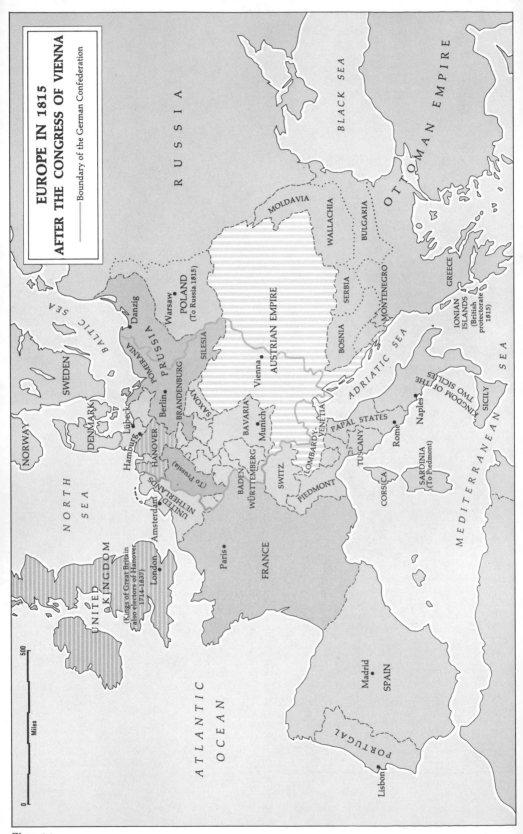

EUROPE IN 1815
AFTER THE CONGRESS OF VIENNA

——— Boundary of the German Confederation

Plate 26

and setting fire to the city. By 1761, Frederick's Epicureanism had turned sour, and his Stoicism was beginning to give way.[27] Yet when peace came in 1763, his Prussia was intact.

In addition to Frederick's courage and persistence, this improbable outcome had two causes: the steadfast support of Pitt and a lucky accident in Russia. The fall of Walpole in the early 1740s had left Britain in the hands of a coalition unskillful abroad and uncertain at home. George II was reluctant to bring the young, immensely popular, William Pitt into the government—had Pitt not denounced the king's ancestral home, Hanover, as a "despicable electorate"? But by the mid-1740s, Pitt was in the government; in 1756 he formed his first cabinet and in the following year, after a few months out of office, he returned, in complete charge of the war. He was a strange man, subject to fits of manic activity and melancholic apathy; especially in his later years he crossed the threshold of madness. But his self-confident boast, "I know that I can save the country and that I alone can" (which every English schoolchild knows as well as every German schoolchild knows Frederick's military exploits), was not the product of mania—it carried conviction. He was bold, original, and charismatic. In 1757 he needed all these qualities; the war was going badly everywhere. By 1759, Pitt's *annus mirabilis*, the world looked brighter: this was the year in which the British took Guadeloupe and Quebec, defeated the French army at Minden in August, and the French navy at Quiberon Bay in November, while continuing their cooperation with Frederick of Prussia. Yet all this would not have been enough to save the Prussian king and the Prussian state. To make things worse, in 1760 George II died and was succeeded by George III, who had little use for Pitt. By 1761, Pitt was out of office, and Lord Bute, the king's great favorite, deserted Prussia in 1762. It was then that Frederick coined the derisive phrase, "perfidious Albion."[28] But it was in the same year that Russia, the source of Frederick's initial distress, became the source of his eventual rescue. In January, the Tsarina Elizabeth died; she was succeeded by the young Tsar Peter III, a fanatical admirer of Frederick the Great. He instantly called off hostilities against Prussia, and thus reduced Frederick's military burdens by half. Prussia was saved.

Since the accession of George III there had been talk of peace: Elizabeth's death hastened negotiations. In May 1762, with the Treaty of St. Petersburg, the Russians settled with Prussia, restoring Prussian territory in Russian hands. In the same month, at Hamburg, the Prussians settled with Sweden. And in February 1763, after some final victories over the Austrians in the field, Frederick concluded the Peace of Hubertusburg with Maria Theresa. It restored Saxony, but—and this is what mattered to Frederick—it kept Silesia in his hands. In the same month, at Paris, Britain and France made peace as well. It was a diplomatic coup for the French, who got back the sugar islands the British

---

[27] For these terms, see p. 13.
[28] For Britain's domestic history in these decades, see p. 443.

had taken, but, abandoning its American holdings in the south to Spain and in the north to the British, the French in effect left the American continent to become part of the growing British Empire. It was a peace of exhaustion; only Pitt and the City merchants of London thought it a disaster.

EIGHTEENTH-CENTURY SOCIETY: PEERS, PIETISTS, AND PEASANTS

The Changing Contours of Religion

While generals maneuvered and ministers intrigued, the essential realities of eighteenth-century European society—habits of piety, patterns of deference, methods of food production, paths of commerce, and techniques of industry— slowly changed. These changes were often anything but radical; in religion especially they represented a return to earlier ways of thinking—or rather, of feeling. The Enlightenment had penetrated wide reaches of educated society; while picturesque tales of atheist bishops in France and deist bishops in England were wild exaggerations, it remains true that especially in the advanced Western countries, the official guardians of piety on the whole favored a tranquil and cultivated religion, derided displays of pious emotion-ality, and concentrated their sermons on the hope of salvation rather than the dread prospects of hell. The Anglican bishop Benjamin Hoadly is doubtless exceptional, but he represents an extreme symptom of a general condition: Hoadly was too busy as Walpole's political agent to attend to his religious duties. When he ascended the pulpit at all, he enunciated a doctrine so worldly and so bland, that the most liberal of Anglicans, the Latitudinarians, were moved to remonstrate with him. In one well-known sermon of 1717, Hoadly argued that since Christ Himself had pronounced His church to be not of this world, it followed that the Church of England had neither the right to meddle with worldly power, nor the obligation to inquire into evidence of religious orthodoxy. This view found apt expression in Joseph Addison's famous ode, which he published in his journal, the *Spectator:*

> The Spacious Firmament on high,
> With all the blue Etherial Sky,
> And spangl'd Heav'ns, a Shining Frame,
> Their great Original proclaim:
> Th' unwearied Sun, from Day to Day,
> Does his Creator's Power display,
> And publishes to every Land
> The Work of an Almighty Hand.

Such tepid, cheerful religiosity, in which respectful contemplation of nature's beauty, benevolence to the unfortunate, and good manners were the keys to heaven, was useful to politicians like Walpole. But it left the traditional religious emotions starved. The striking careers of notorious mountebanks—sellers of medical nostrums, esoteric knowledge, or infallible financial schemes—in the midst of what was supposed to be an age of Enlightenment, testifies to this starvation. So do, even more eloquently, the rise of Pietism and Methodism, the two dominant religions of the heart in the eighteenth century.

Pietism was a response to German Protestantism gone sterile. Luther's complacent heirs had been wholly unable to sustain his crusading spirit and intellectual vitality; they lived comfortably in the certainty that they possessed the truth, and quibbled over trivial theological points. Their congregations were treated to pedantic lectures or vituperative denunciations of heretics; in the parade of erudition and the extravagant name-calling, the meaning of the Reformation withered away for lack of sustenance. Then, in the 1670s, Philipp Jakob Spener spoke, like the proverbial voice in the desert, for a return to a study of the Bible and an increased voice of the laity in church affairs. Not surprisingly, his reforming words, formulated in sermons and, in 1675, in the book *Pia Desideria*, aroused vehement opposition. But Pietism survived the attacks on Spener and Spener's death in 1705; Spener's disciple and successor August Hermann Francke used the University of Halle, which Spener had helped to found in 1694, as a platform from which to preach a revitalized Lutheranism, with an emphasis on practical piety, on works, and on sincere self-searching in contrast with the dry-as-dust scholasticism into which it had fallen.

The impact of Pietism was wide and deep. After Spener's death, its most influential supporter was the count von Zinzendorf, a Saxon nobleman who, under Pietist impulsion, offered refuge to a persecuted Protestant sect, the Moravian Brethren, on his estate at Herrnhut. Under his guidance, the Moravians reconstituted themselves, indulging freely in the very emotional displays that more rational Protestants were apt to regret and ridicule, preaching man's fellowship with man and kinship with Christ. To the Moravians and to Zinzendorf, their bishop after 1737, God was love, His word the Bible, and His injunction to true believers: spread the faith. Accordingly, the Moravians became missionaries, taking their heartfelt, unintellectual Protestantism across Europe and into the British colonies in America. One of their most devoted admirers was the founder of English Methodism, John Wesley.

John Wesley, and his younger brother Charles, first encountered the Moravians in the British colony of Georgia, to which they had gone in 1735 in the company of James Oglethorpe, who was intent on founding a refuge in which graduates of England's debtors prisons could be rehabilitated. Wesley was already a deeply pious, but still a deeply troubled soul; the name Methodist had been conferred on him at Oxford in derision for his forming a club of devout young men intent on praying and studying the Bible. "That such a programme should have provoked ridicule," it has rightly been observed, "is a revealing commentary on the condition of the Hanoverian church."[29] It was not until 1738, a year after his return from Georgia, that John Wesley found the certainty he had prayed for. "In the evening" of May 24, 1738, he noted in his great journal, "I went very unwillingly to a society in Aldersgate Street, where one was reading Luther's preface to the Epistle to the Romans. About a quarter to nine, while he was describing the change which God works in the heart through faith in Christ, I felt my heart strangely warmed. I felt that I did trust in Christ, Christ alone, for salvation; and an assurance was given me that he had taken away *my* sins, even *mine,* and saved me from the law of sin and death." It is a famous moment in religious history, and an important moment in English social history. For Wesley, filled with new knowledge and endowed with enormous energy, discovered that while he trusted in Christ, the Anglican church did not trust in Wesley. Undismayed, and encouraged by the powerful evangelist George Whitefield, Wesley took to the streets and the fields, holding public meetings at any time and in any place that seemed possible. And he traveled, carrying the gospel of his earnest faith across the country; it is not for nothing that his journal has been called a "guidebook to the British Isles." The estimate of two hundred fifty thousand miles traveled, mainly on horseback, and of forty thousand sermons delivered, seems accurate. It was a hard task; crowds were often unfriendly, hurling insults and more damaging missiles as well. Wesley was unafraid and triumphant.

Wesley did not only preach; he organized his followers into societies held together internally by religious seriousness and small dues, and as a group by a network culminating in the Conference. But Wesley had no intention of forming his own church. Like the Anglicanism in which he had grown up, Wesley's Methodism was Arminian in theology; it rejected Calvin's strict doctrine of predestination. Wesley, indeed, was a conservative, both theologically and politically; he wanted to keep his followers in the Anglican communion and away from revolutionary sentiments. He failed in the first: in 1784, he reluctantly constituted the Methodist societies as legal entities, though when he died in 1791, he was still a member of the Church of England. It was only after his death that the English Methodists followed the step already taken in the United States and became an independent church. But Wesley succeeded in the second part of his conservative program. By reaching the unchurched and discontented with his simple and eloquent Christian message, he helped to channel potentially revolutionary sentiments into constructive paths. Methodism, writes the great French historian Elie Halévy, brought "under its influence, first the Dissenting sects, then the Establishment, finally secular opinion." And this helps to explain "the extraordinary stability which English society was destined to enjoy throughout a period of revolutions and crises."[30] Halévy's

---

[29] G. R. Cragg, The Church in the Age of Reason (1648–1789) (1960), 142.
[30] England in 1815 (1913, 2nd English ed., 1949), 387.

famous thesis has recently been disputed, and the essential impact of Methodism remains a matter of debate. But what is clear is that Methodism reached the masses, wholly untouched by the eighteenth-century Church of England. And when Wesley preached, there were more masses in England, and in Europe, than ever before.

Toward the Population Explosion

Probably the most far-reaching of the subterranean changes in eighteenth-century Europe was the increase in its population; the roots of the great population explosion in the nineteenth century go back to the eighteenth. England (with Wales) grew from 5.5 million in 1700 to more than 9 million in 1800; France from 22 million to 28 million in the same period. Other countries offer equally striking figures: the population of the Italian peninsula increased roughly from 13 million to 19 million in the course of the eighteenth century; that of Spain from about 5 million to about 11 million. In Scandinavia, the German States, the American colonies, there were more mouths to feed, more customers to satisfy, more peasants to exploit. All in all, Europe in 1800 had nearly 190 million souls—70 million more than in 1700.

In view of scanty, often maddeningly incomplete statistics, these estimates must remain just that—estimates. The *fact* of population growth remains undisputed; it caused widespread discussion in its own time, and even some dismay, before the Reverend Thomas Malthus painted the grim specter of overpopulation in his famous essay *On Population* (1798). Recent studies suggest that the population of Europe increased nearly 60 percent in the eighteenth century not because the birthrate rose, but because the death rate dropped.[31] The improvements in medicine and sanitation, coupled with the decline of the plague and of smallpox, reduced the number of victims claimed earlier by infant mortality and by epidemics. Improvements in agricultural techniques and in transport reduced the number of victims claimed earlier by famine. Improvements in medicine were chiefly in theory: medical practitioners remained the threat to their patients' lives that they had always been. Smallpox was diminishing, but it haunted men's minds: in 1766, an advertisement offering a consignment of "about 250 fine healthy *Negroes*" duly noted that "the utmost care has already been taken, and shall be continued, to keep them free from the least danger of being infected with the *small-pox*"; indeed, a postscript added, "full one half of the above Negroes have had the *small-pox* in their own country."[32] Nevertheless, in some areas of Europe, notably in England and Flanders, the birthrate actually rose to contribute to the general increase. Even periods of high mortality, caused by bitter winters, bad harvests,

---

[31] For the controversy, and the population explosion, see Chapter 14.

[32] Reproduced in the picture section of Daniel P. Mannix and Malcolm Cowley, *Black Cargoes: A History of the Atlantic Slave Trade, 1518-1865* (ed. 1965).

or local epidemics, had their part to play: when the times of trouble had subsided, deferred marriages took place in large numbers, and the number of births following upon them swelled the population. One significant factor in eighteenth-century population growth was the call for working hands. "What is essentially necessary to a rapid increase of population," Malthus wrote, "is a great and continued demand for labour." Demographic and economic factors reinforced one another; certainly Europe at the end of the eighteenth century was drastically different from what it had been a hundred years before.

Behind these general observations stand concrete, often terrible experiences. Cruelty, destitution, infanticide (a favorite way of disposing of illegitimate babies) remained wholesale killers. "It is not uncommon, I have frequently been told," Adam Smith reported in 1776, "in the Highlands of Scotland for a mother who has borne twenty children not to have two alive." The death of an infant was as common an occurrence among the rich as among the poor. Goethe, who came from a prosperous patrician family in Frankfurt, later could not recall how many of his younger siblings had died in infancy. And the historian Edward Gibbon, writing near the end of the eighteenth century, coolly noted that "the death of a newborn child before that of its parents may seem an unnatural, but it is strictly a probable event: since of any given number the greater part are extinguished before their ninth year." His own infantile constitution had been so weak, he wrote, that "in the baptism of my brothers, my father's prudence successively repeated the Christian name of Edward, that, in case of the departure of the eldest son, this patronymic appellation might still be perpetuated in the family." Gibbon's story is inaccurate, but it testifies to the power the death of the young had over the imagination of the eighteenth century. [33]

The Persistence of Hierarchy

Whatever else it changed, the growth in population did not materially affect the hierarchical structure of society. All across Europe, and in its outposts overseas, government was in the hands of the few who governed in behalf of the few. Republics and monarchies alike were what they had traditionally been— oligarchies. The gap between rich and poor, powerful and powerless, enfranchised and disfranchised, remained wide. It was spanned by a few narrow and precarious bridges bearing the one-way traffic of charity and the two-way traffic of social mobility: the ruin of old and the rise of new families. But this, though spectacular, was relatively light. Some hundreds of enterprising tradesmen and bankers moved upward, their financial success the ticket to social ascent. But to speak of a "rising bourgeoisie" is to neglect a fact of central significance: by

---

[33] See Gibbon's *Autobiography* (ed. Dero A. Saunders, 1961), 53; for a correction of this report, see D. M. Low, *Gibbon's Journal* to January 28th, 1763 (n.d.), xxix.

buying rural properties and marrying his children into the gentry or the aristocracy, the affluent bourgeois did not rise—he disappeared. He himself might acquire a patent of nobility; many merchants, including prosperous slave traders in the French port cities, did. And if he failed, his offspring succeeded. As Daniel Defoe, the vigorous spokesman for the English bourgeoisie, put it in 1726, in *The Complete English Tradesman:* "Trade in England makes gentlemen, and has peopled this nation with gentlemen; for the tradesmen's children, or at least their grandchildren, come to be as good gentlemen, statesmen, Parliament men, privy counsellors, judges, bishops and noblemen, as those of the highest birth and the most ancient families." Even the elder Pitt, the Great Commoner, accepted a peerage after he resigned in 1761. The phrase, "the people," was on everyone's lips: Samuel Johnson, in a well-known epigram, said that unlike Walpole ("a minister given by the King to the people"), Pitt was "a minister given by the people to the King." In statements like these, "people" referred to the merchants of the City of London, to bankers and tradesmen, to some thousands of politically influential country squires and peers, and to a handful of disinterested patriots impressed with Pitt's gift for leadership. Even in England, where discussion was unusually candid and politics a game played by an unusually large number of persons, the political public was a small minority of the total population. The oligarchic, hierarchical nature of social life and political power was all-pervasive. It was evident in vast empires like Russia and in tiny republics like Geneva, in large tracts of countryside with their local lord and in flourishing cities with their commercial patriciate. The free imperial city of Frankfurt rigidly ranked its population by a nuanced dress code—a *Kleiderordnung*—that instantly placed each citizen into his proper social niche. And in Strasbourg, a typical city, the governing legislature "seemed to be a debating society for brothers, cousins, and brothers-in-law." [34]

Politics and power were family affairs. The majority of Europeans were subjects of condescension, fear, or indifference. There were a few exceptional voices, more audible for being so exceptional. Adam Smith, the most brilliant political economist of the century, flatly urged high wages for the working population: "The liberal reward of labour," he argued, "as it encourages the propagation, so it increases the industry of the common people"; where wages are high, "we shall always find the workmen more active, diligent, and expeditious than where they are low." Nor was such "liberal reward" merely a device for ensuring high productivity; it was sheer "equity" that those "who feed, cloath and lodge the whole body of the people, should have such a share of the produce of their own labour as to be themselves tolerably well fed, cloathed, and lodged." But this was the voice of the radical Enlightenment; other, harsher voices were more representative of the age: "Everyone but an idiot knows," Arthur Young, the influential writer on western European agriculture, said in 1771, "that the lowest classes must be kept poor or they will

[34] Franklin L. Ford, *Strasbourg in Transition, 1648-1789* (1958), 15.

never be industrious." Clearly, the time of the "lowest classes" had not yet come.

All across Europe, then, societies were dominated by oligarchies. Nearly everywhere, noblemen monopolized the highest posts in state and church, and there was a tendency for different branches of the aristocracy to coalesce: in France, the old nobility of the sword increasingly intermarried with the new nobility of the robe. Wealth and status attracted each other. In their role as influential courtiers, great landowners, high-ranking bureaucrats, or princes of the church, aristocrats had access to the sources of wealth. While not all nobles were rich—the poor among them were numerous and conspicuous—most of them could afford extensive estates, luxurious styles of life, and impressive gambling debts. And those aristocrats whose resources were failing could replenish them by marrying their sons to bourgeois heiresses. Yet the cosmopolitan splendor of the leading noble houses gives eighteenth-century Europe a misleading appearance of uniformity. In fact, the shape, role, and powers of aristocracies differed from country to country. In Great Britain, the nobility generally lived on the land; though their properties were generally rented to tenant farmers, they kept in touch through their stewards, and many among them actually enjoyed experimenting with new agricultural techniques. These peers governed Britain by superintending local government in association with the local squire and by going to Westminster to sit in the House of Lords. In Britain, only the eldest son inherited his father's title. Thus father and son, older and younger brother, often met one another in Parliament—the one sitting in the Lords, the other in the House of Commons (see pp. 385 and 445). Both in local and national affairs, then, relations between the peerage and the far larger squierarchy were often intimate. This, and a sizable, self-respecting urban bourgeoisie, meant that the higher reaches of English society were not sharply divided, but gently, if subtly, graded and interrelated. One did not have to be a nobleman to get on: the great Sir Robert Walpole was the incarnation of the country squire in politics. As we know, his elevation to the peerage was less a reward for services performed than a sign that his political influence was at an end (see p. 388).

In France, in contrast, the apex of the social hierarchy remained the court nobility. For them, to go back to the provinces was to go into exile. But there were striking and numerous exceptions to this pattern: while French law closed most trades to the nobility as unworthy of their privileged estate, many provincial nobles lived cheerfully enough far from Paris, cultivating their properties and increasing their incomes. For example, at Toulouse, whose nobility has been closely studied, noblemen were thrifty and rational landlords; their "mode of living," writes their historian, "was maintained by adherence to the so-called bourgeois virtues of thrift, discipline, and strict management of the family fortune."[35] High posts were in the hands of aristocrats; by 1789, all

---

[35] Robert Forster, *The Nobility of Toulouse in the Eighteenth Century* (1960), 177.

bishops in France were noblemen, often younger sons combining vast perqui-
sites with no duties, and only one of Louis XVI's thirty-six ministers was a
commoner. The French Revolution, as we shall see, had many causes. But one
of them was the short-sighted self-centeredness of the French aristocracy, alert
mainly to its interests, intent on pleasure, and deaf to the call for social
responsibility, let alone social reform. As the marquise de La Tour du Pin, one
of the most intelligent survivors of this aristocracy, would later put it in her
memoirs: "The Revolution of 1789 was only the inevitable consequence and, I
might almost say, the just punishment of the vices of the upper classes, vices
carried to such excess that if people had not been stricken with a mortal
blindness, they must have seen that they would inevitably be consumed by the
very fire they themselves were lighting." The "famous 'douceur de vivre,' of the
old regime," as Professor John McManners sums it up, "was concocted from a
very simple formula, privilege without responsibility." [36]

Elsewhere, in Prussia, the Hapsburg Empire, Russia, aristocracies were
variations on the English and French models. Nearly everywhere, there were
too many noble courtiers, doing too many useless things. They organized
dances and hunts, they arranged theatricals and card parties, they intrigued to
be close to the duke—or, perhaps better, the duchess—who was the center of
these little universes. "In the Saxon State Calendar," one historian reminds us,
"the list of offices covered fifty-three pages." [37] Most of these aristocracies were
supposedly service aristocracies; they enjoyed a monopoly of high offices in the
bureaucracy and the army, and an almost undisputed right to treat "their"
peasants as they liked, but in return they were obliged to serve their royal
masters all their lives, and with unquestioning fidelity. The reality was a little
more complicated than this; everywhere, nobles sought to escape, or at least
lighten, the burdens that energetic and power-hungry monarchs had imposed
upon them. In Russia they wholly succeeded; [38] even in Prussia—though only
after the death of the omnipresent Frederick II in 1786—they succeeded in part.
Gradually, the Junker bureaucrats became centers of power hard to move and
impossible to dislodge. It is not extravagant to call the eighteenth century a
century of the rising aristocracy.

Europe: A Rural Society

The basis of aristocratic wealth and power was the land. Economic historians
used to date the Industrial Revolution from 1760. There is some reason for their
choice. It was in 1769, after long experimentation, that James Watt patented his

[36] "France," in A. Goodwin, ed., *The European Nobility in the Eighteenth Century* (1953), 29.
[37] J. O. Lindsay, "The Social Classes and the Foundations of the States," in *The New
Cambridge Modern History*, vol. VII (1957), 55.
[38] See p. 378 and, for developments under Catherine II, p. 432.

steam engine—the decisive invention of that revolution, the source of power vastly greater than men, or horses, or waterwheels could provide. What has been called the "invention of invention" multiplied the number of devices used in the production of goods: while in the century between 1660 and 1760, the average number of patents granted in England was sixty, in the years between 1760 and 1790, that number rose to three hundred twenty-five. This was the period in which the factory began to emerge, and the factory—a central building with machinery, on which workers converged for stated periods of time—was an invention like that of the steam engine. The factory demanded something new: the regular employment of labor. It put a premium on what came to be called "industrial discipline"—the workingman's ability and willingness to report for work on schedule, every day, for the machines were voracious and could not stand idle. These moral and psychological requirements went hand in hand with improvements in commercial and banking techniques which eased the transfer of funds, and with the agglomeration of sprawling industrial cities, in which the working population clustered in increasing numbers—and increasing misery.

In some industries, notably in textiles, these spectacular improvements were truly revolutionary. John Kay's flying shuttle, patented in 1733, cut the number of weavers needed to work the loom from two to one. In about 1764, James Hargreaves invented the spinning jenny, a modern mechanical version of the spinning wheel. His first version permitted the simultaneous working of eight spindles; in 1770, when the jenny was patented, it was capable of handling sixteen. The year before, the gifted Richard Arkwright had patented the water frame, and ten years later, in 1779, Samuel Crompton patented the spinning mule. These two inventions permitted the spinning of fine and coarse yarns in unprecedented, hitherto almost unimaginable quantities. And, significantly enough, in 1785 Watt's steam engine was harnessed to these devices, and factory mass production of cloth was under way. Yet, despite all this, the Industrial Revolution was a slow and uneven growth. It began in England: Germany saw its first steam engine in 1785, and factories in France long remained small. And even in England, the factory town did not spring up overnight: by 1790 there were still fewer than a thousand spinning jennies in operation. The old commercial mentality, the old handicraft industries, and the old small-scale enterprise were tenacious survivals. Through the eighteenth century, Europe remained a predominantly rural society.

This in itself was not a sign of stagnation. There was no rigid separation between agricultural and industrial occupations; before the age of the factory, employers of labor depended largely on the domestic system. They engaged workers, rural and urban, to do their work at home. This held true for England, the mother of industrial society, as well as all across central Europe. In the rural districts of Bohemia, there were more than two hundred thousand domestic workers spinning flax; in the Swiss canton of Glaurus there were more than thirty-four thousand domestic spinners across the countryside. Most of these rural industrial workers were women. [39]

Moreover, like the industrial sector of Europe, rural life, too, felt the bracing breath of innovation. Viscount Townshend acquired the nickname Turnip Townshend for his experiments with introducing turnips, which served as fodder for livestock, fed nitrogen to the soil, and facilitated crop rotation; his dual career—politics and scientific farming—is in many ways characteristic of the style congenial to the English peerage. But not all experimental, "improving" farmers were noblemen. Jethro Tull, a gentleman farmer, was something of a crank and professional inventor, who published an important book on the use of deep and straight ploughing for the thorough tillage of the soil. And Robert Bakewell, a tenant farmer still lower on the social scale, proved the immense utility of controlled, selective stock breeding for sheep and cattle alike. Nearly all these innovations took place on enclosed land. The enclosure of common land, on which the small tenant farmer had traditionally grazed his cattle and the rural poor squatted, consolidated holdings and made farming more efficient. Enclosure had been going on since the Tudors, and called forth protests from reformers appalled at the dislocations it produced. But it went on, at a vastly increased pace in the eighteenth century after 1760, while dislocations and protests increased apace. Like so much else in economic life, the enclosure movement illustrates an experience that is almost a law of progress: procedures that benefit some will hurt others; all improvement must be paid for, and it is normally paid for by those least capable of making their voices heard or their will felt.

In England, agricultural improvements were far more noticeable than on the Continent, but even in England innovations moved slowly against massive resistance. The once popular term, "agricultural revolution," is going out of use: the proverbial conservatism of rural life defeated the most impatient projector. Hierarchies of wealth and status remained intact, and in some areas grew more pronounced. In England, the three hundred or so noble families were also the great landlords; their incomes ranged from a comfortable £5000 to a magnificent £50,000. Next in line were the gentry, less than a thousand of them rich enough to approach the peers; three to four thousand solid squires with incomes ranging from £1000 to £3000 a year; and up to twenty thousand ordinary, middling landed gentlemen whose income was anywhere between £300 and £1000 a year. The least affluent of these gentlemen were little more prosperous than that far larger category, the freeholders, whose farms might bring them as little as £30, or as much as £700 a year. This scale, ranging from £30 to £50,000, offers a prospect of vast economic and social distance, from cottage to palace. Yet even this hierarchy, steep as it appears, does not comprehend the whole spectrum of English rural life: below the petty freeholder with his £50 or £75 a year were the mass of tenant farmers, some of

[39] See Anderson, *Europe in the Eighteenth Century*, 65.

them respectable yeomen, many of them sturdy laborers, and many others miserable squatters dependent on casual labor, charity, and poaching. [40]

In France, the hierarchy was steeper still, and the condition of the poor, worse. France's population was far larger than Britain's—about five times larger—and more rural: roughly six out of every seven Frenchmen lived on the land. [41] The church, which made up a vanishingly small minority of the French population—no more than 0.5 percent—owned 15 percent of that land. This was considerably less than aggressive philosophies like to charge, but it was still a great deal, and most church lands were highly desirable soil. The nobility, which totaled 1.5 percent of the French population, owned 20 percent of the land, another striking disproportion. Well-to-do bourgeois, holding farms normally on the outskirts of the towns in which they lived, owned another third. And a final third was in the hands of peasants, a class that made up about 85 percent of France's population.

These bare figures tell only part of the story. A small minority of peasants, the *laboureurs,* were prosperous and proud; a handful of these rural aristocrats could put by enough to finance their children's social ascent; many of them made themselves unpopular with their tight fists and hard hearts, their shrewd dealings with their poorer neighbors and with the government. But many, indeed most, of the peasants who owned land could not really support themselves and their burgeoning families with the returns from their small plots. They therefore hired themselves out to work on the property of *laboureurs* or earned a pittance taking in domestic industry. Nor were these pathetic property owners at the bottom of the economic and social ladder: perhaps eleven million French peasants were sharecroppers at the mercy of their neighbors and the price of bread, and five million more were condemned to a life of intermittent labor, migratory work, banditry, and starvation. Most of these peasants were ridden with onerous obligations: rents to the landlord, tithes to the church, a variety of payments dating back to medieval times for such "privileges" as the use of the local wine press or the local mill, and a host of taxes to the government. When Arthur Young traveled through France in the years from 1787 to 1789 to write his famous comparison between French and English conditions, he was amazed at the low productivity of French agriculture, appalled at the "miserable state of the labouring poor," and constrained to observe that the average French peasant's morale was irremediably low. They were "content merely to live." [42]

If French peasants suffered in comparison with the English yeomanry, they were at least legally better off than the peasants on Prussian, Hapsburg, or Russian lands. While about a million French peasants—less than one in

---

[40] See G. E. Mingay, *English Landed Society in the Eighteenth Century* (1963).

[41] For the French population of the seventeenth century, see p. 291.

[42] See Robert and Elborg Forster, eds., *European Society in the Eighteenth Century* (1969), 108 ff.

twenty—were serfs, the vast majority of east European peasants lived in legal bondage. In Austria, they suffered under heavy and growing exactions from their noble landlords; the nobility sweated the peasantry for increasing contributions, through a variety of taxes and, above all, through *robot*—compulsory labor service. Here, as everywhere else, there were regional and local variations; the lot of the peasant differed with the laxity or efficiency, kindness or cruelty, of individual landlords and their stewards. But in general, conditions were terrible almost beyond description; travelers' reports are notoriously undependable, but visitor after visitor speaks of Bohemian and Hungarian peasants living more or less like animals. It was not until the 1760s and 1770s, when Maria Theresa turned her attention from Silesia—now definitively lost to her—to domestic affairs, and when peasant revolts jogged her elbow, that she placed these conditions on the agenda for state action. She decreed the abolition of some long-standing obligations which had become burdensome abuses on the peasants, established "maxima" beyond which peasants could not be exploited by their lords, and at least in some measure protected common lands from being converted to the landlords' private use. She did much, but, as C. A. Macartney has observed, her decrees "left the peasant position in the monarchy incompletely solved."[43]

In Russia, too, the condition of the serf, though it varied greatly, was in general a life of incessant toil and total dependence, a routine of exploitation and oppression. The law put the peasant into the hands of the landlord, and the gradual emancipation of the Russian nobility from state service was accompanied by its tightening control over its serfs' labor and their very lives. Peter the Great had made the nobility's right to its serf-estates hereditary, so that Russian peasants were handed down from father to son like so much cattle. The law protected a serf from being tortured to death by his master—an ominous prohibition act whose very existence suggests the prevalence of the practice—but the law did not provide specific penalties for those landlords who violated it. "Where the masters took their returns from the peasants in the form of money-dues or *obrok*," Geroid T. Robinson sums up the life of the Russian serf in the eighteenth century, "the average weight of this obligation seems to have increased considerably between the 'sixties and the 'nineties—perhaps even as much as one hundred per cent. . . . On the estates where the principal exaction was in the form of forced labor or *barshchina*, three days' work per week was the amount usually required of adult peasants of both sexes, but four or five days' work was sometimes exacted, and not infrequently the peasant was forced to work continuously for a considerable period in the manorial fields, while his own plot waited for seeding, or his own harvest rotted on the ground. Furthermore, it was customary to require of the forced-labor peasants certain payments in kind—poultry, eggs, meat, honey, homespun cloth, and the like.

---

[43] *The Hapsburg Empire, 1790–1918* (1969), 66. For the reign of Maria Theresa's son, Joseph II, see p. 427 below.

Again, it was this century that witnessed the first considerable development of mining and manufacturing in Russia, and numbers of private serfs were put to forced labor in these industries. Sick and aged peasants who were unable to render the dues and services required by their masters might be 'liberated'— that is to say, expelled from their villages to go where they could."[44] Not surprisingly, most of the serfs were so beaten down by their existence, so dully accustomed to their misery, that they did not even think of complaining, to say nothing of rebelling. "It appears that the spirit of freedom is so dried up in the slaves," the eighteenth-century Russian educator and reformer Alexander Mikolayevich Radichev observed, that they "have no desire to end their suffering."[45]

Radichev's use of the word "slave" should cause only momentary surprise. The Russian landlord could compel his serfs to increase their contributions in labor or products, move them from field to domestic service, force them to marry or to abstain from marrying, and sell them alone or with the rest of their families, with or without the land on which they toiled—completely at will.[46] Slaves were hardly worse off than this.

Slavery

There were few slaves in Europe proper, but slaves were an indispensable ingredient in the European economy. America—North, Central, and South— was a vitally important extension of the European market, and the slave trade formed the basis for the mercantile greatness of port cities like Nantes and Liverpool, Bordeaux and Bristol. Slavery, as we know (see p. 85), was invented long before the eighteenth century, but the slave trade rose to its climax in that century—a depressing commentary on an age of Enlightenment. The argument for slavery was simple and practical: the gold mines of Brazil, the sugar plantations of the West Indies, the tobacco plantations of the southern colonies, demanded labor so hard, in such heat, that free men would never do the necessary work. In 1764, John Pinney, a prominent Bristol sugar merchant, spoke for the British commercial community: "Negroes," he wrote, "are the Sinews of a Plantation, and it is as impossible for a Man to make Sugar without the assistance of Negroes, as to make Bricks without Straw"—and by Negroes he meant slaves.[47] And in 1789, the chambre de commerce of Bordeaux officially declared: "France needs its colonies to sustain its commerce, and consequently slaves to allow agriculture in that part of the world to flourish, until another way is found to achieve this end."[48] These were the arguments

---

[44] *Rural Russia Under the Old Regime* (1932), 27-28.
[45] Quoted in Forster and Forster, *European Society in the Eighteenth Century,* 136.
[46] See Robinson, *Rural Russia,* 27.
[47] Quoted in C. M. MacInnes, *A Gateway to Empire* (1939), 193.
[48] Quoted in Henri Sée, *La France économique et sociale au XVIIIe siècle* (5th ed., 1952), 121.

of mercantile good sense; they carried weight with a substantial majority of Europeans. Antislavery agitation was rising, but the outraged protest of humane philosophes and conscience-stricken Christians were dismissed as the voices of well-meaning but irresponsible cranks. Most Europeans continued to justify the institution, and its lifeline the slave trade, in James Boswell's words, as a "very important and necessary branch of commercial interest." They rationalized it (again in Boswell's words) as kindness to the "African Savages, a portion of whom it saves from massacre, or intolerable bondage in their own country, and introduces . . . into a much happier state of life." Samuel Johnson thundered that slavery is against nature; Horace Walpole passionately and prophetically exclaimed: "I scarce wish perfect freedom to merchants who are the bloodiest of all tyrants. I should think the souls of the Africans would sit heavy on the swords of the Americans." But the antislavery cause was slow to win converts.

Late in the eighteenth century, philosophes added a new argument to the cause. While slavery had long been attacked as inhuman or un-Christian, two Scottish economists, John Millar and Adam Smith, now suggested that it was uneconomical as well: the slave always remains a reluctant and unskilled workman, and slavery by its very existence keeps managers from introducing labor-saving innovations. "The work done by slaves," Adam Smith wrote, "though it appears to cost only their maintenance, is in the end the dearest of any." Recent studies support these eighteenth-century conjectures. In addition to perpetuating inefficient modes of labor, the profits accruing to what were essentially selected luxury industries were purchased at an exorbitant price in health and life. The high mortality of slaves is widely known. Untold black lives were lost in Africa during slaving expeditions and internecine warfare, untold more in America in an unaccustomed environment of exhausting toil, brutal treatment, and endemic disease. In addition, the mortality rate of slaves on board ship averaged more than 13 percent—often it was much higher. What is less well known is the loss sustained by the whites: again and again, more sailors than slaves died in the long middle passage across the Atlantic. Besides, the soldiers, merchants, and officials who went to the disease-ridden slave depots in West Africa perished in large numbers: one estimate suggests that during the first year there one of two Europeans died. And life in the West Indian plantations was little better. The social cost of slavery—to Africa, Europe, and America, to blacks and whites alike—was thus incalculable. Nor can this cost be measured by wasted lives alone; those who survived suffered irreparable moral damage. Captain John Newton, a reformed eighteenth-century slave trader, insisted late in life that the need for dealing harshly with Negro slaves "gradually brings a numbness upon the heart, and renders most of those who are engaged in it too indifferent to the sufferings of their fellow creatures." [49] Slavery degraded everyone, master and slave alike.

[49] Quoted in Mannix and Cowley, Black Cargoes, 145.

Despite these harrowing and familiar realities, the slave trade flourished mightily through the eighteenth century. In the sixteenth century, the number of slaves imported from Africa into all of America—Brazil, Spanish America, and the islands—totaled about[50] two hundred thirty thousand. In the seventeenth century, especially after 1650, when the plantation economies of the Western hemisphere became firmly established, the number rose to over one and a third million, with the largest single contingent, over 40 percent, going to Brazil. In the eighteenth century, the number rose again, and drastically, to about six million, with Brazil still taking the lion's share—almost a third. Most of these imports came from Africa, but by no means all: throughout the eighteenth century, the West Indian island of Jamaica exported as one of its commodities an average of two thousand blacks a year to the English colonies on the mainland. While the trade continued beyond the end of the eighteenth century, it fell off, especially in the north, in the nineteenth. All in all, about ten million black slaves came from Africa to America, to work in the mines and the fields, to enrich the planters and the shipping magnates. The miserable mutilated slave whom Voltaire's innocent voyager, Candide, finds lying on a road sums it all up with bitter felicity: "This is the price at which you eat sugar in Europe."

The price, as we have said, was high, and the trade was risky; but the profits were great. And if there were any doubts, a host of pamphleteers reassured the public: "Our West Indian and African trades," one such writer told his British readers in 1749, "are the most nationally beneficial of any we carry on." The "Negroe-Trade," he concluded, "may be justly esteemed an inexhaustible Fund of the Wealth and Naval Power of this Nation."[51] This is why British merchants fought so hard for the *asiento*, the exclusive agreement that Britain imposed on Spain at Utrecht in 1713, giving British traders a monopoly on the selling of African slaves to the Spanish colonies in America. This, too, is why the British Parliament granted the Royal African Company— a company specializing in the slave trade—a generous subsidy to maintain its forts on the Gold Coast against the unwelcome intrusion of Dutch and French slavers. The profits of the trade were not confined to the returns on slaves alone. What was called the "triangular trade" involved European exports to Africa (payments like beads or firearms to African slave sellers), the transport of African blacks to the West Indies or the Carolinas, and the import of American commodities into Europe. Shipbuilders and importers, therefore, quite as much

---

[50] We use this cautious word advisedly; all discussions on the slave trade, with the complex questions it raises about the origins and destination of slaves, and the fragmentary, often contradictory figures, must depend on intelligent estimates at best. These estimates vary enormously—between 8 million and 25 million as the global figure; detailed estimates (exports from, or imports to, specific areas) differ as well. In this section we are much indebted to Philip D. Curtin, *The Atlantic Slave Trade: A Census* (1969), a brilliant reassessment of all the available evidence, and an invaluable compendium of new estimates.

[51] Quoted in Williams, *Whig Supremacy*, 296.

as shareholders in slaving companies, were deeply involved in the trade and did their utmost to defend it. What with disease, piracy, accident, high costs, and commissions, many expeditions involved losses, but the average profit has been estimated at 30 percent or more—too tidy a sum to permit mere humanitarian or prudential considerations to weigh heavily in the balance. The importance of the trade and its consequences for the mercantile establishment stand revealed in the rising share of Britain's trade with America (which rose from 13 percent in 1700 to 34 percent in 1785) and with Africa (which rose, in the same time span, at the same rate).[52] Only reformers and revolutionaries could make light of such figures.

SELECTED READINGS

For Europe in the quarter century after the Peace of Utrecht, see, in general, M. S. Anderson, *Europe in the Eighteenth Century, 1713-1783* (1961). It largely replaces the older book by Penfield Roberts, *The Quest for Security, 1715-1740* (1947). The appropriate volume (VII) of *The New Cambridge Modern History,* J. O. Lindsay, ed., *The Old Regime, 1713-1763* (1957), is useful.

France after Louis XIV is beautifully and economically summarized in Alfred Cobban, *A History of Modern France,* vol. I, *The Old Regime and Revolution, 1715-1799* (1957). Franklin L. Ford, *Robe and Sword: The Regrouping of the French Aristocracy After Louis XIV* (1953), takes an important sociopolitical problem down to 1748. It can be read in conjunction with Robert Forster's informative essay, *The Nobility of Toulouse in the Eighteenth Century* (1960). On foreign policy, Arthur M. Wilson, *French Foreign Policy During the Administration of Cardinal Fleury, 1726-43* (1936), retains its value. See also the general treatment by G. P. Gooch, *Louis XV: The Monarchy in Decline* (1956). C. B. A. Behrens, *The Ancien Régime* (1967), though up-to-date, is slight; it should be supplemented by Elinor G. Barber, *The Bourgeoisie in 18th Century France* (1955); John Lough, *An Introduction to Eighteenth Century France* (1960); and John McManners, *French Ecclesiastical Society Under the Ancient Regime* (1961)—this last, though it concentrates on the city of Angers, is a masterly account that illuminates life in the France of Louis XV and beyond. For economic history, the brief book by Henri E. Sée, *Economic and Social Conditions in France During the Eighteenth Century* (1927), is useful.

For England during these same decades, see the survey by Basil Williams, *The Whig Supremacy, 1714-1760* (1939), though it is now somewhat old. For a more modern view, the first half of J. H. Plumb, *England in the Eighteenth Century* (1950), short, lucid, and accurate, is excellent; so is Plumb's large-scale biography, *Sir Robert Walpole: The Making of a Statesman* (1956) and *Sir Robert Walpole: The King's Minister* (1960)—these take the great minister down to 1734; a final volume is promised. Plumb's popular *The First Four Georges* (1956) and his brief life of *Chatham* (1953) are also valuable introductions to the period; his *The Growth of Political Stability in England, 1675-1725* (1967) is more technical, but an important reinterpretation. See also John B. Owen, *The*

---

[52] See Jacques Godechot and R. R. Palmer, "Le problème de l'Atlantique du XVIIIᵉ au XXᵉ siècle," *X Congreso Internazionale di Scienze Storiche,* V (1955), 196-197.

Rise of the Pelhams (1957). On social history, M. Dorothy George, *London Life in the XVIIIth Century* (1925), and her *England in Transition* (1931), may be supplemented with Dorothy Marshall's *English People in the Eighteenth Century* (1956) and *The English Poor in the Eighteenth Century* (1926). See also the opening sections of Peter Mathias, *The First Industrial Nation* (1969), and the later sections of Charles Wilson, *England's Apprenticeship, 1603-1673* (1965). John Carswell, *The South Sea Bubble* (1960), explains a complex matter of high finance; Norman Sykes' *Church and State in England in the XVIIIth Century* (1934) is authoritative.

The best survey of the great confrontation after 1740 is Walter L. Dorn, *Competition for Empire, 1740-1763* (1940). Among biographies of Prussia's controversial ruler, G. P. Gooch, *Frederick the Great: The Ruler, the Writer, the Man* (1947), is judicious; Pierre Gaxotte, *Frederick the Great* (tr. 1942), is hostile; D. B. Horn, *Frederick the Great and the Rise of Prussia* (1969), is brief. Hans Rosenberg, *Bureaucracy, Aristocracy, Autocracy: The Prussian Experience, 1660-1815* (1960), and volume II of Hajo Holborn's *History of Modern Germany* (1964), are indispensable here. Chester V. Easum, *Prince Henry of Prussia, Brother of Frederick the Great* (1942), is also useful.

For Frederick's Austrian counterpart, see Edward Crankshaw, *Maria Theresa* (1969), and G. P. Gooch, *Maria Theresa and Other Studies* (1951); for her son, the recent *Joseph II* by Paul P. Bernard (1968) largely supersedes Saul K. Padover, *The Revolutionary Emperor: Joseph the Second, 1741-90* (2nd. ed., 1967). See also Robert J. Kerner, *Bohemia in the Eighteenth Century* (1932), and, also on Bohemia, William E. Wright, *Serf, Seigneur, and Sovereign* (1966), and Edith M. Link, *The Emancipation of the Austrian Peasant, 1740-1798* (1949).

On population increase, see Carlo Cipolla, *The Economic History of World Population, 1750-1918* (1962); M. C. Buer, *Health, Wealth and Population in the Early Days of the Industrial Revolution* (ed. 1968); and above all a number of important essays in D. V. Glass and D. E. C. Eversley, eds., *Population in History: Essays in Historical Demography* (1965). On social structure, in addition to the volumes by Ford, Forster, Barber, and Marshall cited earlier in this chapter, as well as Geroid T. Robinson, *Rural Russia Under the Old Regime* (1932), on the Russian serf, see Albert Goodwin, ed., *The European Nobility in the Eighteenth Century* (1953); G. E. Mingay, *English Landed Society in the Eighteenth Century* (1963); and Robert and Elborg Forster, eds., *European Society in the Eighteenth Century* (1969)—an unusually well-conceived anthology of social history.

On slavery, we (and the historical profession) are much indebted to the researches of Philip D. Curtin, published in *The Atlantic Slave Trade: A Census* (1969). C. M. MacInnes, *A Gateway to Empire* (1939), discusses one slave-trading port, Bristol. Daniel P. Mannix, in collaboration with Malcolm Cowley, *Black Cargoes: A History of the Atlantic Slave Trade, 1518-1865* (ed. 1965), is a sobering survey. For the African side of the trade, see Basil Davidson, *Black Mother* (1961), and Melville J. Herskovits, *The Myth of the Negro Past* (1958). Eric Williams, *Capitalism and Slavery* (1944), treats the question from a Marxist perspective.

10

Reformers and Revolutionaries: 1763-1789

THE VARIETIES OF GOOD GOVERNMENT

The age of Enlightenment was also an age of reform. An impressive array of energetic rulers modified institutions and experimented with policies to meet new demands, to fulfill old obligations in a new way, to bring their states into a new age. These parallel developments—enlightenment and reform—were obviously not unrelated, and since the nineteenth century it has been fashionable to group reforming rulers under the single rubric of "enlightened despots." The fashion persists, at the expense of historical precision, for the name is misleading. It unjustly saddles the philosophes with a principled predilection for progressive despots. It wrongly implies that these "despots" heavily depended on the guidance of philosophes. And, by forcing a striking diversity of ideas and practices into a single category, it imposes on the second half of the eighteenth century a specious uniformity. Frederick II of Prussia dominated and prized his nobility, Catherine II of Russia increased the privileges of her nobility, Joseph II of Austria humbled his nobility as much as lay within his power. While Joseph sought to centralize Hapsburg institutions under his authoritarian control, his younger brother Leopold, archduke of Tuscany, fostered local autonomy. And—to give one more instance—while Joseph II and other potentates of the day lightened the burden of the peasantry, Catherine of Russia increased those burdens until Russian serfdom took on the lineaments of slavery. In light of these far-reaching differences, it would be best to characterize the period as an age of good government, eighteenth-century style.

Sweden, Portugal, and Spain

This search for good—that is, effective—government dominated great powers and small, in the centers of Europe and on its periphery. In Sweden, in 1772, young King Gustavus III abruptly terminated half a century of aristocratic misrule with a picturesque coup d'etat. He forced a new constitution on a cowed Riksdag and then, his hands relatively free, he proceeded on an ambitious program of internal reforms. The first laws introduced by his regime demonstrated the king's devotion to enlightened principles: they ended torture and established a free press. Gustavus' legislation made judges irremovable, abolished extraordinary tribunals, and protected, with a habeas corpus act, the rights of accused persons. Abundantly endowed with vitality and liberal principles, Gustavus battled entrenched abuses on all sides. He reformed the currency and the state's finances; he cleansed the scandal-ridden judiciary in a spectacular trial; he brought a measure of equality to the tax system; he proclaimed religious liberty, modernized the poor law, and fostered free trade. Mindful of Sweden's great enemy, Russia, Gustavus also improved his army and constructed a formidable navy. But after a prolonged period of domestic peace, Gustavus found aristocratic opposition reemerging. It was perhaps an inescapable development: Gustavus, proud to be a noble, had no intention of eliminating the aristocracy from its high social position; he only wanted to keep it from exercising political power. But he could not sustain this policy in the long run without either moderating his own claims or violating the very constitution he had pressed on the country in 1772, for in that constitution, he had deliberately kept the power of the purse in the hands of the Riksdag. The Riksdag that convened in 1786 was practically in mutiny and so Gustavus, who was preparing to engage Russia in war, determined to govern on his own. In 1788, he declared war, and in February 1789, with the support of the non-noble estates, he imposed a new constitution, the Act of Union and Security. This made the king practically absolute in his kingdom.

The French Revolution completed Gustavus' move to absolutism. He had surprisingly beaten the Russians, and in 1790 he concluded an advantageous peace with them; this permitted him to concentrate on events in France. With his customary vigor, he attempted to construct a league of princes against the revolutionaries. But the Swedish nobility, humiliated and infuriated, took a revenge more melodramatic than his accession had been: in March 1792, at a midnight masquerade at the Stockholm opera house, Gustavus was shot to death by a masked aristocrat. The Swedish experiment in good government was over.

At the other end of Europe, in the Iberian Peninsula, enlightened government, too, had its moment. In both Portugal and Spain, legislative experimentation was pragmatic; it was undertaken in behalf not of the anti-Christian Enlightenment but of the commercial revival of the country and the political independence of the crown. In Portugal, the legislative program was the monopoly of Sebastião José de Carvalho e Melo, marquis de Pombal. Joseph I had ascended the throne in 1750, but he disliked the business of government and left it to Pombal, his favorite minister. Pombal ruled almost as though *he* were king—almost, but not quite: when Joseph I died in 1777, Pombal was instantly dismissed, and his reform program limped on without him. Pombal's first concern was to crush competing centers of power; to that end he curbed the Inquisition, kept the Jesuits from the court, and curtailed the powers of the nobility. An attempt on the life of his king, in September 1758, gave Pombal the pretext he needed. He had several leading Portuguese nobles tried and, early in 1759, cruelly executed. Later that year, Pombal gained a unique distinction for his Catholic country: Portugal was the first kingdom in Europe to sequester the Jesuits' property and to expel them from the country and from its overseas possessions. Pombal's regime illustrates the essential ambiguities of reform activities undertaken not under a constitution or with widespread popular support but by the will of a single autocrat. Pombal worked with single-minded concentration to free Portugal from its commercial dependence on Britain, a condition that was profitable to the latter and galling to the former. He built silk, wool, glass, paper, and gunpowder factories; he founded chartered companies to compete with British traders; he reorganized the tax structure and encouraged free trade between Portugal and her overseas possessions. Once his hands were untied by his triumph over the nobility and expulsion of the Jesuits, he moved toward reform in other fields. He cut government expenditures by dismissing useless officials from their sinecures. He abolished the distinction between "old and new Christians" and thus, in effect, extended toleration to Portuguese Catholics of Jewish ancestry. And the departure of the Jesuits, who ran the schools in Portugal as they did across Catholic Europe, compelled him to found new schools on new principles. He succeeded: under his close supervision, Portugal saw the rise of commercial schools, schools of art, and a comprehensive system of primary and secondary education. Yet with no apparent perception of incongruity, Pombal stamped out opposition, actual or potential, without regard to the niceties of the law or the commands of charity. He honeycombed the country with informers; when the new monarch, Maria I, dismissed him in 1777, she began her reign by releasing a horde of Pombal's prisoners.

Pombal's greatest claim to enlightened statesmanship, which fastened his hold on the loyalty of his king and the imagination of his contemporaries, was his response to the Lisbon earthquake. On November 1, 1755, a devastating tremor, followed by a tidal wave, leveled much of the city and left thirty thousand dead. Tirelessly and efficiently, Pombal labored to bring the city out of its shock and panic and to restore it to a semblance of normal life. The famous command attributed to him—"bury the dead and feed the living"— appears to be apocryphal, but it is an apt epitome of his work, and of authoritarian eighteenth-century reform in general.

In neighboring Spain, planning and reform were perhaps less spectacular than in Portugal, but more sustained. Spain's first Bourbon king, Philip V, died in 1746, and was succeeded by his son, Ferdinand VI, pacific in foreign policy and mildly interested in domestic reform. Despite his mediocrity and general lack of initiative, Ferdinand superintended the beginnings of tax reform and, in line with other Catholic rulers of his day, curbed the Inquisition. But it was not until his half-brother Charles, king of Naples, ascended the throne in 1759, that Spain entered the main current of eighteenth-century reform. Experienced and popular as he was, Charles' earliest interventions only served to document the tenacity of Spanish conservatism. His favorite minister, the Sicilian marquis di Squillace, aroused a furor of xenophobia. His edicts ordering the cleaning of streets, lighting of roads, and construction of highways seemed reasonable enough, but they were accompanied by rumors of his private rapacity, and all this in a time of high bread prices. In 1766 Squillace prohibited the wearing of the traditional Spanish slouch hat and long cape (on the ground that the former prevented the recognition of bandits, and the latter concealed their weapons). There was a popular riot, and Squillace was forced into exile. His successors, the counts de Aranda and de Floridablanca, Spaniards both, were more diplomatic than the luckless Squillace. Under their regime, loyally supported by Charles III, a measure of Enlightenment came to Spain. Aranda was an admirer of Voltaire and an acquaintance of the Encyclopedists. Under his eye, and at his urging, Spain expelled the Jesuits in 1767 in the wake of widespread reports that they had been behind the anti-Squillace riots and secretly opposed all reform. Aranda, too, converted the Spanish Inquisition into a relatively innocuous office. But Charles III refused to countenance its abolition: "The Spaniards want it," he is reported to have said of the Inquisition, "and it does not bother me."[1]

The royal remark, whether authentic or invented, expresses the conservative tenor of Spanish reform. Only a handful of the philosophes' writings were permitted to enter Spain; in the censoring of books, the Inquisition retained a certain measure of influence. Indeed, when the French Revolution burst over France in 1789, Spain's panic-stricken response was to prevent its contagion from crossing the borders. Charles III had died in 1788, but Floridablanca, who

---

[1] Quoted in Richard Herr, *The Eighteenth Century Revolution in Spain* (1958), 29. For the origins of the Spanish Inquisition, see p. 104.

survived him and retained office under Charles IV, sealed off Spain with a fair degree of effectiveness. Official newspapers reported nothing at all; news of the fall of the Bastille on July 14, 1789, entered Spain underground and became known to a few only later that month. In such an atmosphere, the sphere of reform was severely constricted. The government built roads, simplified and reduced taxes, encouraged local industry, improved the policing of cities and the administration of justice. The primary and secondary school system was radically modernized, and the universities painfully freed themselves from the Scholastic mold in which they had been frozen for centuries. But such reform was always timid; the Enlightenment that the most radical of the reformers could countenance was the kind that in no way questioned the truths of the Roman Catholic church. Characteristically, it was the *amigos del pais*—societies devoted to disseminating information on agricultural and industrial techniques—that spread across Spain's major cities and, of all new institutions, enjoyed the greatest success. They did not, after all, touch on sacred things. Yet even the *amigos del pais,* with their affronts to traditional ways, found their triumphs at best partial. The societies that need change most usually resist it best.

"Old Fritz" and His Prussia

If the name "enlightened despot" has any application at all, it applies to Frederick of Prussia. Except for participating in the dismemberment of Poland (see p. 488) and a brief flurry against Hapsburg Austria over Bavaria in the late 1770s, Frederick II after 1763 cultivated the arts of peace. In the twenty-three years that remained to him—he died in 1786, venerated and feared by his people as Old Fritz—he sought to heal the wounds his own wars had made. He resumed his interrupted friendship with Voltaire, though never on the old intimate footing; the two depended entirely on correspondence—a safe and distant means of communication. Frederick continued to write poetry, essays, history, and memoirs, all in French, and to despise the burgeoning seeds of German culture all around him. None of the German writers of his day—not even Lessing, not even the phenomenally gifted young Goethe—found favor in his eyes. They were, after all, not French neoclassicists. When all was said and done, they did not write like Voltaire.

Frederick II found it relatively easy to concentrate on domestic restoration; unlike many contemporary potentates, he had no factions to appease or rivals to fear at home. His role as "the first servant of the state" was self-imposed. He would do his duty as he saw it, surrounded by obedient servants. Service to the state, in Frederick's view, was service to reason, specifically to *raison d'état;* it included a conscientious attempt to eliminate subjective motives like pride, ambition, and desire for revenge. As he put it in his Political Testament of 1752, the statesman must realistically concentrate on "the strengthening of his state and the growth of its power." Frederick II tried to run Prussia as if he were running a machine; it worked fairly well as long as the supreme engineer was at the controls. How quickly it could fall apart after he left them became promptly and painfully evident during the Napoleonic Wars, only two decades after Frederick II's death (see p. 515). The king governed alone, from the privacy of his study, from which he periodically emerged on his feared tours of inspection. The French minister to Prussia, Lord Tyrconnel, had reported in 1751: "The King is naturally mistrustful and in general thinks ill of all men. He consequently gives his confidence to none and often plays his own Ministers false by misinforming them on the few subjects which he leaves in their hands. He transacts all his business himself, and seldom allows his Ministers to make representations, especially in foreign affairs."[2] His suspiciousness only increased as the reign stretched into the 1770s and 1780s. Voltaire, who knew his Frederick well, had good cause to deplore Frederick's low estimate of human nature and a cynicism that saw mankind solely governed by fear of punishment and hope for reward.

Yet, cynic though he was, Frederick II was philosophe enough (and found enough enjoyment in the publicity the philosophes gave him) to take his duty to provide enlightened government with the utmost seriousness. "My peacetime activity," he wrote to an admirer as early as 1742, after his first Silesian venture, "must be as useful to the state as had been my concern for the war." After 1763, he had the time to stress this aspect of his self-imposed servitude. From his early days he had been hostile to all organized religions, impatient with theology, and contemptuous of priests of all denominations. Shortly after his accession, he had proclaimed freedom of conscience: "Religions must all be tolerated . . . for here everybody must be saved in his own fashion." Frederick's consistent if limited policy of toleration sprang from this attitude: it was a tolerance born of indifference, even of disdain.[3] The secularism implicit in such a view also governed Frederick's other domestic policies. Three days after his accession, he abolished torture in cases of high treason and mass murder; in 1755 he suppressed it altogether. The state must act not to avenge crime, he thought, but to deter it. In the 1740s, he ordered Samuel von Cocceji, the minister of justice, to prepare a new code for Prussia; after Cocceji's death in 1755, younger jurists, notably Karl Gottlieb Suarez and J. H. von Carmer, carried on his work. While they had not completed it by 1786, the year of Frederick II's death, the direction of their thinking, and that of Frederick's, was plain: the state is a legal institution, not a religious one; its ruler and subjects

---

[2] Quoted in C. A. Macartney, ed., *The Habsburg and Hohenzollern Dynasties in the Seventeenth and Eighteenth Centuries* (1970), 329.

[3] Frederick II's attitude was by no means wholly consistent. Toward the Jews, whom he regarded with even greater contempt than other human beings, he was persistently distrustful; in his Political Testaments he urged his successor to keep the numbers and the economic power of the Jews in check. But Frederick himself used them, as bankers and industrialists, when they suited his own schemes.

have clearly defined rights and obligations; and the whole stands under the sign, not of tradition or churchly regulation, but of reason. It was the reason of Prussian absolutism, not of the philosophes. The code formalized the social structure that Frederick II took so strictly: the nobility, the bourgeoisie, and the peasantry were three distinct estates, with little mobility among them. Thus Prussia's rigid social, political, and legal structures were officially acknowledged and confirmed. This was not what most of the philosophes had had in mind.

Frederick's peculiar mixture of *raison d'état* and enlightened policies emerges most clearly in his economic policy. As a good mercantilist, Frederick gave economic matters high priority and made them, as much as possible, the business of the state. Prussia was poor in resources, in industry, and in population. Frederick husbanded the first, encouraged the second, and enlarged the third. He founded a bank and several trading companies; he offered powerful inducements to foreign workers and capitalists to migrate to Prussia; he improved Prussia's transportation system by constructing a series of canals and new ports. But progress was slow. Frederick was appalled to find Prussian merchants without initiative; yet he would give them neither the economic freedom nor the social prestige that would have developed the kind of high morale their counterparts were displaying in England, France, and the Dutch Republic—the three leading capitalist states of his day. And Frederick faced another difficulty, at the core of his political machine. In his view, the Prussian bureaucracy must be the servant of its ruler just as the ruler was the servant of the state. But actually, bureaucrats, mainly of noble family, generated vested interests and a measure of power of their own. In 1766, not long after the end of the Seven Years' War, Frederick set up an office to superintend the customs and the excise, the *régie;* significantly he entrusted its management to de Launay, a Frenchman. Frederick devised this new institution to bypass the General Directory, which had demurred at levying new taxes in the midst of an economic downturn. In fact, Prussia's bureaucrats affected policies by administrative sabotage. To achieve their aim and protect their colleagues, officials would keep silent about embarrassing incidents, submit misleading reports, manipulate inconvenient figures. However hard Frederick tried to subdue his servants, however furiously he railed at them, they were his "active political copartners" who "limited his powers," for they "possessed, in fact, a tacit veto over royal legislation and executive decrees."[4] Yet, much was accomplished. Frederick had the Oder and the Netze valleys drained and settled thousands of families on the reclaimed lands. In consequence, over fifty-seven thousand families found new homes; by 1786 one in every five Prussians belonged to a settler family. In the last decade of his reign, Frederick could look back on his record with some satisfaction. While industry remained relatively insignificant and foreign trade and shipping small, all were growing at a most gratifying rate.

[4] Hans Rosenberg, *Bureaucracy, Aristocracy, and Autocracy: The Prussian Experience, 1660–1815* (1958), 192–193; the book is a splendid essay to which we are much indebted.

Yet, at the same time, Prussia's collection of revenue, and its war chest, were larger than ever. Even Frederick's detractors could not withhold their admiration from so strenuous a performance.[5] Its hidden, nearly fatal flaws emerged later.

The Hapsburgs: A Family Drama

As in Prussia, so in Austria, too, the rhythm of reform accelerated in the 1760s, but for a different reason—not the end of a war but the death of an emperor. In 1765, after Maria Theresa's amiable, adored, and ineffectual husband, Francis, died, the amble of cautious compromise changed to the gallop of determined innovation. Joseph, Maria Theresa's eldest son, was promptly elected German emperor, and his mother co-opted him as her co-regent. Final authority remained in her capable hands, but Joseph II was far too assertive to remain a mere figurehead. For fifteen years, until Maria Theresa's death in 1780, mother and son argued, cooperated, and clashed. Maria Theresa watched Joseph with motherly tenderness and statesmanlike disapproval; she tried to curb his tongue, give him patience, and teach him tact—in vain. "You are a coquette of wit," she admonished him in a long letter in 1776, "and run after it wherever you think to find it, without discrimination. . . . What I fear is that you will never find a friend, a man attached to Joseph—by which you set such store—for it is neither from the Emperor nor from the co-Regent that these biting, ironical, malicious shafts proceed, but from the heart of Joseph, and this is what alarms me, and what will be the misfortune of your days and will entail that of the Monarchy and of us all."[6] In her fond concern, she exaggerated, but her admonitions were not without point: Joseph's character was at once his greatest asset and his gravest liability. His devotion to work and aversion to frivolity were complete; his supervision of his officials, though effective, approached paranoia; he desired the good of his subjects with a fanatical intensity that ultimately caused great suffering. His edicts, issued from his office in a veritable avalanche, trampled on cherished feelings and ancient, deeply rooted practices. Joseph showed all the callousness of the ruler who combined absolute sincerity with absolute power. He puzzled the philosophes, who watched him with a great deal of interest. "The Emperor is hard to judge," wrote the Physiocrat Du Pont. "When one observes what he has done and is doing daily for his country, he is a prince of the rarest merit. . . . But on the other hand, when one takes a look at his political attitude toward his neighbors, his avidity for war, his desire for aggrandizement, the partition of Poland, the invasion of Bavaria, the plots against the Turkish Empire, his disrespect for old

---

[5] See Hajo Holborn, A History of Modern Germany, vol. II, 1648–1840 (1964), 262–277.
[6] Quoted in Macartney, Habsburg and Hohenzollern Dynasties, 185–186.

treaties, his inclination to decide everything by force, then the noble-minded eagle is only a terrible bird of prey."[7] After 1780, when he ruled alone, these contradictions became more palpable than ever.

Not surprisingly, a potentate of such single-mindedness could brook no opposition and tolerate no independent centers of power. Joseph II was an avid centralizer. He laid his hands on the court chancellery, reorganized the ministries, and constructed new departments. Yet the result was not efficiency but paralysis: Joseph II was too eager to be everywhere to be able to construct a rational administrative system—even had the resistance of established bureaucrats permitted it. Joseph II, all too readily, confused reason of state with his own will. His policy toward subject peoples was no more tactful. Sweeping aside the anxious warnings of his ministers, he replaced self-governing institutions in Hungary and in the Austrian Netherlands with a uniform bureaucracy centered ultimately on himself. More autocratic than his mother, Joseph II broke more promises than Maria Theresa ever had. He was an indefatigable Germanizer; when, in 1784, he decreed German to be the official language, he gravely affronted the Hungarians and sealed the humiliation of the Czechs, who had endured Hapsburg autocracy since early in the seventeenth century (see p. 250). It was not that Joseph II thought German culture somehow superior to all others, but that his rage for uniformity of laws, rules, and regulations knew no bounds. Ironically enough, Joseph avoided the company of philosophes and, quite literally, went out of his way *not* to meet Voltaire, but with his overriding desire to make everyone happy, in *his* own way, he acted like a caricature of a philosophe in power.[8]

In his hostility to institutions competing with the autocratic authority of the state, Joseph II could hardly overlook the nobility in his sprawling domains. Aristocratic clans held vast estates and kept them intact with a strict system of land entail, the *Fideikommiss*. They had a firm grip on ceremonial court offices and a monopoly of high posts, often sinecures with rich emoluments and no duties, in the government, the army, and the church. And they enjoyed extensive, almost unchecked privileges over their peasants. Like Louis XIV a century before, Joseph II broke these noble monopolies by introducing commoners into positions of power: seven members of his imperial cabinet, and three out of every four officials in the ministry of war were commoners. Even the nobles appointed to public place were expected to give their undivided loyalty to the state and to defend it against intermediate interests and lesser allegiances.[9] A related aspect of Joseph's absolutism, his peasant policy, grew

[7] Quoted in Heinz Holldack, "Der Physiokratismus und die absolute Monarchie," *Historische Zeitschrift*, CVL (1932), 533.

[8] This is not to say that he did not get philosophic counsel. He was particularly open to the advice of Joseph von Sonnenfels, grandson of a rabbi, son of a Catholic convert, professor at the University of Vienna, and distinguished theorist of public administration.

[9] See H. G. Schenk, "Austria," in A. Goodwin, ed., *The European Nobility in the Eighteenth Century* (1953), 109.

beyond a mere attack on aristocratic privilege into a characteristic instance of what came to be known as "Josephinism."

Josephinism

Most peasants in the Hapsburg territories were for all practical purposes serfs. Their legal position differed from province to province and was, for the most part, better than that of their Russian counterparts. Yet in practice their dependence was almost unmitigated and certainly inescapable. Peasants were obliged to perform onerous, back-breaking, compulsory labor service, and stood by powerless if their landlord chose to expel them from their meager holdings because he judged he could cultivate the land more profitably in large enclosed farms. Practically the whole tax burden imposed by the Hapsburg government was either borne directly by or passed on to the peasants, while their noble masters lived increasingly luxurious lives at court or in their splendid local manor houses. Maria Theresa had launched some extensive investigations and instituted some pioneering reforms, setting an upper limit to taxation and to *robot.* But it was not until after 1780, when Joseph II attacked the peasant question with his characteristic impatience, that legislation became systematic. Beginning in November 1781, in a stream of edicts, he addressed himself to the peasant's life and turned him from a pliant instrument in the hands of his omnipotent master into a subject of the Austrian government. Here, as elsewhere, Josephinism directed itself against intermediate powers in the state. Joseph's first edicts erased all remaining traces of the *Leibeigenschaft*—personal servitude—still in force after Maria Theresa's initial reforms. They stipulated the kinds of penalties a court could impose on peasants and gave peasants an elaborate procedure for lodging complaints against their lord or their lord's steward. These were only the first steps, and in practice small ones; they were supplemented by further edicts regulating forced labor and limiting the landlord's other exactions. Yet, for all Joseph's furious energy, resistance to all these enactments, especially to a proposed tax reform of 1789, was powerful and, in the end, triumphant. Joseph's liberal peasant policy remained more an aspiration for the future than a guide to the present.

In the area of religious policy, Josephinism was rather more successful. Its rationale was, as usual, complicated. Joseph was anxious to enlist the church in his campaign to make good—that is, obedient—subjects, to curtail its influence in the state, and to reduce its dependence on Rome. His motives were also intensely personal and are therefore hard to fathom. Suspicious as he was of the philosophes, he shared their distaste for the "wasteful" lives of monks and nuns and their fear of priestly control over education and marriage. Joseph claimed to be a good Catholic and advertised his religious policy as an act of purification wholly consonant with adherence to the Church of Rome. His antipapal policy, in fact, owed much to the German prelate von Hontheim, whose doctrines are generally known as Febronianism.[10] In any event, whatever his true convictions, no issue caused greater controversy between Joseph and his doting mother than religion. He profoundly provoked Maria Theresa by urging that "all sects" enjoy "perfect equality" and by insisting on his essential principle, "liberty of belief."[11] He tried to reassure his mother: "I would give all I possess," he told her, "if all the Protestants of your States would go over to Catholicism." But he argued at the same time that a sound state must not seek to do the work of the Holy Spirit, but must confine itself instead to ensuring punctual obedience to the laws. "The word 'toleration,' as I understand it, means only that I would employ any persons, without distinction of religion, in purely temporal matters, allow them to own property, practice trades, be citizens, if they were qualified and if this would be of advantage to the State and its industries. . . . The undisturbed practice of their religion makes them far better subjects and causes them to avoid irreligion." Maria Theresa was appalled at such lax doctrine. The institution of tolerance, she told Joseph, would be a "misfortune, the greatest which would ever have descended on the Monarchy." Her attitude toward the Jews, another issue that divided mother and son, accurately defines her horizons: "I know of no worse plague than this people, with their swindling, usury, and money-making, bringing people to beggary, practicing all evil transactions which an honest man abhors." To her, a tolerant recognition of cultural variety was a betrayal of the true faith, the child—and the father—of religious indifference.

It was therefore only after her death—but very promptly after—that Joseph II found it possible to translate his convictions into legislation. His famous Toleration Edict was issued in October 1781. It extended considerable religious and full civic rights to Protestants, though retaining a visibly privileged status for Catholic places of worship. Protestant churches, the decree specified, "shall not have any chimes, bells, or towers, unless such already exist, or public entrance from the street signifying a church." These were bearable constraints: Protestants were granted the right to worship in peace, to appoint teachers for their parish schools, to choose their pastors, to raise their children in their faith, to buy houses and real property, to practice as master craftsmen, and to be admitted to "academic appointments and posts in the public service" without being "required to take the oath in any form contrary to their religious tenets." In the course of time, issuing separate decrees for each of his domains between 1781 and 1789, Joseph extended some, though by no means all, of these rights to Jews as well; as Joseph explicitly noted, it was his intention not to raise the Jews in his domains to full equality, but to place them "on a footing of near-equality." In a spirit typical of the Enlightenment, he exacted from the

---

[10] The name derives from the pseudonym "Febronius" which von Hontheim used for his critique of the pope, published in 1763.

[11] Quoted material is from Macartney, *Habsburg and Hohenzollern Dynasties*, 145–169 passim.

Jews, in return, a measure of assimilation: "We do earnestly exhort them to observe strictly all political, civic, and judicial laws of the land. . . . We look to their sense of duty and their gratitude" not to abuse "Our grace and the freedom deriving from it to cause any public scandal by excesses and loose living." Many eighteenth-century free spirits, even sovereigns who professed contempt for old prejudices and advocated freedom, found it hard wholly to escape the first and wholly to grant the second.

Yet, limited though Joseph's radicalism was, the bulk of the Catholic hierarchy in his domains and the papacy in Rome found his edicts of toleration extremely alarming. In 1782, Pope Pius VI took the unprecedented step of visiting Vienna to protest against the Toleration Edict. He got no more than a respectful reception. Indeed, some of Joseph's other interventions were even more disturbing. It was one thing to close down all the contemplative orders in the kingdom—that had been done in other Catholic countries. It was a drastic but not unprecedented step to place the surviving monasteries under state control and to establish a series of "general seminaries" in which future priests would be trained uniformly, free from what Joseph called the "fanatical hydra of ultramontanism." After all, Joseph also decreed in 1783 that in areas of his kingdom "where the parochial clergy are too few in numbers, or too far from the communes which they serve," new priests or curates should be sent, and that all shortages of churches and vicarages be promptly repaired as well. Joseph's insistence that all religious policy-makers, including archbishops, look to Vienna instead of Rome was also familiar; during the eighteenth century, many good Catholic rulers claimed the ultimate supremacy of secular over religious authority. Many of Joseph's decrees, including those concerning monastic orders and religious holidays, had been anticipated by Maria Theresa, whose loyalty to the faith of Rome was never questioned by anyone. But Joseph intervened in Catholic practice, and this aroused vehement opposition not merely among priests, but among his population as well. He produced an "order of divine service," which regulated such petty but cherished details as the number of candles proper on the altar; and, in the interest of purifying and elevating the church, he decreed that his subjects be buried not in coffins but in sheets or linen sacks—an edict that was promptly withdrawn. [12] Down to his pathetic end in 1790, Joseph II never learned that it is easier to curtail the power of the few than to change the habits of the many.

From Joseph II to Leopold II

Joseph had a decade of sole government, and in that time he tried to reform everything. He decreed the institution of civil marriage; he simplified and modernized the legal code, removing from the catalogue of crimes such offenses

[12] See Saul K. Padover, *The Revolutionary Emperor: Joseph the Second, 1741–90* (1934), 231.

as apostasy from the Roman church and the practice of magic. He reformed the courts, reducing the jurisdiction of local aristocrats. He wiped out censorship, thus inundating the country with heterodox opinions from abroad. Like his mother, he took an abiding interest in education and in attracting skilled foreigners to his dominions. Yet on balance, as Joseph II himself sadly realized, his rule was a failure. Six thousand edicts in ten years testify to his industry, his energy, and his ubiquity. But he discovered that everything he did aroused opposition, even resistance. It is too easy to criticize his ignorance of human nature and his impatience with the conservatism of custom. Joseph suffered from the dilemma of all radical reformers: he feared that moderate proposals and tactful proceedings would bring no visible results, and he found that the forced pace he set brought only rebellion.

While in the late 1780s there was unrest in his Austrian dominions, Joseph's most pressing problems arose in the south, in Hungary, and in the west, in the Austrian Netherlands. Joseph's rage for centralization and his insensitive disregard for traditional privileges were partly responsible for these rebellions. But in addition Joseph's foreign policy obliged him to raise money from unwilling subjects. In 1778, while Maria Theresa was still alive, Joseph had involved Austria in the brief, almost bloodless War of the Bavarian Succession, which had given him only a small portion of eastern Bavaria—far less than he had plotted to obtain. Later, in 1785, his continued designs on Bavaria led to the formation of the *Fürstenbund,* the League of German Princes, which held Joseph in check. Then, in 1788, Austria joined its ally, Russia, in a war against the Ottomans, and the campaign turned out to be a frustrating and expensive adventure. Hard-pressed for money, Joseph proposed to raise taxes on, among others, the Hungarian nobility, and this without calling the diet that the constitution provided for. Joseph had already mortally offended articulate Hungarians with his language decrees, his refusal to be crowned king of Hungary, and other abrasive measures. In the fall of 1789, the threat of rebellion was very real, while loyal Hungarian officials begged the emperor to change his course. The Austrian Netherlands, meanwhile, were in open revolt, led (in striking distinction from the revolutions all across the Western world) by the forces of conservatism. The application of the Toleration Edict to the Belgian lands and the closing down of the contemplative orders had aroused widespread anger; Joseph's arbitrary, rationalistic intervention in the celebration of religious holidays and time-honored constitutional arrangements brought Brabant to rebellion in late 1787; in December 1789 the Netherlands Estates General proclaimed Joseph deposed. Disheartened, sick, worn out before his time—he was not yet fifty—Joseph II hastened to undo what he had done and, late in January 1790, gave the Hungarians what they had pressed for. He agreed to repeal the most disturbing of his enactments and to convoke a Coronation Diet. He did not live to see it: in February 1790, he died, to be succeeded by his younger brother, Leopold, as Emperor Leopold II. The concessions Joseph had not had time to make, his successor promptly granted.

Leopold II was an extraordinary figure, perhaps the only ruler of the eighteenth century to take the vocation of enlightened monarch seriously. Since 1765, he had governed Tuscany with a consistently progressive program designed to permit the Tuscan people ultimately to determine their own political life. His elder brother's policies, which he derided as "despotism," struck him as the opposite of good government. All his early reforms, he wrote in 1782, had been designed to awaken "in men's hearts the feeling of an honorable civic freedom, and the habit of devotion to, and zeal for, the public good." To that end, he instituted free trade and a humane legal code, reformed local government, and improved the police; then, in 1779, he began to draft a constitution that would sum up his reform work and give the Tuscans political self-determination. His belief in the fundamental rights of the people was exceptional for its radicalism and its consistency. The sovereign, he wrote, is "only the delegate of his people" and must "govern through law alone." If the ruler is granted preeminence, it is for the sake of his subjects, whom he is duty-bound to make happy, "not as he wants it, but as they themselves want it and feel it." This was to take the logic of Enlightenment as education for autonomy to its logical conclusion.

A combination of domestic resistance, administrative sabotage by reluctant officials, and unexpected foreign involvements aborted the scheme for a constitution. And then in 1790, Leopold was called to succeed his brother in Vienna. In his short reign—he died suddenly in March 1792—he repealed much of his brother's hasty and schematic work. He pacified the Hungarians, restored order in the Austrian Netherlands, and withdrew much of the legislation that seemed to him unenforceable or calculated to alienate too many powerful social groups from the monarchy. His partial repeal of Josephinism was based less on fear of the revolutionary forces at work in the West, and less on the growing conservatism of an aging liberal, than on his innate tact, his commitment to constitutional procedures, and his search for stability in a multinational empire. What his role might have been in the decade of the French Revolution is hard to say. He died too soon.

EXTREMES IN EASTERN EUROPE:
RUSSIA AND POLAND

Catherine of Russia: At Home

Of all the eighteenth-century monarchs ostensibly devoted to enlightened government, Catherine II of Russia was doubtless the most spectacular and the most disappointing. The philosophes, most of whom she cleverly kept at a distance, greatly overestimated her; Voltaire in particular acted as her unpaid propaganda agent in the West. In her struggle for security, Catherine needed all the help she could get, and the philosophes' all-too-public adulation could be had at bargain rates. It cost a few pensions and generous gestures, some honeyed letters and some well-advertised obeisances to the principles of Montesquieu; in return, it gave her a good press that helped to establish and solidify her reputation before a skeptical world.

It was the manner of her accession that made Catherine need help and the world skeptical. When in June 1762 Catherine deposed her inadequate husband, Peter III, and took the throne, her dependence on her aristocratic co-conspirators seemed so complete that few observers gave her much chance of survival. "It is certain," the Prussian ambassador reported back to Frederick II soon after her coup d'etat, "that the reign of the Empress Catherine is not to be more than a brief episode in the history of the world." [13] The forecast proved wrong, but it was sensible. Catherine had been born a foreigner and a heretic— a German princess of the Lutheran persuasion. Her title to the throne was weaker than that of Prince Ivan, briefly tsar in 1744, or that of her son Paul. She had come to power by means of a palace revolt, and rulers who owe their accession to intrigues live under the threat of being deposed by the same means. Her passion for amorous adventure, which emerged early and lasted her lifetime, exposed her to public scandal and, worse, seemed to put her at the mercy of her many lovers whom she, in her gratitude, endowed with public posts and great estates. Worst of all, when her husband, the deposed tsar, was assassinated in July 1762, she was rumored to have ordered or abetted the murder; she certainly knew of the act and never punished the actors. Rumor also implicated her in the disposition of her other rival, Ivan, murdered in prison in 1764. Western opinion, no longer callous to political assassination, was shocked; even some of the philosophes—always with the exception of Voltaire, who had unlimited indulgence for his "Semiramis of the North"— declared themselves out of patience with her. Yet there was more to Catherine than charm, sensuality, and ambition. She was able, energetic, and in the midst of her pleasures, hard-working. By about 1770 the English *chargé d'affaires* could report that "the power of Her Imperial Majesty increases every day, and is already arrived at such a degree, that this prudent Princess thinks herself strong enough to humble the Guards, who placed her upon the throne." [14]

That might well be: Catherine soon learned to maneuver among rival factions of Russian aristocrats. But she never made the mistake of alienating the aristocracy as a whole. Her intention was to govern. "The monarch must be sovereign," she wrote. "His power cannot be divided." And, while she made far-reaching concessions to the Russian nobility, it remained a service nobility. Catherine followed her late husband's policy of exempting nobles from

---

[13] Quoted in Leo Gershoy, *From Despotism to Revolution, 1763–1789* (1944), 108.
[14] Quoted in Georg Sacke, *Die gesetzgebende Kommission Katherinas II*, in *Jahrbuch für Geschichte Osteuropas*, Beiheft 2 (1940), 156.

compulsory state service, and a number of them took advantage of this new liberality to return to their country estates or to travel abroad. Yet, as Max Beloff has argued, "service to the State in some form continued to be the normal practice among Russian noblemen. It was encouraged by the State, for instance by sumptuary laws which discriminated in favor of nobles who had done their stint. Nobles who had not served were not received at court," so that at the end of the eighteenth century the Russian nobility "was no less a subservient element in the Russian state than it had been under the masterful Peter one hundred years before."[15] Thus in return for service, the nobles had their privileges confirmed. In 1785, Catherine promulgated a charter of nobility that gave it corporate organization in each province, designed to channel noble officials into local government and to serve as a vehicle for grievances. Freedom from compulsory state service was reaffirmed, nobles were explicitly exempted from the billeting of troops, corporal punishment, and perhaps most important, direct taxation. In addition, they were guaranteed trial by their peers and hereditary status, and were granted the right to enter trade and dispose of their land. Best of all, the charter left the vast and increasing power of nobles over their serfs untouched. While Catherine, the philosophe in power, trimmed the remaining privileges of the Russian Orthodox church by extending toleration to minority sects and secularizing church property, she gave the nobility— especially its richest and oldest families—most of what it wanted. Her reward was peace from that difficult, always troublesome quarter.

While Catherine appeased the nobles, she did little for the peasants, beyond fastening the yoke of servitude more securely than ever. Her "enlightened" regime was punctuated by peasant uprisings. The most notable of these was led by the illiterate, charismatic Don Cossack Emelian Pugachev, a new Stenka Razin (see p. 260). Claiming to be Peter III in the flesh, this latest in a long line of pretenders in Russian history enlisted thousands of aggrieved Cossacks, Asiatics subject to Russian hegemony, and embittered peasants conscripted into factory labor. In 1773, Pugachev's casual but fierce army defeated the tsarina's troops in the Volga basin; in 1774 it took the city of Kazan. Pugachev's inflammatory rhetoric embodied a social program: he told his followers to treat the noble landowners as "traitors to the empire, despoilers of the peasants," and to put them to death—instructions his followers cheerfully obeyed. In the end, Catherine's troops were too much for him: in September 1774, after a crushing defeat, he was betrayed and brought to Moscow, where, in January 1775, he was publicly quartered. Clearly, humanitarianism did not extend to social rebels.

Not all of Catherine's reign was maneuver or repression. She reduced tariffs, imported skilled foreigners, and cultivated the iron industry. In this one industry, indeed, she could boast some remarkable results: dozens of new iron works were built, especially in the rich Ural Mountains, and by the end of her

---

[15] Max Beloff, "Russia," in Goodwin, *European Nobility*, 181–182, 189.

reign, Russia was exporting pig iron to all of Western Europe, including England. But capital was too scarce, the urban bourgeoisie too timid, and domestic consumption too restricted, to permit Russia to compete for long with the more dynamic economic powers of the West. It remained a land of domestic handicraft and an importer of manufactured goods. Yet in the search for economic growth, Catherine made at least some strenuous, if incomplete and often misguided efforts. In other respects, her domestic policy reads like an exercise in duplicity. In 1767, she convened a legislative commission and supplied it with her famous *Nakaz*—Instruction. This *Instruction*, ostentatiously patterned after Montesquieu and Beccaria, provided guidelines for legislation and for a legal code, and even laid down principles of political theory. The commission, which included representatives from the government, the nobility, the towns, the peasants, the Cossacks and other subject peoples, earnestly debated the *Instruction* and submissively praised Catherine. Admirers called it a monument to liberalism, cynics a charade, and in the end the cynics were right: by 1768, most of the representatives had left to serve in Catherine's first war against the Ottomans (see p. 436), and the noble intentions (or, at least, the noble professions) of the *Instruction* were forgotten. Catherine's comprehensive reform of provincial government displays similar ambiguities. In an ambitious act of 1775, Russia was divided into provinces of roughly equal size, each headed by a governor, and each subdivided into manageable districts. But the measure in effect gave the landed magnates a share in the tsar's autocratic authority; like other reforms, it benefited the privileged by securing them in their privileges. By the end of the reign the process of Europeanization begun by Peter was complete; in trade as in international politics, Russia was a power to be reckoned with. But the cost was very high: a deeply divided society.

Catherine of Russia: Abroad

Catherine never absorbed that old and obvious lesson that foreign conquests cost money. The sums she lavished on her entertainments and her favorites were vast; the sums she poured into her wars were vaster. In the thirty-four years of her reign, the outlay of the Russian state quadrupled; the issuing of paper money had caused ruinous inflation; and taxes rose precipitously. Undeterred, the tsarina pressed on.

Catherine directed her aggressive attentions principally to two of her neighbors: Poland to her west and Turkey to her south. Her adventures were linked: Russia's intervention in Poland brought the Ottomans, alarmed at Russia's growing power, into the field. Poland was easy terrain for manipulation and conquest; it had declined in the course of a hundred and fifty years from stability and even grandeur into an international joke. Poland's Catholic ruling oligarchy, the landed gentry, oppressed, and on occasion actively persecuted, its large ethnic and religious minorities. Poland's elective king was a puppet in the hands of the proud and quarrelsome nobility. The work of the Polish Diet was an exercise in futility; a single deputy could force its dissolution and the cancellation of its earlier decisions by exercising the *liberum veto*.[16]

Voltaire expressed the general contempt when he characterized Poland as the plaything of selfish forces. "The nobility and the clergy defend their liberty against their king, and take it away from the rest of the nation." Such a country virtually invited the intervention of its more powerful neighbors. In 1764, Catherine replied to that invitation. When Poland's Saxon king, Augustus III, died in 1763, Catherine bullied and bought Polish support to secure the election of a former lover, Stanislas Poniatowski. At the same time, in concert with Frederick of Prussia, she insisted on perpetuating the anarchy prevalent in Poland and on posing as the champion of its religious minorities. Things did not go smoothly. Once on the throne, Poniatowski aimed at reform, especially the abolition of the *liberum veto*, an improvement in the Polish state that Catherine had no interest in permitting. And her insistence that Roman Catholic Poland grant toleration to the Dissidents—the Greek Orthodox and the Protestants—brought the formation of the anti-Russian Confederation of Bar.

In 1768, the Ottoman's alarm, shrewdly stimulated by the French ambassador, resulted in a Turkish declaration of war on Russia. Catherine converted the war she had not wanted into a convincing demonstration of Russia's stature. Her Polish intervention had worried the Turks; her rapid and convincing victories, dramatically underscored by the operations of Russian naval squadrons that had sailed from Kronstadt around Europe into the Mediterranean, in turn worried the Austrians. By 1771, war between Austria and Russia seemed only a matter of time. But this would be a general European conflict that the great powers rather dreaded. Frederick of Prussia found the way out. Playing on rising sentiments for the partition of Poland, he convinced both Russia and Austria to annex some Polish territory instead of fighting one another. Catherine still adhered to the traditional Russian view of Poland as a useful buffer in the west, but early in 1772, the bargain was concluded, and in August, the first Partition pitilessly cut into the body of Poland. Roughly one third of Poland's territory, and nearly one half of its population, went to its rapacious neighbors: Prussia acquired most of Polish Prussia; Austria received Red Russia, Galicia, and western Podolia; Russia took the Greek Orthodox eastern sections of the country—White Russia and territories to the Dvina and the Dnieper rivers.

---

[16] The member, presumably speaking for the province that had elected him, but actually open to bribery on other appeals by a local magnate or a foreign power, simply rose and said, *"nie pozwalam—I protest."* This was called "exploding" the Diet; for a century nearly all of them had ended in this way. True, the Poles had devised a constitutional alternative, the Confederation, which could substitute for the Diet; here the *liberum veto* did not hold and simple majority ruled. But in practice this meant virtual civil war among contending aristocratic clans. The whole system, ostensibly designed to protect individual liberty and a symbol of the equality of every Polish gentleman, was organized anarchy.

The Turkish War, meanwhile, continued to go well for the Russians. In 1769, Russian troops had overrun Moldavia and Wallachia, and were stirring up revolt in Greece. In July 1770, the Russian navy annihilated the Turkish navy at the battle of Chesme, and by 1771, the Russians were in the Crimea. The affair of Poland and the Pugachev rebellion slowed Russian operations, but the Peace of Kutchuk-Kainarji of 1774 detached the Crimea from the Ottoman Empire and gave Russia the mouth of the Dnieper, freedom to navigate the Black Sea, and the right to make representations in behalf of Christian subjects of the Turks. This last, a vaguely worded provision, laid the groundwork for future Russian interventions.

Catherine's victory encouraged her further. In 1780, she won Joseph II's assent to the "Greek project," which looked to the expulsion of the Turks from Europe; in 1783, on the pretext of restoring order, she annexed the Crimea. Further deliberate provocations on her part drove the Turks into war once more: in 1788, the second Russo-Turkish War began, ending, much like the first, in Russian gains. In 1792, at the Treaty of Jassy, the Ottomans had to yield up the northern shore of the Black Sea. While Catherine's most ambitious plans had not been realized, the Turkish threat was over. She had four more years to reign, to 1796—and in these final years, though distracted by the French Revolution, she continued Russian expansion in Poland. She had not achieved all she had wanted, but she had wanted much. For the German states, in any event, accustomed in the past to look westward in concern, or for support, Russia was now a formidable neighbor, equal in power perhaps to France.

THE FORTUNES OF FRANCE: 1743-1774

Louis XV: Reign of a Disappointment

In January 1743, the aged Cardinal Fleury died, and Louis XV, sounding much as Louis XIV had sounded in 1661, after the death of Mazarin, announced that he would govern by himself, without a first minister. He did not mean it literally, of course; not even Louis XIV, a far more powerful man than his successor, had been able to forego the counsel of ministers or to overcome the resistance of provincial officials. But Louis XV, though he wished to, was not equipped to lead. He was too indolent, too intent on his pleasure, and despite attacks of energy and independence, too uncertain, to emulate his more energetic contemporaries.

Fleury had given both Louis XV and France what they badly needed: calm leadership, pacific policies, a group of competent and diligent royal officials, and a respite from the costly bellicosity of Louis XIV. True, not long before his death, the war party had dragged Fleury into the War of the Austrian

Succession, and in future years, France would continue the old duel with England in the Seven Years' War (see p. 400). But despite serious losses of territories overseas, France under Louis XV was experiencing economic expansion and widespread prosperity. Fleury's program, though his moderate foreign policy did not in the end prevail, had much to do with this gratifying condition. Peace and the government of able and honest ministers proved good foundations for national well-being. They helped to restore profitable foreign trade and to stabilize a once fluctuating currency. Beginning not long after Fleury's accession, France underwent a long-drawn-out and slow inflation, which acted as a stimulus to the French economy as a whole; it ended about the time Louis XV died, in 1774, and its end, as much as anything else, put France on the road to revolution. Cities boomed, as slave traders, financiers, cotton and silk manufacturers, prosperous judges built their town houses. Roads were improved, new canals speeded the transport of goods. There were gloomy spots in this cheerful picture: tenacious French conservatism, especially strong after Law's schemes had ended in disaster (see p. 380), slowed down the rate of investment and kept alive a host of old-fashioned regulations—internal tariffs, gild regulations—that had long been abandoned in Britain and the Dutch Republic. The poor, as usual, remained poor; as in the course of the century the population increased without a corresponding increase in food production, many of them pressed hard upon the margin of subsistence. And there was unrest in the midst of prosperity. In Lyons, in 1744, the silk workers rose up against their masters, only to be callously repressed by the state: their leaders were tortured and executed or sent to the galleys for life. Prevailing social attitudes precluded the expenditure of pity on such workers; they had risen against their natural place in the social order. And in any case, it was well known that high wages only served to corrupt the poor. "I reflected on the terrible drawbacks of the high cost of labor," Restif de la Bretonne, novelist, pornographer, and social observer, wrote, "and thought of this in terms of the noxious effects on the masses, who, like savage tribes, think only of the present. If they earn enough in three days for necessities, they work for three days only and spend the other four in debauchery." [17] This was in 1788. In the cheerful, prosperous days of the 1740s, such views were, if anything, even more pronounced. Life was good and getting better. Why worry about those whose appointed task in life was to labor and be silent?

Rebellious workers and miserable peasants were objects of religious charity, but they did not constitute a serious problem for the state. The need for an attack on privilege on the other hand, was palpable, even to Louis XV. As a young monarch, he had been called *le bien aimé*, but soon he was widely disliked. As popular opinion turned against the king, he was particularly blamed for his mistresses—for the power they were reputed to hold and the

[17] "Les Nuits de Paris or Nocturnal Spectator," in Robert and Elborg Forster, eds., *European Society in the Eighteenth Century* (1969), 264.

money they were reputed to cost. True, the king was an avid womanizer. He had been married in 1725 to Marie Leszczynska, daughter of Stanislas, the deposed king of Poland. But apart from Lorraine, which Stanislas Leszczynski obtained in 1736 as a consolation prize, and which passed to France after his death in 1766, Louis XV had few rewards from his wife. So he occupied himself with hunting and with a shifting gallery of mistresses. The most famous and most interesting of these, Madame de Pompadour, became the king's official mistress in 1745 and remained his friend until her death in 1764, long after Louis' sexual appetites had led him to other mistresses. She was witty and intelligent as well as lovely, and she was a munificent and keen-eyed patron of the decorative arts: the china factory at Sèvres was essentially her idea, and the arts of music, tapestry, weaving, furniture design, and light-hearted painting flourished under her hand. She was doubtless influential and expensive, but her influence was hardly baneful, and her cost, though high, hardly ruinous: "That a lot of money went on palaces, parks, works of art, and even more on places and pensions for courtiers and their hangers-on, is undeniable; but in relation to the whole cost of the government of France the expenditure of the court, excessive as it may have been, does not play a decisive role. The expense, even of a small war, was greater than that of the biggest palace." [18] Still, her reign symbolized a malaise from which Fleury's sensible appointment policies had attempted to rescue France: the prevalence of intrigue, the rule of favorites, the rapid shift of personnel at the top. In such an atmosphere it was hard to devise a rational financial policy, impossible to carry it through.

The Resistance of Privilege

France was a society riddled with privilege—it was burdened with a set of exemptions that Louis XV had not invented, but inherited. Here, more than anywhere else, the legacy of his great predecessor was nothing less than disastrous. The checks on the king's power were not merely personal; many of them were structural. Most official positions—judgeships, army posts, all but the highest government jobs—were private property. They were bought, traded, sold with little interference from the state; their value fluctuated and was regulated by market conditions. This was the so-called "venality of office," an old abuse by which French kings had raised money, but which had become a regular, seemingly irrevocable part of French government early in the seventeenth century. It was rare for the crown to dismiss or to buy out one of its servants; hence judges, bureaucrats, even army officers faced their sovereign with a good deal of independence and with a solid, thoroughgoing esprit de corps which normally put loyalty to one's corporation before disinterested

[18] Alfred Cobban, *A History of Modern France*, vol. I, *Old Regime and Revolution, 1715-1799* (1965), 55.

service to one's country. [19] Resistance to royal decrees was stiffened by appeals for exemptions from this tax or that, granted in the past to nobles, towns, and corporations. The clergy, France's first estate, did not pay taxes, but contributed what it called a "voluntary gift," the *don gratuit*, voted at its quinquennial assemblies. Surviving provincial estates were in perpetual obstructive conflict with royal officials. And while Louis XIV had deprived his parlements of their share in the making of legislation, the regent, as we know, had in effect restored it by restoring their right to remonstrate against royal decrees (see p. 379).

In May 1749, upon the urging of his controller general of finance, Machault d'Arnouville, Louis XV boldly confronted the whole system of privilege. He issued a decree imposing a 5 percent income tax on all his subjects. Machault, former intendant of Valenciennes, had been finance minister since 1745 and had spent the first three years in his office raising money for the War of the Austrian Succession. In 1748, the Peace of Aix-la-Chapelle took that burden off his shoulders and enabled him to address himself to the structure of French taxation. The *vingtième*, that 5 percent income tax, was the result. Resistance was noisy and immediate. The *vingtième* was an equitable tax without exemptions. It thus affronted all those—towns, office holders, nobles, clerics— hitherto exempted, and it endangered the system under which the inequitable indirect taxes were gathered by the farmers general. Worse, it was being levied in peacetime. Under pressure, the parlements registered the decrees, and Louis XV stood firm: Machault, he said, "is the man after my own heart." Officially, the parlements obeyed, but they knew their cause was in capable hands—the clergy. The bishops, highly placed and well connected, mobilized the *dévot* party at court and obliquely threatened to go on strike. Machault, earnest and determined, rallied public opinion in his turn. But his master was too unstable to persevere. In May 1750, the Assembly of the Clergy met in Paris and, in the course of the summer, secured some decisive concessions from a weakening king: in August, he demanded that the clergy deliver up its normal *don gratuit* and add a special gift in the next five years. The principle of a tax without exemptions had been breached. But the clergy wanted more, and in December 1751, Louis XV, thoroughly softened up by the assaults of his own family and of favorite ecclesiastics, withdrew all of his demands. His brave, brief effort at fiscal reform was over.

The parlements had profited from the triumph of the clergy; in the 1750s and 1760s, they took the lead in defending privilege against a vacillating king. In the name of the "French constitution," an unwritten set of precepts with little, if any, legal standing, they preached disobedience and taught it to others. As we shall soon see, their talk led to action, especially in Brittany. With the Parlement of Paris setting the tone, and the provincial parlements providing the

---

[19] Louis XIV had tampered with this system through periodic inquiries into the right of nobles to hold their titles or of office holders to keep their posts. But this had been a kind of blackmail rather than an assertion of absolute power.

echo, the high magistrates sabotaged royal policies and embittered the lives of provincial intendants. The magistrates triumphed all along the line; the expulsion of the Jesuits from France was largely their work, and a sign of their power. The robe nobility of the parlements were Gallican in temper and Jansenist in sympathy; they feared and detested the ultramontane Society of Jesus and schemed to dispose of it, however much Louis XV and his bishops might dislike that. Effective teachers, assiduous collectors of influential personages, subject to stringent military discipline, and slavishly devoted to Rome, the Jesuits, in France as elsewhere, found themselves the targets of dark, unproved, normally untrue charges. The parlements were lucky: the French Jesuits presented them with a solid case. In 1761, a Jesuit commercial house on the island of Martinique had gone bankrupt; a court at Marseilles found the society as a whole financially responsible for the losses its branch had incurred. Whatever possessed them, the Jesuits appealed the verdict to the Parlement of Paris. With unconcealed pleasure, the Paris magistrates seized on the issue and ordered an investigation into the practices and ideas of the Jesuit order. Not surprisingly, they found what they wanted: shocked, they reported that the Jesuits believed in political assassination. In August 1761, the parlement ordered twenty-four Jesuit books burned as irreligious and seditious; in 1762, overcoming royal reluctance, they secured the suppression of the society in France and closed its *collèges;* in 1764, they secured a royal edict officially expelling the Society of Jesus from the country. In 1767, finally, whatever individual Jesuits remained on French soil as secular priests were ordered to leave.

But while they succeeded in their religious politics, in provincial politics the parlements overreached themselves. The parlements' most powerful ally in the royal entourage was the duke de Choiseul, a friend of Madame de Pompadour, who had been secretary of state for foreign affairs since 1758. With his hold on offices and grasp of affairs, Choiseul came closer to rivaling Fleury than anyone else in Louis XV's reign. He had a difficult task: to extricate France from a losing war and to make an acceptable peace. Abler than his British counterparts, tenacious and intelligent, he succeeded to a remarkable degree. Yet, to secure his flank at home, he yielded to the parlements on every point, including the all-important issue of fiscal reform. "Choiseul had willed the end, which was the re-establishment of French power in the world and a war of revenge against England"—to quote Alfred Cobban once again—but "he did not will the necessary means, which was the restoration of royal authority inside France and the reform of royal finances, without which all other reforms would be in vain." [20] Counting on Choiseul, the parlements went too far. In 1764, the provincial estates of Brittany protested against the royal *corvée*—the service due the king for construction and maintenance of roads—as an illegal infringement of its traditional rights; the Breton parlement at Rennes naturally

[20] *History of Modern France,* vol. I, 87.

sustained the estates and suspended the administration of justice. In reply, the royal military commander, d'Aiguillon, had the Breton attorney general, La Chalotais, and five other officials put under arrest. In their newly found unanimity, the other parlements sent vehement remonstrances to Louis XV supporting the strike of their Breton brethren.

The king had had enough. In March 1766, he read the Parlement of Paris a stern lecture on his rights and its duties. He claimed sole sovereign authority and admonished the judges to remember that he was supreme judge as well and that their power depended on his will alone. Besides, the affair of Brittany was none of their business. The magistrates were cowed only for a time. After all, the king had blustered before, only to collapse. In an impudent display of self-confidence, the Breton parlement initiated a prosecution of d'Aiguillon. Paris continued defiant. "This astonishing anarchy," wrote Voltaire, "could not subsist. Either the crown must recover its authority, or the parlement must prevail. In such a critical moment, an enterprising and audacious chancellor was needed. He was found." That chancellor was René Nicolas de Maupeou, a one-time member of the Parlement of Paris, who knew his former colleagues well and detested them thoroughly. Since the mid-1760s, he had enjoyed considerable influence—it is probable that the king's strong language in March 1766 owed something to Maupeou's dour tone and uncompromising views. In September 1768, Louis XV appointed Maupeou his chancellor. In the following year, Maupeou brought the abbé Terray into the government as controller general. Avid for power and intent on his plans, Maupeou knew he could never obtain the former or implement the latter without first ruining his rival, Choiseul. Beginning in September 1770, Maupeou warned the parlements against any further disobedience—in vain. Then, in December, Maupeou and Terray secured Choiseul's dismissal. Maupeou's coup d'etat followed. In January 1771, the members of the Parlement of Paris were dismissed and exiled from the city. In February, Maupeou undertook a far-reaching reform of the judicial system: he abolished venality of office and created six courts in place of the Parlement of Paris, with its extensive jurisdiction. In April, Louis XV publicly declared his unyielding support for Maupeou: "I shall never change."

Actually, the new system, a few minor, much blown-up scandals apart, worked fairly well; gradually, lawyers and judges abated their resistance and agreed to practice before, or sit on, the new courts. At the same time, Terray initiated a reform of French finances as far-reaching as Maupeou's court reforms. His task was, if anything, even harder. He renegotiated the government's contract with the farmers general on better terms for the state, improved the collection and increased the equity of several imposts, and reimposed the old *vingtième*. The aging Louis XV held firm, for once. It seemed as if the counterattack of privilege could be checked and France reformed. Then nature intervened. In May 1774, Louis XV died. He was succeeded by his grandson, Louis XVI. The new king was by no means averse to reform or hostile to reformers, but Maupeou was unpopular, and Louis XVI had no wish to share that "tyrant's" reputation. "What I should like most," he is reported to have said on his accession, "is to be loved." [21] To that end, by late 1774, he had dismissed Maupeou and recalled the parlements. Only a few pessimists recognized that a revolution in France was only a matter of time now. In any event, there was a revolution in the making elsewhere: in America.

THE AMERICAN REVOLUTION

Britain and the American Revolution

In Britain's history, the rebellion of its American colonies stands as a supreme irony. It came after the Hanoverian dynasty had established itself beyond question and after some brilliant British victories in the Seven Years' War. And from the perspective of the colonies, the irony is compounded.

The mercantilist notions of the British government prescribed that the American colonies be subjected to tight economic controls and exploited for the sake of the homeland. But in actuality, the American colonies grew to a measure of political maturity and economic prosperity in an atmosphere of benign neglect. The majority of Englishmen, as J. H. Plumb has put it, "never thought about America at all; to them it was a dumping ground for thieves, bankrupts, and prostitutes," for which England "received tobacco in return." [22] At the same time, British troops defended the American colonies against Indian raids and French incursions, furnishing a far-flung and expensive protective shield that the colonists needed, but ungratefully took for granted.

Colonial government was equally paradoxical. The official powers of each colonial governor were large. He was responsible, and in theory responsive, to the privy council in London, which had the authority to "disallow" colonial laws. When in the 1760s excited demagogues roused up the colonists against the "tyranny" of George III, all these principles were sufficiently denounced. But they did not represent the realities of colonial life. The colonial governor was as much the prisoner of his legislatures as their master; he lived among them and found it politic by and large to listen to them. He had little patronage to dispense, and without patronage, power could rest only on guns, which he did not have and in any event would have been reluctant to use. The board of trade, which from its establishment in 1696 oversaw colonial economic affairs, on occasion placed restrictions on American manufacture and export, but these restrictions were rare and relatively insignificant. And the privy council on the whole left the colonies to themselves and exercised its ultimate veto power with

---

[21] See Gordon Wright, *France in Modern Times, 1760 to the Present* (1960), 42.
[22] *England in the Eighteenth Century* (1950), 124.

the utmost restraint. The impressive growth of American towns, trades, and general prosperity proves that the hand of Britain rested lightly on its American dependencies.

Yet (as subsequent events made abundantly clear) all was not well with Britain's empire overseas, or with Britain's affairs at home. In his long, deliberately undramatic rule, Walpole had given his country deeper tranquility than it had known for over a century (see p. 385). It was only in 1745, three years after Walpole's fall and in the year of his death, that King George II faced one more challenge to his hold on the British crown. Thirty years earlier, in 1715, the son of James II, the Pretender, had launched an invasion to reclaim the throne for the Stuarts. As we know (see p. 383), the "'15" had ignominiously failed. Now the Pretender's son imitated his father, in tactics and in results. The glamorous fables woven around the Young Pretender, Bonnie Prince Charlie and his early successes cannot conceal his ultimate disaster. In July 1745, he landed in Scotland and rallied wide support among the Highlanders. He took Edinburgh, and by fall his rebel troops were on English soil. But while the "'45" enlisted the emotional support of Scotsmen nostalgic for the Stuart dynasty—it was, after all, Scotland's own—the Jacobite cause found practically no supporters among Englishmen. Finally, in April 1746 the Young Pretender's forces were routed by government troops at Culloden, and the Jacobite menace was over. The "'45," intended to overthrow the Hanoverians, only confirmed them on Britain's throne.

From war at home, George II turned his attention to war abroad. And it was foreign war, as we have seen (see p. 401), that compelled George II to turn to Pitt; the outbreak of the Seven Years' War made the immensely popular Pitt the inevitable first minister. Pitt could rightly boast that he had been called into office by his sovereign and "by the Voice of the People." Pitt was first minister during the early months of the Seven Years' War, from November 1756 to April 1757; then, after three months out of office, he returned, with Walpole's old political manager, the duke of Newcastle, as first lord of the treasury. This arrangement remained secure until George II's death in 1760.

The accession of George's grandson as George III changed the shape of Pitt's career and much else in British history besides. George II had disliked Pitt but found he could not do without him for the conduct of the war; George III, who wanted to substitute his old tutor and lifelong favorite, the earl of Bute, for the great war minister, was willing to be consistent. He was ready to close out the war to get rid of Pitt. In 1761, he appointed Bute secretary of state to find ways of making peace; half a year later, Pitt was out of office.

In foreign policy, this turn of events meant the Peace of Paris of 1763, which restored to France at the conference table much that it had lost on the battlefield (see p. 401). At home, it meant a constitutional crisis whose true lineaments did not become clear until a few decades ago, through the magisterial work of Sir Lewis Namier. The critics of George III, and many historians after them, accused the king of seeking to destroy the British

Constitution and to rule absolutely with the aid of his men, the King's Friends. But George III had no wish to subvert the British Constitution; he meant to rule in accord with the constitution established by the Glorious Revolution in 1689. His model was William III, not Charles I. [23]

The king's "aggression" focused new attention on Parliament and on the role of parties in the political life of the nation. While ministers squabbled over the Paris settlement and formed unstable alliances, and while George III envisioned himself as a "patriot king" floating above contending forces, a few perceptive political thinkers reversed the time-honored condemnation of party as mere faction, and praised it instead as an essential element of good government. In 1770, Edmund Burke, a rising Whig politician, articulated this new vision in a famous pamphlet, *Thoughts on the Cause of the Present Discontents*. A party, Burke wrote, "is a body of men united, for promoting by their joint endeavors the national interest, upon some particular principle in which they are all agreed." By implication, a party leader must publicly state his principles and then govern through a firm majority of the House of Commons.

But this raised other and even more pressing problems. When Burke wrote, "parties" were mere coalitions of interest, susceptible to bribery or other pressures from the court. The franchise by which the nation selected its representatives to the House of Commons was notoriously unequal and notoriously open to manipulation. The idea of responsible party government thus could not be divorced from the idea of parliamentary reform, and through the 1760s and 1770s the reform agitation occupied the center of England's political stage. Like all great reform movements, this too enlisted a curious collection of supporters. There was the conservative theoretician Edmund Burke, who believed in "virtual representation"—the government of the rich and powerful in behalf of the lesser orders—but who insisted on the need to eliminate conflicting outside interests among members of Parliament. There was the indefatigable Major John Cartwright, who in contrast to Burke sought to make representation more equal. For fifty years, down to his death in 1824, he campaigned in innumerable pamphlets for the payment of members, for annual elections, for universal male suffrage, for the equalization of parliamentary constituencies, and for the abolition of property qualifications for membership in the House of Commons—the whole program of nineteenth-century English radicals is contained in his energetic writings. And then there was John Wilkes, whose flamboyant style, amorous adventures, and gift for dramatic cases gave the reform agitation a raffish, though by no means absurd, air. Wilkes, known for his ugliness and irresistible attractiveness to women, had

---

[23] See R. K. Webb, *Modern England from the Eighteenth Century to the Present* (1968), 74. Namier's main work bearing on these years of English politics are the classic *The Structure of Politics at the Accession of George III* (1929) and *England in the Age of the American Revolution* (1930). It must be added, however, that his conception of politics has been criticized for being unduly narrow: see Sir Herbert Butterfield, *George III and the Historians* (1957).

entered Parliament in 1757, but was expelled from it in 1764 for seditious libel. What had aroused the government to this extreme act was the notorious Number 45 of the *North Briton,* a newspaper Wilkes had been publishing since 1762. In that number, Wilkes had so venomously assailed George III's speech from the throne defending the Peace of Paris, that he was thrown into the Tower. Wilkes was released, pleading parliamentary privilege, but once released, he republished the offensive Number 45, and into the bargain an obscene poem entitled *An Essay on Woman.* Facing arrest once more, Wilkes fled to France.

This was only the beginning. In 1768, Wilkes returned, stood for the constituency of Middlesex, was elected, arrested and imprisoned, and once again expelled from the Commons. Obviously enjoying this notoriety, Wilkes stood for reelection for Middlesex four more times, defying the House of Commons which continued to refuse to seat him. But then, in 1774, as Wilkes had some supporters in Parliament, his election was allowed to stand, and the principles of majority rule and free criticism advanced by a step. Stirring events overseas, meanwhile, were engrossing Englishmen including the reformers. The American colonies were filled with unrest; there had been clashes with loss of life. The reformers from all quarters—Burke, Cartwright, Wilkes, and the aging Pitt, now earl of Chatham—called for conciliation with America and voiced their sympathies with the rebels' cause. But the British government, stable once more under the guidance of Lord North, had other ideas and made conciliation impossible.

Foundations of American Identity

It is evident that the American Revolution was a great event in the history of Britain. It was also a great event in the history of Europe, reverberating into the nineteenth and even the twentieth centuries. More immediately, its impact on French finances and, with that, on French politics, was enormous. And in the realm of ideas, it seemed like a fantasy realized. The philosophes had long professed their admiration of the American colonies, and made much of those colonials, like Benjamin Franklin, who came to visit them. In fact, Franklin's enthusiastic European followers used him as a model in two opposite ways. He seemed to embody the simplicity of nature and the sophistication of urbanity; he was philosopher and backwoodsman at the same time. America, wrote Turgot in 1778, must prosper, for the American people are "the hope of the human race; they may well become its model." In the same year, as the aged Voltaire returned to his native Paris to be celebrated and to die, he met Benjamin Franklin in a carefully staged public encounter; while spectators shed tears, Voltaire embraced Franklin and blessed Franklin's grandson in English with the significant words, "God and liberty." For its European well-wishers, the American Revolution was a just cause, but it was also more than that: it was the culmination of a development to which enlightened men could look with hope. America was the Enlightenment in action.[24]

American realities were, of course, much more complicated. The British colonies that rose against their mother country in the 1770s were, though geographically and economically linked, politically and emotionally separate. Their official status was unambiguous: they were colonies, governed from England presumably for its sake. Yet these colonies displayed most of the characteristics one expects from developed states. They had far-flung trade, established elites, social conflicts, colleges, newspapers, and an emerging self-awareness. If European states had their serfs, the American colonies had their slaves. Leading colonial cities had achieved respectable size: in 1775, Philadelphia, America's largest and the British Empire's second largest city, had forty thousand inhabitants; New York followed with twenty-five thousand, then Boston with over sixteen thousand, and Charleston with twelve thousand. Through the seventeenth century, American colonials had looked to England as their home, and their attachment reflected more than economic or political dependence. It was a powerful, unquestioned sentiment, not unmixed with the inferiority feelings of the provincial. England set the tone for the Americans: their religious and political convictions, their cultural styles, their most cherished kind of approval came from there. Nothing could better please the Massachusetts Puritan Cotton Mather, professional theologian and amateur scientist, than to be able to style himself "F.R.S."—Fellow of the Royal Society, London. It was not until the eighteenth century that this began to change. Economic self-interest dictated conduct sharply at variance with the needs of the mother country: during the French and Indian Wars, while the British desperately battled against France on three continents, colonial merchants in America coolly and profitably traded with the enemy. While the colonies squabbled with one another over boundaries, and while frontiersmen argued with "easterners" over Indian policy, the American colonists had enough common interests (intercolonial trade) and common enemies (the Indians, the French, and increasingly, the English government) to develop a certain sense of distance from Europe and a certain sense of identity. Yet it is striking how slowly these feelings grew; Americans became Americans with marked reluctance. Through the 1760s, the most discontented and most radical of the colonists continued to think of themselves as Englishmen [25] and borrowed their most subversive ideas from English political writers. When, on July 4, 1776, the American rebels gave the reasons why it had become necessary for them to "dissolve the political bands" that had hitherto connected them with England,

[24] See Peter Gay, *The Enlightenment: An Interpretation*, vol. II, *The Science of Freedom* (1969), 555–568.

[25] The language of the revolution was English, and most revolutionary leaders were of English descent, but by the middle of the eighteenth century, there were numerous settlers of Scotch-Irish and German origins as well. And there were two hundred thirty thousand blacks, practically all of them slaves.

they took care to indict the "tyranny" of "the present King of Great Britain" by citing over a score of "injuries and usurpations." They knew that a declaration of independence was an act of the utmost gravity and, however eager they had become for separation, they felt it as a wrench and needed to explain and justify it.

The special quality of the American experience—what made Americans American—has been debated since the time of the Revolution. "What then is the American, this new man?" J. Hector St. John de Crèvecoeur asked in 1782, in words that have often been quoted. America, he answered his own question, is a land where "individuals of all nations are melted into a new race of men." Anticipating the self-congratulation that would become the envy of Europeans, he added that the Americans' "labors and posterity will one day cause great changes in the world. . . . The American is a new man, who acts upon new principles; he must therefore entertain new ideas, and form new opinions." In good eighteenth-century fashion, Crèvecoeur did not overlook the impact of geography on character: "From involuntary idleness, servile dependence, penury, and useless labor, he has passed to toils of a very different nature, rewarded by ample substance." The American was new in part because America was new. This assertion of American uniqueness itself contributed to the creation of that uniqueness. So did the experience of fighting a war for independence together, under the single command of George Washington.

While, once free and united, Americans strenuously cultivated their sense of a common fate and a common mission, the early history of Britain's colonies on the North American continent differed from colony to colony. Yet some of the common ingredients in the American experience were palpable enough. Settled predominantly on the eastern seaboard and in its adjacent hinterland, migrants to America mainly became farmers. Virgin land was plentiful and agricultural labor scarce—a reversal of the familiar European pattern. Life was isolated, even in the villages of New England or in the Middle Atlantic states; population was thinly scattered, and migrants to America found voyages to their homeland arduous if not perilous. All these factors gave survival value to qualities that Americans later claimed as particularly their own: ingenuity, adaptability, self-reliance, and a certain sense of social freedom, almost egalitarianism. Of course, like the European societies from which they had sprung, the American colonies, too, were socially stratified; the old habits of deference receded slowly. Yet in this vast, largely unexplored and promising new land many traditional guideposts lost their meaning. Social boundaries were more porous, social mobility was easier, sheer ability counted for more than it had at home, in the "old country."

While each colony had its own history, the principal divisions among them were sectional. Indeed, the division that marks (and plagues) the United States to this day—South versus North—emerged early in colonial times. The southern colonies were dominated by large plantations worked by black slaves and white indentured servants. Its great export crop was tobacco; rice and indigo became cash crops only in the eighteenth century. The Middle Atlantic colonies and New England, in contrast, grew tobacco only in a few isolated areas like the southern Connecticut valley. Instead, northern farmers raised corn and wheat and familiar European staples—rye, barley, and oats. In addition, the northern colonies developed a flourishing home industry, weaving linen and making furniture. While the vast majority of Americans even in the North continued to live on, and off, the land, colonial towns grew into flourishing ports, with a lively trade in fish, raw materials, and slaves. In the Middle Atlantic states the iron industry and the export of grain burgeoned. Life here was visibly good and getting better: wages were high, and opportunities for the entrepreneur vast.

In cultural life, too, the distinction between South and North was striking. The South was Anglican and English; the North, far more mixed religiously and ethnically. In New York, Dutch and English settlers learned to live with each other. In Pennsylvania, German settlers (the misnamed Pennsylvania Dutch), descendants of English Quakers, and Scotch-Irish immigrants forged a single society. New England, in contrast, was Puritan, but this much-abused word should be used with care. The Puritans were not puritan. They lived and dressed soberly, they believed in hard work, they taught that few are elected to salvation and many damned. And at least in the early decades, the dominant families kept their communities pure by driving out dissenters. But the Puritans knew how to laugh; they wrote poetry and gave room to sensuality—if normally within narrowly prescribed limits. While the Virginia planter aristocracy produced some educated men in these early times, the center of learning in America was in New England. It is not an accident that Harvard, America's first college, founded in 1636, should be in the Massachusetts Bay Colony.

Despite all opportunities for independent development, the ties between the colonies and the motherland remained intimate to the very edge of revolution. Earthquakes in England caused tremors in America. The Restoration of Charles II in 1660 forced increased tolerance on New England. The Glorious Revolution, after some confusion, produced conditions congenial to the new British government and the colonists alike: James II had briefly experimented with joining New Jersey, New York, and the New England colonies into the single Dominion of New England, but with the accession of William and Mary this unpopular idea vanished, with its author, from the scene. Religious and philosophical movements, too, had their reverberations in the American colonies. As the life of the educated in Europe grew more urbane and secular, so did life in Philadelphia, New York, and even in Congregationalist Boston. By the beginning of the eighteenth century, the survivors of the old Puritan order lamented the disappearance of the fervent sense of mission and charged that Bostonians had grown more interested in making money than in discussing Calvinist doctrine. In England John Wesley had responded to worldliness with his powerful Methodist sermons (see p. 403), and Americans once again followed the home country's lead. In the late 1730s, Wesley's most eloquent disciple, the revivalist orator George Whitefield, toured the colonies to touch off a frenzy of religious enthusiasm and produce thousands of dramatic conversions. The European Enlightenment had a pervasive effect in America; those who would soon lead the American colonies in rebellion were all in some degree philosophes. Benjamin Franklin—printer, moralist, inventor, business promoter, statesman—formed his style on Addison's *Spectator*, his deist philosophy on English writers, his scientific knowledge on Newton, his wit on Voltaire. Thomas Jefferson, principal author of the Declaration of Independence, third president of the United States, and founder of the University of Virginia, was European in every fiber of his intellectual being; John Adams (his predecessor in the presidency) said maliciously of Jefferson that he "drank freely of the French philosophy, in religion, in science, in politics." But Jefferson drank, just as freely, of English sources, too; he was both Francophile and Anglomaniac. And James Madison, the chief architect of the Constitution, and fourth president of the United States, imitated Addison and Voltaire and learned his political theories from Locke, Montesquieu, and Hume. America's separation from England and from Europe came, when it finally did come, with English and with European words and ideas.

From Resistance to Rebellion

Serious tensions began during and because of the Seven Years' War. In 1759, the privy council disallowed several South Carolina and Virginia enactments and announced that henceforth the royal prerogative would be more strictly enforced. Two years later, angered at continued smuggling operations, the government authorized general search warrants in Massachusetts, which permitted searches of warehouses and even private dwellings without court order. Then, in 1763, after peace had come, the British government addressed itself to the Indian "problem" in a manner to anger the colonists further. Beginning with the first settlements, the American Indian tribes had lived sometimes at peace, often at war, with the European invaders. The white newcomers, as in Massachusetts Bay, were sometimes grateful for the help they received; elsewhere, as in Virginia, they accepted help from the local tribes and then unscrupulously despoiled them. A century and a half of experience had taught the American Indians that French masters were preferable to English masters, and when, after their victory over France, the British pressed inland across the Appalachians, Indian tribes, led by the Ottawa chief Pontiac, mounted a vigorous, if futile campaign. "Freed of the restraint imposed by French competition," John A. Garraty sums it up, "Englishman and colonist increased their pressure on the Indians. Cynical fur traders now cheated them outrageously, while callous military men hoped to exterminate them like vermin. The British commander in the west, Lord Jeffrey Amherst, suggested infecting the Indians with smallpox, and another officer expressed the wish that they could be hunted down with dogs."[26] Eventually, caution prevailed over brutality: in a proclamation of 1763, the British government prohibited settlers from crossing the Appalachian divide, an action that was also intended to divert settlement to the colony of Canada, newly acquired from the French. But the English colonists failed to see the statesmanship of the move; speculators in western lands and prospective westerners were furious.

All this was bad enough; the use of general search warrants—the so-called "writs of assistance"—in the absence of a stringent emergency could even be dramatized as an invasion of an Englishman's fundamental rights. But now the British government proposed to invade the colonists' pocketbook, and the outcry became an uproar. For the British, the situation in 1763 was anything but enviable. Victory had brought more problems than it had solved. The national debt had nearly doubled in the course of the war; taxes were high, and the ministry was casting about for ways of reducing them—or at least of avoiding raising the onerous land tax any further. In April 1763, a month after the Peace of Paris was proclaimed, Bute was followed in office by George Grenville, a competent though limited and highly unpopular politician. His course seemed clear to him: across the seas lived nearly two million British subjects who had violated practically every law on the books, manufactured what they were forbidden to manufacture, exported what they were forbidden to export, traded with enemy merchants in time of war, and evaded most taxes for a century. A year after his accession to office, in April 1764, Parliament passed the Revenue Act (popularly called the Sugar Act), which actually reduced tariffs on a number of raw materials but sought to enforce payment. Clearly, the colonists would rather live under high tariffs that were not collected than under moderate ones that were. They exploded, and with a principled argument: the restrictions provided by the Navigation Acts were designed to channel manufacture and trade in prescribed directions, not to raise revenue. The Sugar Act, though, was clearly a money-raising law, and it had been passed without the colonists' consent. In the following year, the same principle was raised by another act, the Stamp Act of 1765, more detested in the colonies even than the Sugar Act. It did not strike Englishmen as a burdensome exaction; they were used to paying small sums on land transfers, licenses, and newspapers. But it so happened that this act, innocuous as it seemed, struck at the most articulate interest groups in America: at lawyers and printers, at editors, notaries, and tavern keepers. With the battle cry, "No taxation without representation," colonists resisted the Stamp Act. Grenville's announced intention to spend all the anticipated revenue on the defense of the colonies made no impression. Popular demagogues became popular heroes. In May 1765, Patrick Henry started a great debate in the Virginia legislature by introducing resolutions declaring Parliament powerless to tax the colonies. And in the summer, mobs looted the houses

[26] *The American Nation to 1877* (1966), 78.

of the officials designated to distribute the stamps. But by then Grenville had been dismissed.

For several years the British government, appalled at the outcry in America, vacillated. For a year—from July 1765 to July 1766—the Rockingham Whigs, including Burke, tried to conciliate the Americans: Rockingham repealed the Stamp Act in 1766, but insisted that on principle Parliament had the right to tax the colonies. The American call for representation was confronted with the British doctrine of "virtual representation"—members of Parliament were held to represent not this district or that, but all of Britain's great empire. The interests of colonials were safeguarded by members of Parliament in the same way as were those of English subjects who did not have the right to vote. The Americans were not impressed. They were impressed even less by the "Townshend duties," imposed in 1767 by the young chancellor of the exchequer, Charles Townshend, even though he had dressed up the new imposts under the guise of "indirect taxes," an absurd distinction that meant nothing to Townshend and nothing to the colonists, even if some orators had proclaimed their readiness to pay taxes as long as they were indirect. Colonists were joining forces to an alarming degree: in 1765, a Stamp Act Congress in New York had brought together delegates from nine of the colonies; in 1768, the Massachusetts legislature circularized other legislatures to discover common ground on the new duties. The atmosphere, already inflamed, fed on its own high temperature. Townshend had died in 1767, and was succeeded at the exchequer by Lord North, who favored repeal, but insisted that, simply to dramatize Britain's rights, one tax—that on tea—be retained. He prevailed, and by 1770, all but one of the Townshend taxes were lifted. In the same year, North became prime minister and brought a measure of stability to English affairs. Blood had already been shed: in March 1770, British troops fired on a mob in Boston and killed five persons. Then, in December 1773, Boston was involved in another incident which was less tragic but more consequential. The East India Company, which, thanks to American boycotts, had stores of tea on its hands, persuaded the British government to remit its duties and grant it a monopoly on the American market. A consignment of their tea, low in price and high in quality, arrived in Boston harbor late in November 1773. Samuel Adams and his fellow agitators inflamed excited crowds with their single argument that to permit the tea to land was to submit, abjectly, to tyranny from overseas. On the night of December 16, "patriots" painted like Indians boarded the vessels and dumped their cargo into Boston harbor. The Boston Tea Party provoked stern reprisals in the early spring of 1774. The Boston port was closed, the jurisdiction of the Massachusetts courts was curtailed, the power of the colonial governor was enlarged at the expense of local government. By an unfortunate coincidence, colonists were further incensed by the Quebec Act, a wise and statesmanlike measure that was directed at providing a form of government suitable to the French Canadians, whose ways were alien to the colonists; it seemed both arbitrary and—in its more liberal aspects—a portentous concession to Roman Catholics. The American response to these "Intolerable Acts" was the first Continental Congress; it met in Philadelphia in September, with twelve out of thirteen colonies—all but Georgia—sending delegates. Samuel Adams had been talking of an "American Commonwealth" since 1773, but conciliation seemed, if improbable, still possible to American and British moderates alike. Lord Chatham, Edmund Burke, even Lord North himself suggested far-reaching concessions. But then large-scale violence frustrated such hopes. In April 1775, General Gage received orders in Boston to repress rebellion; on April 19, his troops clashed with American irregulars, the Minute Men, at Lexington and Concord. There were sharp losses on both sides. The call for independence became irresistible. "The revolution was complete, in the minds of the people and the Union of the colonies," John Adams said many years later, "before the war commenced." But not long before.

The British began to gather troops—including German mercenaries—to restore order, and in January 1776, the English polemicist Thomas Paine published his *Common Sense,* an inflammatory, brilliantly lucid attack on the "Royal Brute," George III, in which he denounced monarchy as corrupt and called upon Americans to become independent. It spoke to, and for, America. The second Continental Congress, which had been in session since May 1775, followed Paine's call, which was being echoed with growing fervor through all the colonies. On July 4, 1776, Congress passed Jefferson's draft of a Declaration of Independence, a mixture of natural-law sentiments and specific grievances. To support this declaration, the delegates mutually pledged their lives, their fortunes, and their sacred honor. The fortunes of war vacillated, but George Washington converted his untrained troops into a respectable fighting instrument, while British commanders, incompetent, self-destructive, and far from home, found the colonists far more formidable than they had expected. In October 1777, General John Burgoyne, failing to split the colonies, surrendered his army at Saratoga; in early 1778, Benjamin Franklin and two fellow envoys concluded a treaty with France, which recognized the independence of the rebellious colonies and provided for troops and supplies; in 1779 the beleaguered colonists obtained further support from Spain. Lord North's belated concessions were rejected, and the Americans, through defeat, desertions, and treason, fought on. After the British took Charleston in May 1780, affairs took a turn for the better, and in October 1781, at Yorktown, Virginia, General Cornwallis capitulated to General Washington. The improbable and the unforeseen had become reality: the American colonies were free and independent.

The Peace of Paris, provisionally complete in November 1782, and signed at Paris in September 1783, exceeded all expectations and astounded the most experienced of European diplomats. Britain recognized the sovereign independence of the "United States," set their frontiers just north of Spanish Florida, at the Great Lakes, and on the Mississippi River—a western boundary remote enough to invite westward expansion. It undertook to withdraw British troops rapidly, and granted Americans fishing rights off Newfoundland. All this was impressive enough. But whether this agglomeration of independent colonies— now independent states—would prosper, or even survive, remained an open question.

From Confederation to Federation

In 1778, Turgot had called the rebels "the hope of the human race"; in 1790, Condorcet paid excited tribute to the new nation that was serving as an inspiration to the old nations of Europe: "Men whom the reading of philosophic books had secretly converted to the love of liberty, became enthusiastic over the liberty of a foreign people while they waited for the moment when they could recover their own." The victory of the colonies proved that free men could, after all, defeat a powerful and entrenched imperial power.

At the beginning, however, the American experiment seemed fragile, exposed to constant danger. The young confederation found itself in conflict with Great Britain over the carrying out of peace terms. American manufacturers, swamped by reasonably priced and well-made British imports, entered a period of depression. Money was first too scarce and then too plentiful; the war emergency had induced both the Continental Congress and the individual states to print paper money, which produced severe inflation and then, as governments responded, even more severe deflation. In this uncertain situation, relations between debtors and creditors, never easy, deteriorated; in 1786, a debtors' rebellion in Massachusetts, let by Daniel Shays, brought actual violence. Benjamin Franklin's famous warning, issued on July 4, 1776, "We must all hang together, or assuredly we shall all hang separately," now acquired new urgency.

The ideal of a United States was obvious, its nature was something else again. The colonies had fought the war of independence under articles of confederation ratified in 1778 by eight of the states, and in 1781 by them all. But the articles, which remained in force after the Peace of Paris had been signed, kept the sovereignty of the individual states intact; it ratified a "league of friendship," suitable to an emergency perhaps, when a common enemy overrides all particular interests, but hopelessly inadequate in a world of great powers, with well-organized and well-financed traders, to say nothing of sizable armies and navies. The states were jealous of their independence and wary of a closer union that might compromise their interests. But in the end, after a long and often acrimonious debate, they preferred common survival to parochial pride. From 1786, strong voices for union were heard, and from impressive quarters: from George Washington, from the Virginia legislature. In September, delegates from five states met at Annapolis; the sparse attendance was a sign of obvious failure, but one of the delegates, the brilliant and indefatigable

New York lawyer Alexander Hamilton, persuaded the others to try again. In May 1787, delegates from nine states accordingly met at Philadelphia, elected George Washington as president, and adjourned in September with a draft constitution. Its preamble, in grave and ambitious words, spoke the language of a new age: "We the People of the United States, in order to form a more perfect union, establish justice, insure domestic tranquility, provide for the common defence, promote the general welfare, and secure the blessings of liberty to ourselves and our posterity, do ordain and establish this Constitution for the United States of America." The delegates dispersed, to lobby in their respective states for its adoption. One of the polemics written in its behalf— eighty-five separate articles by James Madison, Alexander Hamilton, and John Jay, and collected as *The Federalist*—was a masterpiece of persuasion, a model of enlightened sociology, and a monument to the ideal of freedom, eighteenth-century style. The authors were thoroughly aware that the eyes of the world were upon them. "It has been frequently remarked," Hamilton wrote in the opening paragraph, "that it seems to have been reserved to the people of this country, by their conduct and example, to decide the important question, whether societies of men are really capable or not, of establishing good government from reflection and choice, or whether they are forever destined to depend, for their political constitutions, on accident and force." Tough-minded and realistic, the authors saw man in need of government, and government in need of checks. "If men were angels," wrote Madison, "no government would be necessary. If angels were to govern men, neither external nor internal controuls on government would be necessary. In framing a government which is to be administered by men over men, the great difficulty lies in this: You must first enable the government to controul the governed; and in the next place, oblige it to controul itself." In the eyes of Madison, Hamilton, and Jay, the proposed constitution admirably met this double requirement.

Public opinion was deeply divided. The Constitution proposed to substitute energetic action for the paralysis into which the confederation had fallen. That is largely why its advocates won out over the opposition. One other important thing helped. The Constitution was a shrewd compromise among conflicting forces. The proposed government was a secular republic, with guarantees for the civil rights of all its citizens. But it was not a democracy; the manner of voting for senators and for president was designed to weaken, if not eliminate, the influence of the mob. Some of its compromises, as between large states and small, were wise; others, above all the retention of slavery, were disastrous and bore the seeds of grave troubles ahead. Still, the advantages of a strong, yet not tyrannical government carried the day. By June 1788, ten ratifying conventions had approved the new constitution; the last, Rhode Island, fell into line in May 1790. By that time, George Washington, architect of victory, remote but trustworthy, a legend in his time, had been serving as the first president of the United States for over a year. He had been in office since April 30, 1789. Four days after his momentous swearing in, which brought the

American Revolution to a close with official solemnity, the French Estates General met in Versailles to inaugurate, with greater pomp, an even more portentous revolution.

SELECTED READINGS

For a recent, brief general survey of good government, eighteenth-century fashion, see John G. Gagliardo, *Enlightened Despotism* (1967), and the relevant chapters in M. S. Anderson, *Europe in the Eighteenth Century, 1718–1783* (1961). A. Goodwin, ed., *The American and French Revolutions, 1763–1793* (1968), vol. VIII of *The New Cambridge Modern History,* has numerous useful articles. See also Geoffrey Bruun, *The Enlightened Despots* (2nd ed., 1967), and, for a historical account of these years, Leo Gershoy, *From Despotism to Revolution, 1763–1789* (1944). The first volume of R. R. Palmer, *The Age of the Democratic Revolution: A Political History of Europe and America, 1760–1800* (1959), has, in addition to its thesis of a general movement toward democracy, a great deal of interesting material.

For specific countries in the time of reform, see in addition to these general titles, for Sweden, Michael Roberts, "The Swedish Aristocracy in the Eighteenth Century," in his *Essays in Swedish History* (1967), and Ingvar Andersson, *A History of Sweden* (tr. 1956); for Spain, Richard Herr, *The Eighteenth Century Revolution in Spain* (1958), and the appropriate chapters in Rafael Altamira, *A History of Spain, from the Beginnings to the Present Day* (tr. 1949). For Germany in general, W. H. Bruford, *Germany in the Eighteenth Century: The Social Background of the Literary Revival* (1935); Bruford's more specialized but illuminating study, *Culture and Society in Classical Weimar, 1775–1806* (1962); the excellent monograph by Helen P. Liebel, *Enlightened Bureaucracy Versus Enlightened Despotism in Baden, 1750–1792* (1965); the opening section of Leonard Krieger, *The German Idea of Freedom* (1957), a searching analysis; and Klaus Epstein's bulky *The Genesis of German Conservatism* (1966). For Josephinism, in addition to the titles by Bernard, Padover, Kerner, and others listed in Chapter 9, see Henrick Marczali, *Hungary in the 18th Century* (tr. 1910), and Robert A. Kann, *A Study in Austrian Intellectual History: From Late Baroque to Romanticism* (1960).

Catherine of Russia is undergoing reappraisal. Meanwhile, there is G. P. Gooch, *Catherine the Great and Other Studies* (1954), conventional but informative; Gladys S. Thomson, *Catherine the Great and the Expansion of Russia* (1947); the recent Paul Dukes, *Catherine the Great and the Russian Nobility* (1968); and the interesting essay by Marc Raeff, *Origins of the Russian Intelligentsia: The Eighteenth Century Nobility* (1966).

In addition to the titles on the regime of Louis XV listed in Chapter 9, see Shelby B. McCloy, *The Humanitarian Movement in Eighteenth Century France* (1957); Vivian R. Gruder, *The Royal Provincial Intendants: A Governing Elite in Eighteenth Century France* (1968); George T. Matthews, *The Royal General Farms in Eighteenth-Century France* (1958); Franklin L. Ford, *Strasbourg in Transition, 1648–1789* (1966); and Jacques L. Godechot, *France and the Atlantic Revolution of the Eighteenth Century, 1770–1799* (tr. 1965), to be read in conjunction with Palmer, *Age of the Democratic Revolution.*

For England under George III, see the opening chapters of R. K. Webb, *Modern England from the 18th Century to the Present* (1968), and J. Steven Watson, *The Reign* of George III, 1760-1815 (1960). Lewis Namier, *The Structure of Politics at the Accession of George III* (2nd ed., 1957), and *England in the Age of the American Revolution* (2nd ed., 1961), are both classics. But see Herbert Butterfield, *George III and the Historians* (1957), a critique of Namier. To these should be added Richard Pares, *King George and the Politicians* (1953); Herbert Butterfield, *George III, Lord North and the People, 1779-80* (1949); and John Brooke, *The Chatham Administration, 1766-1768* (1956). There is stimulating information on English radicals in George Rudé, *Wilkes and Liberty* (1962); see also I. R. Christie, *Wilkes, Wyville and Reform* (1963); Betty Kemp, *Sir Francis Dashwood* (1967); and Lucy Sutherland, *The City of London and the Opposition to Government, 1768-1774* (1959). On economic history, see T. S. Ashton, *The Industrial Revolution, 1760-1830* (2nd ed., 1964), and *An Economic History of England: The Eighteenth Century* (1955). And see J. D. Chambers and G. E. Mingay, *The Agricultural Revolution, 1750-1880* (1966).

Among histories of the American colonies, see the general treatment by John A. Garraty, *The American Nation to 1877* (1966), which includes helpful bibliographies. Richard Hofstadter's posthumous *America at 1750: A Social Portrait* (1971) is a lucid essay. See also John R. Alden, *Pioneer America* (1960). Bernard Bailyn's *The Ideological Origins of the American Revolution* (1967) and *The Origins of American Politics* (1968) offer important interpretations. See also Clarence L. Ver Steeg, *The Formative Years* (1964). For colonial culture in general, L. B. Wright, *The Cultural Life of the American Colonies* (1957), says the essential. For New England civilization, several volumes by Perry Miller remain indispensable, especially *Errand into the Wilderness* (1956), a collection of stimulating essays, and his informal trilogy, *Orthodoxy in Massachusetts* (1933), *The New England Mind: The 17th Century* (1939), and *The New England Mind: From Colony to Province* (1953). In addition, see Carl Bridenbaugh, *Myths and Realities: Societies of the Colonial South* (1952), and two other books by him: *Cities in the Wilderness* (1938) and *Cities in Revolt* (1955). See also L. B. Wright, *The First Gentlemen of Virginia* (1940).

For the revolutionary period, see Lawrence H. Gipson, *The Coming of the Revolution* (1954), which ably summarizes a far more voluminous work; J. C. Miller, *Origins of the American Revolution* (1943); and Edmund S. Morgan, *The Birth of the Republic* (1956). Richard B. Morris, *The American Revolution Reconsidered* (1967), intelligently surveys the field. Arthur M. Schlesinger, Sr., *The Colonial Merchants and the American Revolution* (1918), has not been superseded. See also Benjamin W. Labaree, *The Boston Tea Party* (1964), as well as Edmund S. and Helen M. Morgan, *The Stamp Act Crisis* (1953). The best biographies of revolutionary leaders include Carl Van Doren's *Benjamin Franklin* (1938) and Verner W. Crane's economical *Benjamin Franklin and a Rising People* (1954); Dumas Malone's *Jefferson: The Virginian* (1948) and Merrill D. Peterson's *Thomas Jefferson and the New Nation* (1970); Douglas S. Freeman's *George Washington*, 7 vols. (1948-1957) and Marcus Cunliffe's *George Washington: Man and Monument* (1958); J. C. Miller's *Alexander Hamilton: A Portrait in Paradox* (1959); and Irving Brant's *James Madison: Father of the Constitution* (1950). On the Constitution itself, Charles A. Beard's controversial *An Economic Interpretation of the Constitution* (2nd ed., 1935) long held the field, but has now been successfully challenged by Robert E. Brown, *Charles Beard and the Constitution* (1956). See also Forrest McDonald, *We the People: The Economic Origins of the Constitution* (1958).

11

The French Revolution

Historians are inordinately fond of resounding terms like "turning point" and "epoch making." The French Revolution fully deserves such language. It confirmed the ascendancy of the modern state and gave birth to the modern army; it served to spread ideas of Enlightenment and mass politics across several continents; it signaled the intervention of new sectors of the population in the political process; it served for decades, and continues to serve, as a rallying cry to radicals and a dreadful warning to conservatives. Modern radicalism, indeed, like modern conservatism, takes its rise from the French Revolution. And it was more than a French revolution; it marked an epoch in the history of France, of Europe, and of the world.

DECLINE AND FALL OF
THE OLD REGIME: 1774-1789
·•·<⊗>·•·

Anatomy of a Reign

When Louis XVI became king of France in 1774 at the age of twenty, he had only his birth to recommend him for his position. He was well meaning, indolent, and incurious. Even the vivacious Hapsburg princess, Marie Antoinette, to whom he was married at sixteen, did not interest him, although her impetuous character and strong will eventually gave her a baleful influence over him. His amusements consisted of tinkering with locks, working at masonry, and hunting. On that imperishable day in 1789, Bastille Day, when Paris was swept by the first wave of the revolution that would cost him his head, his diary, characteristically preoccupied with his hunting, contained the single entry: "July 14: Nothing."

The country that Louis inherited had all the bloom of prosperity, but it was a bloom ill-rooted and ill-nourished. At the end of the eighteenth century France remained overwhelmingly agricultural, and most of its peasants lived at, and sometimes below, subsistence level. In some areas such as maritime Flanders or in the neighborhood of Versailles three-fourths of the peasants owned no land at all, and in most regions they depended heavily on customary communal grazing and forest rights and on supplementary employment to sustain their minimum standard. Every agricultural crisis reduced hordes of day laborers and small landholders to destitution. In Normandy, Arthur Young reported, "most of the dwellings consist of four posts . . . to which a chimney has been added made up of four poles and some mud." The inhabitants of such hovels, he wrote, were "walking dunghills."

Anachronistic as French agriculture was, the French tax structure, with its age-old inequities, was more anachronistic still. As we have seen, the rich, the most obvious source of revenue, were for the most part exempt; by the time of the Revolution, the nobles, despite their vast holdings, were paying a bare 10 percent of the taxes. The nobility justified its privileges with a convenient feudal theory: in exchange for offering their king (the first of the nobles) support in war, they had a right to be exempt from the *taille* (the land tax) and from the *corvée*. Many prosperous members of the urban bourgeoisie escaped most taxation as well; not even Louis XIV had managed to prevent widespread tax evasion. His successors managed no better. The system of turning over the collection of taxes to tax farmers was an inefficient and desperate way of raising money; by May 1789, 60 percent of the revenue the farmers general collected remained with them. The one national tax that was faithfully collected and universally hated was the salt tax, the *gabelle;* the Paris financiers who bought the right of collecting it for three million livres a year had the right to sentence evaders to the galleys or even to death.

On top of the national taxes were piled the seigneurial dues, the *banalités,* payments to the lord for use of the village bakeovens, winepress, and mill, and payments that fell due when property changed hands. Among other irritating, and sometimes costly, vestiges of feudalism was the lord's retention of hunting rights: game was reserved to the nobility, and hunting parties could ride across tilled fields without paying indemnity for any damage to standing crops. This was not yet all. The church retained its ancient rights to the tithe, theoretically a tenth but actually a thirteenth, of the gross produce of the land. Once again the rich generally evaded this supposedly universal tax, which yielded the church some five million livres a year.

With this chaotic and antiquated system of raising revenue, the government was running progressively deeper into debt. Despite its high and inflammatory visibility, the notorious extravagance of Marie Antoinette and her court was a relatively minor drain on French resources: perhaps 6 percent of French revenue in 1788 went to support the royal family and its palaces.[1] The real burden was the cost of the military establishment and of past wars, which had been financed by loans: almost half the national income in the year before the Revolution went to the payment of principal and interest. One of the heaviest charges on the French exchequer was the cost of the American Revolution: French support of this revolution, given less out of love of liberty than from enmity to England, helped to bring revolution to France. Yet, the burdens of the French national debt and current expenditures were no greater than those encumbering other states.

But public morale was low, resistance to reform entrenched, and, to make matters worse, the French economy was in the midst of a rising tide of unemployment, of inflation and a decline in production. The increase in population that had begun early in the eighteenth century amounted by 1789 to six million. This placed an increasing strain on the resources available in the countryside where methods of cultivation had not improved. Those displaced by unemployment or by endless subdivision of landed property drifted to the towns as unskilled laborers or joined the bands of homeless brigands who infested the countryside. One of the major industries employing day labor was textiles, but with increasing unemployment, purchases of textiles fell; by 1789 the quantity of cloth produced in France was half that of 1787. A disastrous harvest in 1788 followed by an only moderately successful one in 1789 carried the crisis into agriculture, while the wine industry, of central importance, faced similar difficulties as a result of an only fair grape harvest in 1788. The economic decline affected not only the poor and landless, but larger landowning farmers

[1] The same, as we saw on p. 439, had held true of Madame de Pompadour.

and master craftsmen as well. The seigneurs, finding their feudal dues worth less and less, sought to recoup by collecting rents in kind rather than in cash or by renegotiating their contracts. The whole century saw a widening gap between the price of food and real wages. After 1730 prices, especially those of necessities, rose while wages limped behind; when prices dropped, as they did in the 1780s, the drop was selective and benefited only a few. Rents and the price of bread remained high.

Population growth, crop failures, cycles of inflation and unemployment: by the 1780s the great question was, Who is to blame? As Frenchmen discussed their hardships in the cafés, they found the cause of the trouble not in the vagaries of nature or the fluctuation of the economy, but in the court. Prices had risen not because of crop failures but because the government did not care for its people—had it not signed a treaty of commerce with the English in 1786 which had let down customs barriers? Other grievances—military service, the burdensome population, the heavy taxes—all seemed to have a political origin, so that the regime itself became the target of popular criticism.

In Search of a Policy

In this lurid light, the reign of Louis XVI appears as a search for the finance minister who would extricate the country from its difficulties and for ways of translating his program into practice. The king's first appointment was his boldest, although his courage did not match his minister's. Anne Robert Turgot, whom Louis XVI appointed controller general of finance only three months after his accession, was a precocious intellectual, a friend of the philosophes, and sympathetic to the physiocratic doctrines of free trade. He had been intendant at Limoges, where he had made a reputation by his attack on old abuses and by a rational road-building program in place of the *corvée*. Now, as controller general, Turgot devised a vigorous plan of reform; radical in its prescriptions and humanitarian in its philosophy, it grew out of his administrative experience and embodied his advanced convictions. He drafted six edicts, which proposed to abolish useless sinecures, internal customs barriers (which had the effect of greatly increasing the price of grain), the gilds (which limited the introduction of both new workmen and new processes) and, most daring of all, the *corvée*, which he planned to replace with a new land tax. In moving language Turgot dwelt both on the irreparable harm to the peasant "who has nothing for his subsistence but his hand," and on the uneconomic nature of the old system.

Louis let himself be persuaded to support Turgot's program; he presented the six edicts to the Parlement of Paris for registration. But he was unwilling to back his minister in the face of outraged criticism. Turgot's edicts did indeed touch upon the practices that were strangling the country, and his recommendations were preparing to overturn usages that had been in effect for centuries.

The members of the parlement were indifferent to the arguments of both humanity and economic theory, and they steadfastly reiterated their belief in the fitness of things as they were: "All public financial burdens," said one member, "should be borne by the lower orders."

The merits of Turgot's policies, combined with his undiplomatic self-confidence, were the causes of their demise and of his downfall. The intransigent Parlement of Paris refused to register the six edicts, and the king, after a brief show of energy, grew tired of the complaints of the nobility and of Turgot's rivals. In May 1776, to restore his own tranquility, he dismissed Turgot. The six edicts were forgotten and the poor continued to labor on the roads, pay most taxes, and accumulate grievances. Voltaire, the gadfly of the nation, then an old man of eighty-two, had followed Turgot's career with passionate interest. When Louis XVI removed Turgot from office, Voltaire saw in it more than the fall of a ministry. "The dismissal of this great man," he wrote, "crushes me. . . . Since that fatal day, I have not followed anything . . . and I am waiting patiently for someone to cut our throats."

There were still some years, and some further changes of ministers, before any throats were cut. Louis temporized. Some of his officials were effective and imaginative administrators: the army, the navy, the church, the Protestants all felt the breath of reform. But reform, where it was not too late, was too little. Essentially uninterested in government, Louis XVI hoped for some magical solution, some sleight of hand that would set all to rights and permit him to pursue, untroubled, his regular pleasures. The minister he chose to perform this miracle was the Swiss banker Jacques Necker, who arrived accompanied by a dazzling reputation as a financial wizard. He assumed the post of director general of finances at the moment when these finances were undergoing particular strain; French support for the American Revolution was placing intolerable burdens on insufficient revenue. The cost of this support was borne by a shaky financial pyramid constructed by borrowing funds for capital outlay and then further borrowing to pay interest on the earlier loans. By the end of hostilities in America in 1781, the French government had accumulated a national debt of 3400 million livres. During Necker's ministry expenditures were outrunning income at the rate of 80 million livres a year; the gap continued to grow until by 1786 it had reached 110 million.

After five years in office, Necker showed his verbal, if not his financial brilliance in a lengthy account of his stewardship, the Compte Rendu of 1781, which glossed over the essential structural difficulties of French finances. In his accounting he chose to treat the war debt as an emergency expenditure to be reckoned apart from the regular finances of the country. He could assure the nation, therefore, that there was actually a "normal" annual surplus of some 10 million livres. Having offered this improbable explanation of his "success," his next act of magic was to resign before he could be dismissed.

The most remarkable among Necker's successors was Charles Alexandre de Calonne, an energetic administrator who had gathered valuable experience as intendant at Lille. He was appointed controller general in 1783 and undertook boldly to attack privilege, the disease of the French state, at its source. He proposed to abolish the *corvée*, reduce the salt tax, increase the stamp tax, and above all, replace the inequitable *taille* with a land tax that would finally tap the rich as well as the poor. Calonne was enough of a statesman to know that such measures could succeed only with the consent of the prospective victims. He decided therefore to bypass the parlements and obtained Louis' agreement to convene an Assembly of Notables, a body that had last met a hundred and sixty years before. It met in February 1787. The Assembly was composed of prominent clerics, noblemen, important land-owners, and officers of state. Here was a splendid chance—it turned out to be the last—for the privileged orders to surrender or reduce their privileges voluntarily, as an act of disinterested statesmanship. But once convened, the Assembly developed a surprising independence of spirit; it refused to ratify Calonne's proposals with the docility he had hoped for. And so, intimidated by Calonne's enemies, including Necker and the queen's entourage, the king let Calonne go.

Louis XVI's weakness had left him in the indefensible position of asking as a favor what he might have demanded as a right. The aristocracy responded by reasserting its prerogatives, notable its right to be exempt from taxation. The leader of the opposition to Calonne in the Assembly, Loménie de Brienne, archbishop of Toulouse, succeeded Calonne. Having unseated a minister and rejected his program, the Assembly retired, but Calonne's proposal for a land tax survived his disgrace. Brienne, compelled to advocate what he had helped to defeat, carried it to the Parlement of Paris. This august body found the proposal no less distasteful than the Assembly of Notables; in an attempt to evade the issue, it argued that such a tax could only be approved by the Estates General, an advisory body representative of the three estates of the realm. Instead of raising money, the Assembly of Notables had triggered widespread expressions of dissatisfaction with the crown; and it was used by the provincial parlements to affirm their independence. From April 1787, when Brienne became minister, until August 1788, when he resigned, he struggled with an increasingly intransigent aristocracy who were closing ranks against absolutism. Abusive pamphlets, offensive declarations of rights, and open disobedience became endemic. Having consistently yielded to the privileged, the government now found itself with a virtual revolt of the privileged on its hands.

This "aristocratic revolution" came at a time when the French state was on the verge of bankruptcy. In a desperate move to find money in the face of an uproar across the country and to restablish harmony—the aristocracy refusing to be taxed, the church refusing to make satisfactory *dons gratuits* to the treasury, and parlements aggressively declaiming against "tyranny"—the king was forced at last into motion. Among Brienne's last acts as minister, he agreed to convene the Estates General for May 1, 1789. Necker, the popular miracle-worker whom Louis XVI had reluctantly recalled to office in August, acceded. The king piously hoped to see the meeting of the three estates as an "assembly of a great family headed by a common father," organized with "essential proportion and harmony in the composition of the three orders." The French Revolution had many causes—loss of respect for the crown, resistance of the privileged, long-range economic decline in the face of population increase, high bread prices in critical moments. But among these causes, the very calling of the Estates General must rank high. It brought and kept together men who took ideas and determination from one another and made the revolution they had been invited to forestall.

The Emergence of the Third Estate

There are times when the tempo of events increases radically; when far-reaching, irreversible changes take place in a matter of weeks, even of days. Remote, deep causes lurk in the background, but a single day may bring the eruption of subterranean forces, long, often silently in the shaping. The French Revolution was such a time—a time of dramatic, revolutionary *journées*. Hence, as the pace of events quickens, the speed of the historian slows down, as he seeks to grasp, and describe, each decisive moment in its turn.

For whom did the three orders speak? How were they to conduct their business? These proved to be pivotal questions, and their discussion began long before the assembly convened. Since the Estates had last been convoked under Louis XIII in 1614, Louis XVI appealed to the learned of the nation to advise him on procedure. His request unloosed such a flood of pamphlets that the censorship office was swamped and in a significant retreat from authority abandoned censorship altogether. Doubtless the most lasting of this literature was *What Is the Third Estate?* by the supple and ubiquitous Abbé Sieyès, published in January 1789. The very title of Sieyès' pamphlet framed the question over which the first revolutionary struggle would be fought. In phrases as memorable as the catechism, Sieyès answered his own question: "1st. What is the third estate? Everything. 2nd. What has it been up to now in the political order? Nothing. 3rd. What does it demand? To become something in it."

By its nature, he said, the third estate contains "within itself all that is necessary to constitute a complete nation." If the "privileged orders were abolished," he continued, somewhat ominously, "the nation would be not something less but something more." The third estate, he reminded his readers, "represents twenty-five million persons and deliberates on the interests of the nation. The two others . . . have the powers of only 200,000 individuals and think only of their privileges."[2] Sieyès' threatening pamphlet sharpened a

---

[2] The best modern estimates of the composition of the three estates differ only slightly from those of Abbé Sieyès: the clergy or first estate numbered about one hundred thirty thousand; the nobility or second estate four hundred thousand. The third estate, twenty-six million strong, thus accounted for 98 percent of the population.

debate that clarified the conflicts dividing French society. The previous September the Parlement of Paris had decreed that the Estates should vote, as in 1614, by order. With one stroke, the magistrates stood unmasked as the spokesmen of privilege. By their stubborn, self-interested resistance to reform, the privileged orders had compelled the king to convene the Estates General. Now, if the three orders were to vote separately the third estate would obviously be outvoted two to one every time, and the rule of privilege would be saddled on France, perhaps forever. As critical pamphleteers did not fail to point out, even if the voting was to be *par tête,* with each delegate casting one vote in a joint session, the third estate needed to double its allotted representation to equal the other two. In late December 1788 the royal council, acting on Necker's proposal, agreed to the "doubling of the Third"; in the end, the third estate elected 610 representatives, the nobles 291, and the clergy 300. The mode of voting remained in the air, but the third estate had scored its first triumph. *What Is the Third Estate?* did not make, it consolidated, that triumph. It is essential to recognize that the third had not secured its victory alone: the leading propagandists at this early stage were liberal nobles and priests, touched by the doctrines of the Enlightenment, even more than discontented bourgeois.

The election of the 610 representatives of the third estate proceeded by a cumbersome indirect process which did not, however, winnow out local grievances. At each level the deputies were sent on with a statement of the needs of the local population. These *cahiers,* of which twenty thousand survive, took the form of addresses to the king beginning with expressions of loyalty and continuing with particular complaints. Taking advantage of this unusual opportunity for a hearing, the writers of the *cahiers* freely voiced political or philosophical theories, sometimes genuinely representative of a district, often reflecting the ideas of a profession, of a special interest, or of the author himself. As usual, the very poor, the most inarticulate, had few spokesmen.

In addition to the expected chronic complaints about taxation, the *cahiers* offered a rich expression of the prevailing desire for a radical reform of the government. The *cahiers* of the third estate called for nothing less than a recognition that authority had shifted from the king to the people. For three decades or more, the parlements had been swamping the nation with constitutionalist, even democratic rhetoric; it was now employed by other men, in a better cause. The vows of loyalty were accompanied by reiterated demands for the abolition of "feudal" dues, an end to the special status that privilege conferred, and a guarantee of the civil rights of the individual. This meant, in addition to freedom of the press, protection from arbitrary arrest at the pleasure of the king or his ministers using *lettres de cachet.* In sum, the *cahiers* of the third estate asked for the transformation of the absolute into a constitutional monarchy. The *cahiers* of the nobility and clergy were equally representative. While the aristocrats also desired a legislative assembly with a voice in taxation, their main concern was to preserve traditional privileges to as great a degree as possible. At the same time, therefore, that they seemed to be accepting a constitutional monarchy, some *cahiers* of the nobility called for the appointment of official genealogists in each province to investigate and clear noble titles. The *cahiers* of the clergy were defensive: they demanded perpetuation of control over the extensive properties of the church and of its traditional authority over education and the registration of births and deaths. Not unexpectedly, they took a conservative—which is to say, dim—view of the widespread demand for greater freedom of the press.

After months of preliminaries—meetings, elections, drafting sessions for the *cahiers*—the Estates General of France convened at Versailles on May 4, 1789, with all the pageantry of a regime accustomed to splendor. The very opening ceremonies, however, were symptomatic of the troubles that had brought the deputies together—the attachment of the king to hierarchy and privilege, his evident indifference to the national interest. The France of the Old Regime was a status-conscious society. Money and ability mattered; birth mattered more. Precisely in the century in which bourgeois—lawyers, physicians, merchants, manufacturers, civil servants—increased their wealth, acquired new self-confidence, and thought of themselves, not without justice, as doing the nation's business, they found themselves subject to certain taxes from which the nobility was exempt, excluded from high posts they knew they could fill, and snubbed at court or in select social circles. The "aristocratic revolt" of the 1780s was a closing-in upon itself of a caste in danger; resentful bourgeois took this defensiveness as aggression. Now, in the ceremonies of May 4, the delegates of the third estate were being gratuitously exposed to indignities they had no intention of swallowing. They were dressed in plain black—as distinct from the gorgeous plumage of the first and second estates—compelled by ancient ceremonial to remain bareheaded when the privileged orders put on their hats, compelled even to enter the hall by a side door while the others entered in front.

With the verification of the deputies' credentials, the question of status merged into the question of power. The nobility saw no difficulty; they convened separately, formally registered their deputies, and on May 11 declared their estate to be officially constituted. The clergy, heavily represented by village *curés* with radical leanings, proceeded more cautiously by beginning a roll call but keeping open a line of discussion with the third estate. The commons, for their part, were tenacious. Their world was not the world of the Bourbons based on ceremony and adherence to medieval ideas of kingship. The revolution in America for which France had paid so dearly, the ideas of the philosophes which had been fermenting legally and illegally for half a century, the sympathies of radical clerics and aristocrats, had created a new temper and a new set of expectations. The deputies of the third estate were men of education and standing: half were lawyers, and the rest were largely professional men, merchants, and officials. They proposed to use the convocation of the three orders to create an Estates General that spoke for the nation. The issue of credentials, therefore, became critical. While the clergy temporized, the commons met for six consecutive weeks and waited to have their claims recognized.

This long period of calculated resistance heightened tempers; at the same time it gave the members of the third estate an opportunity to develop esprit de corps and find leaders, and time to deliberate as a body on their course of action. Abbé Sieyès, deputy from Paris, was once again the catalyst. On June 10, he proposed that the third estate meet to verify not only its own credentials but also the credentials of those members of the other orders who wished to be counted as "representatives of the French nation." On June 13, as the roll call continued, the impasse was broken when three members of the clergy came over to sit with the third estate. In the next three days, sixteen more clergymen appeared and, intoxicated by a sense of precedent-breaking significance, the third estate, on June 17, concluded its verification by proclaiming itself the National Assembly.

Even Louis XVI could not ignore so bold an action; although in mourning for the dauphin who had died two weeks earlier, he emerged to summon a second convocation of the Estates General for June 22, in the very hall which the third estate was then using. The deputies did not receive this announcement in time to forestall their next meeting which had been set for June 20. They arrived in a heavy rain to find the hall closed and stood around angrily until their president, the distinguished astronomer Bailly, led them to a nearby indoor tennis court. Outraged by an affront that seemed to presage their dismissal, the assembled deputies reaffirmed their function as representatives of the nation. In an emotional meeting, they swore, "to go on meeting whatever circumstances may dictate until the constitution of the realm is set up and consolidated on firm foundations." June 20, the day of the Tennis Court Oath, marks the emergence of a new power that set itself up firmly as a counterweight to privilege, royalty, and tradition.

The king's response to this extraordinary declaration was characteristic: he seemed to yield while insisting all the while on the old ways. By June 23, when the Estates General met again, two archbishops and one hundred fifty other clerical deputies had joined the third estate, and two days later, nearly fifty liberal nobles came over. The separation of orders had become obsolete. Louis obstinately continued to insist on that separation in procedural matters and in all questions touching on the personal rights of the privileged classes; he dismissed the joint assembly to their separate deliberation. It was a stupid, and in the long run fatal, move. Amid vehement protestations, the commons refused to move despite a hint of force. Bailly spoke for their new-found determination: "No one can give orders to the assembled nation." Finally alerted to this defiance, Louis decided by June 27 that it was prudent to order the three orders to meet jointly. Of the 1201 deputies, only 371 abstained from the meetings, and emboldened by such numbers the deputies set to work, appointed a constitutional committee, appropriately adopted the title of

National Constituent Assembly, and addressed themselves to "the regeneration of France."

Bastille Day: The Intervention of Paris

Despite their brave words the deputies had cause for apprehension. The king, in the sly way of a weak man, called up troops to help shore up his authority. As the Assembly began to meet, the king secretly ordered up six regiments to Versailles and stationed another ten in the outskirts of Paris. The court factions ready to use force against the third estate were gaining the upper hand. On July 11 Necker was dismissed, and baron de Breteuil, the queen's favorite, succeeded him.

The king had read the mood of Paris correctly. Economic hardship, reflected in the rising cost of bread in Paris, was compounded as hungry refugees from the countryside flocked to the city seeking work and food. The parliamentary activity in the manicured parks of Versailles found a powerful echo in the streets of Paris. The *menu peuple* of the capital—the small craftsmen, journeymen, day laborers, domestics—became the new center of national agitation. The overturn of the traditional order of things had begun with the aristocrats' repudiation of their responsibility at the Assembly of Notables. A loose confederation of lawyers, public servants, radical nobles, and priests then took the lead with their parliamentary demands at the convocation of the Estates General. Now the working men—and women—of Paris moved to express their indignation. "The patricians," said Chateaubriand succinctly, "began the revolution; the plebeians completed it." The patricians began it, one must add, both by their resistance to, and pressure for, change.

In April 1789, before the Estates General had convened, Paris had been the scene of a sizable riot, directed against the wealthy wallpaper manufacturer, Réveillon. It was followed in succeeding months by other riots. These street actions, with their raids on food shops and bakeries, were less political demonstrations than simple, violent searches for food. The price of a standard four-pound loaf of bread had risen to fourteen and a half sous, nearly twice the usual price of eight to nine sous. This was a desperately serious matter; 1789 was not the first time, and would not be the last, that the price of bread would trigger popular unrest. In normal times, a French worker laid out about half of his income on bread for himself and his family; when the price of this, his staple food, rose above ten or even twelve sous, practically all he earned must go for bread. In practice, this was destitution; in the winter, it meant being hopelessly cold; at all times, it meant going hungry.[3] By mid-July tempers were as high as the price of bread. Rumors inflated the numbers of troops Louis had ordered up to the Champ de Mars, and the demonstrable presence of armed men added

[3] See George Rudé, *The Crowd in the French Revolution* (1959), 21, 43.

to the news of Necker's fall aggravated the anxiety of Parisians who now sought arms as well as bread. Every night thousands of people gathered at the Palais Royale to listen to orators like Camille Desmoulins, who formulated popular demands in inflammatory slogans. Words were soon accompanied by actions; shops of armorers and gunsmiths were broken into and arms removed. Forty of the fifty-four customs posts that ringed the city were burned down, only partly as a protest against duties that raised prices on food, firewood, and livestock. Their symbolic significance was even more important at that moment: they stood as a barrier to the free entry of arms and persons into the city.

By the morning of July 13, the electors of Paris who had sent the deputies to the Estates General formed a committee to govern the city. They also sought to balance the indiscriminate demand for arms by establishing an official citizen's militia. The momentum of popular agitation, however, outran even this aggressive program. Crowds closed in on the Hôtel de Ville—the city hall—demanding and getting arms, and in the early morning of July 14, they plundered the Invalides. Then they marched on the Bastille. This old fortress, which held a paltry seven prisoners, was reported to be well armed and manned and ready to fire into the buildings around it.

At first the crowd of some eight hundred persons—mostly small merchants, craftsmen, and workmen—wanted only to negotiate for the gunpowder stored in the Bastille. Then the citizen's militia arrived. After several hours of confused palaver the governor of the fortress, de Launay, grew nervous as the besiegers lowered the outer drawbridge. He ordered his men to fire their cannon; ninety-eight persons in the courtyard were killed and some seventy wounded. The crowd outside brought up more arms and men and penetrated the inner courtyard. The governor then surrendered, and the citizens of Paris surged into the Bastille, taking the troops prisoner. De Launay himself was murdered on the way to the Hôtel de Ville.

The political consequences of the storming of this antique fortress far outran its military significance. In Paris the committee of electors appointed a council to govern the city, named Bailly mayor, and the marquis de Lafayette, a popular figure since his participation in the American Revolution, commander of the citizen's militia, the National Guard. Within three days the king decided that it would be prudent to acknowledge the new city council as the official government of Paris. He then ordered his mercenaries to decamp, recalled Necker, and on July 17 himself came to Paris to receive the national cockade with the colors of the Revolution: the white of the house of Bourbon ringed by the red and blue for the city of Paris. These events gave the National Assembly new, much-needed strength. The *menu peuple* of Paris had saved their "betters" at Versailles. By August, only two months after the Estates General had convened, the locus of authority had been irrevocably moved from the king to the representatives of the nation. July 14, Bastille Day, remains a memorable day in European history.

Great Fear and Great Expectations

The scarcity of grain had had its effect outside restless Paris as well. Wandering, penniless men and women roamed the countryside in search of bread. Just as the bread riots in Paris had brought the respectable bourgeoisie into action, so in the country the bands of famished poor sent the small property-owning peasants into a panic. Their feeling, which rose to a paroxysm during the summer, sprang from their apprehension that the roving bands were actually the instruments of an aristocratic plot to seize their holdings. These suspicions were built upon an old and settled conviction that the high price of bread and the grain shortages were directly caused by the hoarding and the manipulation of supplies by the aristocrats. The farmers' response was to arm themselves. But once armed and organized, in many regions they broke into the châteaux, less to pillage than to seize and destroy the ancient feudal records that spelled out the terms of their indebtedness and their onerous obligations. This infectious hysteria was *la grande peur*—the Great Fear.

By early August the aristocrats in the Assembly at Versailles were beginning to feel the discomfort attendant upon so much attention to their affairs. They heard of rioting in the cities and attacks upon the châteaux in the country; open defiance of authority—refusal to pay taxes, shooting of protected game, and the seizure of cultivated land—seemed ubiquitous. On July 27, 1789, as these alarming accounts were circulating widely, the constitutional committee presented to the Assembly its draft of the Declaration of the Rights of Man and Citizen, and opened the floor to debate. Then, on August 4, one deputy introduced a resolution to enforce the payment of dues and taxes. A number of aristocrats who had been meeting privately used this as an opportunity to make a dramatic counterproposal. Beginning with the viscount de Noailles and continuing with aristocrats from a variety of regions and ranks, one after another—noble deputies and propertied commoners—rose to renounce their privileges and prerogatives. Cynical historians have sought the source of this moving exhibition in the desire for self-preservation: by giving up what they could no longer hold, the privileged deputies hoped to keep the rest. Whatever the reason, by the time the meeting adjourned in the early hours of the morning, French society had been dramatically transformed, at least on paper. The principal target had been the remnants of feudal privilege: serfdom was abolished, as were all forms of personal obligation. True, the peasants who now became owners of the land they tilled, were required to make redemption payments to their former lords, but the events of the succeeding years made these payments unnecessary. Hunting preserves were abolished, as were tax exemptions. The church was not spared either: its tithes and ecclesiastical dues were cut off. This orgy of renunciation went on until August 11, and although a nation and its economic institutions cannot be transformed overnight, officially at least privilege as the basis of a social order had been legislated out of existence; all offices were declared open to free competition based solely on ability, not rank.

Against this background, the Declaration of the Rights of Man and Citizen could only be received with fervent enthusiasm. A spare, almost laconic document of no more than two thousand words, it was saturated with the ideas and the rhetoric of the Enlightenment, and obviously in debt to Jefferson's Declaration of Independence. It broke completely with the tradition that entrusted government to God's anointed and held the state to be a sacred institution. "Men," declared the first article, "are born, and remain, free and equal in rights." The function of the state is to guarantee the inalienable freedoms with which man is born—freedom of thought, freedom of religion, freedom from arbitrary arrest, freedom from taxation imposed without the consent of the governed. Law is the expression, not of the divine, but of the general, will. In essence, the "source of all sovereignty resides in the nation." Disseminated throughout France by the hundreds of thousands, it was posted up for the literate and read aloud to the illiterate; promptly translated into many languages and carried into every corner of Europe and beyond, it stimulated and strengthened ideas that had been fermenting for a century. From its very beginning, the French Revolution was for export.

THE RADICALIZATION OF
THE REVOLUTION: 1789-1793

From Absolutism to Constitutionalism

In the four months between May and August 1789 France was transformed, with the hesitant consent of the king himself, from an absolute to a constitutional monarchy. Louis XVI had demonstrated his symbolic acceptance of this revolution when he went to Paris in July to put on the revolutionary cockade—a shocking act that agitated the crowned heads of Europe as much as the French aristocracy. French aristocrats turned students of politics overnight, calculating the direction of the new government. Since between July and August 1789, some twenty thousand passports were issued, it seems plain that a sizable number of Frenchmen decided to study French affairs in the quiet of some spa abroad. One of the king's brothers, the count d'Artois, was among the first to flee; among those who followed him were not only aristocrats, but also craftsmen in the luxury trades who saw their livelihood disappearing across the borders in the silk clad persons of their patrons.[4] The émigrés, like the

---

[4] According to the best estimates, some one hundred twenty-five thousand emigrated in the course of the revolution. About 25 percent of this number were clerics; 20 percent peasants; only 17 percent nobility. Some working men, and even some members of the Constituent Assembly, disgusted with the radicalization of the revolution and the growing influence of the "mob," eventually emigrated as well. D'Artois' older brother, the count de Provence and later King Louis XVIII, fled in June 1791. See Donald M. Greer, *The Incidence of the Emigration During the French Revolution* (1951).

displaced of every period, clustered together in colonies—in Brussels, in Turin, and particularly in the little German principalities of the Rhineland along the French border. The count d'Artois and his party were untiring in their agitation to win the sympathy of Europe's rulers for the French king and in their attempt to strengthen Louis' resistance to any further encroachment on his powers. The American Revolution had already provided Europe with one object lesson; the French émigrés in the fashionable centers of Europe now increased the sense of alarm among supporters of the old order. Louis XVI's half-hearted acceptance of the Revolution meant either that he was playing for time or that he had resigned himself to the new order. In either case, monarchists everywhere should come to the support of d'Artois to bring about a proper restoration of the Bourbons to the throne of France.

The king was, indeed, besieged in Versailles—as much from within the walls, by the queen and her party of intransigents, as from without by the demands of the Assembly and the people of Paris. The possession of the king's very person was to all parties a symbol of success. While the goals of the revolution remained indistinct, the elimination of the king was not yet among them; on the contrary, the populace of Paris as earnestly desired him to join them as the aristocrats wanted him to flee abroad. By autumn 1789 the king was no longer so complaisant as he had been in mid-July. In the intervening months he had refused to approve the Declaration of the Rights of Man, refused to recognize the abolition of privileges following the renunciations of August 4, and quarrelled with the Assembly over his future veto power. While the Assembly wrangled over the place of the king and the shape of the legislature in the proposed constitution, a harvest at once late and poor was causing a shortage of flour. By mid-September Paris was in ferment. Even in normal times, a bread shortage was a serious affair, and these were not normal times. The municipality fixed a price of twelve sous for the four-pound loaf and maintained it by stationing guards at the bakeries. Crowds of women waiting at the bakeshops, already angry and hungry, were further inflamed by reports of insults offered the revolution by the queen and king in Versailles. Early on October 5, some seven thousand women armed themselves and marched off to Versailles, accompanied by agitators. Their single explicit grievance was the price of bread; their aim, as they marched, became clear: to bring "their" king to Paris.

At first, Louis XVI thought it enough to promise the crowd bread. After the queen's bedchamber was invaded toward morning and several of the royal bodyguard were killed, he decided to yield to the women's demand. On October 6 he permitted himself and his family to be escorted to Paris. The Assembly followed of its own accord ten days later. Under these painful circumstances the king ratified all the decrees of the Assembly to which he had previously refused his assent. At the same time he sent secret dispatches to his brother monarchs in Vienna and Madrid repudiating his apparent acquiescence in the changes taking place in France. His fatal policy of duplicity had begun.

The move to Paris brought Louis to the people and brought the people into politics. Where politics had before been the preserve of the deputies in either formal or informal meetings, once in Paris the business of the Assembly became the business of the man in the street. Parisians attended the meetings either as spectators or as members; in either case they lived with politics close at hand. The chief instruments of popular politics outside the meeting hall of the Assembly were the new political clubs. The most influential of these, the Society of the Friends of the Constitution, had its start as an informal group of prosperous Breton deputies who had begun to meet even before the Estates General convened. When the Assembly moved to Paris they continued their meetings, using the quarters of an old Jacobin monastery, from which their popular name derived. The original Jacobins gradually broadened their appeal by lowering club dues and establishing a network of branches across the country. By December 1790 its membership had reached a thousand. Although the Jacobin Club dominated political discussion in Paris—it formed in effect an unofficial caucus of the Assembly—it had no monopoly. The less exclusive Cordeliers,[5] appealing to workmen and shopkeepers, became the forum of the disaffected where they could give voice to their complaints against the work of the Assembly. With the king under its eye, the Constituent Assembly now addressed itself to its ostensible purpose—the making of a constitution—and to the pressing problems of restoring order and raising money. Its business was too serious not to create factions: revolutions, the offspring of fissions, produce fissions of their own. Those deputies content with the changes made so far— the Anglomaniacs—urged France to imitate the aristocratic English constitution, with its royal veto and its House of Lords. But in September, their adversaries, the radical Patriots—these radicals of 1789 were to become the reactionaries of 1792—induced the Assembly to limit the French king to a suspensive veto, which could delay but not annul legislation, and to establish a single-chamber parliament. France had come a long stretch from a society of distinct orders.

At the same time, the deputies, for all their egalitarian oratory, knew that while men are equal in rights, they are not equal in status. The Declaration of the Rights of Man had insisted on the sanctity of property. A majority in the Constituent Assembly had no intention of placing so sacred a thing as property at the mercy of the profane. The issue of the franchise thus confronted the new men of power with a serious dilemma. The deputies fervently believed in the sovereignty of the people, but, for the most part respectable property owners and well-educated professional men, they had seen, with their own eyes, the utter dependence of servants, the helpless illiteracy of peasants, the violent temper of the unemployed. To include these in the political public seemed

---

[5] Like the Jacobins the Cordelier Club took its popular name from the monastery in which it met—this one Franciscan. Its sonorous official title was Society of the Friends of the Rights of Man and of the Citizen.

sentimentality driven to the point of madness. It was Sieyès—always at hand with the right word—who rescued the deputies from their quandary and satisfied ideals and reality at the same time: he proposed a fundamental distinction between "passive" and "active" citizens. All citizens would enjoy the equal protection of the law, but only active citizens—males of twenty-five who paid direct taxes equivalent to three days' wages every year—could vote. This was a generous franchise; it included over four million adult Frenchmen, three out of every five. These active citizens in turn were to vote for electors whose property qualification was rather higher. Though on paper the franchise remained wide, actually the government of France was not in the hands of the potential electors but of those who could afford to serve in the electoral assemblies which chose both the local and the national legislature. This meant a minority of Frenchmen, about fifty thousand, who acted as electors in these opening years of the Revolution. To radical critics, the new France appeared to be a plutocracy speaking in the name of democracy. Maximilien Robespierre, deputy from Arras, who was acquiring a reputation for his speeches in behalf of democracy, vehemently objected to these electoral arrangements in the Assembly; Jean Paul Marat, a popular Parisian journalist with a flair for name-calling, denounced the proposed franchise as establishing an "aristocracy of wealth."[6]

The Civil Constitution of the Clergy

The succession of dramatic events from May onward and the pervasive uncertainty over the powers still remaining with the king and his ministers had produced a collapse in authority. Taxes were virtually uncollectable. But, however visionary the plans of the deputies and orators in Paris, day-to-day government operations had to be carried on, soldiers and judges and interest paid. The church, with its rich lands and far-flung properties, seemed an inexhaustible source of desperately needed revenue. Acting on the accumulated grievances of centuries, the deputies saw solvency ahead, with the old injustices set right at the same time. By no means all French ecclesiastics were hostile to state intervention in church affairs: to the lower clergy, a guaranteed salary seemed pure gain; to most clerics, steeped as they were in the Gallican tradition, a certain degree of independence from Rome seemed no threat. In fact, it was the bishop of Autun, Talleyrand, who on October 10, proposed the nationalization of the church lands. The proposal became law in November, and on December 19 church lands valued at four hundred million livres were put up for sale. In expectation of new revenue arising from the sales, the Constituent Assembly at the same time issued a mortgage bond, the *assignat,*

---

[6] See Alfred Cobban, *A History of Modern France,* vol. I, *The Old Regime and the Revolution, 1715–1799* (1957), 164, and L. G. Wickham Legg, *Select Documents Illustrative of the History of the French Revolution,* vol. I (1905), 170–175. The epithet hardly seems violent, but it must be remembered that the term "aristocrat" was acquiring some rather powerful connotations.

designed to pay the state's most exigent creditors. For some time, the value of the *assignat* held firm; in July 1790 it stood where it had stood when it was first issued—95 percent of face value. Its decline, first measured, then catastrophic, began later.

In that month, July 1790, the Assembly passed a bill that carefully redefined the relationship of church and state. This was the Civil Constitution of the Clergy. Of all the acts of the Assembly none opened such sharp divisions in the country, not only along the lines of interest but also—perhaps even more critically—along the lines of conviction. It also brought an alarmed pope into open opposition to the Revolution. In effect, the Civil Constitution made the French church into an arm of the French government. The buildings of the church became the property of the nation, its priests and bishops were to be elected by the qualified electors. The parishes and ecclesiastical districts were totally renovated. Here the Constituent Assembly had prepared the ground some months before: in December 1789, in a decisive assault on traditional loyalties and entrenched centers of power, it had destroyed France's historic divisions—its provinces, its *généralités,* its bailiwicks—and created eighty-three new rational regions, the "departments," to carry on local government. Parishes were now redesigned to conform to the new administrative units, and each department was to have one bishop, no more. This move reduced the number of bishops from one hundred thirty-five to eighty-three. These bishops, and all lower ecclesiastics, were placed on fixed salaries and under the attentive supervision of departmental authorities.

Good Catholics were torn. Many sections of the Civil Constitution seemed palatable, even statesmanlike, but the dependence of the church on the state that it decreed was far greater than the most Gallican among churchmen had foreseen. And the Assembly was decreeing the most far-reaching changes without consulting the clergy. While Louis XVI reluctantly approved the Civil Constitution in late July, resistance was open and widespread. The Assembly, seriously annoyed, made the Civil Constitution a matter of conscience; in November 1790, it insisted that each cleric swear to "uphold by every means in his power the constitution decreed by the National Assembly and accepted by the King."[7] The king, helpless, gave his assent to the oath late in December, but only seven of the bishops and less than half of the lower clergy complied. The Assembly promptly struck back: it stigmatized the holdouts as "refractory clergy" and deprived them of all clerical functions. So far, Pope Pius VI had disapproved of the Civil Constitution and the Revolution itself in private. As the division within the French clergy deepened, the pope's anxiety over the new French regime was exacerbated by upheavals in Avignon, long a papal possession where revolutionaries were pressing for reunion with France. In February 1791, Talleyrand, whom the pope had excommunicated the year before, guaranteed the apostolic succession of the constitutional clergy by

---

[7] The Civil Constitution of July, Title II, Article 21, had already exacted the same oath. The decree of November 27 simply prodded the dilatory.

consecrating new bishops. Finally, in March, Pius VI formally denounced the Civil Constitution as destructive of the Catholic religion, and the Declaration of the Rights of Man as a "shocking" establishment of unbridled "natural equality and liberty."

Every practicing Catholic in the country was drawn into the struggle. The conservative elements—women, peasants, and the pious folk of the western regions of France—sought out the refractory priests, fearing the taints of schism and excommunication that hung over the constitutional clergy. The king himself, on the first Easter after the pope had denounced the constitution, attempted to attend mass at Saint Cloud said by a refractory priest, but was held back by angry crowds. Voltaire's posthumous triumph was an ambiguous one: France was split in two.

The Road to War

Through early 1791, the divisions opened by the Civil Constitution of the Clergy renewed royalist anxieties; new contingents of the lesser nobility left the country. The king's brother in Turin, who came to be recognized as the leader of the émigrés, fervently urged European monarchs to mount a military invasion to restore the monarchy. Marie Antoinette's brother, Leopold II, now emperor (see p. 432), was regarded as a natural ally, but he refused to participate in any military adventures. The émigrés found money and support elsewhere. D'Artois moved to Coblenz to be closer to the center of preparations as plans for the attack across the Rhine advanced.

It was under these circumstances in June 1791 that the queen's party finally prevailed on the king to consider flight. It was a cumbersome scheme involving the coordination of officers and men and horses at stations along the route and depending upon the kind of timing that left little room for inevitable delays and mishaps. After a lumbering journey of twenty-four hours across France the royal party was ignominiously taken at Varennes and brought back in a slow procession to Paris. Complete with disguises, passwords, messages misunderstood, troops moved too soon or too late, couriers missing their rendezvous, a cross-country chase by a postmaster who had recognized the king, the flight had all the makings of a ludicrous comic opera. In fact it had terrible consequences. It destroyed the fiction that the king was a willing accomplice or pliant instrument of the revolution.

In the Assembly a moderate group headed by Barnave sought to save the principle of constitutional monarchy by a transparent fiction. The king's flight was described as an "abduction" and, to avoid any further difficulties during the completion of the constitution, now near, the king was temporarily suspended from office. The Assembly came to be no less than the jailer of the king. To outsiders, however, its conduct seemed timid. On July 15, the Cordeliers, headed by Danton, presented a petition to the Assembly asking that Louis be deposed and put on trial. The petition split the Jacobins, some of whom were sufficiently agitated to secede to a moderate monarchist club, the Feuillants; among them were Barnave, Bailly, and Lafayette. On July 17 at the Champ de Mars, some six thousand persons signed the Cordeliers' petition, but the demonstration turned into a massacre when the National Guard appeared. A shot rang out, the guard fired into the crowd, killing at least thirteen persons and wounding another thirty. To the Feuillants and their friends this was the preservation of order; to the radicals it became a cause for revenge—the Massacre of the Champ de Mars. Those who thought it time to stop the Revolution desperately tried to shore up the king; those who wanted to push it further began to talk of a republic.

Meanwhile, ominous news arrived from abroad. Leopold had allowed himself to be persuaded to meet with Frederick William II of Prussia to issue some statement on the French situation. Their famous Declaration of Pillnitz, issued late in August 1791, promised that the two monarchs would "not refuse to employ" the "most efficient means" of enabling Louis XVI to "establish with the most absolute freedom the foundations of a monarchical form of government." The meaninglessness of this guarantee was underlined by an escape clause, which emphasized that the signatories would only take action "if and when" all the other powers of Europe joined them—an event that Leopold, at least, did not expect to occur.

The declaration was received with greater literalness than its signatories had expected. Although Marie Antoinette, realistically enough, saw it as a betrayal, the émigrés took it as an offer of help, while the members of the Assembly chose to read it as a violent threat to the hopes of the infant Revolution. The French response to Pillnitz—aggressive rage rather than indifference or fear—was excessive, even misplaced. But it revealed the confidence with which the revolutionary leadership confronted the wrath of Europe. Indeed, undeterred by domestic division and foreign threats, the Constituent Assembly proceeded to finish the task it had assigned to itself two summers before. On September 3, it accepted the constitution; on September 14, Louis XVI obediently took his oath to it. Then, on September 30, the National Constituent Assembly dissolved. In two years, it had done an astonishing amount of demolition work. It had declared the state to be the guardian of natural rights and the servant of the sovereign people. It proposed to govern with a strong unicameral legislature, a rational, highly decentralized system of local bodies, and a hierarchical scheme of political participation that would protect the rights of all while gathering power in the hands of the qualified—that is, the propertied few. It retained the king, but dependent on annual appropriations and with only tattered remnants of his former authority. His very title—"king of the French by the grace of God and the will of the nation"—was a measure of how far France had traveled in so short a time.

Not unexpectedly, the radicalism of the new regime was circumscribed by the limited vision and the particular interests of the deputies who determined its shape. All wanted freedom, but freedom meant different things to different groups. The Constituent Assembly granted freedom to the press and the theater, full civic rights to Protestants in 1789 and (after some resistance) to Jews in 1791. But in the economic sphere the commitment to freedom and individualism resulted in the outlawing of workers' organizations. In June 1791, the Le Chapelier law forbade employers' as well as workers' associations. This destroyed, or drove underground, those rudimentary trade unions through which workers were seeking to improve their lot; it outlawed strikes as well. The enactment of such physiocratic doctrine into law was perfectly comprehensible: it opened access to all trades to everyone and definitively dissolved the encrusted gilds. Thus it clearly expressed the deputies' ideology of individualism, and their hostility to those intermediate attachments that interfered with the free individual's devotion to the common good. In 1791, it did not occur to anyone, not even the left-wing Jacobins, that this attack on special interests was in itself a form of special interest. [8]

However, when the new legislature, the Legislative Assembly, convened on October 1, 1791, the minds of the deputies were less on economic than on military matters. For the course of its short life, the Assembly was dominated by its most bellicose deputies, the Girondins, who profited from the foolish posturing and bluster of counterrevolutionaries abroad. Anything but an organized party, the Girondins were a faction of Jacobins drawn together by certain personal attachments and a degree of political agreement. Originally an informal gathering of deputies from Bordeaux, led by the silver-tongued attorney Pierre Victurnien Vergniaud, they recruited associates like the mathematician-philosophe Condorcet and the inevitable Abbé Sieyès, who were from other parts of the country. A cosmopolitan flavor was added by the adherence of a prominent Parisian hostess, Madame Roland, whose husband was a civil servant and at whose house foreign revolutionaries, including Thomas Paine, gathered to explore the future of the Revolution. The most remarkable and, from the historian's point of view, most instructive of the Girondins was Jacques Pierre Brissot. Son of a pastry cook at Chartres, Brissot had made a dubious living as a dubious political journalist; the Revolution gave him the opportunity of realizing his political schemes and personal aspirations at the same time. Only a revolutionary situation could have thrust such an ambitious mediocrity—and from a social stratum hitherto denied preferment—into a position of leadership. [9] In September, the expiring Constituent Assembly had annexed Avignon to France, thus trampling on the rights of its legal

[8] In October 1790, responding to a petition from workers in Beauvais, the spokesman of the National Assembly told the municipal officials: "The wages of workers are not within their competence, these can only be fixed by natural laws" (quoted in Alfred Cobban, *The Social Interpretation of the French Revolution* [1964], 63).

[9] Bordeaux, on the Gironde, was located in the department of the same name; hence the name of the faction. But Brissot, its best-known spokesman, after whom they were often called the Brissotins, actually sat in the Legislative Assembly for Paris. Since the Constituent Assembly had adopted, in May 1791, Robespierre's "Self-Denying Ordinance," which denied its deputies a place in the Legislative Assembly, all *its* deputies were new men. This also helps to explain, in part, Brissot's prominence.

sovereign, the papacy. In the same high-handed fashion, it had abolished the historic feudal dues owed to German princes in Alsace. Now, beginning in October, the Brissotins went beyond the provocative policy of these unilateral acts. They clamored against the émigrés, threatened unfriendly foreign monarchs that an aroused, liberty-loving French nation was ready to go to war, and preached a crusade to bring the Revolution to the world. With ingenuous naiveté, Brissot commended war as a medicine, as a surgical act. The Girondins' cry for war brought them surprising support from the government and from some of the Feuillants. The count de Narbonne, minister of war, and outside the cabinet, Lafayette, reasoned that war could only strengthen the executive; it would once again rally the nation behind the king and so restore the prestige of the monarchy. Restoration at home through aggression abroad: if the Brissotins were foolish and shallow, their conservative allies were intellectually bankrupt. Almost alone, Robespierre saw through the scheme and held firm against the rising war fever. In increasingly irritable debates with Brissot at the Jacobin Club, he argued the the émigrés posed no threat and that the Revolution's first business was at home. "No one," he said, in prophetic words, "loves an armed missionary."

Then on March 1, 1792, the queen's brother, Emperor Leopold, died, to be succeeded by his son, Francis II, who was young and eager for war. A defensive Prussian-Austrian alliance had just been concluded. The Girondins forced the Feuillant ministry out of office in March and supplanted it with their own men, including Roland. Narbonne, the advocate of war, went with them, but the dominant personality in the new cabinet, General Dumouriez, was, if anything, more bent on war than Narbonne had been, and for the same reason. Robespierre's warnings went unheard.

France declared war on Austria on April 20, 1792 ill-prepared and in a confusion of purposes: the policies officially prompting it—the liberation of Europe—were to be carried out by officers opposed to the Revolution and by ministers who hoped to use the war for the restoration of the monarchy. Dumouriez, minister of foreign affairs, an ambiguous, even sinister figure, sought to bend the situation to his personal advantage. The fears of counterrevolution which had, in part, provoked the war, had been exaggerated; Robespierre was right. But it did not take long for Prussia to join Austria, and on July 25, 1792, the two powers issued the Brunswick Manifesto, which lent plausibility to Brissot's excited pronouncements.

Ostensibly written by the duke of Brunswick, the allied commander, the document had actually been drafted in Paris, and its language had been made more virulent by émigrés. It stated the entire aim of the allied forces to be reestablishment of the rule of law and aid to Louis XVI "to exercise his legitimate authority." The manifesto warned the populace that if the royal family were harmed, "exemplary" vengeance—death and destruction—would be visited on Paris and on the "guilty rebels." The manifesto did, of course, what such threats of terror do—it redoubled revolutionary fervor and cemented the unity of the republicans. It embarrassed the men it was designed to protect, and strengthened those it was designed to frighten.

The Second Revolution

With the armies of Prussia and Austria on the frontiers of the Rhine clearly planning a march on Paris, the hardships and tensions of a country at war began to tell. As in most war emergencies, food and ordinary domestic necessities like soap and firewood became scarce and expensive. With the paper *assignats* rapidly depreciating, with the government as yet untried and unstable, with confidence in the future shaky, food became the real currency of France. While the peasants could hoard their produce and sell it, city workers with their paper money were at a disadvantage in bartering for the necessities of life. Political tensions rose and agitators flourished; yet the menace of the enemy, and the prospect of a restoration that could benefit only returning émigrés also brought mounting nationalist excitement. Troops from the provinces streamed to Paris, and local *sans-culottes* took their case against the treacherous king to the streets. The *sans-culottes* had entered French politics in July and again in October 1789; now, in the general excitement, they took an ever more active part.

The term *sans-culotte* is a social term that acquired political meaning. It referred originally to the lower, though not the lowest, orders in the cities, to men and women with modest education and modest incomes, to small shopkeepers, artisans, industrial workmen; their name literally referred to their clothing: they did not wear the *culottes,* the elegant knee-breeches. But in the course of the Revolution, *sans-culotte* became a name for politically active, generally passionate revolutionary democrats, no matter what their social origins. For them the slogan *liberté, égalité, fraternité* meant direct participation in politics, usually in endless meetings, and the translation of the new ideals into political, social, and economic reality. Now, in the early summer of 1792, they cheered the troops that marched through Paris on their way to the front, to save the country. [10]

Among these troops were recruits from Marseilles, who marched to a new song, the *Marseillaise.* With its plain denunciation of tyranny, its vivid warning against bloodthirsty foreign soldiers, its heady appeal to patriotism, the *Marseillaise* became the rallying call of the Revolution:

> Allons, enfants de la patrie,
> Le jour de gloire est arrivé,
> Contre nous, de la tyrannie,
> L'étendard sanglant est levé . . .

---

[10] By 1793, a rich, even a once-noble revolutionary could be a good *sans-culotte*. The counterpart was the all-purpose epithet "aristocrat," which came to mean, quite simply, enemy of the Revolution.

There had been sporadic demonstrations all during the early months of the war, as food grew scarcer and popular indignation at hoarders grew with the scarcity. Profiteers in goods imported from the colonies, such as sugar, felt the anger of Parisian housewives who invaded stores and warehouses to seize and resell the sugar at the "normal" price of twenty-five sous per pound instead of the three livres per pound charged by the profiteers. Meanwhile the provincial regiments, the *fédérés,* made common cause with the Parisian *sans-culottes.* The terms of the Brunswick Manifesto were known in Paris by August 1; shortly after calls for the abdication of Louis XVI swept through the city. By August 3, this demand was expressed by forty-seven of the forty-eight sections of Paris. On the next day, the representatives of the working-class sections, the Faubourg Saint-Antoine, threatened force if the Assembly did not depose the king by August 9.

In the early hours of the morning of August 10, representatives of the forty-eight sections of the city met at the Hôtel de Ville, suspended the municipal government, and declared a new administration, the Commune. With this, an alarm gun was fired and the tocsins throughout the city aroused the citizenry. A march on the Tuileries followed, and a sanguinary clash. In the encounter of twenty thousand Parisians and *fédérés* with the Swiss guards, misunderstandings and ill-timed orders exacerbated tensions, already high. In the event, eight hundred of the king's troops were killed, and the attackers lost heavily as well: some three hundred Parisians and ninety *fédérés* lay dead. In the confusion, the king and his family fled from their palace and threw themselves on the mercy of the Assembly. This was the *journée* of August 10, as decisive as the *journée* of July 14 had been three years before. As on Bastille Day, once again Paris had radically altered the course of events. The "second revolution" had begun.

On August 11, the Assembly recognized the Commune, surrendered the royal family to its custody, and called for elections to a new assembly, the Convention. The conditions for voting in the new elections were revolutionary, indeed; they abolished the old property qualifications and granted suffrage to every French male over twenty-one who was neither a dependent nor a domestic servant. With its king as prisoner, embroiled in a war with superior powers, the dying constitutional monarchy marched on a path of no return. Early in July, the country had been proclaimed in danger; late in July, Brunswick's troops had invaded French soil. As more and more Frenchmen enrolled for service in the war, the suspicion of domestic enemies assumed grotesque proportions. It was widely believed—and agitators like Danton and Marat did their utmost to foster that belief—that the prisons were full of royalists and traitors to the Revolution who were only waiting for the volunteers to leave Paris for the front to break jail and destroy the country from within. The grim harvest of this belief came in early September, with an attack upon prisons in Paris and in the provinces. In Paris around twelve hundred prisoners, nearly half its prison population, were summarily slaughtered—and only a quarter of them were priests, nobles, Swiss guards, or political enemies of the Revolution. The rest were ordinary criminals. The "September massacres" ushered in a new phase of the Revolution: the final overthrow of the king, the emergence of Paris under the Commune as the revolutionary vanguard, and the prosecution of the war not as a defensive action, but aggressively to win all Europe for the cause of liberty.

The Convention which met in Paris in September 1792 represented the mandate of one million Frenchmen compared with the fifty thousand who had voted for the deputies of the Legislative Assembly. Yet, despite the broadening of the electorate, the social composition of the Convention did not markedly differ from that of its predecessor. Of the seven hundred fifty deputies, nearly half were lawyers and the remainder were businessmen, doctors, landowners, constitutional clergy, artists, scientists, and local officials. In its three years of life, the Convention had only two members officially classified as working men. What did make the Convention representative was the strong local base of the deputies who came from small villages and returned there after their duties in the capital were over. A striking feature of the representation in the Convention was the invitation extended to distinguished foreigners—naturalized by decree—"whose writing has sapped the foundations of tyranny and prepared the road to liberty."[11]

The first meeting of the National Convention on September 20 coincided with the first French victory over the Prussians at Valmy, in northeastern France. It was an auspicious augury. The engagement was minor; the moral effect, decisive. Goethe, who was there, shrewdly described it as the opening of a new era in history. On September 21 the Convention carried by acclamation the formal proposition "that royalty be abolished in France."

The Convention met in a newly renovated hall in the Tuileries; its very physical arrangement, with its steeply banked seats, gave palpable form to the political division among the deputies. The Brissotins sat at the right in the lower tiers. The radical Jacobins sat to the left in the upper tiers—they were the men of the "Mountain," the Montagnards. The "Plain," a majority of the deputies, less noisy than the extremes, and less dogmatic, sat in the center and held the balance. The divisions in the Convention were, of course, more than physical; they represented sharpening differences among the deputies. The Girondins who had been in the vanguard in the Legislative Assembly urging the war and calling for a republic, now took a turn toward moderation; they grew fearful of mob rule. But they had called up spirits they could not exorcise. Robespierre did not permit them to turn back. Nor did the war: success abroad brought radicalization at home.

The victory at Valmy turned back the Prussian march on Paris and left the French free to take the initiative on other fronts. By October, French troops

---

[11] The decree included such famous men as George Washington, Alexander Hamilton, James Madison, Jeremy Bentham, and the great Swiss educational reformer Johann Heinrich Pestalozzi. But only Thomas Paine, elected deputy for Pas-de-Calais, actually took his seat.

under General de Custine, were in Germany, and on November 6, under General Dumouriez, they defeated the Austrians at Jemappes in the Austrian Netherlands. On November 14, they entered Brussels. On November 19, the Convention, responding to the heady news from the front, enacted a sweeping decree "in the name of the French nation," promising "fraternity and aid" to "all peoples wishing to recover their liberty," and charged the government to order French generals to defend all citizens who "have been, or who might be, harassed for the cause of liberty." [12] On December 15, it followed up this November decree by ordering its generals upon occupying an area to proclaim immediately the "sovereignty of the people, the suppression of all the established authorities," and the "abolition of the tithe, feudalism, and seigneurial rights."

While French armies were spreading justice and liberty according to their lights, the Convention in Paris was attempting to establish a permanent government. The most serious piece of unfinished business was the disposition of the king. Since August 10 he and the royal family had been shut up in a fortress in Paris. For several weeks the Convention debated his fate; hundreds of pamphlets on all sides of the question were printed at public expense and widely circulated. The struggle over the king was, for many, a struggle for power in the Convention; leading Girondins counseled delay, impatient Jacobins pressed for an immediate trial of "Louis Capet." At the end of November, an iron chest was discovered in the Tuileries filled with papers incriminating the king—plans for flight and correspondence with émigrés, refractory priests, and foreign diplomats. Brissotin resistance to a trial collapsed.

On December 3, the Convention decided on a trial and, allowing Louis' counsel ten days for preparation, heard his defense on December 26. In the midst of uproar and after vociferous debate on procedural matters, the deputies found Louis guilty without a dissenting vote and rejected a Girondist proposal for a popular referendum on the verdict by three to two. On the third question, then, by an absolute majority of one, 361 of the 721 deputies present voted for the king's immediate execution. [13] The closeness of the decision brought another vote on January 19 on a respite. It lost, 380 to 310. The Montagnards, the Left, had triumphed. On the morning of January 21, 1793, Louis XVI proclaimed his innocence from the scaffold—*"Peuple, je meurs innocent";* a few minutes later he died under that new, humane device, the guillotine.

---

[12] For the decree, see John Hall Stewart, *A Documentary Survey of the French Revolution* (1951), 381.

[13] If we examine the total vote, the figure seems a little less precarious: of 749 members, 28 were absent, 321 had voted for penalties other than death, mainly imprisonment, 26 voted for death but demanded a debate on postponing the execution, 13 voted for death on condition that there *be* a postponement, while 361 attached no conditions to their vote for death.

THE RISE AND FALL OF
REVOLUTIONARY DEMOCRACY: 1793–1795

The Revolution and the World

The irresistible dynamism of the French Revolution had made it determined enemies from the very start. Orderly change imposed from above was one thing; revolutionary change compelled from below was something else again. The Spanish government, though committed to economic and educational reform, solved the embarrassment of news from the Revolution by sealing its frontiers against France (see p. 423). The king of Sweden, Gustavus III, who had denuded the Swedish nobility of all its power, volunteered to lead a crusade against the French revolutionaries (see p. 420). And Catherine of Russia confronted events in France with mounting fear. The fall of the Bastille won her over to the counterrevolution. After the king's flight to Varennes, she, like the Spaniards, imposed censorship; in 1792, she volunteered to join Gustavus' crusade. The execution of Louis XVI made her sick and completed her conversion. She ordered the expulsion of the French ambassador, supported émigrés, and ordered Frenchmen living in Russia to swear loyalty to "Louis XVII." The Revolution led her to reject the philosophes whose ideas she had claimed to follow and whose friendship she had courted.

Inevitably, many Europeans changed their view of the French Revolution as the Revolution itself changed. Friedrich Gentz, whose name is indissolubly linked with the reactionary years after 1815, greeted its early days as mankind's long-delayed awakening; by 1791, he opposed a Revolution which, he declared, had betrayed itself. The radicalization of the Revolution in 1792 alienated other admirers. The execution of Louis XVI alienated more. William Pitt called it "the foulest and most atrocious deed which the history of the world has yet had occasion to attest." This is significant, for Pitt was no reactionary, no friend of the émigrés. Indeed, in the mid-1780s, he had been something of a reformer, in a moderate, practical way.

The younger son of the great Chatham, Pitt had become chancellor of the exchequer at the age of twenty-two. In 1784, at twenty-four, he became prime minister and, after consolidating his hold on the cabinet and Parliament, introduced proposals for parliamentary reform. His bill provided for the abolition of thirty-six rotten boroughs[14] and for the extension of the suffrage.

---

[14] These historic anomalies were grossly overrepresented districts with few voters; with the growth of industrial cities—underrepresented or not represented at all—they became a scandal.

Finding the opposition too strong, he retreated. He was more successful with the organization of imperial government in Canada and India, spectacularly so in financial and administrative affairs. He abolished sinecures and put officials on regular salaries; he reformed the excise and the customs offices; he clarified the system of taxation. His heart was always in orderly government, notably finance.

Far from being exceptional, Pitt's reform schemes were part of a European-wide movement. Since the 1760s, as we have seen, countries from Spain to Sweden had witnessed large-scale efforts at rationalizing bureaucracies, re-vamping legal systems, and reforming taxes. This was the period of assaults on privileged bodies—on Parliament in England, the parlements in France, the nobles in the Hapsburg domains, in Sweden, in Portugal; these included attempts to widen the franchise, to eliminate noble monopoly or ownership of offices, and to reduce or abolish special privileges. Most of these efforts had been the work of royal autocrats like Joseph II or Catherine II. Elsewhere, the call for reform was sounded by movements intent on winning some political power for what in France was called the third estate. There had been political unrest in Geneva in the 1760s, in America in the 1770s, in the Austrian Netherlands, the Dutch Republic, Ireland, and Poland in the 1780s. [15] Granted that the violence, the extent, and the historic import of the French Revolution were unique; but the French Revolution occurred within a larger, fostering climate.

Not surprisingly, therefore, there were many men in many countries who greeted events in France with unconcealed joy. The great slogan, *liberté, égalité, fraternité,* spoke to an international audience: the Dutch Batavian Republic, established in 1795, was to take these words for its official motto. In England, sympathetic observers noted with satisfaction that the French were finally imitating the English. Late in 1789, the well-known dissenting minister Richard Price, gifted mathematician, rationalist theologian, and reformist political thinker, delivered an address that aroused widespread comment; Price thought that the events of 1789 in France confirmed the lesson of the events of 1689 in England: the source of sovereignty, the people, could by right "cashier" its rulers for "misconduct." Charles James Fox, the great liberal politician, consistently defended the Revolution. Thomas Paine, who had encouraged the American rebels with his *Common Sense,* now, in his *Rights of Man,* eloquently defended the natural right of any people to choose its own government, freely. And in 1792, partly drawing on radical English ideas, but much heartened by the revolution in France, Thomas Hardy, a London shoemaker, founded the London Corresponding Society, which, in alliance with similar groups in the

[15] One distinguished American historian, R. R. Palmer, has grouped these efforts under the collective name of "democratic revolution." See *The Age of the Democratic Revolution: A Political History of Europe and America, 1760-1800,* 2 vols. (1959-1964), to which we are indebted in these pages.

provinces, urged radical reforms at home and reached a wider public than the gentleman-reformers of the 1780s. Those young poets whose fame belongs to the early nineteenth century—Coleridge, Wordsworth, Southey, Landor—saw the Revolution with enthusiasm. German *Aufklärer,* young and old, hailed the Revolution as the dawn of mankind. Even the elderly poet Klopstock, wishing he had "a hundred voices" to celebrate the birth of liberty, wrote an ode to the French Revolution in April 1792. Philosophers like Kant and Fichte, Schelling and Hegel saw it as a new age, the age of philosophy. These poets and philosophers spoke for wide circles in German society. In Saxony and in the Rhineland peasants rebelled in imitation of France; German cities were crowded with more or less authentic copies of French Jacobins. At the city of Mainz, Georg Forster, university librarian and cosmopolitan intellectual, formed a pro-French political club; when in October 1792, Custine occupied the city with his army, Forster and his friends welcomed the French and cheerfully collaborated with them. In the following year, the same group sought to have their land annexed to the French Republic. Elsewhere democrats, radicals, reformers took heart. Dutch "Patriots," defeated in 1787 by a combination of the Orangist oligarchy and Prussian troops, founded underground Jacobin cells at home to prepare their country for a revolution. The Italian states were honeycombed with subversive revolutionary clubs; when Bonaparte marched into Milan in May 1796 (see p. 505), the enthusiastic welcome he received proved how revolutionary the city had become in reaction to Austrian overlordship. In the Republic of Geneva, long torn by civil contention, a radical party significantly called the *égalisateurs* made a successful coup in December 1792, proclaimed civic equality for all, and produced a democratic constitution. In restless Ireland, late in 1791, the young lawyer Wolfe Tone founded the Society of United Irishmen, an association that—true to its name and contrary to earlier Irish reform movements—welcomed Catholics as well as Protestants; it rapidly spread across the island, called for parliamentary reform and for a convention—a name that, by late 1792, reminded conservatives, and was intended to remind them, of France. Most of these movements were eventually suppressed. But they testify to the vitality of the ideas that spread from revolutionary France and to the susceptibility of the thousands who adopted them.

While the Revolution had its slogans, by 1790 the counterrevolution had its Bible: Edmund Burke's eloquent *Reflections on the Revolution in France,* an emotional rejoinder to Dr. Price's notorious address. Burke's book, though melodramatic in its defense of the queen and badly misinformed on French affairs, made an impressive philosophical point: society is not a rational business organization; the social contract is a tacit agreement among the dead, the living, and those yet unborn; long-lived institutions deserve to survive simply because they have lived long; to undo the work of centuries in a year is to overestimate the power of reason and to despise the inestimable value of tradition. The September massacres in 1792 and the execution of the king in

January 1793 seemed to confirm Burke's passionate diagnosis. Early supporters dropped away. The English poets were exceptional. Wordsworth, who had been in Paris during the September massacres, defended the establishment of the republic and the execution of Louis XVI. There were some who saw the years of terror, 1793-1794, not as essential to an evil, but as accidental to a good, thing.

Political Struggles and Civil War

In France, the execution of the king solved nothing. The way a deputy had voted on the king's fate became a political test in the acrimonious days and months that followed. It was not a wholly dependable test: the most prominent Brissotins, including Vergniaud and Brissot himself, who had voted in favor of the death sentence were now, for their earlier delaying tactics, stigmatized as "moderates"—a new word of abuse that the Montagnards used to great effect. Gutter journalists, club orators, ambitious politicians freely threw epithets like "traitor," "counterrevolutionary," "English agent" at fellow revolutionaries they disliked or distrusted. Politics became a matter of name-calling, of appeal to the streets, of outright violence. Anxiety and rage were terrible simplifiers; in May 1793, Robespierre put it very plainly: "There are now only two parties in France, the people and the enemies of the people." [16]

In retrospect, the political struggles of early 1793 came to look like a contest between two gigantic monoliths—Montagnards against Girondins. Actually, the political factions were shifting and relatively small; even on sensitive questions of economic policy, Vergniaud and Robespierre sometimes made common cause.

As usual, military reverses sharpened political animosities. The young republic had proved extraordinarily aggressive; foreign statesmen had been right to find the resolutions of the previous November and December (see p. 483) distasteful and frightening. In November, the Convention had annexed Savoy; French forces followed up their occupation of Belgium by systematically looting it and by applying revolutionary decrees in the occupied territory. In mid-November, the French had declared the Scheldt open to shipping, in clear violation of the international settlement of 1648 (see p. 254). England promptly promised the Dutch aid in case of French attack. On January 31, in an important speech, Danton called for the annexation of Belgium and justified his demand by the doctrine of "natural frontiers": France, he said, was defined by the Atlantic, the Alps, and the Rhine. The next day, Pitt voiced his indignation at France's unilateral actions: "England," he said, "will never consent that France shall arrogate the power of annulling at her pleasure and under pretence of a natural right of which she makes herself the only judge, the political system of

[16] Quoted in M. J. Sydenham, *The French Revolution* (1965), 155.

Europe, established by solemn treaties and guaranteed by the consent of all powers." On the same day, doubtless saving Pitt the trouble, France declared war on England and the Dutch Republic; war on Spain followed soon after, on March 7. Within a short time, Pitt had organized an impressive-sounding coalition against the revolutionary republic; it included France's current enemies Prussia and Austria, as well as Spain, the Dutch Republic, Russia, Sardinia, and, of course, Britain.

The precarious situation of France was made more precarious by the defection of General Dumouriez. Here was the kind of treachery that orators were always declaiming about. Once he had swept through Belgium, the Convention ordered him to move north. But the conquest of Belgium was by no means secure; by March 1, as Dumouriez advanced on the Dutch, the Belgians, incensed by the plunder of their churches, rebelled against their new masters. Within a few weeks, the Austrians had capitalized on this uprising; on March 18, at Neerwinden, and again at Louvain on March 21, they forced the French to retreat and to evacuate Belgium. Later that month, Dumouriez, anti-Jacobin at heart and appalled by the execution of Louis XVI, listened to Austrian overtures and offered to restore the constitutional monarchy under "Louis XVII." But he could not persuade his troops to join him in a march on Paris, and on April 5, followed by a few staff officers, he deserted to the Austrians. Thrown back to their own territory, the French at last made a stand at Valenciennes, while in the east, French troops fell back under pressure from the Prussians. The unconquerable revolutionary forces of the previous fall had become vulnerable armies in the spring. The Revolution was in danger; it was rescued, at least in part, by the greed, the callousness, the myopia of its enemies. Shortly after the execution of Louis XVI, the count de Provence wrote to the count d'Artois, reported their brother's death, and added that the dauphin was not likely to survive him long. "Whilst you shed tears, for those near to us," he said, "you must not forget how useful their deaths will be for the country. Comfort yourself with this idea and reflect that your son is, after myself, the heir and hope of the monarchy."[17] From such unteachable Bourbons the new regime, shaky as it was, had little to fear. Even more helpful was the preoccupation of three of the allies—Austria, Prussia, and Russia— with another partition, the second, of Poland. It came after a brave and highly effective effort on the part of Polish reformers to govern themselves more rationally than before: in 1791, under the leadership of their king, Stanislas Poniatowski, they adopted a constitution which abolished the *liberum veto,* made the kingship hereditary, and gave it adequate executive powers. In May of 1792, her hands freed after making peace with the Turks, Catherine of Russia invaded Poland to keep the old constitution, and thus her hegemony, intact. Partition was only a matter of time. Prussia insisted on its share, Austria, eager

[17] Quoted in J. M. Thompson, *The French Revolution* (2nd ed., 1944), 334. Thompson comments: "How these Bourbons loved one another!"

as ever, was this time kept from the trough. In January 1793 the unhappy Poles bowed to the inevitable: Russia grabbed most of the western Ukraine and most of Lithuania; Prussia grabbed Danzig, Thorn, and Great Poland. A third partition in October 1795, with Austria again a partner, would sweep Poland away. Fighting France took second place to the passion for Polish land.

Still, the Convention had good grounds for anxiety. It called for volunteers and, late in February, for three hundred thousand troops. In the far west, in the region of the Vendée, hilly, rural, deeply pious, the draft call triggered an armed rising, which by March 15 amounted to a full-fledged rebellion. And in Paris scarcity of essentials, rumors of hoarding, and the reality of high prices brought, late in February, direct action: enraged *sans-culottes* stormed the shops and terrorized their owners into selling staples at the old, low price. As the spring went on, politics in the Convention increasingly reflected pressures from the outside. This was the year of *sans-culotte* politics.

While much of the *sans-culottes'* conduct was purposeful and politically rational, the threat of hunger, the dearth of dependable news, and the contagious excitement in the streets made the *sans-culottes* particularly susceptible to radical rhetoric. Marat wrote inflammatory articles against hoarders— *accapareur* became an even more hated name than aristocrat—while a small, extremist faction, the *enragés,* shouted for death to speculators, for rationing, and for a ceiling price on food—the *maximum.*

The Convention (and this included its left-wingers like Marat) was torn. It believed in free trade, and the *sans-culottes* were demanding price controls; it was learning the need for effective government, and the *sans-culottes* were acting out the drama of direct democracy. From then on, the Convention was marked by this tragic tension.[18] By mid-March, it had decided to send eighty of its members to the provinces, to superintend recruitment of troops and to take all necessary measures against the counterrevolution—these were the famous, powerful *représentants en mission.* It also reestablished the Revolutionary Tribunal, on a firmer basis than before, to try counterrevolutionaries with suitable dispatch. On March 19, on the motion of Cambacérès (see p. 507), it officially declared those found obstructing recruitment or engaged in armed rebellion outlawed—*hors la loi.* Two days later, it decreed that each section or commune should elect a revolutionary committee of twelve members. Finally, on April 6, it created the Committee of Public Safety. The lineaments of revolutionary government were emerging, though slowly: the committee, established at the urging of Danton to strengthen the executive, did not secure its ascendancy for a few months; Danton, who dominated it, was busily seeking accommodations with the allies.

This rash of decrees left the economic front untouched. Jacques Roux, chief spokesman for the *enragés,* increased his vociferous propaganda for

---

[18] For a lucid survey of this tragedy, see R. R. Palmer, "Popular Democracy in the French Revolution: Review Article," *French Historical Studies,* 1 (Fall 1960), 445–469.

protection of the poor. At the same time, radical Jacobins appealed to the clubs to purge the Convention of its disloyal members. Both had weighty consequences. Late in April, the leaders of the Mountain swallowed their economic liberalism, made common cause with the sans-culottes, and on May 4 pushed through the first maximum, which left the setting of ceiling prices for grain to individual departments. The Brissotin faction, meanwhile, fearing loss of control in the Convention, drew together in a series of ill-timed and ill-conceived defensive maneuvers. They secured the impeachment of Marat for signing a manifesto that openly accused the Convention of harboring counter-revolutionaries. But Marat was immensely popular in the city, and the Revolutionary Tribunal triumphantly acquitted him; the call to cleanse the Convention of "moderates" only grew in shrillness. It was not softened by the Girondins' success in stirring up the provinces against the Jacobins. In May, the cities of Marseilles, Bordeaux, and Caen joined in a call for a "federalist" revolt against Paris. On May 30, there was a bloody clash in Lyons, and the city fell to the anti-Jacobins. In Paris, in response, the Jacobins rallied the sections to their side. The Central Revolutionary Committee appointed Hanriot, a good Jacobin, commander of the National Guard, and on June 2, after two days of confusion, the Convention, intimidated, agreed to put twenty-nine Girondin deputies and two Girondin ministers under arrest. The Mountain had consolidated the victory it had first won in January. But its leaders acted with circumspection, even generosity; they were not sadists. Most of the Girondins were so lightly guarded that they made their escape to the provinces or, like Vergniaud, stayed in Paris to carry on their fight there.

The summer proved to the Jacobins that their forbearance had been misplaced. Reverses continued: in June, in the Vendée, the rebels took Saumur and compelled the government to transfer badly needed troops from the Rhine to the west. In July, the allies took the fortresses of Condé and Valenciennes and the city of Mainz. Then, on July 13, the enthusiast Charlotte Corday brought the danger home to the Jacobins by murdering Marat. In August, finally, royalists turned the port city of Toulon over to the British. In the provinces, the escaped Girondin deputies inspired a cluster of Federalist uprisings and tried to unite the country against Paris. And in Paris itself, the enragés, unappeased by the maximum of May, continued to harangue the Jacobins. The purged Jacobin Convention responded in all directions. On June 24, it adopted a new constitution—a Girondin draft hastily rewritten by Jacobins—which proclaimed new, more populist principles; it was never put into force, and perhaps was not intended to be, but it stood as a statement of democratic aspirations. In the following month, the radicals in the Convention pushed through a ferocious decree against hoarding. More important, the Convention strengthened the Committee of Public Safety. Early in July, his appeasement discredited, Danton left that committee; soon after, Robespierre and two energetic and experienced soldiers, Carnot and Prieur de la Côte d'Or, entered it. Rapidly now, the Committee of Public Safety turned itself into a cabinet. Its members toured the front; late in August, after some hesitation, it acted to mobilize the resources of France with the celebrated *levée en masse,* which demanded, and specified, the sacrifices all Frenchmen, young and old, must make until the republic was safe. The new government had to survive a fierce challenge on September 4 and 5; a mass demonstration of Parisian *sans-culottes,* led by the demagogic journalist Jacques Hébert and goaded by a new shortage of bread, prompted the committee to co-opt two *enragés,* Billaud-Varenne and Collot d'Herbois, to work for a general *maximum* and to press for the trial of the Girondins. On September 17, as radical pressure kept up, the Convention enacted the ominous Law of Suspects, which authorized the arrest of anyone suspected of counterrevolutionary activity. Legality had given way to the Terror. On September 29, the Convention decreed a general *maximum* to hold down wages and prices alike; a few days later, forty-five deputies—Girondins and their sympathizers—were finally put under indictment. And on October 10, Saint-Just, a flint-eyed young Jacobin speaking for the Committee of Public Safety, introduced a decisive decree that mobilized the government for the duration: "The provisional government of France," declared the first article, "will be revolutionary until the peace."

Revolutionary Government

The Committee of Public Safety, which increasingly acted as the government of France, faced daunting difficulties. "Traitors" proved relatively easy to deal with: on October 9, revolutionary forces recaptured Lyons; a week later, Marie Antoinette went to the guillotine after an indecent, hasty trial, and Bordeaux returned to Jacobin control; at the end of the month, the Brissotins in government hands were guillotined. Even "tyrants" seemed vulnerable: on the day of Marie Antoinette's execution, October 16, French forces beat back the Austrians at Wattigny and thus relieved enemy pressure on the northern front.

But the fratricidal conflict between the revolutionary government and the left-wing opposition was harder to resolve. Robespierre and his associates on the Committee of Public Safety did not intend to overlook the lessons of the Hébertist uprisings on September 4 and 5: the government had to repress its wrong-headed or false friends as much as its open enemies. Freedom must wait until discipline had been reestablished. Here, it would turn out, was the tragedy of revolutionary democracy: the Mountain could not live with its supporters and would die without them. Robespierre, though by no means a dictator, had become the best-known spokesman for the Committee of Public Safety. He never doubted that there were enemies on the left and that the ultrarevolutionaries were the agents of the counterrevolutionaries. In the fall of 1793 he had an opportunity of testing his suspicions in a surprising quarter—against atheists. If there was one important issue on which revolutionaries of all stripes could agree, it was that the "Christian superstition" was at once absurd and vicious. But, if Christianity was the false religion *par excellence,* what was the true religion? Here dissensions arose. On October 5, the Convention had enacted a new revolutionary calendar designed to rationalize the year and to wipe out all traditional associations of the calendar with the hated superstition of the past. Each of the new months had thirty days; that left over five days which were designated as holidays and significantly, if rather hollowly, called *sans-culottides.* The names of the months—Brumaire, month of fog, Thermidor, month of heat—and the new arrangement of the week never became popular, but for some years revolutionary governments insisted on dating events by them. The old Gregorian calendar was not reestablished until 1806, by Emperor Napoleon I. [19] Fanatical de-Christianizers wanted to go further; they wanted to ban all religious ceremonies, compel all priests to marry, close all the churches. Robespierre opposed de-Christianization on personal and political grounds. He was a deist himself, on the Rousseauian pattern: he believed in God the creator and in a guiding providence. This doubtless figured in his opposition, but the danger that antireligious extremism might alienate the large mass of moderate believers was more important still. He ordered the committee's traveling spokesmen, the *représentants en mission,* to reduce their antireligious activities, and on November 17 (we should call it 27 Brumaire, Year II), in a famous speech to the Jacobins, he denounced atheism as the religion of aristocrats. Such fanaticism, he urged, could only aid the enemy. In December, some of the extreme de-Christianizers were arrested. Earlier in the year, Robespierre had already denounced the leading *enragés* as Austrian agents, and Jacques Roux was arrested twice. In September, the government machinery of the Terror speeded up its operations. While before then, trials had been scrupulously conducted and the death sentence handed out sparingly, both the speed of the trials and the proportion of death sentences rapidly increased. There were spectacular collective state trials, "mixed bakings" carefully arranged to

[19] Since the decisive *journées* of the revolution that occurred after October 1793 are still known by their revolutionary nomenclature, here, for the record, is the calendar. The decree of October 1793 named September 22, 1792, the day after the official abolition of the monarchy, the first day of Year I of the republic. The months were:

Name	Meaning of name	Dates
Vendémiaire	Month of vintage	Sept. 22–Oct. 21
Brumaire	Month of fog	Oct. 22–Nov. 20
Frimaire	Month of frost	Nov. 21–Dec. 20
Nivôse	Month of snow	Dec. 21–Jan. 19
Pluviôse	Month of rain	Jan. 20–Feb. 18
Ventôse	Month of wind	Feb. 19–Mar. 20
Germinal	Month of budding	Mar. 21–Apr. 19
Floréal	Month of flowers	Apr. 20–May 19
Prairial	Month of meadows	May 20–June 18
Messidor	Month of harvest	June 19–July 18
Thermidor	Month of heat	July 19–Aug. 17
Fructidor	Month of fruit	Aug. 18–Sept. 16

The *sans-culottides* thus fell on September 17 to 21.

increase public revulsion against the accused: suspect foreigners, unsuccessful generals, rapacious speculators, returned émigrés—and political opponents of the regime. Fouquier-Tinville, the efficient chief prosecutor, had much work to do. In October his Tribunal condemned fifty-one persons to death, in November fifty-eight, in December sixty-eight. In the provinces, meanwhile, government representatives vented wholesale vengeance on reconquered cities. After Lyons was retaken, Couthon, a member of the Committee of Public Safety and Robespierre's close associate, proposed that the houses of the rich be razed and the name of the city be wiped from the earth. It was to be called *Ville Affranchie*. And among the ruins of this "liberated city" a column was to rise bearing the legend, "Lyons made war on Liberty, Lyons is no more." But Couthon was more violent in his speech than in his acts; when Robespierre warned him that humaneness would hatch new conspiracies he asked to be transferred. His successors, Collot d'Herbois and Fouché, ex-priest and violent Jacobin, had no such scruples. Under their administration, firing squads and the guillotine carried out large numbers of executions. In the notorious *mitraillades,* the victims first had to dig their graves and then stand still to be mowed down. At Nantes, Carrier, the *représentant en mission,* had more than two thousand people drowned in the Loire in wholesale and indiscriminate murder.

The government, while reproving the actions of these extremists, acted at the same time against the "indulgents." Danton was one of these; Camille Desmoulins, Robespierre's schoolfriend and fellow Jacobin, was another. But while the extremists were merely recalled, the indulgents were arrested. Other arrests followed. In mid-March 1794, Hébert and his followers called for an insurrection against the government. By the end of March, they had been guillotined. Roux had already committed suicide in prison two months before: the *sans-culottes* had no spokesmen left. On April 5, after a short trial which he dominated until he was ruthlessly cut off, Danton also went to the guillotine. The government, it seemed, had made short work of its enemies. The king and queen were dead; so were the Brissotins, the *enragés,* the Dantonists, and most of the Hébertists. With the execution of Desmoulins, the vigorous popular press was stilled as well. In the provinces, as cheerful killers like Fouché were recalled, the Terror was relaxed; in Paris it was intensified. Attempts on Robespierre's life, coupled with the nagging fear of remaining opposition, induced Robespierre on June 10, 1794 (22 Prairial), to secure passage of a new law that gave the Revolutionary Tribunal supreme power over all "enemies of the people"; the only penalty it could impose was death. This was the beginning of the Great Terror; it led, in Paris, to thirteen hundred seventy-six executions in a month and a half.

Thus baldly summarized, the Terror seems to discredit the whole Revolution as a nightmarish orgy of madmen, a sadistic riot in the name of humanity; Robespierre and his associates seem like so many modern Caligulas, wishing that the French people had but one neck. One is reminded of Dickens' Madame Defarge, calmly knitting as she watches the guillotine do its bloody work; of

Vergniaud darkly speaking of the revolution eating its own children. But the facts are rather more complicated. There can be no excuse for murder—even one. The Terror cannot be justified by pointing out that its victims amounted to "only" about thirty-five thousand—half of them condemned to death, the rest shot or drowned without trial or dying miserably in detention. Yet the figures of the Terror give significant clues to its nature. The largest number of its victims (31 percent) were *sans-culottes;* peasants were next (28 percent), followed by the upper middle class (14 percent), the lower middle class (11 percent), the nobility (8 percent), and the clergy (7 percent).[20] Doubtless, if priests and nobles had not emigrated, the proportions would have been different, but it is clear that the guillotine struck down not merely the king of France; not merely the great chemist Lavoisier—not for being a chemist, but for being a farmer general; not merely a Girondin politician like Madame Roland, or a hapless general like Houchard, but also ordinary Frenchmen and Frenchwomen. The location of the Terror is equally instructive. Most of its victims—some 93 percent—were accused of treason or sedition, and while the laws under which the Tribunals operated were perilously vague, many of the accused had certainly been active in domestic rebellion or in aiding the enemy; it is significant that the victims of the Terror were concentrated in the rebellious west of France and in areas of intense military activity—the north and the southeast.

As these figures suggest, no single explanation will do. We may distinguish four of them, rising in complexity: character, politics, idealism, and emergency. There were Terrorists who greatly enjoyed their work, even if, as with Carrier, their previous career gave no evidence of such inclinations. Men like Fouché and Collot d'Herbois have been called men of blood, with justice. The reports they sent back from their theater of operations reek with pleasure in their ingenuity at killing and with ambitious plans for more killing in the future. Such men found willing subordinates, "drinkers of blood—*buveurs de sang,*" in the provinces to do their work for them. But these killers for pleasure were always in a minority; the legislation that organized the Terror was designed at least in part to take it out of the hands of such freebooters and psychopaths.

Politics, too, played its part. Some politicians were sacrificed to the guillotine to appease other politicians. Perhaps the most prominent instance of such maneuvering was Danton. A powerful orator and energetic official, he was also callous and corrupt; in the dark September days of 1792, when the allied invasion was threatening Paris, his courage had stood France in good stead, but at the same time his connivance in the September massacres shows his character in a less flattering light. Less doctrinaire than Robespierre, he was also more amiable: he would not have fitted into Robespierre's republic of virtue.

[20] These figures add up to only 99 percent; 1 percent could not be determined. We are depending in these pages on Donald M. Greer's careful study, *The Incidence of the Terror During the French Revolution* (1935).

He died ostensibly because he had been involved in shady dealings, but while this was true, he died also because the *enragés* on the Committee of Public Safety insisted on it.[21]

Despite such calculation, the Terror was also the consequence of idealism. Robespierre and Saint-Just, whose power was very great when the Terror was at its height, divided the world into the forces of light and darkness. Their scheme of things had no room for honest error. Policies, or even views, that in their eyes harmed the Revolution were proof of wickedness, of complicity in a royalist plot. Saint-Just was pathologically cold-blooded; Robespierre, though, was far more complex. He was quick to accuse his enemies of treason, without a shred of evidence; he was responsible for the terrible law of 22 Prairial. But again and again he intervened to rescue potential victims from the guillotine. For some time he even supported the call of his friend Desmoulins for moderation. But he believed that terror was necessary until the enemies of virtue had been crushed and the republic of virtue secured. Virtue without terror, he said, is impotent; terror without virtue is disastrous. Robespierre— strait-laced, humorless, suspicious, the great "incorruptible"— has been called the worst kind of idealist: the man who *knows* he is right; the reformer who will sacrifice present generations to the future. There is something in this portrait. But Robespierre was also a statesman steeped in, almost overwhelmed by, practical problems. He was an honest man and a democrat, at a time when dishonesty was rife and democracy was in danger. There were men—he knew them—who profiteered from the war and battened on the poor.

And this brings us to the last cause of the Terror: the emergency. France was surrounded by very real and wholly uncompromising enemies. The Bourbons had made it perfectly clear what a restoration would mean (see p. 479). When the Committee of Public Safety established its ascendancy over the country in the fall of 1793, France had not had an effective government for more than four years. In the midst of unceasing turmoil in Paris and treachery in the provinces, the Committee of Public Safety strove to govern a large nation at war. The work of the twelve men on that committee remains impressive. They had to find new generals (the old ones had gone over to the enemy or had been guillotined), collect taxes, secure recruits, feed a large army, wrest territory from the hands of domestic and foreign enemies. In this grave emergency, Terror was a means of reestablishing control. Besides, not all the talk of treason was the fruit of a heated imagination. Toulon was turned over to the British navy by Admiral Trogoff, commander of the French Mediterranean fleet, after news had reached him that the Girondin uprisings had failed

---

[21] "The execution of the Hébertists," which occurred a week before Danton's trial, "implied that of the Dantonists also. If they were left alive after their opponents had been killed their position would be relatively stronger, and it would appear that the Committee had acted at their command. The unity of the Committee itself was also at stake, for Billaud-Varenne and Collot d'Herbois could not have been expected to accept the suppression of the extremists until the moderates were also destroyed" (Sydenham, *French Revolution,* 212).

in Normandy and Marseilles. And the uprising in the Vendée had begun with the systematic murder of numerous government officials. Radical Terror was often a response to the reactionary Terror. That reactionary Terror was soon to have its second opportunity.

Thermidor and the Thermidorians

On May 7, 1794, while his position seemed unassailable, Robespierre told the Convention that the country needed a new religion—the worship of the Supreme Being. It was essential for the establishment of virtue: "Immorality is the basis of despotism; the essence of Republicanism is virtue. The Revolution is the transition from the regime of crime to the regime of justice."[22] On June 8, in accordance with the decree passed at his instance, Robespierre presided over the first Festival of the Supreme Being. The Great Terror began two days later. In the war, meanwhile, the revolutionary armies were near victory. On May 18, General Pichegru routed the British at Tourcoing, and at the same time, Jourdan pushed forward on the northeastern front. On June 13, two weeks after a pitched naval encounter between French and British vessels, a huge food convoy, slipping past battling men-of-war, reached France unscathed. And on June 26, the French beat the Austrians in a decisive engagement at Fleurus. On July 19 they were in Brussels.

Together, these events conspired to encompass Robespierre's fall. The festival had given him undue prominence and made talk of his dictatorial pretensions plausible. The Terror had become more terrible at the very moment victories in the field made relaxation possible. Victory also permitted the Committee of Public Safety the luxury of quarreling in public. Robespierre, Couthon, and Saint-Just stood against the unreconstructed Hébertists, Billaud-Varenne and Collot d'Herbois; outside the committee, Terrorists like Fouché found themselves under attack by Robespierre and his two virtuous colleagues. A conspiracy began to form; it included moderates, but it was led by blood-stained Terrorists fearful of being outlawed: by Fouché, by Carrier, by Barras, by Tallien—men who had "pacified" the provincial cities in late 1793. Robespierre brought the plot to a head on July 26 (8 Thermidor) with an opaque and menacing speech to the Convention. He darkly spoke of a new conspiracy made up of the old combination—atheists and indulgents. He urged a final purge of traitors; pressed, he refused to give any names. This was to do the work of the plotters for them: any of the deputies might be attainted next. On the next day, the fateful 9 Thermidor, Fouché and his associates prevented Saint-Just and Robespierre from addressing the Convention and had their arrest voted. The "Plain," that silent collection of moderates who had countenanced the decimation of the Gironde, now voted against Robespierre.

---

[22] Quoted in Sydenham, *French Revolution*, 216.

For one day, the issue was in doubt. But the city did not rise: the *sans-culottes* were apathetic. Thus, by default, the people of Paris, weary at last, revenged themselves on a government that had killed their leaders and disregarded their legitimate demands. On 10 Thermidor the Republic of Virtue was dead. Robespierre, Couthon, Saint-Just, and nineteen others went to the guillotine; in the next few days, about a hundred more followed them.

The Convention survived Thermidor for over a year. A number of extremists, even though they were anti-Robespierre, were eliminated from positions of power: Billaud-Varenne and Collot d'Herbois were sent to rot in French Guiana. In long painful trials, the crimes of Carrier and his like received wide publicity. Carrier was guillotined; so was Dumas, the president of the Revolutionary Tribunal, and Fouquier-Tinville, its diligent prosecutor. Fouché barely survived the reaction he had done so much to bring about; he slipped into the protection of obscurity. With deliberate speed, the Thermidorians dismantled the machinery the Jacobins had assembled. They reduced the authority of the Committee of Public Safety, destroyed the autonomy of the Paris Commune, decentralized government, assailed Jacobins, and eventually closed down the Jacobin clubs altogether. In May 1795, they put an end to the Revolutionary Tribunal. Thousands—Girondins above all—came out of the prisons, and some émigrés returned.

The Thermidorians achieved their purposes with a new Terror, less formidable, less official, but almost as destructive as the old. In Lyons there was a small reenactment of the September massacres, as crowds stormed the prisons and lynched about a hundred Jacobin prisoners. In the southeast, at Marseilles, at Arles, at Avignon, royalist bands, self-appointed avengers, attacked whatever Jacobins they could find. One spectacular arm of the new repression was the *jeunesse dorée*. These gilded youths—draft dodgers, law clerks—in ostentatious revulsion against the egalitarian talk and dress of the Jacobins, roamed the streets in affected dress, armed with bludgeons. They invaded the offices of the remaining popular newspapers and intimidated Jacobins. The *sans-culottes* soon had good reason to regret their failure to rescue Robespierre from his enemies. The economic legislation of the Mountain had been unsatisfactory, but there had been at least a measure of price control and supervision of the food supply. The new "liberalism" of Thermidor spelled the doom of such state activity. The *maximum* was first openly disregarded; later, in December 1794, repealed. The withdrawal of the state from business brought back the speculators, the hoarders, in greater number than ever. In a final paroxysm of energy, the *sans-culottes* took to the streets once again. On April 1, 1795 (12 Germinal), a crowd broke into the Convention; significantly, its slogans included calls for bread and for the democratic constitution of 1793. It got neither. As bread supplies tightened and prices continued to mount, the *sans-culottes* repeated their demonstration on 1 Prairial (May 20, 1795). Again they invaded the Convention and briefly held the streets. Stronger this time, they shouted what they had shouted before and were sent away with promises. The next day, they were dispersed by government troops. After receiving swift and merciless punishment, the *sans-culottes* fell silent.

Thus secure, the Thermidorian Convention could address itself to making a new fundamental law for France. The Constitution of the Year III, promulgated in August, was a reminder of France's first modern constitution: the "Thermidorian Reaction" was just that—a return to early revolutionary aspirations. The franchise was as indirect and even narrower than that in the constitution of 1791: the number of electors was diminished to about twenty thousand. Its main architect, the moderate Boissy d'Anglas, candidly explained its rationale: "We must be governed by the best citizens; the best citizens are those who are most educated and most interested in the keeping of the law. Now, with very few exceptions, you will find such men only among those who possess some property." [23] One grave problem remained. The country was in a conservative, even a monarchist, mood; if few wanted the restoration of the Old Regime, most wanted the restoration of some stable order. This put the future of the delegates to the Convention, and even of the republic, in doubt. The Convention decided to protect both with the Law of the Two Thirds: two thirds of the new legislature was to be made up of themselves. This brought new uprisings, this time mainly from the Right. Barras was put in charge of the government troops; among his aides was the young general Napoleon Bonaparte. Freely using his firepower, Bonaparte dispersed the demonstrators with a "whiff of grapeshot." This was the famous "13 Vendémaire"—October 5, 1795. Bonaparte had helped to save the republic and, with it, much of the Revolution. His future role in the history of France would be rather more ambiguous.

SELECTED READINGS

The controversies over the French Revolution begin with its origins. In addition to the titles on the Old Regime cited in earlier chapters, see Douglas Dakin, *Turgot and the Ancien Régime in France* (1939), on the reforming minister of the opening years of Louis XVI; J. H. Shennan, *The Parlement of Paris* (1968), which analyzes one great center of resistance to royal power; and, for the economic origins, the authoritative studies by Ernest Labrousse, notably *La crise de l'économie française à la fin de l'ancien régime et au début de la Révolution* (1944). Labrousse's views, and those of other, mostly earlier interpreters, are conveniently summarized in Ralph W. Greenlaw, ed., *The Economic Origins of the French Revolution: Poverty or Prosperity?* (1958).

Another controversial question, still unsettled, involves the general character of the French Revolution—was it primarily French or was it part of a wider revolutionary stream? The leading proponents of the more embracing interpretation are R. R. Palmer, *The Age of the Democratic Revolution: A Political History of Europe and America, 1760–1800*, 2 vols. (1959–1964), and Jacques Godechot, *France and the Atlantic Revolution, 1770–1799* (1965). Peter Amann, ed., *The Eighteenth-Century Revolution: French or Western?* (1963), gathers these, and dissenting, views into one brief compass. One profitable way of examining this question is by looking at other countries in this

---

[23] Quoted in Georges Lefèbvre, *The Thermidorians and the Directory* (tr. 1964), 216.

era. G. P. Gooch, *Germany and the French Revolution* (1920), remains helpful, but has been largely superseded by Jacques Droz, *L'Allemagne et la Révolution française* (1949). For England, see among a large literature, Alfred Cobban, ed., *The Debate on the French Revolution, 1789-1800* (1950); Cobban, *Edmund Burke and the Revolt Against the XVIIIth Century* (ed. 1960); Thomas W. Copeland, *Our Eminent Friend Edmund Burke, Six Essays* (1949); and Carl Cone, *The English Jacobins: Reformers in Late 18th Century England* (1968).

General histories of the French Revolution are numerous. Among the more recent, the most informative are J. M. Thompson, *The French Revolution* (2nd ed., 1944) (splendidly detailed, it stops with the death of Robespierre); A. Goodwin, *The French Revolution* (1953); Norman Hampson, *A Social History of the French Revolution* (1963); and M. J. Sydenham, *The French Revolution* (1965). A classic account offering a moderate Marxist interpretation of the event as a bourgeois revolution is Georges Lefèbvre's *La Révolution française*, revised after the author's death by Albert Soboul in 1963, and now available, somewhat imperfectly translated, in two English volumes as *The French Revolution: From Its Origins to 1793* (1962) and *The French Revolution: From 1793 to 1799* (1964). Soboul's general histories of the era are not yet in English, but see his own summary, *Précis d'histoire de la Révolution française* (1962). For a general history, complete with survey of conflicting schools of interpretation, see Crane Brinton, *A Decade of Revolution* (1934). Paul Farmer, *France Reviews Its Revolutionary Origins* (1944), is also useful in this connection. The most persistent and amusing challenge to the prevailing radical interpretation of the epoch has come from Alfred Cobban, notably in *Historians and the Causes of the French Revolution* (1962) and *The Social Interpretation of the French Revolution* (1964). Students in search of documents can use Leo Gershoy's brief *The Era of the French Revolution, 1789-1799: Ten Years That Shook the World* (1957), which includes a long introductory essay; the more comprehensive *A Documentary Survey of the French Revolution* (1951) by John Hall Stewart; and J. M. Thompson, *French Revolution Documents, 1789-1794* (1948).

The year of decision, 1789, is brilliantly if a little schematically laid out in Georges Lefèbvre's *The Coming of the French Revolution* (tr. 1947). For Sieyès, see G. G. Van Deusen, *Sieyès: His life and His Nationalism* (1932), and M. Blondel's translation of Sieyès, *What Is the Third Estate?* (1964). J. H. Clapham's *The Abbé Sieyès* (1912), though old, remains valuable. Beatrice F. Hyslop, *A Guide to the General Cahiers of 1789, with Texts of Unedited Cahiers* (1936), is a useful introduction to the grievances expressed early in 1789 in writing. For the prominent early revolutionary leader, Mirabeau, see the biography by O. J. G. Welch, subtitled, *A Study of a Democratic Monarchist* (1951).

For July 14, 1789, see the authoritative study by Jacques Godechot, *The Taking of the Bastille* (tr. 1970); George Rudé's pioneering essays on *The Crowd in the French Revolution* (1959) include Bastille Day, the earlier Réveillon riots, and the most important later instances of mass action. For the Great Fear that swept France in midsummer of 1789, Georges Lefèbvre, *La grande peur de 1789* (1922), remains essential.

The Civil Constitution of the Clergy (1790) must be understood in the wider context of the relations of church to state in France. This context is provided by Alphonse Aulard, *Christianity and the French Revolution* (tr. 1927), which can be supplemented with E. E. Y. Hales, *Revolution and Papacy, 1769-1846* (1960), the first volume of Adrien Dansette, *Religious History of Modern France*, 2 vols. (tr. 1961), and the brief, lucid essay by John McManners, *The French Revolution and the Church*

(1969). Burdette C. Poland treats an important religious minority in *French Protestantism and the French Revolution: A Study in Church and State, Thought and Religion 1685-1815* (1957). Church-state relations bring up the hostility to the revolution. Jacques Godechot, *The Counter-Revolution: Doctrine and Action 1789-1804* (tr. 1971), is a full and judicious analysis; Donald M. Greer's statistical survey, *The Incidence of the Emigration During the French Revolution* (1951), remains useful; while Charles Tilly, *The Vendée* (1964), brings a sociologist's insights to the great counterrevolutionary insurgence in the west of France in 1793. See also, Paul Beik, *The French Revolution Seen from the Right* (1956). Agricultural France, which had its own revolution and counterrevolution, is treated in masterly fashion by Georges Lefèbvre, *Les paysans du Nord pendant la Révolution française* (2nd ed., 1959).

The study of clubs and factions in the Revolution has long been a specialty of French historians. Crane Brinton, *The Jacobins: An Essay in the New History* (1930), offers a well-documented, essentially hostile analysis of what appeared to Brinton as a movement of religious fanatics; Richard M. Brace, *Bordeaux and the Gironde, 1789-1794* (1947), is a detailed specific monograph, while M. J. Sydenham, *The Girondins* (1960), rejects simplified accounts of "Brissotins" as a unified "party." For the extremists, see R. B. Rose, *The Enragés* (1965). Biographies of leading political figures include J. M. Thompson, *Robespierre*, 2 vols. (1935), dependably summarized in Thompson, *Robespierre and the French Revolution* (1952); Louis Gottschalk, *Jean Paul Marat: A Study in Radicalism* (1927); Leo Gershoy, *Bertrand Barère, A Reluctant Terrorist* (1962); E. N. Curtis, *Saint-Just, Colleague of Robespierre* (1935). Marcel Reinhard, *Le Grand Carnot*, 2 vols. (1950-1952), is the definitive biography in French; it may be supplemented with Huntley Dupré, *Lazare Carnot, Republican Patriot* (1940). There are useful biographies by Eloise Ellery on *Brissot de Warville* (1915) and by Gita May on *Madame Roland and the Age of Revolution* (1970).

The time of war, of Jacobin dictatorship, and of the Terror, has been well surveyed. See especially the vivid portraits of those who governed France during crisis by R. R. Palmer, *Twelve Who Ruled: The Committee of Public Safety During the Terror* (1958). Donald M. Greer's statistical analysis, *The Incidence of the Terror During the French Revolution* (1935), is invaluable. To it we may add James L. Godfrey, *Revolutionary Justice: A Study of the Organization, Personnel, and Procedure of the Paris Tribunal, 1793-1795* (1951). Part of Albert Soboul's celebrated thesis on the *sans-culottes* (1958) has been translated as *The Parisian Sans-culottes in the French Revolution, 1793-1794* (1964), while John B. Sirich, *The Revolutionary Committees in the Departments of France* (1943), moves outside Paris. Rudé's *Crowd in the French Revolution* and Tilly's *Vendée*, already cited, are of special importance for this period. Seymour Harris' study of *The Assignats* (1930) traces the role of this revolutionary paper money in a French economy at war. Richard Cobb's important thesis, *Les armées révolutionnaires, instrument de la Terreur dans les départements, Avril 1793-Floréal An II*, 2 vols. (1961-1963), though accessible only in French, deserves special attention; Cobb has summarized his findings in "The Revolutionary Mentality in France, 1783-94," *History*, 17 (1957). Albert Mathiez, *La vie chère et le mouvement social sous la Terreur* (1927), on social struggles in Paris and their political consequences in the Year II has not been superseded.

For the Thermidorian Reaction see especially Georges Lefèbvre, *The Thermidorians* (tr. 1966), a masterly synthesis; two collections of essays by Albert Mathiez: *The Fall of Robespierre and Other Essays* (tr. 1927) and *After Robespierre: The Thermidorian Reaction* (tr. 1965); and Richard T. Bienvenu, ed., *The Ninth of Thermidor* (1968).

12

The Age of Napoleon

The age of Napoleon was obviously larger than the man Napoleon Bonaparte. Yet even the modern historian, averse as he is to the cult of personality, will not hesitate to apply the name of this man to his time. Napoleon left his mark on men of letters from Goethe to Byron to Stendhal, as he left it on European taste, laws, and manners, and on countries from England to Russia to Egypt. Even the irreconcilable reputations that pursue him to this day express his epoch: he was symptomatic of its aspirations, its failures, and its immense variety. He was a liberator to German Jews, an archenemy to English statesmen, an ambiguous benefactor to Italian nationalists. Did he complete, stabilize, or betray the French Revolution? The answer must be that he did all these things in turn.

NAPOLEON'S TRIUMPH:
FROM SOLDIER TO EMPEROR

———————··◦⟨∞⟩◦··———————

The Directory: The Reluctant Republic

The Directory, which owed so much to Bonaparte's timely intervention, was inaugurated in November 1795. Its leaders were the old crowd in new clothes; the statute of the Two Thirds and the restricted franchise made the Directory a self-protective, almost a cozy arrangement. The story goes that when, after the years of turmoil, the old Abbé Sieyès was asked what he had done during the Revolution, he replied, "I survived." The Directory, in which he was to play his accustomed prominent role, was a regime of survivors. The qualities that had had greatest survival value during the previous six years were tenacity, suppleness, and a convenient memory; the most conspicuous figures in the Directory had these qualities in abundance. They tended to be rich and ostentatious, often vulgar, about their riches, for their wealth was normally of recent, usually of doubtful, origin: from profiteering and speculation. Sensuality and opulence were in vogue. This aspect of the Directory was splendidly realized in the viscount Paul François Nicolas de Barras, one of the original five directors. Born into an aristocratic family, he had survived the Revolution by being in the right place with the right remedy; he had helped to bring down Robespierre when it was time to bring him down, and now he was pushing forward young Bonaparte. Indeed, Barras' mistress, Josephine de Beauharnais, was to become Bonaparte's first wife. He was a good soldier with a fine bearing, but unscrupulous, essentially unprincipled, and wholly corrupt. Foreign diplomats discovered to their dismay that to negotiate with Barras—or with Talleyrand, the foreign minister, who matched Barras in shamelessness— meant handing out immense bribes.

Yet, while the spectacular corruptions of the Directory have been much discussed, the very genuine difficulties its directors faced have been underestimated.[1] Most of these difficulties were legacies. True, the war went on, unrest in the Vendée flared again, attempts to stabilize the currency ended in partial bankruptcy, inflation was rampant; necessities commanded fantastic prices, and starvation in the countryside was widespread. Royalists corresponded with

---

[1] This is perfectly understandable; the four years of the Directory (1795–1799) appear like an interlude between the dramatic days of the Terror before and the equally dramatic advent of Bonaparte after. Moreover, Napoleon Bonaparte later found it expedient to denigrate the regime he had overthrown, and his self-serving view was quickly adopted. Recently, historians have been suggesting a more balanced appraisal.

unreconstructed émigrés, while the old radicals—splintered, disillusioned, and powerless—desperately looked for leadership. Still, the government managed to bring prices down (partly because the harvest of 1796 was a good one), alleviate hunger by controlling the price of bread and distributing it in critical areas, effectively reorganize the tax system, pacify the Vendée, win impressive military campaigns, and stave off the powers of Europe. The constitution of the Directory flatly included annexed Belgium in France's domains; it was, thus, a regime constructed on imperialist assumptions. Despite the coalitions against it, the Directory could make those assumptions hold good, at least for some time.

Political instability proved harder to manage than the allies. The first challenge to the Directory—pathetic, but of symptomatic value and historical interest—came from the remnants of the old Left. François Emile "Gracchus" Babeuf, with a small band of fellow enthusiasts, propagated a "conspiracy of the equals." Babeuf wanted a new revolution that would accomplish what the old revolution had so miserably failed to do: break the stranglehold of the rich over the poor by nationalizing the land, imposing on everyone equal duties to work, and abolishing private property. All this was to be done by a "common administration"—which today we would call egalitarian socialism with central economic planning. His conspiracy was scheduled for May 1796; it included nebulous plans for killing the directors and winning over the troops, but it was quickly betrayed and easily suppressed. The leading conspirators were arrested and early in 1797 two of them, including Babeuf, went to the guillotine. The egalitarian fantasies of the *enragés* in the Year II remained fantasies in the Year IV.

The challenge from the Right was more widely based and more dangerous. Royalists appeared more openly than they had done for four or five years. Two of the five directors, the experienced diplomat Barthélemy and the old Terrorist General Carnot, "organizer of victory," showed increasing sympathies for the restoration of a constitutional monarchy. Stringent legislation against émigrés and their families was being relaxed, and many of them drifted back home, to strengthen sentiment for a restoration. Yet the Bourbons never made it easy for their most loyal adherents. In June 1795, the young dauphin—whom the émigrés called "Louis XVII"—died of the maltreatment he had suffered since 1793. This made the count de Provence heir to the vacant throne. With an obtuseness in no way mitigated by his years of exile or by French realities, "Louis XVIII" promptly issued the Declaration of Verona that spelled out the program of the counterrevolution in merciless detail. It called for nothing less than the total restoration of the Old Regime: restoration of confiscated property, of Catholic supremacy, of old institutions like the provinces and the parlements, and of the old privileges—the old dues, the old taxes, the old exemptions. Most French monarchists had acquired a vested interest in the abolition of these institutions and privileges and hoped for a rather more moderate return to the past than this.

Despite the unyielding foolishness of their exiled king, French monarchists scored impressive gains in the free elections held in the spring of 1797. Only a dozen of the one hundred fifty or so members of the old legislature who stood for reelection were returned; they were replaced for the most part by moderate royalists. The republic was in danger of disappearing, more peacefully than it had come. In this emergency, three of the directors, Reubell, La Reveillière-Lépeaux, and Barras, decided to forgo even the shadow of legality for the republic's sake—and their own. On 18 Fructidor (September 4, 1797), they occupied Paris, had Barthélemy arrested (Carnot eluded them), annulled most of the inconvenient election results of April, imposed censorship, and sent opposition leaders into exile. Once again Bonaparte helped to shape the course of events. He was leading the French armies in Italy, but alarmed at the prospects of a restoration—which meant an unwelcome peace—he sent General Augereau to Paris as his deputy, to guarantee the success of the coup d'etat.

The Directory: Dictatorship, Victory, Demise

Fructidor was designed to keep the old survivors in power, but its ultimate beneficiary was its servant in Italy: General Napoleon Bonaparte. Even in these early years, when little was clear to him except his unmatched ambition, there was something of the stuff of legend about him. For all his short stature he towered over other men. Born in August 1769 into the minor, impecunious nobility of Corsica, not long after France had annexed the island from Genoa, he liked to boast of his French origins ("I was born free"); but he was a Corsican nationalist and, until 1796, spelled his name in the Italian fashion: Buonaparte. A soldier's career was in his mind from his earliest days; after attending French military schools both in the provinces and in Paris, he obtained a commission in an artillery regiment in 1785. His reading in the philosophes and his youthful involvement in the cause of Corsica made him a convinced Jacobin; his moment of glory came in September 1793, when he distinguished himself in the recapture of Toulon, which counterrevolutionaries had turned over to the British. A grateful government made him a brigadier general. After a brief eclipse during Thermidor for his Jacobin associations, he emerged at Vendémi-aire (see p. 498), and in March 1796, after his marriage to Josephine, he set off for Italy, in command of the French army.

The Directory, desperate for success, was the kind of regime in which a Bonaparte could flourish. In March 1795, in one of the last diplomatic triumphs of the Convention, France had breached the First Coalition, formed against her in 1792, by concluding a peace treaty with Prussia. Lesser German states followed suit; the left bank of the Rhine was retained by France, and Prussia promised neutrality. In the same year, in June, Spain also dropped out of the war. The Directory was now left with two formidable enemies: Austria and Britain. The German campaign remained inconclusive, but in Italy, Bonaparte scored lightning successes. Napoleon's Italian campaign has the breathless speed of the Revolution; and one must account for it by weeks and days, not months. He defeated the Austrians at Millesimo on April 13, 1796; the Piedmontese at Mondovi on April 22, knocking Victor Amadeus out of the war and gaining Nice and Savoy for France. On May 10, the French defeated the Austrians once again, at Lodi, and on May 15, they were in Milan. The next day, Bonaparte proclaimed the first French satellite state in Italy, the Lombard Republic. Austria's Italian allies—the papacy, Parma, Modena—were held up to ransom; priceless works of art and large sums of money made their way to Paris. Then Bonaparte's extraordinary pace slowed—a little. The fortress of Mantua held out for half a year, but the Austrians were defeated again at Arcola in November 1796 and at Rivoli in January 1797; early in February, 1797, the garrison at Mantua surrendered. By April, Bonaparte had negotiated a preliminary peace with the Austrians at Leoben. The British, meanwhile, disheartened by the cost of the war, domestic unrest, naval mutinies, and an Irish uprising, were negotiating with the French at Lille. The coup d'etat of Fructidor encouraged the negotiators to try to force stiff terms on the British, and the negotiations collapsed. Soon, in October 1797, Britain found herself alone: the Hapsburgs made peace with France at Campo Formio. It was a triumph for the Directory; the Austrians got only Venice, treacherously occupied and now just as treacherously bartered off by Bonaparte; the French got Austrian recognition of their hold on Belgium and of their new Italian creation, the Cisalpine Republic; they also got the Ionian Islands off the coast of Greece, and a promise of a congress at Rastatt to settle the complicated shifts of sovereignty consequent on French conquests on the Rhine. Italy now became a French sphere of influence arranged in a string of satellite republics: the Cisalpine, including Milan, Bologna, Ferrara, Modena, and the Romagna; the Ligurian, essentially the old Republic of Genoa; the Roman, created in early 1798; and the Parthenopean, including southern Italy, formed in January 1799. Switzerland had been turned, for good measure, into the Helvetian Republic in April 1798, and Geneva was annexed to France.

Only Britain was now left. In November 1797, Bonaparte returned to Paris, to be hailed as a conqueror and to prepare the invasion of England. Upon a reasonable assessment of British naval strength, Bonaparte soon decided that such an invasion must fail; he persuaded the directors to let him take Egypt instead. An expedition to Egypt seemed an oddly roundabout way of crippling Britain, but Bonaparte was not the only one in France to think the plan reasonable: Talleyrand, too, thought that a French conquest of Egypt might cut off Britain's trade with the East and threaten her lifeline to India. On May 19, 1798, Bonaparte sailed with a fleet of four hundred ships, a small army, and a contingent of scientists. On June 12, he surprised and took Malta; on July 1 he landed in Egypt, and on the next day, Alexandria was his. On July 22, he took Cairo: the whole expedition looked like another Italian campaign. But Napoleon found his match in Admiral Horatio Nelson. On August 1, 1798, Nelson, having missed the French fleet in the Mediterranean, surprised it anchored at

Abukir, outside Alexandria, and annihilated it. Bonaparte's campaign against the Ottomans in Syria, and further victories in Egypt in the summer of 1799, did not end his embarrassment. He seemed cut off from France.

The directors in Paris had mixed feelings about his plight. In his Italian campaign, Bonaparte had displayed unwelcome tendencies toward independence. He was conducting himself like a foreign minister with his own army and his own supplies; he put his notions into action and informed Paris later. The instrument of policy was rapidly becoming its master. That was bad enough; the impermanence of his triumphs was worse. In December 1798, Tsar Paul I—Catherine's erratic and adventurous son, who had succeeded his mother in 1796—concluded an alliance with Great Britain, and by 1799 the Second Coalition against France was in the field; it included the Austrians and Ottomans, and it scored quick victories: by May, the Russian general Suvorov was in Turin; in June, the Austrians defeated the French at Zurich; in August, at the disastrous battle of Novi, Suvorov routed the French once more. These defeats brought the specter of an invasion and, with that, troubles at home. The government found it equally difficult to raise troops and money; Jacobins were agitating on one side, royalists on the other. Then the danger of invasion receded as General Masséna drove the Russians out of Zurich in September. But the Directory faced an even more insidious danger from within. In May, Abbé Sieyès had been elected one of the directors, and he immediately began to conspire against the government he was sworn to uphold. He now wanted a regime with an energetic executive, and soon his principle, he said, was "confidence from below, power from above." This meant a coup d'etat. All he needed was a general to carry it out; in early October, Bonaparte suddenly appeared on French soil—he had left his army behind in Egypt. Clearly, he was the man, though he nearly lost his opportunity by losing his nerve for once. His coup d'etat, badly bungled, took two days to accomplish; on its second day, November 9, 1799—18 Brumaire—Napoleon Bonaparte's brother, Lucien, managed to rally the troops against the government by inventing a plot that had to be put down. The troops dispersed the legislature, and the Directory was at an end. It had been ruined by the immense costs of continued warfare, its failure to enlist the support of most Frenchmen, and its unhappy choice of leaders, like Sieyès and Bonaparte, who were more anxious to serve themselves than their government. By December, a new government, the Consulate, had taken its place. And General Bonaparte was in control.

The Consulate

Once in control—of himself and of the country—Bonaparte did not lose it again. His egotism—admirers called it self-confidence—grew beyond all bounds as flatterers told him what he needed to hear; if he believed himself to be a man of destiny, others believed it too, at least at first. Bonaparte showed a remarkable capacity for giving the nation what it wanted—peace both on the battlefield and in domestic affairs. From the beginning, he compounded his rule of the traditional, the recent, and the original so subtly that he pacified the longings of most Frenchmen and disappointed only principled Jacobins or irreconcilable émigrés. The constitution of the Year VIII, promulgated in December 1799, is a tribute to his political instincts. Its franchise was extended to universal manhood suffrage, but voters chose only "notables" whom the government could then invite to serve in some public capacity; its tribunate debated but did not vote; its legislative body voted but did not debate; its conservative senate selected the two chambers and passed on the constitutionality of proposed legislation; and its council of state actively advised the first consul. This complex structure of the French state barely concealed, behind its Baroque facade, the concentration of autocratic power in the hands of one man—the first consul. Those sturdy classical words—tribune, senate, consulate—evoked the manly patriotism of the Roman Republic; the appeal to "notables" was a reminder of the hierarchical Old Regime; universal suffrage combined with the indirect voting and reliance on a written constitution were devices borrowed from the Revolution; and the use of a mock constitution to screen a dictatorship links Bonaparte directly with popular dictatorships of the twentieth century. His mode of securing popular approval for this charade, the plebiscite, was another foretaste of the future; beginning in December, in open voting across the country, the French people passed on their new constitution. To no one's surprise, the plebiscite approved Bonaparte's handiwork by the overwhelming majority of 3,011,007 to 1,526. [2] Bonaparte was the heir of Sieyès' principle: *he* exercised power from above; confidence from below flowed to *him*. In selecting his closest associates, Bonaparte underscored his express desire to forget about experimentation and achieve the restoration of order: Cambacérès, a lawyer who had sat in the Convention and voted for the execution of Louis XVI, became second consul; Lebrun, an elderly public servant with a gift for financial matters (he had assisted Maupeou in his coup d'etat against the parlements in 1771 [see p. 442]) and with a generally liberal reputation, became third consul; the sinister Joseph Fouché, a born conspirator, an old Terrorist who had turned on Robespierre just in time and who had ingratiated himself by his part in the plot of 18 Brumaire, became minister of police; while the inevitable Talleyrand reappeared as minister of foreign affairs.

One of the first acts of Bonaparte's statesmanship was to write a personal letter to George III on December 26, 1799, offering peace. The Russians, annoyed at the conduct of their allies, had already withdrawn from the Second Coalition, but neither George's ministers nor Emperor Francis II were inclined to bargain with the Corsican upstart. The war went on; Bonaparte rebuilt his

---

[2] The device is worth keeping in mind; Bonaparte would use it again, as would later rulers like Napoleon III and twentieth-century dictators. The plebiscite made it possible to combine a democratic appeal to the people with dictatorial manipulation of its timing and conduct.

army and in May 1800 rushed across the Alps into Italy; in June, in a long, bloody encounter at Marengo, the French finally carried the day against the Austrians. General Moreau meanwhile piled triumph upon triumph in the German theater; in December, at Hohenlinden, he routed the Austrians completely. The Treaty of Lunéville followed in February 1801. Substantially, it confirmed the Treaty of Campo Formio and expanded French hegemony over Italy and western Germany. Having much to lose and, for the moment, little to gain, and aided by Pitt's fall from office on a domestic issue, Bonaparte entered serious negotiations; in March 1802, he concluded the Treaty of Amiens with Britain. It returned Britain's recent conquests to France; but the islands of Trinidad (taken from Spain) and Ceylon (taken from the Dutch Batavian Republic) remained in British hands. In the eastern Mediterranean, Britain agreed to restore Malta to the Order of the Knights of Malta and to respect its independence; France in return recognized the republic of the seven Ionian Islands, returned to Turkish control. For the first time in many years, all Europe was at peace.

Bonaparte did not wait for this armistice to pacify France. He repressed the royalists in the west, independent newspapers in Paris, and for good measure, Jacobin radicals, who were no real danger to him; all this with a typical mixture of clemency and utter ruthlessness. Bonaparte was the perfect pragmatist in the derogatory sense of that word: as long as he thought measures would work, he took them. His rule is pervaded with crimes coolly committed and kindnesses well advertised. One early step, a decisive one in reducing France to order, did not require ferocity at all. The Revolution had begun with an experiment in extreme administrative decentralization; the decrees on local government of December 1789 and January 1790 had assigned wide powers to France's new departments and considerable autonomy to localities. This trust in local self-government had not survived the wars and the civil wars of the Years II and III. Now, in February 1800, Bonaparte confirmed and completed the process of centralizing administration by creating the office of prefect. The prefect headed a department; the subprefects and lesser officials were responsible to him, while he was responsible to Paris. And, in place of popular selection of public officials, Bonaparte put appointment by the central government. The ideal of local autonomy was sacrificed to the ideal of orderly administration.

The establishment of the prefects proved the first consul's most enduring achievement; his concordat with Pope Pius VII, signed after tortuous negotiations in July 1801 and ratified in September, proved the most controversial. Bonaparte's own religious convictions remain a matter of discussion; this only means that they were not strong. He was a rationalist, probably a deist. But he approached religion, as he approached everything, pragmatically. As he told his council of state: "My policy is to govern men as the great majority wish to be governed. . . . It was as a Catholic that I won the war in the Vendée, as a Moslem that I established myself in Egypt, and as an Ultramontane that I won the confidence of the Italians. If I were governing Jews, I should rebuild the temple of Solomon."[3] Bonaparte wanted a settlement with the Vatican because he judged the refractory clergy to be popular and dangerously influential in France; most Frenchmen, despite years of philosophic propaganda, remained good believers. Peace with the church would be part of the general pacification, and a religious settlement would compel many obstinate clerics to renounce their adherence to "Louis XVIII" and to rally around the Consulate.

His calculations proved correct. The concordat gave the French practically all they had asked for: the pope recognized the sale of church lands and the right of the French government to nominate bishops. France's acquisition of the old papal enclave of Avignon was passed over in silence, and since the French negotiators refused to call Catholicism the "dominant" religion or to surrender freedom of conscience, the pope had to be content with the pious declaration that "Catholicism is the religion of the great majority of French citizens"— which was true enough, and the main reason why Bonaparte had desired a concordat in the first place. The pope for his part secured repeal of some of the anticlerical legislation passed in the revolution: the French church was allowed, once again, to hold public services and to establish cathedral chapters and pious foundations. While the church had lost its land and its tithes, it had gained and kept guaranteed salaries. Thus, the church in France, the pope had reason to believe, had returned to the Roman discipline. But Bonaparte, to quiet domestic opposition to the concordat, subverted its spirit with a set of Organic Articles, published later, in April 1802. They spelled out the supremacy of the state over the church and insisted on civil marriage. To add injury to insult, the Organic Articles applied indiscriminately to Catholics and Protestants; this underscored the first consul's intention of keeping the privileges of Catholicism at a minimum. The concordat, thus unilaterally amended, was solemnly celebrated on Easter Day 1802, at Notre Dame, and Bonaparte compelled his Jacobin generals to accompany him to mass. Muttering defiance, they obeyed.

There have been interminable debates over just when Napoleon's career was at its height. One could make a strong argument for choosing the early spring of 1802.[4] Bonaparte was secure in power, self-appointed as the sole dominant figure in France for ten years. There was peace; France itself was quiet. The Consulate was seriously addressing itself to a variety of domestic matters: early in 1801, the government had begun to discuss a civil code; in April 1802, the first educational reforms went into effect. The Bank of France, founded in early 1800, helped to stabilize the currency. The distribution and collection of taxes, following reforms first laid down in the Directory, were more equitable and more efficient than before. Polite society reemerged, visitors thronged the city of Paris, prosperity was widespread. The Old Regime was dead; for most Frenchmen, this Consulate seemed like the realization of the

[3] Quoted in J. M. Thompson, *Napoleon Bonaparte* (1952), 188.
[4] One historian, at least, Thompson (*Napoleon Bonaparte*, 200-201), argues for this date, persuasively.

Revolution without its defects. There was no terror, no civil war, no bankrupt-cy. The abuses that had so long pervaded the fabric of French society—offices for sale, high positions monopolized by the nobility, taxes loaded on the poor and escaped by the privileged, commerce stultified by internal tariffs and manufacture by gild restrictions—had vanished, it seemed, forever. The Revolution had effected a vast redistribution of property with the confiscation of émigré lands, the sale of church properties, and the emergence of new wealth born of war and inflation. The Consulate, having made peace with England and the Vatican alike, appeared as the guarantor of this new order. In April 1802, the Consulate marked the new ease with a sweeping amnesty that included most of the émigrés. But the government made it plain that émigrés who took advantage of the amnesty and came home to swear fidelity to the Consulate would have no claim to those of their properties that had been legally handed to others. The revolutionary settlement must remain untouched.

The nation was grateful. In May 1802, prodded by Bonaparte's most assiduous courtiers, it was given an opportunity of expressing its gratitude. The Senate proposed that the first consul be reelected for another ten years; but on May 10, the Council of State proposed instead a new plebiscite to determine whether Napoleon Bonaparte should be chosen as consul for life. Bonaparte declared himself willing to sacrifice himself once more for the nation. A few outraged generals and republican intellectuals were sent off on remote assignments or kept out of Paris, and on August 2, the result of the plebiscite was announced. It allowed Bonaparte, by a vote of 3,568,885 to 8,374, to make his new sacrifice. Two days later the just-created life consul appeared with a new constitution that empowered him to appoint the other two consuls and the senators to the newly enlarged Senate. The details hardly mattered: Caesarism was at the door.

The new Consulate persisted in domestic reform. It was often of dubious quality: the civil code, developed with Bonaparte's diligent, often passionate participation, and promulgated in March 1804, was hastily drawn by relatively ignorant men. It was a supremely rationalist document, sweeping away a multiplicity of local laws and the authority of tradition in favor of general principles. It was relatively short and eminently quotable; it strengthened the laws of property in behalf of property owners; it decreed religious toleration and civil equality; it even permitted divorce. But it hedged reason and equality with conservative provisions, many of them at the insistence of Bonaparte: it gave the father extensive rights over his children, and men considerable authority over women. All were equal before the civil code, except women— and workers. The code specifically declared that in disputes over wages, courts would take the word of employer rather than that of employee. [5] This code, the

---

[5] The penal code of 1810 reiterated this inequality by strengthening the Le Chapelier law of 1791. That law, it will be recalled, had forbidden associations of labor and management alike; despite its ostensible evenhandedness, it operated mainly against workers, whose strongest weapon, the strike, it outlawed.

first of five, meant retreat from the egalitarianism of the revolution. Those who call Bonaparte a betrayer of the Revolution may appeal to these provisions. The consul retreated from republican equality in other ways. Late in May 1802, he founded a new Legion of Honor, designed to reward civic and military achievement. The legion was headed by the first consul and a grand council and was carefully organized in hierarchical, military fashion, with graduated pay and other privileges. In March 1790, the Constituent Assembly had solemnly declared the abolition of "all honorary distinctions, all power and superiority resulting from the feudal system," and in June, it had abolished hereditary nobility altogether. Now, twelve years later, Bonaparte founded new distinctions. It was Bonaparte's way of interpreting the Revolution's call, and his own, for careers open to talent.

In foreign affairs, the life consul proceeded with his celebrated energy. The fragile web of peace was soon torn. Despite the Peace of Amiens, British suspicions of Bonaparte remained acute. By late summer of 1802, suspicions had grown into tensions. The Consulate's foreign interventions had begun in 1800 in the Dutch Republic; in January 1802, Bonaparte graciously accepted the presidency of the new Italian Republic. All this activity could be justified by existing treaties. Then, in October 1802, Bonaparte turned his attention to a Switzerland torn by civil war. The British warned him; in November, George III pointedly referred to "certain states"—meaning Switzerland and Holland— in whose independence Britain had the most emphatic interest. In reply, in February 1803 and again in March, Bonaparte berated the British ambassador in violent language; Britain meanwhile refused to carry out its agreement to evacuate Malta; in May 1803 Britain declared war. Once again, French troops and ships were got ready to invade England. And in the following year, Consul Bonaparte transformed himself into Emperor Napoleon.

The Early Empire

Napoleon Bonaparte had made himself consul with a lie; he made himself emperor with a murder. He had never been above using, or even inventing, plots to advance his interests. Fouché and his secret police diligently ferreted out conspirators and exploited popular concern for Bonaparte's safety to dispose of unwelcome, if innocent, members of the opposition. On the evening of December 24, 1800, when Bonaparte was on his way to the opera, a bomb went off, killing a number of bystanders, but sparing the intended victim. The authors of the bombing were royalist extremists, but Bonaparte took this opportunity to crush the remnants of the Jacobin party. In 1804, he played the same game for higher stakes. Since the summer of 1803, an oddly assorted collection of exiled royalists, discontented republicans, and police spies had been discussing ways of overthrowing the "tyrant." Beginning in January 1804, the police made a number of arrests; by early March, most of the conspirators were in Fouché's hands. As the interrogators pieced together various confessions, it emerged that the plotters were counting on some unknown Bourbon prince to lead them to a glorious restoration of the Old Regime. But who? Suspicion fell on the young duke d'Enghien, a royal prince, the grandson of the prince de Condé, who was living in exile in Baden, not far from the French frontier. With Bonaparte's assent, he was kidnapped on March 14, brought to Paris, and secretly tried. Baden was foreign territory and the kidnapping an invasion of sovereignty; the reports brought in about the duke d'Enghien—his stealthy trips, his mysterious associates, his suspicious correspondence—were all proved palpably false at his trial, and Bonaparte knew they were false. Yet in the early morning of March 21, d'Enghien was shot.

It was easy enough to represent the event as a desperate act of self-defense—there was, after all, a genuine conspiracy, even if d'Enghien had no part in it. And as long as Bonaparte was in danger, so was France. To make his rule hereditary seemed the safest step to take. While a handful of principled republicans objected, public opinion, partly spontaneous, largely manipulated, called for Bonaparte's elevation. On May 18, the Senate, using a device reminiscent of the wily Caesar Augustus (see p. 16), combined the imperial reality with republican rhetoric. The second clause of the new constitution called Napoleon Bonaparte "First Consul of the Republic" and "Emperor of the French" in a single sentence. The inevitable plebiscite followed. It showed 3,572,329 for, only 2,569 against, the new regime. A smaller majority would have been more impressive.

Bonaparte—we must call him Napoleon I now—dramatized his accession on December 2, 1804, at Notre Dame de Paris, with a great coronation ceremony. Pope Pius VII came all the way from Rome to act his part in the rehearsed charade. He held up the imperial crown, Napoleon grasped it and placed it on his own head. It was a splendid moment for the little Corsican: Charlemagne, too, had crowned himself so. Domestically, the change of title made little difference. From 1803 on, Napoleon had surrounded himself with a court; from 1804, it became merely larger and more lavish. The new emperor created a series of resounding dignities and new titles, and a new nobility. The civil code, another product of the Consulate, was followed by related codes in the following years—a code of civil procedure, a penal code, a code of criminal procedure, and a commercial code. From 1807 on, the civil code, the most important, was deferentially called the *Code Napoléon*. For all its paternalism, this was the code by which French troops brought modernity to Europe—for what was retreat from some revolutionary principles in France was radical rationalism elsewhere.

Europe, indeed, preoccupied Napoleon I in these years as much as did France. In May 1804, while Bonaparte was preparing to make himself emperor, William Pitt had returned to office in England. He was worn with care and sherry, but he gave his remaining energies to the formation of a new coalition—the third—against French aggression. He found sympathetic support from the idealistic young Tsar Alexander I. Alexander had succeeded his unstable father,

Paul I, after a violent palace revolution in 1801. Soon, he came to think of himself as Napoleon's eastern counterpart. Bonaparte's high-handed actions in Germany, Italy, and elsewhere, and, even more, his murder of the duke d'Enghien, made Alexander all the more eager to defend Europe. In November 1804, the Russians signed a defensive treaty with the Austrians; in April 1805, they came to terms with the British. In May, Emperor Napoleon I crowned himself king of Italy and made his stepson Eugène de Beauharnais, viceroy. This was enough for the other powers; by August 1805, the Third Coalition was in being.

Napoleon, who had been ostentatiously assembling troops and ships at Boulogne for a descent on England, now just as ostentatiously turned eastward. With his troops commanded by his celebrated marshals—Ney, Davout, Lannes, Soult, Murat in Germany; Masséna in Italy—Napoleon planned to break up the coalition with lightning marches and rapid victories. He succeeded. On October 17, he compelled the Austrians under General Mack to surrender, with a large army, at Ulm, and marched on Vienna. But at sea, he faced Lord Nelson—his equal. In a melodramatic chase, the French and the allied Spanish navies had escaped British patrols in March and gathered in the West Indies, with Nelson in hot pursuit. The French plan was to draw the British navy across the Atlantic, dash back, gain control of the English channel and thus enable French troops to invade England. The scheme was risky, and Nelson too quick to let it mature. By August, Nelson had the French bottled up at Cadiz. Disappointed, Napoleon now turned his main attention to land warfare, and on October 21, 1805, after brilliant maneuvering on a sunny day, Nelson virtually destroyed the French-Spanish fleet off Cape Trafalgar. The British lost not a single ship, and only a few men, among them the national hero, Nelson himself. Napoleon made light of the debacle, but it was nothing less. Trafalgar guaranteed England the supremacy of the sea, put a permanent end to any notion of invasion, and as events were to show, frustrated Napoleon's later attempts to isolate Britain from the world (see p. 516).

On land, Napoleon had every cause for confidence. In November, when he learned of the defeat at Trafalgar, he was in Vienna, and on December 2, at Austerlitz, in Moravia, he scored his greatest victory. The French battered the allied troops, inflicting over thirty thousand casualties upon them. Austerlitz always remained Napoleon's favorite battle. With good reason: it kept the Prussians, who had been on the verge of abandoning their neutrality, out of war, and it led, in late December, to the advantageous Treaty of Pressburg with Austria.

As in other battles, so at Austerlitz, Napoleon's military prowess stemmed not from technological innovation but from tactical insight. Napoleon had a rich heritage to draw upon: his devices—the combination of line and column, for instance—and his rhetoric—the invocation of the nation in arms—belonged to the eighteenth century and to the wars of the Revolution. But Napoleon possessed unequaled skill at disposing and manipulating his forces and unsurpassed capacity for choosing the right spot to attack and to attack quickly. His insistence on mobility brought him victory after victory; he preferred light to heavy cavalry, and his armies lived off the country. Beyond his tactical skills lay his emotional appeal: he called out all the self-interest, and all the loyalty, of which his officers and men were capable. Better than anyone else, he exploited that new slogan—the career open to talents. Demonstrated fighting ability brought promotion; in Napoleon's army a private could quite literally become a field marshal. Napoleon was brilliant enough as a commander to wrest admiration not only from his associates, but from his enemies as well.

Now, at Pressburg, he used his charms on the Austrians. He got full sovereignty over Italy: Austria recognized him as king of Italy, ceded the Venetian territory they had acquired at Campo Formio eight years before, and permitted France to annex Piedmont, Parma, and Piacenza. In addition, Austria ceded important territories to Napoleon's German ally Bavaria, and agreed to recognize Bavaria and Württemberg as kingdoms, and Baden as a grand duchy.

Pressburg hastened the reorganization of Germany which had been underway for some years. In March 1803, following the provisions of the treaty of Lunéville of 1801, and at French prodding, the imperial Reichstag had simplified the map of their crazyquilt territories in an imperial recess, with the resounding German name of *Reichsdeputationshauptschluss.* It reduced the number of free cities of the empire from fifty-one to six; only two ecclesiastical principalities survived this drastic surgery. In all, some one hundred twelve sovereign units of the Holy Roman Empire disappeared and were merged into larger units. The recess was concluded under the eye of Consul Bonaparte, after undignified wrangling of German princes in Paris—a scramble for territories that made Talleyrand even richer than he already was. It benefited middle-sized states like Bavaria and Baden, made them slavishly dependent on France, and virtually destroyed the empire. Then, in 1804, anticipating its demise, Emperor Francis II officially took the title of Austrian emperor as Francis I, hoping thus to strengthen his hand in domains he could realistically control. Pressburg, as we have seen, further extended the territories of the middle-sized south German states and increased their dependence on France. In July 1806, Napoleon formed the Confederation of the Rhine and acted as its protector; it included the two new German kings—Maximilian I of Bavaria and Frederick I of Württemberg—the archduke of Baden, and most other west German rulers, tied to France by treaty and pledged to supply France with troops. In August 1806, after the members of the confederation seceded, Francis II surrendered his imperial crown, and that great anachronism, the Holy Roman Empire of the German Nation, was dead. This is what makes Napoleon Bonaparte's impact so hard to judge: abroad, however self-centered his motives, his actions often had progressive consequences.

The events of 1806 brought Prussia into the war against France. Neutral— embarrassingly so—since 1795, Prussia had been enjoying a modest age of reform under her king Frederick William III. Upon his accession in 1797, he had greatly simplified his court and given his ministers leeway for administrative changes. By 1805, the peasants on Prussia's crown lands were free, and the national debt was greatly reduced. But the foreign policy of Frederick William III was as timid as the man himself. Its only consistent point was neutrality. But in October 1806, after numerous provocations, Prussia finally went to war. A week later, at the battles of Jena and Auerstädt, the Prussian armies, those admirable instruments of Frederick the Great, were quickly and totally routed. As the French advanced across Prussia, garrison after garrison surrendered with indecent haste. By late October, Napoleon was in Berlin; by December, he had made a separate peace with the elector of Saxony; by early 1807, French troops had occupied German territory from Silesia to the Hanseatic cities. Their first check—almost unprecedented in Napoleon's stunning military career—came in early February, when Russian troops fought them to a standstill at Eylau. But in mid-June, at Friedland, the French forces compelled the Russians to retreat, and Napoleon entered Königsberg. The Treaties of Tilsit were the result. In a dramatic meeting on a raft in the middle of the river Niemen, Tsar Alexander and Emperor Napoleon decided the fate of Prussia on July 7; two days later, the Prussians meekly acceded. Prussia was reduced to half its laboriously amassed territories; only Alexander's insistence kept it on the map at all. Prussian lands between the Rhine and the Elbe were handed to Napoleon for his disposal; Saxony acquired the region around Cottbus; a new duchy of Warsaw was carved out in part from Prussian acquisitions in Poland. And both Russia and Prussia recognized the extensive redrawing of the map of Europe that Napoleon was undertaking elsewhere. In a magnificent gesture of family affection, Napoleon placed his brothers on established and yet-to-be established thrones: Joseph Bonaparte became king of Naples, Louis Bonaparte king of Holland, Jerome Bonaparte king of Westphalia;[6] and to all this, to the Confederation of the Rhine, and to Napoleon's diplomatic activities in Turkey, the signatories assented. Finally Prussia (and, in secret articles, Russia) agreed to aid France in the war against England. Napoleon's position was enviable; his control over central Europe, complete.

FROM TILSIT TO VIENNA

The Mastery of Europe

Tilsit marked an epoch in the history of Europe. Before 1807 the emperor had proved irresistible; after 1807 French successes were won against a counterpoint of resistance that would ultimately conquer. Yet the existence of that counterpoint is more apparent to historians than it was, at least immediately, to

---

[6] One brother, Lucien, was denied a kingdom; Napoleon had never been on good terms with him and had broken with him over what Napoleon regarded as an unsuitable marriage.

contemporaries. For three or four years men continued to be dazzled by the emperor's skill and good fortune. In 1809 the Austrians prematurely and overconfidently rose against him and in July were crushed at Wagram. By the Treaty of Schönbrunn, worse even than Pressburg four years earlier, Austria ceded territory to the client kingdoms and to Tsar Alexander I, who, despite his alliance with Napoleon, had remained calculatedly inactive. The principal Austrian negotiator, the new chancellor Count Klemens von Metternich, once ambassador in Paris, thereupon bought time for his country by a French alliance.

That alliance was confirmed in 1810 by a new Napoleonic triumph, his marriage to the Austrian princess Marie Louise. Josephine had proved incapable of bearing the emperor a child, and he had divorced her at the end of 1809; the hard-headed affection between the two was reflected in Josephine's successful demands for a handsome pension and the retention of her title. Napoleon's new empress gave him his heir, a son born in April 1811 and called the king of Rome, in tribute to the imperial city, which Napoleon had seized from an imprisoned pope in 1808 and incorporated, with the Papal States, into his empire the next year. Napoleon now went further in cultivating the imperial style. He flattered some of the old nobility, multiplied the new Napoleonic nobility on whose loyalty and self-interest he depended, and proclaimed his glory in monumental architecture.

The client states were kept in line. When convenience or necessity demanded, they were rearranged, and Napoleon's royal relatives and allies were shunted about. In 1808 Joseph was sent from Naples to Spain, replaced in his Italian kingdom by Caroline Bonaparte and her husband, the opportunistic and flamboyant Marshal Joachim Murat, who had ruled the grand duchy of Berg, pieced together from territories on the lower Rhine that had come to Napoleon after Austerlitz. The grand duchy of Warsaw, Napoleon's modest and not entirely sincere gesture to Polish independence—created from Prussia's Polish territories in 1807 and increased by some Austrian territory in 1809—was given Napoleon's dependent, the king of Saxony, as its puppet ruler. And when the emperor's brother Louis proved too sympathetic to the Dutch over whom he had been placed, he was unceremoniously chased from his throne in 1810. The client states were not mere conquests; they were the cutting edge of French ideals and of modernity, and to a greater or lesser degree the changes in law and institutions inspired or imposed by the French struck root. But the subjects of this vast empire also paid tribute to Napoleon—in money, in art treasures carried back to Paris, and, mercilessly, in troops.

Consolidation was the major internal task facing the Napoleonic Empire in the years after Tilsit, but, despite the victories in the field, the external challenge persisted. Great Britain, resourceful and determined, was now secure from direct assault by invasion. Napoleon was necessarily respectful of British skill and daring at sea, and he was fascinated by the casual, hard-drinking aristocrats who commanded the British army. But he comprehended British government not at all and was appalled by the freedom and scurrilousness of the British press. One thing, however, he was sure he understood: that Britain was a nation of shopkeepers.[7] Now a nation of shopkeepers was surely vulnerable to economic pressure; and, from the time of the Directory, desultory and not very effective attempts had been made at bringing Britain to its knees through economic warfare. Napoleon proposed to regularize this strategy in the Continental System.

The policy was inaugurated with the Berlin Decree in November 1806, which closed all Continental ports to British ships and goods. The British responded the next year with orders in council requiring neutral ships to be licensed in an English port, where they might also take on British goods to run the blockade. Napoleon countered with the Fontainebleau and Milan Decrees of October and December 1807, warning that any neutral ships complying with the orders in council would be treated as English. There were, in fact, few enough neutrals. The only important uncommitted maritime power caught in this paper war was the United States, and in 1807 President Jefferson tried to force France and Britain to back down by carrying an Embargo Act, which so hurt American merchants and shippers that it was soon repealed. Napoleon, playing the American card more effectively than the British, declared his readiness to make concessions, but never had to make them because the British were intransigent. The British insisted, moreover, on boarding neutral ships to find deserters from their navy, thus causing an additional grievance to the Americans, for American citizens were sometimes seized in these searches. In 1812 the United States and Britain drifted into a ridiculous and futile war, marked by some American military successes and by a British victory of sorts in the burning of Washington; but the peace that concluded this incidental embroilment in 1814 settled none of the outstanding issues between the two English-speaking nations.

British society in these years was subjected to unparalleled stresses and strains—from war, taxation, inflation, and the terrible dislocations of rapid and unplanned industrialization. French strategists calculated that a drop in English exports would provoke unrest and perhaps revolt: they were not wrong. When exports fell precipitously in late 1807 and early 1808, there was real hardship in Britain. When a newly stringent enforcement of the blockade was undertaken in 1810-1811, the difficulties within Britain triggered the savage, quasirevolutionary outbursts of violence and machine-breaking in the industrial districts known (after their mythical leader, General Ludd or King Ludd) as the Luddite riots. Had the French had the resources or will to enforce the blockade effectively and regularly, the Continental System might have gone far toward bringing Britain into negotiations. But in the end it failed.

---

[7] This famous phrase, reportedly uttered by Napoleon in his exile on St. Helena, may have originated with the Corsican patriot General Paoli; but it was also used by Adam Smith in the *Wealth of Nations* and by the American patriot Samuel Adams, both in 1776.

The British economy was far more resilient than the emperor or his advisors knew. The rapid progress of industrialization in the years when the French were preoccupied with revolution made British goods cheaper and more abundant, and increased demand for them throughout the world. Not only did the importance of the North American market continue to grow, but the Napoleonic invasion of Portugal and Spain opened the colonies of South America to British enterprise. And to a remarkable degree the Continent itself, though its importance to British commerce had been declining for more than a century, was kept open. The Baltic trade was maintained by the British seizure of Copenhagen in a daring naval raid in 1807 and by the capture of the tiny island of Heligoland in the North Sea for use as a trading base. Even the territory most directly under Napoleon's control needed British goods: internal transport on the Continent was too rudimentary and slow to allow overland supply to be substituted efficiently for transit by sea, and the coastline was too long to be regularly and closely supervised. The smugglers had a field day. In time Napoleon had to consent to a licensing system that allowed the import of colonial produce, which England was getting in increasing amounts in exchange for her stepped-up shipments to the New World. But other goods made their way through the blockade as well. Even French troops wore English cloth.

The Continental System failed in another respect. It was intended not merely as wartime strategy but as a way of strengthening the long-term prospects of the French economy against the British, but the French pursued this goal narrowly, looking on the other nations of Europe as tributaries. Had French policymakers learned from Adam Smith, they might have implemented a mutually beneficial free-trade area on the Continent. As it was, French policy offended precisely those aggressive and informed groups in the growing middle segment of European society who were, on other grounds, the best and most loyal supporters Napoleon could claim.

The Beginning of the End: Spain

Efforts to consolidate the French hold on the Continent and to bring Britain down by economic pressure dictated further French expansion. Spain had been allied to France since 1796; far overestimating Spain's strategic and economic importance, Napoleon insisted on its adherence to the Continental System. Priest-ridden, backward, and mysterious, Spain was wretchedly ruled by King Charles IV, his queen, and her favorite Manuel de Godoy. Godoy was not entirely illiberal or unenlightened, but he was fatally compromised by his taste for intrigue, his reputation (probably undeserved) as the queen's lover, and the suspicion of self-serving, even royal ambitions. Constantly working against this strange triangle was the heir to the throne, Ferdinand, who was implicated in a riot that forced his father to abdicate early in 1808. Napoleon thereupon summoned the whole royal family to Bayonne in southwestern France, badgered both Charles and Ferdinand into giving up their rights, and created a new kingdom of Spain, which he conferred on his brother Joseph. The result was a genuinely popular uprising throughout the kingdom. Joseph fled from Madrid at the beginning of August; to restore him, Napoleon had to occupy the country. Although they were successful in this immediate goal, the French found themselves facing constant guerrilla activity they could not understand. French forces had already been sent, late in 1807, to occupy Portugal, which had refused to abandon its long-standing alliance with Britain. British forces had landed and, under the command of Arthur Wellesley—later famous as the duke of Wellington—drove the French out of Portugal at the battle of Vimeiro in August 1808. A British force under Sir John Moore, sent to aid the Spanish insurgents in Madrid, was nearly cut off by the French and retreated with heavy losses to be evacuated at Corunna. But Wellesley stayed in the mountains of Portugal and let the superbly mobile French troops hurl themselves futilely time after time against his lines at Torres Vedras. Wellesley's careful preparation and patience, and a war of position, not movement, puzzled and exhausted the French; then slowly, systematically, Wellesley began to move forward into Spain. The Peninsular War had begun. "It was the Spanish ulcer," Napoleon later said ruefully, "that ruined me."

The creation of the Napoleonic kingdom of Spain brought more than an uprising and military defeat: it caused a sharp, self-conscious rejection of the cosmopolitanism for which France had come to stand and the institutions in which the French embodied their ideals. From the middle of the eighteenth century the smaller number of educated, forward-looking Spaniards to whom the term *liberal* was coming to be affixed, had been loyal to the enlightened monarchy of Charles III (see p. 422), and they had even managed to live with a church that, though unenlightened, was pervasive and popular and in which the highest places could still be reached by men of lowly origin. But when Napoleon dethroned the Bourbons in 1808, he forced a crisis of loyalty on the liberals. Some, the so-called *afrancesados*, saw collaboration with Joseph Bonaparte—an attractive, liberal-minded, though largely ineffectual man—as the best way of preserving a semblance of national independence and at the same time of regenerating Spain. But more of the liberals veered toward the republicanism affected by younger radicals, and in time, as they became aware of the total resistance of the church to reforming ideas, toward anticlericalism. This new radicalism, bitterly opposed to Napoleon, was grafted onto a genuinely national resistance.

In 1810, while Spain was still occupied and the British were biding their time in Portugal, the Spaniards elected a new Cortes; in it for the first time the representatives of the third estate outnumbered the nobles and clergy. In 1812, as the peninsular campaign moved forward, a constitution was adopted, which combined equality before the law, the defense of property rights, and a severely limited monarchy in a grand rhetorical scheme for which no country in Europe was ready. Taken far more seriously by liberals elsewhere than they deserved to be—the word "liberal" as a political term entered the English language from the Spanish—the Spanish reformers bequeathed a model to a generation of radical constitution-makers. But the alliance between this reforming impulse and the national resistance could not coexist for long, and ignorance, xenophobia, and clericalism proved stronger. The radical regime was threatened from the outset by opposition from the church and from a coalition of officers and conservatives, and military victory over the French doomed the reforms. In 1814 Ferdinand VII, a national hero in spite of himself, returned to rule his country with an unimaginative stupidity that provoked by turns new revolutions, French intervention, and a dreary civil war. Still, despite the confusion and cross-purposes of Spanish patriots, the Spanish example in these years is instructive. Whatever the success of reformers, whatever their obligations to native tradition, French example, or imported ideas, the struggle against Napoleonic domination and against the institutions and armies by which it was enforced, welded a new sense of nationhood, of a common culture and a shared pride, that was a potent legacy to the nineteenth century.

National Regeneration: Britain, Russia, Austria, Germany

Great Britain, the chief, most energetic, and most effective of Napoleon's enemies, changed little during these years in political and administrative structure, less perhaps than any European nation except Austria. Yet change there was; the war dictated reforms in the central administration and carried further the quest for efficiency and the reduction of useless but remunerative offices that gave the crown a major means of exerting political influence. In the income tax—instituted in 1797, revised in 1802, and heartily hated throughout the war—the government had found a modern instrument that, though it had to be given up in 1816, would be restored a quarter of a century later to remain the chief financial mainstay of British government to the present day. But William Pitt, the principal architect of such administrative reforms as were carried through, was out of office from 1801 to 1804, and in his brief second ministry from 1804 to 1806 he was completely preoccupied with the renewed war against France. In 1806 he died, exhausted, at the age of forty-seven.

The Whigs—or the most liberal-minded remnant of them—out of office since 1783, offered the only basis for a government, and, much against his will, the king agreed to a coalition known as the Ministry of All the Talents. Its most prominent figure, Charles James Fox, died late in the year, and the single notable legislative accomplishment of the ministry was the act of 1807 abolishing the slave trade, a response to a national agitation of humanitarian and religious reformers led in Parliament by Pitt's friend, the merchant and Evangelical politician William Wilberforce. An attempt to secure the traditional Whig goal of Catholic Emancipation—the right of Catholics to hold offices in the state and to sit in Parliament—the issue on which Pitt had been driven from office by the king in 1801, brought the downfall of the Talents in 1807. The governments that succeeded were made up of men who considered themselves heirs of Pitt; as they had worked his system effectively, they saw little need to change it. Headed first by an ineffectual peer, then by the colorless but competent Spencer Perceval, the government picked its way through political difficulties and somehow fought the war. Its worst political threat appeared in 1810, when King George III was declared irretrievably mad and a regency was conferred on the dissolute and incompetent prince of Wales; the prince had long dallied with the Whigs, but over the next year he rejected their claims on office, showing himself an opponent of all meaningful change. When Perceval was assassinated in 1812 (by a bankrupt who blamed his troubles on the government), his successor was another of Pitt's lieutenants, the earl of Liverpool. Liverpool's ministry was to carry Britain into the liberal era, but it was to be ten years before that promise would become apparent.

The reforming impulse that had been at work in the 1770s and 1780s and the full-blown radicalism of the early years of the French Revolution were driven underground by repressive legislation in the nineties. Among working men it survived in clandestine trade-union activity, disguised often as benefit clubs to get round the Combination Acts of 1799 and 1800, which made unions illegal. This activity in turn underlay the working-class agitations that in 1811–1812 gave rise to those episodes of machine-breaking and violence against employers associated with the effects of the Continental System. A new, more respectable, middle-class movement for parliamentary reform was organized in the city of Westminster, adjacent to London, in 1806–1807 and grew steadily throughout the remainder of the war. It drew not only on the tradition of the 1780s but on the frustration felt by some educated and ambitious men, particularly among manufacturers and members of the more radical Dissenting sects, who added dislike of the war to resentment of their continued exclusion from political participation. But neither the working-class agitation nor the Westminster movement reflected the real mood of the country. The vehement reaction against the French Revolution—so superbly if unfairly expressed by Edmund Burke in 1790—was easily transmuted into hatred of "Boney," replete with overtones of the xenophobic pride that had always characterized English patriotism.

There is, however, a more important explanation of the willingness of most Englishmen to tolerate a society so imperfect in so many ways, an explanation that goes beyond invoking patriotism, fear of radicalism, or the undoubted diffusion of prosperity in the wartime boom: England had had her revolution and was in the last analysis, as the greatest historian of nineteenth-century England has put it, a free country, "a country of voluntary obedience, of an organization freely initiated and freely accepted."[8] That lesson the entire Continent had yet to learn.

Across the Continent, in Russia, the Napoleonic era seemed to hold out greater promise for reform. The brief reign of Catherine the Great's son Paul I,

---

[8] The quotation is the concluding passage of the first volume (1913) of Elie Halévy's *A History of the English People in the Nineteenth Century,* a superb recreation of England in 1815.

from 1796 to 1801, had verged on the disastrous. Paul had come to the throne hating his mother and all she stood for. He released her prisoners, incarcerated his own, and played the autocrat in the most extreme fashion, in petty details as well as in high policy.[9] He extended the geographical sway of serfdom and harshly suppressed agrarian troubles; at the same time he offended the gentry whom his mother had cultivated by imposing limitations (scarcely enforceable but nonetheless galling to the gentry) on the amount of labor a serfowner could exact. He entered the Second Coalition precipitously at the end of 1798 and as precipitously left it in 1800, allying himself with Napoleon. When fighting the French he had extended Russian power to the Ionian Islands in the Mediterranean, where a Russian-protected republic was created under Turkish suzerainty, and to the island of Malta, when he accepted election as grand master of the Knights of Malta who had ruled there from the sixteenth century until Napoleon turned them out in 1798. When Malta was lost to the British in the tsar's change of front, he sent off an army of Cossacks to invade India. But in March 1801 a revolt of the palace guards ended in Paul's assassination; the new tsar was Paul's twenty-three-year-old son, Alexander I.

The change in rulers was received everywhere with relief. Alexander at once replaced his father's belligerency with a policy of peace, and it seemed likely that sweeping domestic changes would follow as well. The young tsar was charming, intelligent, well-informed, and ambitious to better his country. He had been educated by a Swiss philosophe, Frédéric César de La Harpe, and he early gave an earnest of his liberal intentions by declaring an amnesty for his father's political prisoners and by relaxing the censorship. He met regularly with an "unofficial committee" of liberal-minded advisors to plan how Russia might be reformed. But there was another side to Alexander's nature: he was emotional, unstable, and as prone to discouragement as he was to enthusiasm. And there was much in that huge, ungovernable country to discourage even the most determined of men. Overwhelmingly agrarian, Russia lacked any significant middle class, that source of enterprise and vision on which so much of western European progress depended. Alexander's initial hope to do something about serfdom quickly vanished when confronted with intractable reality; only a law of 1803 permitting voluntary emancipation resulted, and little was done under it. The gentry, who had hated Paul, wanted only such alterations as would restore the privileges they had gained under Catherine the Great and maintain the autocracy as they thought it had existed in the eighteenth century. There was no significant demand at any level of society for fundamental change in either society or government. And so the initial reforming impulse died out by 1804; the unofficial committee had already ceased to meet. In government some useful, even important, administrative alterations were made—the establishment of the Senate as the supreme administrative and judicial body,

---

[9] He is reported to have said that the person speaking to him was the only important person in the country—and only so long as the conversation lasted.

and the gradual transformation of the collegial system of administration into ministries, each with a single head. But the one lasting, broadly significant reform was in education: a number of new universities and schools were founded, and by the end of the reign the essentials of a rational, nationwide system were laid down.

Between 1807 and 1812 there was another burst of reforming activity, this time centered on the astonishing activity of M. M. Speransky. The son of a priest, Speransky had absorbed the best that could be had from the old-fashioned Scholastic education in Russian seminaries and had gone on to immerse himself in the ideas of the Enlightenment. A consummate bureaucrat and a far-sighted statesman (though entirely within the confines of autocracy), Speransky had a clear sense of the need for a rational institutional and legal structure to replace the confusion and arbitrariness that passed for tsarist autocracy. But Speransky's sense of what needed doing was better than his sense of what could be done. For all his brilliance, he had to plan and administer too much. He tried but could not carry through a codification of Russian law on the model of the French code. In 1809 he drafted a complete constitution providing for a series of legislative assemblies culminating in an indirectly elected state Duma; for a judicial administration culminating, as in the past, in the Senate; for a reformed system of local government; and for an executive capped by a Council of State made up of the tsar's most intimate advisers. But only the last survived the planning stage. Brilliant civil servants, especially when they are innovators, are rarely popular. Speransky was hated for some of his measures—notably his effort to impose written examinations or university training as qualifications for the higher ranks of the civil service. He was suspected of undue admiration for France. Above all the gentry resented his plebeian origins. In 1812 he fell, exiled to the Urals as if he were a traitor. And while he returned to St. Petersburg later in Alexander's reign, having done remarkable administrative work in Siberia, he was never again to attempt reform on so grand a scale.

Nor was Alexander. On occasion the tsar still showed signs of his early dedication to liberal ideas, but he was preoccupied with foreign affairs and sought political counsel chiefly from the reactionary Count Arakcheev, who had been his boyhood friend. His increasing withdrawal into religiosity finds its most celebrated evidence in his brief infatuation with the famous mystic, the Baroness Julie de Krüdener. In short, Alexander's fragile temperament could not bear the strains he himself had placed upon it—in vain. It is tempting to see his quarter-century's rule as a succession of lost opportunities; it is wiser to see the reign as a demonstration of futility. Liberal ideas could work marvels where the way for them had been properly prepared; they could do little to break the harsh, resistant ground of Russian society and culture.

In Austria the inclination to do nothing (or as little as possible) was superbly distilled in the outlook of Francis I, who had come to the throne in

1792, at the age of twenty-four, following the unexpected death of his father, the able and statesman-like Leopold II; he ruled until 1835. Although he maintained most of the compromises by which Leopold had sought to reverse or temper the Josephine revolution,[10] little in Francis's Austria was touched by a liberal or enlightened spirit. The serfs, with whose status and lords Joseph II had dealt so drastically, remained personally free; but because Francis had decreed that only the lord's consent could make it possible to escape the obligation of forced labor, the serfs still fell short of true peasant status. Intellectuals, especially suspect in the reaction against revolutionary ideas, were kept in hand by censorship and by strict control of schools and universities. Radical activity, like everything else, was supervised by a pervasive and, for its time quite sophisticated, police apparatus. There were breaks, however, in this cover of social and constitutional monotony. Hungary, glad enough to be freed from the hated Josephine program of Germanization, was loyal to the emperor, but a degree of patriotic independence survived in fairly regular meetings of the Hungarian Diet down to 1811, even though few grievances ever reached the stage of discussion and still fewer brought executive action. Similarly, demands for the recognition of Magyar as the language of official life and education in place of Latin and German got nowhere.

The reforming impulse flickered briefly in Austria itself in the three years after the disastrous defeat by Napoleon at Ulm in 1805 and the humiliating Peace of Pressburg. Count Philipp Stadion, a transplanted Rhinelander who was foreign minister, envisioned a national uprising among all the German peoples based on a patriotic revival and a program of genuine, if limited, reform. No solid foundation for this goal had been assured, however, when the Austrians tackled Napoleon in 1809, to end in defeat at Wagram and Schönbrunn. Stadion was at once dismissed, and reform was dismissed with him. He returned to serve under Metternich,[11] but his experiment was not repeated.

In the German lands outside Austria the situation was far different. There the French example, directly or indirectly, had a powerful impact. The parts of Germany on the left bank of the Rhine were incorporated directly into France in 1797, divided into seven departments, and ruled from Paris; much of the right bank went to make up the duchy of Berg in 1806. That the Rhineland was well prepared to welcome and retain much that was done, however alien its source, is indicated by the fact that Stadion and Metternich in Austria, Nesselrode in Russia, and the leading reformers in Prussia all came from the Rhineland—long a progressive region, it produced civil servants of fortune needed by backward states as desperate earlier rulers had needed soldiers of fortune. In northern Germany, the Napoleonic kingdom of Westphalia was intended as a model of enlightened government; though much was restored in 1815, the process was irreversible. In the south, new states were created around established nuclei—Bavaria, Württemberg, and Baden were the most prominent—not merely by the accretion of petty principalities but by the ruthless ignoring of traditional boundaries and customs, by centralization, and by enlightened administration on the French model. In these parts of Germany there had been some sympathy with the efforts of Joseph II to wrench Austria into the modern world, and reforms were quickly absorbed, the more so perhaps as they were the work of native dynasties and bureaucrats who were at once enlightened, autocratic, and German. But these new creations were not undertaken as the first steps toward a united Germany; rather they were expressions of pride and ambition in separate, and for the time viable, middle-sized states. Thus the chaos of Germany was rationalized under Napoleon but not reduced to uniformity; even within the Confederation of the Rhine, that loose agglomeration of southern, western, and central German states, the variety was startling. In contrast to Bavaria or Baden, Saxony and Mecklenburg, which kept their independence by timely alliances with Napoleon, remained almost totally unchanged, even though the Saxon king, Frederick Augustus I, was required to implement the usual reforms in the grand duchy of Warsaw, which he also headed. [12]

National Regeneration: The Prussian Case

Looking back on his career, Napoleon regretted that he did not eliminate Prussia at the time of Tilsit. By detaching Prussia's western territories, leaving only its backward eastern lands, and confronting the country with occupation and a huge indemnity, he stimulated the desire for recovery and revenge; the means to attain those ends were sought in fundamental political and social reforms. In time, a reconstructed Prussia formed the base on which the ultimate solution of the German problem was founded.

Given the Prussian tradition of autocracy, a formidable civil and military bureaucracy, and a passive people, these reforms could be imposed from above. [13] Prussia's king, Frederick William III, was well-meaning but timid, preferring to rely for advice on his most intimate counselors, the cabinet secretaries, rather than on his ministers. The most prominent of his ministers was the Freiherr vom Stein, the proud descendant of a family of imperial

[12] Hence the wits of Warsaw poked fun at Frederick Augustus by calling him (alluding to the Molière farce) "*le médecin malgré lui*—the doctor in spite of himself."

[13] The late nineteenth-century English historian Sir John Seeley said, in a somewhat superior way, of the local government reforms, that the Prussian people "were commanded, not allowed, to govern themselves." A few decades later, an English historian would have been quite aware that many of the forms of English local government had originated in the Middle Ages owing to exactly the same imposition of self-government by the king, in his own interest, upon an unwilling people.

knights in the Rhineland. Stein had entered the Prussian service in 1780; by 1804 he was in charge of the general supervision of revenues, commerce, and manufactures, a task to which he brought a close knowledge of Adam Smith and the French Physiocrats and a general admiration for England. Convinced of the need for sweeping change and impatient with Frederick William's temporizing, Stein led a virtual revolt among the king ministers in 1806 and was dismissed early in 1807 for his insubordination. Stein's colleague Count Hardenberg, less imaginative and more diplomatic, persuaded the king to rely on his ministers and, in October, to recall Stein as his principal adviser. In a little over a year in office Stein initiated a series of major reforms, though he was prevented from seeing them through by Napoleon's insistence on his dismissal at the end of November 1808. [14]

During his brief hold on power, Stein reorganized the central government by removing the informal cabinet and by reorganizing the administrative structure into five ministries—interior, foreign affairs, finance, justice, and war—all organized on the French model. He wanted to unify the action of the ministries through a state council that would give collective advice to the king, hoping thus to avoid the dangers of power concentrated in the hands of a single minister—a device that surely reflects an Anglophile's awareness of the hostility in eighteenth-century England to the notion of a "prime minister." Stein was unable to carry through this second stage of his reorganization, and in 1810 the king, who temperamentally needed one man on whom he could rely, appointed the indispensable Hardenberg (a good eighteenth-century absolutist) as chancellor, an office that, later revived on a wider national level by Bismarck, has remained the pivot of German politics and administration right down to the present. Stein also increased the powers and responsibilities of provincial governments, again preferring to confide those powers to boards rather than to single officials. He did, however, provide for "high presidents" to represent the central government in the provinces, and these officials became an important part of Prussian government following 1815. Stein also initiated a sweeping reform of town governments in 1808 and hoped that at the level of the rural districts as well as in towns some representation of all ranks of society might be included. Again his departure—or perhaps the realities of the situation—prevented implementation of notions for which he was clearly indebted to his admiration of English local government.

These governmental reforms, restricted though they were in Hardenberg's politic application of them, were supplemented by military reforms carried through by Generals Scharnhorst and Gneisenau to rebuild the army so thoroughly discredited at Jena in 1806. The clear remedy for the manpower problem lay in abandoning the canton system, by which regiments could draw only on small recruiting districts—a system hampered by wholesale exemptions—and replacing it with a national system of universal service. Partly

[14] After a brief stay in Austria, Stein was summoned to become an adviser to Tsar Alexander I.

because of political problems, partly because the French put strict limits on the size of the Prussian forces, this sweeping change was postponed until 1813. But the barbarous discipline of the old Prussian army gave way to a more humane and regular system of military justice in 1808; the officer corps was opened to others than aristocrats; a new emphasis on ability and training dictated a reorganization of the war schools and a concentration on theory and planning that foreshadowed the creation of a general staff; there was, moreover, a wholesale revision of the organization of army units and of tactics. [15] Thus these years of abject defeat produced a state and an army that could cope more effectively than could the old Prussian institutions with the Napoleonic challenge. But, in Stein's view, far more sweeping social reforms were essential to a real marshaling of the nation.

The gradual reduction of ancient restrictions on the economy had gone on from the accession of Frederick William III; early in the reign, moreover, serfs on the royal estates were freed, an example followed by a handful of great landowners in East Prussia who could see the advantage of ridding themselves of the obligation to maintain their serfs and relying on hired instead of forced labor. In 1807 Stein drafted an edict decreeing the emancipation of serfs throughout what the French had left of Prussia; but his dismissal meant a less sweeping implementation and extension of these reforms than he had anticipated or might have been able to carry into effect. The serfs obtained their legal freedom—they could, for example, now marry without the lord's consent—but their labor obligations were only gradually removed, and they were prevented by lack of capital from using more intensive agricultural techniques. The aristocratic landowners, moreover, retained special privileges through much of the century. Indeed, it was they who profited most from the reforms, not only because their estates tended to grow larger with land the peasants could not maintain, not only because the state was solicitous of their welfare and prejudices, but because what was done opened the way to more effective capitalistic exploitation of the land. And, if landowners chose not to be better capitalists, middle-class entrepreneurs could take over, for Stein did away with the old monopoly of the aristocrats on the purchase and holding of land. Far more than had been anticipated, the changes converted serfs, not into landholding peasants, but into landless laborers. A process that had taken several centuries in England was accomplished by fiat in Germany within a decade or two. The complete freeing of the industrial system, however, was not attained in practice until midcentury and later, although edicts of 1808–1811 recognized the principle, allowed most trades to be practiced by anyone who could pay the entry fee, regulated few of them, and left the gilds to survive only as voluntary institutions.

[15] The outstanding figure in this transformation was General Karl von Clausewitz, who, after helping with the reforms and serving in the field, returned to head the Kriegsakademie (war academy) from 1818 to 1830. He was the most influential military theorist of the century. His true teacher, of course, was Napoleon.

The German revival was far more sweeping and constructive in the realm of the spirit than was possible in the touchier areas of money, land, and rights. Heirs to the imposing legacy of the German Enlightenment, with its ideals of tolerance and its notions of the distinctiveness of Germany and the centrality of culture, the educated middle class and the professional classes were given a new range of educational institutions through which these ideals were propagated in ever more nationalistic forms. Stein's nominee to oversee the educational reorganization of Prussia was Wilhelm von Humboldt, the brother of the distinguished naturalist and traveler Alexander von Humboldt, and himself a literary figure of considerable importance. Humboldt remained minister of public instruction for only a little over a year, but in that year Prussia was provided with a system of *Gymnasien*, secondary schools that prepared boys for examinations for university entrance by giving them the essentials of a liberal education and rigorous intellectual discipline. In 1810, because the university at Halle had been absorbed into the Napoleonic kingdom of Westphalia, a new university was founded in Berlin; in the fields of philosophy, religion, and science, the new university was to have profound effects throughout Europe and the rest of the world. An approach to education that would nourish a distinctive German spirit had been called for in 1807–1808 in the powerful *Addresses to the German Nation*, delivered by the philosopher J. G. Fichte, who had been converted by the revolutionary and Napoleonic experience from a cosmopolitan and Francophile enthusiasm to a fervent German nationalism. Fichte saw Germany as increasingly unified by aggressive national educational institutions and by the traditions and ambitions of a common culture. To those raised in the French or English tradition, however, this fact suggests a strange and disturbing flaw: Fichte appealed to a cultural, not a political, nation; in German politics, the state still decreed, even when it was reforming, and the subject received, neither knowing nor valuing meaningful participation. Thus the legacy of the unpolitical German was transmitted in altered form, with profound effects, to the new century and to ours.

Napoleon's Fall and the Making of the Peace

After his victory over Austria at Wagram in 1809, Napoleon determined to crush Spanish resistance and to "drive the English leopard into the sea." But after Masséna's failure to penetrate the English lines in Portugal, Wellington, with deliberate initiative, attacked the French armies and in the battles of Salamanca and Vitoria in 1812 and 1813 drove them out of Spain. Wellington's way was eased by the deflection of the emperor's attention—and of a great many troops—to more pressing concerns in the east. Despite the initial show of enthusiasm, the alliance between Alexander and Napoleon concluded at Tilsit had proved little more than nominal. Neither party was particularly trustworthy, and each resented bad faith in the other. Napoleon's seizure of

Holland was in violation of the Tilsit agreements; nor did Napoleon help the tsar against the Turks, as he had promised. Worse, he had offended Alexander by supporting an independent Polish state in the grand duchy of Warsaw and by concluding an alliance and a marriage with Russia's hereditary enemy Austria. For his part, the tsar had stayed neutral during the Austrian campaign of 1809, had connived at violations of the Continental System, and was in fact consistently working against his nominal ally. By 1811 the last shred of pretense to a Franco-Russian alliance had dissolved. Metternich had noted as early as 1807 that Napoleon seemed to regard moderation as a "useless obstacle"; now the Russian impasse drove the emperor once more to a military solution. On June 24, 1812, Napoleon launched an invasion of Russia, with his Grande Armée built around a core of veterans, both officers and men, but filled out with raw recruits and unwilling draftees from occupied territories. The total number in Napoleon's forces may have reached six hundred thousand at their peak, but the ranks were quickly depleted by desertion, disease, and casualties. Napoleon could still show his old brilliance, but his leadership was sporadic. And while he could appear in Poland as a liberator, he could not imagine turning that powerful weapon—exporting the Revolution—to account in Russia: the serfs struck him as subhuman, and he feared that their liberation would touch off dreadful massacres.

The Russians made a show of resistance at Smolensk in August; early in September, at Borodino, west of Moscow, was fought the most savage and costly battle of the Napoleonic era: the French lost a quarter of their army—nearly thirty thousand—and the Russians counted casualties of twice that number.[16] But pitched battles were not to win the war for the Russians. Retreat—imposed by necessity rather than clever calculation—proved the successful strategy. On September 14, the emperor began the occupation of Moscow, the old holy city of Russia. There he planned to spend the winter and to secure reinforcements from the west. Almost at once fires broke out. "I had no idea of the wonders of this town," Napoleon wrote to his empress a few days later. "It had five hundred mansions as fine as the Elysée, with French furniture and incredible luxury, a number of imperial palaces, barracks, and magnificent hospitals. The whole place has disappeared. . . . All the small middle-class houses are of wood, and catch fire like matches. . . . The respectable inhabitants, 200,000 of them, are in despair, and are reduced to wandering wretchedly in the streets. However there is enough left for the army, which has found all kinds of valuables; in the present confusion everything is for loot."[17] Moscow was in

---

[16] A French officer wrote: "When it was all over I saw Napoleon riding over the battle-field; I followed him everywhere; he was beaming and rubbing his hands: 'There are five dead Russians'—he said it repeatedly with satisfaction—'to every Frenchman.' I suppose he took Germans for Russians" (Thompson, *Napoleon Bonaparte,* 333). Or perhaps generals simply prefer favorable body counts.

[17] Ibid., 335.

fact untenable. Napoleon made peace offers and waited for answers that never came. In mid-October he decided to evacuate the city. The better route to the south was barred by Russian armies; burdened with booty and short of food and transport, the remnants of the Grande Armée straggled back through Smolensk, by the route over which they had come, pursued by the Russians and harried by Cossack raiders. By skill and good fortune Napoleon escaped a trap that was closing on him at the Berezina River in November. But then the winter, long delayed, set in in earnest. Napoleon, having heard of attempts to overthrow him at home, hurried back to Paris in early December: the legend of his suffering with his troops has little foundation in fact. The ravages of cold and starvation on the army he left behind were appalling. Fewer than a hundred thousand men found their way to safety in the west. Napoleon had suffered his first major defeat.

Alexander decided to pursue the French into central Europe, a strategy encouraged by the British, who wanted certain victory; by Stein, who wanted to unify Germany; and by Alexander's own ambition to rule over Poland. Russian forces entered Prussia as liberators, and in late February and March 1813 Frederick William III was persuaded to desert his enforced alliance with the French and to join with the Russians. In June Metternich overcame his scruples against breaking the Austrian alliance with Napoleon and conquered his distrust of British goals of total victory, and the Grand Alliance was created, heavily subsidized with British money. Napoleon managed to defeat the allied armies at Dresden in late August, but in mid-October, near Leipzig, took place what has come to be known as the Battle of the Nations, in which two armies of a quarter of a million men each were engaged. Decisively defeated, Napoleon reentered France, turned on at the last moment by his Bavarian allies. The pursuit continued, and on March 30, 1814, the allied armies entered the capital, followed next day by Frederick William III and the new hero Alexander.

Piecing together the Grand Alliance had involved a number of shifting and contradictory agreements among the allies; soon after Leipzig, negotiations were begun with Napoleon. But it was not only the emperor's obstinacy over terms or his awareness of what he could and could not legitimately or politically offer France that prolonged the confusion. From the first the allies were in conflict over goals. The main outlines of the settlements finally arrived at were laid down by the British foreign secretary, Viscount Castlereagh. Castlereagh's first aim was to ensure the defeat of Napoleon so completely that neither the emperor nor France could again disturb the balance of power. Along with his political associates at home, Castlereagh preferred a restoration of the Bourbon dynasty, dethroned in 1792, though he was more willing than most British opinion to negotiate with Napoleon. Castlereagh wanted, also, to maintain a European coalition that would prevent the distortion of the balance by any single power. He was flexible on central Europe and even on Italy. But he was adamant on the restoration of Spain and Portugal and on a European guarantee of their protection from France. Like all English diplomats for at least four centuries, he insisted that territories directly across the Channel must not be allowed to fall into the possession of a major power that might threaten British security; to that end he proposed that France be kept away from Antwerp and that the southern portion of the Low Countries be given to a restored kingdom of Holland. For further security he proposed to marry Princess Charlotte of Wales, the daughter of the prince regent, to the heir to the Dutch throne. If these basic principles were granted, Britain stood ready to provide subsidies and to cede, as compensation, most of the colonies picked up during the war—from France, Holland, and Spain—to serve, in good eighteenth-century fashion, as bargaining counters. But certain strategic prizes Britain kept—Ceylon in the East, the Cape of Good Hope in southern Africa, Malta, and a protectorate over the Ionian Islands in the Mediterranean—assuring the security of the routes to India.

Metternich played a cool and cynical diplomatic game to maintain the integrity (if that is the word) of his ramshackle empire. He was won over to Castlereagh's side because of the threat posed by the willingness of Frederick William III of Prussia to defer to Alexander. Prussia was, of course, determined to regain the territory it had lost and to be compensated by territorial gains for the humiliations it, more than any other power, had suffered: to Hardenberg, the principal Prussian negotiator, it was a matter of flexibility, if not indifference, whether those gains were at the expense of the Poles or the Saxons. It was rather Alexander who posed the profound enigma and the greatest danger to allied unity. The acknowledged leader of the alliance, well advised and undoubtedly intelligent, Alexander was the only European statesman then able to grasp the importance of liberal and national movements; hence the relish with which he played the role of liberator in central and western Europe. At the same time, as he said, the burning of Moscow "had enlightened his soul," and he was entering on a deeply mystical and religious phase that was not without its impact on the Vienna settlement. Liberal and conservative, enthusiastic and calculating, generous and rigid by turns, he was predictable only when certain national or personal goals were involved, above all in Poland. He felt a personal mission to take moral charge of Poland, and he was supported by some Polish nobles who preferred him to a restoration of the Austrian or Prussian rulers they had escaped by collaborating with Napoleon. In this collision of Russian with Prussian and above all Austrian policy lay the toughest problem of the peace.

The making of a French settlement was centered on two main points: the future of Napoleon and the boundaries to which the defeated nation would be confined. In general the allies were disposed to be fairly generous. The Frankfurt Proposals were drawn up by Russia, Prussia, and Austria shortly after Leipzig and assented to by one of Castlereagh's subordinates. Castlereagh found the offer of frontiers at the Alps on the east and the Pyrenees on the south acceptable, but could not agree to a France extending to the Rhine and encompassing the Low Countries. Napoleon, hoping for better terms, remained noncommittal too long, and when his foreign minister Caulaincourt finally accepted the Frankfurt Proposals, the allies turned him down. Castlereagh was determined that no such error would be made again; negotiations brought Metternich over to the idea of limiting French frontiers more stringently, and the tsar was willing to consider that possibility, given the success of the military operations that continued during negotiations. But Napoleon would still not accept the ancient frontiers, and the tsar wavered; Castlereagh therefore gave his attention to cementing the alliance more effectively than had been done so far.

This goal was accomplished in the Treaty of Chaumont, signed on March 9, 1814. Secret articles set down specific goals that conformed to Castlereagh's intentions, above all an expanded Holland. Of more general importance was the construction of a Quadruple Alliance, to last, according to the treaty, for twenty years: the allies would act in concert to preserve the balance of power. The alliance secure, Castlereagh could return to the problem of Napoleon, whom he would allow to remain on the throne only if the chastened emperor would accept the boundaries of prerevolutionary France. At the end of March the allies were in touch with representatives of the Bourbons, and there were signs that opinion in France, or parts of it, was growing more favorable to restoration; most symptomatic and important of all, Talleyrand, that astute master of the art of surviving, had come to their aid. [18] This show of support for the Bourbons helped to convert Alexander from his enthusiasm for the candidacy of Prince Bernadotte, one of Napoleon's marshals who had been named heir to the Swedish throne, but he magnanimously agreed to offer Napoleon sovereignty over the island of Elba in the Mediterranean, a promise that Castlereagh and Metternich much disliked but that was written into the Treaty of Fontainebleau, signed on April 11. Napoleon abdicated, and on May 3 Louis XVIII entered Paris. Negotiations for a peace treaty had been opened with the Bourbons after military operations ceased in late April, and on May 30 the first Peace of Paris was signed. The French agreed to accept the frontiers of 1792 (a more generous settlement than Castlereagh had earlier insisted upon) and the main heads on which the allies had agreed at Chaumont: free navigation of the Rhine, a big Holland, an independent Switzerland, a German confederation, a divided Italy under Austrian domination, and British retention of Malta.

The French problem settled, the allies could then turn to more general European problems. Preliminary conversations were held in Paris and in London, but nothing had been made firm when the talks opened in Vienna in mid-September. Shortly thereafter the four major powers decided that all decisions would be kept in their hands; the only plenary session was the final one at which the terms were ratified. Much time was spent in discussing the organization of the congress with other, smaller powers, and those in attendance were kept under elaborate police surveillance while they were treated to

---

[18] On Talleyrand, see p. 474.

extensive festivities that kept them from paying close attention to business. The postponement of formal actions reflected deep divisions among the four great powers, above all over the conflict of Prussian, Russian, and Austrian ambitions concerning Poland and Saxony, ambitions on which the entire settlement of the German situation depended. The result of the deadlock was that Britain drew closer to France; when in late December the tsar insisted on beginning formal conferences on the Polish question, Castlereagh and Metternich demanded the admission of France, represented by Talleyrand, into the inner councils. Prussia was outraged and even went so far as to threaten war and to mobilize her army; the result was a treaty of alliance among Britain, Austria, and France, signed early in January 1815. Acceptance of the tsar's modified ambitions for Poland (in which some Polish territory went to both Austria and Prussia) brought him around to supporting a compromise on Saxony. France was admitted to a reconstituted committee of five; the five worked their way through to a division of Saxon territory that left part of it an independent kingdom and annexed part of it to Prussia.

While the negotiators were making gradual progress on specific provisions of the treaty, the congress was shaken by the news that on March 1 Napoleon had crossed from Elba to France and had begun a triumphal progress toward Paris. Old soldiers flocked to his standard, and by the middle of the month he was in the capital, forming a new government. Louis XVIII fled to Ghent. Of Napoleon's former allies, only Murat in Naples, who had long been negotiating with the Austrians to preserve his throne, rallied to the emperor—a decision that was to cost Murat his life. In Paris, despite the enthusiasm that had greeted him, Napoleon found much opinion dead set against the resurrection of the Napoleonic autocracy, especially since what passed for a liberal constitution had been drawn up at Alexander's insistence by the Bourbons. Napoleon responded with his own very similar constitution and assured the world that he intended to live at peace with his neighbors.

The assurance was lost on the allies at Vienna. Armies were hastily summoned, Napoleon took the field against them, and on June 18, near the Flemish village of Waterloo, Napoleon was beaten after a three-day battle. It was a narrow decision: Napoleon just failed to drive out Wellington's army and was finally routed with the last-minute help of a Prussian army under Marshal Blücher. The defeat was decisive, and after briefly toying with the idea of a dictatorship, Napoleon abdicated in favor of his son, Napoleon II. The child-king was not without supporters, but the threatened descent of the allied forces on the capital put a stop to any hesitation, and on July 8, Louis XVIII was back in his palace. Napoleon was allowed to escape to the west-coast port of Rochefort where he surrendered to the English, throwing himself on the mercy of the prince regent. After a few days on board ship in Plymouth, he was embarked on H.M.S. *Bellerophon* for the lonely island of St. Helena in the south Atlantic, where he survived a prisoner until 1821, reviewing his errors and triumphs, and spinning a legend that would stir France for fifty years and more.

The Hundred Days necessitated a new treaty of peace with France. The feelings of generosity that had inspired the first Treaty of Paris were gone from the second, concluded on November 20, 1815, which reduced France to the frontiers of 1790, transferred the Saar to Prussia, and required that France be occupied by one hundred fifty thousand troops for three to five years and pay an indemnity of 700 million francs. The new treaty was reinforced by a renewed Quadruple Alliance among the four big victorious powers. Two months earlier, however, Alexander I, from the depths of his religious conviction, had persuaded the emperor of Austria and the king of Prussia to join him in a Treaty of Holy Alliance. It was no more than an agreement that the public acts of the monarchs would be in accordance with the principles of Christianity; Castlereagh called it a "piece of sublime mysticism and nonsense." The Holy Alliance had no direct practical effect, but the fact that it was signed by the three reactionary rulers of eastern Europe made it a bogey to most liberal-minded men, the more so as they saw those rulers often acting together. The Quadruple Alliance (later expanded by adding France) was the real basis for the Concert of Europe in the postwar years, but confusion of the Concert of Europe with the Holy Alliance—by contemporaries and by historians since—gave the postwar settlement an evil reputation it did not deserve.

It has been common to discuss the provisions of the Congress of Vienna in terms of principles, some honored, some honored in the breach, and some ignored. Talleyrand, naturally, argued the case for the principle of legitimacy—the restoration of rightful rulers—which was applied in France and Naples, but legitimacy was not enforced in the many small states that simply disappeared, particularly in Germany. The force of nationalism was clearly flouted by many arrangements and is often evoked by critics of the congress; but to have recognized it would have required superhuman imagination from statesmen raised in the eighteenth century.[19] That the balance of power should be restored, that France should be isolated, that states which had lost territory to settle European problems should be compensated are not so much principles as the practical essentials of diplomatic negotiation. To be sure, there were some forward-looking provisions—an agreement on internationalizing rivers and another to put a stop to the slave trade, though the latter had to be fought for by Castlereagh, under pressure from home, and extracted from an unwilling France. The first and only plenary session at Vienna, held just before Waterloo, ratified a series of decisions that were eminently pragmatic. Taken within the limitations of the age, they were directed to solving one great problem—to destroy the Napoleonic threat and ensure against its revival—and a host of refractory conflicts of the kind that arise in any reconstruction after a major war. Some solutions worked, others did not. But the shape of Europe was by and large determined for more than a generation, and men were enabled to turn their attention to the far more novel and perplexing problems of a world at peace.

[19] For a discussion of nationalism, see Ch. 16.

SELECTED READINGS

The most extensive survey of the Napoleonic era is Georges Lefebvre, *Napoleon*, 2 vols. (1935, tr. 1969), by one of the modern masters. A briefer work of the same vintage is Geoffrey Bruun, *Europe and the French Imperium, 1799–1814* (1938), in the Langer series. More recent, though with the disadvantage of composite works, are the relevant chapters in *The New Cambridge Modern History*, vol. 9, *War and Peace in an Age of Upheaval, 1793–1830*, ed., C. W. Crawley (1965).

The best biography of Napoleon is J. M. Thompson, *Napoleon Bonaparte: His Rise and Fall* (1952). J. C. Herold's *The Mind of Napoleon* (1955) is drawn from the emperor's own words, and the same author's *Bonaparte in Egypt* (1962) deals with an episode of unusual interest. On the military side, David G. Chandler's massive and authoritative *The Campaigns of Napoleon* (1966). The fascinating legacy of Napoleon is dealt with in A. L. Guerard, *Reflections on the Napoleonic Legend* (1924) and, from a different perspective, Pieter Geyl, *Napoleon: For and Against* (1949), a study of changing views among French historians.

Owen Connelly's *Napoleon's Satellite Kingdoms* (1965) is a useful survey, and the same author has written a biography of Joseph Bonaparte under the apt title *The Gentle Bonaparte* (1968). Eli Heckscher, *The Continental System* (1922), is a study by a major economic historian. Narrower but highly sophisticated and absolutely conclusive is a formidable statistical study of the effect of the system on Britain by François Crouzet, *L'économie britannique et le blocus continental, 1806–1813,* 2 vols. (1958); it has not yet been translated. For Spain, in addition to the Connelly books, G. H. Lovett, *Napoleon and the Birth of Modern Spain*, 2 vols. (1965), is the fullest treatment, but the appropriate chapters in Raymond Carr, *Spain, 1808–1939* (1966), are excellent. On Austria, besides the general surveys of Macartney and Taylor, there are two European works on Metternich: H. Ritter von Srbik, *Metternich, der Staatsmann und der Mensch*, 2 vols. (1925), a favorable view not translated; and G. Bertier de Sauvigny, *Metternich and his Times* (1959, tr. 1962), which places that key Austrian statesman in his European setting.

On the German situation, beyond the chapters in the second volume of Hajo Holborn's general history, the best starting place is H. A. L. Fisher, *Studies in Napoleonic Statesmanship: Germany* (1903, reprinted 1968)—detailed, charmingly written, and, despite its age, authoritative. Gerhard Ritter's *Stein, eine politische Biographie* (1931, 3rd ed., 1958) remains untranslated; for an English life of the great reformer one must go back to Guy Stanton Ford, *Stein and the Era of Reform in Prussia, 1807–1815* (1922). There are valuable institutional and critical studies of Prussian reforms of more recent date: Walter M. Simon, *The Failure of the Prussian Reform Movement, 1807–1819* (1955); W. O. Shanahan, *Prussian Military Reforms, 1786–1813* (1945), and Peter Paret, *Yorck and the Era of Prussian Reform* (1966). On the intellectual background there are the chapters on the period in Leonard Krieger, *The German Idea of Freedom: History of a Political Tradition* (1957); see, too, Klaus Epstein, *The Genesis of German Conservatism* (1966), both cited before.

For Russian history in the Napoleonic era, the greatest need is for a major study of Alexander I, but much can be learned about him as well as about his principal servants in Marc Raeff, *Michael Speransky, Statesman of Imperial Russia, 1772–1839* (1957) and Patricia Kennedy Grimsted, *The Foreign Ministers of Alexander I* (1970). E. V. Tarlé, *Napoleon's Invasion of Russia, 1812* (1938, tr. 1942), is by a Soviet scholar. E. J. Knapton, *The Lady of the Holy Alliance* (1939) is of interest for the religious history of the period, but this life of the Baroness de Krüdener also touches an important side of Alexander's complex personality.

No better introduction can be found to Britain at the opening of the new century than Elie Halévy, *England in 1815* (1913, tr. 1924, and reprinted under this shortened title in 1949); it is the first volume of his masterpiece, *A History of the English People in the Nineteenth Century,* and provides a superb retrospective view of the nation and its institutions as well as a provocative interpretation of English stability in a period of revolution. The old two-volume biography of William Pitt by J. Holland Rose is now being replaced by a new life by John Ehrman, but only the first volume, *The Younger Pitt: The Years of Acclaim* (1969), covering the period to 1789, has appeared. Elizabeth Longford's *Wellington: The Years of the Sword* (1969) is the most recent biographical essay, but Wellington still awaits a major, definitive study by the lucky scholar who has a lifetime to give to the subject. The best starting point for radicalism in the period is E. P. Thompson's passionate and partisan *The Making of the English Working Class* (1963), to which should be added Carl B. Cone, *The English Jacobins: Reformers in Late 18th-Century England* (1968), cited above.

Studies of the 1815 settlement—in addition to E. Saunders, *The Hundred Days* (1964), an account of the momentous interruption of negotiations—must begin with C. K. Webster's remarkable sketch, *The Congress of Vienna, 1814-1815* (1919). A more recent work, E. V. Gulick, *Europe's Classical Balance of Power: A Case History of the Theory and Practice of One of the Great Concepts of European Statecraft* (1955) is helpful in disentangling some of the intricacies of the settlement and sets them in a schematic context.

Index

Birth and death dates are given for all persons mentioned in the text, including a few historians whose works have attained the status of classics. Dates are also given for the reigns of kings and the pontificates of popes, but regnal dates are given only for queens when they ruled in their own right. A query (?) indicates an approximate but reasonably certain date; to avoid ambiguity it appears after a birth date but before a death date. Where dates are less certain, c. (for circa) is used, and occasionally we can only note a date of death or (with fl., for *floruit*, flourished) the time when the person comes to our attention.

Names are given in the form that is most convenient with respect to usage in the text. It is not possible to take into account variations in spelling or (save very occasionally) translation. Titles of nobility present great complexities that vary from country to country; they are given here in the simplest form consistent with the text and common usage. Fuller information for most names in this index can be derived (as can pronunciation) from *Webster's Biographical Dictionary* or the *Columbia Encyclopedia*. Beyond those handy brief references one may resort to the great national encyclopedias or biographical dictionaries.

The index is constructed to facilitate reviewing as well as the usual checking of references. The absence of identification other than birth and death dates for an individual allows a student to test his knowledge and to check back if his memory has slipped. For more important subjects a student can easily construct little informal outlines by using index entries to help fix in his mind what he has learned. To that end, analytical entries are provided for certain key concepts like bureaucracy or centralization or armies, making possible a review outline or an essay cutting across national boundaries. Entries for major countries or institutions—such as France, England, the Roman Catholic Church—are handled somewhat differently. Every substantive entry in the text is noted in the index, but identifying phrases are used only for major references; these phrases and the pages to which they pertain appear in chronological sequence, set off by semicolons from the briefer or secondary references.

Printer and Binder: Kingsport Press